ENTANGLED IN FEAR

ENTANGLED IN FEAR
EVERYDAY TERROR IN POLAND, 1944–1947

MARCIN ZAREMBA

TRANSLATED BY MAYA LATYNSKI

INDIANA UNIVERSITY PRESS

This book is a publication of

Indiana University Press
Office of Scholarly Publishing
Herman B Wells Library 350
1320 East 10th Street
Bloomington, Indiana 47405 USA

iupress.org

© 2022 by Marcin Zaremba

All rights reserved
No part of this book may be reproduced or utilized in any form or by any means, electronic or mechanical, including photocopying and recording, or by any information storage and retrieval system, without permission in writing from the publisher. The paper used in this publication meets the minimum requirements of the American National Standard for Information Sciences—Permanence of Paper for Printed Library Materials, ANSI Z39.48-1992.

Manufactured in the United States of America

First printing 2022

Library of Congress Cataloging-in-Publication Data

Names: Zaremba, Marcin, author. | Latynski, Maya, translator.
Title: Entangled in fear : everyday terror in Poland, 1944-1947 / Marcin Zaremba ; translated by Maya Latynski.
Other titles: Wielka trwoga. English | Everyday terror in Poland, 1944-1947
Description: Bloomington, Indiana : Indiana University Press, [2022] | Includes bibliographical references and index.
Identifiers: LCCN 2022011697 (print) | LCCN 2022011698 (ebook) | ISBN 9780253063083 (hardback) | ISBN 9780253063090 (paperback) | ISBN 9780253063106 (ebook)
Subjects: LCSH: World War, 1939-1945—Psychological aspects. | World War, 1939-1945—Atrocities—Poland. | Psychic trauma—Poland. | Terror—Poland. | Violence—Poland.
Classification: LCC D744.55 .Z3713 2022 (print) | LCC D744.55 (ebook) | DDC 940.53/1—dc23/eng/20220328
LC record available at https://lccn.loc.gov/2022011697
LC ebook record available at https://lccn.loc.gov/2022011698

CONTENTS

Acknowledgments vii

    Introduction: Before There Was Fear 1
1. In the Labyrinth of Fear 10
2. Fear in Interwar Culture: The Bolsheviks and "Jewish Communism" 19
3. The Trauma of a World War: Psychosocial Effects of the Second World War 38
4. In the Beginning Was Chaos 65
5. "Out of the Frying Pan and into the Fire": The Dreaded Red Army 69
6. The Demobilized 94
7. Looting Fever 135
8. Outlaws: "The Dishonored Soldiers' Peasant War" 155
9. It Was More than Just Travel Nerves 175
10. The Politics of Fear 182
11. The Phantoms of Transience 200
12. The Three Horsemen of the Apocalypse: Hunger, High Prices, and Infectious Diseases 253
13. Ethnic Phobias and Violence 275

    Conclusion: "The Boogeyman" 325

Bibliography 327
Index 347

ACKNOWLEDGMENTS

This book would not have been written had several things not happened. Marcin Kula helped me to overcome my "ante-fear" of studying fear. He read the whole manuscript, for which I am eternally grateful. I would also like to thank Błażej Brzostek, Jerzy Kochanowski, Łukasz Krzyżanowski, Jolanta Tokarska-Bakir, Antoni Sułek, Bożena Szaynok, and Joanna Wawrzyniak for being so kind as to read the whole manuscript before it was published and to give me their comments. Andrzej Friszke, Joanna Hytrek-Hryciuk, Bartosz Kaliski, Adam Leszczyński, Piotr Osęka, Andrzej Paczkowski, Krzysztof Persak, Dariusz Stola, Paweł Śpiewak, and Marek Wierzbicki read sections. I presented some of the chapters in seminars and discussions chaired by Andrzej Paczkowski at the Institute of Political Studies of the Polish Academy of Sciences; by the late Włodzimierz Borodziej, Jerzy Kochanowski, and Marcin Kula in the Faculty of History of the University of Warsaw; and by the late Jerzy Jedlicki at the Institute of History of the Polish Academy of Sciences. The tips about sources and the comments made on these occasions were of great help. A warm thank you to Padraic Kenney.

This publication would have been much shorter had it not been for a grant I received from the State Committee for Scientific Research [Nr 1 H01g 031 2 for "Fear in People's Poland (1944–1989)"] and a two-month fellowship in 2005 at the Institute of Human Sciences in Vienna, where an Andrew W. Mellon Foundation grant allowed me to conduct research. The interviews with former prisoners of the Mauthausen concentration camp by Piotr Filipkowski and Jarosław Pałka of the Oral History Archive, to which I was given access, were invaluable. Translation of the book has been funded by the Ministry of Science and Higher Education, Republic of Poland, National Program for the Development of Humanities, grant no. 0126/NPRH3/H31/82/2014.

My wife was the book's first reviewer and editor, and without her help I would not have dared show it to anyone. I spent several years living by fear and in fear. My family could not avoid sensing it, and I would like to thank them enormously for their patience.

ENTANGLED IN FEAR

INTRODUCTION

BEFORE THERE WAS FEAR

The period after the war ended was a strange time, so difficult to pigeonhole. A time of Roger Caillois's universal pairs of complementary opposites: celebration, carnival, and great hope as well as feelings of defeat, privation, and dread.[1]

Poland's changing postwar reality was filled with contradictions. With peace came a natural rebirth and joy.[2] The poet Konstanty Ildefons Gałczyński wrote in 1946, "One has spent six years wandering the world. And out of the blue: Poland is there and an Aeolian harp is there, what a musical miracle."[3] People were thrilled that they had survived, that they were reuniting with their families, starting businesses, and tackling the challenges of rebuilding.[4] The writer Stefan Kisielewski reported, "I went to Warsaw recently. They're all keeping busy as hell among all that rubble. Business is booming. Work is thriving. There is no shortage of humor. In the streets, the throngs are brimming with life; you would never know that all these people have only just been rescued from a catastrophe and are now living in conditions unfit for humans."[5] The Poles were celebrating, living it up. It was carnival time.

The slightest signs of normalcy—a shiny new windowpane, clean water flowing from a faucet, a tram coming down a rubble-free street—made people happy as never before. In the summer of 1945, a street scene encapsulated this mood: A funeral procession moved down Ząbkowska Street in Warsaw. "An ordinary procession with a small group of mourners followed the hearse. Suddenly, a tram emerged from the distance in Ząbkowska Street (most probably coming from the Kawęczyńska Street depot). It was a real red Warsaw tram, a vital component of the cityscape being reborn. The sight of the tram sparked universal enthusiasm. Pedestrians stopped in their tracks, some came running toward it, cheering loudly and clapping. Oddly, the funeral procession came to a halt, too, and the living who were accompanying the dead turned to look at the tram and, then, swept by the mood, they, too, began to clap."[6]

In 1945, the Poles were making merry, and any national, state, or church ceremony would serve as an excuse. There were parties and weddings everywhere. According to a Pomerania Province civil servant, "a party fever" had gripped the population.[7] A peasant memoirist in Cracow Province noted, "Calm gradually returned after the war. A good feeling was back, especially among the young people, who are always eager to enjoy themselves and who are now putting on dances almost every Sunday. People dance to exhaustion to simple tunes played by a violin. Sometimes, dawn was surprised to see boys in sweat-drenched shirts, clouds of dust rising from under their feet, whirling zealously to the rhythms of a polka, an oberek or a sztajerek.

Progress was just around the corner, as people learned to dance to modern (much deformed) hits."[8]

A mad frolic also gripped the cities. Never again would people dance so much in streets, squares, and parks. The children of the intelligentsia preferred to put on parties at home and dances at school, and in the summer they dispersed to the countryside.[9] "The night before last, I went to yet another ball," wrote Jan Józef Szczepański, a student at the time.[10] During the hot days of July 1946, the banks of the Vistula in Warsaw were literally "caked" with "thousands of beachgoers," wrote the daily *Express Wieczorny*.[11] Manners relaxed, and sexual relations suddenly became quite easy. The end of the war made people want to marry and have children. The second half of the 1940s was the beginning of the postwar baby boom, which peaked in the early 1950s. This was also a time of great political hope, which was linked to the non-Communist Peasant Party leader Stanisław Mikołajczyk and the expectation that the West would intervene and expel the Soviets.

But there was another side to this hopefulness—fear and trepidation.

Georges Lefebvre called the state of deepened peasant unrest in some parts of France on the eve of the revolution the Great Fear of 1789.[12] Fear of hunger and of brigands and bandits was pervasive. Rumors traveled about the aristocrats conspiring to raise food prices or to bring in foreign armies. People felt threatened by a "hunger conspiracy," and a mass panic swept large swaths of the country. Hatred between the estates and fear combined with hopes of improving the lives of the peasantry led to a great outburst of grassroots violence. Another wave followed: the storming of castles and seignorial homes, the ousting of drifters, hunger tumults and anti-Semitic riots. Many similar surges of local fear exploded all through the history of Europe. Jean Delumeau wrote about them in his *La peur en Occident XIVe–XVIIIe siècles*.

Poland in 1945 was obviously not France in 1789. In Poland, peasant animosities were based more on ethnic enmities and less on class differences. Still, the Polish peasantry's response to collectivization was rooted in its fear of a brand-new incarnation of the feudal system being imported from the Soviet Union. After the Second World War, thieves and looters supplanted bandits and vagrants. Despite these and other differences, the intensity of emotions, the states of fear and anxiety, show that the time coming in the wake of the war was one not only of celebration and hope but also of Great Fear.

THIS BOOK'S GOALS AND RATIONALE

This book's main ambition is to sketch out a broad panorama of the Poles' apprehensions in the immediate postwar period. What were people afraid of? What made them anxious? The book is not interested as much in events and their origins as in identifying and describing the emotions these events generated. In other words, it focuses on what the people watching a public execution felt rather than on the execution itself. But in writing about the insecurities brought on by repression, it is difficult to omit describing the repression itself, as well as the authorities' role in stirring up fear.

The government prototype based on the Soviet model was accompanied by a "centralized" fear. In the first couple of years after liberation, however, most people suffered from their own "decentralized" fears.[13] These included dread of Soviet marauders and attacks by native bandits, hunger, typhus, and the uncertainty brought on by having no home and no work. It's easy enough to assemble a list of the looming menaces, but the dynamics of the emotions involved are much more complex. Creating a spatial and sequential map of the Polish postwar fears, which would yield indicators such as the routes along which rumors traveled and the localities that experienced panic about inflation, is an important goal here. While this book attempts to draw such a map, it inevitably cannot be comprehensive since many sources are scattered and available narratives are laconic.

This study aims to be more than a catalogue of the postwar fears. The relentlessly elevated feeling of insecurity had the social consequences of waves of rumors, panic, and violence. In a word, what matters is not only what people feared but also how they expressed their fears and how they tried to calm them. Thus, the book's second goal is to create a narrative of the mental and behavioral manifestations of fear and the strategies people used to manage them.

Three phenomena dominated this period: an eruption of dangers, feelings of uncertainty and impermanence, and, especially early on, a weakening of social control, including loss of the fear of punishment. In the absence of new institutions to take over the functions of the prewar state organization, feelings of impunity escalated, culminating in anarchy. An accumulation of fear in the special conditions of decay and dramatic change mingled with perceived license can engender violence against social and ethnic groups other than one's own. The chaos, anarchy, and feeling of impermanence united Poles against Jews, Germans, Ukrainians, or Belorusians, and thus the pogroms were embedded in that period's Polish state of mind. The fear-soaked emotional climate combined with the atrophy of social control made people want to take part in hateful and violent acts or at least to champion them. If we observe the fear and the individual strategies used to overcome it, which also helped to solve the problems of everyday life after the war, a powerful force shaping the postwar reality emerges. The atmosphere, dominated by tension and fear, generated aggressive behaviors. The lessons of violence learned during the war and fear-based prewar prejudices also played a crucial role. In writing this book, I was inspired by a desire to understand the mechanisms of these behaviors, particularly toward the Jews. And this is the book's third goal. Because the book was written in the humanistic spirit, it should not be interpreted as attempting to excuse the Poles for their crimes against Jews, Belorussians, Germans, and Ukrainians.

This study of fear and terror was motivated by two beliefs. The first was the conviction that emotions are an inextricable part of human life. A history that focuses solely on events and leaves out the emotional significance that people attach to them is self-limiting and lags behind the other social sciences. This fallacy has been boosted since September 11, 2001, as scores of publications about fear have filled bookstore shelves. The subject of fear also became trendy for sociologists and social psychologists, who had until then rarely researched it.[14] But missing from their avalanche of publications were works in contemporary history.[15]

The second belief was that this white spot in the historiography of the postwar years in Poland needed to be filled. Vivid colors dominated pre-1989 studies about constructing the new order. Since 1989 most writings have introduced much darker colors and concentrated on political history—a natural reaction. But the doyen of social historians, George M. Trevelyan, long ago predicted the unintended consequences of this slant: "Without social history, economic history is barren, and political history unintelligible."[16] Historians have begun to focus on politics and thinking about social phenomena outside the comprehensive context of society's life, freezing Polish society in its heroic resistance to Communist rule. Where are the new books about land reform, demobilization, the revolution in class structure, women's roles during and after the war, orphans and social assistance, popular culture, and changes in social mores brought on by the war? We do have some studies of the wartime and postwar resettlements of populations, although little is known about the consequences of migrations to urban areas.

Historians have almost completely ignored the universe of the collective imagination, of thoughts and emotions. Since it is the historian's mission to narrate human history—including emotions—he or she should try to re-create the central emotions and to think about where they came from and how they influenced behaviors and views. Events become fuller and can be understood better when they are placed in a broader context. The time has come to depoliticize the immediate postwar period and to turn to its social trends, its everyday life.

SOURCES AND OTHER ISSUES

This author's emphatic belief that social emotions must be studied cannot conceal his uncertainty about the available methodology and sources. To put it more directly: the title of this introduction, "Before There Was Fear," communicates the author's own fear of facing fear as a field of research. Numerous traps lie in wait. Bringing together sociology, psychology, and history is a daredevil enterprise. Each of these disciplines is governed by its own laws, and each uses its own language, methodology, and questionnaires. For example, the frequent demands to combine history and sociology may lead to painful bifurcations, but it is still worth a try. Studying past fears is accompanied by another hazard: sociologists and social psychologists have not developed a template that historians can use. Medievalists have long studied fear, but the uniqueness of twentieth-century source materials makes it difficult to take advantage of the medievalists' experiences. We are left with the trial-and-error method, which does not sound encouraging.

Yet another challenge is the very nature of fear. As I have discussed my research topic in various venues, I have been asked by other scholars about tangibles, about facts. As historians focus on writing the history of events and institutions, they have not developed a methodology for studying something as amorphous as fear, which is illusory and chimerical and rarely leaves a trace behind. Eventually, as I asked, "What am I really looking for?" the subject became clearer. Fear is always experienced individually, and few experiences are as personal. There can be no collective fear without individual fear preceding it. A society's fear is born out of the convergence of individual experiences, when dozens, hundreds, thousands, and millions of people are afraid of the same thing at the same time. Fear has led, also after the Second World War, to mass panic, escapist behaviors, and panic buying. But the real problem occurs only when action, whether individual or collective, does not come out of the sensation of fear. The literary critic Maria Janion, discussing the inexpressibility of death and existence noted that "there are vast areas that have not been named or expressed."[17] These areas also include anxiety and fear.

Let's take the fear of authority. The most common reaction to this fear is retreat. How can a historian use historical materials to show it? The disintegration of an organized opposition is certainly one indicator, but it is inadequate for explaining the experiences of millions of people. Since in postwar Poland no sensible person would have written that he was afraid of, let's say, the secret police, it is difficult to find documentary evidence of this fear. In this and similar situations, the historian's preferred method is to focus on describing the instruments of fear, such as the language the government used in its fear policies, and to presume that the governed reacted similarly to oppression. It is much the same with the greatest fear of all: the fear of hunger. As had frequently been the case earlier, after the war it was mostly the poor and uneducated who went hungry, and these were people who tended not to write memoirs or letters. Time and again, the only indication of their emotional state was their behavior: strikes or hunger protests. This is not much to prove the existence of insecurity stemming from food shortages, all the more so since this form of dissatisfaction can alternately be interpreted as an expression of public resistance. For these reasons alone, fear is the elephant in the room of historical research, which makes the question of sources crucial.

When fear surfaces as collective action, it becomes rumor, flight, panic, mass violence, or large-scale hoarding, and evidence of it can be found in official documents. Traces of fear are also present in personal records such as diaries, memoirs, and letters. Many postwar Polish diaries survive, including those of Maria Dąbrowska, Jarosław Iwaszkiewicz, Adam Kamiński, Zygmunt Klukowski, Joanna Konopińska, Anna Kowalska, Wacław Kubacki, Zofia Nałkowska, Hugo Steinhaus, and Jan Józef Szczepański.[18] The problem here is that their authors were all intellectuals, and they shared their group's specific perspective on reality. Memoirs come to the rescue but are problematic because most were written many years after the events, and they rarely discuss moods and emotions. This is particularly true of memoirs written by men, as women usually have an easier time being in touch with their feelings, including fear.[19] Fear appears frequently in the peasant memoirs written a short time after the events of interest here, in 1948, and collected by Krystyna Kersten and Tomasz Szarota.[20] Entered in a contest organized by the Czytelnik Press Institute, they are a terrific source of information about many aspects of life in the countryside, including collective perceptions and worries. What the peasant memoirs lack, however, is any credible analysis of their authors' political fears, as a result of self-censorship.

Bulletins of the Main Censorship Office (Główny Urząd Cenzury, renamed Office "B" of the Second Department of the Ministry of Public Security in December 1947), which relied heavily on excerpts from private letters, remain a valuable source of knowledge about public emotions. Wartime Censorship, created as a discrete office by an order of the commander in chief of the Polish Army on October 8, 1944, was a unit of the Ministry of Public Security.[21] It initially had four branches but grew at lightning speed as the people's government expanded its reach. In June 1945 it had a presence in eleven provinces and seventeen district offices and employed more than 300 censors.[22] In November 1944, for example, its staff was able to read 700,000 letters and telegrams.[23] By May 1, 1945, they had inspected nearly 4,400,000 pieces of mail and over 178,000 telegrams; correspondence between troops and their families was only a fraction of this total.[24]

The censorship office believed that the great majority of this sea of letters was unexceptional. They divided "unfavorable" statements into twelve categories including testimonials of an "anti-government, pro-fascist, provocative [nature], which disseminated defeatist attitudes" (by May 1945, the censorship office functionaries had logged more than 19,000 letters of this type); those discrediting the Polish People's Army and the Red Army (8,142 letters); those "about reactionary elements and H[ome] A[rmy], N[ational] A[rmed] F[orces] and other groupings" (6,860); those "about disorder in our country: banditry, looting, hunger, epidemics, high prices, speculation, catastrophes, explosions" (51,972); those about desertions (944); and those "about repressions, group repressions of the civilian population, the work of the organs of P[ublic] S[ecurity], alerts about arrests, house searches and pursuits" (6,323).[25]

These letters, which are a rich resource for us today, served two purposes. First, they were used in "security" operations to eliminate underground organizations and capture deserters. Second, they helped the authorities keep tabs on the public mood. In addition, censors quoted letters in their "special reports" tailored to the handful of officials at the very top of the Communist power structure. The sociological studies conducted by the censorship office as it catalogued and analyzed these private letters were unprecedented in scale—in April 1945, the average censor went through 276 letters in an eight-hour workday. Indeed, it is solely thanks to the censors' hard work that we can learn today about the population's fears of banditry or hunger.

But roses have thorns. First, the censors' bulletins excerpted only the most spectacular fragments of the letters and rarely reproduced them in full. Second, the picture of reality that emerges from them is overly dark. People (perhaps especially the Poles[26]) sit down to write letters when something terrible has happened to them and when they want to complain. Third, probably all soldiers, as well as many civilians, knew that their letters would be read by censors.[27] In those days, envelopes and postcards were stamped "Screened by military censorship." It would thus be inaccurate to use critical statements from these letters about the new government to draw conclusions about the government's legitimacy. Fourth, only a dozen reports out of more than 2,600 produced by the Main Censorship Office before August 1946 have been found. It is likely that the others were destroyed in the several episodes of document destruction conducted by the government. Fifth, the censorship machine's institutional growth was interrupted by the Council of Ministers decree of June 22, 1945, abolishing postal censorship. While the censors continued to read mail from and to soldiers as well as international correspondence,[28] some district censorship offices were shut down and the staff of its provincial branches cut. Still, the changes must have improved the censors' efficiency, for in the three months preceding the national referendum of 1946 (April–June), they read nearly nine million pieces of mail. In this period, the Main Censorship Office prepared forty-nine "Special reports."[29] Unluckily, none has survived. This book quotes abundantly from the surviving reports for 1944–46. Since the letters were private, their senders' and addressees' names and addresses are left out.

Introduction

Official documents are another source used here. Their archival categories are listed at the end of the book. It is noteworthy, though, that because of the nature of the new government, the low skill levels of its cadres, and the absence of a bureaucratic ethos, these government documents are of low professional quality.

Materials that have not yet been used by historians include reports coming from the provincial commands of the Citizens' Militia. Their contents vary, yet the facts they present are closer to reality than the central government reports.

The analyses of the public mood that the Underground State conducted on behalf of the Government Delegate's Office are far more sophisticated. But their quality steadily declines over time, probably because many of the analysts voluntarily came out of the underground or were arrested.

As for newspapers, some analysts subscribe to the stereotype that they should be used solely to learn about the new regime's ideology, as they do not reflect the views of the opposition—and this is true. They undoubtedly contain much valuable information about everyday life in the wake of the war, but one needs to keep in mind that the overall image of the postwar reality that emerges from the press smacks heavily of retouching.

HOW THIS BOOK IS ORGANIZED

Because the Great Fear was a spontaneous and short-lived phenomenon, it was difficult to find the right point at which to begin a cohesive analysis. The first three chapters prepare the background by defining key concepts, trace the origins of some of the postwar angst, and argue that the Great Fear would not have gone off had it not been for the population's dramatic experiences in the war.

The core of this book, beginning with chapter 4 about chaos, brings together several themes that meet at the turbulent moment in 1944–45 when the front moved across Poland. The plague of Soviet marauders and the birth of Balkanization are covered in chapter 5. Chapter 6, which discusses demobilized troops, seems to depart from the earlier theme, as it addresses not only emotions but "the expendable people." The reason this chapter fits here is that the fear these people experienced—and the fear they triggered in others—contributed significantly to the atmosphere of the Great Fear. A discussion of plunder and banditry follows in chapters 7 and 8, then the short chapter 9 describes what it was like for millions of people to be on the move.

After discussing the new regime's policies aimed at generating fright in the population in chapter 10, the book moves on to examine the psychosocial consequences of these policies, which included a sense of impermanence, in chapters 11 and 12. After the war, many Poles experienced a feeling of suspension and instability in their lives. Not all their fears could be attributed to the government's policies, however, since hunger, inflation, infectious diseases, and epidemics were rampant.

The book's final chapter analyzes the Poles' fears of other ethnic groups, of the Other. It examines the myth of ritual murder. The fear of Jewish cannibalism was one of the main reasons behind the eruption of pogroms after the war. But in the big picture, the sources of the pogroms were both an expression and a consequence of the Great Fear.

WHAT THIS BOOK IS AND IS NOT ABOUT

Entangled in Fear examines the psychological atmosphere of the postwar period, what people dreaded, and how they coped with their distress. A reconstruction of this mood should help to explain group attitudes, the roots of that era's many instances of unrest and protest, hunger riots, and anti-Jewish pogroms.

The book covers the period 1944–47, but these years were not all filled with fear. Since no human can endure this crushing burden for so long, no terror known to historians lasted three years, and even after the Second World War ended in Poland, days and weeks of intensified feelings of insecurity alternated with periods of relaxation. Still, these three years can be perceived as a self-enclosed era that opened with the arrival of the Red Army and closed with the January 1947 elections to the Sejm. Even though fear and terror did not govern alone, waves of anxiety recurred, as did numerous outbreaks of panic and anti-Semitic pogroms (the latter exclusive to these years). The year 1948, which marked the beginning of collectivization and accelerated Stalinization, opened a new chapter in the history of Polish fear.

While the origins of this era's collective behaviors cannot be explained by just one factor, many behaviors were rooted in the peasant mentality. Assuming that the rural population experienced these postwar anxieties and fears more powerfully, how can this be explained? On the one hand, the institutional infrastructure had been impaired (in some regions outright toppled) by the war, which in turn weakened or eliminated social control. On the other hand, the roots of these fears may have been deeper, buried in peasant fatalism, a characteristic feature of this culture.

The postwar waves of hearsay are a case in point. Hearsay as a form of social communications initially thrived during the war, not only in Poland but also in countries lacking a peasant culture, such as Germany and the United States. The potency of rumors can be explained by the unavailability of information, a mood of endangerment, and people's desire to grasp the world's complexities. In the peasant culture, gossip and rumor are primary tools of social transmission.[30] Accepting potentially contradictory pieces of news uncritically is another feature of the peasant culture. The explosion of magical thinking, a source of the anti-Semitic pogroms in Poland, can be linked to traditional thinking and the important role of magical beliefs and practices in it.[31] Clearly, people were pushed to commit crimes by poverty, encouraged by the absence of social control and motivated by wartime demoralization. Yet city dwellers also engaged in pillaging in Lvov, Radom, and Warsaw. Plunder happened on a mass scale, and, at least initially, most looters came from the countryside. This can be explained by what anthropologists describe as the characteristic peasant social awareness, which is based on the double ethics of needing to be absolutely honest within one's own group and lacking inhibitions when stealing from groups of others. And when the other was a Jew or, after the war, a German, killing or robbing them was a virtue, taking back what one was owed. Looting can also be interpreted as a symptom of rural territorialism.

We also cannot call the postwar violence (unlike the violence organized by state institutions such as the NKVD and the Security Office) modern, to use Zygmunt Bauman's definition.[32] It did not form in the minds of bureaucrats and was not rationally planned but happened mostly spontaneously and chaotically. If we take into account the anti-Semitic pogroms, in which the myth of ritual murder played a key role, the more fitting adjective describing this violence is *traditional*.

In covering the postwar Great Fear, this book does not imply that the war had been trouble-free for the Poles. Chapter 3 is devoted to the war's significance and social consequences. The year 1945 was indeed an important watershed in terms of people's impressions, experiences, and psychological reactions. The end of the Second World War was also the end of an era in the history of Polish fear. The sources of fear were qualitatively different, and fear diminished, rarely reaching the levels of the wartime psychosis. People no longer needed to look up to the sky anticipating air strikes, and city dwellers no longer had to dread random street roundups. Despite everything that would come later, most Poles stopped experiencing the paralyzing fear for their own and their dear ones' lives.

This book is about the terror that descended on Poland. That is not to say that the Polish terror was exceptional, since Belorusians, Germans, Ukrainians, and Jews experienced it, too. It is impossible to measure who felt most threatened—a Jew by a pogrom, a Pole by the secret police, or a Polish, Ukrainian, or German family by expulsion and drifting without a home. To use Jan T. Gross's term, it was a "ghastly decade."[33] Poland can serve as a case study to help us understand the forces shaping the postwar reality elsewhere, to get to the core of conflicts and tensions, including ones between ethnic groups.

To say that the postwar "mental space" was filled solely with fear and terror would be an oversimplification.[34] Not everyone experienced them, and those who did felt them in different degrees and not necessarily at the same time. As in prerevolutionary France, in Poland terror was not distributed evenly. In some areas of the country, its floodwaters were still rising, while in others they had already receded, and an aura of security had settled in. It seems there was less anxiety in the native Polish lands that had earlier been annexed by the Third Reich, which may be explained by the lesser destruction and better provisions in some areas, for example in Greater Poland. The traditions of these territories, which during the Partitions had been governed by Prussia, such as greater conformity and adherence to the legal order, may have played a greater role here. Perhaps the rural population was more afraid than city dwellers, especially in the larger conglomerations, because of roaming gangs, passages of troops, requisitions, and the threat of pacifications in the countryside. This is one of the ways in which the postwar period differed from the time of war, when the countryside not only had been relatively safer and served as a refuge for "hot" underground activists but also had greater supplies of food. Different social groups experienced fear differently, too. The intelligentsia, tending to judge reality rationally, probably did not dwell on it as much as the less-educated social strata, but those individuals and groups who remained active underground or feared repression and harassment because of their provenance, such as landowners, entrepreneurs, or prewar political elites, were an exception.

TRADITIONS

The concept of the Great Fear helps to address some of the issues facing scholars interested in topics such as postwar Polish–Jewish relations. But it is not an original concept, as it tweaks and merges earlier theses and research traditions. At the top of the long list of thinkers to whom I am indebted are the French historians Georges Lefebvre and Jean Delumeau. Their books inspired me to begin my research on fear. Krystyna Kersten's work sets a high standard for nonjudgmental history. Her contribution to our knowledge and understanding of the postwar period is enormous.[35] Andrzej Paczkowski's many publications about the security apparatus are equally important.[36] Tomasz Szarota was the first historian to write about wartime fear in his book about everyday life in occupied Warsaw.[37] *Entangled in Fear* is a continuation of his thought.

There are many publications about Polish–Jewish relations after the war. Were it not for their authors' findings, I would be floating on the surface of my subject like a cork on water. Most outstanding are works about the Cracow pogrom by Anna Cichopek[38] and about the Kielce pogrom by Bożena Szaynok,[39] Stanisław Meducki, and Zenon Wrona.[40] In 2018, after the Polish version of this book was published, Joanna Tokarska-Bakir published her book about the Kielce pogrom: *Pod klątwą. Społeczny portret pogromu kieleckiego*, Warszawa 2018.

I am hugely indebted to Łukasz Kamiński for his research. His book about social resistance after the war is the best example of social history of this period to have come out since 1989.[41]

This book does not attempt to debate with Jan T. Gross's *Fear*, which appeared when my research about fear in the People's Republic was already underway.[42] On the contrary, I deeply respect Professor Gross's writings and draw on his books extensively. But we disagree on some issues.[43] His work on the sources of the Poles' violent acts directed at the Jews does not sufficiently take into account the Poles' psychological and material condition, and it treats anti-Semitism as the key and adequate explanation of aggression against the Jews, while I believe that this violence had many causes.

NOTES

1. Caillois, *Man and the Sacred*.
2. Świda-Ziemba, *Człowiek wewnętrznie zniewolony*, 125.
3. Gałczyński, *Wiersze*, 204.
4. For a recent discussion of "private rebuilding," see Markiewicz, "Prywatna odbudowa Warszawy," 213–64.
5. Kisielewski, "Ci z Warszawy."
6. Pacho, *Życie silniejsze*, 15.
7. "Sprawozdanie wojewody pomorskiego za miesiąc listopad 1945 roku" in Borodij, Kutta, and Kozłowski, *Rok 1945*, 140.
8. Kersten and Szarota, *Wieś polska 1939–1948*, 312.
9. Świda-Ziemba, *Urwany lot*, 77–81.
10. Szczepański, *Dzienniki 1945–1956*, 52.
11. *Express Wieczorny*, July 29, 1946.
12. Lefebvre, *The Great Fear of 1789*.

13. Shlapentokh, *Fear in Contemporary Society*, 6.

14. Vladimir Shlapentokh notes sociology's and social psychology's disinterest in the question of fear; Shlapentokh, *Fear in Contemporary Society*.

15. Joanna Bourke, *Fear. A Cultural History* (London: Virago Press, 2006), and Bernard Greiner, Christian Th. Müller, and Dierk Walter, eds., *Angst im kalten Krieg* (Hamburg: Hamburger Edition, 2009), fill some of this gap. The most recent Polish-language works include Zbigniew M. Osiński, *Lęk w kulturze społeczeństwa polskiego w XVI–XVII wieku* (Warsaw: DiG, 2009).

16. Trevelyan, *English Social History*, 15.

17. "'O, i tak,' z profesor Marią Janion rozmawia Barbara N. Łopieńska," *Wysokie Obcasy*, October 16, 2004.

18. Dąbrowska, *Dzienniki 1914–1965 w 13 tomach*; Iwaszkiewicz, *Notatki 1939–1945*; Iwaszkiewicz, *Dzienniki 1911–1955*; Kamiński, *Diariusz podręczny 1939–1945*; Klukowski, *Zamojszczyzna 1944–1959*; Konopińska, *Tamten wrocławski rok. Dziennik 1945–1946*; Kubacki, *Dziennik (1944–1958)*; Nałkowska, *Dzienniki 1945–1954*; Steinhaus, *Wspomnienia i zapiski*; Szczepański, *Dzienniki 1945–1956*.

19. Barbara Szacka analyzed autobiographical research and reached similar conclusions: "Polish women, like German women, focus more on the threats and basic needs that need to be satisfied for their families and children to survive." Szacka, "II wojna światowa w pamięci rodzinnej," in Kwiatkowski et al., *Między codziennością a wielką historią*, 117.

20. Kersten and Szarota, *Wieś polska 1939–1948*.

21. Archiwum Instytutu Pamięci Narodowej w Warszawie (hereafter AIPN), Polski Komitet Wyzwolenia Narodowego (hereafter PKWN), Resort Bezpieczeństwa Publicznego (hereafter RBP), sign. 31. Sprawozdanie Kierownika Wydziału Cenzury Wojennej, November 4, 1944, k 1–2.

22. AIPN, Ministerstwo Bezpieczeństwa Publicznego (hereafter MBP) 3378, k. 10–20. Sprawozdanie z pracy Wydziału C.W. Ministerstwa B.P. za cały okres swojej pracy od X 1944 do 1-go V 1945.

23. Kochanowski, "Listonosz nie doniósł"; Kochanowski, "Lubelskie czarne gabinety," 325–37; Drygas, "Perlustracja," 89–125.

24. AIPN, MBP 3378, k. 10–20. Sprawozdanie z pracy Wydziału C.W. Ministerstwa B.P. za cały okres swojej pracy od X 1944 do 1-go V 1945.

25. AIPN, MBP 3378, k. 11, 12.

26. Piotr Szarota recently noted "a negativity norm" in viewing the public space as evil in the Poles' thinking. "Polaków zmagania z uśmiechem" in Skarżyńska and Jakubowska, *Społeczeństwo po przejściach*, 143–56.

27. During a discussion at a district teachers' congress in Warsaw in July 1945, a teacher observed, "What sort of freedom and democracy is this if before I write a letter to a [student's] mother I must spend an hour thinking about what I'm allowed or not allowed to write." IPN, Zespół Wolność i Niezawisłość [hereafter WiN] 92, k. 87. Raport WiN-u z VIII 1945.

28. It is not clear who in the Committee for Public Security decided that all letters should be read, thus breaking the law, and when this happened. The "special reports" doubtless became more secret from then on, and it is likely that they were later scrupulously destroyed for this very reason.

29. AIPN, MBP 3353, k. 2–7. Raport o pracy Głównego Urzędu Cenzury za okres kwiecień, maj, czerwiec 1946.

30. Dobrowolski, "Chłopska kultura tradycyjna," 85.

31. Dobrowolski, 90–92.

32. Cf. Bauman, *Modernity and the Holocaust*.

33. Gross, *Upiorna dekada*.

34. Kurt Lewin came up with the concept of life space in his *A Dynamic Theory of Personality*. Tomasz Szarota introduced it into Polish literature in *Okupowanej Warszawy dzień powszedni*, 455.

35. Some of Krystyna Kersten's books: *The Establishment of Communist Rule in Poland, 1943–1948*; *Polacy, Żydzi, komunizm. Anatomia półprawd 1939–68*; *Między wyzwoleniem a zniewoleniem. Polska 1944–1956*; *Pisma rozproszone*.

36. Including Andrzej Paczkowski's two chapters in Courtois et al., *The Black Book of Communism*.

37. Szarota, *Okupowanej Warszawy*....

38. Cichopek, *Pogrom Żydów w Krakowie 11 VIII 1945*.

39. Szaynok, *Pogrom Żydów w Kielcach 4 VII 1946*.

40. *Antyżydowskie wydarzenia kieleckie 4 VII 1946 roku. Dokumenty i materiały*, vol. 1, Stanisław Meducki and Zenon Wrona, eds.; vol. 2, Meducki, ed.

41. Kamiński, *Polacy wobec nowej rzeczywistości 1944–1948*.

42. Gross, *Fear*.

43. More in Zaremba, "Sąd nieostateczny." Other voices in the discussion were collected in Gądek, *Wokół strachu*.

1

IN THE LABYRINTH OF FEAR

As the historian begins to research fear, he gradually begins to experience it himself. Of the six universal emotions—happiness, sadness, anger, surprise, disgust, and fear—fear takes pride of place, with the largest body of literature, dozens of theories, and major studies devoted to it. The only way to escape from this labyrinth is to ignore all its side corridors and stick to the main route, the main goal. This goal, which is described in this chapter, is to explain the key ideas in the study of fear and to examine fear's role in a community's life and the consequences of its escalation. The chapter wraps things up by analyzing the differences between a Great Fear and a Great Terror.

Most psychologists define fear as a distinct emotional state brought on by the presence of a tangible, direct threat or by the anticipation of such a threat.[1] Fear is a reaction to external stimuli that leads us to experience extreme internal agitation and shock, usually preceded by surprise and an understanding of the danger. We try either to escape the fear or to confront it. The sympathetic nervous system reacts inside our bodies, making our hearts beat faster, releasing adrenaline and sugar into the bloodstream, and causing our bodies to shiver and sweat profusely. Intensive fear may even lead to death. During the 1991 Iraqi scud missile attacks on Israel, about one hundred people died of heart attacks, most probably caused by fear and tension.[2]

Some fears may be inherited genetically, such as atavistic fears of the dark, of spiders and snakes, and of death. Scientists hypothesize that the amygdala is the part of the brain that governs the emotion of fear. When the amygdala is damaged, we may stop being afraid.[3] But not all types of fear are inborn; most are acquired. For a specific fear to surface, its memory must be recorded in our brain. Psychologists believe that a permanent association needs to be made between the initially neutral stimulus heralding danger (conditional stimulus) and a specific aversion or pain factor (unconditional stimulus). Such associations become imprinted in our emotional memory and determine our quick defensive reactions, which recur even when only a shadow of the danger appears.[4] Thus, even a minor impulse and a minor risk translate into fear, which may grow into a lasting component of a person's life. To use an example from history, if the announcement of war is defined as a conditional stimulus and the painful experiences of war as an unconditional stimulus, in postwar Poland the mental association of these stimuli brought on the defensive reaction of panic buying. At times, a single aggressive speech by a politician that did not even mention the word *war* sufficed to trigger a run on the shops. But the size of a threat an individual or a group feels is conditioned not only by their negative experiences (both their own and others' relayed as warnings) but also by a person's character and temperament,[5] which define different responses to the same threat. In other words, people react differently.

Since a large number of people may experience a danger—for example, a contagious disease—at the same time, there is such a thing as collective fear. When an abrupt, uncontainable, and unfounded fear materializes, it becomes panic. It may sweep small and large groups, and the individuals who are panicking may be physically close or they may be dispersed.[6] A panic usually lasts fifteen to thirty minutes, sometimes an hour or longer.[7]

A definition of the "disease" of fear should also include its exceptionally high degree of contagiousness. The "infection" usually spreads down the social hierarchy[8] from those the community respects and considers to be well informed. For this reason, *Angstträger*, the carriers of fear, be they journalists, scientists, railroad employees, priests, or policemen, play a crucial role in generating fear and panic. Indeed, the contagiousness rule applies to all collective behaviors, including religious and ethnic persecutions. This book examines many such cases, but for now two should suffice as examples. In 1938, after the play *The War of the Worlds* by H. G. Wells was broadcast on the radio in the United States, a huge panic broke out. In 1946 in Paris, people panicked after hearing a radio program about an imaginary nuclear disaster. In both cases, millions were infected in under an hour.

People who are panicking typically resist rational arguments and tend to flee and to follow others. Those who have already experienced trauma and who are living in uncertain times are most likely to panic. Previous experiences of fear do not make people more resistant to panic; on the contrary, the greater the dose of fear a person received earlier, the greater their susceptibility to panic later. This rule aids in understanding the later parts of this book, where we learn that experiences of the war of 1939–45 prompted instances of panic after the war. Someone who is mentally and physically exhausted and lives through recurring threats may become indifferent to danger or succumb to depression. A similar reaction may occur after a person has already experienced fear.

When a major threat persists, states of mobilization and apathy alternate repeatedly. In Poland, public moods fluctuated for several years after the war.

Today's mass media eagerly seize on and publicize dangers, sometimes fabricating them and often using stereotypes to explain them. London School of Economics sociologist Stanley Cohen has coined the term *moral panic* to describe the public anxiety brought on by the media. Arousing and sustaining anxious tension in cases such as the bird flu or mad cow disease turns people's attention away from the real problems of the day. Political authorities may demonstrate their ability to subdue such a threat in order to legitimize themselves.[9] The invention and long life of the "Jewish Communist" stereotype in interwar Poland illustrates the phenomenon Cohen described.

Thanks to the internet and television, the postmodern "moral panic" differs from its earlier incarnations by its global reach. New epidemics of fear roll across the world again and again.[10] New types of social fear specific to industrial societies range from climate change and oil shortages to terrorism. Security agencies announce alerts—red, orange, yellow—that become the colors of our fears. In *Risk Society*, an apt diagnosis of contemporary life, Ulrich Beck notes new threats: accidents in nuclear power plants, the poisoning of food supplies, global warming, and financial crises.[11] The spirit of our era emanates anxieties, fears, and phobias according to the principle "tell me what you're afraid of and I'll tell you what era you live in (and vice versa)." Fear reflects the intricate tissue of human relations, value systems, beliefs, and levels of civilizational development. People have been frightened of various phenomena according to where and when they lived. But this does not mean that today they are more fearful than they were in the past or that fear is a feature of the early twenty-first century. The sociologist Kenneth Thompson believes that panic has become a feature of the modern world.[12] This is not the place to challenge his thesis; suffice it to say that his statement reveals an ignorance of history.

In the past, a rumor was the most effective carrier of the fear virus, and no proper panic started without one.

Hearsay may become the emanation of fear—as Klaus Thiele-Dohrmann calls it, a release valve for human fears and aggressions.[13] Rumors may take on the form of irrational joy and mad hope but usually augur misfortune and thrive in a climate of despair and disaster. It was no coincidence that shortly after the Japanese attack on Pearl Harbor, fear rumors swept the United States, and until the end of 1942 they comprised one-quarter of all the rumors.[14] This corroborates Jean Delumeau's observation that "a rumor is born on top of an existing layer of accumulated anxieties and is the result of mental conditioning stemming from the confluence of various threats or misfortunes whose effects build up."[15] Thus, spreading a rumor also spreads fear.

Anxiety is commonly considered a more general, sublimated emotional state than fear. The danger is only vaguely defined, and mental mechanisms produce or exaggerate it. While fear is invariably linked to concrete objects or events and is proportional to the threat, anxiety is exacerbated out of proportion, born in the imagination of emotions. It is hidden and unconscious. It makes us feel uncertain and powerless. It is accompanied by waiting for an uncertain future.[16] Hence, it often materializes together with a sense of impermanence. When society faces a threat, anxiety is less intensive than fear, although it usually lasts longer, and its persistence can be lethal. Adrenaline emitted continually in small doses can damage the heart slightly, increasing the risk of coronary disease.[17] Karen Horney explains the difference between fear and anxiety thus: "When a mother is afraid that her child will die when it has only a pimple or a slight cold we speak of anxiety; but if she is afraid when the child has a serious illness we call her reaction fear. If someone is afraid whenever he stands on a height or when he has to discuss a topic he knows well, we call his reaction anxiety; if someone is afraid when he loses his way high up in the mountains during a heavy thunderstorm we would speak of fear."[18] To borrow Antoni Kępiński's idea, with fear a person knows what is threatening him (objective anxiety) while with anxiety he does not know what he is afraid of (subjective anxiety).[19]

Despite these distinctions, anxiety and fear are so closely related that they are often used interchangeably. In real life, it is frequently difficult to know where fear ends and anxiety begins. It happens that the former is imperceptibly transformed into the latter. For instance, the emotion stemming from food shortages in preharvest is fear, which manifests itself in an instinctive hoarding of food at times of plenty, an expression of anxiety.

With all this in mind, how do we define terror? We generally see it as a state of intensified fear and hence tend to treat terror and fear as synonymous. However, with its vagueness and uncertainty, terror can also resemble anxiety. Psychologists have little interest in it. The invaluable Jean Delumeau wrote, "Fear has a well-defined object one can face. Anxiety hasn't one and one experiences it as a painful anticipation of danger, which is all the more terrifying that it hasn't been clearly identified, creating a total feeling of insecurity. Thus, it is more unbearable than fear."[20] Yet terror and fear are not the same. Individual and subjective, anxiety is difficult to experience collectively. Even though psychologists distinguish between different types of social anxiety, they have in mind an individual's unwitting unease with, for instance, public speaking[21] and not the anxiety of a group experiencing it at the same time and in the same place. Terror has therefore become synonymous with collective anxiety.

Anxiety, fear, and terror are considered negative emotions. They are associated with unpleasantness that can be at times painful and troubling. But they can also play a positive role. Fear is like the red light and the alarm signal that put a ship's crew on alert in times of danger. Then again, fear is also a looming hurricane, iceberg, or reef: danger lurks there. The red light—that is, fear—makes the individual or the group react by either rising to the challenge or fleeing it. If we did not experience fear, we would not feel the need to practice self-defense, and our species would perish.

Some philosophers believe that fear is an expression of an ancient *conditio humana*—"the more anxiety, the more sensuousness," wrote Søren Kierkegaard in *The Concept of Anxiety*. Anxiety is an indispensable component of human life, as it is crucial to our emotional and moral development.[22] We associate its absence with

Peter Pan, delusion, and immaturity. From a dialectical point of view, happiness loses its flavor and its value without a touch of fear.[23]

For a long time, sociologists did not keep track of fear's positive functions. Despite the fact that one bibliography of works about the sociology of emotions is over two hundred pages long,[24] there is little in it about the role of fear in the lives of societies. The sociologist Vladimir Shlapentokh comments on this gap in *Fear in Contemporary Society*: "My experiences in the USSR familiarized me with the complex nature of social fear. First, I saw how fear can demoralize people, how it can degrade even the finest human beings and the closest human relations."[25] Shlapentokh calls this kind of fear generated by totalitarian states "centralized" while democratic societies suffer from numerous "decentralized" fears: of unemployment, discrimination (racial, ethnic, religious, or gender), bankruptcy and not being able to afford health care or an education, and, of course, crime.

Drawing on his own experience, Shlapentokh argues that fear is a pillar of the social order. But the history of sociology lacks any such affirmation of fear's positive role. Talcott Parsons's revolutionary 1937 book *The Structure of Social Action* contends that in the dominant paradigm the social order is rooted in the internalization of values and norms in childhood and subsequent stages of socialization. The belief that *The Social Construction of Reality* (to borrow the title of the classic work by Peter Berger and Thomas Luckmann) takes place as society creates and agrees on meanings is now firmly entrenched in sociology and social psychology textbooks. According to Shlapentokh, the role of the state, with its structural controls and the fear it instills in the population, has been underestimated while the role of internalized positive values in sustaining the social order has been overestimated. Indeed, many people internalize negative attitudes and behaviors such as alcoholism, drug addiction, violence, xenophobia, corruption, and anti-intellectualism. Their role comes into the open when people discover that they are outside the control of, for instance, state institutions.[26] Of course, the presence of external controls and the fear of them do not rid societies of these behaviors, but they prevent the behaviors from taking over. The disintegration of the social and institutional order brought on by a catastrophe, usually a war, liberates instincts of impunity and augments chaos and anarchy. In such a case, the conditions are perfect for antisocial behaviors such as crime, unrest, and lynching to multiply and for social relations, including actions aimed against religious and ethnic minorities, to become more violent. One of this book's theses holds that the demoralization triggered by the war and the turmoil of the first postwar months and years lay at the roots of pathological behaviors in Poland. Thus, the limited but real fear of the socially legitimate state may have positive effects.

There are other examples of the beneficial role of fear. As a mobilizing force, only the drive for success matches fear. Rulers in all kinds of political systems have used and abused fear. As Napoleon reportedly said, "There are only two forces that unite men: fear and interest." In political races, a negative campaign that demonizes opponents and sows fear of them among voters becomes just as valuable as a candidate's own program. The slogans used by various types of social campaigns—for example, anti-smoking—intend to frighten. In the family, fear and anxiety have always helped to hold up the patriarch's dominance. The fears of loneliness and divorce serve as an important glue in relationships. Conformity goes hand in hand with fear. Doctors employ fear to push patients to agree to treatments they recommend.[27]

In everyday life, fear has a bad reputation, but it is sometimes necessary. Some people actually seek it out and derive excitement, an adrenaline rush, from overcoming it. Postmodern culture satisfies the thirst for fear with films, computer games, and extreme sports. But it is difficult to define just how much fear is acceptable, since an overdose becomes pathological, securing blind obedience, a lack of scruples, and failed moral brakes.

Persistent fear is a sort of illness. Simone Weil wrote:

> Security is an essential need of the soul. Security means that the soul is not under the weight of fear or terror, except as the result of an accidental

conjunction of circumstances and for brief and exceptional periods. Fear and terror, as permanent states of the soul, are wellnigh mortal poisons, whether they be caused by the threat of unemployment, police persecution, the presence of a foreign conqueror, the probability of invasion, or any other calamity which seems too much for human strength to bear.... Even if permanent fear constitutes a latent state only, so that its painful effects are only rarely experienced directly, it remains always a disease. It is a semi-paralysis of the soul.[28]

But these are not all the charges that must be pressed against fear.

In a key psychological concept, fear is a source of aggression. Some scholars follow in the footsteps of Sigmund Freud and Konrad Lorenz to underscore the biological conditioning of aggressive behaviors and the aggression instinct, which have been formed in the course of evolution. Another school of psychology stresses the psychosocial aspects of the mechanisms that formed them. Thus, Rowell L. Huesmann's *Aggressive Behavior: Current Perspectives* focuses on the learning process as the foundation of antisocial and aggressive behaviors. Increased aggression in the wake of the Second World War, including violence against ethnic minorities, is a case in point. Yet another concept accepted by psychologists is aggression as a way to overcome the anxiety and fear brought on by a threat. Antoni Kępiński has promoted the thesis that anxiety and anger are inseparable. They can make people flee, but when there is nowhere to flee, when the only option is aggression against oneself or against others, fear may generate behaviors aimed at reducing the perceived threat to oneself. If this fear is sufficiently powerful, aggression is either transferred or transformed. Transferring aggression is redirecting it onto another object, which will entail a lesser penalty. Similarly, transforming the nature of aggression consists of replacing it with another aggressive action that will bring a lesser punishment.[29]

Fear produces aversion, hostility, hatred, and prejudice. We dislike, indeed despise, the person who makes us fearful. Where there is no fear there is no hatred; there can be only indifference and disrespect or contempt.[30] The outcomes of some recent experiments in social psychology trace a direct link between racism and our anxiety over coming in contact with "the Other." This anxiety may also be biologically conditioned.[31]

Fear has played both direct and indirect roles at the origins of many ethnic conflicts. The most obvious direct role is an ethnic group's fear of another ethnic group. Thus, the ancient Romans feared the barbarians, in early modern times the Europeans feared the Turks, in the First World War the French feared the Germans, and so on. Just like the Catholic and Protestant propagandists in the wars of religion, twentieth-century Nazis and Stalinists promoted fear in order to mobilize people to hate. Under fear's influence, our thoughts and actions lead us to eliminate the adversary, and the group that presents the greatest threat becomes the target of ethnic violence.

Yet acts of violence aimed at ethnic and religious minorities—such as the Night of Saint Bartholomew in 1572 or the pogroms in Jedwabne and Radziłów in 1941 or Kielce in 1946—are difficult to explain with a real and direct danger. The causes of the 1941 pogroms included a yearning for revenge, ingrained anti-Semitism, and anticipation of the wishes of the feared Germans but not a threat coming from the Jews themselves, who became the victims of the pogroms. In situations of this kind, when the minority does not present a threat, fear acts indirectly. When unrest is brought on by a disaster (famine, war, economic crisis, unemployment, revolution), magical thinking grows, exaggerating the causality of irrelevant factors. These blown-up delusions further increase anxiety, which in a vicious cycle further amplifies the alleged threat.[32] "Fear has big eyes," says the proverb. In times of war, famine, or even financial crisis, the whole world becomes mysterious and threatening, and demons come alive. Jan Mitarski writes, "Anxiety, especially long-lasting anxiety, may lead to regression, a return to primal behaviors, intensifying man's latent attraction to archaic, magical thinking."[33] This is when legends thrive, telling us that "the Others" are responsible for the catastrophe. It is no coincidence that research reveals a growing hostility toward foreigners during the financial crisis of 2008.[34] The amplified sense of threat brought on by the attacks of September 11, 2001, gave birth to a new American nationalism.[35] After the April 10, 2010, airplane crash at Smolensk, which killed Poland's president and a host of others, the wave of patriotic elation included contentions that Moscow's agents were to blame.

People living under constant threat feel hemmed in, uncertain, and often frustrated. Since they usually do not understand the complex reasons behind their situation, they seek someone to blame, a scapegoat to allow them to chase away the evil forces or just to "do something" when it seems that nothing can be done. Sometimes they want to release their pent-up aggression by transferring it onto "the Others." The violence directed at Belorussians and Jews in postwar Poland can be explained partly by the state of terror and transferal, since neither minority actually presented a threat to the Polish majority. There are numerous similar cases in history; one of the most spectacular is the expulsion of the Jews from fifteenth-century Spain, which was staged during a prolonged recession. Fernand Braudel drew up a correlation between shifts in economic and demographic conditions on the one hand and oppression, pogroms, population expulsions, and forced conversions, which add up to the history of the persecution of the Jews, on the other.[36] The Vienna stock market crash of May 1873, which launched a lengthy crisis, proved an important catalyst for a period of anti-Semitism in the Habsburg monarchy. Pioneer of prejudice research Gordon W. Allport draws on other scholars' work to point to similar causal relationships between the economic deterioration of the cotton industry in the American South and a surge of lynchings of Blacks.[37] Changes stemming from the processes of modernization and transformation gave rise to anxiety when the familiar world was being cast aside for a nebulous future. The rise of nationalism played this role in the nineteenth century, and Ernest Gellner argued that it eased the birth pangs of modernity.[38] The growing alienation between ethnic groups, which was produced by anxiety, was also due to accelerated demographic changes, urbanization, and the rapid inflow of immigrants. The immigration of Lithuanian Jews into the Kingdom of Poland at the turn of the nineteenth and twentieth centuries coincided with the birth of Poland's modern anti-Semitism. Similarly, in the spring of 1946, the return of Polish Jews from Russia to a ravaged Poland may have been a factor behind Polish anxieties. Today, many analogous examples of anti-immigrant reactions combine with majorities' apprehensions about joblessness, the arrivals' cultural otherness, and being overwhelmed by flooding by a "foreign element." The planned wall on the US–Mexican border best symbolizes this fear.

But not everything can be explained with the fear reflex, which is a typical consequence of a crisis of state and society. The causes of religious and ethnic persecution are many, and collective anxiety may not always be the dominant one. Psychological factors may be more decisive in these types of behaviors. Intolerance of minorities may also emerge in periods of relative stability. Marie-Françoise Baslez, who studies persecutions in antiquity, notes that explosions of anti-Christian violence were not closely synchronized with invasions, civil wars, or other disasters.[39] Roger D. Petersen's studies shed a new light on the mechanisms that govern ethnic violence and discrimination, emotions relevant to this book. Petersen names four culprits—fear, hatred, resentment, and rage—and asks which of them made the greatest contribution to the twentieth century's ethnic conflicts in Central and Southern Europe. He chooses resentment but uses fear to explain the motivations behind only some forms of ethnic violence.[40] Undoubtedly, there is also the cultural explanation based on existing religious antagonisms, deep-rooted stereotypes and ideologies, resentments, and prejudices, which in times of terror and anxiety grow like muscles on steroids.

Most often, the terror category is used to describe collective behaviors such as pogroms, witch hunts, and peasant riots. The story of terror appears to stop in the nineteenth century. Or at least historians of the modern era do not mention it, likely believing that it belonged in the premodern era, and they tend to devote themselves to studying the concept of the Great Fear. The Polish historian Andrzej Wyrobisz used this term recently in his analysis of homophobia in fifteenth-century Venice and Florence.[41] Some also see it in a more recent Great Fear: the second half of the 1930s in the Soviet Union and the Soviet occupation of the Polish Eastern Borderlands in 1939–41. English-language literature uses the term *Great Fear* for the prerevolutionary mood in France and some later situations. In contemporary US history, it appears in at least two contexts, to describe American society's racial prejudice and,[42] more often, the growing belief in a Soviet threat in the late 1940s–early 1950s. Senator Joseph McCarthy made a career out of it, steering Americans' anxieties and apprehensions into an anti-Communist near-hysteria.[43]

Determining the differences between a Great Fear and a Great Terror is a difficult, perhaps even unattainable task. One reason is that we are actually dealing with metaphors, which are often enclosed in quotation marks, suggesting haziness and imprecision. Another obstacle is that the two are so closely related that they are almost synonymous. But as they must be differentiated for the sake of clarity, we must remember that their outlines are imprecise and their definitions generalized.

To this author, a Great Fear is a social situation dominated by a single powerful, tangible, paralyzing fear, which usually ruptures social ties. The Russian sociologist Pitirim Sorokin notes that in situations of this kind, people focus all their cognitive processes on the threat (be it famine or terror) and become increasingly insensitive to everything outside it. Flight, rather than fight, is the dominant reaction, accompanied by progressive social atomization. A Great Fear does not lead to chaos and a disintegration of state structures. On the contrary, in times like this the government draws power from the atmosphere of fear and often exploits it or even contributes to it. Hence, this concept would be most appropriate to describe human emotions in times of persecution, dictatorship, intensified repression, and terror, such as the Great Purge in the USSR, the Cultural Revolution in China, and the occupations of Poland during the Second World War; it appears in at least partly modernized and urbanized societies rather than peasant ones.

A Great Terror, on the other hand, can be defined as a unique, collective, fear-induced stress that manifests itself in mass unrest, disruptions, turmoil, or panic. It is not individuals who are paralyzed by fear but a whole populace. Its leaders are usually amorphous and impermanent and the authorities weak or not interested in restoring order. The most likely moment for terror to explode comes after the abrupt breakdown of the existing social order, usually brought on by a disaster such as a famine, epidemic, war, or revolution. It is an instant of suspension, disintegration, interregnum, and uncertainty about what the future will bring. The weakening of the political center makes institutional barriers snap, which means to some joyous impunity and to others increased anxiety. Terror is related to anxiety. It is associated with an atmosphere of uncertainty, often nondescript and elusive fears, and rumors—setting it apart from fear, which always has a precise source. Even though concrete fears may produce an atmosphere of terror, terror is something more than the sum of individual fears. It is a social fact that manifests itself as rumors, panic, pogroms, and lynching, or hunger strikes. The Great Terror also differs from the Great Fear in that it is ambiguous. Jean Delumeau wrote:

> Like fear, terror is ambivalent. It is the presentiment of something strange and an expectation of something new, a giddiness of nothingness and hope for abundance. It is fear and longing.... On the psychological level, terror, a phenomenon that is natural to man, an engine of his evolution, is positive when it can anticipate dangers, which, even when they are still imprecise, remain real. It stimulates a person to mobilize. But a terror that lasts too long may also create a state of disorientation and inadaptability, an emotional blindness, a dangerous explosion of the imagination, it may release a backward mechanism by introducing an interior climate of insecurity. It is especially dangerous when it becomes a guilty terror because the subject turns forces that should be mobilized against external aggression on himself and becomes the focal object of his own fears.[44]

It is probably only because of established research traditions that the concept of the Great Terror is more applicable to the behaviors of peasant societies than of modern ones. In Polish history, the Galician Slaughter of 1846 was a terror, as were the anti-Jewish pogroms that engulfed northern Mazovia and the Białystoks region in June and July 1941. To English-language readers, the term *Great Terror* is immediately associated with Robert Conquest's book about Stalin's purges of the 1930s. Evidently, the terror that reigned in the Soviet Union at the time surpassed in scale anything else that happened in the terrible twentieth century. And yet, the popular frame of mind during other periods in modern history, including Poland in 1944–47, makes this term equally appropriate.

In 1944–47, chaos ruled some parts of Poland after the Germans fled. State institutions were slowly beginning to operate but, lacking social capital, long remained weak. Large groups of people persisted in a state of postwar anomie, governed by a feeling of impermanence and suspension. The Poles had great hopes for starting a new life without war, but they also experienced anguish and uncertainty about their future. Real dangers, such as hunger, the Red Army, the secret police, and banditry, interfered with their happiness that the occupation had ended. Anxiety and fear led to not only spatial but also vertical migrations as the social structure was transformed. Accruing fears pushed individuals to stage protests and hunger strikes. Some found a balm for insecurity by joining crews of bandits and plunderers. The situation of terror brought out demons, circulated prophecies and apocalyptic gossip, and spread rumors about ritual murder. Aggression against the "Soviets" (the NKVD, Red Army, or Office of Public Security) was redirected onto the Jews. Everyone was trapped in the labyrinth of fear now.

NOTES

1. See, among others, Ramachandran, *Encyclopedia of Human Behavior*; Klichowski, *Lęk, strach, panika*; Reber, *Słownik psychologii*; Kazdin, *Encyclopedia of Psychology*; Siuta, *Słownik psychologii*.
2. Cowley, "Our Bodies, Our Fears."
3. Kossobudzka, "Straszne życie bez strachu."
4. Werka and Zagrodzka, "Strach i lęk w świetle badań neurobiologicznych," 20.
5. Strelau, "Miejsce lęku i zbliżonych konstruktów w badaniach nad temperamentem," 211–30.
6. Smelser, *Theory of Collective Behavior*.
7. "Panic Disorder," *New York Times Health Guide*.
8. Kępiński, *Lęk*, 303.
9. Cohen, *Folk Devils and Moral Panics*; Ungar, "Moral Panic versus the Risk Society."
10. Cf. Zarembina, "Strach się bać"; Gibbs, "Shadow of Fear"; Maćkowiak, "Panika w mieście?"; Walewski, "Epidemia strachu."
11. Beck, *Risk Society*.
12. Thompson, *Moral Panics*, 3.
13. Thiele-Dohrmann, *Unter dem Siegel der Verschwiegenheit*.
14. Allport and Postman, *Psychology of Rumor*, 3, 13.
15. Delumeau, *La peur en Occident XIVe–XVIIe siècles*, 174.
16. Kępiński, *Lęk*, 14.
17. Żuradzki, "Strach się bać."
18. Horney, *The Neurotic Personality of Our Time*, 41.
19. Kępiński, *Lęk*, 247–49.
20. Delumeau, *La peur*, 15.
21. Leary and Kowalski, *Social Anxiety*.
22. Kierkegaard, *The Concept of Anxiety*, 89.
23. For a praise of anxiety, see Bielik-Robson, "Horror, Horror!," 19–29.
24. Jasińska-Kania, "Socjologiczne odkrywanie emocji," 44.
25. Shlapentokh, *Fear in Contemporary Society*, 2.
26. Shlapentokh, *Fear*, 7, 85, et al.
27. For an elaboration, see Pratkanis and Aronson, *Age of Propaganda*, chapter 24, "The Fear Appeal."
28. Weil, *Simone Weil*, 114.
29. Frączek and Zumkley, *Socialization and Aggression*; Pietrzak, *Agresja indywidualna i zbiorowa w sytuacji napięć i konfliktów społecznych*; Zagrodzka and Kowaleczko-Szumowska, *Psychospołeczne i neurobiologiczne aspekty agresji*; Kacprzak, *Przemoc i agresja a oddziaływania społeczno-wychowawcze*.
30. Klichowski, *Lęk, strach, panika*, 20.
31. "Rasizm to zwykły lęk przed obcym?" *Gazeta Wyborcza*.
32. Kępiński, *Lęk*, 223.
33. Mitarski, "Demonologia lęku," in Kępiński, *Lęk*, 335.
34. "Czas niepewności," interview with Ulrich Beck, *Forum*.
35. See, for example, Neier, "America's New Nationalism."
36. Braudel, *The Mediterranean and the Mediterranean World*, 820.
37. Allport, *The Nature of Prejudice*, 218–19.
38. Gellner, *Nations and Nationalism*.
39. Baslez, *Les persécutions dans l'Antiquité*.
40. While I agree with Petersen about the importance of emotions in interethnic conflicts, I am at least skeptical about his emphatic rejection of fear in such explanations. In some situations, fear plays a crucial role, while in others it is anxiety, which

Petersen ignores altogether. Thus, according to his theory, the passing of the German–Soviet front in June 1941 evoked no stronger emotions in people than crossing a street, and it was absent in the anti-Semitic pogroms in Lithuania, Ukraine, and Poland. Petersen, *Understanding Ethnic Violence*.

41. Wyrobisz, "'Wielki strach' w Wenecji i we Florencji w XV wieku i jego możliwe przyczyny."
42. Nash, *The Great Fear*.
43. Caute, *The Great Fear*; Stein, *The Great Red Scare*.
44. Delumeau, *La peur*, 16.

2

FEAR IN INTERWAR CULTURE

THE BOLSHEVIKS AND "JEWISH COMMUNISM"

"We believed in the Masons, we believed in the Jews. . . .
And now we believe in Them. Any faith whatsoever will do."
    Stanisław Ignacy Witkiewicz, *Them*, 1920

"Despite the late hour, the prison was alive. Its repulsive, violent sounds actually drowned out the thuds of the horrific harvest of death the Communist oppressors were meting out so generously. Ardent pleas and laments could be heard escaping heavenward out of the tiny windows, some begging to live, others calling for help and redemption for the exhausted Motherland. These sighs, moans and prayers blended with the soldiers' brutal profanities and barks and, together with the echoes of gunshots coming from the courtyard and the town, made for hell itself, terror-filled and petrifying."

These words may seem like a depiction of a Polish Security Service prison in 1945. In fact, it comes from a 1927 prophetic novel by Edmund Jezierski, *A gdy komunizm zapanuje* (When Communism takes over).[1] The novel was one of the countless manifestations of the Poles' fear of Communism, which they tended to portray as an absolute evil. In the public imagination of the interwar years, Bolshevism became a prominent antihero. It was the subject of research studies (some of them very sound),[2] reportages, newspaper articles, and novels. The historian Paweł Jasienica argued many years later that someone should write a history of fear, adding that in the interwar period the Poles had experienced several stages of it.[3] What were these stages? The first one had to do with the Polish–Bolshevik War. The second one exploded during the Great Depression. The third one had several causes, which included the radicalization of rightist anti-Semitic political views in the second half of the 1930s and news about the Moscow show trials. The fourth stage stemmed from the growing war scare, which had been growing since the outbreak of the Spanish Civil War. Polish catastrophism thrived in them all.

Eric Hobsbawm called the twentieth century the age of extremes,[4] and it would be difficult to disagree with him. While one of the century's faces could boast progressive inventions such as antibiotics, universal social insurance, and artificial fertilizers, the other face wore a grimace twisted in horror. Soldiers at Verdun and the Somme committed suicide out of fear. In the wake of the First World War, masses of people were haunted by the specter of death by poison gas in unimaginable torments. The command "masks on!" could be heard during exercises all over Europe. Workers in the Ruhr Valley, Warsaw, and Chicago lived in fear for the duration of the Great Depression. Germany's Drang nach Osten made the Poles extremely apprehensive, especially at the beginning and end of the interwar period. Only the Bolsheviks terrified people more, and side curls were added to depictions of them so as to confirm that they came from hell. After the Second World War, the fear of the Bolsheviks and of "Jewish Communism" would continue to influence people, serving as the emotional backdrop to events.

THE BOLSHEVIK HELL

The salvos from the *Aurora* that launched the October Revolution did not kick off the Poles' fear of the Bolsheviks. It evolved instead from an earlier stereotype of Russia as Asia: barbaric, savage, and foreign. The origins of this thinking date to *Letters from Russia* by the Marquis de Custine,[5] which is only one of the meanders of a much longer story. According to Andrzej Kępiński, a scholar of the Polish stereotype of the Muscovite, the outlines of the Poles' negative image of Russia and the Russians emerged in the second half of the sixteenth century. Sustained by subsequent literary generations, this image reached the pinnacle of artistic expression in the works of the Romantics.[6] Henryk Sienkiewicz's novel *Ogniem i mieczem* (*With Fire and Sword*), whose influence on the Poles' worldview has been colossal, compiles ready-made clichés about the "eastern savages."

This stereotype acquired a new dynamic and modern, proto-scientific features in the late nineteenth century from the first theoreticians of racism, including Arthur de Gobineau, and the fad of using the natural sciences to explain the lives of societies. Their racial theories are built on three theses. First, humans can be divided into races that are characterized by their anthropological features and—even more importantly—the resultant cultural characteristics. Second, no matter how intensively a lower race (i.e., the black or the yellow) is subjected to the civilizing process, the stains (today we would call them genes) of barbarism, savagery, and primitivism cannot be purged. Third, mixing races leads to the deterioration of each one's features.[7]

The racial theories' directness and pseudoscientific aura helped to fix them in the language used to describe reality. *Dżingis-Chan zmartwychwstały: Studia z psychopatologii rosyjskiej* (Genghis Khan resurrected: Studies in Russian psychopathology) by the Slavicist Stanisław Zdziarski, begun in 1907 and published in 1919, is a good example of a text that uses this theory.[8]

"How do you say to sort a person out in Russian? It means to slug him in the mug so hard that he sees all the stars, to knock out his teeth, to split his guts the way the Russians do it. The Russians are governed by bloodthirsty instincts inherited from their ancestors who once roamed the steppes." And, "What is morality for a 'pure-bred' Russian? 'Morality,' he will answer, 'is when our wives and daughters give themselves to others in exchange for bling and riches.'" It was no accident that "pure-bred" was put in quotation marks since Russian veins also carried the blood of Turks, Tatars, and Finns. We will find "irrefutable evidence" in anthropometric measurements as well as in the economic situation, language, folk beliefs, and the absolutist form of government: "They are all undeniably of Asian origin *par excellence*."[9]

According to Zdziarski, Bolshevism emanates Russia's past; it is the specter of Genghis Khan born of "degenerated blood," disintegrating in the "organism that is still alive," a horrific monster governed by a destructive impulse. Its animal instincts fuse with demonic elements. But perhaps this combination of animalistic features, "bloodthirsty instincts," "beastly urges," and metaphors of hell is nothing new, as it goes back to medieval depictions of the devil. Zdziarski's message was clear: we must fear the Bolsheviks because they are not human, and definitely not human like us. But this was not all: the Jews, "many of them freshly baptized," were to blame for the Bolshevik hurricane.[10]

At the turn of the nineteenth and twentieth centuries, racial theories of this kind were all the rage across the globe. During the First World War, competing nationalisms stepped up their production.

In 1917, the French psychologist Dr. Edgar Bérillon "discovered" that the Germans' intestines were nine feet longer than other humans', which made them more susceptible to polychesia (excessive defecation) and bromidrosis (foul-smelling perspiration). In 1915, William Simmons, an itinerant preacher from the US state of Georgia, founded the Ku Klux Klan. What all these views had in common was (and remains) the linking of two abstractions: a group of "Others" with a threat to society. According to Gavin I. Langmuir, a scholar of anti-Semitism, "a xenophobic assertion affirms the existence of a social peril that can be connected with the existence of the outgroup because some of its members have in fact been involved in the events considered threatening."[11] In other words, Zdziarski's beliefs say more about the Poles' fears of the Russians and the Bolsheviks than about the Russians and the Bolsheviks themselves.[12]

Later in the interwar period, many publications featured sets of analogous attributes associated with the image of the "Bolshevik," the "Communist." (More about this later.) It is noteworthy that fear of the "reds," fed by reports coming from a Russia embroiled in a civil war, spread easily and flourished because it was supported by a very real threat. This fear peaked during the Polish–Bolshevik War of 1919–20.

At first, the universal nervousness was vague. But as the armed conflict between Poland and the Soviet Union escalated and Poles fleeing westward brought with them frightening stories about rape, murder, and slaughter, the collective anxiety took on the tangible characteristics of fear. Little is known about the differences in how various social groups experienced it, but most likely the fear spread from the privileged elites, who feared the proletarian revolution the most, down the social ladder to its bottom rungs, the peasants and workers, some of whom voiced hopes that it might lead to an improvement in their situation. Russia was on everyone's lips. As it came to dominate the front pages of Polish newspapers, public hysteria grew. In 1919, the writer Jan Parandowski, organizing his notes taken during the few years he had spent in Russia, wrote about the "Bolshevik specter circling over Poland":

> We can see it everywhere, in ourselves, in our neighbors near and far. This specter haunts us day and night, peering out from behind all national, political and social questions. We paste the Bolshevik label on extremist views, radical takes on common issues, everything down to the lowliest criminal act. This is the worst possible state of affairs. People fear the unknown the most, since behind the unknown lurks something that is mysterious, and therefore alluring. Let's tear the curtain off this unfamiliar deity and maybe, just as in Egyptian sanctuaries, nothing but wild beasts will emerge from behind it.[13]

The overwhelming feeling that the end of the world was near overcame the religiously orthodox communities in the Polish countryside. In 1919, the writer Paweł Jasienica stopped in the city of Białystok on his way back from Russia. There, a villager asked him, her voice tinged with fear, "Will those Bolsheviks be passing through Poland?"[14]

Reports from the front brought stories of supreme bravery but also of nervous breakdowns and terror.[15] Soldiers wearing the characteristic Soviet pointed caps evoked terror not only because they were difficult, victorious adversaries. The atmosphere of growing threat intensified as news about these soldiers' ruthlessness arrived and was passed from person to person, sometimes exaggerated. Adam Bień, who would later be sentenced in the Trial of the Sixteen, wrote in a letter on July 14, 1920: "We, secondary-school pupils, have been assigned to the Machine Gun Company, and in two weeks we will most likely be going to the front. . . . There is no point in getting captured because, they say, the Bolsheviks kill volunteers."[16]

Semyon Budyonny's First Cavalry Army exceeded all standards of ruthlessness. Its men executed both officers and privates who did not follow orders. They murdered prisoners of war and civilians with relish; burned down hospitals with their patients and staff inside; leveled entire towns and villages; plundered churches, palaces, and manor houses; and raped women. Melchior Wańkowicz, a young writer, described the horrors: "This vague 'something' . . . an ordinary Bolshevik counteroffensive, gradually gels in the soldiers' minds until all of a sudden one day a single word trickles out of all their mouths: 'Budyonny!' A terrifying warlord emerges from the Savage Steppe and moves down to the Dnieper River at the head of his hordes. Denikin's vanquisher, fast as lightning, chief of the swift and savage bareback riders, rolls his tested regiments from Taganrog, and with every step his ranks grow, and with every viorst he draws more men, more horse herds."[17]

Fear can paralyze defenders. In this war, it became as effective a weapon as the *tachanki*, the horse-drawn machine-gun platforms that Budyonny introduced into battle. The Polish side understood this. The governor of Lublin Province, Stanisław Moskalewski, attributed the enemy's successes to the huge numbers of his "wild hordes, spreading panic and terror."[18] Indeed, during the Russian offensive, the Polish troops panicked and repeatedly yielded the field, the numbers of deserters growing. This happened during the fierce fighting on the Niemen River when some units of the Eleventh Infantry Division abandoned their positions in a panic and left behind their heavy weaponry. In August 1920, during the dramatic fighting at Radzymin (where the Russians were eventually stopped), officers of the Forty-Sixth Regiment used threats and pistols to compel their men to remain at their positions—often in vain. Even a gendarme platoon sent out to capture deserters fled. One of its commanders, Major Matczyński, grabbed a dead man's gun, confronted a column of soldiers, and cried, "Boys, are you afraid of the Bolsheviks? Onward!"[19] But some of the officers also surrendered to the psychosis of fear. Many of the highest ranked of them would tear off their insignia, knowing that the Bolsheviks habitually executed the officers they captured.[20] Budyonny's army produced panic even deep behind the Polish frontlines. Sometimes all it took for a marching column to panic and break was the cry "Cossacks!" Hence, the refrain of a popular *Żurawiejka* cavalry song—"Lances at the ready, hands on the sabres! Go after the Bolsheviks, go, go, go!"—was a sublimated tool for fighting fear.

Collective fear, which is what this was, can lead to irregular acts that often result from an inaccurate assessment of reality, even suicide. The year 1920 saw a mass flight syndrome. The roads were crowded with panicked civilians fleeing west. As Marshal Mikhail Tukhachevsky's armies approached Warsaw, some locals, especially the wealthy, fled the city "as far away as possible," even to Zakopane in the Tatras, over 400 kilometers away.[21] But fear can also serve to fuel aggressive behaviors, mutinies, and pogroms. William W. Hagen writes about the anti-Jewish pogrom in Lvov in November 1918 as a carnival of victors, the Poles drunk on their defeat of the Ukrainians.[22] The carnival motif was absent in later pogroms, when people were most clearly reacting to terror. In April 1919, there were pogroms in Lublin and Radom. The anti-Semitic mood escalated in 1920 with the retreat of the Polish armies, and incidents of targeting Jews, mainly by men of the Poznań regiments, were many. There were stories of robberies, Jews' beards being cut off, beatings, and even killings. The chaos of war and the weakening of discipline combined with widespread poverty and frailty of the civilian administration to promote behaviors of this type. The press, chiefly the National Democratic papers, helped to build up a mood of revulsion and hatred, as did the gossip about Jews supporting the Bolsheviks, which was brought by people fleeing from the east. This sense of endangerment played a crucial role in hatching these moods. The rising fear sought a release and was at times taken out on captured troops and Jews. This was not the first time—and not the last—when acting on the call to "thrash the Jews!" was to cure fear.

As it mobilized its population to defend the country, Polish propaganda also fanned fears of the Bolsheviks.[23] Articles in the press as well as flyers and posters presented the commissars' Russia as submerged in unimaginable chaos, spiraling into violence and terror. Bolshevism allegedly transformed humans into "beasts" who were ready to conquer the world to satisfy their "animal instincts" and who could not be restrained by civilized norms. "The enemy, wild and terrifying, is murdering, stealing everything in his path, not only property and life but, worse, he also wants to soil our dignity, to despoil the honor of our mothers, wives and sisters. This gory and enraged monster wants to drown our freedom in tears and a sea of blood."[24] V. I. Lenin was described as the executioner of millions and a psychopath. Another Soviet revolutionary leader,

Leon Trotsky, who was Jewish to boot, appeared in this propaganda as an attractive antihero.

Most often the Bolshevik was discussed as an invader. His presence in the Polish lands translated into charred remains, ruins, and cemeteries. A flyer read, "He murders men and pregnant women, slaughters children, burns, robs, and he will snatch the last cow, the last breadcrumb."[25] According to Henryk Lisiak's article about defense propaganda, the Red Army soldier was universally depicted as a barbarian who differed from civilized man not only intellectually but also morphologically. "The caricature of the 'Bolshevik' staring out of posters, comics and newspaper illustrations did not always possess the classic features of the *Homo sapiens*: mental retardation clearly radiated from his face's Mongoloid features. Savagery and ruthlessness were characteristic of these eastern features."[26]

Fear of the Bolsheviks was expressed most tangibly in the stereotype present in the language of flyers, propaganda brochures, and newspaper articles. Irena Kamińska-Szmaj analyzed the language used to transmit emotions associated with this stereotype. She points out that the Bolsheviks were not depicted as individuals but as a huge and dangerous collectivity, a "horde" or an "onslaught." In these texts, the word *Bolsheviks* most often connoted cruel and ruthless enemies of all civilization, beasts inhabiting human bodies or raging savages who raped, murdered, robbed, and plundered.[27] The language of these reports also included words that evoked the tsarist regime: *terror*, *oppression*, *yoke*, and *dictatorship*. They argued that "Moscow's Bolshevism is a direct descendant of the tsarist Okhrana." Writing about the "Bolshevik hell," the plunder of churches, and the destruction and trampling of crucifixes and religious paintings, their authors wanted to terrify readers. This brings to mind the medieval and modern charges that Jews desecrated the Host. Some caricaturists endowed Trotsky with Semitic features. Maria Kamińska remembered the streets of Warsaw plastered with such posters and the fear-filled reactions of passersby: "Pasted on walls were enormous posters with a pile of skulls and a revolting, savage bandit sitting on top, a knife between his bared teeth, a Red Army cap on his disheveled head, a degenerate's face, repulsive and vicious. His features were strikingly Semitic. Intimidated, people stopped. A Jew, a Bolshevik, they would say. Some whispered cleverly, It's Trotsky."[28]

The Jewish theme was frequently woven in to explain the phenomenon of Bolshevism, as evidence of its cunning and ignoble intentions vis-à-vis Poland. Because of its importance in constructing this atmosphere of danger, the next section of this chapter is devoted to this Jewish theme.

Emphasizing that the Germans had helped the revolution triumph also reminded people that Bolshevism was foreign. A brochure argued that "the current Bolshevik government is not Russian but German, and it works exclusively for the benefit of Germany and cheats the Russian nation much like it cheats Russia's natural allies solely in the interest of the imperial German government."[29]

Such publications did admit that apart from the Russians, Jews, and Germans there were also Poles in the Communist movement (Feliks Dzierżyński), but because the presence of "our" people could spoil the picture, their role was marginalized. These texts emphasized the Bolsheviks' racial foreignness by pointing to the allegedly numerous Chinese "mercenaries" in their ranks and compared the Bolshevik threat to past Mongolian and Tatar invasions. The image of social terror that emerges from the literature of 1919–20 resembles emotional states that today would be called a moral panic, comparable to the mood in Europe at moments when it was threatened by Tatars or Turks.

Research in church archives and the religious press would likely clarify the role played by the Catholic Church in the explosion of fear of the Bolsheviks. There is no question that the church contributed to the anti-Communist propaganda, most often by accusing the Bolsheviks of behaving immorally and disseminating atheistic propaganda. Father Antoni Szymański, professor and later rector of the Catholic University of Lublin, wrote that "Bolshevism has also declared war on Christian morality in the areas of respect for others' property, raising children, the family, authority and fairness in relations between people. Soviet decrees that forcibly socialized women were the pinnacle of violating this morality."[30]

The Bolshevik revolution's anti-Christian nature was underscored insistently and continually. Its victorious march across Poland would wipe out all of Christian Europe. The propagandists therefore called on people to resist this evil collectively as a nation all the more so because Poland was considered the rampart of Christianity.[31]

State propaganda, party publications, and the Catholic Church instrumentalized the terror, presenting a case of successful modern "fear management."[32] But the spiral of fear unleashed then did not stop. The war of 1920 was a founding war that affirmed the ties between Polish society and the state being reborn and shaped the national consciousness, but it also planted fear of the "plague from the East." This fear was repeated and reinforced, and until the Great Depression and the anxieties that accompanied it no other fear would match it. The role of the emotions attached to it was so colossal as to make it a distinct current in the culture of the interwar years: the culture of fear. This is such an enormous topic that it cannot fit into a single chapter, and hence three examples of literature must suffice, one each from the top, middle, and bottom categories.

The highbrow book was, of course, *Przedwiośnie* (*The Coming Spring*) by Stefan Żeromski, a novel that all eighteen-year-olds sitting for the end-of-school examination were expected to be familiar with. What did its readers retain? Was it the chaos of the revolution, the "new class" appropriating houses and flats, the stench of decomposing corpses being transported on a cemetery cart by the protagonist? Or was it the lofty slogans about social justice and the momentum of revolutionary reconstruction? Żeromski gave no easy answers.

The middlebrow example was *Pożoga* (Conflagration), Zofia Kossak-Szczucka's 1922 autobiographical novel, which lacks Żeromski's ambivalence. For our purposes, it is a canonical work.[33] It picks up many of the author's earlier theses and motifs, for which she found a new form of expression, which made the book's message all the more powerful.

The novel, whose subtitle is "our historical mission in the East," takes place in the Eastern Borderlands, which early on in the book resemble scenes from English and German colonial novels. The author transports her readers to a lost Eden governed by work and virtue, well-being and culture. Outside lurks a "deplorably uncultured and ignorant" people. Kossak-Szczucka restates her belief that this people's degeneration is due to the mixing of blood. The Ruthenians have been given a "sizeable additive" of Tatar blood and are immersed in "the stigma of the Tatar East, which our race does not possess." They are lethargic and lazy but carry inside them a lurking desire to destroy; once this desire is awakened, it explodes in a "fire that subdues all other psychological drives."[34]

In her critical analysis of *Pożoga*, the critic Ewa Pogonowska writes that the book's frequent evocations of the cataclysms of deluge, storms, and fire bring to mind negative connotations from the Bible. The elements of water and fire are the attributes of hell, and it is they, in their fury, that will bring about the annihilation of the Eastern Borderlands. Repeating these kinds of metaphors entrenches a view of the historical players as demonic "Satan's children."[35] Kossak-Szczucka is exceptionally hostile not only to the Ruthenians and the Bolsheviks but also to the Jews ("a rabble of disgusting little yids," "ragged Communist jewlings," "the Polish people [are] crushed, the jews [sic] sassy and merry"), but more about this later.[36] Yet she was able to rise above her bias to write with empathy about an anti-Jewish pogrom by Symon Petlyura's men.

The annihilation of the Eastern Borderlands and the Bolshevik revolution in *Pożoga* resemble the fall of ancient Rome and the invasion by the barbarian Huns, who brought with them chaos, savagery, and anarchy and left behind charred buildings and dread. The cataclysm arrived in stages: the fall of tsarist rule, the first Bolshevik agitators, the initially hesitant first raids on manor houses and their people, pogroms and lynchings by peasants. Incidentally, their progression was almost identical to both the anti-Jewish pogroms of 1941, 1945, and 1946 and the plunder that took place during the Second World War and afterward. "As usual, [the plunder] was started by soldiers, who were also egged on by the country women who craved the pillows, bedding and any household wares they could lay their hands on. . . . The men came last."[37] In 1918, the most powerful motivations were hatred based on class and nationality, since the landowners were mostly Polish, and centuries-old feelings of material deprivation. It was all taking place—this is important to remember in order to understand these behaviors—while an increasingly violent civil war was spreading. Out of this chaos and commotion emerged the Bolsheviks.

Their depiction is unequivocally negative. Kossak-Szczucka uses various stylistic devices—including, importantly, animalization—to attain the effect of terror. "They were unpredictable and horrific, lacking all rationality. . . . Bloodthirst would become an addiction for them, just like tobacco or vodka, and these people could not live without murder. . . . Their singing resembled the howling of animals."[38] This depiction is built on impulsiveness, and their unreasoned animalism is a force of nature. As the critic Pogonowska notes, "This animalistic concept fit in perfectly with the writer's vision of the enemy, and once more was used to justify the mistreated race's superiority to the race that had brought on the 'horrific hecatomb,' to 'the Russki mob' with its cruel mentality flavored by the East."[39] The Bolsheviks are quintessentially Asian or, to use the language of their twin Nazi ideology, subhuman. (How curious that these ideologies were born at precisely the same time.)[40]

"The Bolsheviks have come to town" is the final circle of hell that Kossak-Szczucka brings us into. They launched their rule with the murders of political adversaries, robberies, and a victors' orgy. "Executioners who axed convicts, blood dripping from their whole bodies, who coerced people to serve them, to bring them water and towels. Women were dishonored, men beaten up." Organized chaos followed the chaos of war. Food disappeared from the shops as the culture of shortages arrived and with it an increasingly horrific famine. The Bolsheviks requisitioned books (they did start a public reading room, but Kossak-Szczucka discounted it as an indoctrination tool), then household items, bedclothes, and furniture. Catholic and Orthodox priests were persecuted. Plans were made to turn a Catholic church into a bathhouse and an Orthodox church into a hospital. Now it was no longer only anxiety and fear that ruled, for they had been in charge for some time now, but also numbness and lethargy. She repeats Dante's words—"abandon all hope"—and defines Communism: "One of the reasons the Soviet Union is hell is that it leaves no room for hope."[41]

It is easy to gauge *Pożoga*'s reception in the interwar years by the number of its editions (four prior to 1927), the number of its copies in libraries (this author owns one that belonged to the Young Women's Catholic Association in the tiny town of Mszana Dolna), and the number of times it was checked out. Let it be enough to guess that Kossak-Szczucka's novel would shape the image of the Bolsheviks for a long time and link them with fear in the Polish emotional memory.

On the bottom tier stands a lowbrow novel: Edmund Jezierski, *A gdy komunizm zapanuje* (When Communism takes over). This book did not play the same role in promoting fear as did *Pożoga*, but its author did try. He is very open about his fear of Bolshevism, as if he were teaching young people the facts of life. There is another reason to inspect this book carefully: its anti-utopian nature. Its year of publication, 1927, should be declared the year of this literary genre, since at least two analogous books were published then: *Gdyby pod Radzyminem* (If near Radzymin) by Edward Ligocki and *Triumf żółtych* (The triumph of the yellow race) by Bogusław Adamowicz. This coincidence concealed more than a fad for conventions and literary genres. Lying in wait behind it was also catastrophic fear.

Some commentators view this interwar catastrophism as a discrete mindset, others as a worldview or theory. But the answer probably lies in emotions including the anxiety stemming from the expectation of imminent annihilation, the unavoidable destruction that was threatening Europe, especially its traditional spiritual values (Christianity). The anxiety evolved from the experiences of the First World War, the Russian Revolution, the birth of Fascism, the belief in Asia's biological flexibility ("the yellow peril"), the Great

Depression, and the theories of Oskar Spengler and his Polish counterpart Florian Znaniecki, who wrote *Upadek cywilizacji zachodniej* (The fall of Western civilization). These feelings were most fully in evidence in the works of Stanisław Ignacy Witkiewicz, the poetry of Czesław Miłosz and Józef Czechowicz, and the writings of Aleksander Wat. Many interwar commentators and journalists suffered from catastrophic fears, and catastrophism had many faces.[42] Fears of a new phase of the Bolshevik revolution, which would wipe the old world off the face of the Earth, predominated.

Jezierski's portrayal of the Communists is schematic and lacking in nuance. He seems not to have tried very hard and to have been interested less in the plot and the characters' psychological motivations than in the question "what would have happened if the German and the Russian Communist armies and the 'mercenary, well-paid' Chinese units had invaded Poland?"[43]

After the 1918–19 revolution in Germany, Poland stood in the way of a supranational Communist empire. Favoring an invasion were Poland's economic successes in winning new markets, which made it competitive with German industry. Poland was attacked from both east and west. The Poles put up a heroic fight. But local Communists, "supplied abundantly with gold by the Soviets,"[44] conducted a dynamic propaganda, winning over people, especially the underclass, and promising that if they won, looting would not be punished. In these circumstances, the Polish Armed Forces commander-in-chief General Stanisław Okonicz decided to abandon the capital. The government, together with the remnants of the army, moved to the mountains. Partisan warfare began. All the European enemies of Communism, including the Germans, were drawn to serve under Polish banners in the growing resistance against Bolshevik rule. But let's skip ahead and calm down: Poland, like Moses, would save Europe from the flooding red sea.

Crucial in Jezierski's novel was the theme of Promethean and Polish Messianism merging hope with fear, with a vision of Armageddon looming over it. Before the Communist armies would march into Warsaw, "Everyone was immersed in a bottomless fear, they all ran home and, locked in illusory safety, waited for what would happen next.... Red flags, manufactured on the spot, appeared on many buildings, especially in the Jewish district, like talismans to stave off misfortune."[45]

In Jezierski's book, Warsaw, declared the capital of the Polish Soviet Republic, was in an appalling state. The population had shrunk by half. Thousands had been forcibly transported to Russia and Germany to work in factories, and thousands had died of starvation. The only unrationed product was vodka. Churches of all denominations were first robbed, then nationalized and transformed into barracks, warehouses, soldiers' clubs, and cinemas. A statue of Leon Trotsky, "his full-blooded Semite's smile mockingly surveying the conquered city," replaced the monument of Prince Józef Poniatowski. A statue of Marx replaced the statue of Adam Mickiewicz, and Feliks Dzierżyński's column supplanted King Sigismund's.[46] Jezierski's novel proved somewhat prophetic, since a statue of "Iron Feliks" Dzierżyński would indeed be put up in Warsaw.

But *A gdy komunizm zapanuje* did not become a best seller like *Pożoga*, which cannot be explained by low demand for catastrophic tales. Soon, other prophecies of mass destruction swept in from the East. In 1930, S. I. Witkiewicz published *Nienasycenie* (*Insatiability*). The fear in culture matched the fear in politics.[47] The sentiment of the "red peril" affected relations with Soviet Russia,[48] and creating a "calm external atmosphere" became one of Poland's main foreign policy goals.[49] As for the domestic situation, fear implied defensive actions, hence the army's influence in the interwar period. The domestic "war on terror"—on the internal enemy, the native Communists—also boosted collective anxiety. We don't know much about this, regrettably, as little has been written about the premises, decision-making processes, tools, and key actions of this war. The program of the officially banned Communist Party of Poland included handing Silesia over to the Germans and the Eastern Borderlands to the "homeland of the proletariat" and establishing the rest of Poland as the seventeenth Soviet Republic. The party therefore enjoyed marginal support, and in many social circles its members were treated as out-of-touch traitors.[50] After several attacks by its raiding parties, they were labeled dangerously subversive. At that time, violence, including acts of terror, was a tool used by all the political players. The assassination of President Gabriel Narutowicz in December 1922 is its most extreme example. Surprisingly, it does make sense to compare that era's attitude toward the Communists with today's public opinion about terrorism. The Communists had at their disposal an underground organization, a network of activists and underground printers, and the Comintern controlled their party. Officially the party was viewed as a subversive force that threatened the foundations of the state order. On October 12, 1931, a typical piece of news from *Ilustrowany Kuryer Codzienny*, the most popular interwar newspaper affiliated with the Sanacja regime, about "the liquidation of a huge nest of subversion in Warsaw" read:

> In recent days, the security authorities conducted a number of searches in Warsaw, which led to the arrests of many Communist subversives. At the same time, the search of a flat belonging to Sara Puterman yielded an archive of the central committee of the CPWB [Communist Party of Western Belorussia]. A modern printing press used to print the CPWB's underground Communist publications was found in the flat of one Gelenter. The list of arrestees: Hanna Fryman, E. Wolfowicz, H. Golfeder, M. Jezierska, J. Kajzer, F. Menkus, S. Puterman, M. Biter, St. Manikowski, Ch. Rabinowicz, E. Konman, R. Zylberman, W. Rutkiewicz, Noech Lend, R. Gwicman.

Mug shots of the detainees accompanied the article. Dozens of similar news stories about the capture of "Communist cells" played a role in creating this unique, fearful attitude toward the Communists in the interwar years.[51] Soviet books were available in bookshops, Soviet films ran in cinemas, and Soviet art was occasionally exhibited. Julian Tuwim and Antoni Słonimski would meet with Vladimir Mayakovsky when he visited Warsaw, their prominence permitting them to do so.[52] But generally speaking, anyone who traveled in Communist circles risked being ostracized and losing their job. Party members and collaborators were under constant surveillance, and their newspapers and periodicals were censored, although—notably—so was the National Democratic press.[53] In the latter, the mood of threat coming from the "reds" verged on anti-Communist hysteria, especially in the 1930s. Some of its writers maniacally stalked anyone who held Communist views, imagining that they detected such views even among those who had little to do with the left, let alone with Communism. The cancer of Communism grew under the skin, they argued, and its harmful substances, such as liberalism, moral relativism, and atheism, infected "society's healthy parts." Hence, we should fear not the external enemy but the internal one:

> We . . . should not be afraid of the Communism and godlessness that are out in the open, but of covert Communism and godlessness, crypto-Communism and crypto-godlessness, which are disseminated by free thinkers, Freemasons, Socialists and some of the organizations that insinuate themselves into the ranks of workers, peasants, youth and even the intelligentsia. One must be alert here and resist the birth of evil, so it is not too late. Here, too, Moscow's Comintern is operating with the "Trojan horse method." The Communists are inserting themselves into various organizations, even Catholic ones, in order to disseminate their principles slyly and to blow up Catholic organizations from the inside.[54]

Waves of anti-Communist hysteria came and went. One came in the early 1930s hand in hand with Marshal Piłsudski's system of escalated repressions that followed the formation of the Centrolew coalition of center and leftist parties. At the same time, the political and intellectual elites attacked its alternative, anticipating a decline in the population's faith in capitalism during the economic crisis. This also coincided with news coming from the east about collectivization and the Ukrainian famine. The all-purpose message from the government and the right-wing press was: We are experiencing only temporary difficulties, but they have their "Bolshevik hell." Evidently, cultivating alarm about Communism in Poland would serve to cure concern about domestic unemployment. Two days after the article previously quoted, *Ilustrowany Kuryer Codzienny* ran an interview with a man who had just come from Russia: "Since I survived the hell over there, I will certainly feel better here. Misery greater than theirs cannot possibly exist anywhere. I see laughing faces here, but there I never saw a sober person smile."[55]

The next wave of anti-Bolshevism, in 1936, was much more powerful than the previous one for several reasons. In March strikers occupied the Semperit rubber factory in Cracow, and this led to unrest in which eight people were killed by police bullets. Solidarity strikes and protests were staged across the country. The police arrested Communist activists it had long been keeping an eye on.[56] In this extremely tense atmosphere, a Congress of Employees of Cultural Institutions was held in Lvov, with many leftist-leaning intellectuals taking part. The government and right-wing press exclaimed in a united voice of outrage: How could this be happening? Where were the police? Who allowed this Bolshevik demonstration to take place? The words of Henryk Dembiński, editor of the Vilna newspaper *Po prostu*—"Long live Lvov, the capital of Ukraine"—were cited as an example of treason and of the growing threat, as was the gathering's singing of the Internationale and its farewell "Next year in red Warsaw."[57] There were more arrests. Throughout this period, the relatively liberal Sanacja regime was becoming rightist and nationalist. Newspapers brimmed with news about the show trials in Moscow, which soon also became one of the main topics of discussion. Polish minds boggled at the spectacle of charges against yesterday's Soviet leaders—and this confirmed their belief in the Bolshevik regime's civilizational foreignness. One commentator prophesied an attack on Poland by Jews and Mongolian Russia, which is "spiritual for now, but given favorable circumstances may also become physical." He urged, "As for the spiritual atmosphere in Poland, we must introduce a permanent anti-Semitic and anti-Russian mood."[58]

The writer Paweł Jasienica compared Poland's atmosphere to the Great Fear of the McCarthy era in the United States: "They pigeon-holed Daszyński and Stalin together and saw those who promoted reforms, even ordinary liberals, as the precursors to a native Cheka."[59]

Falanga, the National-Radical Camp's newspaper, called for the death penalty for Communists.[60] But Stalin's dissolution of the Communist Party of Poland and the growing threat of war stemming from the Munich Conference shifted public fears in a different direction. Fear lived on, albeit deeply buried; it surfaced in the general panic in the Eastern Borderlands as the Red Army crossed the border into Poland on September 17, 1939.[61]

THE CHIMERA OF THE JEWISH–COMMUNIST CONSPIRACY

The depictions of the "Bolshevik hell" in the culture of the interwar period merge the grotesque with the horrific. The fear lying at the roots of these depictions was real, drawn from the historical experiences of the revolutionary period and of the Polish–Bolshevik War of 1920, as well as from the real threat the Soviet state, the prime manufacturer of fear, posed to the world. Soviet representations of the imperialists were abundant and surreal, related to a characteristic persecution complex, spy-mania. "Imperialist plotting" was used to explain shortcomings in the construction of Socialism: empty shop shelves, industrial accidents, and agricultural shortages. The imperialists' alleged designs on the first workers' and peasants' state were to encourage the Soviet people to make sacrifices and push themselves to work more efficiently. Concealed behind this propaganda, apart from self-interest, were xenophobic fears poorly masked by internationalism. Mikhail Bulgakov's *The Master and Margarita* captures this xenophobia brilliantly in a conversation between Berlioz, the Homeless, and the foreigner. In analyzing the roots of this vigilance, we should not forget Stalin's own obsessive distrust and belief in conspiracy theories, which thrived in a closed society. From the perspective of social psychology, this was a collective paranoia imposed from the top.[62] But the Western world did not stay far behind in creating its own: "Jewish Communism."

Léon Poliakov, the author of *The History of Anti-Semitism*, called Jewish Communism a madness that swept all of Europe. It was predicated on the assumption that the shocking and total overthrow of tsarist rule was made possible by secret forces, certainly Jewish ones, since an undefined percentage of Bolsheviks were Jews.[63]

But the belief in Jewish Communism was not a purely European invention. "The politics of insecurity are contagious," wrote Tony Judt.[64] In 1917–20 the Red Scare reached the United States. Even President Woodrow Wilson believed that "the Bolshevist movement had been led by the Jews."[65]

President Wilson was not insane. Like many others, he was drawing conclusions from insufficient information. After a visit to Moscow in 1934, Poland's foreign minister Józef Beck remarked that Mikhail I. Kalinin was one of the few ethnic Russians in the Soviet leadership.[66] Nothing proves that Beck believed in a Jewish-Communist conspiracy. During Wilson's presidency, several hundred leftists, many of them Jews who had come to America from Russia, were kept under surveillance and detained. Some of them were deported back to Russia. The Jewish press in the United States was censored.[67] Clearly, the US government had begun to associate people of Jewish origin with the Bolshevik threat.

It would be difficult to pinpoint the instant when flawed reasoning ended and the anti-Semitic stereotype began. The Communist movement was popular among some Jews, much like among some Poles, Latvians, or Georgians, not to mention Russians or Chinese. One could hardly accuse the Sanacja historian Władysław Pobóg-Malinowski of believing in stereotypes: "'The Jews' outstanding role in the Russian Revolution and in the Soviet state, the names of Trotsky, Kaganovich, Radek and Litvinov, who were on the team that governed 'one-sixth of the Earth' and represented the 'red power' to the outside world by openly taking part in the 'great game' of world politics, must have served as a magnet for psychological factors such as Jewish national pride or tribal solidarity."[68]

We need to disconnect two issues: some Jews' adherence to Communism, a familiar event in the sociology of excluded groups, and the political myth that it was the Jews who had conspiratorially invented and established Communism and branded it with their indelible mark. There is a vast body of literature about the generation of Jewish Communists in Poland.[69] But there is virtually nothing about the Jewish Communist stereotype, as André Gerrits notes,[70] which seems odd in view of the fact that millions of people in the twentieth century believed in the Jewish conspiracy.

The deeper roots of the belief in a Jewish conspiracy are as old as the religiously oriented anti-Judaism with its topos of Jewish betrayal. The germ of the stereotype of Jewish Communism is present in *Nie-Boska komedia* (The undivine comedy) by Zygmunt Krasiński, written in 1833, which painted a powerful, menacing image of the revolution and assigned a particularly perfidious role to converts. In it, philosophers and artists, too, take part in the overthrow of the traditional European Christian world order. They are steered by Jews who appear to have converted to Christianity, assimilate, and pretend to be "one of us." It is they who drive events. Here is what they have to say:

> THE CONVERTS' CHOIR: Jehovah is our lord, there is no other. He scattered us everywhere. He used us to bind the world of the worshippers of the Cross, our stupid and illiterate masters, as if with an enormous reptile. Spit thrice for their doom, curse them thrice...."
>
> CONVERT: We shall build Israel's might on the unruly freedom, never-ending killings, arguments and anger, on their ignorance and pride, for now only these few masters, these few must be pushed down, their corpses covered with the shattered Cross.[71]

The Polish elites of the first half of the twentieth century were quite familiar with Krasiński's vision. But his vision does not explain the rise of the stereotype of the Jewish Communist conspiracy, since it operated also in countries where this Romantic poet's work was not known. His superposition of several clichés, however, may have appealed more to the Poles. Subsequent clichés were linked to the birth of modern political parties in the late nineteenth century. At that time, people already argued that the Jews had cosmopolitan leanings and leftist tendencies.[72] The full-blooded stereotype of

Jewish Communism was born in 1918–20 of generalizations based on actual news from Russia about Jews' mass participation in the Bolshevik revolution. The stereotype was supported by false conclusions drawn from the Jews' support of leftist organizations in Poland such as the Bund and Poalej Syjon.[73] To borrow Gavin Langmuir's definition of a chimera, the mythological monster with the head of a lion, the body of a goat, and the tail of a snake, the stereotype of Jewish Communism was made up of logically incompatible, empirically unproven beliefs.[74] Here they are, beginning with the tail.

The snake claims that Communism is the work of an international Jewish conspiracy whose members want to rule the world. The Bolsheviks undeniably operated in secret, and their determination and a stroke of luck permitted them to take power in Russia. Those who believe in an ordered and rational world cannot comprehend that it could be governed by chance. Thus, as people search for explanations and find none, they look for clandestine forces and interests lying behind events. From there it is only a tiny step to believing in a universal Jewish conspiracy as its prototype, as the recently "discovered" Protocols of the Elder of Zion show. To Daniel Pipes, conspiracy theories represent the fear of nonexistent conspiracies.[75] The founder of Poland's National Democratic Party, Roman Dmowski, wrote, "There is plenty of evidence that it was the Jewish capitalists in the West who facilitated the Bolshevik revolution's success in Russia, and that this revolution treated Jewish capitalists differently from non-Jewish ones."[76] Yet there is no historical evidence to show that the "Jewish financial class" funded the Bolsheviks, nor that the Jews as a whole aspired (or aspire) to rule mankind.

Dmowski's claim that even non-Jewish Communists are "in a sense proselytizing Judaism" confirms the lion's belief that the Communist movement is steered by the Jews.[77] Undeniably, many of the Soviet leaders were Jewish. According to Jaff Schatz, they may have brought into this movement the baggage of some traditional Jewish values, such as the love of learning, intellectualism, and Messianic yearnings. Schatz believes that Jewish Messianism played a crucial role in shaping the Communist worldview. It is also true that cultural traditions can be conveyed indirectly, intangibly, and imperceptibly, even through denial.[78] For instance, to some Jewish Communists in Poland, assimilation meant a total break with their Jewish roots. Hence, the Communist Party's national nihilism may have partly reflected a denial of national identity on the individual level.[79] It would be impossible to prove empirically that the Semitic nature, however defined, influenced the nature and direction of the Bolshevik revolution, the creation of the Gulag, or collectivization. As Stanisław Krajewski fittingly notes, "The goals of the Communists' activities did not correspond to their ethnic origins, for Jews were in power not as a collectivity but as individuals, not as Jews but as Communists."[80]

The goat believes that the Jews killed Jesus, and now, flying the red flag, they continue to disseminate hatred of Christianity. We know that the rulers of all the countries building Socialism, from Albania and China to the USSR, were hostile to all religions and associations based on faith. But there is no evidence of any connections, influences, or dependencies between Jewish religious orthodoxy and the Communists' fanatical hatred of Christianity, which should not prevent anyone from looking for similarities between religion and the quasi-religion that is Communism.

To recap, Jewish Communists did exist. By one estimate, they numbered between one-quarter and one-third of the Polish Communist Party's membership—a significant number. But, to look at it differently, only a handful of Polish Jews adhered to Communist ideals. According to Jaff Schatz, among Poland's Jewish minority of more than three million, only 0.16 to 0.29 percent were Communists.[81] In an analysis of party support in the Polish parliamentary elections of 1928 by Jeffrey S. Kopstein and Jason Wittenberg, only 7 percent of Jewish voters opted for the Communists. Of the 830,000 votes the Communists obtained, only 14 percent were cast by Jews. Thus, not only were most Jews not Communists, conclude Kopstein and Wittenberg, but the Polish Communist movement had only a marginal presence in the Jewish community.[82] Jewish Communism is thus an invective, a stereotype, and a fantasy. Only the belief in it can be proven empirically. Here is an example from the time when the chimera was born.

The booklet *Bolszewizm i Polska* (Bolshevism and Poland) was published in Vilna in 1920. Its author, Wincenty Lutosławski, was a lecturer at the University of Vilna and a commentator with conspicuously National Democratic views. He keenly promoted the snake's view that the Jews had instigated the Russian Revolution. He believed that the Jews were bad spirits, virtual vampires whose bite made monsters out of humans: "They transformed humble residents into wild beasts, who will tear them to pieces when they run out of food."[83] In Lutosławski's view, the Jews had only one goal: to bring about a social revolution in Poland and then to subordinate Poland to Russia. Standing in the way of this revolution was the Polish state, one of the oldest in Europe, the continuator of its nationhood, which made it "the refuge of the most ancient Aryan tradition."[84] Hence, the war with the Bolsheviks was racial, a clash between the Aryan Poles and the "Bolshevik plague" led by Jews.

Lutosławski shared the goat's view that the Polish–Bolshevik War also had a fundamental religious dimension, that it should be viewed through the prism of the ancient conflict between Christians and Jews. "This hatred of theirs stems mostly from the race of its leaders, who as jews [sic] have inherited from their ancient ancestors a hatred of Christ, whom they crucified, and furthermore they burn with hatred because of all the persecution they have experienced on the hands of Christians."[85] There could be no lasting peace between Jewish Bolshevism and Christian Poland. The only "solution to the Jewish question" was Jewish emigration to Palestine. Only strengthening the nation spiritually and religiously, "ordaining our soldiers as knights who will protect the sacred laws and truths of Christianity," could save Poland from the Bolshevik onslaught.

These "chimeric" beliefs are omnipresent in the literature of propaganda during the war of 1920, as well as in pamphlets and newspapers of the interwar period published by the right and the Catholic Church.[86] Opinions that the Jews had infected Communism and strove to rule the world appeared in the right-wing and Catholic media even more frequently than the interwar period's omnipresent slogan "sugar makes you strong." A brochure published by the National Democrats reads, "Jews are taking a very active part in today's Bolshevik revolution. They are the heart and soul of this movement, its leaders, and they occupy the leading positions in the government of the soviets as a majority of its commissars, the executive organs of its absolute will, its organizers and creators."[87]

This text's key motif was a private eye's anti-Semitism, exposing past and current Communist leaders who were Jewish. This was driven by at least two forces. First, discovering someone's true identity produced proof of the eternal Jewish deceptiveness. Second, finding out that a Jew was hiding behind an assumed name served as conclusive evidence that the Communist movement was a conspiracy and had a Jewish leadership. Since this was practically the only "evidence," it was used ad nauseam. Thus, *Żydowskie ugrupowania wywrotowe w Polsce* (Jewish revolutionary groups in Poland) reads:

> The Jews play a leading role in all revolutionary movements.... With this leadership role in the age of the "dictatorship of the proletariat," the Jewish element is able to steer the policies of a given State in the direction it desires. This is what happened in Hungary during the dictatorship of Béla Kun (the jew [sic] Kohen) (1919), this is how it was in Bavaria during the dictatorship of Kurt Eisner (a jew) [sic] (1919), and this is how it was and still is in Russia under the rule of Radek (Sobelson), Zinovev (Apfelbaum), Trotsky (Bronstein) etc.[88]

The key message was: Bolsheviks are Jews who scheme and entangle the world in a spider web of intrigues. In point of fact, behind every threat to the world today lurked a Jewish–Bolshevik conspiracy, which was present in religious sects, "Bolshevism's *yacheykas* [cells],"[89] in "the Methodists' diluted Christianism,"[90] and in the "pan-Judaic power."[91] The quintessence of the image of the chimera and of conspiracy theories can be found in the popular interwar publication *Zmierzch Izraela* (The Twilight of Israel, three editions by 1933) by Henryk Rolicki (pen name of Tadeusz Gluziński, the chief ideologue of the National Radical

Camp [ONR ABC]). Rolicki argued on more than four hundred pages that for centuries the Jews' politics had stood out with their conspiratorial methods, that "the dictatorship of the proletariat was to be the Jews' salvation," that "the Jewry greeted the Bolshevik revolution in Russia with an explosion of jubilant wildness," and that "quite simply, the Jewish financiers gave money for the revolutions."[92]

Jędrzej Giertych, whose *O wyjście z kryzysu* (To emerge from the crisis) was treated as the National Democrats' informal political program, also believed in the existence of the "Jewish Communist" chimera.[93] For him, fear was the Jews. They were a threat because "at any instant they may stab us in the back by organizing revolutions in our key cities." They were a "great power"; they played a "huge role in world politics" and messianically strove to rule the world. They owned "British, American, Soviet, French and former Prussian battleships and airplanes" thanks to the money they had amassed.[94] They had at their disposal a network of influential agents in the world financial elite, among journalists and writers, and in the *Wiadomości Literackie* literary weekly. We can argue that this was anti-Semitic gibberish, but it did mask genuine fear.

According to the historian Ernst Nolte, to Hitler the word *Jew* was a concrete term that meant something much broader and much more abstract—namely, the globalization or homogenization of the world. Giertych shared Hitler's anxiety, which lives on, albeit in altered form. The Communism introduced by the Jews, with its slogans of internationalism, strives for a *Gleichschaltung* of nations, for doing away with state borders and national identities. Their plan had allegedly come close to being put into practice earlier, as the eighteenth-century partitions of Poland had "to a large degree" been the work of Jews and Freemasons. Now, the "Communist action in Poland has the Jewish population as its main base of support." Had Poland lost the war of 1920, it would have been made a Soviet republic with a Jewish ruling class. It would have staged mass executions of Poles and brought in Jews from the USSR and America to make Poland totally Jewish.[95] Nolte compares Hitler's and Giertych's fears to our contemporary worries about Islam.[96] The fears of the first half of the twentieth century were clearly more obsessive and much more widespread, but also, with the looming Stalinist threat, more real.

In the second half of the 1930s, Giertych-style anxieties spread like a virus. The National Radical Camp's leader and *Prosto z mostu* commentator Jan Mosdorf diagnosed this period's mood among the younger generation as an anguish that a "fourth partition" by the Jews loomed over Poland.[97] *Falanga*, a radically anti-Semitic newspaper, never doubted that Marxism emerged from the "Jewish spirit" and the Judaic tradition, and even believed that Karl Marx had conceived his doctrine in order to destroy the Aryan nation and to benefit the Jews. But, as the writer Jan Józef Lipski noted, this clashed with another claim by *Falanga* that capitalism, too, had its roots in the "Jewish spirit."[98]

The writer Antoni Słonimski challenged this chimera in *Wiadomości Literackie*. Mocking the editor in chief of *Prosto z mostu*, he wrote, "Mr. Piasecki claims that it was the Jews who invented Communism. But if he recognizes that the Jews also invented capitalism, it would seem that as far as we are concerned they are even. One might add that it had also been the Jews who came up with Christianity, but let's not complicate Mr. Piasecki's already complicated ideological situation."[99]

As psychologists know, stereotypes are rigid and not easily modified,[100] all the more so in a general mood of growing intolerance and state-sanctioned anti-Semitism. Słonimski's arguments didn't have a snowball's chance in hell of shaking up society's belief in the chimera of Jewish Communism. But it was also not swayed by news of more and more Jewish victims being annihilated by Stalin in the Great Purge. The *Falanga* people held up their shaky theory of a Jewish conspiracy and its crucial role in producing Communism with another conspiracy, this time a Jewish–Masonic one.[101] Mieczysław Czerski wrote in an article on "Kryzys bolszewizmu w Rosji" (The crisis of Bolshevism in Russia), "A battle is raging between Lejba Bronsztajn's Jewish–Masonic Communism and Stalin's Soviet imperialism. Its victims, Kamenev, Zinovev, Piatakov and Serebriakov, and their comrades were sentenced to death. Only Radek aka Sobelsohn came out unharmed, with a ten-year sentence. He was saved by the Masonic Order of the Eastern Star, which intervened via the French prime minister, the Jew Léon Blum. Sobelsohn aka Radek was a representative of the Jewish–French 'brothers in aprons' in the USSR, and it was on their behalf that he had enormous influence on Soviet domestic relations."[102]

There is no need to give more examples of the pro-chimera arguments. More important are answers to these questions: Why were Semitic features attributed to Bolshevism? Or, to put it as a metaphor, out of what was the chimera of Jewish Communism hatched? Stanisław Krajewski is wrong to claim that fighting Jewish Communism was unique to the Polish political scene, since this stereotype was also juggled around elsewhere, including the Third Reich. But it is true that it was particularly vicious in Poland. Why? Certainly, this stereotype's genesis lay in Poland's prevalent anti-Semitism whose fanatical extreme held that all the evil in the world, therefore also Communism, came from the Jews.

What also mattered was the flawed interpretation of what motivated the Jews' joyous welcoming of the Bolshevik armies marching into the areas earlier occupied by Symon Petlyura's troops. The Poles understood it as support for Communist ideas when in fact the majority of the Jews were actually rejoicing that they had come out alive from the pogroms. From then on, it sufficed to repeat the rumor that "sassy, merry jews" were supporting the Bolsheviks and that Trotsky's real name was Bronsztajn.

A sociological hypothesis may link the eruption of Polish nationalism brought on by the recently regained sovereignty and a real chance of losing it with the growth of xenophobic tendencies. The Second World War saw a similar mindset when the national feeling deepened and the distance to others widened.

Also influential was the singular mood of panic, combined with an eschatological terror, that grew in August 1920 as General Tukhachevsky's divisions approached Warsaw. Mass gatherings there and in other Polish cities prayed for deliverance. On August 8, processions from all of Warsaw's churches headed toward Zamkowy [Castle] Square, where several bishops celebrated a Mass for the Motherland.[103] A few days earlier, a camp had been set up at Jabłonna outside Warsaw to hold the more than seventeen thousand Jews who had been discharged from the army for allegedly rooting for the Bolsheviks.[104] Negative stereotypes not only preach anxiety but are also born of it, and in this way Jewish Communism is no different. Marc Bloch's study of wartime rumors cites the fear-fed story that made the rounds in the German army about acts of cruelty (such as poking out eyes) reportedly inflicted by Belgian Catholics on German soldiers in 1914.[105] Thus, the birth of Jewish Communism may be interpreted as a reaction that combined hysteria and anxiety brought on by the prolonged state of threat. But unlike the fable about bloodthirsty Belgians, the story about the Jewish Communists was not quickly forgotten.

Another factor in the growth of xenophobia was self-serving motivations and a genuine fear of the Communist slogans among some in the Polish elite. These slogans appealed to the public, which had been exhausted and pauperized by the First World War. News coming from the Eastern Borderlands about the rebellious peasantry's assault, lynching, and pogroms of landowners and the bourgeoisie naturally gave rise to alarm that this might be repeated in central Poland. Thus, promoting fear by debasing the image of the Bolsheviks and retelling events in Russia by giving them a mask of the neophyte Jew was a public relations tool. The Polish rightist elites' intellectual impotence and inability to express themselves in a language that could describe the phenomenon of the Russian revolution are striking. This new situation required rationalizing and "getting people used to" it, for which the anti-Semitic clichés and diagnoses, tested in the course of the ongoing political battle, were most useful.

In order to discredit the Communists, the Sanacja regime and the right-wing newspapers emphasized Jewish names among the Communists, transparently suggesting, Look, they're all Jewish! The Piłsudski faction had built its legitimacy on the legend of its legions' feats, the Polish–Bolshevik War, and the dangers of Poland's "cursed location" between Germany and Soviet Russia. New waves of anti-Bolshevik hysteria in the media did

Figure 2.1. "What threatens Poland? Communism with its mask off," *Falanga*, February 24, 1937

not incline people to listen to rational arguments or promote taking a more sober look at the Jewish question. As we know, fear, especially when it is powerful and protracted, muddles people's thinking. It is difficult to know just how many people had problems seeing this type of chimera or, to put it differently, how widespread the belief in it was.

"Every normal Pole is an anti-Semite," claimed Maria Rzętkowska, a *Falanga* author, in April 1937.[106] The historian Anna Landau-Czajka believes that slogans urging people to boycott Jewish businesses or books by authors of Jewish ancestry did not kindle aggressive behaviors. The frequency of such calls would suggest that they were not very successful and that the Poles were resistant to anti-Jewish arguments.[107] But of course public opinion does not change overnight. Looking at 1939 alone makes us miss instances of collective aggression, such as the wartime and postwar pogroms, which were the delayed effects of the prewar anti-Semitic propaganda. Indeed, this mood began to ripen already in the late 1930s when Jan Szczepański, at the time a young sociologist, could see it clearly, even though he believed that the growing anti-Semitism was caused mainly by poverty. After returning from a fellowship in Denmark in the summer of 1938, he wrote:

We are back in a savage country. Comparing Warsaw to Copenhagen, it's difficult to call it anything but that. It's difficult to give it another name when one sees juveniles bumping into old Jews, knocking over market stalls, pedestrians jumping out of the way of automobile wheels, the chaotic and unregulated traffic, and Warsaw's simply indescribable, appalling riverbanks. So it is difficult not to compare it to Danish cities and towns. Stink, filth and desperate destitution, which disfigures people's faces and bodies into those of freaks, a destitution which emanates savagely from their eyes and facial features. We are nowhere near the prosperity and human kindness that lies at the bottom of everyday culture, guaranteeing that no one will beat up old people in the street and destroy others' property! We are a country of paupers whose everyday life is governed by the laws of the jungle.[108]

On the other hand, interwar Poland was a mosaic of attitudes and viewpoints, not all of them hostile to the Jews.[109] The anti-Semitic obsession appeared only in some newspaper headlines. When *Prosto z mostu* became "infected" with it, some of its writers, including Tadeusz Kotarbiński, Maria Dąbrowska, Adam Próchnik, and Jerzy Andrzejewski, stopped writing for it in protest. The obverse of the fear of the Jews was the equally powerful fear of the National Democrats, which electrified the liberal and left-wing milieux.[110] They tried to do battle with anti-Semitism,[111] even though certainly by the second half of the '30s it was a defense in depth.[112]

"On the third hand," in the interwar period everyone was familiar with the stereotype of Jewish Communism, which, much like the cliché about the dumb blonde, was popular prior to the feminist revolution. It is clear from a reading of the interwar newspapers that this stereotype was imprinted in people's minds, which is not to say that everyone shared it. Some would say there was something to it and, like Foreign Minister Józef Beck, point out Communist leaders who were Jewish, while others tended to see every Jew they came across as a potential Bolshevik. Czesław Miłosz recalled that in Vilna, May Day was called a "Jewish holiday."[113] The most extreme form of the stereotype was to exclude and expel: the best solution to the Jewish problem would be to rid Poland of the Jews, preferably by having them emigrate of their own volition.

Beginning in the mid-1930s, intensifying anti-Semitism powered the vicious circle of a self-fulfilling prophecy. The more the Jews felt discriminated against in Polish society, the greater their hope that Communism would liberate them from class and ethnic oppression. According to Jaff Schatz, the stereotype of Jewish Communism meant that "because anti-Semitism was one of the main forces that drew Jews to the Communist movement, Zydokomuna [*sic*] meant turning the effects of anti-Semitism into a cause of its further increase."[114] To repeat William I. Thomas's famous maxim, "If men define things as real, they are real in their consequences."[115]

As fate would have it, much like in 1918–20, circumstances seemed to confirm the stereotype of Jewish Communism. Again, in September 1939, many Poles viewed Polish Jews' enthusiasm at finding themselves under Soviet occupation and escaping Nazi oppression[116] as conclusive evidence for their support of Communist ideals. This cognitive bias, partly understandable in view of the circumstances of the panic and shock of September, was a cause of the mass murders in Jedwabne and Radziłów.

NOTES

1. Jezierski, *A gdy komunizm zapanuje*, 30.
2. Kornat, *Polska szkoła sowietologiczna 1930–1939*.
3. Jasienica, *Pamiętniki*, 110.
4. Eric Hobsbawm, *The Age of Extremes*.
5. For a discussion of de Custine's fear, see Grudzińska-Gross, *The Scar of Revolution*, especially 80–81.
6. Andrzej Kępiński, *Lach i Moskal. Z dziejów stereotypu* (Warsaw–Cracow: PWN, 1990), 41.
7. For a recent discussion of this theory, see Krzywiec, *Szowinizm po polsku*, 79–120.
8. Zdziarski, *Dżingis-Chan zmartwychwstały*.
9. Zdziarski, 9.
10. Zdziarski, ix.
11. Langmuir, *Toward a Definition of Antisemitism*, 330.
12. Andrzej Garlicki supports this: "Stereotypes say a lot about those who have produced them, about their thinking, their knowledge and their geographic horizons. An analysis of the features ascribed to foreigners allows us to understand the worldview of those who focus on those features." *Sąsiedzi i inni*, 5.
13. Parandowski, *Bolszewizm i bolszewicy w Rosji*, 2.
14. Jasienica, *Pamiętniki*, 82, 110.
15. Odziemkowski, *15 wiorst od Warszawy*, 5.
16. Bień, *Listy z wojny 1920*, 11.
17. Wańkowicz, "Ogniem i mieczem."
18. *Front: Żołnierskie Pismo Codzienne*, July 22, 1920.
19. Odziemkowski, *15 wiorst od Warszawy*, 33, 34.
20. "When I joined my regiment, I found a handful of officers who were not wearing their insignia and I concluded that they

had taken them off out of fear, since the Bolsheviks execute the officers they capture." Letter from Józef Jaklicz to his wife in *Rok 1920*, 177.

21. Kamińska, *Ścieżkami wspomnień*, 200.
22. Hagen, "The Moral Economy of Popular Violence," 124–46.
23. See, inter alia, M.B., *Jak powstała armja bolszewicka?*; Dąbrowski, *Prawda o bolszewikach*; Dąbrowski, *Precz z carską i bolszewicką Rosją!*; Orczewski, *Rządy bolszewickie*; Rokicki, *Bolszewizm wobec kultury i cywilizacji i ludzkość wobec bolszewizmu*.
24. Lisiak, "Propaganda obronna w Polsce w rozstrzygającym okresie wojny polsko-sowieckiej 1920 r.," 12. On this topic see also, inter alia, Korzeniewski, "Wróg nadchodzi," 467–84.
25. Lisiak, "Propaganda."
26. Lisiak.
27. Kamińska-Szmaj, *Judzi, zohydza, ze czci odziera*, 133–67.
28. Kamińska, *Ścieżkami wspomnień*.
29. *Spisek niemiecko-bolszewicki*, 3.
30. Szymański, *Bolszewizm*, 55.
31. Bojomir, *Chrześcijaństwo a bolszewizm*, 14.
32. Bauman, *Liquid Times*, 55ff.
33. Kossak-Szczucka, *Pożoga*.
34. Kossak-Szczucka, 5, 6, 84.
35. Pogonowska, "*Pożoga* Zofii Kossak-Szczuckiej," 45.
36. Kossak-Szczucka, *Pożoga*.
37. Kossak-Szczucka, *Pożoga*, 49–51, 75, 82–84 et al.
38. Kossak-Szczucka, 324.
39. Pogonowska, "*Pożoga* Zofii Kossak-Szczuckiej," 37.
40. The author of *Pożoga* and *Krzyżowcy* held deep-seated racist views. She wrote in the mid-1930s, "Converting to Christianity would inevitably change the Jewish psyche, restore it morally and plough it through, but it would not change their race.... The Jews are so terribly foreign to us, foreign and unpleasant, because they are of a different race. All their characteristics annoy and irritate us: their Eastern quick temper, petulance, that specific type of mind, the way their eyes are set, the shape of their ears, the way they squint, the form of their lips, everything. In mixed families we try to sniff out suspicious traces of these characteristics down to the third, fourth generation and further" (Kossak, "Najpilniejsza sprawa").
41. Kossak-Szczucka, *Pożoga*, 299–321.
42. For more on catastrophism, see Wyka, "Wspomnienie o katastrofizmie," 347–66; Wojnowska, "Katastrofizm," 428–29; Werner, "Katastrofizm," 445–53; Gawor, *Katastrofizm w polskiej myśli społecznej i filozofii 1918–1939*.
43. Jezierski, *A gdy komunizm zapanuje*, 7.
44. Jezierski, 8.
45. Jezierski, 14, 15.
46. Jezierski, 44.
47. More in Zackiewicz, *Polska myśl polityczna wobec systemu radzieckiego 1918–1939*.
48. More in Materski, *Na widecie*.
49. Pobóg-Malinowski, *Najnowsza historia polityczna Polski, 1964–1945*, vol. 2, part 1, 507.
50. For the Communist Party's national program, see Zaremba, *Komunizm, legitymizacja, nacjonalizm*, 72–80.
51. Aleksander Wat writes about a very similar press campaign after he and a group of friends (including Władysław Broniewski and Jan Hempel) were arrested:

> The absolutely fantastic publicity our arrest was given by the entire press—not just the gutter press, but the Catholic press too. The day after our arrest there were enormous front-page stories and for two or three days our pictures were in the paper, with our numbers, of course. People always look like criminals in mug shots. I think they turned everyone, with the exception of Broniewski, into Jews. So Hempel was turned into Szloma—I don't remember what it was—Grynhorn or Grynwasser. They went wild with the story, writing that some incredibly big fish had been caught, and material evidence of an international Comintern conspiracy had been found and an enormous sum of money, dollars. God only knows (Wat, *My Century*, 70).

52. Cf. Shore, *Caviar and Ashes*.
53. For more, see Paczkowski, *Prasa polska w latach 1918–1939*, 10–16, 219, et al.
54. Kwiatkowski, *Źródła dzisiejszego bezbożnictwa*, 81, 82.
55. "O kraju, gdzie ludzie zapomnieli się śmiać."
56. Paczkowski, *Prasa polska w latach . . .*, 35.
57. Piasecki, "Front sowiecki i front polski."
58. Nowosad, "Timiakow i trockiści."
59. Jasienica, *Pamiętniki*, 110.
60. Rościszewski, "Nasza walka z komuną."
61. Wojciech Jaruzelski acquired this fear:
> I saw the first ones outside Grodno. We hid in a small wood. They drove around in their tanks, fired. I saw dead Polish soldiers. I saw them again in 1940 in Lithuania. They appeared out of the blue in the swampy meadows near the town of Kalvarija. There were swarms of them. Swarms. In gray greatcoats, pointy *budenovka*s with red stars. I was in shock. I was under the impression that this enormous mass would submerge us instantly. I was very afraid of them. What I knew about the Soviet Union, my awareness and upbringing then made me think of them as virtually devilish beings ("Mówi generał, z generałem Wojciechem Jaruzelskim rozmawia Teresa Torańska").

62. Cf. Kramer, "Collective Paranoia," 1–18.
63. Poliakov, *The History of Anti-Semitism*, 4: *Suicidal Europe, 1870–1933*, 67–134.
64. Judt, *Reappraisals*, 16.
65. For more on this subject, see Szajkowski, *Jews, Wars, and Communism*, 7.
66. Beck, *Ostatni raport*, 66.
67. Szajkowski, *Jews, Wars, and Communism*, 11–15, 30–31, et al.
68. Pobóg-Malinowski, *Najnowsza historia*, 618.
69. Mishkinsky, "The Communist Party of Poland and the Jews," 56–74; Kula, *Narodowe i rewolucyjne*, 175–227; Schatz, *The Generation*; Schatz, "Świat mentalności i świadomości komunistów polsko-żydowskich—zkic do portretu," 43–55; Kersten, *Polacy, Żydzi, komunizm*, 76–88; Pragier, *Żydzi czy Polacy*, 34–44,

78–105; Brun-Zejmis, "National Self-Denial and Marxist Ideology, 29–54; Krajewski, "Fakty i mity," 90–104; Zaremba, *Communism-Legitimacy-Nationalism*, 66, 67; *Żydzi i komunizm*, 2000; Nalewajko-Kulikov, *Obywatel Jidyszlandu*, 45–7, 67–76; Paczkowski, *Trzy twarze Józefa Światły*, 28–41.

70. Gerrits, "Antisemitism and Anti-Communism," 49–72; see also Pufelska, *Die "Judäo-Kommune" ein Feindbild in Polen*.

71. Krasiński, *Nie-Boska komedia*, 50, 51.

72. More on the prehistory of Jewish Communism, its ties to the beginnings of Romanticism, and the emergence of Polish nationalism in the nineteenth century, see Pufelska, *Die "Judäo-Kommune,"* 25–46.

73. Tomaszewski, *Najnowsze dzieje Żydów w Polsce*, 148.

74. Langmuir, *Toward a Definition of Antisemitism*, 328ff.

75. Pipes, *Conspiracy*.

76. Dmowski, *W kwestii komunizmu*, 13–15.

77. Dmowski, 13.

78. Schatz, *The Generation*.

79. Zaremba, *Komunizm, legitymizacja, nacjonalizm*, 73, 74.

80. Krajewski, "Problem żydowski," 71.

81. Schatz, "O micie 'żydokomuny,'" 76.

82. Kopstein and Wittenberg, "Who Voted Communist?," 87–107.

83. Lutosławski, *Bolszewizm i Polska*, 10.

84. Lutosławski, 24.

85. Lutosławski, 1.

86. Cf. Friszke, "Naród, państwo, system władzy w myśli politycznej Związku Ludowo-Narodowego w latach 1919–1926," 65, 66.

87. J. K., *Bolszewizm a mesjasz żydowski*, 3.

88. Korsch, *Żydowskie ugrupowania wywrotowe w Polsce*, 13, 14.

89. Skrudlik, *Sekty żydujące w Polsce*, 24.

90. Skrudlik, *Agentury obce*, 43.

91. Delacroix, *Masoneria i bolszewizm*.

92. Rolicki, *Zmierzch Izraela*, 353, 384, 387, 398.

93. Giertych, *O wyjście z kryzysu*.

94. Giertych, 238.

95. Giertych, 133, 235–63.

96. Nolte, "Auschwitz zrodził się z gułagu."

97. Mosdorf, "U źródeł. Pokolenie Niepodległej Polski."

98. Lipski, *Antysemityzm ONR "Falangi"*, 17–19.

99. Słonimski, "Kroniki tygodniowe."

100. Cf. Kurcz, *Zmienność i nieuchronność stereotypów*.

101. Already in the 1920s, Antoni W. Kwiatkowski pointed out the absurdity—one could say chimeric nature—of the alleged Bolshevik–Freemason conspiracy, clearly with no effect. See Starodworski (A. W. Kwiatkowski's pen name), *Bolszewizm a masoneria*.

102. Czerski, "Kryzys bolszewizmu w Rosji."

103. Wawer, "Miasto niepokonane," 22.

104. *Najnowsze dzieje Żydów*, 149.

105. Bloch, *Strange Defeat*.

106. Rzętkowska, "Czy chcecie walki z żydami?"

107. Landau-Czajka, *W jednym stali domu*, 19.

108. Szczepański, *Dzienniki z lat 1935–1945*, 60.

109. Cf. Bronsztejn, "Stosunki polsko-żydowskie przed Holocaustem we wspomnieniach okresu międzywojennego," 125–42.

110. Stefan Arski remembered, "There were also brawls at my university, the Warsaw School of Economics, but, you know, the point is that it was not everyone who started these brawls. We of the P[olish] S[ocialist] P[arty] did not feel isolated also on this issue" (Pragier, *Żydzi czy Polacy*, 55).

111. Zaremba et al., "O Żydach i antysemityzmie" (made available to this author by Andrzej Friszke). More on this subject in Friszke, *Adam Ciołkosz*, 200–203 et al.

112. For leftist newspapers' take on the Jewish question, see Landau-Czajka, *W jednym stali domu*, 79–82.

113. Miłosz, *Native Realm*, 95.

114. Schatz, *The Generation*, 95.

115. Patton, *Qualitative Research and Evaluation Methods*, 121.

116. Teofila Weintraub reminisced, "I can remember how happy we were to have crossed the border and left the Germans behind. And I can also remember a Russian soldier standing nearby, surprised, watching us being so happy" (Pragier, *Żydzi czy Polacy*, 89).

3

THE TRAUMA OF A WORLD WAR

PSYCHOSOCIAL EFFECTS OF THE SECOND WORLD WAR

Not even the most apocalyptic visions dreamed up in the 1920s, such as the Jezierski passage about a prison quoted at the beginning of chapter 2, could match the tragic image of Warsaw as the Second World War drew to a close.[1] In January 1945, the writer Vasily Grossman was one of the first war correspondents to arrive in the freshly liberated capital of Poland. He wrote, "When we arrived, liberated Warsaw was looking majestic and sad, even tragic. City streets were filled with heaps of broken brick"[2] The Polish hearts and minds fared no better than their devastated capital.

The chaos, organizational decay, and demoralization that go hand in hand with war, especially in lands very recently occupied by foreign powers, cannot but produce terror. This terror is, first of all, created by the state of suspension and uncertainty, when no one knows what is going on, when everything eludes control, when for an instant all boundaries disappear. Often, this condition is accompanied by anarchy and weak political power, or else that power's lack of interest in restoring order in lands without a functioning state administration.

Most of the terrors in history exploded in the wake of wars, disastrous harvests and starvation, and plagues. Some regions of Poland experienced one such terror in 1918–20. There is no question that the Polish terror would not have appeared had the Second World War not taken place. The Poles had only just lived through the demise of their state, the chaos of one war, and two foreign occupations and witnessed the annihilation of the Jews. They, too, suffered racially motivated violence. It is impossible to understand the Polish state of mind in the postwar years without taking into account its sociopsychological dimension.

In his analysis of the social consequences of the twentieth century's wars, the social historian Arthur Marwick distinguishes between two sociological approaches, which are also useful to the historian.[3] The first one centers on the participation in the war effort of previously nonprivileged groups, which leads to the replacement of earlier class structures. War creates an opportunity to build a new solidarity, socialization, and, in the Polish case, grassroots organization within the Underground State. Marwick describes the Underground State's institutions (underground educational or court systems) and the resistance movement, which help the nation to survive by opposing the occupier and strengthening the national identity. This paradigm presents the community as united in struggle, self-sacrifice, and shared suffering. Often, the national community is represented as sacred, and its struggle and resistance as heroic. The majority of Polish publications about the Second World War, memoirs as well as analyses, fall into this pattern, as do all forms of commemoration.

There is another interpretation of war: as an event that in some ways resembles a natural disaster, with an analogous social and psychological impact on the people living at its epicenter. Hence, the Second World War should be interpreted as a multidimensional natural catastrophe whose social and psychological consequences have not yet been adequately recognized.[4] This book attempts to put some order into these consequences, focusing on those that best served as the subsoil for growing fear. It does not intend to demystify or to play down the heroism of the Polish wartime experience but instead to make a sociological generalization about it, especially about those events that do not fit into the category of heroism. The overview it offers will thus unavoidably be incomplete, as it will omit some issues, including some aspects of politics. And one more caveat: while this book is mostly interested in the end result—i.e., the state of the Polish society in 1945—it does not delve into the impact of the Red Army's arrival in the Polish lands.

Two theories will serve as points of reference for this analysis: Pitirim Sorokin's sociology of catastrophes[5] and Piotr Sztompka's sociology of trauma.[6] Even though sixty years divide their publications, and neither specifically addresses Poland's experiences in the Second World War, they can be used mutatis mutandis to search for the wartime sources of the Great Fear.

To paraphrase the title of Sztompka's book, the Polish wartime experience can be called "the trauma of a world war," a particular type of the "pathology of society's agency."[7] It was shaped by the drawn-out, destructive trauma, the collective experience of terror and shock, horror and fear, disintegration and devastation. For Sztompka, trauma is related to the experience of social change, especially change that is sudden, unexpected, and related to various areas of social life, as well as cultural disorganization, affecting the personality of the people who experience it. Change of this type results in institutional disorder in public life and cultural disorganization, which affect the personalities of the people experiencing it.[8] This type of social disruption accompanies wars, revolutions, and abrupt modernization. There is no question that Poland in 1945 was totally transformed from what it had been in August 1939. It had only just experienced dramatic change and faced the new transformations resulting from the Communist takeover of power. The war had acted as the revolution's destructive phase.[9] Commenting on the outcomes of his study of postwar young people, Stefan Baley said, "We have the right to say that their collective soul is infected with the war complex."[10] What inroads did this infection make into the Polish "collective soul," and what havoc did it wreak inside?

SOURCES OF THE TRAUMA

The omnipresence of death was the first and most powerful source of psychological scars. In 1945, human and animal bodies remained scattered where carpet bombings and fighting had taken place: Silesia, East Prussia, the Pomeranian Wall, and the sites of partisan skirmishes. In April and May, the stench became unbearable. Flies of an unprecedented size grazed on the corpses and swarmed above the bodies of the dead. In his memoir, the first Polish mayor of Kołobrzeg (Kolberg), Stefan Lipicki, remembered the unburied bodies still lying in the streets of his town in the early summer of 1945: "The sanitary conditions in Kołobrzeg were abominable, dried pools of blood covered the streets, swarms of flies nested. I located a storeroom with barrels of insecticide in Ząbrowo near Kołobrzeg and had it strewn in the streets, and the flies began to disappear; they were gone at last, what a relief. The corpses were the other plague, as the summer was exceptionally hot, and they were decaying rapidly. Outdoors, the reek of the cadavers was so powerful that you had to hold your nose."[11]

The same smell wafted over towns in Lower Silesia. The Citizens' Militia Provincial Command reported in May 1945 from Trzebnica, "Many human corpses, and of other animals [sic] are lying around, unburied."[12]

The reek of corpses also prevailed in Warsaw. People felt like they were walking through a cemetery: "I had the impression that I was treading on dead bodies, that blood was going to gush out from under my feet."[13] According to a spring 1945 estimate, some 12,000 of the

150,000 Warsaw Uprising dead continued to lie in the streets, inside houses and cellars, or under a thin layer of soil. The *Życie Warszawy* daily reported that "in some streets, there are hundreds of provisional graves, and an unbearable stink emanating from them." The paper even launched the idea to "make it your motto: For May Day, let not a single corpse remain unburied in Warsaw."[14] Fears of a cholera epidemic appeared in Warsaw, for good reason. The year 1945 saw a proliferation of mice and rats, which continued into 1946.[15]

Across the whole country, bodies of the fallen and murdered were being dug up. While the exhumations prolonged the war psychologically, they were also an attempt to put a symbolic end to the trauma. Most families dug up their dead themselves—provided they knew where to find them. The composer Andrzej Panufnik had no problem finding the grave of his brother, a fighter in the Warsaw Uprising. Their father had buried the body with a bottle with a piece of paper inside it, on which he wrote, "Lieutenant Mirosław Panufnik, nom de guerre Witel. Killed on 16 September 1944, age 36."[16] Those who had been interred in a hurry during the Warsaw Uprising, as well as the victims of mass executions, usually had no identification marks.

When the exhumations became public, curiosity gained the upper hand over revulsion:

> A disinterment is taking place in Puławska Street, on the lawn outside the Wedel house. Spectators fill the windows. Onlookers crowd the pavement, surging closer and receding as the wind changes direction. Every now and again a passerby, stung by a sudden terror, looking for familiar facial features, moves closer. But there is no face. The uniform has rotted away, but it still holds the body's youthful shape, even though everything else is a slimy mass. A girl, the embodiment of good health, all pink inside her white gown, leans over the corpse and pats it down expertly. Another one is making an official list. They are doing their duty with a perfect, dreadful calm and a smile on their faces.[17]

The body of the poet Krzysztof Kamil Baczyński was not dug up from its temporary Warsaw Uprising grave until January 1947, two and a half years after its burial. Processions of thousands accompanied his reburial.[18] The atmosphere of mourning persisted for several years, something that was evident in Polish cemeteries every All Souls' Day.

Still, the final death count evades us. A pioneering study of the war's psychological impact on children and adolescents conducted by psychologists from the State Institute of Mental Hygiene in Warsaw gives us some idea of the scope of human losses. In June and July 1945, the psychologists interviewed over five thousand fifteen- to twenty-three-year-olds. A sample of the 1,500 questionnaires filled out by pupils in Warsaw, Cracow, and Lublin reveals that 73.2 percent of them had lost someone close to them, often more than one person, in tragic circumstances. Thirty-six percent of the interviewees had lost one person, 24 percent had lost two, 16 percent had lost three, 12 percent had lost four, 5 percent had lost five, and 2 percent had lost six persons. Some had lost seven, eight, or as many as thirteen people from their immediate and extended families.[19]

Shortly after the war ended, the Office of War Compensation set the number of victims at 6 million, but this figure was inflated for political reasons.[20] We now know that the numbers of people who died in Auschwitz and during the Warsaw Uprising were lower than assumed immediately after the war. The most recent death estimates of Poland's prewar populations of Polish and Jewish nationalities are about 5 million, 2.9 million of them Jewish.[21] Yet even this lowered figure is too low because the final count should include citizens of the Second Republic of Belorussian, German, and Ukrainian nationalities who died as a result of the war, or about 800,000 people.[22] Thus, if we take into account Poland's August 1939 population of 35 million, a conservative estimate would yield about 20 percent who did not live to see the end of the war. Adding all those who did survive but dispersed around the world, both east and west, the war reduced Poland's population by nearly a quarter. No other European country suffered losses on this scale.

While all social groups suffered, the intelligentsia's losses were the highest. The political, intellectual, and cultural elites were decimated; it has been estimated that 37.5 percent of individuals with a university education and about 30 percent of those with a secondary education lost their lives in the war.[23] To look at it differently: if we also include top civil servants, the officer corps, and members of the free professions who left Poland in 1939 and for the most part chose not to return, this translates into a Poland in 1945 with a population of not quite 24 million, with 60,000 to 70,000 individuals with university degrees and fewer than 300,000 secondary-school finishers.[24] In other words, lost in the wartime migrations, exterminations, and battlefields was the "Poland A" of educated people, opinion makers, and civil servants who upheld the Second Republic's values and symbols. Today we would call it the middle class, the foundation of a stable social order. It must therefore have been extremely difficult after the war to restart the institutions that are crucial to public life and to the economy. The cadre revolution that took place after the war was imposed from the top and by the realities of the moment. Another reason for the enormous significance of these human losses was that only the intelligentsia would know how to define the postwar reality, to put an end to the chaos and confusion that naturally accompanied postwar life, and to plot the way forward to reconstruction.

Left on the battleground was "Poland B," impoverished and uneducated, well aware of its deficits, governed by anguish and trauma. It identified more closely with the Catholic Church, was more conservative and traditional, and lived predominantly in villages and in small towns. Poland's Communists placed their hopes for modernization on this group and sought in it the functionaries to run their system. The base of this revolution from above was made up of people who were marginalized and "expendable." The new regime flung open the doors to upward mobility before them and took advantage of their energy, using them to target the remnants of "Poland A," which was inclined to oppose the new system.

The second trauma-producing factor was hardship. In 1939, many German officers, certain of their cultural superiority, photographed what to them was the exotic poverty of eastern Europe. Yet as they fled from the Polish lands in a panic in 1944 and 1945, and often carried on their plunder until the very last instant, what they were leaving behind was incomparably worse. The war had ravaged Poland—and also Germany and the Soviet Union—to a far greater degree than any other country. The GNP of 1945 was only 38.2 percent of the 1938 level,[25] which translated directly into daily life. Several million people had lost all their belongings, jobs, and sources of support. During the 1946 preharvest, people spoke openly about the specter of national famine. But it was not only food that was in short supply. The six years of war had deprived hundreds of thousands of families of even the most basic possessions. In the words of Stanisław Szwalbe, vice chairman of the State National Council (KRN—Krajowa Rada Narodowa), "There are families that don't own a single pair of shoes, and when they want to go out they borrow some from neighbors. We have families of seven with one pair of shoes and three shirts between them."[26] It is thus not surprising that after the war the most frequently stolen items were clothing, shoes, and pork fat. Wrocław, which the mathematician Hugo Steinhaus saw as a city of paupers, could have described all of Poland: "Wrocław: the Battle of Grunwald is taking place again in Grunwald Square. On the one side are thousands of people in rags and on the other Germans wearing white armbands, German women wearing trousers, who inspect the goods, hand them back, turn around, pack and shove; Europe's hugest bunch of beggars on Europe's largest heap of bricks and rubble."[27]

Pauperization, destitution, and degradation focus all of a person's cognitive processes on survival and on dulling sensitivity to everything external to the individual, writes Sorokin.[28] The human being who finds himself in these conditions becomes more egotistical, less sensitive to the suffering of others—and therefore prone to aggressive behavior. Wartime and postwar assaults, murders of Jews, looting, and banditry had their roots in the material deprivation of large segments of the population. The postwar migrations from central Poland to the so-called Regained Territories were also driven by hardship. Material destruction was accompanied by other, less tangible cultural consequences, such as the destruction of thousands of micro-traditions preserved in items of everyday use, trinkets, photographs, and family libraries. The prewar past, with its symbols, values, and rituals, abruptly receded into the distance and became out-and-out foreign. The writer Jan Parandowski, whose Warsaw flat had burned down during the Uprising, wrote, "We now own nothing. Continuity and our family traditions have ruptured, and everything that comes now will be new, and a lot of time will pass before we take possession of it, before it became permeated with the easy familiarity exclusive to inherited objects that have been living with us for a long time."[29]

The third source of the trauma was disintegration and atomization, the consequences of wartime deportations and expulsions, which in the lands incorporated into the Reich had begun already in the autumn of 1939. By the time the war was over, the Germans had expelled over 860,000 people, mostly from Greater Poland and the area around Łódź. Two hundred eighty thousand Poles were forced to leave their homes in the General Government, and 500,000 were driven out from Warsaw in the wake of its uprising. All in all, under the German occupation, 1,650,000 people were forced out of their homes. Furthermore, about 2 million Polish citizens were sent to Germany as laborers.[30] Even though fewer Polish citizens, about 300,000,[31] were deported from the areas annexed by the Soviet Union, the trauma of the transport and time spent in exile and the feeling of being cut off and lost were greater. The social consequences of deportations and expulsions on midlevel ties (occupational, local, milieu) were similar, and for forced laborers and prisoners of war these traumas also affected family ties, since they often involved the disintegration or disappearance of entire social groups and communities.

"For the majority of people in occupied Poland," wrote the historian Czesław Łuczak, "many existing social ties, which had often been the source of occupational, political, social, cultural and religious activity, and also of complex personal and cultural development and mental health, suddenly ceased to exist."[32]

In effect, Polish society had already begun during the war to resemble magma, which turned into liquid after the war ended and people returned en masse to their prewar homes and migrated elsewhere as a result of the decisions made at Potsdam to redraw borders.

The fourth trauma-inducing factor was the disintegration of the universe of institutions. According to sociologists, institutions by their very nature form a system of social control, keeping human behavior in check and imposing norms of conduct from the top, as well as creating a predictable space and a sense of security.[33] Hence their importance. Absent in 1945 were not only the prewar elites but also the structures of authentic, recognizable organizations, associations, and institutions that—as in the West—could instantly act to hinder anarchy or smother it at inception. The war almost totally disorganized public life, severed ties, and destroyed most institutions and organizations.

In 1945 an anonymous columnist wrote, "The war and occupation disturbed the pre-war order so profoundly that everything was simply turned upside-down. The world stood on its head, turned a dozen somersaults, and after we've finally landed on our feet, we are still dizzy, reeling like drunks."[34]

The destruction of the state in 1939, accompanied by the collapse of institutions, was the first traumatic assault. There is only one word that can convey the psychological experience of the time: *shock*. "In other words, the most abrupt, unexpected, surprising political, social and moral quake," wrote the author Kazimierz Wyka. "A quake extending across all the areas of public life, over all beliefs that had only recently, on the thirty-first of August and the first of September, underpinned actions and expectations."[35]

The breakdown of the state diminished social control and led to what would probably be the greatest panic in Polish history, when hundreds of thousands of people fled east before the advancing Germans. Wartime diaries as well as postwar memoirs and literature are filled with memories of the September trauma. But the destruction of the universe of institutions did not stop in that month. Virtually all institutions and organizations were banned in the lands occupied by the Third Reich and most of those in the areas annexed by the Soviet Union. In the latter, universities, theaters, and schools were also shut down after Germany invaded the Soviet Union in 1941. The Central Welfare Council and the Polish Red Cross were the only organizations the Germans allowed to operate.

In response to the German policy of disorganizing and atomizing Polish society, the resistance, aiming to preserve its social well-being, re-created the most important state institutions within the Underground State, including clandestine schools, courts of law, and various forms of social assistance. Political parties carried on, and an extensive publishing movement did its best to satisfy the hunger for information and even leisure. New bonds and a new solidarity were born underground. In the sociologist Jan Strzelecki's words, "The team, connected by ties that can best be described as brotherly, was the form of our existence. This existence, which we experienced as we lived under permanent threat, understanding that together we are walking on the precipice of life, that every time we meet increases the likelihood that we are saying good-bye forever, taught us the meaning of the word 'community.'"[36]

Thousands of such communities formed a first-of-its-kind social movement underground, which above all strengthened the Poles' belief in themselves and their hope for ultimate victory and gave them the feelings of having bonds and of being masters of their own fate. Even though the majority of those who were active underground were not formally sworn in, the movement was socially legitimate, and the population felt that it belonged to it. But mutual support was not enough. The Underground State established a code of sanctions for treason and banditry, which generated a system for overseeing the population's behavior and attitudes.[37] Because it was forced to operate underground, the structure had to limit its activities to some behaviors and geographically to those places where it could be effective. But it is clear—for all the deep engagement, social determination, self-organization, and courage of thousands of people—that these underground ties and organizations were an insufficient stand-in for a "normal," stable state and society.

The second traumatic assault on institutions came when this universe of underground institutions was wiped out in 1944. The defeat of the Warsaw Uprising significantly weakened most forms of clandestine self-organization, so crucial in sustaining society's agency during the German occupation. The next stages in society's disintegration were marked by the invasion by the Red Army and the arrests of sixteen leaders of the Underground State. As the underground ethos disappeared, an institutional vacuum persisted until the creation of the Polish Peasant Party (Polskie Stronnictwo Ludowe). Missing in 1945 were sovereign authority figures and centers of local government, judicial, and economic power. Prewar political parties, labor unions, business associations, and local societies and clubs did not resume their activities.[38] On the other hand, the Union of Polish Teachers, Polish Western Union, Sea League, Society of Children's Friends, veterans' organizations, national academic societies, and scouting movement resumed their activities fairly quickly. The Polish Peasant Party instantly grew into a nearly one-million-strong entity, especially in Lesser Poland. As the incoming government advanced its single-organization system, many organizations and associations active in 1945–48 were closed down. Yet it seems that the Communist system did not create a "sociological vacuum," a term the sociologist Stefan Nowak coined in 1979 to define the disappearance of midlevel ties and cooperation.[39] This was yet another consequence of the war and the two occupations, which made it much easier for the Communists to take power.[40] The immediate postwar scarcity of institutions translated into an absence of social control, leading to chaos and lawlessness.

Now the Catholic Church remained the only widely respected national institution. It, too, had suffered enormous losses, not only human but also material: damaged churches, asylums, hospitals, archives, and libraries. Still, it continued to govern hearts and minds. But the problem with it was that by cultivating the memory of the treatment of the Christian churches in the USSR, it spread that fear to those who opposed the "offensive of godlessness" rather than becoming a collective psychotherapist who would reduce public stress and anxiety. To use a metaphor, one could say that in organizational and institutional terms, postwar Poland resembled Cologne after the Allied carpet bombings: a sea of rubble with an almost untouched cathedral emerging out of it.

The fifth factor that caused trauma was the deformation of the existing strata-forming hierarchy. The war had reduced hierarchies and stereotypes of social roles to rubble. The anonymous columnist quoted earlier remarked, "A famous actor began to work as a waiter, the waiter began to write poetry, the poet went into the business of smuggling prosaic pork fat, and the ex-butcher was appointed theater director. Professors and scholars clad in prison uniforms worked with shovels, with former criminals serving as their guards. Mr. Kowalski suddenly sensed the pure Germanic blood flowing in his veins, while Mr. Miller and Mr. Schmidt were dying for Poland."[41]

The war economically downgraded many formerly privileged groups, including managers of state companies and proprietors of large and medium-size enterprises, which the Main Trustee Office for the East (Haupttreuhandstelle Ost—HTO) had taken over on behalf of the Third Reich in the occupied lands.[42] In the Polish Eastern Borderlands, the "government of workers and peasants" seized property belonging to the middle and upper classes. To "aryanize" the economy in the former and in the name of historical justice in the latter, thousands of people would be deprived overnight of their ownership status, which often went back generations. Existing political, scholarly, and cultural elites—politicians, civil servants, university lecturers, artists, journalists, writers—were also downgraded. Previous honors, knowledge, and offices meant nothing in this era of potato and coal shortages, and they could even be used as a pretext to persecute a person. This meant the social pyramid was steamrolled and class antagonisms lightened. The war imposed democratization on a society that had retained its pre-twentieth–century class system. But these changes also meant that the existing social order had collapsed, giving rise to anxiety due not only to social degradation but also to the social and economic ascent of small groups. Here, it is important to remember how the extermination of the Polish Jews affected the nation's social structure. The Jews were replaced by a new bourgeoisie that lacked an ethos and was rootless and insecure about its future and its property. This group had pulled itself out of the fire of war by looting and scheming with the Germans and unavoidably suffered more and more burns as the war drew to a close.

The rural population was also structurally flipped over. The ancient order, sitting firmly on the three pillars of "master, local governor and parish priest," had collapsed once and for all. In the interwar years, despite the civilizational changes that had also reached the rural areas, one could still hear people say, "There must be a master, so that when you are humble, you will earn a living and win his favor. Just like in the army. If there was no master, you would be ordered around by a boor, when you are one yourself, and nothing good will come of it. The Lord made things this way, and this is how they must be. This is the eternal, ancient order. You are not allowed to spoil it. The people were better, more obedient in the time of serfdom."[43]

In the Eastern Borderlands and the territories annexed by the Reich, the landowning class had been exterminated already in 1939. Elsewhere, its slow death dragged out until 1945. During the war in the countryside, the manor house lost its importance as a focal point of the social order, and its inhabitants were subjected to the persecution that was a cornerstone of the German policy of eliminating the Polish elites.[44] The rural population's opinions about this change were divided. Especially for older people, the fall of their feudal lord may have engendered fears of "what will things be like without the landowner, who will pay us?"[45] The younger and the unemployed, who had been given land in accordance with the land reform of 1944, feared the "return of the masters." To them, the destruction of the manor house may have represented social justice and an end to barriers and to the ancient oppressive order. Their fears, analyzed as a symbol, would later be turned into a key source of legitimacy for the postwar social order.

The importance of the second pillar of the rural communities, the *wójt*, a government clerk, and the *sołtys*, the elected chair of the village council, was also reduced, albeit for different reasons. During the war, as both functionaries of the German administrative apparatus and representatives of local communities vis-à-vis the occupation authorities, they needed to navigate nonstop between following the authorities' orders, thereby harming the community, and lying to the German authorities to protect the community's interests, thereby risking penalties. Many would cross the line between the necessary cooperation and collaboration, which would turn the village population against them and make them lose their authority.[46] The sołtys of Prudno in the Wołkowysko township remembered, "No one wanted to understand that we were living under foreign occupation, and they were all shouting to the sołtys: 'It's your fault!' There was revenge and complaints to the partisans and the bands, who then beat up even the best sołtys for bad people's lies. No one wanted to be a sołtys to avoid getting killed."[47]

Several hundred were executed after being tried by courts of the Underground State. The number of collaborators sentenced after the war is unknown. But it was not only the manor house or the village officials who helped to stabilize life in the prewar countryside. Already before the war, traditional hierarchies and relationships had begun to modernize, and a large group of rural leaders—social activists, politicians, teachers, and forest workers—was created. During the war, many of them led various formations of rural self-defense, foremost among them the Peasant Battalions. Rural solidarity clearly grew stronger as the war went on. Thanks to the war, the countryside became important as the supply network for the underground and the partisans and, most importantly, to feed the hungry towns. Yet the effects of the policies of disintegration and the collapse of social ties were most visible in rural communities. Furthermore, many peasant leaders, who could have served as leaders and focal points of social stability in postwar reconstruction, died or were exiled by the occupying powers. In sociological terms, in many rural areas the traditional community, *Gemeinschaft*, collapsed while the emerging modern society, *Gesellschaft*, had for the most part been put to death. This upset and loosened the system of power and social control in the countryside, which in turn brought on postwar chaos, anomie, and the plague of score-settling. Crime, which was partly a reaction to the wartime destabilization of the ages-old peasant world, must be added to this list.

SYMPTOMS OF THE TRAUMA

Wartime trauma manifested itself in different ways, with three of them most prevalent. The first was near-universal fear. It took over lives, affecting behaviors and outlooks. This war was exceptional in that pervasive fear was not limited to soldiers, who experience it in all wars, but affected whole civilian populations, especially in eastern Europe. This war erased whatever feeling of security had survived the Great Depression. Throughout the six years of hostilities, the Poles almost continuously felt that their lives were in danger. According to Tomasz Szarota, the psychological threat was constant.[48]

Henryk Vogler noted in his *Introduction to the Physiology of Fear* that "wherever I look in the past of our generation and of our social class that I am familiar with, I come across traces of fear. The most learned botanist knows fewer types of native plants than we knew types of this native sensation."[49] Each source of trauma mentioned above was accompanied by its own distinctive fear. The main one was fear of death, followed by distress about the fortunes of one's nearest and dearest, and there was also the fear of arrest, torture, and breaking down during an interrogation. People were living under enormous stress. The Germans could arbitrarily declare anyone guilty of anything, especially since they did not adhere to laws and could act unpredictably. To force people to obey them, they would use blind force, creating an atmosphere of terror. Stepped-up repressions put people in a state of collective psychosis, which led to escapism, atomization, and waves of apocalyptic hearsay.[50] A November 1943 diary entry by the writer Maria Dąbrowska conveys this mood: "Horrific rumors among people in Warsaw. Everyone is talking about gas chambers, that the Germans want to kill us all like the Jews. That they are doing it already."[51]

Public executions by firing squad, hanging, or guillotine (in the lands annexed by the Reich) made it seem that history had reverted to barbarian times. After the war, young Poles answered the question "what event has had the greatest impact on you?" with "the Warsaw Uprising (22 percent), their own or a friend's or relative's arrest (16 percent), execution by firing squad or hanging (14 percent), and roundups to procure hostages or forced laborers (11 percent)."[52]

An eighteen-year-old female resident of Lublin recalled, "I can remember as if it were yesterday the innocent people, their mouths filled with plaster, in groups of ten, who were made to stand up on the embankment to be shot in the backs of their heads. The next group had to move the dead out of the way to make room for themselves. A mother's piercing cry in the crowd topped it all. I was a nervous wreck for weeks."[53]

A nineteen-year-old from Warsaw: "I was there when a drunk gendarme on Kierbedź Bridge in Warsaw grabbed a little Jewish kid, stopped a passerby and told him to throw the kid in the river. The man begged for mercy for the child, the little boy was covering his shoes with kisses, but it didn't help. The German pointed his gun to force the man to act on his bestial whim."[54]

Aerial bombardments and artillery shelling of towns and villages produced borderline situations. Soviet and German deportations and resettlements gave rise to a new type of insecurity, fear, and trauma. Following the first deportation in February 1940 in a Soviet-occupied area of Poland, "the fear got to everybody. People were doing everything the Bolsheviks ordered them to do because they knew that otherwise they would land in Siberia."[55] From then on, people would spend months sleeping with food supplies and ski clothing packed by their beds. Some, unable to endure the suspense, simply wanted to be deported already.[56]

The great fear is the writer Julian Stryjkowski's term for Soviet rule in the Eastern Borderlands. The years of German occupation obfuscated some of the memories of that fear, but not enough to prevent it from feeding the postwar anguish. Words such as *Siberia* and the *Soviet Union*, *roundups* and *deportations*, *Oświęcim* and *Majdanek*, the *Gestapo* and the *NKVD*, which people uttered with terror in their voices, came to symbolize Polish fear, the national martyrology. Pauperization and the difficulty of finding food were also major sources of constant distress. It was not only Jews in ghettos and concentration camp inmates who feared hunger and infectious diseases.

The end of the war did not liberate people from the rule of fear; it did not automatically make them stop being afraid. Fear was transformed into a less tangible, often unarticulated anxiety with roots that could not always be identified. It should be added to the long list of the aftereffects of the war that were crucial in shaping the Poles' mindsets and reactions of fear.

The Poles came out of the war psychologically devastated, but it is difficult to weigh the baggage of fear they were bringing with them. Postwar estimates had sixty thousand people with mental handicaps.[57] But it is very likely that had current psychiatric and psychological tools been available then, a far greater number would have been diagnosed as suffering from the "war syndrome." The symptoms would have been many: emotional instability, stress, major depression, and phobias. Living in fear for long periods of time can also lead to conformism, social apathy, and passivity. This is how an Underground State publication described the postwar mental condition of people in Greater Poland in June 1945: "The local population's mental state continues with unextinguished fear and passivity, and a characteristic camouflage, legalism. People have not yet recovered internally, the feeling of wellbeing has not returned. The Poles do not feel that they are fully valuable human beings, they are smothered and apathetic, as they struggle full-time with daily material problems. It is difficult to awaken them from their sluggishness."[58] Observations such as these undermine the common myth of the Poles' universal postwar euphoria.

It was not only underground analysts who were interested in the Poles' psychological condition. Shortly after the war, a group of psychologists led by Stefan Baley, Stanisław Batawia, Maria Kaczyńska, and Maria Żebrowska launched an extensive study of the war's psychological impact.[59] Much later, US psychologists studying the experience of the Vietnam War diagnosed a discrete category of health problems, post-traumatic stress disorder,[60] whose most frequent symptoms include recurrent phobic reactions, phobias, psychosomatic disturbances, and addictions. Notably, in the aftermath of the Second World War, Polish psychologists observed the same symptoms in their subjects, which they called "the war complex." It included various neuroses and phobias brought on by, for instance, the howling of factory sirens or sounds made by airplanes. Diaries and memoirs also go into phobias of this type. Jadwiga Krawczyńska wrote in her memoir, "To this day, the sound of a diving plane makes me, and not only me, feel extremely unpleasant. In the immediate post-war and post-occupation years, it was very difficult to stomach the air's constant vibration and the whizzing! So many things reminded me of the horrors of September 1939 and of the Warsaw Uprising of 1944, the daytime and nighttime air raids."[61]

These psychologists also addressed the aftereffects of the war on dreams. Of the 1,005 accounts of dreams they collected, the contents of 28.5 percent of them were related to the war and occupation.[62] Wanda Półtawska wrote in her memoir *I boję się snów* (And I fear my dreams), "I came home on 28 May 1945 after a 20-day journey, and I realized a horrifying thing on the very first night: every day, or rather every night, I had dreams about Ravensbrück. To make things worse, they were so clear and lifelike that I could not tell whether I was dreaming or still in the camp."[63]

The state of emotional dejection was most visible in children, especially Jewish children. In *The Girl in the Red Coat*, Roma Ligocka remembered the first postwar lessons in a Jewish school in Cracow: "The atmosphere in the classroom is so tense. Hardly a minute passes when someone doesn't break down in tears. The teachers and the pupils cry at almost anything. Everyone is nervous, almost hysterical."[64]

Non-Jewish children in Poland also tended to be weepy and irritable. Their stories and drawings brought to light the trauma of war. "Fearfulness, timidity, distrust of strangers are often young children's chronic reactions to the horrors of war," wrote Stefan Baley.[65] Poll findings also reflected emotional problems. Asked in 1945, "Have you observed neuroses in yourself or in someone close to you?" 64.7 percent of Polish youths answered in the affirmative, with 31 percent having observed them in themselves and 69 percent in others.

A twenty-year-old man living in a village: "I have observed neuroses that were caused by pacification in myself and my whole family. We had to dig a ditch for ourselves, then to lie on the edge from 8 at night to 5 in the afternoon, we were only called out for interrogations, during which we were beaten, many were hanged. Father was hanged high up in the barn, we were forced to look at father all covered in blood."

A sixteen-year-old boy: "Father died during the uprising, mother died in the street, she was hit right in the heart. I have dreams about the uprising, sometimes horrible fears."

A twenty-year-old woman: "I am suffering from a nervous breakdown. I had a German boss who used any excuse to hit me in the face or with a belt, or he kicked me. Every knock, every sneeze, loud talk give me a fright now."[66]

Not even the passage of time could free some people from fear. Memoirs and journals written in People's Poland, as well as literary works, films, and art, testify to the long life of individuals' wartime trauma. The author of a memoir describes the post-traumatic stress syndrome as "the sickness of ruins," from which she suffered for "many years" after the war:

> I can remember more than just the first days of being back in Warsaw, when I would gag on my tears every time I saw the city—abused, wrecked, burned. I spent the next few days wandering around, crying and no longer embarrassed by the tears flooding out of my eyes. When I passed houses in which friends who were now dead or in exile had lived, memories about the ruthless occupiers would come back, and I could not stop sobbing. This lasted for a long time, a very long time, years. My breakdowns would manifest themselves with varying intensity, and the nervous shocks would recur unexpectedly. For instance, after the occupation I could not stand hearing young people laugh out loud, and I myself was no longer laughing, not even smiling. This was contrary to my usual disposition and temperament. I was irritated

by people who had booming voices, and in the street I would turn around to glare at others who were laughing, even though I knew it wasn't right.[67]

Long after 1945, psychologists would uncover layers of wartime fear. Studying the health of former German concentration camp inmates and their families, they would diagnose the "concentration camp syndrome."[68] In an early 1960s study of former inmates, only one-third of those interviewed had no major mental disorders. Studies conducted nearly thirty years after liberation showed that symptoms of the concentration camp syndrome persisted in various degrees of intensity in all former prisoners.[69] In the words of Jan Chodakowski, after his stay in Mauthausen, "the fear was still there. I was afraid of doing anything that would get me in trouble with anyone. At work, I was always afraid of talking to anyone, I was afraid of asking for my wages. This fear stayed with me almost all my life. I constantly had doubts: what if they fire me, what if something happens."[70] Psychologists found the same symptoms of fear, depression, and problems with relations with others in those who had lived through forced exile in the Soviet Union. A study by Ewa Jackowska conducted in the late 1990s shows that unpleasant, obsessive memories bothered 66 percent of those who had spent time in Siberian exile, and 33 percent of them continued to have nightmares about it. Even though over fifty years had passed since then, 30 percent of the victims suffered evident post-stress symptoms, which manifested in apprehensive reactions (fear of hunger and war, anxiety) and neurotic personality traits (feelings of inferiority, timidity, distrust).[71]

Aggression was another symptom closely correlated with war trauma. The growth of aggression in interpersonal relations was an important consequence of the war, also as expressed in the violence and the readiness to use force in even a minor social conflict. Indeed, prior to 1939 Polish society was already plagued by aggression, which exploded with exceptional brutality during labor strikes and political and ethnic conflicts. "Everybody beat up everybody else," wrote Tomasz Marszałkowski in his study of riots and demonstrations in Cracow in 1918–39.[72] In the interwar period, the escalation of violence occurred in two stages. The first, which lasted until the May 1926 coup d'état, is a good example of how aggression grows after an armed conflict, in this case the First World War. The second phase began in the early 1930s and was a symptom of both the radicalization of the political struggle and social tensions stemming from the Great Depression. Rural areas were far from bucolic then. They, too, suffered not only from the brutalization of the political struggle, whose pinnacle was the peasant strikes, but also from the patriarchal violence of everyday life, present in the home among family members and used to solve problems between neighbors and to release frustration.

The war made this type of rural violence commonplace. A village teacher remembered, "Every single village dance ended with a fist fight."[73] Other village teachers interviewed in 1946 pointed out their pupils' growing tendency to engage in fighting.[74] Solving conflicts with physical force became quite normal. Here, the ownership of firearms, which was especially prevalent in the countryside, played an important role. Setting peasant homes and farm buildings on fire remained a feature of the Polish landscape for many years after the war. But to become accustomed to using firearms, people needed a new model of socially acceptable behavior, a struggle aiming to eliminate the adversary physically. According to Citizens' Militia statistics, 8,411 murders were committed in Poland in 1945. But this is a gross underestimate.[75] It likely did not include all the killings by the police, militiamen, Security Office functionaries, Internal Security Corps, and soldiers, nor the killing of Germans or Ukrainians. Every shallow grave on the edge of a forest somewhere is also an aftereffect of the war.

There are many answers to the question about what stamped such violence on public life. A general answer is: immediately after an armed conflict, the number of murders grows. A study by Dane Archer and Rosemary Gartner views the causes as the legitimation of murder by the state and the devaluation of moral standards. "Wars provide concrete evidence that homicide, under some conditions, is acceptable in the eyes of a nation's leaders. This wartime reversal of the customary peacetime prohibition against killing may somehow influence the threshold for using homicidal force as a means of settling conflict in everyday life."[76] But the demoralization brought on by war does not explain everything. There was also the population's emotional state. Again, some psychologists believe that aggression and hostility are reactions to primal fears. The growth of individual and collective aggression can be seen as a symptom of trauma, the aftermath of living with terror and fear for a long time.

Archer and Gartner use statistics to show that wars leave behind a legacy of a growing coefficient of killings. But they do not come up with a causality between that figure and the nature of the war, whether little or big, ending in victory or in defeat. It is also remarkable that their study did not take into account Poland, Yugoslavia, and the USSR, countries that simultaneously experienced total war and partisan warfare. We could venture the hypothesis that in the case of Poland, the threshold of the argument of murder was lowered by the exceptional violence, unprecedented in centuries, of the war staged there. And here we stumble on the next reason: psychologists believe that aggression begets aggression.[77] In spite of the hopeful expectations voiced in the war's early days, the war did not have the effect of purging, of collective catharsis. On the contrary, the spectacle of hatred and German brutality eliminated all inhibitions. Even with the underground press reminding its readers about the cultural distance between the Poles and the barbarian Krauts, for some groups in society the war nonetheless launched the process of learning how to be violent and merciless. An example of this lesson appears in the wartime diaries of the writer Jarosław Iwaszkiewicz. A neighborhood boy learns to solve problems overnight: when someone starts to bother you, you just grab a gun, take the person aside—and it's done. The youth discovers this effortlessness as he watches German gendarmes, who do not hesitate to execute three Jews they arrested in the train station.[78] This lesson is also visible in collective behaviors. It would appear that the murderers of the Jews of Jedwabne were aping the Germans' burning of seven hundred to eight hundred Jews in a synagogue in Białystok in late June 1941.

The Poles responded to the occupying powers' violence by escalating their own. Aggression became a facet of the wartime way of life, a unique set of norms and behaviors that included drunkenness, disregard for human life, cynicism, and a perspective shortened to the coming days, even hours. According to a diary, "Most of those who experienced 'the forest' no longer valued human life, they became accustomed to an effortless and unconstrained life, to moonshine and all that."[79] The blade of aggression could also turn against members of one's own national group. As a result, public life became increasingly brutal over the years, which could be seen in the growth of criminal behaviors, brawls, and brutal murders. Nazi terror also created an atmosphere favoring another type of terror: the lawlessness and armed attacks by political or quasi-political groups. According to psychologists, when suffering and premature death are everywhere, scruples about inflicting suffering and death evaporate.[80] Incidents of torturing adversaries once the war ended would probably not have occurred had the war not increased aggression. Once Berlin was captured and the war was over, it would probably not have occurred to any commander to order a village or small town pacified had he not witnessed pacifications during the war.

The process of internalizing aggression was most significant in the General Government and in Volhynia, where the Germans went to great lengths to treat civilians ruthlessly, to a degree comparable only to their acts in Yugoslavia and the USSR, but in Poland this treatment lasted the longest. The significance of this experience becomes clear when one compares the morale of the men of the First Polish Army, most of them from the Eastern Borderlands, with that of the men who joined the Second Army from lands earlier belonging to the General Government. After studying hundreds of reports coming from Military Information and political commissars, this author would venture the hypothesis that soldiers who originally came from central Poland more frequently treated German prisoners of war and civilians cruelly and were tried by drumhead courts-martial for attacking their countrymen more frequently.

The nature of partisan warfare, long known to have been exceptionally bloody and ruthless, also contributed to the rise of aggression. Underground fighters had no inkling about prisoner-of-war laws (the soldiers in the Warsaw Uprising were an exception), which usually meant that regular units would execute prisoners; the partisans usually took no prisoners, if only because they had nowhere to hold them. What is more, the underground soldiers' aggressive behaviors were rewarded since they were treated as heroes and decorated, in contrast to aggression by civilians. A blatant example is that of a Home Army saboteur near Rzeszów who carried out hundreds of death sentences. Today, we would call him an executioner. In a unit of hundreds, he was one of four men to be decorated for bravery with the Cross of Valor. There is no question that he was a courageous and disciplined team player, but he was also cruel and merciless. He was rewarded for executing a fellow fighter accused of collaboration by being transferred to a sabotage unit. Subsequently, as "Żbik I," he killed Poles, Germans, and Ukrainians, most of them men, but occasionally also women. "I shot at people as if they were practice targets, feeling nothing. I enjoyed looking at their terrified faces before they were liquidated, I enjoyed looking at the streamlets of blood gushing out of their shattered skulls."[81] In operation "Storm" he killed at least a handful of German prisoners of war who had no military identity documents on them with shots to the backs of their heads. As revenge for being humiliated and robbed by Soviet soldiers, he hammered a nail into the head of a random drunk one. "The little Soviet only sighed gently and stiffened in some strange convulsions, which were over in no time. I got back on my bike and set off on my way, without emotions or scruples."[82] "Żbik I" was involved in murdering fifty Ukrainians. "As I looked at their bodies, I thought of myself as a hero who is working hard for his Motherland and admiring the fruits of his labor."[83] He killed several members of the Polish Workers' Party and wrote about the soldiers of leftist formations: "We executed them on the spot, closely following orders from Home Army Headquarters."[84] His memoirs illustrate wartime aberration, contempt for human life, aggression, and sadism.[85] They are one of the many symptoms of the anomie, the demise of existing norms and disruption of social relations during the occupation.[86]

The third symptom of wartime trauma, as well as a strategy for coping with it, was alcoholism. Little of it is visible in postwar photographs, even though it was an effect of the war, which also contributed to the postwar mood. City dwellers drank alcohol, usually moonshine, en masse. In the countryside, it ceased to be an item to be drunk festively in pubs and instead became a key feature of daily life. Now, women also drank—something that before the war would have been scandalous—as did adolescents and children. A postwar study of seven- to fifteen-year-olds in Lublin found that of its 1,000 interviewees, only 264 had never tasted vodka, while 27.9 percent drank regularly and 47.4 percent occasionally. In 90 percent of the cases, their parents served as suppliers.[87] In some villages, moonshine was produced in nearly every farmer's house. A farmer who lived near Augustów remembered, "As the parents drank, they even gave vodka to their underage children, would turn them into drunks, what a scandal. Of the 50 families that remain in our village only four did not produce vodka, and all the others had distilleries at home.... I often saw with my own eyes parents plying their own young children with vodka. As blood poured at the front, vodka poured inside our homes."[88]

During the war, producing and selling moonshine turned out to be an exceptionally profitable occupation. Inflation turned alcohol into a crucial commodity. After the war, vodka was used also, perhaps primarily, to barter with Soviet troops. The unexpected currency devaluation introduced in January 1945 left millions penniless. The new bills began to arrive in many regions of the country, especially in the Regained Territories a few months later. Until then, even factories and institutions such as the militia paid their employees' and functionaries' salaries in bottles of vodka.

Drinking became a part of the wartime lifestyle that did not disappear after the capture of Berlin. People often committed theft and looting after the war under the influence of alcohol or in order to acquire it. Typical militia reports of the era included information about distillery holdups. An inhabitant of Pomerania noted, "Observation leads me to conclude that the reasons for alcoholism here were an indeterminate occupation, existence and domicile, since alcohol was needed to awaken courage, made it easier to make friends and to bribe people, and was the universal, often irreplaceable currency in all dark affairs."[89]

Alcohol was the stimulant for the postwar anti-Semitic unrest. Many of the executioners in the Cracow pogrom of August 1945 acted under its influence. Inebriated invalids started anti-Semitic brawls in Zduńska Wola in November 1945 and in Cracow in March 1946. Drunk soldiers, Citizens' Militia, Security Service, and Internal Security Corps functionaries initiated many incidents of this kind. A drunk launched a pogrom in Kielce in 1946. Another pogrom participant, later sentenced to death, testified that before he joined the crowd, "I went home and drank a quarter of a liter of vodka and had a snack."[90] It is conceivable that inebriated individuals were also responsible for many postwar murders, both political and criminal and many of them exceptionally cold-blooded. Losing oneself in drink and cruelty often merged.

Moralists have accused the Germans of driving the Poles to drink, since they did often pay with alcohol. But because of alcohol's high caloric content, people also drank during the war to deaden hunger. And its therapeutic value was even more important. "Confronted with bitterness and a sense of entrapment, vodka offered instants of solace and, what was most important, of forgetting; it relieved frustration and neutralized tension and thoughts about pain."[91]

THE CULTURAL CONSEQUENCES OF THE TRAUMA

The trauma of the world war also disturbed culture, both its normative (values, norms, rules, principles) and cognitive (convictions, beliefs, opinions) components. Here, the changes were the most substantial, enduring, and inert, much like postwar anxiety. War had upset the old world's most crucial values, putting into question its strategies and behaviors, and the occupation's unreality forced people to look for new behavioral strategies to soothe their trauma. The sociologist Pitirim Sorokin wrote in 1942, "Calamities generate two opposite movements in different sections of the population: one is a trend toward unreligiousness and demoralization; the other is a trend toward extreme religious spiritual and moral exaltation."[92] Three pairs of complementary opposites best represented the Polish situation during the occupation. First, on the one hand were the growth of religious faith and the lure of magical thinking, which may have brought with them elevated moral standards, and on the other were alienation from the church for some and for others a process leading to the atrophy of moral bonds and an anomie. The second pair of opposites defined family ties: they were both strengthened and weakened. The third pair of opposites was the reinforcement of national ties and solidarity that transcended class divisions and the emergence of an exclusive definition of the national "we," which included a deeper, or at least persistent, anti-Semitism. These three dichotomies should not be labeled as good and bad. While increased piety could be strongly correlated with an aversion to Jews, the strengthening of family ties may have led to family-centrism and indifference toward others. To put it differently, there was no nook or cranny in the Polish collective soul that could resist becoming infected by the complex of war.

For a large part of the population, stronger religiosity was a natural reaction to the fear and horror of the war. Attending church daily also gave people a chance to meet, as a substitute for other ties and social activities that had been destroyed by the occupying powers. In the autumn of 1939, Poland's churches were already crowded like never before. "People prayed ardently, churches were saturated with exultation and hope."[93] When street roundups multiplied and people became afraid of going out, group prayers were held in small chapels in the courtyards of apartment complexes. Ties to the church became stronger, despite the fact that Primate August Hlond had fled the country; after the war,

The Trauma of a World War

mass participation in religious ceremonies continued.⁹⁴ But anti-clericalism, which had been fairly widespread in the prewar peasant movement, definitely weakened as a result of the feeling of community of the equally persecuted nation and church, as well as the worsening of the church's economic situation in the countryside. Maria Kaczyńska, the author of a mid-1945 study of youth attitudes, noted an increase in religiosity. Fifty-four percent (65 percent of girls and 43 percent of boys) believed that their faith had deepened during the war while 26 percent stated that it had not changed and 19 percent confessed that they had left the church. They said, "'The war had a positive impact on my faith. As a result of all the misfortunes that befell our nation, I became more religious' (boy, 16 years old). 'I stopped going to church and became an atheist' (adolescent, 18)."⁹⁵

People reacted to the trauma by subscribing to magical thinking as well as to prophecies and predictions, especially those foretelling the imminent fall of both the Soviet Union and the Third Reich. The downfall of the state, the annihilation of the known world, uncertainty, and lack of information combined to serve as fertile ground for the atrophying of critical thinking and blossoming of magic. The anthropologist Bronisław Malinowski wrote, "The function of magic is to ritualize man's optimism, to enhance his faith in the victory of hope over fear. Magic expresses the greater value for man of confidence over doubt, of steadfastness over vacillation, of optimism over pessimism."⁹⁶ His thinking was backed up by Karolina Lanckorońska's observation after she stayed for a few months in Soviet-occupied Lvov:

> As there was no good news, the most fantastic prophesies proliferated, passed from person to person or, worse, many copies were written out and hidden in people's apartments.... First was the rhymed prophecy, according to which the war would last four years, which sometimes troubled even those who repeated it, but it did not mean that the war in Europe, and particularly in Poland where it had begun, would last so long, and this prophecy promised that "the fouled cross will fall together with the hammer" and that Poland will extend from sea to sea. During the winters, especially popular was Saint Andrew Bobola's reported prophecy, which promised that the Russians would leave Poland on 7 or 9 January, something schoolchildren told one another at school, only to be arrested for it. [Legendary Cossack bard] Wernyhora also continued to worry us constantly with new revelations. It was difficult to challenge these prophecies because people yearned for them like drugs, a habit that, as we know, is difficult to break.⁹⁷

The end of the war did not free the Poles from their addiction to magical thinking. Prophecies about the timing of a conflict between East and West were much repeated. The messianic predictions helped people to find a new source of hope and faith for the future, to give meaning to the present, which was unstable and bad. The myth about alleged ritual murders of Christian children by Jews, which began to spread like wildfire beginning in the spring of 1945, was similarly magical. The reasons for the relentless repetition of this myth can explain the civilizational regression brought on by the war and the human need to explain a world that evades explanation.

Religious extremism may have helped to raise moral standards. But there are reasons to believe that this dimorphism of values, a duality of moral attitudes and values (high in the closest circle of family and friends and low vis-à-vis anyone outside that circle), which was later also characteristic of People's Poland, had surfaced already during the war. This was the wartime schizophrenia or, as Kazimierz Wyka described it, the wartime "living as if," which embodied the deep split between reality and the normative system.⁹⁸ While standards of "what is not done" survived, the war left no choice but to steal and kill in order to survive. There is no question that thousands of people adhered to prewar principles and norms, which they demonstrated with the utmost heroism, self-sacrifice, and empathy toward others. But the majority entered a gray area of morality and vacillated between a selective depreciation of some values ("because a person has to survive somehow") and a total atrophy of morality, which led to a deterioration of binding obligations to others and an extreme egotism. The sociologist Piotr Sztompka believes that there are three manifestations of this atrophy: a culture of cynicism, which means constant suspicion, distrust, and belief that others are guided by the basest motivations; a culture of manipulation, which consists of lying and cheating and taking advantage of others' trust and gullibility; and a culture of indifference, or a socially accepted radical self-interest, egotism, and indifference to the suffering of others.[99]

The war favored all three types of culture, and the wartime way of life allowed them to coexist. A person's chances of survival diminished drastically without the weapon of deep distrust. The culture of cynicism was a defensive strategy. The individual might either fight or flee the threat by, for example, cutting himself off from the outside world he distrusted. This strategy, indispensable when facing a permanent threat, proved useful also after the war. But it carried a price: growing social atomization, severed ties, unwillingness to engage, passivity. The passive attitude and apathy of the "local population," in conjunction with distrust, often appears in reports by representatives of "people's power," who are often bitter about it. This distrust and fear, however, appeared not only in the population's relations with the authorities but also in everyday interactions, especially in rural areas, where it became a new layer on top of the peasants' earlier, universal distrust and distance. Numerous Polish Jewish memoirs recount instances during the occupation when peasants denied them assistance. Without downplaying that anti-Semitism, we also need to know that there were stories about Mazovian peasants avoiding Varsovians coming out of the Warsaw Uprising so they would not need to help them, a behavior that can be partly explained by their ancient defensive strategies.[100] Postwar peasant memoirs also discuss behavior of this kind. People barricading themselves inside their homes, hiding weapons, and not venturing outside after dark are only a few extreme examples of behaviors guided by fear. For many years after the war, psychologists remarked that a major problem for the victims of German persecution was their loss of trust of their surroundings and difficult relations with others stemming from the collapse of the psychological mechanisms of adaptation.[101]

The war also taught people the culture of manipulation. Lying and cheating, especially in relations with the Germans, was practically encouraged. A report from the Government Delegate's Office dated late April–early May 1942 reads, "Social phenomena that have recently become more pronounced include an unsettling increase in the demoralization of many strata of society, a demoralization that in some of its manifestations must necessarily be tolerated now, and sometimes even endorsed."[102]

The most drastic deterioration of moral standards occurred in work ethos and business ethics, and it unexpectedly became the Poles' second nature. The authors of the report cited above further noted, "Illicit trade, which consumers support out of necessity and which the pro-freedom organizations recommend as the only way to stave off hunger, is, however, usually the same as the black market, which does not care about poverty, hunger and the growing material ruin of compatriots."[103]

The culture of manipulation also expressed itself as corruption. Paying bribes to Germans made it easier to function and saved many underground activists' lives. But it soon became the norm in the German administration's[104] dealings with Poles—as another symptom of society's degeneration.

An underground report to the government in exile captured the demoralization:

> We have recently reached the point in the public services where often and in many places nothing gets done without a bribe. Almost universal corruption, bribery and definitely illegal methods as sources of income now reign among the Polish staff of many departments of the self-government, institutions that have replaced the old economic self-government and many branches of public administration. Taking care of a matter relatively quickly, efficiently and successfully in this or that administrative, economic or treasury office, to secure officially a desired apartment or shop, a rail pass, to find a seat on that train, to send cargo by train, to extend the hours of

access to electricity, to connect or fix a telephone, to repair a gas installation, etc. in Poland today, all this requires is bribes of different amounts.[105]

Like the cultures of manipulation and corruption, the culture of indifference was also required, as it guaranteed mental health. The problem? It led to an exclusivity of moral ties, reducing human solidarity to small groups.

The most visible sign of the atrophy of moral ties was the spread of antisocial behaviors and an increase in crime. A tendency toward anomie and aberrant behaviors survived from the war; behaviors that before the war had been generally deemed criminal were now considered the norm, even a source of pride. In the study mentioned above of 1,500 young people, over half (60.6 percent) answered yes to the question "Have you stolen, cheated, lied, etc. to Germans?" Maria Kaczyńska, the author of the study, noted, "Although only 10 percent of the young people state clearly that stealing from and cheating Germans had a negative influence on their characters, we nonetheless must assume that wherever and for whatever reasons such an act occurred, it must have had a negative influence on the psyches of those who committed it. And 60.6 percent of the youth in the study had committed such acts, according to their own statements; 20 percent did not respond, and only 19.4 percent clearly stated that they had not committed them."[106]

The teachers interviewed in 1946 noticed behaviors in their pupils including a lack of respect for others' property, an interest in weapons, lowered moral standards, drinking, and an inclination to brawl.[107] Those young people who were mostly weakly rooted in prewar values were most prone to these pathologies. But the problem also affected adults. In observing the impact of the war on older generations, Maria Kaczyńska predicted, "If we take into account the fact that almost the entire adult society committed such acts against the occupiers and that the lack of respect for others' property was well-developed in our psyches (probably as a result of captivity and demoralization by the oppressors), we can predict that now, after the war, dishonesty toward others' property will become catastrophic for our public, community and private life."[108]

Even though this is not altogether obvious from militia statistics,[109] in reality crime grew exponentially, especially among juveniles. Stanisław Batawia, a postwar crime researcher, noted that:

> The psychological climate in those countries [once occupied by the Third Reich] is saturated with an extreme hatred and aggression that we do not come across in countries that were not occupied. In the countries occupied by an enemy force, children and adolescents continue to dwell in an atmosphere of persistent fear, uncertain of the fates of their nearest and dearest, often also their own, cheek by jowl with death. They are witnessing the occupier's total annihilation of fundamental legal and moral principles. Daily life teaches them that once axiomatic ethical norms are relative. Nazi propaganda poisons them with contempt and hatred for people who belong to particular races and nations, encouraging and provoking crimes with impunity against those the occupier has condemned to annihilation. For many years, the underage population witnessed the legalized mass murder of hundreds of thousands of helpless people, bottomless cruelty and constant pillaging of murder victims' property.[110]

In contrast to the experience of observing the annihilation of the Jews, stealing their property was not considered a crime. The fragility of postwar institutions responsible for maintaining order favored impunity. The end of the war did not interrupt the progress of anomie, if only for this reason, and it was heightened by postwar migrations.

During the war, and with particular intensity immediately afterward, people already wrote about the advancing pathology of moral ties, then usually called "demoralization." Newspapers called for combatting it, as did the Catholic Church. For instance, Bishop of Łomża Stanisław Łukomski, whose sermons of 1940–44 have been analyzed by Jan Żaryn, noted deep changes in his flock's behavior. Of the new pathologies in public life, the bishop listed women's excessive submissiveness to the occupiers, disrespect for others' property, the rise in crime, and the resultant insensitivity to witnessed death.[111] The Episcopate's pastoral letter for Lent 1946 focused on the downfall of "private and public morality."[112] It is only when people witness and experience events of this kind as problems in need of a cure that trauma appears. According to Sztompka, "It is the most visible manifestation of trauma when people talk about it and want to do something about it."[113]

The phenomena discussed here, most importantly the culture of cynicism and indifference, as well as increased crime and other deviant behaviors corresponded closely to the processes affecting the family as an institution. It is a challenge to assess these changes. Unquestionably, there was the effect of closing ranks. It can be explained only partly by the overcrowding brought on by resettlements ordered by the occupier and the destruction of housing stock. Far more important causes included life under constant threat as well as pauperization, which was growing exponentially. Faced with the catastrophe of war, the family really did become an oasis of safety in which to survive, a place of psychological respite. The family also became more important economically. "People owed their living conditions to their parents," wrote Kazimierz Wyka.[114] In the 1945 youth study, 61.1 percent of respondents believed that the war had boosted solidarity within their family. "Family relations became tighter because we began to understand each other" (youth, eighteen). "As I watched my mother worry about me, that nothing bad happen to me in this time of roundups, executions and other dangers, I just had to love her more" (young man, twenty). "I realized what parents are, and I feared for their lives" (girl, nineteen).[115]

But the strengthening of family ties could lead to the atrophy of all other types of ties, which were already weakened by the occupiers' disintegrative policies. Social ties were disintegrating in two ways: from top and bottom. The whole organizational and institutional infrastructure was being destroyed from the top. From the bottom, the horrors of daily life forced people to narrow down the concept of society to one's own family and friends, and the home became the supporting institution and focus of life.[116] The family's interests became supreme, establishing the framework for everything people did. Not everyone belonged to the "Columbus generation" of Second World War fighters who were guided by the national interest and built the community that sociologist Jan Strzelecki wrote about. The huge majority of people, living in constant danger (not only of roundups and pacifications but also hunger, typhus, and tuberculosis) were unable to act on behalf of larger groups or even of individuals—including persecuted Jews. Memoirs written by those who survived concentration and labor camps tell us about becoming apathetic, desensitized to the suffering of others. The culture of indifference was also present on the other side of the barbed wire, although not in all groups and all milieux. It would seem that this was decisively affected by the degree of one's impoverishment. A widow bringing up her child in the city or a father of five in the countryside needed to focus all their efforts on survival. This kind of broadened individualism or egotism, which sociologists call "family-centric,"[117] shrank the social space in which an individual traveled, and thus had a disintegrating effect. Already before the war, social solidarity did not thrive in the impoverished Polish countryside, and after the war family-centrism, especially in extremely pauperized areas, became the dominant modus vivendi.

A secondary-school pupil described the relationships in his village in Nieszawa District after the war: "I am ashamed to admit that communal activity in our village is pretty weak. There is none of that community feeling and unity. Usually people aren't eager to help their neighbors, but they also don't ask for help themselves. Often people are envious of someone who is doing better, and sometimes are even happy at the misfortunes of others. You can see the missing sense of community especially, for example, when a road needs to be fixed together, when trucks need to be sent out or when money contributions are needed. Everyone avoids it and makes excuses for himself."[118]

An opposite tendency weakened or outright broke family ties. Husbands and fathers were killed; landed in prisoner-of-war camps, concentration camps, prisons, or forced labor; and fought at the fronts.[119] Their absence accelerated the process of women's and young people's emancipation, but it also increased women's fear of being alone. Hardship forced young people to earn a living, which influenced their relations with their parents. "My attitude toward my parents changed under the occupation. I don't listen to my parents, I became independent and began not to care about anything" (girl, eighteen). "I noticed that I strangely don't care about my parents and my siblings, which is probably due to my nervous exhaustion" (young man, nineteen).

Many young Poles' abrupt entry into adulthood had an impact on the social order. A new generation that could not remember the prewar years appeared.[120] The connections between the old and young generations weakened, especially in the countryside and in the urban working class. According to Czesław Madajczyk, the occupation favored a changing of the guard: "Many of those who survived were quickly able to take on difficult and mature tasks in public life after the war."[121] But there is another diagnosis. The teachers polled in 1946 about the war's influence on their students' psyches listed the "loosening of discipline" (66 percent of answers) second.[122] The absence of fathers upset the old patriarchal model of upbringing, which in turn further weakened social norms. Many of those who survived developed a distorted idea of good and evil, which then led to postwar violence and some of the pathologies of the Stalinist years. A changing of the guard did indeed happen, but it is questionable whether it was a good thing.

National ties became stronger. The world at war was described almost exclusively in ethnic categories. Class or group identities became less important, and what mattered was belonging to the national community,[123] which largely decided whether a person survived the war. For most Poles, the national identity became stronger. Wartime poetry, brimming with national themes, attests to this. Such nationalization was most visible in the countryside. In September 1939 in some areas of Poland, the Germans were already virtually greeted with bread and salt:

In the evening strode in the enemy, whose external as well as internal character did not at all turn out to be that of the executioner, as the slogans had told us, but he turned out to be of the utmost goodness. So the population of our village was very happy about their arrival. People who fled to the forest are now coming back happily to see these new arrivals. Seeing them and their behavior, the peasants said that they were liberators, not some sort of enemies. Because right after they entered our village, they turned out to be so good that no one could even imagine. Right after they came, as they handed out chocolate, sweets and oranges, lemons and many other things to the children, and whole loaves of bread, canned meat and various soups to the poor population.... Straight away then, a few people from the village left voluntarily to work in Germany, thinking that they will live in paradise.[124]

As the war drew to a close, everyday "individual collaboration" of this kind was rare.[125] A peasant memoirist from the Kielce region admitted, "The occupation made us politically conscious, and we learned the meaning of freedom, of the Motherland, of politics."[126] This patriotic zeal was evident on the battlefields.

British pilots described their Polish comrades fighting in the Battle of Britain, who had been trained before the war, as courageous, filled with bravado, and hateful toward the Germans. Compared to the more restrained British and Americans or the outright skeptical French, Belgians, and Norwegians, the Poles stood out with their exceptionally patriotic attitude. But this deepening and intensifying of their national identity had its price.

First of all, Polishness turned out to be exceptionally possessive: it overrode all other identities and identifications. A sociological vacuum arose not only because there were no authentic institutions or organizations to engage civil society but also because national and family bonds reigned supreme. This accelerated and forced patriotic education lacked positive messages and often boiled down to a rift between us and them, friend and foe. There is an anachronistic term for this type of thinking: *tribal*. It imposed a readiness to sacrifice oneself, mandated idealizing the national past and feeling proud—but it entailed an isolation and a sense of being besieged and threatened. The war forced people to divide the world into "ours" (Poles, Allies) and "theirs" (Germans, Ukrainians, Soviets) and created a sense of community by augmenting the feeling of otherness and antagonism vis-à-vis others.[127] It left a deep anti-German scar and an extremely negative image of the Germans. As the war was ending, the desire for revenge for "our wrongs was widespread among the Poles."[128] Relations with the Ukrainians, based on fear and deep wounds, also brimmed with hatred. The Polish–Belorussian disagreement was fired up in the Białystok region. The annihilation of the Jews also helped to bring together the Polish national community. But as the historian Krystyna Kersten frequently remarked, the consequences of the Holocaust went wider and deeper.[129] The division into those who had been marked for immediate execution (the Jews) and those whose sentences were delayed and who were allowed to live fairly normal lives under the occupation (the Poles) inevitably had consequences. The war strengthened the Poles' national consciousness but left deep scars on it, which took the form of national phobias, wounds, and prejudices. The circumstances of the occupation did not promote openness toward other ethnic groups or stigmatizing anti-Semitism, which inevitably formed a xenophobic national community. The process of shaping the national identity and strengthening national ties influenced attitudes toward the Jews, just as it fortified piousness.

Anti-Semitism. The war and occupation bared the full spectrum of Polish attitudes and behaviors toward the Jews, from altruism and heroic, selfless assistance[130] to self-interested help or indifference toward the Other (which initially did not preclude a Christian emotional reaction) to open hostility in denouncing and turning in Jews, and even murdering them. This last type of behavior tended not to be motivated solely by anti-Semitism but rather by a combination of anti-Semitism, fear, anomie, family-centrism, and material incentives. On the other hand, it cannot be denied that in some circles, including nationalist ones, the Holocaust paradoxically did not make people abandon their anti-Semitic vocabulary[131] but fortified anti-Semitic views. Underground State analysts noted that, "the venom of the collaborationist press has seeped into the young people," that young people are "convinced that the Germans have liberated Poland from Jewish oppression."[132] The Underground State's Stefan Grot-Rowecki wrote in a report in September 1941 that "anti-Semitism prevails" in Poland.[133]

Several factors—there is not enough room to examine all of them in detail here—explain the reinforcement of anti-Semitism or its persistence on the existing level.[134] The most significant factors were the general surge of nationalist emotions in 1939–45 and the growing gaps among ethnic groups and among all groups of "others." The nationalism of eastern Europe has always been highly correlated with anti-Semitism, and so there is no reason for things to have been different during and immediately after the war. Blaming anti-Semitism on the war does not hold water. We must remember that ill feeling toward the Jews was almost omnipresent in Poland before 1939, that anti-Semitism had been growing since about 1930, and that its quantitative wartime leap continued prewar trends. It was brought on by the great material deprivation and frustrations of many people, a result of the dramatic economic crisis of the early 1930s. "Many ethical concepts and certitudes collapsed," noted a Polish Socialist Party leader in 1937.[135] Incidentally, it is not out of the question that had the Second World War not occurred, the most important traumatic event the Poles would have remembered from that era was the Great Depression.

German models of political culture, which the Polish extreme nationalist right emulated, also strengthened anti-Semitic attitudes. The effect of Nazi propaganda appeared to grow under the occupation, especially early on, when the "unvanquished Third Reich" could still impress. It is always difficult to analyze the perceptions of propaganda messages, but we can assume that before the war they reached mostly simple, uneducated lowest earners with authoritarian tendencies who were pleased that "Hitler will clean things up."

Under the German occupation of Poland, vulgar propaganda, which was hostile to Jews, reached unprecedented proportions. It was omnipresent: in the cinema, on posters, in Polish-language brochures and newspapers published by the occupation authorities. It was rooted in two cultural codes, which often merged. The first, which had appeared already in the writings of Herodotus, was the fear of the East perceived as synonymous with chaos, barbarism, and bloody and savage ruling methods. The second was religious fear, which powerfully saturated medieval and Renaissance thought, and fear of the Last Judgment, Armageddon, and Satan. Paradoxically, the totalitarian state's modern propaganda apparatus revived these archaic fears. *Nowy Kurier Warszawski*, a Polish-language German collaborationist newspaper, wrote in January 1944:

> Today, the Polish nation is facing the direct horror of the Bolshevik yoke. We can already see the bright eyes of the red beast, which tenses up to pounce at our family hearths, our temples, our peaceful workshops. We can take only one of two roads: to understand the enormity of the threat, to unite in a joint effort with the German rampart of Europe and of the Christian faith or to stand, with arms folded and fear in our hearts, and wait, in vain, to be rescued by someone.... As an ancient Catholic nation, let's join the camp of the defenders of Christ's teachings against Satan's looming rule.[136]

The Jews were allegedly Satan's agents, as they directed the NKVD and purportedly aimed to implement "Bolshevik law," or the rule of fear, in Poland through arrests, expulsions, collectivization, and Sovietization. The last issue of *Nowy Kurier Warszawski*, dated January 17, 1945, reads, "The red hordes are coming to grab all the Polish lands, to hand over all Poles to Moscow's rule. We know what this rule means: stamping out all Polish national aspirations, serfdom for the peasants in the yoke of kolkhozes, economic and currency chaos, hunger, forcible recruitment into the red army, deportations of millions of Poles to Siberia or the Central Asian steppes."[137]

We will never know how the Poles reacted to this propaganda. There may have been two diametrically opposed answers, both sociologically unsound: they outright rejected it or, on the contrary, fully internalized it. After studying rumors, bits of legends and myths that circulated in the immediate postwar years, and, most important, the powerful stereotype of the "Jew-Communist," we can venture the hypothesis that this propaganda did leave an imprint on the political awareness of some Poles, which persisted all the longer since it had an intellectual foundation in the interwar period.

The message of the Third Reich's anti-Semitic propaganda distanced the Poles from the Jews mentally and boosted the negative image of Jews in Polish minds, making them into abstract non-people: "no dogs or Jews allowed," as the sign would have it. This image was accompanied by the physical isolation of the Jewish population in ghettos. "Evidently, moral inhibitions do not act at a distance. They are inextricably tied down to human proximity. Commitment of immoral acts, on the contrary, becomes easier with every inch of social distance," wrote Zygmunt Bauman.[138] In the symbolic sphere, moving the Jews into ghettos meant objectifying them and expelling them from the human world. In practice, as it limited the mingling of the two groups and each group's space, it reduced empathy toward the Jews and even increased hostility toward them. Thus, the ghetto walls, much like prison walls in Philip Zimbardo's experiments, became mediators of anti-Semitism.

Anti-Semitism was able to grow stronger because the voices that censured it were not loud enough. The problem certainly lay in the varying degrees of anti-Semitism of some in the Polish elite, which can be found in the underground press.[139] On the other hand, the empathy toward the Jews who were being exterminated voiced in the Home Army's *Biuletyn Informacyjny* and in the Communist underground newspapers could not possibly sway the masses of uneducated, poor people who before the war had been expendable. If today we complain about the catastrophic state of readership, seventy years ago, during the war, it must have been infinitely worse.[140] While owning a radio carried the penalty of death under the Germans, prior to 1939 few people living in the countryside or in working-class districts owned one. Only a loud public outcry against hostility toward the Jews and negative stereotypes of them could have reduced them, but under the German occupation such an outcry would have had no chance of reaching those it should have reached. When these views and behaviors could not be sufficiently censured, and in the absence of social control, they became social fact.

Another reason for the growing hostility toward the Jews was the psychosocial condition of the Polish national group. It had at least two components. First was the Germans' degradation of the Poles in the socioeconomic hierarchy to the position of *Untermenschen*. Some people could feel satisfied or comforted, even superior, at seeing that another minority was being mistreated even more.[141] The second factor was the growing collective fear and anxiety.[142] These feelings are the psychological component of every nationalism, including the anti-Jewish one. Antoni Kępiński wrote, "Perhaps (because the enemy is invisible) wars are becoming increasingly cruel and ruthless. For this reason, anxiety and aggression are unloaded mostly on the innocent—children, women and old people. As one panics in fear of losing one's life, everything turns into an enemy, not only people but also nature, and so one destroys and burns everything in one's way, fearing that otherwise one will be destroyed."[143]

There was another way in which Polish fear was associated with the Jews. When Jews were being hidden, everyone living in the hiding place, including children, risked death. Thus, Jews became the carriers of a literally biological anxiety and fear. This had always been the case, but during the war the threat the Jews personified reached a pitch that some could not bear psychologically. Refusing to help or even denouncing Jews helped to reduce that fear, to put the source of danger at arm's length.

And finally the last factor, perhaps one of the most crucial: unlike the western Europeans, the Poles, especially those living in the General Government, had been taught not only the theory but also the practice of hatred as they watched their Jewish neighbors being murdered. It is a matter of consequences, writes Michael C. Steinlauf, "the subjective nature of the witnessing." Steinlauf quotes Robert Jay Lifton's idea that "the heart of the traumatic syndrome" is "psychic numbing." Anger, fury and aggression may accompany it as its victims attempt to regain their vital powers.[144] It would seem that the concept of the observers' "psychic numbing" explains well the images of Poles murdering their Jewish neighbors in Jedwabne or Radziłów in a stupor, or of Jewish policemen beating their own people as they walked onto the ramp in the *Umschlagplatz*. The experiences of living in the General Government may thus have increased not only aggression but also the distance from others. In this context, an important observation comes from Lieutenant Colonel Minecki, an officer of the Polish Army's Main Political–Educational Department. In the wake of the Cracow pogrom of August 1945, Minecki commented on the characteristic differences in attitudes toward Jews between troops originally coming from the areas east of the Bug River and those from the General Government: "For the former, the anti-Semitic movement is little known and sometimes they have difficulty coming to terms with the fact that it may have motivated the bloody violence. Many of them have close friends and battle comrades who are Jews," he wrote. On the other hand, "among the soldiers from the [General Government] there is a deep hatred toward the Jewish population as a whole, which has been fed by the occupying power and is the cause of all social ills."[145]

The literary critic Kazimierz Wyka made a similar observation, though not in the Jewish context. He pointed out a difference between the population of the General Government on the one hand and on the other the forced laborers and even Poles from the areas annexed by the Reich, who were free of the "typical contamination by the occupation."[146] Perhaps the fact that they did not directly witness the Holocaust made their distance from the Jews significantly smaller than that of the Poles from central and eastern Poland. If this were the case, it would mean that the trauma of experiencing the German occupation in the General Government may have played a key role in shaping pathological attitudes and behaviors, not just in relations with outsiders.

SUMMARY

"Modern war is total not only in terms of arms and destruction, but in sociological terms," wrote Kazimierz

Wyka.[147] It is undeniable that large numbers of Poles went into 1945 "infected with the war complex," sociologically shattered, with a pathological value system, apprehensive. Indeed, in most European countries, especially those that had been occupied by the Third Reich, societies were in similar shape. Everywhere, chaos and a sense of uncertainty came in the wake of military operations. Millions were anxious about the future. The postwar migrations, crime, the settling of accounts, and some violent acts of revenge inflicted on collaborators and Germans did not encourage rapid stabilization.[148] In many countries, violence and aggression—whether civil war, national conflict, or state violence against opposition—were endemic.[149] The rise of juvenile crime was noted in statistical data even in the United States, Britain, and Finland.[150] In Germany, the years of Nazism, war, defeat and loss of *Heimat*, Allied military occupation, rapes, and political repression collected as a vast reservoir of hatred in both the public and private spheres. There, too, social pathologies, underage crime, and prostitution grew.[151] Everywhere in the West, intergenerational ties weakened, and with them connections between past and present.[152] Nowhere could the specter of hunger be shooed away. In Great Britain in 1943, civilian consumption dropped by 20 percent.[153] Two years later, the fear of unemployment, linked with the transition to a peace economy, manifested itself in England and the United States in the form of weakened work discipline and strikes.[154] And it was not only in Poland that the distances among ethnic groups grew. Thus, British prejudice against people of color arriving in the British Isles escalated. In 1943, Los Angeles and Detroit witnessed unrest brought on by an influx of Mexicans.[155] In Chicago in 1945, whites attacked black car owners. In 1945 in Czechoslovakia, mass pogroms and anti-German lynchings occurred. Yugoslavia was the venue of bloody ethnic purges. Anti-Jewish sentiments were observed not only in Poland, but it was probably only in Poland that the anti-Semitic mood reached the level of collective psychosis. The range of behaviors was wide, from unfriendly indifference to verbalized resentment to demonstrated hostility.[156] Holocaust survivors heard fear-driven words such as "why did you come back here?" "no one needs you here," and "no one asked you to come" in many countries, including France, the Netherlands, and Ukraine. An anti-Semitic pogrom took place in Kiev in September 1946. In Slovakia, synagogues and Jewish cemeteries were desecrated. In September 1945 in Topol'čany, forty-nine people were injured in a pogrom, and similar acts of violence occurred in other localities. In Hungary, too, pogroms and anti-Jewish incidents transpired.[157] Twenty-two percent of the US troops stationed in Germany believed that the Germans had been right to get rid of the Jews.[158]

Again: the war destabilized social relations and brought pauperization and trauma to many countries. Europe's Jews experienced it uniquely. But right behind them in this sad ranking placed the Poles, Ukrainians, Belorussians, and Russians[159]—the peoples of Timothy Snyder's *Bloodlands*.[160] In no other part of Europe were nations so psychologically ravaged, and it was probably only here that the processes of atomization and anomie went so far. Polish society was damaged, robbed of its elites and institutions, swaying this way and that as never before. It was a society in chaos, a collection of family communities that resembled tribes rather than a society. The consequences of the trauma of the war spread out over time, and it took time to rebuild social ties, to normalize and stabilize, and to forget. The wartime way of life, which suspended customary moral and legal norms, established itself so deeply that it survived for many years after the war ended. Some fears and wounds, habits and behaviors entered the nation's cultural bloodstream for an even longer time. They survive to this day and reveal themselves as returning "ethnic allergies." The Czech philosopher Jan Patočka wrote, What is most important is that the war is not over. It has been transformed into a specific state, neither war nor peace."[161] Even though he was writing about the time after the First World War, his thought can also serve as the gist of these reflections.

NOTES

1. The first version of this chapter appeared as Zaremba, "Trauma Wielkiej Wojny," 2, 3–42.

2. Beevor and Vinogradova, *A Writer at War*, 313.

3. Marwick, *War and Social Change*, 10.

4. There is an enormous body of literature about the war and the occupation. But its social history is scarce, and the majority of post-1989 studies are devoted to daily life. The most important books include Madajczyk, *Polityka III Rzeszy w okupowanej Polsce*; Łuczak, *Polityka ekonomiczna Trzeciej Rzeszy w latach drugiej wojny światowej*; Łuczak, *Polska i Polacy w drugiej wojnie światowej*; Gross, *Polish Society under German Occupation*. First on the list of works about everyday life is Szarota, *Okupowanej Warszawy dzień powszedni*. And: Hryciuk, *Polacy we Lwowie 1939–1944*; Lewandowska, *Życie codzienne Wilna w latach II wojny światowej*; Chwalba, *Kraków w latach 1939–1945*; Czocher, *W okupowanym Krakowie*. The classics give us another type of analysis: Wyka, *Życie na niby*; Strzelecki, *Próby świadectwa*. Noteworthy psychological and sociological works about the Second World War are Jackowska, *Psychiczne następstwa deportacji w głąb ZSRR w czasie drugiej wojny światowej*; and Rokuszewska-Pawełek, *Chaos i przymus*.

5. Sorokin, *Man and Society in Calamity*.

6. Sztompka, *Trauma wielkiej zmiany*.

7. Sztompka, 20.

8. For more on trauma, see Kapralski, "Trauma i pamięć zbiorowa. Przypadek Jedwabnego," 631–33.

9. Cf. Gross, *Geneza społeczna demokracji ludowych o konsekwencja II wojny światowej w Europie Środkowej*, in *Komunizm*, 40–58 (Gross, "The Social Consequences of War," 198–214); Gross, "War as Revolution"; Abrams, "The Second World War and the East European Revolution," 623–24.

10. Baley, "O pewnej metodzie badań wpływów na psychikę młodzieży," 37; Baley, "Psychiczne wpływy drugiej wojny światowej," 12.

11. Wspomnienia Stefana Lipickiego, prezydenta miasta Kołobrzeg w okresie 1 VI–31 VIII 1945, 100.

12. AIPN, Komenda Główna Milicji Obywatelskiej (henceforth KG MO) 35/922. Sprawozdanie od dnia 15 IV do 15 V 1945, Wojewódzka Komenda MO Dolny Śląsk, k 1.

13. Godycka-Cwirko, *Lata klęski 1944–1973*, 40.

14. "Przyspieszyć ekshumacje," *Życie Warszawy*, April 15, 1945; "Poprawa stanu sanitarnego miasta sprawą najpilniejszą," *Życie Warszawy*, May 2, 1945.

15. *Dziennik Powszechny* of September 17, 1945, reported in the article "Plaga szczurów w Kieleckim" (A rat plague in Kielce Province): "The Provincial Health Department was recently alerted about a huge plague of mice and rats in the districts that suffered destruction. There are localities on the so-called bridgehead, where mice have literally stripped all the cereals that have been harvested, leaving chopped-up sheaves. And rats are swarming in huge numbers in the bunkers and mud huts in which people who lost their homes are living, sowing diseases and fear among the locals. If the rat plague is not stopped, we can expect reports of rats biting babies and children."

16. Panufnik, *O sobie*, 148.

17. Osińska, "Warszawa, maj 1945," *Tygodnik Powszechny*, July 1, 1945.

18. More in Wawrzyniak, "W cieniu śmierci," *Polityka*, September 29, 2005; Zaremba, "Malborków wiele," *Polityka*, February 21, 2009.

19. Kaczyńska, "Psychiczne skutki wojny wśród dzieci i młodzieży," 54.

20. The office initially estimated losses at 4.8 million (not counting the decreased birth rate of ca. 1.25 million), but Communist leader Jakub Berman ordered this number raised to 6 million (Gniazdowski, "'Ustalić liczbę zabitych na 6 milionów,'" 99–113).

21. Łuczak, "Szanse i trudności bilansu demograficznego Polski w latach 1939–1945," 9–15. The same issue of *Dzieje Najnowsze* includes articles on this subject by Jerzy Z. Holzer, Franciszek Piper, Józef Marszałek, and Krystyna Kersten; Materski and Szarota, *Polska 1939–1945 straty osobowe i ofiary represji pod dwiema okupacjami*.

22. *Polska 1939–1945*, 15.

23. Szarota, "Upowszechnienie kultury," 412.

24. According to Krystyny Kersten, the number of people with a university education was no higher than 65,000. Kersten, "Polskiego inteligenta życie po śmierci," 54.

25. Jędruszczak, *Miasta i przemysł w okresie odbudowy*, 279.

26. *Dziennik Powszechny*, February 14, 1946.

27. Steinhaus, *Wspomnienia i zapiski*, 348.

28. Sorokin, *Man and Society in Calamity*, 25–35. Banfield, *The Moral Basis of a Backward Society* elaborated on these observations.

29. Parandowski, *Luźne kartki*, 14, 15.

30. Detailed data can be found in Sienkiewicz and Hryciuk, *Wysiedlenia, wypędzenia i ucieczki 1939–1959*.

31. The total figure for people who settled in the East was actually at least twice that, since we must add men forcibly recruited by the Red Army and construction battalions, Gulag prisoners, people expelled from the border zone, and others. More in Ciesielski et al., *Masowe deportacje ludności w Związku Radzieckim*. For a narrative and analysis of the consequences of ethnic cleansing in this part of Europe, see Ther and Siljak, *Redrawing Nations*.

32. Łuczak, *Polityka ludnościowa*, 507.

33. Berger and Luckmann, *The Social Construction of Reality*, 72–73.

34. *Dziennik Powszechny*, May 19, 1945.

35. Wyka, *Życie na niby*, 81.

36. Strzelecki, *Próby świadectwa*, 14.

37. Gondek, *Polska karząca 1939–1945*.

38. In Szczebrzeszyn, a small town in eastern Poland, the following associations (not counting political parties and ethnic-minority organizations) existed at some point: Fire Department, "Sokół," St. Vincent a Paulo Christian Mercy Society, Catholic Polish Women's Association, Association of Polish Youth, Association of Democratic Young Countryside, Women's Military Training Organization to Defend the Country, Polish Red Cross, Society for the Protection of Animals, Friends of the Scouts Club, Riflemen's Union, Society of Rifleman's Friends, Union of Women's Civic Work, Union of Reserve Officers, Reservists' Union, Polish Military Organization Union, Legionnaires' Union, Union

of Elementary School Teachers, Society of Secondary School and University Teachers, League of Air and Anti-Gas Defense, Sea and Colonial League, and Society of Poles Abroad. There were also professional organizations, credit unions, and funeral unions. Klukowski, *Zamojszczyna 1918–1943*, 48.

39. Nowak, "System wartości społeczeństwa polskiego," 155–73.

40. Jan T. Gross (*The Social Consequences of War . . .*, op. cit.,) and Bradley E. Abrams (*The Second World War . . .*, op. cit.) note that the disappearance of the Polish and Jewish bourgeoisies during the war was beneficial to the Communists. But the authors did not detect the significance of the destruction of mid-level social ties.

41. *Dziennik Powszechny*, May 19, 1945.

42. More in Madajczyk, *Polityka III Rzeszy*, vol. 1, 515–95.

43. Chałasiński, *Młode pokolenie chłopów*, vol. 1, 71

44. Jasiewicz, *Lista strat ziemiaństwa polskiego 1939–1956*; Jasiewicz, *Zagłada polskich Kresów*.

45. Kersten and Szarota, *Wieś polska 1939–1948*, 483.

46. Madajczyk, *Polityka III Rzeszy*, 194; Łuczak, *Polityka ludnościowa*, 511.

47. Chustecki, *Byłem sołtysem w latach okupacji*, 117.

48. Szarota, *Okupowanej Warszawy*, 457.

49. Vogler, *Wstęp do fizjologii strachu*, 18.

50. Gmitruk et al., *Pro memoria (1941–1944)*, 465.

51. Dąbrowska, *Dzienniki 1914–1965 w 13 tomach*, vol. 5, 71.

52. Kaczyńska, *Psychiczne skutki*, 55

53. Kaczyńska, 55–58.

54. Kaczyńska, 55–58.

55. Gross and Grudzińska-Gross, *W czterdziestym nas matko na sybir zesłali . . ." Polska a Rosja 1939–42*, 67.

56. Lanckorońska, *Wspomnienia wojenne*, 55.

57. Kersten, "Społeczeństwo polskie wobec władzy komunistów," 8.

58. AAN, Delegatura Rządu, 202/III-36, k. 171. Raport o sytuacji na Ziemiach Zachodnich. Wielkopolska (od 15 V do 15 VI 1945).

59. Stalinism unfortunately prevented them from writing a conclusion, and some of the unexamined material was scattered. But by 1948 several articles discussing some of their findings did appear.

60. Cf. Lis-Turlejska, *Traumatyczny stres*; Dudek, *Zaburzenia po stresie traumatycznym*.

61. Krawczyńska, *Zapiski dziennikarki warszawskiej 1939–1947*, 304.

62. Baley, *Psychiczne wpływy drugiej wojny światowej*, 13.

63. Półtawska, *I boję się snów*, 2.

64. Ligocka, *The Girl in the Red Coat*, 119.

65. More on this subject in Baley, *Psychiczne wpływy drugiej wojny światowej*, 13.

66. Kaczyńska, *Psychiczne skutki wojny*, 60.

67. Krawczyńska, *Zapiski dziennikarki warszawskiej*, 304.

68. Kępiński, *Rytm życia*, chapter on "KZ-syndrom."

69. For the most recent review of this research, see Jackowska, *Psychiczne następstwa*, 61–84.

70. Madoń-Mitzner, *Ocaleni z Mauthausen*, 328.

71. Madoń-Mitzner, 327, 328.

72. Marszałkowski, *Zamieszki, ekscesy i demonstracje w Krakowie 1918–1939*.

73. *Wieś polska 1939–1948*, vol. 1, 421.

74. Baley, *Psychiczne wpływy drugiej wojny światowej*, 21.

75. The numbers of recorded murders went down in subsequent years. The militia recorded 7,146 in 1946; 2,812 in 1947; 1,345 in 1948; and 1,068 in 1949. *Przestępstwa zameldowane Policji w latach 1924–1938 oraz przestępstwa zameldowane Milicji Obywatelskiej w latach 1945–1964*, 33.

76. Archer and Gartner, "Peacetime Casualties," 113.

77. Pietrzak, *Agresja indywidualna i zbiorowa w sytuacji napięć społecznych*, 30–2; Geen, Stonner, and Shope, "The Facilitation of Aggression by Aggression," 721–26.

78. Iwaszkiewicz, *Dzienniki 1911–1955*, 223.

79. *Wieś polska 1939–1948*, 105.

80. Pinker, "Żegnaj przemocy."

81. Dąmbski, *Egzekutor*, 23.

82. Dąmbski, 49.

83. Dąmbski, 89.

84. There was no such official order. Still, it is just as important that the belief about the headquarters supporting murders of this kind was widespread.

85. Dąmbski, *Egzekutor*.

86. Let me emphasize that the majority of the underground's commanders attempted to stop this kind of behavior, to prevent the buildup of a group of "professionals." But the disintegration of the underground's organizational structure after the defeat of the Warsaw Uprising made it increasingly difficult to keep their men under control (Gondek, *Polska karząca*, 145 et al.).

87. As quoted in *Dziennik Powszechny*, March 14, 1946, but without the authors or dates of the study. Dreszerowa and Handelsman, "Alkoholizm u młodzieży szkolnej," *Zdrowie Psychiczne*, 2–4, 1948, 112–18, confirm these data. Their findings include data that before the war there were half as many children who drank alcohol, often 10 percent fewer who did not drink than after the war. For more information, see Kosiński, *Historia pijaństwa w czasach PRL*.

88. *Wieś polska 1939–1948*, vol. 4, 11, 12.

89. *Wieś polska 1939–1948*, vol. 1, 241.

90. *Antyżydowskie wydarzenia kieleckie 4 VII 1946 roku*, 122.

91. Buryła, "Wojna i alkohol," 207.

92. Sorokin, *Man and Society in Calamity*, 161.

93. Wyka, *Życie na niby*, 231.

94. Kersten, *The Establishment of Communist Rule in Poland, 1943–1948*, 211–12.

95. Kaczyńska, *Psychiczne skutki wojny*, 66.

96. Malinowski, *Magic, Science and Religion, and Other Essays*, 90.

97. Lanckorońska, *Wspomnienia wojenne*, 35.

98. Wyka, *Życie na niby*.

99. Sztompka, *Socjologia analiza społeczeństwa*, 188.

100. Godycka-Cwirko, *Lata klęski 1944–1973*, 19, 20.

101. Jackowska, *Psychiczne następstwa*, 77.

102. "Pro memoria o sytuacji w kraju w okresie 16 IV–31 V 1942," 157.

103. "Pro memoria o sytuacji w kraju w okresie 16 IV–31 V 1942," 157.
104. Madajczyk, *Polityka III Rzeszy*, vol. 1, 500, 501.
105. *Pro memoria*, 157.
106. Kaczyńska, *Psychiczne skutki wojny*, 62.
107. Baley, *Psychiczne wpływy drugiej wojny światowej*, 21.
108. Kaczyńska, *Psychiczne skutki wojny*, 62.
109. According to militia statistics, of the 265,962 crimes committed in 1945, 26,471 were robberies, 10,073 bodily injuries, and 121,729 thefts. In 1946, the militia recorded 239,954 crimes and 227,175 in 1947 Comparing these figures to prewar statistics, researchers consider them much too low. Thus, in 1936 State Police recorded over 200 percent more crimes: in 1936 they recorded 597,779 crimes; in 1937 they recorded 586,409; and in 1938 they recorded 545,905. Yet there are two reasons why comparisons of prewar and postwar crime are flawed: first, fewer than 20 million people lived in the area covered by the militia statistics in 1945, compared to 35 million in the prewar period. Therefore, the coefficient for reported crimes per 100,000 people may have been close. Second, after the war, many crimes were not recorded. In other words, militia statistics for 1945 do not convey the scale of lawbreaking, which should have been considered catastrophic. Majer, "Zapomniana formacja."
110. Batawia, "Wpływ ostatniej wojny na przestępczość nieletnich," 27.
111. Żaryn, "Hierarchia Kościoła katolickiego wobec relacji polsko-żydowskich w latach 1945–1947," 77.
112. "Panowanie Ducha Bożego w Polsce. Wielkopostny list pasterski Episkopatu," 35.
113. Sztompka, *Trauma wielkiej zmiany*, 36, 37.
114. Wyka, *Życie na niby*, 7.
115. Kaczyńska, *Psychiczne skutki wojny*, 63, 64.
116. Cf. Łukaszewicz, "Funkcje domu w okresie okupacji niemieckiej," 67–82.
117. Tarkowska and Tarkowski, "'Amoralny familizm' czyli o dezintegracji społecznej w Polsce lat osiemdziesiątych," 263–82.
118. *Wieś polska 1939–1948*, vol. 1, 223.
119. The abridged first census of February 1946 revealed a huge deficit of men—2.3 million fewer than women. There were 121.5 women for every 100 men; in the remaining prewar territory the figure was 117.8, and in the western and northern areas it was 137.1. The distorted ratio was greater in the towns and cities (130.8) than in the countryside (117.4). *Rocznik statystyczny 1947*, 19.
120. Wyka, *Życie na niby*, 128.
121. Madajczyk, *Polityka III Rzeszy*, vol. 2, 100.
122. Baley, *Psychiczne wpływy drugiej wojny światowej*, op. cit., 31.
123. Krystyna Kersten wrote extensively about this—for example, in "Ruchliwość w Polsce po II wojnie światowej jako element przeobrażeń społecznych i kształtowania postaw," 178. See also Kłoskowska, *Kultury narodowe u korzeni*, 299–321.
124. *Wieś polska 1939–1948*, vol. 2, 24.
125. For more on collaboration, see Madajczyk, "Kann man in Polen 1939–1945 von Kollaboration sprechen?," 133–48; Madajczyk, "Między współpracą a kolaboracją"; Friedrich, "Problem polskiej kolaboracji podczas II wojny światowej (1939–1944/45)," 46–52; Friedrich, "Collaboration in a 'Land without a Quisling,'" 711–46; Connelly, "Why the Poles Collaborated so Little—and Why That Is No Reason for National Hubris," 771–81; Paczkowski, "Polska ofiarą dwóch totalitaryzmów 1939–1945," 13–17; Gross, "O kolaboracji," 407–16; Szarota, *Karuzela na Placu Krasińskich*.
126. *Wieś polska 1939–1948*, vol. 2, 70.
127. Kersten, "Polska—państwo narodowe," 462.
128. Cf. Dmitrów, *Niemcy i okupacja hitlerowska w oczach Polaków*.
129. Kersten, "Polska—państwo narodowe."
130. Bartoszewski and Lewinówna, *Ten jest z ojczyzny mojej*; Urynowicz, "Stosunki polsko-żydowskie w Warszawie w okresie okupacji hitlerowskiej," 537–626; Paulsson, *Secret City*.
131. Szymon Rudnicki, "Mogą żyć, byle nie u nas … Propaganda NSZ wobec Żydów," *Więź*, April 2006, 111.
132. As quoted in Chwalba, *Kraków w latach 1939–1945*, 161.
133. As quoted in Kersten, *Polacy, Żydzi, komunizm*, 15, 16.
134. For more see Kersten, *Polacy, Żydzi, komunizm*; Gross, "'Ten jest z Ojczyzny mojej,'" 25–60; *Wokół Jedwabnego*; *Polacy i Żydzi*; *Prowincja noc*.
135. As quoted in Friszke, *Adam Ciołkosz*, 175.
136. *Nowy Kurier Warszawski*, January 12, 1944.
137. *Nowy Kurier Warszawski*, January 17, 1945.
138. Bauman, *Modernity and the Holocaust*, 192.
139. Cf. Szapiro, *Wojna żydowsko-niemiecka*; Friszke, "Publicystyka Polski Podziemnej wobec zagłady Żydów 1939–1944"; Friedrich, "Nazistowski mord na Żydach w prasie polskich komunistów (1942–1944)," 54–75.
140. According to Andrzej Paczkowski, near the end of the interwar period, about 2.5 million people bought the daily papers, and therefore 5 to 7.5 million read them. There were huge regional and hence language-nationality differences. For example, people in majority-Belarusian regions did not read newspapers at all while the German figures were well above average. Paczkowski, *Prasa polska w latach 1918–1939*, 412–43. So far no one has attempted to measure the readership of underground newspapers in the General Government. Circulation estimates are fragmentary and address only individual publications. For example, the Underground State's *Biuletyn Informacyjny* had a maximum print run of 50,000. Jarowiecki et al., *Prasa polska w latach 1939–1945*, 49. Paczkowski estimates that at its peak in the first half of 1944, a total of several hundred thousand (400,000 to 500,000 or perhaps 700,000 to 800,000) copies of all underground publications may have appeared. (Letter from A. Paczkowski to the author.) Publications were passed from person to person, so the numbers of readers must have been much higher. But it is unlikely that it went over a million at the time of the intensified extermination of the Jews.
141. "How did the Poles react to us? With laughter? With scorn? With some satisfaction that must have made them more self-assured: some people are lower than them." "O tym, jak z wewnątrz getta patrzono na stronę aryjską. Z profesorem Israelem Gutmanem rozmawia Barbara Engelking," *Zagłada Żydów. Studia i materiały*, 230.

142. I agree with Jan T. Gross when he challenges the single-cause explanation of fear for why the Poles did not help the Jews enough, since fear did not stop people from, for example, engaging in clandestine work. But he forgets that the huge majority of the population was involved in no underground activity. Their lack of engagement can be explained with conformism and fear, which were highly correlated. Gross, "Ten jest z Ojczyzny mojej," 34–38).
143. Kępiński, *Lęk*, 275.
144. Steinlauf, *Bondage to the Dead*, 57.
145. Cichopek, *Pogrom Żydów w Krakowie 11 VIII 1945*, 227, 228.
146. Wyka, *Życie na niby*, 135.
147. Wyka, 27.
148. Cf. *The Politics of Retribution in Europe*; Frommer, *National Cleansing*; Mazower, *Dark Continent*.
149. Judt, "Preface," 7.
150. Batawia, *Wpływ ostatniej wojny na przestępczość nieletnich*, 25.
151. Bessel, "Hatred after War," 195–216; see also Bessel, *Germany 1945*; for a study of German youth after the war, see Redding, *Hitler's Shadow*.
152. Hobsbawm, *The Age of Extremes*.
153. Hobsbawm, 50. See also Zweiniger-Bargielowska, *Austerity in Britain*.
154. *Praca i Opieka Społeczna*, 113–15.
155. Allport, *The Nature of Prejudice*, 219, 221.
156. Aleksiun-Mądrzak, "Sytuacja Żydów w Europie Wschodniej w latach 1945–1947 w świetle raportów przedstawicieli dyplomatycznych Wielkiej Brytanii," 65–75.
157. Kersten, *Polacy, Żydzi, komunizm*, 134–35.
158. Stouffer et al., *The American Soldier*, vol. 2, 571.
159. The Soviets, especially in the western republics, also lived through a trauma, although victory made them proud and strengthened state institutions. Weiner, *Making Sense of War*.
160. Snyder, *Bloodlands*.
161. Patočka, "Wojna XX wieku oraz wiek XX jako wojna," 150.

4

IN THE BEGINNING WAS CHAOS

For all intents and purposes, chaos and war are virtually conjoined twins. Virtually because it is not war itself that creates chaos—some bureaucratic war machines have managed very well in wartime—but the fighting. The battlefield rarely resembles an orderly board game but instead usually the haphazard clashing of electrons. When political power dies, chaos thrives. And chaos thrives not only when centers of government die but also when there are too many of them or when they are constantly changing. Thus, people living in areas that have changed governments as a result of military operations, often more than once, experience the pain of chaos.

The onset of chaos may be gradual when a regime weakens or abrupt when we wake up to see an empty lot where the police station used to stand. This kind of situation leads to various often contradictory psychological reactions. According to Jean Delumeau, "A power vacuum is ambiguous. It releases forces that were cooped up as long as power was strong. A time of permissiveness arrives. It brings hope, freedom, abandon and feast. But it invariably also produces something other than fear. It also releases its opposite number: the undeniable cargo of anxiety hiding inside it. The head spins; we have broken off with continuity, hence with security. Now, tomorrow is uncertain, maybe better or maybe worse than yesterday. The new anxiety and nervousness can easily lead to violent unrest."[1]

Order helps us to orient ourselves and therefore to feel secure. Chaos deprives us of this point of reference. When chaos takes over, social control—both in terms of a system of generally followed norms and principles and as an institutional infrastructure used to punish those who violate these norms—wanes. When the fear of getting caught diminishes, a wave of asocial behavior follows in the form of crime, the settling of scores, or explosions of interethnic resentments. For some, this is a time of successes, for others of excruciating uncertainty.

In September 1939 the Poles experienced chaos as they fled the invading German armored columns in a panic. In 1943 they again lived through chaos, with the lawlessness of random street roundups in Warsaw, nicknamed "Mexico," and in areas of concentrated German pacifications: Kielce Province, Lublin Province, and Volhynia. According to an assessment by the Government Delegate's Office for Poland:

Confusion and chaos have been growing in the General Government for several months now. Amid this confusion, alongside operations by authorized Polish organizations aimed against the occupying forces are operations organized by political groups that are not subordinated to the Polish authorities, various semi-political and semi-private groups, Soviet sabotage units and, finally, proliferating ordinary gangs of bandits. All these heavily armed groups are becoming increasingly active, and for this reason it is often difficult to know who was responsible for an operation. Altogether, this makes the current life of our province appear to be a universal revolt of bloody confusion and total economic chaos."[2]

All this creates the impression that the German occupation authorities decided that in some regions, especially in the Eastern Borderlands, it was less costly to govern by chaos than to strive to restore order.

One thing is certain: the longer the state of chaos prevailed, the greater the numbers of people who tried to take advantage of it and tried to adapt to it. It turned out that the central force generating chaos was the passing of the front line and the new occupation, this time Soviet. "Liberation" was an exceptional moment: boundless joy combined with surprise at the abrupt end of brutal German rule. Roman Loth, who was living in Radom then, remembered, "Excitement and joy that it's all over became the dominant emotions. But uncertainty and worry came alongside it. Paradoxically, as the military action moved away from us, as we could count on some degree of calm, we felt helpless, trusting in vague hope, lost in the new world emerging out of Chaos, as it had in the early days of Creation."[3]

Widespread anxiety about the uncertain future—what next?—accompanied these emotions. How would life sort itself out? In his diary, Zygmunt Klukowski described this state of powerful anxiety—panic, actually. On July 19, 1944, he wrote, "People are afraid, even though there is universal joy across the city that the Germans are gone. People are passing on gossip about forced evacuations, men being taken away, robberies and so on. Some are burying and hiding their most expensive possessions, food, while others have left the city for a while."[4]

It turned out that in some areas there were no Germans and no Soviets; Red Army units either had not yet arrived or had passed through quickly leaving clouds of dust in their wake. There was Delumeau's power vacuum for an instant, an hour or a few days. The philosopher Józef Tischner recalled, "I can clearly remember not even the day, but the instant when one power had left and the other had not yet arrived."[5]

The sudden arrival of freedom inebriated some. Others took advantage of this power vacuum. Here came looting and the bloody settling of accounts, some of it having been put aside for this very moment. "And then, the horrific hunt for kapos began": this is how Stanisław Dobosiewicz, a prisoner of the Mauthausen-Gusen I concentration camp, remembered liberation.[6] Back home in Poland, people were taking revenge on neighbors who had collaborated. Newspapers were calling for public executions of "the nation's traitors."[7] Some Jews coming out of hiding, who had witnessed Poles informing, betraying, and even assassinating, were now murdered. Women accused of having had intimate relationships with Germans became the victims of group violence, had their heads shaven. This punishment, which had been sanctioned in 1943 by the underground Home Army, was now being implemented spontaneously on a mass scale. In Kielce shortly after liberation, a number of women had their hair shorn, then were told to march through the streets to face taunting crowds.[8] In June 1945 an unheard-of underground group invaded the small town of Sterdyń near Sokołowo Podlaskie and shaved the heads of women who, according to the Citizens' Militia, "used to maintain close relations with germans [sic] and now the soviets [sic]."[9] "They are still shaving girls' heads and telling them to pay 300 zlotys each," wrote a man from the environs of Płock in a letter to a friend or relative.[10] In Żurawica in May 1945, ten months after the town was liberated, an anonymous group "performed executions on women by shaving their heads and cutting off their hair."[11]

With the Germans gone, the people of the underground became unemployed. Some engaged in vengeance for what had happened during the war; punishing those believed guilty of treason became a popular occupation. In his diaries, Klukowski recorded a handful of executions of alleged collaborators. Most likely in a majority of the cases the punishment was out of proportion with the crime. First, because real collaborators had long fled with the Germans, and second, because the avengers also murdered relatives of people they had accused of treason. For some of the avengers, killing became effortless: they set their minds to it and became addicted to it, compensating for the shortage of German blood by turning against anyone who had spent the occupation in the "gray zone" and not been "one of us." A child wrote to its father about its mother's murder, which had probably been brought on by the father's taking the wrong side in a political conflict: "Daddy dearest, do not despair that mommy has died. . . . It's done, she won't be back. Mommy was killed out in the field. . . . As they were taking her to beat her up in the cemetery, mommy begged them so much, sirs, please don't kill me and make my children orphans, they paid no attention, and when she got to the cemetery she fell down and prayed to God to forgive her sins, they picked mommy up and took her to the cemetery and shot her in the left side of the head three times."[12]

It was not only the Polish "forest people" who adhered to the principle of collective responsibility but often also Lithuanian and Ukrainian partisans. All partisan movements liquidate their nation's suspected and real traitors,[13] and the Polish Communists were no exception. Władysław Gomułka told Bulgarian leader Georgi Dimitrov about the situation in Poland in May 1945: "We have armed our party members, but after they were armed the kangaroo courts began. Party members went and killed people without asking anyone's permission. At times they would simply kill someone and leave their body in the street to make a point."[14] The spiral of violence reached a level comparable to wartime. Someone wrote from Busko-Zdrój, "Things are not so great in Busko because brothers are killing brothers, shamefully, with gun butts, breaking their arms, legs, poking out their eyes, cutting up their innards. Two people from the Polish Workers' Party, from the militia, have been murdered thus, this is a very sad picture, even the Hitlerite bands didn't perform such feats."[15]

To observers, this war, which had all the attributes of a civil war, only deepened the impression of chaos. This impression was changed little by the appearance of the first centers of authority, mostly because in 1944 in the "liberated" area reaching from Białystok to Przemyśl in the east, many localities were ruled by the triumvirate of Red Army war commissar, delegate of the government in exile, and the starost and mayor appointed by the Polish Committee of National Liberation (Polski Komitet Wyzwolenia Narodowego). In some areas, four or even five power centers—adding local Polish partisan leaders and, in the southeast, Ukrainian partisans—claimed that they were in charge. Whether they liked it or not, in such situations the locals had to serve many masters. The structural establishment of the new power solved nothing, at least initially, since the population did not support it. As they acquired the tools of power, the new authorities remained very weak. In mid-June 1945, a correspondent wrote from the village of Mordy near Siedlce, "Things are getting worse and worse here. They come into town at night and kill innocent people, beat them up, murder and steal whatever they can, and during the day they lurk on the roads outside towns and kill people all the same, drag their bodies into the cereal fields, and people find the bodies a week or so later. Things were pretty calm until April, but now they are awful. This wouldn't be happening if the army was here, but we only have a few militias, who just aren't managing."[16]

The chaos of war blended with administrative and economic chaos, especially after the January 1945 replacement of the occupation-era currency with a new one. Historical literature tends to describe the year or so after the war as a time when the new order was being constructed. The poet Zbigniew Herbert wrote about the beautiful human longing for rational arrangements that would explain dark events, as it did when the Siennese beat the Florentines. "On 4 September 1260, Siena lived its finest hour—routing the strong Florentine army of thirty thousand men near its walls at Monteaperti, *'che fece l'Arbia colorato in rosso.'* The river flowed with blood, sang the poet amidst the many contradictory accounts of the battle, as the chaos of combat is systemized *post factum* by generals, politicians and chroniclers to provide rationalizations for dark events. All the bells tolled in Siena."[17]

Actually, this time Poland was even more chaotic, disorderly, "dark," made up of events that observers could not organize into a logical sequence. A sense of disorder, anarchy, and uncertainty dominated. Several factors contributed to this. First, the arrival of millions of Red Army troops, whose behavior—robbery and rape—significantly prolonged the rule of chaos. Second, the presence of the "demobilized," hundreds of thousands of people made redundant by the war. Bandits and looters were recruited for gangs that roamed in search of loot. Pillage and banditry were the third and fourth sources of chaos. The fifth, an especially traumatic one, was the great migrations. Each factor needs to be analyzed individually because of their social consequences and their impact on collective emotions.

NOTES

1. Delumeau, *La Peur en Occident*, 157.
2. "Pro memoria o sytuacji w kraju. Generalne Gubernatorstwo i Ziemie Wschodnie w okresie 22 V – 19 VI 1943," in Gmitruk et al., *Pro memoria*, 394.
3. Loth, *Wspomnienia Kochanowskie*, 16, 17.
4. Klukowski, *Zamojszczyzna 1944–1959*, vol. 2, 71.
5. Michnik, Tischner, and Żakowski, *Między Panem a Plebanem*, 8.
6. Archiwum Historii Mówionej, Relacja Stanisława Dobosiewicza. Wywiad przeprowadził Piotr Filipkowski.
7. Rawicz, "Publicznie karać zdrajców narodu!"
8. Massalski and Meducki, *Kielce w latach okupacji hitlerowskiej 1939–1945*, 305.
9. AIPN, KG MO 35/897, k. 126. Raport milicji, n.d.
10. AIPN, MBP 3378, k. 83. Specjalne doniesienie dot. działalności dywersyjnych band.
11. It is possible that sexual violence in the area of Przemyśl was not so much a "splinter" of the old war as a manifestation of the new Polish–Ukrainian one (AIPN, MBP 3378, k. 77. Specjalne doniesienie dot. działalności dywersyjnych band).
12. AIPN 3378, k. 79. Specjalne doniesienie dot. działalności dywersyjnych band.
13. Grzegorz Motyka, *Od rzezi wołyńskiej do akcji "Wisła,"* 359.
14. *Polska—ZSRR: struktury podległości. Dokumenty KC WKP(b) 1944–1949*, Warsaw, 118.
15. AIPN 3378, k. 81. Specjalne doniesienie dot. działalności dywersyjnych band.
16. AIPN 3378, k. 83. Specjalne doniesienie dot. działalności dywersyjnych band.
17. Herbert, *The Barbarian in the Garden*, 52.

5

"OUT OF THE FRYING PAN AND INTO THE FIRE"

THE DREADED RED ARMY

Marching and billeting armies have always frightened people.[1] The saying "out of the frying pan and into the fire"[2] illustrates this fear. People experienced it in Poland on many occasions since the Great Northern War of the eighteenth century. The population would go into hiding in the forests to evade marching armies and the marauders coming in their wake like locusts. The partitioning powers would treat the quartering of soldiers as a punishment, a way to pacify moods of rebellion. During the Polish-Soviet War of 1920, the cry "Budyonny is coming!" would make civilian populations fall to pieces. In September 1939, the panic that preceded the approaching front made thousands of Poles flee east. Many terrified people would go into an anti-German hysteria, imagining that they could see fifth-column saboteurs in every nook and cranny. Some Poles with German names were interned, and several thousand were killed. During the September 1939 defense of Warsaw, General Walerian Czuma needed to issue an order forbidding "such harassment, which is based on nothing more than someone's foreign-sounding last name."[3] The Red Army's invasion on September 17 terrified the people of Poland's eastern provinces just as much. The more prosperous hid their valuables, and the cautious stocked food. Those who felt hopeless obtained poison.[4] Those who had experienced the first Soviet occupation of 1920 subsequently thought that their September fears had been justified, and these fears lived on, especially in the lands east of the Bug River.

Thus in 1944, the Polish population facing the approaching Red Army was torn between hope and anxiety about the future. On the one hand, people could not wait to be set free from the Germans, but on the other, very few rejoiced that they were being liberated by forces coming from the East. In the spectrum of apprehension, those living in the lands annexed by the Soviets in 1939 were typically more fearful than those in central and western Poland. The dominant mood was one of anticipation and a general belief that "come who may, as long as it's not the Germans." The reaction of people in Tarnopol to its German commander's order to move to neighboring villages is a good example: most ignored it. Some people in Lvov panicked on the eve of the Red Army's arrival, not because they feared a second Soviet occupation but because they heard a rumor that men were being murdered by the Germans and the Ukrainian SS.[5] An April 1944 report from the Government Delegate's Office reads, "The Polish people do not currently want to leave the places where they are, and,

69

if the Ukrainian terror did not complicate matters, they would not be evacuating with the Germans. Only some people who fear being separated from their families are leaving, as are small groups of the intelligentsia who experienced the previous Russian occupation and do not want to relive it in the same place."[6] But there was no mass panic of the kind experienced by the Germans in East Prussia and Silesia.

In 1944 and 1945, the German occupation authorities failed to force the Polish population to evacuate ahead of the approaching front as the Poles feared the Germans and the Ukrainians more than the Soviets. In 1943 and 1944, some two hundred thousand to three hundred thousand Poles left their homes in Volhynia, fearing Ukrainian terror. A Government Delegate's Office February 1944 report read, "The Poles in Volhynia, despite the forced evacuation, are escaping en masse in fear of not only the Soviet army, but also of Ukrainian bandits."[7] At times, the Poles were very fearful of the approaching Red Army, but it appears that now, confronted with the "German plague," of the two evils, they seemed to prefer the "Soviet flu."

The Soviet army's occupation of Poland came in two phases. The first one stopped at the Vistula in September 1944 and the second, in January–February 1945, quickly pushed the German armies out of the rest of Poland. The population greeted the incoming Red Army with genuine joy. The war correspondent Vasily Grossman would hear from many Poles he encountered that they had been waiting for the arrival of the Red Army: "We waited for it like for God."[8] General Nikolai Kirillovich Popel remembered how the people of Sandomierz welcomed the Red Army: "Even though it was winter, the Poles were just bombarding us with flowers. I don't know where they got them.... Must have been an orangery."[9] The same happened in Łódź. According to letters written in January 1945:

> We welcomed the passing Red Army troops with ovations and flowers, our eyes filled with tears of joy, for which they thanked us and asked that we leave the flowers for the Polish Army, which came to Łódź in their wake. The Red Army thus won the hearts of the people of Łódź, for they are truly kind people, not wild beasts like the Nazis, who at the last minute still burned the Radogoszcz prison outside Łódź with about 3,000 Poles inside. Make haste, and death to the germans [*sic*]. We have been yanked out of this cruel captivity, we have thrown off our shackles, the chains of German captivity. Beloved Poland, which we've been waiting for over 5 years, is here.... The people welcomed the troops warmly, offered them food and cigarettes. But they wanted nothing, they already had everything. When the townspeople gave the russians [*sic*] bread, they would pull out sausage and give it to us to eat with the bread, for the people to eat, because they want nothing, they have everything.

And a letter from Parczew in Lublin Province: "First let's thank the Lord and the Holy Mother for protecting us, and also the Red Army for protecting us from that Nazi enemy. Had they come three hours later, the Nazi Satan was ready to burn us all. The petrol was ready, and the teutons had positioned themselves in the city and the villages nearby, and they were prepared that night to burn us all. Lord, we thank you and the Red Army liberators so ardently for keeping us so providentially alive."[10]

People often expressed gratitude to the victorious troops, even though many suspected that Poland might end up under Soviet domination. Initially, the troops' demeanor was not objectionable. But soon enough, as contacts with the Soviet soldiers multiplied, dislike, and then hatred, replaced gratitude. On January 22, 1945, the writer Maria Dąbrowska noted in her diary, "Four days of nervous stress, anticipation, hope and fear are behind us. Finally, everything has settled into a stultifying boredom."[11] But anxiety, at first vague, thickened into fear. Franciszek Starowieyski remembered from January 1945, "The Bolsheviks began to hang around the kitchen entrance. There was the soldier who fell asleep from exhaustion at the front, another was banging on the door. Fear came. Small for now.... This was the beginning of the first, most chaotic week, without any norms of behavior."[12]

The Red Army troops scared people for two reasons: because they engaged in political subjugation and because they requisitioned, stole, raped, and even murdered. They became a nightmare for the population, especially in the first year following the German occupation. The first reason requires a separate treatment (see chap. 10, "The Politics of Fear"). As for the second, these crimes occurred everywhere the Soviet military appeared, especially their second wave. Placing these incidents on a spatial and chronological map will tell us where and when fear was the greatest and what exactly evoked the greatest terror.

In 1944, crime and requisitions in the native Polish lands rarely began right at "liberation." As a rule, they started after a while, after the welcoming flowers and the cries of "hooray" and "long live!" had stopped. These crimes and requisitions were often organized and overseen by quartermasters, and thus people rarely associated them with aggression and brutality, despite the fact that the total figures for food, farm animals, and all sorts of movables for the needs of the army far surpassed the quantities seized by individual marauders. The Red Army had inferior equipment and scarce food supplies, and thus its men often went cold and hungry.[13] It therefore waged war by sending out special teams led by officers to seize food from villagers, even after the war was over. The Soviets also took Polish state property, including at least one thousand factories and large numbers of small artisan workshops.[14] But these confiscations seemed to make their victims feel helpless rather than fearful. Fear came from having a farm stripped of its food supplies and its buildings destroyed just before winter. What mattered was not only what and how much was taken but how. It was bandit-style invasions, often at night, with weapons and shouting that gave people the greatest fright. In 1944, populations living closest to the front were in greatest danger of these raids. The situation in the area of Augustów in northern Mazovia, at the Sandomierz bridgehead, and in some districts of Rzeszów Province resembled the Thirty Years' War. Civilians were forced out of their homes to live in mud huts and burned-out houses, often after having been robbed blind by Soviet troops, whose own situation—let's not forget—was not much better. Somehow, they needed to survive the autumn and winter in trenches. Their reaction to the experiences at the Eastern Front was natural: cold and hungry, often deeply traumatized, they saved themselves by assaulting the locals, stealing food, underwear, warm clothes, bed sheets, and vodka. Rzeszów Province militia reports give an idea of the scale of this behavior:

> On 7 October 1944, four Soviet soldiers robbed Kopczyk, Marian, resident of Golcowa, Brzozów District, at gunpoint robbing him of 2 pairs of shoes, and departed in an unknown direction."
>
> On 14 October 1944, ca. 23.00 hours, several Soviet soldiers stormed into the flat of Konieczny, Tomasz, resident of Hawłowice, Jarosław District, and after terrorizing the inhabitants with firearms, took their clothes, underclothes and shoes.
>
> On 15 October 1944, a Soviet soldier stole a coat belonging to Smeda, Kazimiera, resident of Dynów, Brzozów District, and was stopped during the chase, the coat was seized and returned to the victim, and the soldier was delivered to the War Commander's Office in Dynów.[15]

The Soviet soldiers' impunity also surfaced in larger towns such as Białystok, Rzeszów, and Przemyśl, where they attacked people in the streets and broke into homes. "Cases of theft and robbery by Red Army troops of private homes in Rzeszów and nearby proliferate, and the garrison command does not react to them at all."[16] Localities close to major roads were most likely to be attacked. In October 1944 in Biłgoraj, food, animal feed, bedding, and undergarments were seized as well as "all kinds of household equipment, in other words, anything that could be stolen." As had happened throughout history, women and children, fearing rape and pillage, fled to fields and forests. According to a report by the *starost* (district official) of Biłgoraj, "When people escape to the forest they are not there to meet the compulsory deliveries of grains, potatoes and other articles. The army responds with threats and insults.... At night, drunk soldiers try to barge into homes, bother people by firing their guns and acting aggressively."[17]

"Out of the Frying Pan and into the Fire"

These first contacts shaped a negative stereotype of the fearsome Red Army men, which became universal among the Poles. Were someone to conduct a national opinion poll about reasons for this apprehension then, the most common response would most likely have been "because they drink, steal and rape." The writer Maria Dąbrowska added gloom and distrust to the list. She noted in her diary in January 1945, "They have already seized all the horses, the cow, two pigs, many hens and eggs. They, especially the officers, drink gallons of vodka, which they demand by the glassful. They are so suspicious that they make the farmer try it first—what an insult to the Polish nation, which has never had poisoners in its midst. They are glum and rude, and have nothing of the spirit of liberators."[18]

The mathematician Hugo Steinhaus, who had had direct contact with Red Army men and officers, was generally less critical but also pointed out their drinking and their tendency to steal. In January 1945 he wrote:

> They robbed and stole whatever they could get their hands on. They took pots, spoons, flour, hens from the Szcześniewicz family, destroyed their beds, bedclothes and the piano.... The first wave gets food from the farmers' cottages because the kitchens and supply train don't even try to keep up.... They drink and steal, and when they are drunk, they even rob and rape women. "We can't execute everyone for plunder," a major told us. "They have stopped declaiming about Lenin and Marx, about the Soviet Union and the capitalists, and have simply turned into a Russian army. As for the Jews, they know that they are hiding in the staffs and supply offices, and they will settle scores with them after the war. They put crosses on the graves of their dead. They promise that after the war things in the Soviet Union will be the same as in Poland, just like in England and America. They've been around."[19]

Anxiety and fear arrive by degrees. It seems that those emotions caused by robberies had not yet reached their apex in the second half of 1944. Then, the soldiers with red stars on their helmets were still relatively well-disciplined as they would have been harshly penalized for such crimes, even executed. Indeed, taking into account the fact that initially over two million troops were stationed in a small area of Poland, the scale of the marauding does not seem extreme. It appears that the powerful fear arrived later, in late spring and summer of 1945, as the Red Army became demoralized, primarily as a result of the Kremlin's tolerance of the rapes and robberies of German civilians. The Soviets' intoxication with their victory over Germany, and the ensuing relaxation and loosening of discipline, something normal when fighting ends, were also psychologically significant. A third and equally important reason for the Soviet troops' corruption was the fact that looming ahead of them was their return to the hardships of life in the *kolkhoz*. As they traveled across Poland, those who had not managed to acquire possessions in Germany now saw their last chance to get rich. The situation was worst in the lands that had earlier belonged to the Reich and along the major routes between East and West. In some ways it resembled what was going on in the Soviet occupation zone:[20] a continuation of wartime chaos and fear of robbery, beatings, rape, and even murder.

"KEEP AN EYE ON YOUR PACKAGES"

The "Regained Territories," the German lands annexed by Poland in 1945, had a special place on the map of fear.[21] The Soviet troops did not always understand the territories' ethnic complexity nor the Polish resettlement operation underway. They tended to treat the area as German, and hence to loot. For this reason, the dimensions of both organized and spontaneous stealing by groups of soldiers were greatest there, and the Poles' sense of security was the lowest. An envoy of the Polish underground sent there in the autumn of 1945 described it thus: "The area is packed with the Red Army, but it is hard to tell how many of them there are. The city is full of soldiers, villages are occupied. Destruction, burning, pillage, whether intentional or not, is in any case an extremely shocking example of raucousness that is impossible to curb."[22] A Citizens' Militia officer in Gliwice noted that in Silesia, plunder, thefts, and rapes occurred "daily," and that "not an hour passes without an incident."[23] A Polish soldier wrote in August 1945 that "here in Gliwice they are stealing. Terrible things are happening. Robbery, theft in broad daylight, break-ins, and they steal in the streets, too. When a well-dressed man, carrying a suitcase too, appears in the street, they will follow him. If he goes into a side street, it's all over. I witness incidents of this kind every day."[24]

The situation was similar in Lower Silesia. According to the district Citizens' Militia commander in Trzebnica, "The Polish population is living in constant anxiety and fear." There were "assaults and robberies, beatings and mistreatment by Soviet soldiers every night and every day."[25] A woman from Lower Silesia described one such incident in a letter dated August 13, 1945:

> I had a brawl with the Bolsheviks. I saw a crowd outside our building from my window. My children yelled to me not to go out because he will shoot me. But one came from downstairs, broke down the door and came into our apartment, rummaged through everything, and I was afraid that he would steal all the clothing, so I went downstairs. He threw himself at me and screamed that I would be held responsible that he, a *"russki soldat"* [Russian soldier] had got his whole hand cut up when he was smashing a window. He blocked the door, struck me a few times between the eyes with his fist. "You, *Polachka* [little Polish woman] will feel our hard hand," he kept screaming. I wonder how much longer this rabble will oppress us. Maybe forever? But you, of course, are well-disposed to these allies.[26]

A similar situation persisted into 1946 in the whole coastal region from Szczecin to Elbląg. Everywhere, civil servants repeated the mantra "the issue of security is beneath contempt." The people of Szczecin, the farthest point in the Wild West, as western Poland was called then, experienced this kind of fear most frequently. In 1946, there were still seventy-two Red Army units stationed in the city, mostly non-frontline ones, therefore less disciplined. The area also played host to a camp for Soviet forced laborers repatriated from Germany, who were allowed to go outside whenever they wished. The stories from that time recall Westerns, except that they were real. On March 20, 1946, a group of a dozen or so Soviet soldiers fired on a passing tram as a warning, surrounded it, confiscated the passengers' valuables, and disappeared into the ruins. The security authorities estimated that Red Army troops were responsible for the majority of killings in the Szczecin area.[27] People living in and around Gdańsk also felt extremely insecure. In the first year or so after "liberation," the city was marked by vandalism, a devastated urban infrastructure, arson, and robbery. Some people were robbed repeatedly. Someone writing from Gdańsk-Wrzeszcz complained in April 1945, "The soviets [*sic*] took everything.... No one has any clothes left, the soviets [*sic*] have taken everything.... If you miss two days of work, the soviets [*sic*] take you away wherever they like."[28]

Such experiences seem to have been widespread all along the Baltic Coast, as another correspondent complained: "I have nothing left because the russkis took everything, and if the Russians are robbing and destroying this much where you are, thanks but no thanks."[29]

People in Elbląg feared robberies by Soviet marauders as much as people did in Szczecin, and as late as September 1945 few dared go outside unarmed.[30] A worker at the Schichau factory in Elbląg remembered:

> We moved in together in Elbląg and joined the militia. Very often we had to defend Polish homes and shops from the russki army. We often also stood guard outside government buildings. There was a constant battle with the russki army, and there were nearly 40,000 of them. The Soviet Army is gradually leaving Elbląg. But the Russian army still often sabotages. They have destroyed some buildings. All their wartime loot is being taken to Russia. There are many battles with the escorts of trucks that transport various useful things, and they often take all the machines out of the factories. They take food, cows, horses, sheep and pigs. All the equipment, even window frames, doors, windows and furniture.[31]

A Soviet *komendatura*, a military command, governed Malbork for many months, and several Red Army units were stationed there. A Polish settler described a typical incident in a letter of August 7, 1945:

The night Gośka arrived, Friday, they stole her cow and a hen each from her and me. Three of them came. It was daylight still, they stood on the road talking with german [sic] women, and we were no longer sleepy. They began to break down the door to Daddy's pigsty, and one of them stood by the door and says that he won't let us in. He started to argue with dad to let him out or else he would shoot, and he even rattled the house lock until dad came out through the window and ran to get someone, and when he came running back, they were gone. Then they took the cows to Fadus. Something happens every night, and they even came to Janek Ostrowski's during the day, opened a cupboard and took 8 liters and some clothes.[32]

In Bydgoszcz, the "locals live in fear, what with all the news about the Soviet army's violence in these lands, which makes it virtually impossible to settle down and work in peace," wrote the governor of Pomerania about the collective emotions in June 1945.[33] Fearing robberies, some shopkeepers would spend the night in their shops and hide the most valuable items in the back.[34] Not wanting to bump into Soviet soldiers, people avoided going out also in Warmia and Masuria. An inhabitant of Olsztyn wrote in August 1945 in a letter intercepted by the War Censorship Office:

The worst now is that they are stealing horses, sheep, pigs even individually in the daytime, even one at a time. You have to keep an eye on everything. They got Zenka Kodłobowska's cow, she only had one, no other ones. And even though there is a police station here, it can do nothing, because there are only 4 of them, that's nothing. When they say "*shto tebya nuzhna*" [what do you need], there is nothing even the police can do. When they come at night, shouting "*davai vodku*" [hand over the vodka] or "*krivai dveri*" [open the door], the women will run to the police in their nightgowns, but the police station is meaningless because whoever there is more of wins.[35]

Włodzimierz Lubowicz, material benefits inspector in Sławno District, wrote in a report that this was a "drunken occupation." Many of the disturbances, robberies, and rapes were either motivated by drunkenness or driven by the desire to find alcohol. In the early summer of 1945, the army, intoxicated with victory and having lost its discipline, became slackened and demoralized. On the Baltic coast, things were worst in small towns, where the local Soviet commanders ruled like sovereign princelings. An untouched distillery fell into the victors' hands in Sławno, near Słupsk: "After taking over food-processing plants, including a distillery, the Soviet garrison persists in a state of perpetual drunken stupor. Since then, you cannot find a sober commander or soldier. Since then, the power has been in the hands of the drunken soldier and the sober German and Vlasov saboteurs, who are undermining the cohesion of the Red Army like moles and efficiently conducting disintegration work."[36]

Governing the town, according to Lubowicz, was a "Hitlerized ataman," Colonel Borovikov. Baseless arrests, harassment, and constant disputes with the Polish settlers over former German property and harvests were an everyday occurrence. "The Red Army is absent from this district, only one drunken soldier and a commander, both of them don't give a damn about faraway Moscow and their supervisors, since they have nothing to lose except their intoxicated heads. They are defending the distillery and the crops with machine guns, and they will not hand them over without a fight." Official reminders and pleas were useless. Lubowicz suggested organizing a "punitive expedition" to "put an end to the tribal rulers' lawlessness."[37]

The map of postwar fear should have communications routes marked in a very bright color. Hundreds of thousands of Polish forced laborers, prisoners of war, and camp inmates were making their way home from Germany. Many were robbed even before crossing the border, and many women, even former prisoners, were raped. The "Grande Armée" was crossing Poland on its way back to the USSR. Some of its soldiers' actions gave the word *Reisefieber* (travel nerves) a new meaning. Traveling in the vicinity of Szczecin meant having your heart in your mouth, since Red Army units were crossing the border from the Soviet occupation zone in Germany into Poland on a roll, and they continued to steal. Soviet soldiers searched train passengers, took away their luggage, and attacked train stations. For example, on August 7, 1945, they stopped a train from Stargard to Scheune (today, Szczecin Gumieńce) and robbed all its passengers, then raped several women in the station waiting room. Many terrified Polish railway employees resigned from their jobs and left Szczecin Pomerania.[38] Marian Bogusz, a railroad worker in Szczecin, lived through such an attack on September 10, 1945. He could remember clearly that a train from Gdynia had pulled into the station at 10:00 p.m. Suddenly, he heard shots. He heard "incredible shouting, women and children crying" in the train cars. He was so petrified that he hid in the station's attic. When he came out in the morning, he saw that "the passenger train had stopped. Lots of smashed suitcases, women's, children's clothing strewn on the ground, wrappers with food, etc. on the tracks and platforms. The cars are quiet. The baggage attendant was lying in the doorway to the baggage car... murdered. Two dead individuals in Soviet uniform are lying in the orchard next to the station building."[39]

Even people living in towns along railway lines deeper into Poland could not sleep well. The Citizens' Militia Command in Poznań reported that "the march of the Polish Army's front units and of Red Army units evokes a widespread psychosis of apprehension and anxiety among the local people, which manifests itself in people in all the different districts taking their possessions out of their houses or hiding them lest the marching military units take them. The rise in crime in our province is also connected to the army's march from the front."[40]

People were at greatest risk of being attacked in and around train stations and on the trains themselves, where Soviet soldiers would push out passengers who were unwilling to hand over their baggage even as the train was moving.[41] On July 28, 1945, soldiers raped a woman, slit her throat, and threw her body out of the train onto the tracks of the Radom–Skarżysko line. Before she died, the woman identified her assailants. Also in late July, drunk Soviet soldiers threw a Polish railway worker and his wife out of a moving train between the Jedlina Letnisko and Radom stations. The train's wheels cut off both the man's arms and one leg, and the woman was killed on the spot.[42] These are extreme examples, but brutal beatings often accompanied theft. In a private letter dated April 15, 1945, a man described his experience of changing trains in Poznań: "This was the worst, three russki soldiers robbing us at night in Poznań. As we changed trains, Renia and I went to buy tickets, and those russkis assaulted some older ladies and struck one of them on the head with a metal object so she fell down, and they grabbed my suitcase and Kazimierek's shirts and the lady's package and ran off between the train cars. After the lady got up, we went with her to the ticket office, and the NKVD came. The russkis went running after them, but they didn't catch them."[43]

On August 7, 1945, someone recounted his relative's or friend's "adventures" in a letter: "When Czechu was going home, the Russkis robbed him. They took two suitcases from him. They rob everyone going to Germany and there, too. They're not allowed to do this, but they still rob, and whoever resists will be shot.... We're praying that the Russkis will leave, our lives would be so different, but we don't know when they will leave Poland."[44]

Fear escalated and spread, carried by wandering Poles who disseminated warnings. A letter dated August 26, 1945, read, "If you should come here, keep an eye on your baggage because the Russkis are stealing a lot. And when the train is moving at night, they jump on and take whatever they please."[45]

In the summer of 1945 there were many instances of soldiers jumping out of transports traveling east. At times, entire villages, even towns, were their victims, such as Koszyce in Kielce Province, which was ransacked on July 31. The starost of Łódź Province informed his governor that on July 3, 1945, "Large groups of Soviet soldiers from a 2-train transport stopped in Olechów station and committed armed attacks on the villages of Zalesie, Olechów, Feliksin and Huta Szklana, stealing farmers' property and raping Polish women. Fifty German women were raped in a German camp in Olechów.

"Out of the Frying Pan and into the Fire"

Terrified, the population fled from their houses, abandoning everything."⁴⁶

The escalation of "operation train," especially in the second half of 1945, was associated with the Red Army's departure. But incidents continued into 1946. In early December 1946 some Soviet soldiers escaped from their transport, which had stopped at Pionki station in Kielce Province and, freezing, dispersed, going into houses and stealing underwear, bedclothes, and clothing; they also plundered shops. From then on, knowing the times when their transports would be passing through and learning from experience, shopkeepers would lock up their businesses and the locals would barricade themselves in their homes.⁴⁷

The Red Army also traveled from west to east by car and truck. Its garrisons, redeployment stations, supply bases, and hospitals were located in many places, not only in western and northern Poland. This significantly stretched out the map of fear across virtually the whole country. Someone wrote from Łomża, "There are incidents here all the time, they are constantly attacking. They drive through, take everything, and they even . . . killed a woman and took everything. They had to borrow clothes for the funeral because they had been left just like that in their night clothes, even their poultry was taken. Today they robbed Kowalczyk in the field . . . . They came in daylight and took everything."⁴⁸

It would be possible to go on with the list of reports of thefts and associated incidents. They usually sounded insignificant: "On 31.7.1945 [at] 18.00 a lorry with 8 russki soldiers came to Dąbrowa to see Czesław G. of Polish nationality, and they demanded that he prepare supper, butter, cheese, milk and vodka, and beautiful women."⁴⁹ As their victims would complain to the militia, invasions like this one made people panic. Many such incidents had even worse endings. On July 13, 1945, a Soviet military column went through Ostrów, on the road from Jarosław to Przemyśl. It stopped outside thirty-eight-year-old Józef Czyż's house. The column included Captain Kokhachin, First Lieutenant Pankov, Sergeant Proskoronov, and two privates, Sidelnikov and Tymakhovich. They unceremoniously proceeded to rob the house and tried to rape Czyż's wife. Czyż attempted to defend them, and Tymakhovich shot him. The militia at the station in nearby Radymno arrested the soldiers and officers, but their commander released them later that night, maintaining that otherwise they would be court-martialed. No documents have been found to confirm that Poles ever served as witnesses in Soviet military courts.⁵⁰

Bicycles and watches were stolen most frequently. The cry "*davay chesy!*" (hand over your watch), often heard during robberies, became one of the symbols of the postwar period. Often quoted by Poles, it was psychologically important, since it devalued the "invincible ally" and improved the national self-confidence. Hence the popularity of the verse "take the watches and the bikes/and go to hell as fast as you like."

But no one who was stopped in the street and ordered to hand over their watch was in a laughing mood. A woman who had been assaulted, probably in April 1945, recalled in a letter:

> Two Russkis came up to me and first attacked me to get my watch, I'm to give them my watch, and when I told them that I haven't got one, they threatened to shoot me if I don't give it to them, and they began to look for it everywhere. And when they didn't find it, they took my bike, a box with tobacco in it and a cigarette box, and then they wanted to take my shoes off my feet and my coat. When I didn't want to give them the coat and the shoes, they said that they were going to shoot me. So I agreed to everything, and I say to them, shoot me, I don't care. Then, each one shot in the air next to my head once and I still wasn't afraid, and when they saw that I wasn't afraid they left the coat and the shoes and told me to go.⁵¹

Peasants complained about what they had to suffer when millions of "trophy" cattle, horses, and sheep were herded from Germany to the USSR. They feared hunger not only because their crops were destroyed but also because their livestock was stolen, and so they hid their cattle in forests. There were instances of collective self-defense—for example, in the village of Apolonki near Częstochowa. In August 1945, Soviet troops, pretending to be looking for their captured animals, began to requisition cows from villages, inciting peasant protests. One person was shot, another wounded, and the Citizens' Militia and the Security Office were forced to intervene.[52] Many similar conflicts, some more bloody than others, occurred in this period.

Inhabitants of larger towns and cities, perhaps with the exception of Warsaw (where the Soviet garrison was relatively small and, most important, disciplined), also learned to fear Soviet troops' banditry. An analyst of the Government Delegate's Office reported from Cracow, "The hordes spent the first few days wandering around Cracow drunk and brazen, ripping watches and jewelry off people in the street and demanding vodka and cash to buy vodka."[53] While the number of assaults and rapes in Cracow gradually dropped,[54] the actual threat posed by the presence of Soviet garrisons in cities like Białystok, Częstochowa, Łódź, and Poznań, remained steady from early 1946.[55] Near the Western Train Station in Poznań, an all-out battle featuring hand grenades broke out between the local militia and Soviet soldiers. Six militiamen and four Red Army men died.[56] In Szamotuły near Poznań, ten civilians were wounded, one militia officer died, and there were five dead and six wounded on the Soviet side.[57] The fear brought on by the rise in crime by bandits in Red Army uniforms was also widespread in Łódź. The population had nowhere to turn for help, since the militia, too, were afraid. A woman wrote:

> You can't imagine what is happening here now. Russki and Polish soldiers are going around together and stealing. They also came to our house, at 3 a.m., robbed us and almost used rape. In this house we are all weak women. They robbed us so thoroughly that we had no clothes to wear outside. First, a Polish soldier knocked and told the owner to open up because they were looking for weapons and soldiers. She opened the door and only Russkis came in and went for us straight away. But let me tell you, we couldn't say much because they'd immediately say, shush, shush, and if we didn't want to give them what they wanted, they would aim their rifles at us. They would release the safety lock, hold the gun in one paw, and take all our things with the other. The huge one was the worst, let me tell you, a giant, very young and didn't look like a Muscovite. I think that someone must have sent [him] because they were asking for people's names and addresses. As soon as they left, Mommy ran to the militia station and the militiamen came, but what could we do? Since they come to our street every night at 2, we told them to do a manhunt. But they can't be bothered.[58]

In Częstochowa and the surrounding area, very high crime rates, and not only by the Red Army, caused extreme anxiety. "The population has been greatly intimidated by robberies and murders. Stories about every incident spread like wildfire and come in different versions," reported the Provincial Office of Information and Propaganda.[59] The city was a stopping-off point for Soviet troops of the northern group as well as the home of a Soviet military hospital. This alone made Częstochowa the leader among the towns of central Poland in individual and organized crime statistics. The monetary losses from theft and devastation committed by the "fraternal army's" soldiers quartered there made the municipality suffer over fifty-one million *zlotys*, a huge sum for those times, in January 1945–June 1946 alone. Between January 16 and July 27, 1945, 22 murders and 50 attempted murders during robberies, 36 robberies, 11 rapes, 18 shootings and 136 thefts were noted. In the second half of 1945 (from July 28), there was a drop to 8 confirmed murders, 42 robberies, 9 break-ins that included robberies, 11 rapes and 2 attempted rapes, 11 shootings, 56 robberies, 2 beatings, and some cases of arson by Soviet soldiers.[60] The municipal authorities felt helpless and could not count on assistance from the militia. The people of Częstochowa defended themselves as best they could. At night, they would pass warnings door to door that the "Russkis" were coming,[61] and during the day they tried to stay out of their way. "Furthermore, in numerous instances Red Army officers and men speak contemptuously of Poles in general in public and elsewhere, which leads the civilian population, in part out of physical caution and in part from disappointment, to leave these ... public places when the Red Army officers and men arrive."[62]

In July 1945 in Kielce, people became greatly agitated when a Soviet officer shot Antoni Nowicki in the street after Nowicki refused to give him his watch. "The people who crowded around the corpse did not hold back their comments about the Red Army and even stopped superior officers, explaining to them the reasons for the murder and demanding an explanation," the governor described the incident, which almost ended in a lynching.[63] The situation in Częstochowa region was no better, as some villages were stripped of their belongings. To avoid being robbed, people traveled by bicycle in groups. To preempt rapes, women would also move in large groups.[64]

"I'M AWFULLY SCARED OF THEM"

Fear of rape by Soviet soldiers was a central emotion in the postwar era. Because it was mostly a feminine fear, it did not make it into the Polish "masculine" historiography of the war.[65] Even before the Red Army occupied the Polish lands, it simmered, with the raping Bolshevik a cliché of Nazi propaganda. It would not allow anyone to forget the name Nemmersdorf, the first East Prussian village occupied by the Soviets in October 1944, which was subsequently taken by the Wehrmacht. Sixty-two women and girls were reportedly raped and murdered there by Soviet troops. Some were nailed to barn doors.[66]

Taking into account the number of Soviet soldiers present in Poland, in the second half of 1944 the number of rapes by Red Army men remained constant, as violent as this may sound.[67] Janina Godycka-Cwirko, a young girl living with her family in Ostrowia Mazowiecka near the Polish-Russian border, remembered, "As I rushed about my town, twice I saw girls being raped by Soviet soldiers on sidewalks. I would shout: *"Vy khuzhe Germantsov!"* (You are worse than the Germans!). One of them jumped at me, but I managed to hide behind a farmer's door. Then the second one let the girl go."[68]

During the Second World War, men of all armies, even the more civilized British and American ones,[69] committed rape, in Italy, Normandy, and later Germany. There is documentation of 501 rapes by US troops in Germany in April and 241 in May 1945. There are estimates as high as 94,000 of *Besatzungskinder* (occupation's children) born in the American occupation zone.[70] But the women living in the western occupation zones did not experience the panicked terror felt by all women in the Soviet occupation zone, and to a lesser degree in Poland.

There are several explanations for these mass rapes.[71] The most prosaic is that Red Army troops, unlike the Germans or the western Allies, did not go on leave and therefore spent years without seeing their wives. Also, to put it diplomatically, women of the countries they were liberating tended to view them differently from British, American, or Polish soldiers: as unattractive or, to put it plainly, as primitive and boorish. In other words, Allied troops in Italy or France did not need rape to win sexual favors, but Soviet men could rarely count on wartime romance. American soldiers, due to the malnutrition of the civilian population in Italy in 1944 and in Germany in 1945 and 1946, did not have to rape—they used food to buy sex. Also, all soldiers can become demoralized and go wild. Rape can be a component of conquerors' comportment, especially as they capture the enemy's cities.

Freud also suggests another answer. The lack of sexual satisfaction for millions of Soviet men may also have had neurotic roots in the earlier quashing of all eroticism in official Stalinist culture, which deplored human drives and emotions. It even considered the sculpture *Venus de Milo* "pornographic."[72] Also, the brutal treatment of women may have relieved psychological stress more than satisfied a real sex drive. It is also not out of the question that raping and demeaning women stemmed from the need to dominate, which people who were debased every day, and not only fighting men, felt. Some psychologists use empirical data to show that sex drive often rises in conditions of elevated fear.[73] The Eastern Front, of all places, was just such a place. Furthermore—and this may be crucial—Soviet commanders of all ranks, including at the very top, consented to such behavior by their men.

Joseph Stalin, commenting on the rapes by Soviet troops in northeast Yugoslavia, told Milovan Djilas:

> Do you see what a complicated thing is a man's soul, a man's psyche? Well then, imagine a man who has fought from Stalingrad to Belgrade, over thousands

of kilometers of his own devastated land, across the dead bodies of his comrades and dearest ones. How can such a man react normally? And what is so awful in his having a fun with a woman after such horrors? You have imagined the Red Army to be ideal. . . . One has to understand the soldier. The Red Army is not ideal. The important thing is that it fights Germans—and it is fighting them well, while the rest doesn't matter.[74]

Djilas heard Stalin's opinion of the murders of German civilians in East Prussia by Red Army troops. Stalin reportedly said, "We lecture our soldiers too much; let them have some initiative!"[75]

Revenge on the enemy was certainly one of the most important motivations for rape. Notably, Soviet troops' brutality against women in the Allied countries—Poles, Czechs, Slovaks, and Serbs (incidentally, fellow Slavs)—never attained the scale of their violence against German or Hungarian women. But Norman M. Naimark, historian of the Soviet occupation of Germany, is wrong to believe that Polish women were only sporadically the targets of sex crimes.[76] The revenge argument also does not explain the rapes of concentration camp inmates or forced laborers, many of them Russian. Vasily Grossman realized quickly that the rape victims were not all German. "Soviet girls liberated from the camps are suffering a lot now." One of the stories he heard was "about a breast-feeding mother who was being raped in a barn. Her relatives came to the barn and asked her attackers to let her have a break, because the hungry baby was crying the whole time."[77]

It is possible that for some soldiers the rape of a Polish or a Ukrainian forced laborer played the role of not so much revenge as a reward for liberating them. "We spilled our blood for Poland," they said, implying that "we deserve something in return." Because many officers and noncommissioned officers were quartered in Polish homes, they might have considered forced sexual relations with a Polish woman not as attempted rape but as an expression of hospitality and gratitude toward the liberators. But even if this was different from the brutal, often gang rapes that took place amid ruins or in barns, a woman's fear was still the same. Janina Godycka-Ćwirko, whose house was chosen to accommodate Soviet troops, experienced this:

> The next guest inflicted on us was a young, 26-year-old captain coming from the front, a very handsome Georgian. He believed that his wartime experiences and his epaulettes and his beautiful figure entitled him to everything. . . . Like all the rest of them, the captain brought with him rationed vodka and canned food. Because he had no drinking companions for him in our house, he brought a mate. Terror was in the air. . . . After drinking a bottle of vodka with his adjutant, the captain was left alone. He sat on his bed for a long time, and stared at the other bed non-stop, where I was to sleep. I could not wait any longer. I undressed under the blanket and lay close to the wall, with Krysia on the edge. Mom placed her head at the other end of the bed, so that my feet were next to Krysia's head. An instant later, we heard the captain's easy breathing: tiredness and vodka had done their job. I whispered to Mom that I was afraid and that she should take my place. We swapped places quietly. The captain stirred. He sat up. I thought that my heart would jump out of my chest from fear. We lay still. We were afraid. We missed having father home so much. . . . After napping for a bit, the officer got up. Mom pulled the blanket over her head so he wouldn't discover our switch, even though the room was dark. The captain yanked off the blanket and began to kiss. At first Mom defended herself, but the strong young man easily held back her hands and locked his mouth with hers. But the kiss was not enough, and he tried to drag her to his bed. I lifted my head and shouted loudly: *"Ty khuzhe Nemtsa!"* [You're worse than a German!] The officer acted like a wolf who had snatched a sheep. . . . He let Mom go, and went back to his lair, repeating restlessly: *"Ya tebe pokazhu, ty staraia vedma, khuzhe Nemtsa, khuzhe Nemtsa."* [I'll show you, you old witch, worse than a German, worse than a German.][78]

German women could not use these words to defend themselves, but the answer to the question of why they

"Out of the Frying Pan and into the Fire"

were raped can also be found in their perspective. In occupied Warsaw, the cleverer *szmalcownicy* (extortionist) recognized Jews not so much by their appearance as by the fear emanating from their eyes and their body language, which predisposed them to victimhood. Naimark is right to note that Soviet soldiers may also have sensed fear in their victims' faces, which may have made them more likely to attack.[79] Godycka-Ćwirko knew instinctively that it was not advisable to project anxiety in public: "Before, I walked with my head down, not paying attention to anyone, but now I learned to carry my head high and to look down on the annoying soldiers, which worked to some extent. I never went out alone. My youngest sister always came with me."[80]

A laughing, triumphant Polish woman walking in the streets of Katowice, Wrocław, or Gdańsk thus had a better chance of avoiding rape than a German woman who was crushed by defeat and fear. But as the front line passed, fear was visible in all women's eyes regardless of nationality. They were raped because many Soviet soldiers simply could not tell a German from a Polish woman. Soviet Central Asian soldiers, Kyrghyz, Uzbek, or Tajik, for whom the ethnic differences in eastern Europe were indecipherable, were in the most difficult situation. Alcohol and the Soviet troops' universal drunkenness also had a huge impact on their perceptions and boosted their propensity to be violent. Indeed, in this respect, these men did not differ from the Poles.

Again, in the second half of 1944 Polish women were raped sporadically, but following the winter offensive of January 1945, these rapes assumed epidemic proportions. The closer the front came to Berlin, Gdańsk, and Elbląg, the more frequent and cruel the sexual violence became. Rapes had already been occurring in Cracow and during the capture of Festung Poznań. In Poznań there were cases of Soviet soldiers luring young women by asking their help with dressing the wounds of allegedly injured men. But the wave of rapes in the spring and summer, coming from the Baltic, East Prussia, and Silesia, primarily represented the transfer of brutality from German women onto Polish women. A Polish woman complained in a letter sent from Gdańsk on April 17, 1945, that she had been raped seven times, probably as she sought work in a Soviet garrison: "They were eager to have us because we could speak Polish. But I was scared when I heard that all these women were being raped 15 times, and I went back. . . . I was raped once that night, this disgrace occurred as my father watched. . . . I was raped 7 times, it was horrific."[81]

Other letters from Polish and German women in Gdańsk intercepted by the War Censorship Office also describe this fear. On April 21, 1945, "when the Russians came, every girl got it." On April 22, 1945: "So far, I've been protected by Our Lord. Is this what they did to women there? . . . I'm afraid because there are lots of Russkis here and it's horrible how they are still grabbing women. I go outside very little, we are spending most of our time in the cellar." From Gdynia on April 24, 1945: "What women went through with these Soviets in this war. They raped, very many were martyred by them."[82]

Women in Warmia and Masuria went through a similar ordeal. Even after the front had moved, German and Polish women were frequently raped there. As reported from Olsztyn in March 1945, "virtually no woman was spared"[83] and, the writers stressed, age made no difference. According to eyewitnesses, even ten-year-old girls and seventy-year-old women were assaulted. Someone remarked in a private letter, "And most importantly, women are allegedly women from 9 to 80, and there was even the case of an 82-year-old."[84] It would happen that a grandmother, mother, and granddaughter were raped at the same time. There were very many gang rapes committed by a dozen or even several dozen soldiers. "These things are still happening right now. Because of this, Polish female workers are in an especially difficult situation since the Soviet authorities continue to force them to work. They are desperately begging for help to get out of this ordeal."[85]

Polish women forcibly taken to Germany to work were raped frequently.[86] Natalia, twenty, landed in East Prussia after her father had been shot to death by the Germans who were pacifying their village in Białystok Province. At liberation she was living in the village of Petersdorf near Templin on the road from Berlin to Szczecin, where she had been evacuated with the family for which she worked. The first Soviet soldiers she saw began with looting. Their commanding officer, a captain, demanded milk. Afraid that he would be poisoned, he made the girl taste it. He walked around the house, told his men to leave, and said to her in Russian, "Lie down! We're going to sleep." He raped her twice, violently. After he fell asleep, she continued to lie next to him, afraid that he would shoot her if she moved. She felt "nailed to the wall." The next afternoon, a soldier came to get her and take her to another house. She was served tea, then she was told to go to a room where an undressed major was waiting for her. He was gentler than the first man. After the second time, he told her that his wife was a doctor. The girl was shocked: "I thought that these guys were ruffians." Fyodor Andreevich Molodchikov was next: "He stank of petroleum." He talked about how great it was that the war was over. Again, she heard, in Russian, "Let's go, lie down!" The fourth time she was raped in the street. She was walking past small groups of Soviet soldiers, who were looking at pornographic photographs. One of them suddenly grabbed Natalia, pushed her down on a bench, and began to fondle her. She started to cry. He told her to take off her underpants. She did, and he raped her on the bench as the other soldiers watched. Some civilians walked by. Natalia remembered this rape as the most humiliating one of all. After the soldier was done, another one came up to her to console her, telling her that he could not do what his mates had done. He placed a watch on Natalia's wrist, introduced himself, and left her his field post address. His name was Ivan Belmasov. The girl became pregnant but did not have an abortion like many other raped forced laborers. She was fortunate not to have been gang-raped, like a young Danish woman who worked with her.[87]

Other Poles were less lucky. A May 1945 conference of delegates of repatriation offices declared, "Masses of people returning from Germany travel through Stargard to the east, toward Szczecin, and they are the object of non-stop attacks by individual Soviet soldiers and groups. All along the route, these people are being relentlessly assaulted and robbed, and the women are raped. Asked whether the rapes are isolated, those supervising a stretch of the route, basing their opinion on their steady contact with people on their way back from Germany, declared that women who are not attacked are the exception."[88]

The chief of the militia station in Trzebiatów in Western Pomerania Province advised women not to go out at all, since the company of a man or even an armed militia officer could not guarantee their safety. Soviet troops frequently disarmed militia officers.[89] There were incidents of men who attempted to defend bullied women being shot dead by the attackers. Reports from the Government Delegate's Office confirm the critical situation in Pomerania: "Numerous cases of death resulting from mass rapes have been recorded. Pomerania's northern districts have experienced exceptionally difficult times in this respect, since the Bolsheviks organized formal orgies there." A soldier tried to rape a twenty-year-old woman in the Bydgoszcz train station, and when she tried to defend herself, he stabbed her with his bayonet in front of her mother. In Bydgoszcz, soldiers organized hunts for Polish girls. "According to unconfirmed data, some of them are kept as concubines in the *kommandaturas*."[90]

Because of the numbers of rapes, the situation in Silesia, much like in Pomerania, can be described only as a natural disaster.[91] In Dębska Kuźnia, Opole District, 268 rapes were recorded by the end of June 1945 alone. There, too, soldiers organized hunts for women. In March 1945, a dozen drunken Russians barged into a linen-weaving workshop in a town near Racibórz. They abducted some thirty female employees to the nearby village of Makowo. One of the women testified, "The soldiers locked us up in a house and raped us, threatening to shoot us. I was raped by four soldiers." A woman on her way back home to Katowice in June 1945 testified that when her train stopped at a station at nightfall, "Russian soldiers began to chase women. I was caught by three soldiers, and all of them raped me."[92] Women in Silesia could not feel safe anywhere, at any time. Soviet soldiers raped women in roadside ditches, in fields and woods, robbing and beating them, at times killing them. They would also capture women in daylight in the streets of Katowice, Zabrze, and Chorzów: "On 16 June

'45, I was coming home by tram from Bytom to Katowice with a friend. The tram broke down after Chorzów, and we began to walk toward Katowice. Four Soviet soldiers in a drunken state stopped us near the Chorzów stadium. These soldiers forced us to go with them into a nearby field. When I tried to defend myself, I was hit in the jaw with some hard tool. The soldiers threw me on the ground and committed rape on me."[93]

Train stations and trains were especially dangerous for women. At times, when a troop transport stopped, a dozen or so soldiers would run out in search of women, "as if they were in need." A teacher in Szprotawa requested time off:

On 8 January (1946) at 1, as I was returning from Christmas holidays from Radom to Szprotawa, between Legnica and Szprotawa masses of bolsheviks [sic] marched into the car in which I was traveling, and into other cars, and began to torture and beat the men, steal suitcases and rape the women, of whom not one escaped shame and rape. Their bestiality and unruliness reached unimaginable levels, with several or even a dozen of them hurling themselves like beasts at their victims, the women. At some point, amid the confusion and tumult, albeit after the beast had satisfied himself, I managed to escape and jump out of a train window. The Bolsheviks then stopped the train and began to hunt for us. Scratched, wounded, beaten up, after this train left I crawled to the next station and reached Szprotawa only the next day.[94]

Although sexual violence was most widespread in the Regained Territories, it also occurred in Częstochowa, Białystok, Gniezno, Łódź, and Poznań—basically everywhere Soviet war veterans appeared, although they must have realized, even when they were drunk, that they were in Poland and not in Berlin or Frankfurt an der Oder. Second worst after the winter offensive must have been June 1945, which Norman Naimark associates with the demobilization order releasing older soldiers. Younger ones who disbanded in Ukraine and Belarus, regions that had experienced a brutal occupation, were more likely to rape than older soldiers.[95] Ostrów District (Poznań Province) alone recorded thirty-three rapes.[96] The militia station in Olkusz received reports of twelve rapes in only two days.[97] In July in Kielce, the rapes of about thirty women and girls were registered (fifteen of them suffered from venereal diseases). Five of them, aged nine to twenty-eight, landed in the town hospital. The district starost set off alarm bells: "There have been a dozen or so cases of rape in Kielce recently, of older women but also totally underage ones, the victims were bestially bitten, had chunks of flesh literally ripped out, and in one case a bite through her larynx. The Soviet army has been terrorizing the population and destroying property in all of Kielce District."[98]

According to assessments of the underground Freedom and Independence Association, August in Pomerania Province was the worst when it came to rapes. While reportedly 49 women had been raped in June, in July the number was 103 and in August 379.[99]

Certainly only some of the victims reported to the authorities that they had been raped. There were probably two types of situations when rapes were reported: when the sexual violence was accompanied by beating and the victim landed in the hospital, and when the rape resulted in a pregnancy. In Toruń, for example, where fifty rapes were reported in February through October 1945, most women who reported being raped did it only in order to obtain permission to have an abortion. The historian Mirosław Golon concludes on the basis of these figures that many more rapes must have been committed.[100] A husband's complaint in Pińczów gives us an idea: "I am reporting that in the night of 26–27 of this month in '45, two Russian soldiers barged into my house at 47 Bednarska Street. After barging in, the soldiers terrorized me by putting a gun to my head and threatening to have me sent to Russia, and accused me of having an unfriendly attitude toward them, since when they requested my daughters, I resisted them. The soldiers claimed that they had been fighting for Poland for three years, and so they have a right to all Polish women and that they came here on their commander's orders. They whipped my younger daughter with a belt for being afraid of them and crying as she saw them terrorize me. They wanted to force the older one to give herself to them, but my six-year-old son stood up for her, shouting and crying, as did my wife. They then began to terrorize my wife, put a gun in her mouth, kicked her, pulled her hair and demanded that she hand over our daughters. When my wife announced that she would absolutely not hand over our daughters, they pulled her outside by the hair and raped her brutally after hurling her on the ground. Let me note that my wife was ill then, suffering from the flu, she is 52 years old, and they still did this."[101]

Militia reports noted numerous abductions and rapes of girls as well as sexually motivated murders. These are only a handful of such reports from June 1945:

> From Cracow Province: "On 25 June of this year, at 2 o'clock, two individuals in Soviet army uniforms armed with automatic weapons murdered B. Ludwik, his daughter Helena age 3 by shooting, and raped B.'s wife, Agnieszka, and then beat her up and punched out her eyes. The individuals furthermore stole clothing and fled."
>
> "In the night of 25 June of this year, at 2, two Soviet soldiers barged into K. Wincenty's apartment in Cracow District, committed rape on a 4-year-old girl and then stole clothing."[102]
>
> From Białystok Province: "On 3 June [19]45, 4 driving Soviet soldiers, including the War *Kommandant* in Żydków, attacked Cit. Jakubowski and his wife and neighbors, who were returning from Germany to the village of Wersale. Cit. Jakubowski was murdered in a bestial way (they poked out his eyes), Cit. Raczydło had his cheeks sliced with a knife, was shot and then hanged. After committing the murders, the soldiers stole 3 horses, 3 carts and went off toward Gołdap."[103]
>
> From Poznań: "A Soviet soldier who attempted to rape an 8-year-old girl by taking her into a rye field was arrested by District Militia Station XI and sent to the War Comm[and]."[104]

Blinding or murdering victims was intended to eliminate eyewitnesses. Murderers and rapists in Red Army uniforms feared execution, but there are no figures of how many were punished this way in Poland, nor in which months of 1945 military courts issued the largest numbers of such sentences. In spring and summer, the numbers of abductions and rapes of girls reached their peak, although they continued in 1946 and even 1947.[105] It is possible that these numerous accounts gave rise to a national panic about the disappearances of children in the spring of 1945. This panic was a factor in producing an atmosphere for pogroms, which led to the anti-Jewish pogroms in Rzeszów, Cracow, and Kielce.

But these were not all the effects of the wave of rapes that crossed Poland then. No one has even tried to estimate the number of "kraut children" born from the rapes, and there is no way to know how many women opted for abortions. A rare indication comes in an excerpt of a pastoral letter issued in October 1945 by the Polish Episcopate, which mentions "the proliferation of the crime of abortion."[106] In 1945–47, the Institute of Forensic Medicine in Cracow noted an annual figure of dozens of cases of abandoned newborns, de facto acts of infanticide.[107] We do not know how many women attempted suicide after being raped.[108] One indicator of the scale of the rape phenomenon was the pandemic of venereal diseases (which was also the result of Polish soldiers' and militia officers' sexual hyperactivity as well as the general postwar loosening of moral standards). In some districts in Pomerania and Silesia, the majority of women were infected with venereal disease. The schoolteacher quoted earlier applied for leave because she was infected. In Tucholski District in Pomerania alone, 1,700 women were in the same situation.[109] The number of infected women in Masuria reportedly hovered around 50 percent.[110] According to a militia estimate in Gniezno (where numerous Polish and Soviet army units were stationed), the percentage of women infected with venereal diseases approached 40. The deputy commander of the Citizens' Militia even issued an order for all women found outdoors after 10:00 p.m. to be examined by doctors.[111] These estimates, which were not based on empirical research, may have been inflated. Still, according to the Ministry of Health, immediately after the war about 10 percent of the Polish population may have had syphilis.[112] In some areas, research showed as many as 90 percent.[113]

"Out of the Frying Pan and into the Fire"

It would be difficult to use the figures for venereal diseases to determine the numbers of women raped in 1944–47. The biggest obstacle is the question of their nationality, which the reports did not always take into account. There is no doubt, however, that the largest subgroup were German women who did not manage to flee before the approach of the front line. Patient data from two Berlin hospitals estimated the number of rapes at 95,000 to 130,000. According to Antony Beevor, as many as two million German women may have been raped by Soviet soldiers as the war drew to a close.[114] Often, women were raped repeatedly, a dozen or even several dozen times. James Mark estimates that during the capture of Budapest, about 50,000 Hungarian women may have been raped,[115] but higher figures, between 75,000 and 120,000, have also been mentioned.[116] Generally, Red Army men treated Slavic women better than non-Slavs. But they did commit rapes in Czechoslovakia, where the number of raped women has been estimated at 10,000 to 20,000.[117] It appears that the number of Polish women who were raped must have been higher, if only because of the larger numbers of troops passing through Poland on their way to Berlin. The estimate of 40,000 or higher should be used as a hypothesis.

Rape generated fear, hatred, and, at times, years of trauma. Some victims felt that they were witnessing a new barbarian invasion. A Polish woman living near Wrocław wrote (August 8, 1945), "I'm very apprehensive of traveling far. I'm afraid of those Russian devils, those animals, who would devour any young woman with their eyes. I'm so terribly scared of those brutes. Because I know what they did to the German women, what savages. The Dark Ages in the Caucasus, Asians, morons, sickening. I'm awfully afraid of them because they are still lurking around here."[118]

The fear of Red Army troops increased not only geographically but also in people's minds, where the army became increasingly demonic. It had four faces: those of the Red Army, the Soviets, the Soviet Union, and Communism. People believed them responsible for all sorts of evils: threats to the Polish national and Christian identities and national sovereignty, murders, exile to Siberia, theft and depleting supplies, and conspiracy. All sorts of stories were told about them, most, alarmingly, based on actual experiences and facts. Imagination filled in the gaps. The Soviet Union's ill intentions toward Poland were allegedly proven by the injections of Poles with poison-laced vaccinations, guaranteeing infertility.[119] These stories' antiheroes were Russians and Jews, which may mean that the collective imagination transferred the role of poisoning wells and carrying epidemics, historically reserved for the Jews, to the Russians. One of the most terrifying rumors had Soviet soldiers impaling girls on their way to First Communion on bayonets.[120] Who knows whether this was the invention of a scheming propagandist or, on the contrary, an authentic expression of the views of at least some Poles. Whichever is true, it is important to remember that similar stories about the kidnapping and murder of children appear more than once across history. It was not much earlier that people believed that Jews, Jesuits, Turks, or Roma—whatever group was feared the most at a given time—committed them.

"THE PSYCHOSIS HAS EVEN OVERWHELMED THE CIVIL SERVANTS"

How did the plague of robberies and rapes influence behaviors and attitudes? People were afraid—this we already know. But how did they manage their fear? What did they do to minimize their feelings of being in danger? First of all, in the first months following "liberation," the thinking about the Red Army had already changed fundamentally.

In Pomerania: "The political situation in Gdańsk Province worsened in August. Anti-Soviet sentiments continue to deepen as a result of the constant disturbances caused by individual Red Army soldiers. Assaults and robberies have recently shifted to towns which until recently had been relatively calm, such as Sopot."[121]

In Greater Poland: "The attitude of the population of Greater Poland toward the Red Army, which so far had been indifferent, has taken on intense forms: it would not be an exaggeration to say that an anti-Soviet frond, inactive so far, is forming in Greater Poland. Even . . . Red Army enthusiasts now take a hostile stand toward Soviet soldiers (tragically equating the soldier who fought with the undisciplined tramp or deserter!). Instances of disputes and fist fights between Soviet soldiers and the Polish population are happening with increasing frequency."[122]

In Silesia: "The Polish population's ardent friendliness and sympathy toward the Red Army ... has cooled down significantly. Robberies and rapes committed by bands in Red Army uniforms are the reason."[123]

In Rzeszów: "Individual Soviet army units, which for a long time now have been committing assaults, robberies, murders and other such crimes against the local population with impunity, have turned it against them. At the present time, the very appearance of Soviet soldiers in the area brings out anxiety and a hostile attitude to every one of their actions."[124]

The growing dislike of Red Army troops turned into hatred, which was manifested even by the lowest-level Polish Security Office functionaries. There were many ways to conquer fear, which can be explained by both the high level of threat and the low effectiveness of at least some of those ways. Hiding one's possessions and barricading oneself in one's home and farm buildings was the first method. At times, people constructed virtual fortresses. Fearing Soviet robbers, one settler moved into such a fortress, abandoning a house he had moved into earlier, whose position made it more vulnerable to attack. "Thieves would not be able to capture the fortress. Its high window in the attic could only be reached by ladder. We made a hole in the attic ceiling through which we inserted a second ladder. We bolted the doors from the inside with heavy bars, and brought both ladders inside. We moved into one room, which had just enough space for two beds and a small table. We felt secure."[125]

To feel safer, the pioneers of the settlement operation ostentatiously stressed their national identity by wearing red-and-white armbands and displaying Polish flags on their houses (Allied prisoners of war and forced laborers returning home signaled their nationality in similar ways).[126] This did not always bring the desired results. It is possible that other methods, such as branding Germans with a red letter *N* on their backs in Kluczbork; with white armbands in Wrocław, Głogówek, Zabrze, Wołów, and many other localities; and elsewhere with a swastika painted on their backs aimed to redirect the Red Army's aggression.[127] The Poles were thus making the Germans their scapegoats, anything to be left alone, throwing them to the Soviet dragon to devour. This seems not to have worked, especially since the letter *N*s or the armbands may have been incomprehensible to the Soviets, at least initially. But Polish women did not dress in a way to suggest that they were ill, something German women tried unsuccessfully as the front line passed.[128] Some unmarried women, believing that Soviet soldiers did not rape married women, wore scarves on their heads, the traditional mark of a married woman in the Polish countryside.[129]

The simplest way to escape the threat was to flee. The settlement operation in Poland's western and northern areas slowed down. Many of the arrivals would return to central Poland, usually after having been robbed several times. In Złotoryja in Lower Silesia, "the settlers ... are leaving their jobs, explaining that they do not want to risk their lives and possessions, which are threatened by Soviet soldiers."[130] In Pomerania, "the district's greatest problem is security, and, if it's not resolved, the town of Elbląg and the district will empty out completely."[131] But the settlers from the Eastern Borderlands could not afford to go back home. When leaving their new homes in the endangered areas was out of the question, all they could do was flee into fields and forests. At times, a local panic would break out. Desperate families, fearing rape and robbery, would leave their homes in the evening and camp out in safer places until dawn. Rumors, the carriers of fear, often preceded such panics. Hearsay about armies on the march and their expected quarters was among the most often repeated rumor, which translated directly into behaviors. It was built on the experience of the "road to Berlin" and evoked fear of the Red Army crossing Poland, which would again lay waste to everything in its path. In the summer of 1945, there must not have been a single place in Poland, other than Warsaw, where this rumor was not repeated—and every time it gave rise to terror.

Greater Poland experienced such terror in June 1945. "A mad panic gripped the inhabitants of southern Greater Poland along the routes from Ostrów to Leszno and Ostrów to Kępno as a result of unconfirmed reports that the army commander in Ostrów Wielkopolski had announced that the returning 1.5-million strong Soviet army might threaten the calm and safety of the population. Property was secured, women were hidden away because, as people repeated, the military commander had said that women are most imperiled. The suggestions were so convincing that everyone believed this announcement."[132]

In mid-July 1945, a short-lived terror also touched Cracow. Since Soviet front units were to pass through the city, the starost banned the sales of alcohol.[133] So far, no one has attempted to count the number, reach, and duration of the explosions of this kind of panic in Poland at that time. But it would appear that the most common strategy spurred by gossip about the passage of Soviet armies, especially outside the cities, was to hide livestock and all sorts of possessions, clothes, and food, and at times to barricade the family indoors. To shield them from rape, men looked after women and girls especially well. When in March 1946 the Red Army was to come to the town of Pisz (whose inhabitants had been assaulted and women raped, repeatedly, in 1945[134]), the starost reported, "A panic has gripped the population living in the district. Settlers are abandoning their places and intend to move back to Central Poland with all their possessions. In the town of Pisz itself, the psychosis has even gripped the civil servants so powerfully that for this and other reasons four department heads have handed in their resignations to me."[135] Rumors about troops on the march returned with great force in the last quarter of 1946. They traveled across all of Poland. Its Grudziądz version was "the people of Grudziądz have been living under the stress of whispered propaganda, namely: ca. the 15th of this month, 2 Russian army battalions will pass through Grudziądz in the direction of the Łaba and Nysa Rivers. They will be allowed to do whatever they like, i.e., rob, kill, etc. Others are saying that 2 Russian army battalions will come to Grudziądz with their whole families. They will have the right to remove inhabitants from their homes without granting them the right to take anything, and will shoot anyone who doesn't want to leave."[136]

There was the expectation that as many as three million soldiers might march through Poland. Stories of this kind fed public anxiety. In Łódź Province, peasants were said to be getting rid of their livestock.[137] People saw projected requisitions as the cause of food price increases.[138] In late 1946, the tale that a "grand army" would be marching through Poland arrived together with another tale that Soviet troops would settle in areas along the border and expel the Polish population. People would also be forced out of sections of towns or out of entire towns. Also repeated was the claim that the majority of Polish products were being sent to the USSR. Transports of coal to the Soviet Union were invariably used as an example of such economic exploitation of Poland. Food, including potatoes, flour, vodka, salt, and sugar, was also allegedly transported there, as were twenty million pairs of shoes, which explained, people believed, shoe shortages in the shops. Food price increases were explained by the Red Army buying up food, and the Red Army was also thought to be grabbing UNRRA assistance destined for Poland. Money being collected to rebuild Warsaw was said to have been transferred to Moscow. There was also gossip about Poles being murdered or exiled to Siberia. The accumulation of alarmed gossip on the eve of the January 1947 parliamentary elections confirms the high level of collective anxiety.

"MARIAN, PLEASE . . . GET ME A . . . RIFLE OR REVOLVER, PLEASE"

Barricading oneself indoors, fleeing, panicking, and rumors represented different expressions of fear and of overcoming it. People also tried to fight it, literally. The Poles armed themselves, even if their weapon was an ax hidden under a bed. The habit of hiding one under a bed or close to the front door started during the war, and the situation after the war did not allow people to abandon it. In October 1945, some desperate inhabitants of Nowy Sącz who had been attacked repeatedly by patients from the local military hospital organized a system of self-defense. Much like during the Swedish invasion of 1655–60, they grabbed their "axes, pitchforks and iron crowbars to defend their property and their lives." As they faced never-ending raids, their despair and aggression, a common reaction to fear, intensified. "In view of the fact that new Soviet units were stationed yesterday near Nowy Sącz, ... we fear a rise in robberies and despaired self-defense of the agitated citizens."[139]

Someone writing from Western Pomerania in early September 1945 pleaded with the letter's addressee, "Marian, please, when you come to see us during your leave, will you get me a German rifle or revolver please? If you can, please do it because I need one to defend us. The red bandits are roaming around here and they steal whatever they see. They just stole our cow, which is our whole livelihood."[140]

Historical forms of local self-defense were used in many villages and towns. At times only a night watchman was posted, but more often large groups of men, rural militias, were organized. They were usually an extension of the Home Army and the Peasant Battalions, which took on new names as their members gathered again to protect their communities. According to a man from Greater Poland:

> I was [in] the [volunteer] militia beginning on the first day after the front passed. There were 30 or 40 of us watching to protect our women, our villages, our houses from the Russkis. We patrolled in groups of six, otherwise you couldn't stand up to the Russkis. They would be stationed with their guns in farmers' courtyards, all of them drunk. We had no uniforms, only red-and-white bands and weapons. We thought it was good that the Russkis beat the German. But they should leave now. It's been almost half a year, and they're still here, all over the place.[141]

Fear, hatred, and aggression awakened by the war were just the right backdrop for lynching to proliferate. Yet most of the available information about the lynchings is very fragmented. Most often the victims were military men caught at a crime scene. At times, a quarrel sufficed to start a lynching. In Jerzów in Łódź Province, a dispute ended in a lynching. On October 24, 1945, a group of Soviet soldiers went to shop in the farmers' market. They were not happy about what they thought were inflated prices, and they started a quarrel, attracting a mob. The mob, "egged on by reactionary elements," began to shout aggressively. People tussled, then clashed. The soldiers, outnumbered, decided to leave town. People hurled stones at them, and their retreat quickly turned into a chase. One of the soldiers began to shoot, and another threw a hand grenade, injuring seven people. Someone in the crowd fired a gun, hitting the soldier who had thrown the grenade, and the mob probably killed him. Two others were wounded.[142] In Wola Duchacka, today a district of Cracow, on November 22, 1945, two drunk Soviet soldiers accompanied by two women attempted to break into a home. One of the women was caught and almost killed by the crowd, which the militia allegedly prevented.[143] A few days later in Szczytno, men of the Fifteenth Infantry Division and the Soviet Thirty-Fifth Infantry Regiment scuffled. A Soviet officer was killed. The crowd captured two Soviet soldiers and ostentatiously herded them through the streets, then beat them and put them against a wall, pretending to execute them.[144] We do not know how many people were in the crowd and what its social and gender makeup and attitudes toward military service may have been. It is reasonable to assume that if at least three incidents of this kind took place in such a short time in different places across Poland, there must have been many more in the first two postwar years. If this were the case, it would reveal the despair of the population, as it was tormented by assaults, fear, and hatred of the Soviets, as well as the time's tendency to behave in extreme ways. Also, as US researchers have noted, lynching is often a way to reaffirm domination.[145] People who had been pushed down to the "subhuman" category for five years and were now being humiliated by the Soviets may have used lynching to assert their position. Still, the deep feelings of insecurity and absence of outside help were equally significant.

In the spring and summer of 1945, the Polish authorities were indeed helpless. Militia reports described their attempts to chase Soviet marauders and even armed skirmishes with larger groups of Soviets. But in view of the scale of the problem, these attempts made no impact on the Poles' overall sense of security, especially for those living in small towns and rural areas. The new government's functionaries, especially lower-level ones, themselves lived in fear. This was the case especially with the militia, whom the Soviet soldiers would disarm, then they would steal their bicycles, ransack their stations, beat them, and even murder them. It happened that the militia would barricade themselves inside their stations, afraid to come out when veterans returning from Kursk or Berlin prowled nearby. A symbolic incident occurred in Stargard. Three men from a Soviet tank crew were enjoying themselves in a restaurant, shouting "*davay chesy*" to the German women working there. The militia arrested two of them, but the third one got away. Shortly, a tank rolled into Joseph Stalin Square and fired a warning shot at the militia station, whose whole staff fled. The tank crew liberated their mates and rode off to their barracks.[146]

Soldiers with red stars on their helmets were not even afraid of the "Polish NKVD," as an incident in Sandomierz showed. In early September 1945 a group of men led by two lieutenants went into town to rob shops. They shot at several functionaries of the District Office of Public Security who were trying to restrain them. One of them died, and three Soviets were arrested. An hour later, their colleagues drove up to the District Office of Public Security and fired at it from a heavy machine gun, stormed it, and probably freed their comrades.[147]

The new regime's inability to guarantee basic protection from soldiers of the "fraternal army" had a huge impact on its lack of social legitimacy.[148] This was one of the reasons why it attempted to put pressure on Soviet Marshal Konstantin Rokossovsky[149] and lower-level Red Army commanders stationed in Poland as well as the Kremlin[150] to put an end to the Soviet marauders' lawlessness—when this problem did not officially exist. It appeared only rarely in reports from the Polish Army's Main Political Office and the Security Office. Militia reports sometimes underplayed it, writing that "individuals in Soviet uniforms" were committing the crimes. In some reports, wording of this kind was even crossed out. In Trzebiatów in October 1946, the funeral of a fire chief murdered by a Soviet officer turned into a public demonstration. The head of the Provincial Security Office attended, complaining that people were not allowed to say that Russians were responsible for attacks and murders; instead, they had to say it was Vlasov's people, forest bands, and werewolves.[151]

This interpretation was in force in all media except underground publications.[152] Władysław Gomułka stammered about it in a speech at the Polish Workers' Party congress in December 1945: "Every army has some soldiers who commit marauders' disturbances. The Red Army is also not free of such soldiers, but to paraphrase a well-known proverb, let me say, 'you have to see a whole healthy and beautiful forest, not only the feeble, individual trees in that forest.' Such individual disturbances of marauding and theft also occur in the Polish Army."[153] Gomułka was partly right: demoralization had also had a significant impact on the ranks of the Polish Army.

Plundering had already occurred during the winter offensive. "Discipline has collapsed in all units," read a report of the Main Political-Educational Department of the Polish Army in February 1945.[154] A few months later came more reports about moral decay in some units.[155] It fully revealed itself during the resettlements of Germans and during operation "Vistula." Soldiers also did not spare their compatriots, as many of the bandit attacks, which had been attributed to the "forest people," turned out to have been the work of Polish Army soldiers and officers. In February 1946, a group of men of the Forty-Ninth Infantry Regiment forced every inhabitant of the village of Dubno (Białystok Province) to hand over one hundred zlotys and a kilogram of lard. Because the village did not deliver this tribute, the soldiers seized three children and carved crosses on their stomachs.[156]

Polish military men also raped German women. Most guilty were soldiers of the Second Army, although those of the First Army also indulged. Lower-ranking officers not only turned the other way but outright approved this behavior. One of them saw nothing wrong with it, as he would admit years later: "A drunken soldier chased after some old woman, who, in his stupor, he probably thought was young. The old woman locked herself inside a toilet in the courtyard, and the soldier banged on the door wildly. I told her that I was ready to defend her from the soldier's passion, but that she should consider this her last chance ever, what with the war and the dead-drunk soldier, and that she may not get another chance like it. As I didn't manage to persuade her, I convinced the soldier to redirect his inclinations toward some pretty young thing. I succeeded."[157]

But higher-up commanders did not approve of rape. One difference between Polish and Soviet troops was that the former were reportedly tried by military courts. There is much information in both documents and oral accounts about these trials as well as the military morale. In a trial for the rape of two German women, Second Lieutenant Jelowej was sentenced to be demoted to sergeant and to serve eight years in prison, and Gunner Nowak to five years in prison. Both were sent to a penal company. Officer witnesses at the trial expressed their disappointment and tried to explain the defendants' actions with their hatred of "germans" [sic], which they had been fed over several years. They did not understand why someone could be tried for raping a German girl and asked whether German officers had also been put on trial for raping Russian or Polish women.[158]

A colossal rise in infections with venereal diseases was noted in some Polish Army units, especially those stationed along the western borders. Concerned, the head of the Political-Educational Department of the Tenth Infantry Division issued a pertinent regulation. In it, he claimed that "the Germans are purposely serving up ill persons to our soldiers, aiming to diminish our army's fighting ability, wanting to weaken us morally and physically." He claimed that "associating with german [sic] women is a dishonor, a stain on the uniform of a victorious Polish soldier."[159]

The victors' behavior and the "trophy" atmosphere prolonged the war psychologically. The Red Army's banditry, rapes, and murders sowed fear and a feeling of powerlessness in the population; in some Poles it brought a desire for revenge, in others a desire to emulate the culprits. Hugo Steinhaus was right when he defined the consequences of the Red Army men's behavior as "the growth of Balkanization."[160]

NOTES

1. Delumeau, *La peur en Occident*.
2. The first version of this chapter, Zaremba, "'Jak nie urok, to . . . ,'" 235–62.
3. Cieplewicz, *Obrona Warszawy w 1939 r.*, 324; as quoted in Borodziej and Lemberg, *Niemcy w Polsce 1945–1950*, vol. 2, 19.
4. Gross and Grudzińska-Gross, "W czterdziestym nas matko na sybir zesłali . . . ," 242.
5. Tomaszewski, *Lwów 1940–1944*, 205, 206.
6. AAN, Zespół Delegatura Rządu na Kraj (dalej DRnK), 202/VIII-4, k. 52. Sytuacja społeczna w miesiącu kwietniu 1944.
7. AAN, DRnK, 202/III-23, k. 13. Sytuacja społeczna w miesiącu lutym 1944.
8. Beevor and Vinogradova, *A Writer at War*, 279.
9. "Jak 'uwalniano' Polskę, wspomnienia generała-porucznika N.K. Popiela," 228.
10. AIPN, MBP 3378, k. 45, 46. Doniesienie specjalne dotyczące wypowiedzi o marszałku Stalinie i o Armii Czerwonej, April 3, 1945.
11. Dąbrowska, *Dzienniki*, vol. 5, 137.
12. Uniechowska, *Franciszka Starowieyskiego opowieść o końcu świata, czyli reforma rolna*, 88.
13. For more see Merridale, *Ivan's War*.
14. For Białystok Province, see Kułak, *Białostocczyzna 1944–1945 w dokumentach podziemia i oficjalnych władz*, 161–64. Western Pomerania Province: Wojtaszek, *Źródła do dziejów Pomorza Zachodniego*, 53, 74, 87, et al.; Dziurok and Musiał, "'Bratni rabunek,'" 321–49.
15. AIPN, KG MO 35/2038, k. 15–17. Raport sytuacyjny nr 3 za czas od dnia 15 X 1944 do dnia 22 X 1944.
16. Centralne Archiwum Wojskowe w Rembertowie (henceforth CAW) III.2.87, k. 42. Raport o sytuacji w Rzeszowie.
17. AAN, Zespół Krajowej Rady Narodowej (dalej KRN) 187, k. 1. Starosta Powiatu w Biłgoraju do Biura Ekonomicznego Departamentu Aprowizacji Pana Wojewody, October 28, 1944.
18. Dąbrowska, *Dzienniki*, 137.
19. Steinhaus, *Wspomnienia i zapiski*, 300, 301.
20. Naimark, *The Russians in Germany*; MacDonogh, *After the Reich*, chapter on "Life in the Russian Zone."
21. For more on Soviet policy and situation in this area, see Magierska, "Ziemie Zachodnie i Północne w okresie komendantur wojennych i kształtowanie się polskiej administracji cywilnej," 231–50; Łach, *Ziemie Odzyskane pod wojskową administracją radziecką po II wojnie światowej*; Mochocki, "Przestępstwa pospolite A. Czerwonej na Środkowym Nadodrzu (1945–1947) w przekazach urzędowych administracji terenowej i centralnej," 37–52; Grabiec, "Postępowanie Armii Czerwonej wobec miejscowej ludności w świetle pisemnych sprawozdań sytuacyjnych wojewody śląsko-dąbrowskiego z 1945 r.," 207–16; Golon, *Polityka radzieckich władz wojskowych i policyjnych na Pomorzu Nadwiślańskim w*

latach 1945–1947; Bazior, "Stacjonowanie jednostek Armii Czerwonej na terenie woj. gdańskiego w latach 1945–1947," 161–67; Bazior, *Armia Czerwona na Pomorzu Gdańskim 1945–1947*.

22. AIPN, MBP 1406, k. 1. *Ziemie Odzyskane. Fakty mówią za siebie*, opracowanie przygotowane prawdopodobnie na zlecenie Delegatury Rządu na Kraj.

23. Neja, "Problemy z sojusznikami," 61.

24. AIPN, mf. 01265/752, k. 2b. Specjalne doniesienie dot. bezpieczeństwa w kraju według opisów w listach cywilnej ludności.

25. AIPN, KG MO 35/922, k. 39. Raport sytuacyjny od dnia 27 VII 1945 do dnia 5 IX 1945.

26. AIPN, MBP 3378, k. 112. Specjalne doniesienie Wydziału Cenzury Wojennej MBP, October 13, 1945.

27. AIPN, 1572/734, k. 9. Raport dekadowy Kierownika Wojewódzkiego UBP w Szczecinie za okres 10–20 III 1946, n.d.

28. AIPN, MBP 3378, k. 60a. Specjalne doniesienie dotyczące prowokacyjnych pogłosek, May 14, 1945.

29. CAW, III.2.200, k. 87. Specjalne doniesienie dotyczące nadużyć żołnierzy Armii Czerwonej, May 10, 1945.

30. AAN, Ministerstwo Informacji i Propagandy [henceforth, MIiP] 78, k. 27. Sprawozdanie z inspekcji przeprowadzonej w Powiatowym Oddziale Informacji i Propagandy w Elblągu w dn. 20 IX–24 IX br. przez ob. Skowrońskiego, n.d.

31. Pichór, "Byłem robotnikiem Schichau'a," 23.

32. AIPN, MBP Mf 01265/752, Specjalne doniesienie dot. bezpieczeństwa według opisów w listach cywilnej ludności, October 12, 1945, n.p.

33. Borodij et al., *Rok 1945*, 109.

34. AAN, URM 5/640, k. 15. Raport Narodowego Banku Polskiego o sytuacji gospodarczej kraju.

35. AIPN, MBP 3378, Specjalne doniesienie Wydziału Cenzury Wojennej MBP, 13 Oct. 1945, k. 112.

36. AAN, Prezydium Rady Ministrów, 2/16, k. 70–71. Raport, 4 VIII 1945. I would like to thank Prof. Andrzej Paczkowski for alerting me to the existence of this document.

37. AAN, Prezydium Rady Ministrów, 2/16, k. 70–71.

38. AAN, URM 5/776, k. 14. Dyrekcja Okręgowa Kolei Państwowych w Szczecinie do Ministerstwa Komunikacji w Warszawie. See also Wojtaszek, *Źródła do dziejów Pomorza Zachodniego*, 126.

39. Białecki, *Drogi powrotu. Wspomnienia mieszkańców Pomorza Szczecińskiego*, 18, 19.

40. AIPN, KG MO 35/888, k. 8. Raport sytuacyjny MO w woj. poznańskim za czas 16 V–5 VI 1945.

41. Wojtaszek, *Źródła do dziejów Pomorza Zachodniego*, 130.

42. Śmietanka-Kruszelnicki and Wróbel, "Przestępstwa żołnierzy Armii Czerwonej na Kielecczyźnie 1945–1946," 125.

43. CAW III.2.200, k. 87. Specjalne doniesienie dotyczące nadużyć żołnierzy Armii Czerwonej, n.d.

44. AIPN, MBP 3378, k. 112. Specjalne doniesienie Wydziału Cenzury Wojennej MBP, October 13, 1945.

45. AIPN, MBP 3378, k. 112.

46. Wróbel, "Wyzwoliciele czy okupanci? Żołnierze sowieccy w Łódzkiem 1945–1946," 41.

47. AAN, URM 5/776, k. 48. Wyciąg ze sprawozdania inspektora CKW-PPS tow. Butlowa Gustawa z inspekcji przeprowadzonej w dn. 21 i 22 XII 1946 w PK Pionkach i MK Radom woj. kieleckiego, n.d.

48. AIPN, mf. 01265/752, k. 5b. Specjalne doniesienie dot. bezpieczeństwa w kraju według opisów w listach cywilnej ludności.

49. AIPN, KG MO 35/920, k. 16. Doniesienie nr 15, n.d.

50. AIPN, KG MO 35/895, k. 22. Wypadki nadzwyczajne za czas od 10-go VII br. do 25 VII [1945], Zastępca Pow. Kom. [MO] dla Spraw Polit.-Wych, Rzeszów.

51. CAW III.2.200, k. 87. Specjalne doniesienie dotyczące nadużyć żołnierzy Armii Czerwonej, n.d.

52. APK, Wojewódzki Urząd Informacji i Propagandy 27, k. 294. Ważniejsze wypadki na terenie powiatu częstochowskiego, n.d.

53. The underground report from which this quotation is drawn goes on:

> The Soviet army, which came later to serve as the garrison, is behaving properly. But it is still fairly dangerous to walk in the empty streets after dark, and watches are in especially high demand. There have been a few incidents in Cracow where pedestrians were made to undress in the dark in desolate streets, and their coats and other clothing were confiscated. . . . The arbitrary taking over of living quarters is an even worse plague in towns and villages. Single soldiers often come into homes using any kind of excuse and request vodka, and when they're denied they search the home and take watches, expensive items, jams and juices, often also suitcases, when they are full and packed (AAN, DRnK 202/III-36, k. 53. Sprawozdanie sytuacyjne z kraju za okres od 21 XII 1944 do 21 II 1945, n.d.).

54. As late as September 1945, pedestrians were robbed and raped night after night (AAN, MIiP 80. Sprawozdanie z wyjazdu służbowego do Wojewódzkiego Urzędu Informacji i Propagandy w Krakowie, 10 IX 1945, k. 8). On the situation in Cracow, see Chwalba, *Kraków w latach 1939–1945*, 441–43.

55. In Poznań in only two weeks in June–July 1945, Soviet soldiers without a doubt committed eight robberies and one murder. A boy was shot dead by a Soviet officer. There was also the attempted rape of an eight-year-old girl (AIPN, KG MO 35/888, k. 19, 20. Raport sytuacyjny za okres od 20 VI do 5 VII 1945, n.d.).

56. AAN, KC PPR 295/VII 267, k. 3. Wyciąg ze sprawozdania Urzędu Informacji i Propagandy woj. poznańskiego za sierpień 1945.

57. AIPN, KG MO 35/2260, k. 114. Raport sytuacyjny nr 20 za drugą dekadę VIII 1945, n.d.

58. AIPN 01265/752. Specjalne doniesienie dotyczące bezpieczeństwa w kraju według opisów w listach cywilnej ludności, n.d., n.p. (microfilm).

59. APK, Wojewódzki Urząd Informacji i Propagandy 27, k. 326. Kwestionariusz sprawozdawczy za wrzesień 1945, n.d.

60. Majzner, "Bilans radzieckiej obecności w Częstochowie w latach 1945–1946," 275–99.

61. AAN, KC PPR 295/IX–19, k. 57. Sprawozdanie instruktora Szafrańskiego z wyjazdu do Częstochowy, n.d.

62. APK, Urząd Wojewódzki II 1337, k. 323, 325. Sytuacyjne sprawozdanie miesięczne za lipiec 1945, n.d.

63. APK, Urząd Wojewódzki II 1337, k. 323, 325.

64. APK, Wojewódzki Urząd Informacji i Propagandy 27, k. 326. Kwestionariusz sprawozdawczy za wrzesień 1945.
65. Zaremba and Zarembina, "1945 rok kobiet upodlonych"; Ostrowska and Zaremba, "Kobieca gehenna."
66. Grossmann, "A Question of Silence," 42–63; Fisch, *Nemmersdorf, Oktober 1944.*
67. "I must add here," remembered Franciszek Ryszka, "that our front units, and I mean mostly the Soviets, behaved rather decently toward the Polish population, if one may even use this word for soldiers at the front. I didn't hear about mass rapes or robberies then, even though fresh memories, such as a field in Czyżkówek covered with corpses, left no illusions about what the Soviet were capable of" (Ryszka, *Pamiętnik inteligenta. Dojrzewanie,* 263, 264).
68. Godycka-Ćwirko, *Lata klęski 1944–1973,* 26.
69. Some historians estimate that beginning with operation "Overlord," US troops committed at least seventeen thousand rapes (*Gazeta Wyborcza,* June 7, 2004).
70. MacDonogh, *After the Reich,* 240.
71. To read more about the reasons for the rape wave, see Norman M. Naimark, *The Russians in the Germany,* 70–140 et al.; Merridale, *Ivan's War,* 312ff; MacDonogh, *After the Reich,* 26–27.
72. Merridale, *Ivan's War,* 314.
73. Dutton and Aron, "Some Evidence for Heightened Sexual Attraction," 484–97.
74. Djilas, *Conversations with Stalin,* 110–11.
75. Djilas, 110–11.
76. Naimark, *The Russians in Germany,* 107.
77. Beevor and Vinogradova, *A Writer at War,* 327.
78. Godycka-Ćwirko, *Lata klęski 1944–1973,* 26.
79. Beevor and Vinogradova, *A Writer at War,* 110–11.
80. Godycka-Ćwirko, *Lata klęski 1944–1973,* 26.
81. CAW, III.2.200. Specjalne doniesienie dotyczące nadużyć żołnierzy Armii Czerwonej, n.d., k. 86.
82. CAW, III.2.200.
83. AAN, KRN 797, k. 13. Raport nr 2 prezesa Wojewódzkiego Urzędu Ziemskiego w Olsztynie, n.d.
84. CAW, III.2.200. Specjalne doniesienie dotyczące nadużyć żołnierzy Armii Czerwonej, n.d., k. 86.
85. AAN, KRN 797, k. 13, 14. Raport nr 2 prezesa Wojewódzkiego Urzędu Ziemskiego w Olsztynie, n.d.
86. Hugo Steinhaus wrote in his diary on May 11, 1945: "The Poles are coming back from Germany. You can meet people from Saxony, Potsdam, Vienna walking on the roads. They often bring horses. The Soviets rob them on the way; they say that the women are raped en masse, and that Polish identity cards don't help. They kill many Poles, and they take almost everyone's belongings.... They rob people on the trains, often throw passengers out of moving trains. They did this to a woman on a bridge on the Wisłoka" (Steinhaus, *Wspomnienia i zapiski,* 316).
87. Account in the author's possession.
88. Stenogram z konferencji sprawozdawczej odbytej w dniu 25 V 1945 w Dyrekcji PUR w Łodzi z objazdu delegatów Centrali Pomorza Zachodniego, Ewakuacja 1945. Doniesienia z etapów, 72.
89. AIPN, KG MO 35/922, k. 39. Raport sytuacyjny od dnia 27 VII do dnia 5 IX 1945, n.d.
90. In some localities in western Poland, illegal brothels and harems opened and employed mostly German women. AAN, DRnK 202/III–36, k. 141. Sytuacja na Pomorzu (do 10 VI 1945), n.d.; AAN, DRnK 202/III–36, k. 219. Sytuacja na Pomorzu (luźne informacje za czas 10–23 VI 1945r.), Kronika PAT, n.d.
91. Cf. Wodecka, "I nadeszli barbarzyńcy."
92. Neja, *Problemy z sojusznikami,* 59.
93. Neja, 59–63.
94. AAN, MZO 60, k. 114.
95. Naimark, *The Russians in the Germany,* 90.
96. AIPN, WiN 92, k. 80. Niepodpisany raport WiN, n.d.
97. AIPN, KG MO 35/793, k. 9. Raport sytuacyjny od dnia 15 VI 1945 do dnia 30 VI 1945.
98. Śmietanka-Kruszelnicki and Wróbel, *Przestępstwa żołnierzy Armii Czerwonej na Kielecczyźnie,* 124, 125.
99. Raport informacyjny nr 21 ZG WiN za okres 15–30 września 1945, in *Zrzeszenie "Wolność i Niezawisłość" w dokumentach. Wrzesień 1945–czerwiec 1946,* vol. 1, 344.
100. Golon, "Polityka radzieckich władz na Kujawach i Pomorzu w 1945 roku," 87, 88.
101. This most likely happened in May or June. AAN, KC PPR 295/VII-268, k. 19. Pismo do Pana Starosty pow. pińczowskiego w Pińczowie, n.d.
102. AIPN, KG MO 35/2260, k. 90. Raport sytuacyjny Komendy Głównej MO nr 17 za pierwszą i drugą dekadę VII 1945.
103. AIPN, KG MO 35/2260, k. 73. Raport sytuacyjny Komendy Głównej MO nr 16 za trzecią dekadę VI 1945.
104. AIPN, KG MO 35/888, k. 20. Raport sytuacyjny MO w woj. poznańskim za czas 6 VI–20 VI 1945.
105. Zgwałcenie 15-letniej dziewczyny w Małych Polanach, gm. Kunice, przez dwóch żołnierzy radzieckich (AAN, Delegatura rządu RP przy PGWAR 14, k. 261. Wykaz przestępstw popełnianych przez żołnierzy radzieckich za czas 1 VIII–8 XI 1947 w Legnicy i okolicach, n.d.).
106. Żaryn, *Komunikaty Konferencji Episkopatu Polski 1945–2000,* 49.
107. Konopka, "Śmierć na ulicach Krakowa w latach 1945–1947 w materiale archiwum krakowskiego Zakładu Medycyny Sądowej," 145.
108. A reference was found in the newspaper *Ziemia Pomorska.* Its reporter examined the logs of the emergency room in Bydgoszcz. "The majority of suicides are women (middle-aged). Only a few suicides of young women brought on by disappointment in love were registered. The reasons for the attempted suicides are usually poverty and venereal diseases. The majority used gas or Lysol to kill themselves" ("Ponure cyfry," *Ziemia Pomorska,* May 13, 1946).
109. AAN, DRnK 202/III–36, k. 219. Sytuacja na Pomorzu (luźne informacje za czas 10–23 VI 1945), Kronika PAT, n.d.
110. Baryła, *Okręg Mazurski w raportach Jakuba Prawina. Wybór dokumentów 1945 r,* 81.
111. AIPN, KG MO 35/888, k. 15. Raport sytuacyjny MO w woj. poznańskim za czas 6–20 VI 1945, n.d.

112. Borkowski, *Choroby weneryczne szerzą się*, 34, quoted after Barański, *Walka z chorobami wenerycznymi w Polsce w latach 1948–1949*.
113. T. Stępniewski, "Zwalczanie chorób wenerycznych na wsi," *Zdrowie Publiczne*, 1 (1946), 119, as quoted in Barański, *Walka z chorobami wenerycznymi*.
114. Beevor, *Berlin*, 410; Beevor, "They Raped Every German Female from Eight to 80."
115. Mark, "Remembering Rape: Divided Social Memory and the Red Army in Hungary 1944–1945," 133.
116. Janos Tischler, data in the author's possession.
117. The daily *Mladá Fronta Dnes* published these data based on information from British and US observers, quoted in *Rzeczpospolita*, May 9, 2005.
118. AIPN, MBP 3378, k. 112. Specjalne doniesienie Wydziału Cenzury Wojennej MBP, n.d.
119. Gronek and Marczak, *Biuletyny Informacyjne Ministerstwa Bezpieczeństwa Publicznego*, vol. 1: *1947*, 145.
120. AAN, MIiP 95, k. 77. Wyciąg ze sprawozdania, n.d., 18.
121. AAN, KC PPR 295/VII–267, k. 23. Odpis sprawozdania politycznego za sierpień 1945 województwa gdańskiego.
122. AAN, KC PPR 295/VII–267, k. 2. Wyciąg ze sprawozdania Urzędu Informacji i Propagandy woj. poznańskiego za sierpień 1945.
123. *Sprawozdanie sytuacyjne Urzędu Wojewódzkiego Śląskiego w Katowicach za czerwiec 1945 r.*, as quoted in Jarosław Neja, *Problemy z sojusznikami*, op. cit., 60.
124. AAN, Ministerstwo Administracji Publicznej 121, k. 48. Unsigned, first page missing. Probably report by Rzeszów Province governor for August 1945.
125. Sobków, "Do innego kraju," 64–65.
126. Scholz, *Dziennik niemieckiego księdza*; Kowacz, "Miejsce przechodnie," 77, 94.
127. Pollok, *Śląskie tragedie*, 47.
128. I was able to find only one report about this. In Sieraków, Poznań Province, right before the Red Army arrived, a Polish mother smeared her fifteen-year-old daughter with substances that would make her look dirty and ill. In 1939, Sieraków had been annexed by the Reich, and many Germans continued to live there. The Polish woman was probably copying German women.
129. AHM, AHM_0089. Wspomnienia Leokadii Słopieckiej.
130. AIPN, KG MO 35/920, k. 2. Wyjątek z raportu sytuacyjnego Komendy Powiatowej MO w Złotoryi, n.d.
131. AAN, MIiP 78, k. 27. Sprawozdanie z inspekcji przeprowadzonej w Powiatowym Oddziale Informacji i Propagandy w Elblągu w dn. 20 IX–24 IX br. przez ob. Skowrońskiego. See also Wojtaszek, *Źródła do dziejów Pomorza Zachodniego*, 140, 141, 154, 162.
132. AAN, DRnK 202/III-36, k. 154, 155. Raport o sytuacji na Ziemiach Zachodnich. Wielkopolska (od 15 V do 15 VI 1945).
133. "Zakaz sprzedaży i podawania alkoholu," *Dziennik Polski*, July 16, 1945.
134. AAN, MZO 1115, k. 15. Protokół z odbytej inspekcji w Starostwie Powiatowym w Jansborku w listopadzie 1945.
135. Brenda, "O bandytyzmie na Warmii i Mazurach w pierwszych latach powojennych," 95.
136. AAN, MIiP 365, k. 62. Meldunek sytuacyjny Powiatowego Oddziału Informacji i Propagandy w Grudziądzu z dnia 11 X 1946.
137. AAN, MIiP 184, k. 15. Dane o propagandzie szeptanej nr 10, December 20, 1946.
138. AAN, MIiP, k. 1.
139. AIPN, KG MO 35/88. Telefonogram, Kraków, October 6, 1945, n.p.
140. AIPN, MBP 3378, k. 112. Specjalne doniesienie Wydziału Cenzury Wojennej MBP.
141. Krzysztof Gozdowski, "Wielkopolski ataman," *Karta*, 10 (1993), 82.
142. CAW IV.502.1.247, k. 150. Raport w związku z zajściami, jakie miały miejsce w m. Jerzowie, woj. łódzkie.
143. AIPN, KG MO 35/878, k. 78. Meldunek, n.d.
144. CAW III.2.212, k. 71. Meldunek dzienny nr 8 GZPW WP, n.d.
145. McGovern, *Anatomy of a Lynching* (Louisiana State University Press, 1982), 4.
146. "Wspomnienia Stanisława Jarmieńczuka," in *Stargard moje miasto*, 33.
147. Śmietanka-Kruszelnicki and Wróbel, *Przestępstwa żołnierzy Armii Czerwonej na Kielecczyźnie*, 126.
148. The Politburo of the CC PPR (AAN, KC PPR, 295/V–5, k. 40–44) noted the delegitimizing effect as "our Party is paying for this state of affairs politically" in September 1945.
149. AAN, URM 2/16, k. 53–54. Sprawozdanie specjalne z rozmowy Aleksandra Zawadzkiego z marszałkiem Rokossowskim, July 30, 1945.
150. Jakub Berman discussed this with Stalin in September 1945. His notes from the discussion read, "The [Red Army's] diminished popularity stemming from the loosened discipline of the rear units spread across all of Poland and the units crossing Poland, the lack of security especially in western regions linked to the numerous roaming bands of marauders and Vlasovites touch peasants and repatriates deeply. This impunity primarily burdens the [Polish Workers' Party] and weakens its authority among the masses" (AAN. Jakub Berman—spuścizna 325/33, k. 11, Notatka z rozmowy ze Stalinem, n.d.).
151. AAN, URM 5/776, k. 40, 41. List Wacława Lubarskiego, Trzebiatów November 18, 1946.
152. Newspapers rarely covered Soviet marauders. For this reason, one article is worth quoting:

> The Government of National Unity has reached an agreement with Marshal Rokossovsky that a higher-up officer (general) of the Red Army with a full mandate and an army unit at his disposal will be stationed at every provincial-level office. All manifestations of marauding will be among this officer's duties. The lawless taking of cattle, grain etc., and ordinary robbery are also considered marauding. Because of this, the Ministry of Public Administration has imposed on starosts the duty to inform provincial offices about the marauders present in their districts and to report all complaints about marauding to provincial offices. Complaints are to be based on a precise statement of facts because every case will lead to action by the Soviet command at the provincial office ("Walka z wybrykami maruderów," *Sztandar Ludu*, October 11, 1945).

153. Gomułka, *Artykuły i przemówienia*, vol. 1, 499.
154. CAW III.2.174, k. 28. Sprawozdanie Wydziału Organizacyjnego Głównego Zarządu Polityczno-Wychowawczego za luty 1945.
155. CAW IV.502.1.70, k. 17. Sprawozdanie miesięczne Głównego Zarządu Polityczno-Wychowawczego WP za okres od 1 XI do 31 XII 1945.
156. AIPN 00835/68, k. 7. Informacja o stanie moralno–politycznym w jednostkach Wojska Polskiego w lutym 1946.
157. Drabienko, *Jedno życie. Wspomnienia z lat 1942–1951*, 75.
158. CAW III.2.204, k. 180. Meldunek dzienny Głównego Zarządu Pol.-Wych. WP, 13 IV 1945.
159. Borodziej and Lemberg, *Niemcy w Polsce 1945–1950*, 163, 164.
160. Steinhaus, *Wspomnienia i zapiski*, 318.

THE DEMOBILIZED

The people who will be discussed here are missing from existing pictures of the postwar period. They do not make appearances in diaries and memoirs or monographs about the heroic resettlement of the Regained Territories or the rebuilding of Poland. With effort, it is possible to understand why political studies leave them out. But it is difficult to explain their absence from works analyzing the period's interethnic conflicts. It is impossible to explain why analysts of the socioeconomic situation do not include them. In fact, the demobilized, deserters, vagrants, beggars, invalids, orphans, unemployed, and profiteers—for it is they who are being discussed—were often in the forefront of events. They hid in forests and lay around in streets and bazaars, milled around in throngs. They emanated anxiety and often gave others a fright.

Like the sociologist Stefan Czarnowski, we can call them "the expendables."[1] Robert Castel's term "the dangerous classes" fits them to a tee.[2] Both authors discuss individuals who, because of a crisis or accelerated economic progress, are excluded, unintegrated, and deprived of a "useful function." They stand out by closing themselves off inside the family group, being averse to strangers and very accepting of pathologies. A social perspective that has been narrowed down to one's own group implies a lack of engagement in politics combined with disgust with and even a hostility to all sorts of "them"—political, intellectual, or business elites.[3] But their lack of interest in politics is not symmetrical. Especially during tensions and crises, the "expendable" were exploited in short-term political competitions. According to Czarnowski's apt descriptions, they "served violence." Their services were employed by political parties in republican Rome and in the cities of medieval northern Italy. Nineteenth- and twentieth-century political parties recruited them for their raiding parties. The authors of *The Communist Manifesto* affirmed that the *lumpenproletariat* could be sold as a "bribed tool of reactionary intrigue."[4] Totalitarian movements also swept them under their wings en masse. In Poland, the landless nobility and the urban plebs were not needed. According to the author of an eighteenth-century memoir, Poland was "chockfull of loafers and vagrants."[5]

Czarnowski, who died before the Second World War, included among the "expendable" people who were suspended between structures the jobless, those who had lost their social position; youth from working-class and peasant families who were searching for an occupation in vain; people without a vocation or money; the homeless, vagrants, and beggars; and all those who in eras of stability lived one day at a time, taking temporary jobs that others often looked down on. In Poland the "expendable" were most troublesome in rural areas. Before the war, Ludwik Landau, Jan Pański, and Edward Strzelecki estimated the number of unproductive people aged fourteen to fifty-nine at nearly 2,400,000, with

900,000 of them in central Poland. This meant that they made up 30 percent of the peasantry.[6] Small towns in the interwar period all had their "bad" streets while larger ones such as Częstochowa, Gdynia, Łódź, and Katowice had entire "bad" parts of town, and Warsaw had several. The people living in them, immersed in the culture of poverty, developed specific behaviors as well as social norms and attitudes different from those prevailing in the "good" areas. But during the 1920s economic crisis, these traditional social divisions blurred, as civil servants and the intelligentsia also lost their jobs and their social position. In 1933, the Warsaw poor were a permanent feature of the urban landscape: "The homeless are sleeping in entryways, at night, under boats, on the banks of the Vistula, on piers and in changing cabins. You will encounter them on benches in stairways, in attics and cellars, into which they slipped before the front doors were locked for the night."[7] In the late 1930s, as the economy emerged from its crisis, the numbers of urban unemployed dropped. Still, by 1939, about 450,000 people who played no "useful role" may still have been vegetating in the cities.[8]

During the war, contradictory processes pulled at these "dangerous classes." On the one hand, they became smaller as hundreds of thousands of mostly young men were mobilized and thousands landed in prisoner-of-war camps. Over two million men and women were deported to the Reich to perform forced labor. Indeed, initially this group was made up of volunteers, as the writer Kazimierz Wyka observed, primarily the rural underclass lured by the myth of working abroad.[9] The extermination of the Polish Jews had a direct influence on the job market. But the war also helped to create groups of potential "new expendables"—all kinds of hawkers, smugglers, and moonshine makers and those living hand to mouth, "as if."[10] Tomasz Szarota, a historian of everyday life during the war, believes that the number of people living outside society was much larger during than before the war.[11] Swelling their ranks were people who lost their social positions as a result of the occupying powers' policies. Single mothers and old people who lost those who had once taken care of them struggled. Also adding to the "dangerous class" were young people who had interrupted their education and had their entrance into adulthood accelerated by wartime conditions. Cultural processes were as important as numerical changes, most important among them the proliferation of the wartime way of life.

The next wave of "expendables" came after the war ended. In 1945, the rural "expendable" population was estimated at nearly a million in Lesser Poland, especially in Cracow and Kielce Provinces, and in Mazovia.[12] The zones of extreme poverty grew on the social maps of Polish cities, spilling out of the outskirts and taking over downtowns, which until then had been elite. In the poor Łódź districts of Bałuty and Widzewo, people were living just like before the war: jam-packed, and without running water, plumbing, or electricity. But now, people were also living in similar conditions, in overcrowded cellars and stairwells, in the showy Piotrkowska Street. In January 1947, the Łódź daily *Echo Wieczorne* rang the alarm bells about this situation:

> Clean air! People of Łódź! You often complain about the poor quality of air in your city. About bad smells, dust and filth. How about the next time you're especially bothered by the Łódź air, go into one of these houses, their gloomy stairwells with their rational "overhead lights," spend half an hour inside, chat with one of the wax-faced children, a child who is born, lives and dies without air, and then come out on Piotrkowska Street. Then, the Łódź air, filled with sweat and smoke as it is, will smell like balsamic pine trees and flowery lawns. It will seem ever so clean, pleasant and refreshing.[13]

Many Polish cities, tormented by permanent power cuts, smashed windows, leaking roofs, lack of heating, and filth in the streets, resembled favelas. In the autumn and winter of 1945, voices begging for coal resounded across the country. A quarter of the temporary barracks built in Przemyśl were intended for people from nearby burned-down villages. Repatriated people camped out along train tracks in Greater Poland, Lesser Poland, and the Regained Territories.[14] With a shortage of habitable space in bombed-out Wrocław, Gdańsk, and especially Warsaw, people slept in ruins and moved into half-burned or half-bombed buildings. The crowding boggled the mind.

"The pits of human misery: homelessness, cold, rage," Anna Kowalska wrote after spending time in the train station in Nowy Sącz in December 1944.[15] The "dangerous classes" grew and became radicalized in the course of the next year. Repatriates, refugees, demobilized troops, deserters, profiteers, invalids, and orphans inflated the group for a total of hundreds of thousands of people who had been hurled into marginal existence by the war, who were struggling to return to ordinary life. But their return was made more difficult by the postwar chaos, the weakness of the institutions supposed to enforce the law, demoralization, and the socially legitimized use of violence—the opportunity makes the thief. But, on the other hand, other processes were underway that made it easy to reject these "dangerous classes." The rebuilding economy required a larger workforce. Land reform and the resettlement of landless peasants from central Poland to the Regained Territories reduced social tensions in the countryside and made it more livable.

The new regime also recruited its functionaries from among the "expendable" people. It promoted them en masse since it had few existing cadres and was operating in a social vacuum. As they owed their undeserved promotions, positions, and prestige to the regime and the regime only, its clerks became more loyal and accepted the ruling party's policies. Jan T. Gross is right to claim that the system's social backbone was constructed out of the native lumpenproletariat and not the Jews.[16] In other words, some of the "dangerous class" acquired a new consciousness and became a new class—a real social revolution was underway. In the first postwar months and years, the former "expendable" people ruled provincial Poland. The intelligentsia, for the most part, opposed to the regime and tended to believe that the government was made up of "people from nowhere," quarter-illiterates. As Hugo Steinhaus noted acerbically in his diary in April 1945, "pipsqueaks from the militia, motley former bar-keepers, loafers are in power; if you want a certificate or a permit, you need to dictate it to them because they won't be able to put the words together by themselves."[17]

Of course, the "expendables" were not the only group from which the Communist regime recruited its people. Not all of them ended up working for the Citizens' Militia or the District Offices of Security, and some joined thieves' gangs. Some lived by violence in a less organized way, taking part in pogroms and lynchings, stealing, settling of scores, and raping. Unemployed, vagrants and beggars, they had the anxieties of the hungry and destitute. As they drifted, they added to the atmosphere of chaos and transience, but when they began to serve violence, they evoked fear and terror. (Later parts of the book will analyze these fears and terrors.) Here, as a kind of introduction, let's take a closer look at some of the groups of the "expendables"—the demobilized and invalids, beggars and vagrants, profiteers, and jobless, and the one occupational group for which they were often recruited: the militia. The ideas presented in this chapter are only introductory also because, as we know, the postwar "expendable" people have not yet been analyzed.

THE DEMOBILIZED, INVALIDS, DESERTERS

Demobilization was one of the most central social processes of the postwar period. It had an effect on many aspects of life ranging from collective moods and crime statistics to the job market. It involved hundreds of thousands of men, soldiers of the Polish Army and of the Polish Armed Forces in the West, of the underground Peasant Battalions, and, most important, of the Home Army. Each one of these formations had experienced a different farewell to arms accompanied by different hopes and frustrations. It might seem at first that the underground fighters had it worse than official soldiers, since they had no rights and were not welcomed by people bearing flowers. They all felt defeated and anxious lest harassment and persecution continue, while the average private and officer of the Polish Army would allegedly have a relatively soft landing. And yet, all were damaged to some degree.

To understand the scale of the problem of demobilization, we must remember the numbers of people involved. In May 1945 some four hundred thousand men remained under arms in the regular army. In the summer of 1944, at the culmination of operation "Tempest," the Home Army may have had similar numbers. As the war drew to a close, the Polish Armed Forces in the West were made up of about two hundred thousand men, but relatively few of them would return to Communist-ruled Poland. Demobilization does not comprise only numbers, laying down arms, taking off one's uniform, and putting on civilian clothing. It also means a preceding easing of discipline and a relaxation as well as suffering from the demoralization of war—obstacles to becoming professionally active, especially for those whose only skill was killing.

Demobilization was announced on June 3, 1945, by order 111 by the commander in chief of the Polish Army, with promises that included "the family of every Polish Army soldier is guaranteed a ten-hectare plot. The families of Polish soldiers will be first among the millions of Polish families to settle the Western Territories in the next few months."[18] The soldiers learned about the form, nature, and rules of demobilization only from a decree of August 1945 (Dz.U. 1945, nr 31, poz. 187), whose provisions included full uniforms for retiring men and officers, who otherwise would have had no clothes. They also obtained severance pay in keeping with their military rank. All government offices, institutions, and state and private enterprises and factories were to hire these men according to their qualifications to make up at least 5 percent of their staff. A demobilized man with the same professional qualifications as a civilian was to be hired first. The decree also gave priority to soldiers rebuilding farms belonging to soldiers, building up their livestock, and bringing in building materials. The promise to those willing to settle on the ten-hectare plots of medium-quality soil in the Regained Territories or to obtain a workshop was the decree's most important provision. But these promises were not always kept.

Demobilization happened in phases. The largest number of men, about 135,000, left their barracks in September–December 1945. The next wave of discharges, brought on by the state's economic difficulties, came in the spring of 1946. By June 1946, a total of 200,000 privates and officers had been decommissioned.[19] As it turned out, the speed of demobilization affected its conditions, as did the job market, which could not absorb so many new workers.

It was especially privates and noncommissioned officers who greeted the announcement of release enthusiastically. They wanted to return to civilian life, to put order into their lives, and to help their families. Many, especially farmers originally from the Eastern Borderlands, were interested in the military settlements. But their enthusiasm was cooled by news about the comportment of Soviet marauders in the Regained Territories.[20] They hesitated and felt anxious for other reasons, too,[21] most having to do with concern for family members remaining in the formerly Polish lands that had been annexed by the Soviet Union. Still, thousands of soldiers successfully ended up starting new lives in the Regained Territories with their families. By mid-1948, about 170,000 families of discharged soldiers (also the widows and orphans of soldiers who had been killed) had settled in western and northern Poland. Of them, 130,000 took over farms and 40,000 moved into urban areas.[22] Those coming from central Poland and/or those who had no experience in agriculture were worse off. And only 10 to 15 percent of soldiers over the age of forty expressed an interest in settling in the Regained Territories in the military settlement operation.[23] The rest had to find something else to do. As the first groups left their barracks in October 1945, the official newspapers encouraged the public to treat them with special care. For example, the Lublin *Sztandar Ludu*:

> It's not easy for a soldier to come home after being away for a few years. We need to reach out to him. Every factory, every enterprise and every institution should prepare itself to hire a number of demobilized troops. Among them are many specialists who will work productively. Our countryside, too, has a shortage of specialists, able administrators, of whom there are many among the demobilized. What is more, let us stress emphatically, it is these

very demobilized people who should have priority in assuming the posts of village administrators, etc. They have learned many things in the harsh military service. They have been toughened and are highly idealistic and moral.²⁴

But it quickly turned out that there were no jobs waiting the former soldiers and that public help was scarce. The governor of Rzeszów Province noted in November 1945 that giving assistance to the demobilized surpassed the public's capacity.²⁵ Local self-governments lacked resources and were unable to meet the commitments of the decree. The professional officers' lack of education and professional skills was also an obstacle, since many knew how to command a company or battery but not always how to manage an office. In the end, the majority of state and private companies put no former military men on their payrolls.²⁶ Even the mayor of Warsaw asked the prime minister to be released from the obligation to hire them.²⁷ The situation was worst in the winter of 1945 and spring of 1946 when the newest group encountered a widespread bad mood caused by the worsening of the economic situation in enterprises. In November, about twelve thousand soldiers and officers were fighting for survival in Warsaw. A story in *Ilustrowany Kurier Polski* serves as a good illustration of their mental state:

> This is the office of the Society of Friends of the Soldier at 1 Żurawia Street, apt. 3. The room is furnished modestly with a table and a handful of chairs. There is no glass in the windows. Every time the door opens, the draft sends pieces of paper flying. Conversations are constantly interrupted by soldiers walking in. One of them says: "I was discharged two weeks ago. I'm looking for something to do. I'm not strong enough to clear rubble, but this is the only work I've been offered." Another one says: "This is my third day in Warsaw. I wanted to find my family, but I hear that they've all been killed. I've eaten nothing since I arrived, I spent the night in the ruins. . . ." A third one: "I was told to leave the military hospital because there was no room, even though my wounds have not healed yet. I am unable to work."

Hundreds of cases, hundreds of people: officers, non-commissioned officers, privates. Their faces are pale, tired, their uniforms in tatters, some are holding humble bundles, others nothing. They show documents, try to explain, point to their orders and decorations. Their eyes are asking: "Help me!" Some have been traveling from office to office for a long time, from institution to institution, and you can tell that they have repeated their arguments again and again. Some speak in quiet voices as if they were embarrassed about their situation, being forced to seek protection, while others make demands: "We fought for you. We risked our lives so that you could build in peace. We deserve a piece of bread and a roof over our heads." People who survived six years of a horrific war have nerves that are too tattered to defy panic.²⁸

No psychological studies of former fighting men were conducted right after the war. But we can assume that some of them, especially those without family support and without work, suffered from universal war-related stress. Their sets of beliefs, feelings, and attitudes included the conviction that a soldier's experience predestined him to a higher professional position and social status, combined with a profound regret that "we spilled our blood, and what's in it for us?" Most believed that they deserved something for defeating the "Nazi beast," for their blood and suffering, including a "better life," a job to fulfill their ambitions, and significant government assistance.²⁹ Going from being called "sir" to standing in line as yet another job seeker must have been an especially painful experience, a degradation, accompanied by frustration and anger, especially for midlevel commanders. Some blamed the Jews for this situation, something studies by US social psychologists confirm.³⁰ This resembled the growing intolerance observed among demobilized German and Italian officers in the wake of the First World War. The Polish Army's Military Information office noted "anti-Semitic statements coming mostly from people disposed that way prior to 1939 and during the German occupation or from those who envied the higher positions occupied by jews [*sic*] in some units."³¹ Professional officers who were let go against their will for political reasons must have been especially bitter. The head of the Main Directorate of the Information of the Polish Army was open in his report about officers who were dismissed from the army for having political views "hostile" to the new regime. Consequently, he wrote, "every month the fear of demobilization has yielded a systematic reduction of hostile statements by the officers."[32]

Many veterans who were accustomed to military discipline may have had trouble relating to others in everyday life and preferred to use force in situations of conflict. Some entered civilian life with a small severance pay and a baggage of behaviors and values, including some very authoritarian ones. The soldier Franciszek Ryszka remembered that "many of us wearing those uniforms carried the brute barbarism of war inside."[33] Deprived of a "useful function," they grabbed random jobs and drank. In March 1946 in Wrocław, "demobilized Polish Army troops from the east caused a huge disruption in collective life. They claim that they were promised a lot when they were demobilized, but that now they have to beg for every last piece of bread. In Wrocław one comes across very many of them in the streets and squares selling old stuff, but very few of them working."[34]

There was chaos, especially in larger towns where the discharged troops, suffering from being anonymous and jobless, wandered the streets, idled in bazaars, and crowded into restaurants and bars, often frustrated and annoyed. An analyst of the underground organization Freedom and Independence working for the Olsztyn magistrate's office wrote:

> The demobilized left their military units pumped up with propaganda and promises. Arriving here, they demand, often insolently, that these promises be fulfilled. Consequently, the central authorities have come up with absolutely no means of implementing their own directives on assistance to the demobilized. The discharged soldier says: "We were told in our unit to ask for assistance everywhere because we won Poland's freedom, but when we come in we are told that there is no money." Some of them come with handwritten letters from [Defense Minister Rola-]Żymierski requesting assistance. . . . Many demand that people who have moved into a house leave and that they are given it instead, claiming that they have priority because they won our freedom.[35]

This attitude of entitlement must have irritated many people, not only civil servants. Those released from military service, on the other hand, may have believed that people were turning their backs on them, not understanding their trauma. "We learned then," recalled Franciszek Ryszka, "that Cracow didn't like and didn't respect Berling's men. This naturally formed the belief that 'if you don't like us, you should at least fear us.'"[36] Indeed, a great many thefts and robberies, or even ordinary street incidents, were caused by men who were still in the service or those who had been discharged.[37] Militia reports from that time always included crimes committed by unidentified men in uniform. This expanded the chasm between them and civilians, and the sight of begging soldiers gradually augmented popular distaste rather than compassion. For example, in the summer of 1946:

> Literally everywhere you go in Lublin, and in other urban centers, on trains, you can see demobilized Polish Army men in military uniform (often decorated), usually invalids, begging. The public advocates for them, but they complain about the way things are, saying that they didn't fight for the Motherland to become invalids, hands held out to good people. Others still (also with decorations) are forced to go into smuggling and fencing, soiling their uniforms, their decorations and the honor of the Motherland for which they fought. But they also soil their uniforms by begging—even though the Society for the Care of Soldiers is there for them.[38]

The men returning to Poland after serving in the Polish Armed Forces in the West (32 officers, 1,612 noncommissioned officers, and 10,661 privates by December 1945) were in a comparatively better situation.[39] Because most brought some foreign currency with them, they were probably a little better off materially, and yet this is not why they were popular and felt needed. In contrast to "Berling's people," those who had fought for Generals Maczek or Anders in the West were seen as heroes. Men wearing Allied battledress in public were respected by all and admired by women. They usually had an easier time finding work, all the more so since many of them had been Polish citizens mobilized by the Wehrmacht, some 375,000 men. But life was a little more difficult for men from Pomerania, many of whom, unable to find work, became bitter in the winter of 1946.[40]

Life was very different for underground fighters returning to civilian life. It was not the same for all of them, depending on how much time they had spent in the forest, where they came from, and how intense the civil war had been in the area where they had fought. Those originally from the other side of the Curzon Line had it even worse, since returning to their prewar homes was not an option, and no decree promised them land in the Regained Territories. Sometimes, when a unit remained intact and its network was still functioning and, just as importantly, it had some money left, the fighters could find a place to live and a job somewhere. Lower Silesia became home for many of them. Those who came from central Poland and had been mobilized late, only for operation "Tempest," which began in January 1944, were in a better situation. As only a small number of underground fighters had carried arms and worn uniforms throughout their time of service, most could stay in touch with their native area, and it was easier for them to return to civilian life. Thus, despite the large size of the underground army, its demobilization was infinitely easier than the regular Polish Army's. But the situation was different for those who had become professional underground fighters and were paid and remained in the forest until the end of the war or longer. They were different from regular troops in that they were more nervous about being among civilians and became more demoralized and violent. Stefan Dąmbski, a young Home Army soldier in Reszów Province, who performed executions, recalled, "So in a week or two free Poland will be here, the day will come that I've been longing for. And now, when everything was so close, I became frightened. Maybe I'd have to lay down arms, become a civilian, and then what? Finish my studies? Start earning an honest living?"[41] The road from being "forest people" to "expendable" people was probably shorter for them than for any other social group. Many of those who had fought in the People's Army moved to the Citizens' Militia or Security Service. Their political adversaries from the Home Army, Peasant Battalions, and National Armed Forces, on the other hand, either continued to fight, often as bandits, or came out of hiding after two amnesties. For the purposes of the present analysis, the most interesting were those who ceased to play a useful role for either the underground or society and opted for a life of violence. Zygmunt Klukowski observed this process as he experienced the violence of autonomous underground soldiers during a robbery. He wrote, "Our boys were not allowed to join Berling's army, no one took care of them properly, they could go free, and especially those who like to have a drink and have some fun were not paid enough to support themselves. Thus, those with morally weaker constitutions, who were not used to ordinary work but to violence easily let go of their scruples and became real bandits. This is why robberies of this kind committed by former sabotage soldiers have recently become almost an everyday occurrence. And, regrettably, they will no doubt become more frequent."[42]

And, regrettably, Klukowski was right.

The legacy of life in the forest, low pay, and lack of supervision by their commanders made many partisans join the "dangerous classes." And there was another force that shaped their state of mind: a profound sense of defeat. Most Poles, especially those fighting underground, had imagined the end of the war very differently. The "forest people," like all nonprofessional soldiers, would ask each other: What will you do when this is all over? There would be flowers, decorations, girls, victory parades in Berlin and Warsaw, postwar honors, and great personal and professional opportunities. But instead, those in power called them "the reactionary drooling dwarfs" and persecuted and imprisoned them.[43] The first reaction of someone who hears that they are on the losing side is rejection, rebellion, and anger. The greater their investment in victory, the greater their anger. Behaviors became desensitized in

1944–45, partly in reaction to this feeling of defeat. This also applied to Polish–Jewish relations; although certainly anti-Semitism had preceded this sense of defeat, it was nonetheless indispensable for the anti-Jewish conflict to appear. A typical example: on September 21, 1945, in Kałuszyn, Mazovia Province, a Jewish gunner and warrant officer of the First Artillery Regiment of the First Kościuszko Infantry Division were beaten up by thirty young men leaving a restaurant. When the officer was struck in the face, he shouted, "How dare you lift a hand against an officer of the Polish Army?" "You're no Polish Army! We are the Polish Army!" was the answer.[44] We know nothing about the roots of this particular incident other than that one of the civilians said something strongly anti-Semitic, and the warrant officer asked to see his papers. We also do not know the identities of the aggressive young men. One might guess that the men in the restaurant were underground fighters, for whom the arrival of Jews in Polish Army uniform by car worked like a red cape on a bull. The war had undermined previous social roles and terminated plans and hopes. Some could not handle it and looked for scapegoats.

A similar psychological mechanism governed the behavior of invalids, but even more harshly. Of all the "expendable" groups, they probably felt most acutely excluded, disillusioned, and angry. But their feelings were not uniquely Polish. Soviet invalids could become at least as furious and aggressive, especially those missing both legs, who moved on a sort of skateboards. Andrzej Mandalian's memoirs from Moscow in the last year of the war include this observation:

> They lay around in marketplaces on the outskirts of towns and in train stations, belching aggression and later also alcohol, but it was the appearance of an officer's uniform that made them go nuts. They moved as a group, attacked in line formation, silently. Their attack technique was to block the enemy's path, trip him up and give him a deathly threshing. Actually, the one-eyed or one-armed ones were not handicapped, since they would counterattack when any charge whatsoever came from men in active service who ventured near their prosthetic. But those on the boards were the guard, choice units, the true Decembrists in this war, who owed their return from Europe/Volhynia/Podolia/Masuria solely to the missed shots of the barrage battalions and, of course, to a serendipitous verdict of the field doctor. No wonder they were loaded with the ideals of universal freedom, they were no *homo sovieticus*, but another human species. What was worse, their voices, hurling sewer-quality insults at their motherland, the flag and the generalissimus, were not voices crying in the wilderness, but resounded in very public and very crowded places. They were terrifying.[45]

In Poland, too, the mutilated were literally everywhere. They begged outside churches and on public transportation, peddled whatever they could lay their hands on, and wandered through bazaars and marketplaces. Two years after the war, "we quite often met the huddled figures of the war wounded, their hands stretched out for handouts, in the streets of Warsaw and of other Polish cities. Many musicians, also war invalids, collect donations in the streets, on trams and trains. Many of them are missing an arm or a leg. People are moved by their sight and take pity on the victims of the war, throw them alms."[46]

In late 1945, the disabled swelled into a real army. The Union of War Invalids had about 300,000 members, or more than the population of Cracow at the time.[47] The total number of invalids, both military and civilian, was estimated at 650,000.[48] According to local government authorities, in Chełmno in Pomerania about 50 percent of the population was unable to work.[49] The situation across the Regained Territories may have been similar, since many old and infirm Germans were living there, too. The numbers of landmine victims, who included children playing with unexploded ordnance, continued to grow. For injured soldiers, the first months after leaving hospital were psychologically among the worst. They struggled with adjustment, self-acceptance, and organizing their personal and professional lives. There was no such thing then as mental health counselors, psychologists, physical therapists, or even volunteers who could help, advise, or simply console. No wonder they felt abandoned and excluded. "What hurts us most," one of them reported to the *Dziennik Bałtycki* daily in June 1945, "is that many of our fellow citizens think of us as parasites and intruders who are gratuitously inserting themselves into a society of healthy people."[50]

They could become a part of society only by having a job, but no one wanted to hire them. An article on "The operation of employing invalids is limping" read, "There are many well-dressed and well-fed women working in every office, and maybe they don't need their jobs as much as the invalids do."[51] The invalids' material situation verged on the tragic. A blind soldier's monthly pay, including a supplement for his wife, was 425 zlotys in 1945, when at midyear the estimated monthly cost of groceries per person was about 1,500 zlotys.[52] The chairman of the Union of War Invalids wrote to the prime minister, "In this situation, with what the food prices are on the free market, with insufficient or, in some areas, non-existent food rations, with the wartime destruction of homes, the invalids', widows' and orphans' situation is desperate, especially for the most disabled of them. They have been condemned to be hungry, cold and destitute, with diseases raging in their midst, and death which is reaping a rich harvest among those who defended the Motherland."[53]

The mood among invalids, especially those without family help, could thus not have been worse. They were enraged at the army, until recently their whole universe; at their command for abandoning them; and at fate for punishing them so harshly. In November 1945, an inspection was conducted of a Polish Red Cross vacation home for the war wounded in Zduńska Wola, where 110 men, including 12 officers, were staying. The report read:

> The invalids are generally embittered, claiming that they are no longer needed, that no one is taking care of them, that they've been "cheated." They are so embittered that they are accusing the Commander in Chief of having promised them "the moon," but that now no one is lifting a finger to do anything for them. They are asking for military assistance since they are still soldiers, not yet having been demobilized. . . . They are incapable of taking care of problems that are important in their lives, such as bringing their families from the areas now belonging to the USSR (nearly all the invalids come from the other side of the Bug River), or obtaining a business concession or a farm.[54]

The frustrated invalids who felt cheated often got drunk and started fights. We have no information about cases of unloading aggression on officers, the way it happened in Moscow, but such incidents did probably occur. The Jews became a preferred target, and several postwar anti-Semitic incidents were started by invalids. In Chełm, Lublin Province, on August 13, 1945, a group of four invalids accosted Jewish passersby, demanded money, and injured them when they refused to give any. The invalids entered the offices of the Jewish Committee and beat up several Jews inside. The next day, the same group joined forces with a Red Army sergeant and some civilians to launch what the document describes as a pogrom, which reportedly lasted six hours. Its victims included five who were gravely beaten and many more lightly beaten.[55]

In Zduńska Wola in early November 1945, some of the war wounded from the convalescent home were drinking alcohol in a "Jewish restaurant." They were expelled for not wanting to pay and, with the assistance of some friends they called in as reinforcements, retaliated by trashing the restaurant. When Security Office functionaries arrested some of them, the others stirred up the crowd and, armed, stormed the jail, disarmed the Security Office functionaries, freed the prisoners, and ransacked the District Security Office headquarters.[56]

On October 18, 1945, anti-Jewish riots took place in Lublin near the Lubartowska Street bazaar.[57] Little information about it survives, but it probably included invalids, if one is to believe an article in the local paper that appeared a few days later, titled "An Invalid May Not Be Treated as a Beggar." The article discussed a conference on the situation of invalids that was held after the incident. The two events could not have been a coincidence. According to the article, "Rumors have been flying for some time now that war invalids are not being treated well, that they are being harmed, that the Polish Red Cross shelters for them are not fulfilling their mission. This state of affairs led to the staging of a special conference devoted to invalid issues.... The conference showed that, indeed, these matters are being neglected. There are numerous institutions that take care of invalids, and as a result of this multi-track approach the invalid issue is not only not treated appropriately but, making things worse, and the invalid is disoriented."[58]

Cracow, too, experienced anti-Semitic incidents (not only the pogrom of August 11, 1945) in which some war wounded took part. Invalids tended to spend a lot of time in the Market Square around the Sukiennice Cloth Hall. Zofia Nałkowska noticed them in the crowd and recorded this in her diary (September 11, 1945):

> Disabled soldiers wander in the crowd, most of them on crutches. On our way back, we see a throng lined up. A piece of a man is sitting in a wheelchair playing a harmonica, which is affixed with wire at mouth level to the wheelchair's armrest. He has no arms, he has no legs and he is so short that it looks like there is only a part of his trunk left. He has a pleasant, serious, young face, with well-defined lips, which say politely "thank you, Ma'am." The sight of him makes you want to black out from nausea, to faint. I turn around, thinking that I should give him a piece of cake or a pear, but I would have to feed him. People put money next to his body, at the foot of the wheelchair. He must have some family that brings him here. Someone who got him back from the war in this shape.[59]

By the end of January 1946, there were 970 invalids registered with the Cracow Province Invalid Audit-Medical Commission. At least 1,300 more were waiting to register.[60] Witnesses described the living conditions for some of the disabled in the invalid shelter at 14 Lenartowicza Street as "very primitive." The most basic equipment was in short supply, the food was inadequate, and their uniforms were in such shabby shape that they wore German uniforms when they went outside. "No wonder that the disabled living in such conditions were bitter and got up to all sorts of trouble."[61] The most violent incidents occurred on March 19 and 20, 1946. On March 19 the men shattered a Jewish man's head with a crutch. According to the Citizens' Militia, Polish currency dealers working in Market Square had egged them on, but their motivations were not clear. The man was either a secret police collaborator, which was made likely by the fact that he was holding weapons issued by the Office of Public Security in Rzeszów, or he was competition for the currency dealers and had been given a gun to protect himself, although this would have been rare prior to the July 1946 Kielce pogrom. The Freedom and Independence report indicates that one of the invalids, wanting to buy dollars, approached a Jew who was selling them. He agreed to the transaction, but when it was being finalized, he showed his Security Office identity card and tried to make the case seem "criminal and official." The invalid reacted by saying, "You louse, you Yid.... Didn't the Germans kill enough of you?" and struck him with his crutch. The Jew responded by shooting the attacker. Next day, a group of tipsy invalids again started a brawl and "began to thrash citizens who looked Semitic"[62] doing business in the Market Square. The militia managed to capture five of the attackers, but a Soviet patrol joined in, freeing the men and paying the militia back by painfully beating two of them.[63] After more militia arrived, the invalids retreated to their shelter in Lenartowicza Street and threw all kinds of objects at the attacking militia. According to an underground report, "The incident gave rise to a new wave of outrage at the Jews and the security authorities for even thinking about taking revenge on honorable invalids and going wild."[64]

Anti-Semitic brawls that included the war wounded also occurred in Lower Silesia. On October 10, 1946, in Duszniki, seven disabled men overturned a kiosk "operated by a citizen of Jewish nationality" and two days later destroyed it completely, seemingly "not for robbery purposes." They also ransacked the hall in which the Jewish Committee was putting on a dance.[65] Looking at a map, it is clear that attacks by the war wounded were migrating westward. Looking at a calendar, it is striking that most such incidents occurred between August 1945 and

The Demobilized

July–August 1946. Why? There are three possible explanations. First, after the events in Zduńska Wola, Lublin, and Cracow, both the civilian and military authorities attempted to improve the situation of those injured in the war. Perhaps these attempts were successful enough for manifestations of frustration to abate. Second, as a result of the attacks and murders and all the other anti-Semitic incidents, many Polish Jews either emigrated or moved to Lower Silesia, reducing the numbers of potential scapegoats. Third, the invalids had gradually begun to learn how to be "expendable."

Deserters also joined the "dangerous classes." According to Polish Army data, in 1943–48 some 24,069 soldiers deserted.[66] Scholar of social resistance Łukasz Kamiński argues that the number was actually closer to 30,000, of whom 80 percent deserted between September 1944 and the end of 1945.[67] If we add the approximately 50,000 recruits who did not report for duty after receiving a Polish Underground State summons, it becomes clear that in the period covered in this book, tens of thousands of young men persistently evaded the military. Attempts by various institutions of the new regime to capture them through roundups in marketplaces and streets added to the public fear by disrupting the rhythm of everyday life, especially in the second half of 1944. An underground flyer called out, "Hide! Your hiding place is your own farm and watching closely what's going on around you. Organize watches in your villages, warn your neighbors. Don't fear terror, since even traitors can't afford it. You will build a better tomorrow by being loyal to Poland and Her Government."[68]

Those in hiding must have felt like hunted animals, outlaws, which may have made it easier for some of them to continue breaking the law. While Kamiński is right to treat the motivations behind soldiers' desertions as one of his main research questions, his typology of motivations is questionable. In his *Polacy wobec nowej rzeczywistości* (The Poles in the new reality), he lists three kinds of reasons for desertions—political, personal, and material—and makes the first the most important and neglects the other two.[69] Instead, the role of the first group, while indeed the most important, should be reduced some, while the second and the third should be made more prominent; a fourth group, fear, should be added. We must begin with fear, since the largest numbers of desertions occurred at times of the most intensive fighting by the Polish Army, between July 1944 and the end of May 1945. (Kamiński notes this fact but does not draw the correct conclusions from it.) After Japan surrendered, there was a marked drop in the numbers of deserters. In early summer of 1945, there was widespread talk about sending Polish armies to the Far East. "Now, Wikcia, we will be moving on, so please send me food. They're going to train us for a few weeks, and we will fight Japan and Turkey," wrote a soldier in a private letter intercepted by censors in May 1945.[70] Most people also believed that the Red Army would spill its soldiers' blood inconsiderately, and that the marches on Berlin and then on Tokyo were paid for with copious numbers of dead. The end of the war terminated these worries, which was immediately reflected in the drop in the numbers of desertions. On the other hand, the concerns remained very significant because large numbers of Poles distrusted both the Soviet Union and the Red Army enough to send their sons and husbands enthusiastically to serve in the "allied army." A letter read by the war censors presents the political motivations: "Yesterday, 1,700 men left here for Warsaw [they may have been recruits—MZ], but they will only deliver half of them, since the guys are running like crazy into the forest [unclear—MZ], to the army they call partisans, and I'm doing this, too, I'll wait for the first chance when things get easier. Please don't worry about me because nothing bad can happen to me. And I won't be serving in that Soviet army."[71]

Soldiers escaped the army also for personal reasons, primarily to help their families, and for material ones. There were shortages of uniforms and shoes,[72] and the quartermasters weren't always able to feed the privates, especially in the spring of 1945. The important research question is not only why the soldiers fled but what happened to them once they took flight. Most important, how many began to serve violence? And, how much did the presence of thousands of men in hiding add to the tensions in society, influence the scale of banditry? Nina

Assorodobraj notes that in the late eighteenth century, desertions were one of the ways to join the "freewheeling population."[73] Was it the same in the wake of the Second World War? Since no research has been done in court documents, we can only guess.[74]

BEGGARS AND HOBOES

Poland in 1944–47 was a country of beggars, vagrants, and various other "free particles" who had been forced out of their routines by the war, who drifted, camped out in train stations, and begged for alms in soup kitchens and shelters. The Cracow daily *Dziennik Polski* ran an editorial titled "The Begging Plague":

> Begging has invaded everything, it appears everywhere you look. In the form of the concierge who wakes us up in the morning or evening holding a list of payments to be made, of the "unemployed man" or "someone who has just been released from the hospital" or of another wretch who interrupts us with an alarming door bell at work, assaults us in the street, a large can in his hand, invades our field of vision with his arm stubs and crutches asking for alms, punctures our ears with his fiddles and mouth organs or with his pathetic singing and a whisper, begging for mercy, for help. This person won't leave us alone not only at home and in the street, but also lurks in parks as a ragged old woman or a pushy gypsy, on trams as a young boy exploiting his compatriots' emotions by singing "patriotic" songs, as all kinds of "musicians," in restaurants, pff—even inserting himself into schools, churches and offices.[75]

In November 1947, a department director in the Ministry of Public Administration gauged that "because of its steady rise, combatting begging and vagrancy has become a significant challenge, which calls for the most urgent solutions."[76] This diagnosis was late in that the phenomenon had reached its zenith in 1945–46.

Today, it is difficult to estimate the dimensions of panhandling at that time. If we count all the people who sought assistance from the state and from church institutions (both Polish and foreign), the number of beggars would reach millions. These millions were one of the most important consequences of the war. In Kielce Province alone in January 1946, the state provided assistance to about 180,000 people.[77] The Provincial Committee of Social Assistance oversaw 271 soup kitchens, 25 of them in Kielce, in which 39,655 children were given meals.[78] In August 1945 in central Poland, the total spent on people receiving some form of state assistance (vouchers of all kinds, hospitals, student residences, boarding schools, retirement homes, orphanages) reached 10.2 million zlotys. (This assistance was also for Germans and repatriates, but they received a negligible amount.) It reached almost 800,00 zlotys in the Recovered Territories.[79] If we narrow down the definition of panhandling to those who try to stay afloat and obtain a part of their income from individuals or institutions (standing outside churches, going door to door to homes and shops), the number of beggars would be in the thousands. But it, too, fluctuated. It paradoxically declined in the most heavily destroyed areas, where people were living in shanties and mud huts (in some districts of Kielce Province and in northern Mazovia), because there, a huge majority of the population came close to death by starvation. Begging tended to appear in communities with a differentiated income, with a spectrum of rich and poor, and not in areas where the majority of people had almost nothing to eat.

For these reasons, the postwar phenomenon of begging was especially visible in areas that attracted repatriates, resettlers, and those who had lost everything when their homes burned down. They often owned no property whatsoever and were worse off than the locals, from whom they tried very hard to get help. This was the situation in the winter of 1944 in Nisko District, Rzeszów Province, where a militia report read, "Because of the mass influx of people who have been expelled from areas near the front, there is rampant begging by old people, women and children who, deprived of food, resort to public charity and even, given a chance, commit minor theft to satisfy their needs, and for this reason the people living in villages and towns complain about the local authorities' lack of interest in helping the expellees."[80]

But beggars were most interested in cities, even ones as severely destroyed as Warsaw. In April 1945, a single Polish Red Cross shelter at 75 Nowogrodzka Street put up 473 people, most of them either very old, disabled, or very young, all of them homeless, hungry, unwashed. Most were originally from Warsaw, had fled to the countryside after the Warsaw Uprising of August–October 1944, and left again in the spring, pushed by the traditional peasant preharvest angst. The *Życie Warszawy* daily exclaimed, "Give up on Warsaw, old people, invalids and children, if you have no one and nothing to return to! You heard that Warsaw is in the process of rebuilding, it is a 'fortress of work,' and has no room for the weak, the ill and the infirm."[81]

The cities of medieval and modern Europe experienced many such invasions of beggars, most of them propelled by hunger. When hunger came, "armies of the poor," mendicants, hungry peasants, and vagrants flocked to urban areas hoping to find help more easily and, then, since they usually failed to find it, took to begging in streets and squares and outside churches.[82] The pauperized population was similar after this war. Even with inflated food prices, in the city it was easier to find a roof over one's head, if only in a train station, to obtain a warm meal, to beg a little, and to spirit this or that away.

As areas of poverty grew massively also in the cities, the beggars were not all coming from incinerated villages. Urban dwellers were also pauperized and permanently hungry as they faced sky-high food prices and obstacles to finding work. Even society ladies in Cracow, squeezed by hunger pensions and low disability payments, would beg for whatever a passerby could spare. Begging was not for only the old and the infirm but also for invalids, children, and women supporting large families.[83] In Cracow, the phenomenon reportedly surpassed its prewar size and became an "abnormal, unhealthy fact."[84] In Warsaw, too, according to *Express Wieczorny*, in the autumn of 1946 there were beggars everywhere: "At the door to your apartment, in the street, on the church steps, on the tram, at the train station. Everywhere. They are insistent, impertinent, unrelenting. They have a way of blackmailing people passing in the street, flaunting their wounds and their indigence, using those special whiny-weepy intonations to extract alms."[85]

The newspaper gauged that there was now a large group of tricksters and swindlers who preyed "perfidiously on people's goodheartedness, naivete or simple human stupidity." Two castes of beggars reportedly fought over handouts. The first were the "proverbial old church beggars of both sexes. They permanently plant themselves at the same church, which has a defined, predetermined hierarchy of spaces on the steps, at the doors and so on. The least breach of the 'living space' by any of the women beggars leads to a brawl, sometimes ending in a fistfight. The church beggars live in an almost permanent atmosphere of envy, intrigue and animosity. But this caste of beggars recruits itself almost entirely from old people."[86]

The second caste was made up of women, apparently strong and healthy, who, "as numerous police investigations have found," rented children for their time at "work." Friday begging was a discrete category, originating with the prewar custom of giving alms on Fridays. Anyone who came into a shop, regardless of age, would receive a small donation, usually of fifty groszy. "For this reason, starting in the morning, the beggars are exceptionally excited. They tirelessly and feverishly race from shop to shop, 'cashing in' the small donations, which after a day's roaming add up to a fine little sum. We observed one such trail in a shop at Marszałkowska Street. It is always more or less the same. A hunched woman in rags comes into the shop. She begs, her voice brimming with pain: 'whatever you can spare.' The woman working in the store gives her a five-zloty note. 'I'd like 4½ zlotys back.' The beggar is instantly transformed. She straightens out, grabs the 5-zloty note, swiftly hands back the change and in two leaps is outside."[87]

The authors of the article interviewed a few shop workers. Their answers were all the same: every Friday, between 150 and 200 zlotys went to the beggars. If we are to believe the *Express Wieczorny* reporters, on a Friday, over three hundred beggars visited every shop. So how many phony or real beggars were active in Warsaw at that time? The reporters began by admitting that in Warsaw "there is a very large number of real paupers, who support themselves almost exclusively by begging."[88]

In the Regained Territories, Silesia and Łódź, Germans who had been pushed into the streets by reduced or nonexistent food rations formed a discrete caste. In the summer of 1946, the Łódź authorities conducted an "operation to purge the city of the plague of intrusive beggars roaming the streets." The group of 222 people who were rounded up included 54 Germans.[89] At the time, the population of Łódź was 537,000, with a German minority of 29,000.[90] In Szczecin, "dirty German children hang around in the streets, stubbornly repeating Polish words they've memorized, 'Mister, give zloty, Mister, give bread.'"[91] The public at large very rarely heard about such incidents, as German-speaking panhandlers had become so much a fixture of the urban landscape that the Poles barely noticed them. They had become invisible.

Yet another effect of the war was the prevalent panhandling by children. They had their precincts, mostly around train stations, cafés, and outdoor markets. On the eve of the Warsaw Uprising in August 1944, they ruled the city's Three Crosses Square.[92] A *Ziemia Pomorska* reporter, clearly raised on Hans Christian Andersen's and Maria Konopnicka's fairy tales, wrote about a visit to Warsaw in December 1945: "Anyone who has spent time in Warsaw in the first days after the temperature drops below zero would have seen crowds of children selling cigarettes and matches. The cold iced over their small faces, chilled their feet, shriveled their hands, and the snow drizzled on the rags wrapping their little heads. The kids floated among the hurrying pedestrians, their frail shapes getting in the way as they beckoned them in their hoarse voices to buy their wares. . . . Many were seven or eight at most."[93]

After the war, similar scenes could be observed also outside Warsaw.[94] In Cracow, Łódź, and Katowice, emaciated children in rags panhandled, "distrustfully eyeing pedestrians." Some sold looted cigarettes.[95] A journalist accosted by a begging boy in Bydgoszcz in December 1945 reported on an apparently typical scene: "'Mister,' he said, 'a donation, please! My sister is ill, my mother hasn't got the money to take her to the doctor. . . .' I instinctively put my hand in my pocket to get rid of the pushy kid. But an instant later, I said to him: 'Come with me, young man!' On the way, I learned that the boy was 11, that his mother had tuberculosis and his father had been killed in 1939. The kid does go to school and begs after school."[96]

The war put many children in this situation. The Ministry of Labor and Social Welfare estimated the number of orphans and half orphans under the age of twenty at over a million, 150,000 of them orphans.[97] Kielce Province, for example, registered about 1,000 orphans and 34,000 half orphans after the war.[98] Even if these estimates were somewhat exaggerated (the thinking at the time was dominated by a megalomania of martyrdom), the problem was enormous. Before some of their fathers could be found, and before adoption programs were put in place and existing orphanages expanded, some of these children could be found in the streets. Gangs of children and adolescents, formed already during the war in Warsaw or Lvov, plagued the cities. They targeted the weakest: Jews and especially Jewish women.[99] After liberation, on a freezing winter day in Lublin, a sixteen-year-old girl deposited a one-year-old in the entrance to a building, undressed him, and sold his clothes. Younger gang members specialized in robbing shops, often bakeries,[100] while older ones often attacked adults, especially solitary pedestrians. The bands had their beats, ruled the streets, and found hiding places in the ruins. People feared them. The writer Julian Stryjkowski remembered the cities of Łódź, Katowice, Wałbrzych, and Warsaw in 1945 being run by bands of adolescents, who mugged pedestrians, especially at night: "These cities, as destroyed as they were, were ruled by fear. At night, as if in a nightmare, posses of wild boys and girls roiled through their dark streets."[101]

The militia stopped a boy at the Bydgoszcz train station in September 1945: "He is 13. He came here from Starogard and is staying with a friend, but he doesn't know the friend's address. He forgot it, poor guy. He carries parcels at the station, he explains arrogantly. But he can't answer several questions. Finally, he breaks down and admits, repenting, that a few times, but only a few, he took something out of someone's pocket."[102]

The seaside cities of Gdynia and Sopot attracted these children like magnets. Sea voyages and faraway lands appealed to a child's imagination, especially then. It was only in January 1946 that the Provincial National Council alerted all the municipal offices in the province to the imperative of combating underage begging by placing children of this kind in reformatories.[103] Unlike the Germans at the time, the Polish children were not "invisible" and generated special concern. There was even a peculiar psychosis, a hypersensitivity in the public's focus on children's fortunes. Newspapers often wrote about them, and priests' sermons discussed their situation and upbringing.[104] It was unquestionably a topic of public concern. The memoir of a boy whose mother failed to find a job in postwar Cracow tells about the kindness of strangers to panhandling children. He wrote:

> One day as my mother went out to search for work, I was sitting on the steps outside a closed shop, and a passing man who looked like a beggar gave me a small piece of white bread after he cut off a tiny piece of it for himself. I thanked the good man for sharing his bread, but I didn't take it from him since we had white bread at home that day. Another time, as I sat waiting for my mother and brother on a rock outside Saint Adalbert's Church, another man approached me and gave me a five-zloty bill. . . . I was a bit worried that I looked so bad that compassionate people were taking pity on me.[105]

Already during the war, a type of Polish homeless children emerged—mostly boys and orphans, but also those who had parents but ran free and took advantage of public assistance as they traveled from city to city. Franciszek Gil likened them to prewar seasonal workers who followed work from place to place. The children were vagabonds: they managed to obtain money for train tickets in social assistance committees and meals in State Repatriation Office branches in train stations. "They were given money by committees, then scolded for getting some from another institution. Life taught them quickly to stir up pity, to earn money by going coatless and to ignore or look down on others' indignation."[106] They often joined gangs of looters or pillaged themselves, and the older ones committed more serious crimes. The August 1945 pogrom in Cracow began with a group of adolescents throwing stones at synagogue windows.

Still, even though underage crime grew exponentially, begging children were not seen as "expendable," unlike adult beggars and vagrants. Fledgling People's Poland was not a historical exception in criticizing the "expendables." The arguments being used to exclude vagrants from society were also not new. According to historian Bronisław Geremek, in the Middle Ages there were two reasons why vagrants were viewed as criminals: because they evaded the duty to work, a divine obligation, and because thieves, bandits, and hired thugs were recruited in their midst.[107] Burghers did not like beggars and tramps especially in times of hunger, as they feared their insurgencies and assaults and reduced food supplies for others. Hence the various legal measures that were used against them, including banishment and forced labor.

History repeated itself after the Second World War, when people did not like hoboes but did not flaunt it, preferring to evoke the fear of God or threaten to send thugs after them. Most important, people reproached them for being parasites instead of taking part in rebuilding their destroyed country. People also thought of them as serving as a source of manpower for the world of crime—which was quite true. The drifter category included those running three-card tricks or other gambling schemes popular at that time, who moved from one outdoor market to the next, as well as prostitutes, bandits on the run, and people without families or homes who could not settle down. The last group included demobilized soldiers, many of them quite possibly suffering from mental damage brought on by the war.

Anatol Wieliczko, who was arrested by the militia in January 1947 in Legnica in the operation of purging the city of "criminal elements," can serve as a good example of a drifter. After being demobilized, Wieliczko wandered around Poland and in each place obtained assistance from the local State Repatriation Office. In

Wrocław, he eventually went to a Special Commission office, which categorized him as someone who was "touched by the drifting disease, looking for something in the wide world. Wieliczko is an individual who has been totally demoralized by his experiences at the front, who does not want to follow normal rules. He believes that his army service should free him from all obligations, he is self-assured, arrogant and he considers his arrest by the militia a trespass."[108]

The war threw many such human shards into the air. After the war, unaccustomed to life and deprived of support, they tried to find a place for themselves. Those who were unable to, like Wieliczko, ended up in work camps.

The battle against vagrancy began directly after the war. Already in June 1945, the Gdynia city authorities decided to "cleanse the city of undesirable elements."[109] The local newspapers cheered, suggesting plans of action: "The vagrants should be assembled into work crews for the harvest, to thresh, build roads, bridges, and many other kinds of work." And in the spirit of *Ordnung muss sein*, "We must put an end to the repatriates' drifting."[110]

Rzeszów Province in southeastern Poland also could not contain vagrancy. It was noted in December 1945 that the inflow of the demobilized, repatriates, and hoboes who roamed from town to town, searching for a place to sleep and lining up outside soup kitchens, was growing. In October the Citizens' Militia arrested one Władysław Roman, who later confessed to the Special Commission that "since returning to Poland from a camp in Germany he had been professionally playing the 'three-card monte' in markets and fairs in Rzeszów and Lublin Provinces, and that he supported himself this way."[111] People like him repulsed others and sometimes even made them afraid. The head of the Provincial Committee of Social Assistance in Rzeszów had a similar idea as the people in the coastal cities about how to fight this "plague": "We believe that these professional travelers should be made to stay put and to work. Leaving the place where one lives without permission should be punished. This is the only way to eliminate vagrancy and panhandling, which will protect the working people from theft and assaults."[112]

Calls about fighting vagrancy resounded across Poland. It seemed that for some towns it was a point of honor to eliminate the problem, and regional newspapers supported them. *Kurier Szczeciński* adopted an exceptionally principled position on May 31, 1946, when it called mass drifting "the plague of our time." It was everyone's duty to fight it: "We must be ruthless in stamping out drifters and all shady types." There was also talk of an operation by the social services "to eradicate drifting" and "eliminate" people who scorned work and exploited their fellow citizens.[113] This was typical of the language of the twentieth century's totalitarian ideologies, which were based on the cult of work and contempt for all those without "useful roles." It treated itinerants and the panhandlers as demoralized swindlers:

> As they move from town to town pretending to be looking for work or for their family, they first assault the Social Services, [the State Repatriation Office] and the Polish Red Cross, often alleging their more than doubtful merits and suffering during the occupation. At times they have no documents, as these were allegedly robbed, stolen and so on. This makes one suspect that we are dealing with ordinary fraud. It is not out of the question that more than one *Volksdeutsch* is hiding in this mass of the "gravely mistreated." Unfortunately, these professional "swindlers" who are repelled by work often come upon gullible people and use all sorts of tricks to get cash out of them, harming others who truly deserve effective and speedy help.[114]

This article leads to two conclusions and one hypothesis. First, vagrancy was an enormous social problem after the war. Especially cities in the Regained Territories, primarily those on the coast (Szczecin, Słupsk, Gdynia-Gdańsk-Sopot), faced this problem as masses of "expendable" people drifted into them,[115] as did persons with a dark wartime past. There was also a strong wave of migrants (for more, see chap. 11) who swept into cities including Cracow, Łódź, Rzeszów, and Warsaw. These cities attempted to control the problem by branding and excluding beggars and vagrants. Second, the thought schemes expressed in the vocabulary and

The Demobilized

constructions such as "stamping out," "eliminating from society," and "installing order" testify to the deep roots in collective thought of the Nazi attitude toward the "expendable" and the "other." The fact that the same newspapers focused on fighting every last Germanism shows that such thinking was unconscious, embedded. And, finally, the hypothesis, which appears to contradict only the first conclusion: Perhaps this ostentatious eagerness to stamp out vagrancy concealed a desire to distract the public from the behavior of Red Army bandits and marauders, which newspapers were not allowed to cover. Someone had to be blamed.

Following the examples of Gdynia and Szczecin, in August 1946 Łódź launched a campaign to "clear out" beggars, but apparently it was unsuccessful since another one was announced in November. "Our goal: Not a single person in Łódź should be begging." Promises were made that "everyone will be given a roof over their head and bread." A 1946 article from *Echo Wieczorne* also describes the beggars' strategies of going door to door in apartment buildings and shops, as well as people's generosity to them: "The people of Łódź are making the campaign against panhandling difficult by supporting various people who are 'hot' and those returning from Camp."[116] The authorities believed that the problem of begging would be solved not only by sentencing those who engaged in it to labor camps but also by creating a network of workhouses for the young and homes for the old. Orphanages, despite at least some of their staffs' genuine desire to help, added to the numbers of "expendables." All these institutions would become a part of the system of "institutional exclusion" for a long time—a system that the people living in People's Poland consented to.

THE JOBLESS

And now for a scene from a church in Bydgoszcz: Sunday mass, January 1946. A girl wearing a military coat is weeping loudly. After a while, the women praying around her ask why. The girl answers, "I can't find a job!" A reporter comments, "Until recently we were pleased that unemployment was done with in Poland. So far, in fact, it did not exist. But you must all admit that it's becoming more and more difficult to find work."[117] This commentary exemplifies a wider phenomenon: a tendency that was common after the war not to notice real social problems and to engage in myth creation and wishful thinking. There were at least two compatible explanations for it. First was the widespread postwar optimism, a belief in the end of history, which had supposedly come with the fall of the Third Reich. Since the greater Evil had been finished off, lesser ones, such as unemployment, were also supposed to be done. Second, the Ministry of Information and Propaganda most likely issued an order for unemployment to be discussed only in the past tense. In fact, the conditions on the job market had little to do with the myth of work growing on trees. The postwar social landscape also included the unemployed.

The problem of unemployment had appeared already during the war, with the growing imbalance between the supply and demand of work. In larger enterprises, defined as employing more than fifty people, employment dropped to one-quarter. According to analysts in the Government Delegate's Office, this trend resulted from the exhaustion of raw materials.[118] Other factors played parts om this as well: the reduced trade between the General Government and the territories annexed by the Reich; the typical wartime degradation of some branches of industry (e.g., paper and furniture); the German occupation's typical closing down of institutions such as state administration, education, and culture, which eliminated thousands of white-collar jobs; and, finally and possibly most importantly, the top-down slowdown of pay raises alongside a steady rise in living expenses. In these conditions, work lost its income-generating purpose. The legal labor market shrank while the black market, and especially noninstitutionalized trade, expanded. The end of the war changed little of this.

Many factories had difficulties restarting production. Severed cooperative ties, enormous communications difficulties, the impossibility of obtaining investment credit, and machinery that had been destroyed or stolen by the Red Army all meant that everywhere there was a shortage of work. People in Warsaw reported on difficulties with finding work in March 1945: "I have come to look for work, but unfortunately it's extremely difficult to find any because life has been interrupted by the terrible destruction, and it will not get going anytime soon. Everyone is fleeing to other towns because there is no life here for cultured people and there won't be any for a long time." People relied on people they knew to find work: "It is terribly difficult to find a job—unless you have connections."[119]

In May 1945, the *Dziennik Powszechny* daily published in Kielce and Radom asserted, "The inability to restart all enterprises creates the fear of unemployment."[120] Also, wages were very low, insufficient to support one person let alone a family, and people did not always find it worthwhile to work full time. The same newspaper discussed the wages in a tobacco factory in Radom. The average pay, including the payment in kind in cigarettes, after all taxes and insurance were deducted, amounted to about one-fourth of the minimum amount considered necessary to support a family of three.[121] The situation in Cracow was similar. According to a questionnaire distributed by the Industrial-Trade Chamber in ten industrial enterprises there, the real wages of blue- and white-collar industrial workers (including pay, cafeteria meals, food allocations, and bonuses of various types) were far below living expenses.[122] "Pie in the sky" was the term someone living in Warsaw used to describe the likelihood of surviving on the average salary. As an anonymous individual from Warsaw wrote in a letter, "Life here is extremely hard and looks as if someone had turned a piece of clothing inside out."[123] As a result, the group of people unable to find jobs expanded to include those who had become unaccustomed to showing up for work every morning during the war and/or saw no financial benefit in doing so.

This did not happen just in Poland. "The war and the occupation unhinged Europe," noted Jan Szczepański in May 1945. "People are demoralized, not used to working, earning money and living normally. Everyone wants to make a living effortlessly, by wheeling and dealing or by stealing. And not only in Poland."[124] The question is this: can this group of people be called unemployed if they did not work because they could not be bothered to or because they would have earned no more than starvation wages? Some of the realities of that time evade definition. For our purposes, let's accept the definition that the unemployed were all those who would have been capable of being regularly employed but were not either for objective reasons or because they were unwilling. The former were unemployed by necessity and the latter by choice. The former are of interest here because they feared hunger and hardship and the latter because others often feared them, thinking that they stole or engaged in shady business. Even though they were visible then, those unemployed by choice are difficult to find in statistics (which were not very reliable on this matter) as employment offices registered only people searching for work. Still, many of them pursued the prewar practice of registering at an employment office but then, after learning about the low wages, not taking the job being offered.

In 1945, the unemployed of both kinds were especially ubiquitous in central and southern Poland; the situation was especially bad in the Sub-Carpathia region. In Rzeszów individuals without a regular occupation, who often went hungry, wandered the streets.[125] The situation in Kielce Province was even worse. In 1945, in only five of the province's districts, the "economically expendable" rural population was estimated at 250,000. About 30,000 jobless were living in towns, not counting Kielce. In the small town of Pionki, which before the war had one large employer, the State Gunpowder Works, 4,000 people out of a population of just under 9,000 were jobless. In Sandomierz and nearby towns, there were 6,000 jobless.[126] "Everything is extremely expensive here, you have no idea, but, tough, we have to work, except that work is hard to come by," read a letter from Radom in March 1945.[127] In May in Kielce, where the population neared 50,000, the employment office registered 2,299 people looking for work; 599 of them obtained jobs, and 1,700 continued to wait. The majority of the job seekers were women and unskilled workers.[128] Comparing these unemployment figures to those in Sandomierz and estimating those who had not registered, the number of jobless in Kielce may have been as high as 10,000. In the summer of 1945, the

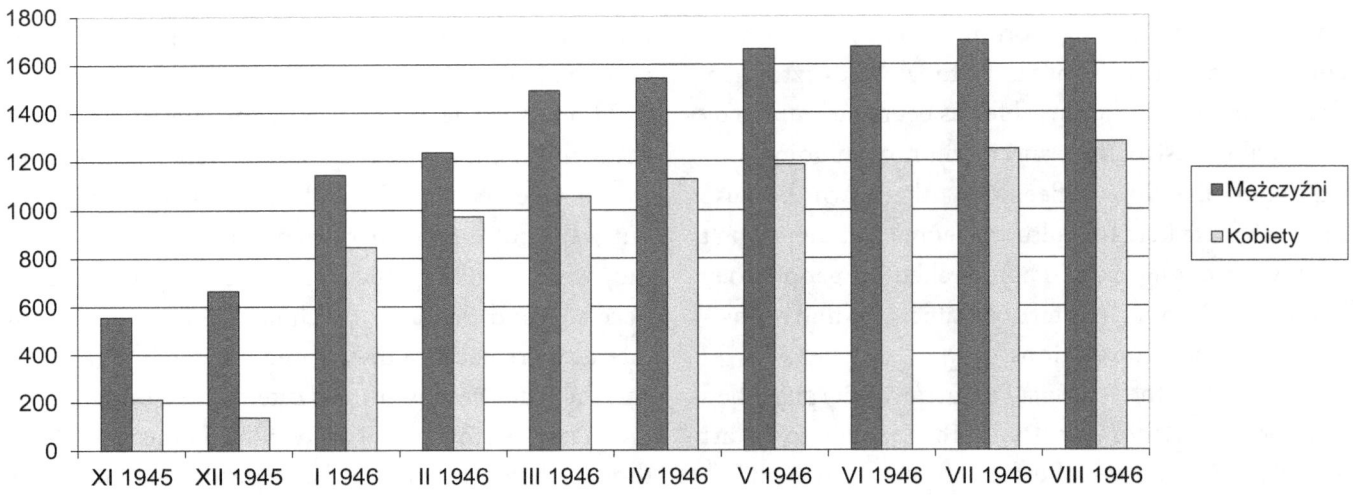

Figure 6.1. Growth in numbers of unemployed in Kielce

militia estimated the number of unemployed in Kielce Province at 40 percent.[129] This figure should have gone down as people migrated to the Regained Territories and as factories reopened, and yet the data kept by the employment offices shows the opposite trend. In March 1946 in Częstochowa, 244 men and 405 women registered as job seekers. By July these figures rose to 1,427 and 1,887, respectively. The increase in the figure for men was nearly sixfold.[130] Figure 6.1 shows the increase in the number of unemployed who signed up at the Kielce employment office.[131]

Across Kielce Province, the number of the registered unemployed rose by nearly 500 percent from September 1945 to July 1946.[132] There were many reasons for this. Apart from the ones already mentioned, which were related to the overall economic situation, the decree about registration and obligation to work (Dz.U 1946, nr 3, poz. 24), issued on February 5, 1946, is noteworthy. It made it compulsory for all nonworking men eighteen to fifty-five years of age and women of eighteen to forty-five to register with employment offices. Another reason was that in the autumn of 1945, over 135,000 men of working age left the army. In Radom, the rise in the jobless figures was linked to the arrival of repatriates.[133] Furthermore, between the autumn of 1945 and late spring of 1946, there was a nationwide economic slowdown, which influenced the unemployment figures but also depended on the location of factories. In some cases, reopening a single factory could change the local employment situation drastically.[134] In September 1945, a man living in Opatów in Świętokrzyskie Province bragged in a letter to France about the situation in Poland: "Some of our factories are operating already, as is the factory in Chmielów, where the workers are making quite good money and receiving allocations and items from UNRRA."[135]

The work situation in the region improved in the second half of the year. The Ludwików Steelworks in Kielce began to hire new people,[136] and its workforce grew from 1,167 in April to 1,391 in July.[137] In October 1946, the Kielce branch of the National Bank of Poland declared, "The issue of unemployment in this region is non-existent."

The problem persisted in Cracow but was not reflected in the statistics kept by the local employment office. Immediately after liberation, out of a population of 284,700, 73,300 people were officially working. If we subtract the ill (ca. 4,000), those under 18 (ca. 70,000), and the old and infirm (ca. 20,000),[138] joblessness was over 50 percent. We must keep in mind, however, that before the war many women, and not only in the middle class, did not work full-time because they took care of the home. "There is no smoke drifting from factory chimneys," *Dziennik Polski* reported in mid-February

1945 about Zabłocie, an industrial district of Cracow. But the workers who stood around outside factories were optimistic.[139] A few days later, a newspaper quoted the deputy minister of communications as saying that "too many young people are going for walks instead of working."[140] The editors of *Dziennik Polski* received a letter from some young people who confirmed that it was indeed easy to meet large numbers of young people out in the streets. They saw involuntary unemployment, which they believed affected the majority of young people, as the main reason for it. They would be told in offices and factories that prewar employees had priority. The newspaper commented, "Until our whole industrial machine resumes its normal rhythm, for now the young people must at least give the impression of being 'voluntarily unemployed.'"[141] It is difficult to gauge the size of this group. In March 1945, 45 men and 320 women signed up at the employment office. In May, the numbers were only slightly higher. The office emphasized, however, that "in reality, since the Office of Labor and Social Welfare expends large sums on taking care of people, whether those who are older or those not managing on their own, there is a shortage of work and significant indigence, and the jobless young and those who are enterprising engage in commerce, which is more profitable than a paid position in a factory or an office."[142] In January, the sales of cigarettes looted from German warehouses became a source of income for many people not only in the city but also across Poznań Province and in Pomerania. In July, the official number of job seekers in Cracow grew to 401 men and 407 women.[143] But there are indications that the real numbers of "freewheeling people" must have been many times higher.[144] One of those indications is the Cracow City National Council's decision in autumn 1945 to expel from the city people refusing to work and to make their homes available to the "working multitudes."[145] If we extend the estimate to the whole region of Lesser Poland, it is very likely that this number was hundreds of thousands.[146]

Poznań also experienced anxiety about the prospects of unemployment. An article in *Kurier Kaliski* in October 1946 reported, "We have observed with trepidation that unemployment is growing in Poznań. This looks like a bad forecast at this time when many branches of the economy are being rebuilt in our city. Theoretically, the unemployment problem should not appear for many decades to come, and for this reason the situation that is beginning to emerge here calls for the quickest intervention of all state, economic and social players."[147]

In late August 1946, Poznań Province registered 4,155 jobless, and in September 2,131 people were looking for work in Poznań. The huge majority, 1,282, were women, 90 percent of them 18 to 30 years old, 70 percent single, and 1,045 unskilled. A discussion about how to resolve this crisis was held in the Poznań employment office, and one voice spoke up as the swan song of bourgeois culture. It suggested "creating the positive aspects of the nature of maids' work, which would lead to a strong decrease in the number of unemployed."[148] But the coming era would bring Soviet five-year plans as the sole method of attaining full employment.

The joblessness in Poznań Province was a marginal problem. The situation was worse in the northeast and in Pomerania. In August 1945, the employment office in Olsztyn enrolled 1,000 people without steady jobs in a public works program.[149] In September a report from Olsztyn read, "Sadly, many people remain unemployed for pleasure because the rascals think that work is not worth doing."[150]

In January 1946, 1,200 of the 4,000 inhabitants of Augustów could not find work.[151] Włocławek in central Poland had 500 jobless in March 1946.[152] In May 1946, in the Pomeranian town of Grudziądz, which had been severely damaged in the war, there were 3,500 unemployed. In Czersk, for every 400 workers there were 1,000 jobless. In Kruszwica, there were 400.[153] According to official data, in Bydgoszcz, population 145,000, only 11,000 people were legally employed and over 12,000 were unemployed.[154] This meant that more than 10,000, both Poles and Germans, either were working illegally or belonged to the "dangerous classes."[155] A man from Bydgoszcz described the situation in his city in a letter to someone in England in August 1945: "There are terribly high prices, and earnings are quite low.... Here there is nothing to do for people who are not working, they are supposed to croak. Only those who are working count. I would like to work very much if I could, and there are thousands like me, but the law is the law [unclear—MZ]. There are plenty of people who don't feel like working, but survive by selling stolen property and cheating, they're in heaven."[156]

The municipal authorities in Bydgoszcz, like those in Cracow, even considered resettling 30,000 of the city's people in the Regained Territories, which caused panic.[157] City hall was also following in the steps of Toruń, which tried to solve the problem of unemployment by creating a special resettlement committee but found no volunteers for resettlement. According to the local paper *Ziemia Pomorska*, "This situation is troubling. An unwillingness to settle outside their native area is fixed in the psyches of the people of Pomerania. The Pomeranian thinks that he must remain in the same place where his father and grandfather worked and lived. He is not even enticed by the prospect of better material conditions elsewhere. The native Pomeranian prefers to sit at home and complain."[158] It seems that the locals were more realistic about the slim prospects of finding work in the Regained Territories than the officials. Also, people from this area tended to fear the return of the Germans.

The situation on the job market was more dynamic on the Baltic coast, between Szczecin and Elbląg, than elsewhere in Poland. Migration played an important role here. A single trainload of repatriates from the east was enough for a queue to form outside the employment office on Starowiejska Street in Gdynia. Between April 6 and May 12, 1945, 473 women and 1,359 men signed up, and 410 women and 1,073 men found work through the office. Conspicuously, the majority were white-collar workers, for whom there were no jobs on the coast in the spring of 1945, while employers were unable to find enough blue-collar workers.[159] In October, the number of official job seekers was 1,533 (Gdańsk) and 1,113 (Gdynia).[160] Repatriates also had difficulty finding jobs in Szczecin. An article in *Kurier Szczeciński* of 29 January 1946 titled "A Pole Moving to Szczecin May Not Remain Unemployed" analyzed:

> Defying predictions, the winter months did not reduce the inflow of settlers into Szczecin. Every day the State Repatriation Office receives 200–300 persons, individually or in groups, from Warsaw, Przemyśl, Kielce Province and other areas. Every day, long queues of arrivals sit in the hallways of employment offices waiting for job referrals and housing allocations. There are many obstacles to employing this incessant flow of hundreds of people, despite the efforts of the State Employment Office and the Trade Union Council. This concerns primarily women, who often spend as long as two weeks in the employment office unable to find an occupation.

Wanting to solve the problem of women's unemployment, on November 22, 1945, the authorities of Szczecin Province issued a directive to prohibit stores, restaurants, and other commercial enterprises from hiring Germans. But this did not produce the desired results since having Germans work virtually for free was profitable for employers, and as long as no one forced them to, they did not even consider hiring Poles.[161] Now, unable to appeal to them with economic arguments, the authorities tried patriotic propaganda, issuing instructions for shops to display notices reading "We only hire Poles." This smacked of the prewar economic nationalism targeting Jewish businesses.[162]

In the first half of 1946, employment offices registered 343,148 job seekers nationally. Various employers submitted 281,455 job announcements, and 244,940 persons were hired.[163] This meant that nearly 100,000 persons remained jobless—a huge drop compared not only to the prewar period but even to the 30,000 in Kielce Province alone. The main reason was the large migration of the landless and jobless from central and southern Poland to the Regained Territories. But these figures were official and did not take into account the gray zone, which must have employed many times more people than official figures indicate. In the second half of the year, the demand for work increased across Poland, for reasons that included the end to plundering trips.

This was evident in Poznań and in Pomerania. In 1946, there were 868,654 people actively looking for work. Of these, 567,164 found it while 217,779 registered but then "abandoned their search for other reasons."[164] They may have been "jobless by choice" who were disappointed by the offers and preferred to remain unemployed, or those who found work on their own. The May 1947 jobless estimate was 110,000. But an increase was expected: 30,000 jobs were to be cut, and the next wave of repatriates was estimated at 500,000.[165]

It is time to draw some conclusions. First, the nonexistence of unemployment in the postwar period was a beautiful myth in a reality that was not so charming. Work was difficult to find, but not everywhere. There are indications that in 1945, central, northeastern, and southern Poland had the biggest problems. In Silesia and Lower Silesia the problem was virtually nonexistent, and there was a permanent shortage of workers. To attract workers, factories offered housing and good wages.[166] In Pomerania, there was constantly great demand for work. Second, in the course of 1946 there were at least 900,000 people looking for work, at least for some time, who registered with employment offices, and over half of them found jobs. Third, at the end of the year, at least 83,781 "unemployed by necessity" were still looking for jobs (30 percent of them were unskilled and about two-thirds were women). Fourth, the size of the group of "unemployed by choice" remained constant; they were mostly rural and working-class youths living at home and traders, looters, moonshine producers, and those performing odd jobs in restoration or construction. Historians have estimated the pool of surplus workers in the countryside at 500,000.[167] This figure may have topped a million in urban areas. Fifth, since unemployment was a social fact, it is very likely that it was also accompanied by the fear of unemployment, which increased the overall sense of threat after the war.

This fear was present in most countries of western Europe and in North America. Polish newspapers wrote about it extensively.[168] Everyone who had lived through the First World War as an adult was aware of the pitfalls of the shift to a peace economy. It was expected that the shrinking job market could not absorb the thousands of men leaving the armed forces. Jerzy Zagórski wrote in the Catholic weekly *Tygodnik Powszechny*, "The world's anticipated gigantic demobilization will make us face the problem of a surplus and not a shortage of hands that want to work in mechanical jobs."[169] Local authorities in some parts of Poland attempted to solve this problem by creating temporary jobs, mostly removing rubble and starting local enterprises. But this was not implemented more broadly for lack of resources, nor did it significantly improve the public mood. An inhabitant of Grudziądz working on a rubble-removal brigade complained in a private letter in September 1945, "The times are very critical, and no one knows how to keep working and living here . . . I am working right now with rubble, the work is fairly strenuous and I make hunger wages because now everything is too expensive: in a word, I will perish together with my children."[170]

Migration to the Regained Territories was seen as a primary solution to the unemployment problem. Newspapers reported enthusiastically, "The joyous moment has arrived when 'jobs are seeking people.'"[171] The mass resettlements led to chaos, often caused by the government's rushed decisions made in part to prevent social unrest motivated by joblessness and hunger. Despite encouragement, some of the unemployed, probably the older ones and those afraid of moving, could not make up their minds to leave. They often stayed, frustrated, and continued to moonlight as if the war were still on. A letter from Radzymin, near Warsaw, dated April 1946 read, "Depression and dissatisfaction are due to the shortages of work and of supplies. Moving west will not stem unemployment since a larger number of people than anticipated have left Radzymin. Two large home distilleries have been shut down, but the remaining ones are working to exhaustion."[172] Similarly, in Pomerania in late spring of 1946, the provincial authorities reported that joblessness was causing "depression and bitterness in the population."[173] A year later in Gdynia, the government's information and propaganda office noted "dissatisfaction among the 3,000 unemployed."[174] This feeling sometimes turned against the Germans living in the Regained Territories. Poles who could not find work were outraged when Germans were hired and employers insisted on keeping them. A woman in Katowice complained in a private letter dated April 10, 1945, "I've been looking for work for 3 months, and I can't find any, yes, also because I don't have the right connections. Regrettably, the *Volksdeutsche* have priority, they were here first, they grabbed everything, they cover for one another, and there is no room for us Poles, who were expelled from Silesia and from Warsaw. It's terribly painful."[175]

Dissatisfaction similarly grew in Gliwice, where in July 1945 people complained about the large numbers of people "of a strongly Germanized nationality" who were working for the administration. There allegedly were very many "pure-blooded Polish men and women" looking for work in vain.[176] In Wrocław, too, people complained that Germans should be blamed for the shortage of jobs.[177] According to research by Sebastian Ligarski, the problem was especially acute in Opole Silesia, where the resettled were unable to understand why locals employed in factories, whom they identified as Germans, had not been fired.[178] People also redirected their dissatisfaction with joblessness at repatriated Jews, who heard views such as "that's because they're not moving the Jews to Pomerania."[179] We have no information whether a similar fear of unemployment was felt on the eve of the anti-Semitic pogroms in Rzeszów in June 1945, two months later in Cracow, and in July 1946 in Kielce. It is noteworthy that in the spring of 1946 a large number of Jews arrived from the Soviet Union, with 136,579 coming between January and the end of July alone.[180] As Gordon W. Allport notes, a growing immigrant population in an unstable period—for example, one with widespread unemployment—increases the likelihood of conflict.[181]

PROFITEERS

In postwar Poland, the "profiteer" was an enemy, not much better than a "reactionary" or an "Anders man." In the official newspapers, he played the crucial role of scapegoat to be blamed for all ills: rising prices, shortages, and every other economic problem. Thus, he was an ersatz Jew, and we should compare this perception to what appeared in anti-Semitic texts. The newspapers created the impression that the "profiteer" was still the "Jew," even without the stereotypical Semitic facial features, props, manners, and speech. Most important, just like the Jew, he lacked human features. He was usually represented as an insipid merchant secretly intending to wipe out the collective effort of reconstruction and to strike at the working class, acting in collusion with his kind, naturally. Just like "the Jew," he represented the threat of destabilizing the market, introducing panic, demoralizing people, and spoiling the work ethic. The language used in this witch hunt was similar, bringing similar negative associations. This was especially visible when the newspapers exploited resentment, branding "profiteers" for the riches they were undeservedly earning, and fabricated hostility, hatred, and rage toward them. The message was: profiteers are bloodsuckers who get rich at our expense. As was typical of this kind of thinking, this part of their representation had them living and dealing in filth. In Radom in January 1946, for instance, "rooted in the occupation, illicit trade survives, selling bread and cold cuts out of baskets and bags, in the street, in a doorway, in a market, all in conditions that violate even the most primitive standards of hygiene: dusty, dirty, straight out of the gutter."[182] To a writer in *Dziennik Bałtycki*, profiteers were "vermin." And: "Gdynia is swarming with vermin of all kinds, suspect profiteers and wildly peddling little ladies who lack even a tad of merchant qualifications, who would like to compensate for all their wartime losses in a flash and to 'make' millions on sewing thread, matches, cigarettes, bacon, looted sheets and so on."[183] There were public appeals to "stamp out" this "vermin" and promises that this would happen imminently. When in the autumn of 1945 prices soared and nothing was available for ration cards, many newspapers carried on about the working class insisting on setting up people's courts for profiteers.[184] Just like in the Middle Ages, "we are demanding harsh punishments for usurers."[185] This time there was no threat of burning in hell, though, only of the much more real work camps to which the "profiteers" were indeed being sent. The anti-profiteer campaigns are comparable to today's moral panic, with the difference that in the former the propaganda pressure was incomparably greater. The "war on profiteering" crested in the spring of 1947 during the "battle over commerce."[186] The emphatic front-page demands for harsh punishments and subsequent reports on the sentences handed down served to distract the public from the real sources of economic problems. They intended to serve as evidence of the new regime's organizational proficiency, of its sensitivity to "the voice of the people." They were a permanent factor in the power game in the early years of People's Poland and would also be used successfully later.

Yet the "profiteers" were not just a propaganda icon, markers of an alleged social gangrene, as in the slogan "the profiteer and the loan shark—social pests."[187] They were also an authentic phenomenon at times of economic revolutions and complications. Here it would be difficult to see them as a group, and even less as a social stratum, since they were not connected to one another and did not have a cohesive identity. They shared many characteristics with a mob, being heterogeneous, haphazard, and varying in gender, age, and social origin. The group was made up of all kinds: children selling cigarettes, prematurely aged adolescents, the wives of prewar army officers and teachers selling off their book collections, and workers. Both the man selling chopped-off bones with bits of meat on them and the shark of the occupation-era commercial underground were labeled profiteers. Immediately after the war, there were two types of definitions.[188] The broker who buys up goods, holds on to them, and then sells them for a higher price, who could thus be blamed for inflation, was thought of as a profiteer. The scalper selling movie tickets he had bought earlier would be the most typical example. The profiteer also lacked institutional ties.[189] He was usually an independent merchant (but not a farmer driving into town to sell the fruits of his labor) who had no rights, no shop, and no stand or warehouse, and who paid no taxes. There were tens of thousands, perhaps hundreds of thousands, of such people after the war. They were called unlicensed traders, illegal merchants, loan sharks, or smugglers. A foreigner traveling through a Polish town or city in 1945 may have come away with the impression that just about every Pole had become a profiteer.

This metamorphosis had taken place already in the first few years of the war. No doubt every armed conflict brings with it economic pathologies and empowers dark deals and gigantic profits from, for example, sales to the armed forces. But this obvious fact does not fully explain the reasons for the swelling of the black market, the profiteers' realm. There is also the threat of hunger in the cities caused by food shortages.[190] Food prices rise steeply in the black market, and at the same time wages freeze at prewar levels, forcing people to seek alternative ways of making a living. According to a Government Delegate's Office report of June 1941, "Often, work is not worth doing when the workers are absolutely unable to feed themselves on their wages. So they move to the countryside where the prices are even higher, they trade and smuggle goods into the Jewish district."[191] With looming hunger and very small rations, the demand for food from outside the official ration system grew. In 1942, according to estimates by Wacław Jastrzębowski, in urban areas the black market satisfied 70 to 80 percent of the demand for food.[192] This meant that hundreds of thousands of people were employed in illegal businesses, which became their principal occupation not only as a source of income but also because it took up the majority of their time. The psychologist Tadeusz Tomaszewski observed this in Lvov in August 1941: "People are buying and selling more and more. More and more people are selling things that are not theirs. With their social contacts giving them many opportunities to sell things, 'society ladies' are going into business."[193]

A long chain of middlemen between the producer and the consumer was established. In Cracow, it was not only the local population that was interested in the workings of the black market. Since they could sell their products at much higher prices than before the war, peasants were also interested in it as a chance to improve their material situation. Thus, whenever they could they avoided making compulsory deliveries to the state and slaughtered their animals illegally. Those who bought up products from a number of peasants were the next link in the chain. The largest group were those who carried the goods themselves in giant bundles to the city. Most of these smugglers-transporters were women, and city dwellers relied on their resourcefulness and courage as they risked persecution from the Germans. The saying in Warsaw that after the war a monument should be built for the "unknown merchant woman" gives an idea of their crucial role. Sometimes they would deliver their wares directly to homes. At other times they would sell them in the streets, which they lined, standing by their baskets with flour, kasha, vegetables, bread, meat, butter, and all sorts of other merchandise. When a "fat German" or a navy-blue policeman appeared, they were always ready to flee. Wacław Jastrzębowski wrote immediately after the war, "These were huge complexes of stalls, with basket sellers, informers and brokers gathered around them. It was a sort of a bourse, where one could buy anything, regardless of what was available on the official market. These outdoor markets were vibrant, and in Warsaw the largest one was the 'Kercelak.'"[194]

Another reason why the black market grew like a polyp was that the official market, constrained by unrealistic German regulations, such as the ban on sales of white bread and meat, stopped playing its regulatory role. A new middle class was born, especially after the Jewish population was expelled from economic life—and then from life altogether. Smugglers, freewheeling merchants, middlemen, and artisans replaced the Jews, not only metaphorically but at times also by adopting their customers and at other times taking over a sewing machine or a workshop. Thus, an illegal market sprang up in the General Government, which Tomasz Szarota believes was the largest and most important one in all of occupied Europe.[195] Wacław Jastrzębowski compared it to "an anthill in the forest, teeming with feverish activity, which appears not to be organized into any evident system and yet is an efficient and cohesive organism, thanks to the ongoing communications among everyone inside it and the constant improvisation to take on new challenges. The illegal market also seemed chaotic, but in fact comprised a sound system, one that was best adapted to life under the occupation, at odds with everything that had long been considered normal, permanent and indispensable."[196]

But once the war was over, the conditions conducive to a thriving black market persisted—or even improved. People remained in their ruts, having become psychologically dependent on the wartime ways of life and work. According to a reporter for the Łódź daily *Kurier Popularny*, "Commerce is a disease, epidemic and, regrettably, chronic. Its microbes have penetrated us too deeply, have eaten through us, and we are no longer able to live normally."[197] But the black market continued to roll on more than just momentum. Hunger, comparable to the spring 1945 hunger and the subsequent winter hungers, thrust people into shady dealings. Furthermore, people who had earlier worked in it only part-time now—with their former places of employment destroyed or not yet running for a lack of raw materials or because their employer, lacking funds, had simply stopped paying their wages—were forced to make it their principal source of income. Hence, the wartime saying "he who doesn't trade won't survive." Letters from Warsaw reported in March 1945:

> The conditions are horrific, you need to bring your own water, prices are through the roof. You can get 2 kg of wholegrain bread and 2½ kg of wholegrain flour with ration cards twice a month, but you really pay a lot. To survive in these hard times, people support themselves by trading, or else by selling their possessions. There is terrible destitution in Warsaw because no income is to be had, there is nothing to live on, and only those who trade stay alive, and those who work go hungry. How can a person live when they pay you 800–1,000 zlotys a month?[198]

The arrival of stolen goods boosted the black market. A stolen German dining set, a radio, or a raincoat needed to be sold somehow, and someone had to do it. It is not necessary to explain that there was huge demand for these types of luxury goods in this pauperized society.

By unexpectedly introducing a currency exchange in January 1945, the state also gave a boost to profiteering. The exchange was ordered in a hurry, chaotically, and for a time stopped the turnover of money, favoring a thriving barter trade instead. A letter from Łódź promoted the obvious solution to this shortage of food and of money:

> Things are worst with making a living. Because all the shops have been raided and shut down. There are also no markets in the squares. There is only barter trade because they don't want to sell anything for money, no food, only for all kinds of rags and materials. Black bread has appeared for sale in the street, so they're asking 120 zlotys for 2 kg, and 60 zlotys for 1 kg of white. In a word, horrendous prices. . . . In a word, to get food you have to go to the countryside and bring a bunch of rags with you.[199]

Furthermore, the powerful fears that the economy would be nationalized, which came on top of the overall uncertainty, also did not make most people want to establish more institutional forms of enterprise. The bedlam in administration and treasury offices also did not encourage anyone to advertise their economic activities. Because the new regime maintained compulsory farm deliveries, the rural population was also interested in selling their products on the black market. In October 1945 a newspaper reported that illegal slaughter was proliferating again.

The overall economic situation, with enormous transportation problems and a shortage of warehouses and shops, also favored profiteering. In the first postwar months and even years, people simply could not survive without the smugglers and merchants who delivered goods that would otherwise not have made it to the markets. Thousands of families, even entire towns, relied on the proverbial countrywoman with veal (at that time only lard) for their meals. On November 22, 1945, militia, Security Office, and rail protection guards encircled the train station in Słupsk. They were there to catch looters, who were expected to arrive by train from Gdynia. But, instead, the train was jam-packed with food merchants. A local wrote to *Dziennik Bałtycki*, "Even though the above-mentioned traders are not our benefactors, nor are they welcome in Słupsk, we must remember that they deliver food to our towns, since the local cooperatives are not yet able to meet even half of the city's grocery needs, even though their activities are expanding, significantly improving the supply situation."[200]

In 1937, over 33,000 commercial enterprises, many of them Jewish, were registered in Lublin Province. In December 1945, only 9,392 were officially registered.[201] Even with some of them grouped into cooperatives, the difference was enormous, but profiteers filled that gap successfully. Thus, even though they could be called independent, should they be included in the category of "expendable" people? This is what they were to the authorities, who made a huge effort to remove the profiteers from the economy. This way, as the state did not wait for self-regulating economic mechanisms to kick in, it increased the sense of "expendability" and fear of the future, and enhanced frustration. Streets, markets, bazaars, trains, and train stations emanated these collective feelings and moods. In all of them, especially in 1945, one could meet illegal dealers, smugglers, and profiteers as well as ordinary swindlers, fences, and thieves.

Every town of any size had at least one bazaar, also called a *szaberplac*. In the Regained Territories, the largest one operated in Grunwaldzki Square in Wrocław. The looters' routes from all of today's southwestern Poland intersected in it. Joanna Konopińska wrote in her diary on December 1, 1945, "What a sight! The merchants spread out their wares on the ground. China, undergarments, clothes, shoes, cutlery, paintings, carpets, toys, thousands of random items. The merchants are mostly German women, but not only. The square empties out in the evening, only piles of rubbish remain, and no one cleans up. Next morning, new vendors assemble and the trading continues. Bartering is king. Money has no value. There is no militia in the churning crowd, people shove each other, shout, steal, often there are fights. The nearby streets are empty and dead, only in the '*szaberplac*' does life thrive."[202]

In Szczecin the bazaar occupied Grunwaldzki Square and the neighboring streets. There was also a market in Cegielskiego Street. Lublin's markets were in Lubartowska and Świętoduska Streets.

The Polish Workers' Party reported from Silesia, "The so-called free markets, where one can buy anything, plague the towns. They are the gathering places for all sorts of swindlers, slackers, fixers and thieves. Much of the merchandise comes from thieving and robberies. The black market also operates there. Every day a dozen people are pickpocketed. Robust young men loaf from morning till night. Tolerating this state of affairs gives rise to great dissatisfaction."[203]

The author of the report also mentioned that the young men who came to the bazaars in Silesia included many Soviet soldiers who sold "trophies" they had brought from Germany. Also in Bydgoszcz, "Lots of Soviet soldiers traded, and at times they occupied a whole street in Gdańsk. They brought various goods from the front and exchanged them, usually for vodka."[204]

In Cracow, trading in used goods occupied squares and markets. The main area was the commercial passage stretching from Sienna Street through the Sukiennice Cloth Hall all the way to Szewska Street. Its whole length was populated by "one-man shops" with their wares dangling from them while women ran stalls; it was a trading place for currency dealers, looters, and fences.[205] Whispers could be heard all around: "Gold, gold, I buy, I sell." The markets were a sort of casino or promenade where three cards, dice, or other scams were played,[206] bigos or pierogis from an itinerant merchant were eaten, vodka was drunk, and news and gossip were exchanged. What a cacophony of sounds and smells, with a multiplicity of human types and nationalities, including Jews and even Italians. They included Primo Levi, who remembered that the "whole city made its way there: bourgeois residents sold furniture, books, paintings, clothes, and silver; peasants padded like mattresses offered meat, chickens, eggs, cheese; children, their noses and cheeks reddened by the frigid wind, sought smokers for the rations of tobacco that the Soviet military administration distributed with peculiar generosity (three hundred grams a month for everyone, even newborns)."[207]

In Płock, the most important market was located in the main square. The local magazine *Jedność* wrote in June 1945, "Now, again, huge crowds of smugglers of different ages and genders have appeared in the main square in Płock. The local population barely manages to buy anything, and then at extremely inflated prices. The smugglers shamelessly raise prices, virtually snatching products being bargained over out of the hands of the honest population."[208]

In Białystok most business moved to three bazaars because of the city's destruction and because people feared assaults by Soviet soldiers.

In the summer of 1945 the commander of the local garrison complained that Warsaw was one huge bazaar.[209] Illustrating his view is a report in the daily *Dziennik Bałtycki* by a reporter who visited Warsaw in early August 1945:

> Right now many people are making a living trading in the streets. The stretch of Marszałkowska Street from the train station to Wspólna Street has been transformed into an enormous bazaar, which truly disgraces Warsaw. Here is a little wooden table with fancy silver-plated dishes, silverware, elegant knick-knacks, right next to banged-up metal bits, dirty scraps of paper, leftover straw, glass trailing on the ground, in a word: a trash heap, which contrasts crassly with the items on the dealer's makeshift counter. It's difficult to squeeze through the stretch of Poznańska Street by Nowogrodzka, for it is filled with food stalls, vegetable carts and pedestrians eating hot soup at flying restaurants. The wind scatters a rusty dust from the ruins all over the bread, sausages and fruit laid out by the merchants, every now and again making the merchants wipe off the food with a dodgy rag.[210]

These images of the postwar bazaars comprise a metaphor for the condition of Polish society, or rather of what was left of it after the cataclysm. Despite their triviality, terms such as *bazaar society* or *Poland, the great bazaar* convey something very important: a piece of the spirit of the time, a crucial component of the postwar popular culture. Its most important feature was the poverty of people who owned one of every item, whether a coat or a shirt, a dress, or a pair of shoes. Families with many children were worse off, and the children had to share clothing. Upper-class or German leftovers made this poverty even more blatant and made a caricature of the tragedy of the pauperized population. Their surroundings, homes, streets, and parks were also unattractive and impoverished and ravaged the city's iconosphere. All privation depraves, but the privation of bazaars and streets does it with great force. Standing for hours next to one's piles of clothes, uncertain that one can hawk them, endlessly bargaining over the price of pork fat or eggs may have humiliated some. The few postwar years brought on a civilizational regression, and not only in commerce. People began to expect less from life.[211] Their needs were limited to the basics. When the windows in one's house have no panes, no one would think about hanging up curtains. When one is hungry, standards of hygiene are secondary. Lying in ruins were not only houses but also value systems, including the merchants'. Fraudulent street gambling proliferated with scams such as the three-card monte, *blaszki* [bits of tin], *cukierki* [candy], and various forms of the wheel of fortune. A morally switched-off economic conglomerate was created, wrote Kazimierz Wyka.[212] Even though they seem chaotic, bazaar collectivities are usually structured and have an internal hierarchy invisible to the outsider. In the streets' and bazaars' fluid postwar reality, this hierarchy was skeletal or only just forming. The community of the postwar bazaar was an assembly of freewheeling people, accidental, lacking mutual ties and at the same time exceptionally mobile, trying to secure their present existence at almost any price. Even though the majority dreamed of stability, chaos reigned, and many became accustomed to it and even learned to draw benefits from it. This may be the reason why the profiteers irritated the planning-obsessed Polish Communists so much. Their planning utopia was waging a war against the postwar bazaar chaos.

Another feature of bazaar society surviving from the war, with its uncertain future, was a perspective that was shortened to a single day. Chance, mobility, fluidity, and "freewheeling" feature in a report about the Green Market, one of the bazaars in Łódź (which also had the Water Square and Geyer's Hall markets):

> There are people on the sidewalks, alongside buildings and even in the road. They are moving along lazily, sleepily, or they stand in one spot. They are loaded down, as if they were being evacuated from an endangered city. Heaps of clothing over their arms. Men's suits, women's dresses, underwear, curtains, shoes, watches, hats in their hands. They walk a few steps, stop, look around. Every now and again, for an instant, they become animated. They say something to someone, shout something heatedly, flutter their loaded arm like a wing. They sometimes gather together and confer, stretch out their necks to look at something in their midst. You would think that the whole world has ceased to interest them, and that all that matters is this one little skirt that some lady just brought and is now unwrapping.[213]

Street vendors, profiteers, and smugglers who traveled the country may have been the most important channel of social communications at the time. The channel came into being during the war, when it played the dual function of providing information and sustaining faith and hope. It represented another manifestation of the civilizational regression brought on by the war, when society, deprived of newspapers and radio, learned to trust oral dispatches, a feature of premodern societies. Peace changed little of these habits. Official reports produced by various institutions determined that peddlers were the source of all sorts of rumors. There is no doubt that postwar markets and bazaars, as well as trains transporting smugglers, were crucial venues for public opinion to form. Thus, we can draw the outlines of collective beliefs, opinions, and moods in this group on the basis of the gossip circulating then. Most of these beliefs concealed unease. For all these people, the postwar economic stabilization, the re-creation of networks of wholesalers and shops and improved transport meant the end of their way of making a living. It is likely that their psychological state resembled the reactions of small shopkeepers today when their bazaars are closed down or when a chain announces plans to open a supermarket nearby. The only difference is that then the change threatened a much larger group. And, the new government made it one of its priorities to "stamp out" this "vermin."

Initially the profiteers came out on top in the war on the chaotic street trade. Wartime practices, such as bribing the militia, came in useful. Militia officials admitted that "they could not vouch for their people's integrity because their difficult conditions force them to take bribes as they fight illegal commerce or drivers."[214] No wonder, then, that subsequent campaigns failed to yield the expected victories. For example, in Bydgoszcz Province, "the operation to eradicate profiteers revealed that our militia and security organs are incapable of conducting such an operation, that people, especially the Citizens' Militia, are demoralized and can be bribed."[215]

Over time, the authorities gave up on using the force of argument alone—something that had never worked particularly well—and ever more implemented the increasingly harsh argument of force: confiscating merchandise, raiding train stations, chasing the merchants away, and detaining them in work camps. The Special Commission for Fighting Economic Abuses and Economic Sabotage was created by a decree of November 16, 1945.[216] Piotr Osęka compared the commission to the Inquisition, as both used holistic methods: the commission tracked down profiteers, indicted them, judged them, and oversaw the execution of their sentences.[217] The first show trials were staged in the spring of 1946, presumably to defuse the very poor preharvest atmosphere. In March, the commander in chief of the Citizens' Militia ordered his people to confiscate tobacco and cigarettes stemming from illicit sources.[218] The liquidation of the "black bourse" in Poznań began in August 1945; things may have gone better in the lands formerly belonging to the Reich because of the underdevelopment of the underground economy and the traditionally smaller number of "expendable" people there. Warsaw did not surrender without a struggle, and in June 1946 several major street fights broke out between street vendors and the militia. "Fighting against the Citizens' Militia are illegal traders and profiteers, who are being harshly eliminated, as well as students and the army, which in the unrest takes a stand against the Militia and stirs up the throngs. It is a consolation that there are no workers and working intelligentsia in the crowd," reported the militia.[219] The authorities announced that they would put a definitive end to street trade in August 1946, and yet its remnants survived outside the bazaars much longer. Szczecin city authorities launched an action to eliminate street trade on March 18, 1946: "Beginning on Monday, the wild trade in Cegielski Street, Grunwald Square and the surrounding streets will be ruthlessly stamped out by the security authorities. We thereby warn all those seeking an opportunity to 'buy something on the cheap' not to spend time in that area, since they will face bothersome and unpleasant consequences."[220] Nothing came of these announcements. According to *Kurier Szczeciński* daily in June 1946, "Just as in the old days, all kinds of characters continue to trail in the streets of the 'bazaar,' peddling clothing, watches, cigarettes etc."[221]

Is there a cause-and-effect relationship between the psychosocial state of this profiteers' microcosm and the fact that at least two anti-Semitic disturbances and one pogrom took place in these bazaars? The pogrom took place largely in a market in Cracow on August 11, 1945. There were also disturbances in Lublin on October 18, 1945, in the market at Lubartowska Street and in Warsaw, probably in the summer of 1946. An undated note tells us how in Szembek Square, near one of the largest outdoor markets in Warsaw, a mob began to accuse Jews living in the Home for Repatriates on Garwolińska Street of murdering a Polish railroad worker. The Internal Security Corps dispersed the gathering.[222] It is difficult to know the relationship between this microcosm and the anti-Semitic incidents, since virtually no information is available on the collective ideas and emotions of the lowest social strata, but there seems to have been a correlation. Behaviors of this type may have been based on this group's feeling of endangerment, its fear of becoming "expendable." Thousands of people had become accustomed to working on the black market and could not imagine any other way of life, especially at a time when it was impossible to earn a living with a regular job. We can only imagine the impact of the news, coming a month before the Cracow pogrom, that informal trading would be banned. The city administrator threatened that he would "act pitilessly" against anyone who resisted.[223] The authorities announced that they would reduce the area available for trading, fine and arrest, and confiscate the wares.[224] The militia staged growing numbers of raids and arrests in the markets.

The distinctive exchange of ideas at the bazaar, which was made up of simple news and lacked critical thought, was another factor. People with this mindset could easily be fired up by even the most irrational piece of gossip, such as hearing that Jews returning from the camps drank children's blood to restore their health. The bazaars' anti-intellectualism was the best possible environment for anti-Semitism to thrive in. Finally, we cannot forget that in all the incidents, the anonymous throng of sellers, traders, and profiteers who had experienced the war and the postwar time of roundups and other harassment easily panicked and gave in to collective emotions, probably also negative ones. People without a past, often exhausted from standing in the street for hours at a time, who included "pure" representatives of the "dangerous classes," people living on the border of the law or constantly violating it, various three-card monte scammers, bootleggers, thieves, and fences, could turn on Jews. As Jerzy Zagórski described them in *Tygodnik Powszechny*, they were "flammable material."[225]

Kazimierz Wyka brilliantly examined the mechanism of tumbling to "expendability" and saw in it the genesis of the Cracow pogrom:

> One would have a hard time finding a more sociologically marginal milieu than the throng that buys and sells, sniffs out every business, floods Miodowa and Szeroka Streets, Bawół and Rybny Squares. The Cracow used-goods market. This crowd is marginal from every point of view. It's made up of people who are selling curtains, bedclothes, tattered children's coats and shoes and feeling ashamed, with latent impatience ("I'm being squeezed"—I need to sell one more bedcover). You will recognize them by their gestures, which are more of a plea to the passerby to deign to buy it than the middleman's confidence that if you don't want to buy it someone else will. This standing around is an unpleasant and demeaning margin of life, which they would finally like to be normal, but they can't. But these very same streets feature margins that are far broader and truly worthy of the name. People who during the occupation were accidentally thrown into this kind of trade and who are trying to stay in it for good. They are skittish and still constantly on their guard. He spent five years dealing and listening out for an approaching roundup. And now, finally, since the liberation of Cracow, no one is rounding anyone up, chasing them away, confiscating their wares. This winter and spring the same people were inebriated with the incredible prospect of selling looted goods. Their golden age has come, as the wave of plundered goods from Silesia floods Cracow. The middlemen, the easy-price specialists have arrived. Their golden age has come, but it's nearly over. The [German-built] anti-aircraft ditch across from Saint Mary's Basilica is my barometer. In the spring, it was the main rug-dealing center. . . . Now it is empty. The wave of stolen goods has dried up. The prices are dropping. This [middleman] won't acquiesce to this easily, and he is growing irritated and impatient. They're not arresting or expelling anyone, but business is faring worse and worse. Worse than in the spring. There must be something to it, some dark machinations. This marginal middleman is feeling threatened today, a mere instant after he could see Eldorado: to make money just like in wartime, but without the wartime risks.[226]

The "war on profiteering" did not end in 1946 but in the spring of 1947 was renamed the "battle over commerce." Now, it was not only the "freewheeling" vendors who were defined as profiteers but also virtually all private businessmen, even those who were established as shopkeepers, wholesalers, and transportation entrepreneurs. Manhunts took place regularly in markets and bazaars. Between June and December 1947, some 77,000 civil servants inspected over 200,000 shops and bazaars, fining 20,000 people a total of 5.5 million zlotys.[227] In 1950, Warsaw's Różycki bazaar was nationalized, but inside it independent merchants were allowed to operate. Photographs of the many small-town markets taken in the 1960s reveal how little the survivors had changed.

Small-time profiteers also survived simply because they had always been there. Even in the 1980s, the presence of old women selling sweets or countrywomen bringing veal to the cities at dawn demonstrated that People's Poland was a sort of deep-freeze for some of the behaviors and customs rooted in the war and in the immediate postwar period.

THE BAD MILITIA

It was not only profiteers, deserters, and invalids who were "expendable" but also militia officers, especially the low-ranking ones.[228] The sociologist Stefan Czarnowski calls them "expendable people serving the oppressors." Some examples: On May 14, 1945, *Gazeta Lubelska* reported on the death sentence and execution of a militia officer charged with killing two people.[229] In the spring of 1947 in Wiśniowo, near Ełk, local Citizens' Militia commander Konstanty Uliasz raped two Polish and one German women, two of them in his office. He was expelled from the militia and arrested.[230] On July 4, 1946, the largest of the postwar anti-Semitic pogroms took place in Kielce. A group of local militiamen were crucial in starting and executing it.

The Citizens' Militia were important players in postwar Poland.[231] They did not bring order but instead fostered public insecurity and promoted chaos ("the militia are introducing anarchy"[232]). Participating in pogroms and lynchings made them feel brazen and above the law. Not only did their behavior demoralize others, but some of them also committed the most violent crimes. Not all of them, of course. Provincial Command reports sometimes included a section on "cases of militia heroism." We have already discussed their clashes with Soviet marauders. But here, it is the bad militia officers who are of interest to us. Who were they, and what were their motivations?

The largest age group in the militia were twenty- to twenty-five-year-olds, uneducated, many of them infected with the wartime lifestyle and demoralized. In Kielce Province, 50 percent of Citizens' Militia officers were of "farming extraction," 30 percent working class. Of the noncommissioned officers and privates, 65 percent came from rural areas while 22 percent declared themselves of working-class origin.[233] These percentages were similar in other parts of the country—for instance, in Rzeszów Province, where 70 percent had been born to peasant families.[234]

Many militia functionaries had only a few years' elementary education, and therefore more than a handful of illiterates must have been based in every station. Their reports say a lot about the intellectual caliber of the people who served in the militia: they are written in casual language and contain numerous errors of spelling, logic, and style. And yet the best writers in the office must have written them. These men's unsophisticated learning and cognitive abilities were the result of their scant elementary education after the six-year war, when many had spent a long time in the forest as partisans. The men of the District Command in Mielec did not know the name of the chairman of the State National Council, the head of state, or the commander in chief of the Polish Army.[235] The jokes and anecdotes about the militia that were very popular in People's Poland had to come from somewhere.[236]

As for their political affiliations, most militia officers declared themselves members of the Polish Workers' Party (8 to 10 percent), but a large majority of noncommissioned officers and privates were unaffiliated. Many had served in the non-Communist underground during the war; soldiers of the Communist underground tended to go directly into the militia. Many District and Municipal Citizens' Militia commands, including those in Lublin, Kraśnik, Rzeszów, Siedlce, Garwolin, and Częstochowa, were formed by People's Army units.[237] Some fighters from the Peasant Battalions and the Home Army also found their way into the militia's ranks. In some districts, Home Army people accounted for up to half of the militia.[238] Some, following their underground commanders' orders, infiltrated the militia to serve as a source of information for the surviving underground. According to Rafał Wnuk's *Atlas polskiego podziemia niepodległościowego* (Atlas of the pro-independence underground), "in 1944–47 a quiet co-existence developed between the militia and the underground."[239] Some historians believe that the

Communist underground's moral standards had been very low. During the war, many forest units—including the Home Army's—had committed robberies and murders, stealing from locals or killing hiding Jews instead of fighting the Germans. Some may have joined the militia to evade the justice system, on the principle that beneath the lamp is the darkest place. Thus, in August 1946 alone, six functionaries of Wrocław Province militia were sacked for a variety of misdeeds, including desertion, signing a *Volksliste*, belonging to Ukrainian SS units, and serving as a German policeman.[240] According to a Government Delegate's Office report, "District militias, both in towns and the countryside, are always headed by people who have dirty hands. Many are pre-1939 thieves and bandits or wartime smugglers."[241] The Wyszków militia commander was a former prisoner who had served a sentence for killing a woman he was trying to rape.[242]

There were also men in the militia who preferred this seemingly safe work to military service, but joining the militia was also a kind of desertion, avoiding fighting at the front. For some, it must have been a logical choice since they had earlier belonged to local self-defense groups. Others joined because they lacked skills other than handling arms and patrolling, and they could remember the status of the prewar State Police, its relatively good salaries and social prestige, especially in small towns and villages.

The Polish Committee of National Liberation manifesto of July 22, 1944, ordered the police instantly dissolved, and the decree of October 7, 1944, replaced it with the Citizens' Militia (Dz.U. 1944, nr 7, poz. 3). Behind these decisions hid crucial political and moral reasons, as the new government needed a new and obedient tool of coercion,[243] and the wartime navy-blue police was—rightly—charged with collaborating with the Germans. Still, dissolving an experienced formation and replacing it with a totally new one in the postwar chaos ended up causing more harm than good. Only a handful of the navy-blue police found their way into the ranks of the Citizens' Militia. In Rzeszów Province, for instance, it was only 3 percent. Everyone else was a greenhorn.

But their origins alone, these men's earlier "expendability" and wartime experiences, cannot explain the reasons for all of the militia's postwar behaviors: why they committed so many crimes and participated in anti-Semitic pogroms. A few other pieces complete the puzzle. The biggest one was the enormous material deprivation of most of the men. An ordinary militia officer was paid 500 to 550 zlotys per month in 1945–46, a starvation wage. All provincial commands received complaints from their men about having to go without shoes, uniforms, or food.[244] "To the locals, because of the poverty of his family, the militia man is a laughing stock," read a report from Poznań.[245] The situation was similar in Warsaw: "The militia are bitter because of their miserable material conditions, shortages of uniforms, inability to support their families, etc. Hence their aversion to service . . . [and] numerous cases of desertion."[246] The saying at the time was "a patch in the front, a patch on his back, there goes a democrat."

Taking into account the numerous grievances submitted to the Provincial Command of the Citizens' Militia in Kielce, its functionaries must have suffered from an extremely high sense of deprivation and resultant frustration. An official report in November 1945 even intimated that a revolt might be looming, if not openly then as a work-to-rule action. "There is generally significant bitterness among the militia related to winter and the shortage of coats. Uniforms, warm underwear and shoes. . . . The issue of the militia and their families must be taken over by a stronger hand and it should not be ignored because otherwise the militia lets their work slide, which leads to a rise in crime, and then the public suffers, and it therefore undermines the authority of the Government of National Unity."[247]

This motif returned in later reports.[248] In March 1946 in Kielce, the militia's delegates to a Polish Workers' Party conference presented a resolution demanding an explanation for why their allocations of food, fuel, textiles, and UNRRA packages were not the same as the industrial workers'.[249] But their unsatisfactory material situation brought on more than a bad mood.

The militia's resentment of the Security Office, which added to their frustrations, was another piece of the

The Demobilized

puzzle. In the mechanism of relative deprivation, there is a reference group to which we compare ourselves and whom we perceive as being better off than us. This comparison makes us feel more dissatisfied at being undeservedly worse off. The militia found it frustrating not that they had nothing but that they had less than the security functionaries. In Cracow, "recently, the militia have been raising the fact that Public Security Office functionaries all got coats and they did not."[250] The militia resented the security people not only for having coats, good shoes, and much higher salaries but also because they bossed them around, or, to put it in sociological terms, they flaunted their higher position on the ladder of power and their status. The militia believed themselves deprived of the honors and privileges that came with secret police jobs. Conflicts that stemmed from this asymmetry between members of the two groups happened all the time. The militia in Cracow reported on the secret police's "tactless" behavior toward them, as "they mistakenly thought they were better."[251] In Kielce Province in 1945, "some State Security Office units are treating the Citizens' Militia tactlessly, believing themselves to be the overseer element."[252] In 1945, fights, shootouts between the two, and conflicts over responsibilities were common. In Wodzisław, Jędrzejów District, a drunk Security Office head of department attempted to resolve a dispute by throwing a hand grenade at the feet of some militia officers.[253]

Adding to the tensions were the clashing pressures from, on the one hand, the political authorities, and on the other, the grassroots. The militia were supposed to guard the government of the people and the alliance with the "fraternal Soviet Union," to fight underground gangs and to enforce the system of compulsory deliveries for farmers. Some of the militia, peasants' sons, assented to the restructuring of relations in society and supported the agricultural revolution. But the majority of the population endorsed neither those in power nor their methods, putting the militia in a psychologically uncomfortable position. Siding with the authorities meant becoming estranged from society, being thought of as collaborating with the despised Security Office and as traitors. This made some of the militia functionaries into ideological fanatics ("I will defend the people's government from the reactionaries") and others into conformists. Those who outright sided with the people deserted from the militia and helped the underground while the less extreme ones sabotaged their superiors' orders and maintained informal contacts with the population. They tried to meet popular expectations as guardians of order by providing protection from Soviet marauders and by being anti-Soviet. According to a militia report from Cracow, "the militia officers' attitude toward the Soviet Union and the Red Army is not positive. The militia as a whole does not comprehend the big picture of the Polish–Soviet relationship, does not have a precise understanding of the fact that Poland was liberated by the Red Army, and develops its opinion of the Soviet Union and the Red Army on the basis of seeing Soviet marauders."[254] Another report warned that "we must accept the mood among the civilian population, which will always be echoed and reflected in the mood of the militia."[255]

An anti-Soviet stance could be punishable by being bypassed for promotion or dismissed. But there was some understanding with the public, which was safer since, at least initially, it entailed no harsh consequences at work, making it possible for militia officers to manifest their distance from the authorities, and that was anti-Semitism. This was another important aspect of the emerging situation. The incidence of anti-Semitism in this occupational group could be seen in the purges in the militia in Cracow in 1945 and in the Lower Silesia, Kielce, and Poznań provinces following the Kielce pogrom and the incidents in Kalisz. It was most likely a local militia officer who threw a hand grenade into a Jewish orphanage in Rabka. In July–August 1946, two militiamen from the District Command in Dzierżoniów pelted the local synagogue with stones and shot at the guard at the Jewish Committee office.[256] There were more such anti-Semitic incidents across Poland. With the tensions between the militia and the Security Office, it is possible that it was actually the militia who fit the stereotype associated with Security Office officers: "The

Jews are in charge." A lecture on "Racism and anti-Semitism" was given in September 1945 for the staff of the militia station on Wilcza Street in Warsaw. Comments from the audience included, "As long as Jews hold [top] positions, things will be bad in Poland," "we have been harmed by the Jews, our and the workers' low wages are the Jews' fault, this is their scheming," and "the Jews need to be done away with and chased out." Loud whispers could be heard: "Down with the Jews" and "Jews out of the security office."[257]

The puzzle reveals a psychological image of the "bad militia," who were peasant sons, often primitive and poorly educated, corrupted by the war; they were convinced that they deserved more because of their functions and the real dangers of risking their lives and damaging their health, and frustrated that "the Security Office Jews are better off" and unable to handle these contradictory pressures. Adding to it was the civil war in Poland's east, south, and center and the aggression that came from all these sentiments, which at the time was expressed by flaunting their power and the prestige of owning weapons and taking part in robbery and plunder as well as in pogroms.

The militiamen dealt with the hardships of life after the war as well as they could, and there was a lot they could do. "The militia and the Security Office do not receive rations, and so they steal," admitted Aleksander Zawadzki, a member of the Politburo of the Central Committee of the Polish Workers' Party and governor of Śląsko-Dąbrowski Province.[258] Looting or confiscating goods from the looters they detained was the best method to fill an empty wallet in the Regained Territories. "The militia are very weak, poorly equipped and represent an extremely low moral level," assessed an inspector in Opole region. "The militia take part in robberies, and often have a quiet agreement with the looters."[259] Bribery was common, rising steeply from a street vendor's small sums to the black market sharks. In rural areas, they took bribes from farmers who wanted to avoid making compulsory deliveries. The mood in the Citizens' Militia is typified so powerfully by corruptibility that they are surprised when someone comes to a district from headquarters for an inspection and leaves without requesting anything."[260] By regularly requisitioning food and clothing, the militia was mimicking the partisans' behaviors. Someone complained in a letter to the starost: In Niedrzwica, near Lublin, "the militia conducted searches of the teacher's and other district inhabitants' homes, looking for allegedly suspect persons, at that time they took clothing and other objects of civilian origin and drove them off on trucks to Lublin.... The militia give the things taken from private people to Piotrkowska and Bednarzowa, who inhabit Niedrzwica, to store. The militia later share these things with them."[261]

In "moonshine" areas, such as the outskirts of Warsaw, criminal groups of militia forcibly protected illegal distilleries and also took over the distribution of the alcohol. There were cases of militia shooting "from behind a fence" at those who dared disrupt the chumminess in "their stills."[262]

Militia drinking and abuse of power were everyday occurrences in the postwar period. "I have personally ascertained that some militias abuse large quantities of alcohol (moonshine) and because of this drunkenness are incapable of performing their work functions," the commander of the district station in Brzeg told his men.[263] Some localities were plagued by demoralized staffs who robbed the local population and practiced extortion, robberies, and banditry. An officer who conducted an inspection in Warsaw Province requested that "legal action be taken against the thieves and bandits who remain in the Citizens' Militia."[264] Drunk militiamen started fights. Near Chełm in 1944, the militia "are taking vodka, getting drunk and then start pursuing not property but real people."[265] Most were violent and boorish, and their behavior worsened the general feeling of oppression and insecurity. A private letter dated March 1, 1945, reported, "Our life now cannot even be called squalid vegetation; it is something distorted, absurd and unworthy of the word life. The eastern culture has found some enthusiasts in the local democracy and pushed them into the top positions as represented by the People's Militia."[266]

A party took place on May 4, 1947, in the village of Mały Płock, Łomża District, during which a young man, Edward Cytrian, was shot by a militia officer. Cytrian's father testified:

> The [Citizens' Militia] commander gave the order to stop everyone and search for the bandit. . . . I said to the Commander: "Why did you kill my son, what have you done?" The Commander put his gun to my head and said that he would kill me, too, right there. They carried my son's body into the courtyard. The Commander's order was that he should lie there till morning. The boy's despaired mother got a few kicks from the Commander and was torn off her son, pushed away. . . . When I, the father, drove my own wagon to get my murdered son's body . . . the Commander didn't want to give me the body, and when I in despair said that I would just take it, then the Commander, Corp. Woźniak, hit me in the face several times (my despair was boundless) and then took out his revolver and shot three times right over my head, so that the fire sprayed into my eyes, and then he hit me several times with the revolver.[267]

The government shut down a dozen corrupt militia stations, or maybe dozens. Several operations to investigate the militia cadres took place in the whole country in this period. They included Gdańsk, where 3,000 employees were fired in 1945, 1,600 in Śląsko-Dąbrowski Province, and over 2,000 in Lower Silesia Province.[268]

National minorities, who had no one to complain to, were easy targets. In the Regained Territories they were the Germans and in Rzeszów Province the Ukrainians. During the forced expulsions, unfounded arrests, rapes, and robberies were everyday occurrences. In this context, we may understand better the militia's motivations for taking part in the anti-Semitic pogrom in Kielce. Frustrated and furious, they probably wanted to conduct a "routine" robbery, pretending to search a building occupied by the Jewish community. They used a story about the Jews' alleged kidnapping of Christian children as their cover. They may also have been indulging in the Freudian mechanism of transferring their aggression from the secret police, which they thought of as Jews and could not get at, onto Jewish civilians.

NOTES

1. Czarnowski, "Ludzie zbędni w służbie przemocy," 421–29.
2. As quoted in Bauman, *Liquid Times*, 69.
3. See Geremek, *Litość i szubienica*; Geremek, *Ludzie marginesu w średniowiecznym Paryżu*; Palska, *Bieda i dostatek*; Tarkowska, *Przeciw biedzie*; Karwacki, *Błędne Koło*.
4. Marx and Engels, *Manifesto of the Communist Party*.
5. Assorodobraj, *Początki klasy robotniczej*, 42.
6. Landau et al., *Bezrobocie wśród chłopów*, 146.
7. Wrzos, *Oko w oko z kryzysem*, 323. See also *Pamiętniki bezrobotnych*, intro. by L. Krzywicki.
8. Kaliński and Landau, *Gospodarka Polski w XX wieku*, 143.
9. Wyka, *Życie na niby*, 146.
10. The group on society's margins also grew in occupied Paris. See Szarota, "Dwie okupacje—ewidentne różnice, ale i podobieństwa," in Szarota, *Karuzela na placu Krasińskich*, 233.
11. Szarota, *Okupowanej Warszawy dzień powszedni*, 182.
12. AAN, Centralny Urząd Planowania 698, k. 119. Problem konsumpcji w Polsce współczesnej.
13. "Piotrkowska od strony podwórza," *Echo Wieczorne*, January 7, 1947.
14. "Here and there on the sidetracks stand open cars, some of them beat-up, dripping dirt, manure and distress. There are lots of these cars, dozens and hundreds." "Tragiczna karta repatriacji—Bieżanów," *Dziennik Polski*, 13 Oct. 1945.
15. Kowalska, *Dzienniki 1927–1969*, 85.
16. Gross, *Neighbors*, 167.
17. Steinhaus, *Wspomnienia i zapiski*, 313.
18. "Rozkaz osiedleńczy nr 111 naczelnego dowódcy WP o osadnictwie wojskowym na Ziemiach Odzyskanych," *Polska Zbrojna*, June 8, 1945.
19. Frontczak, *Siły zbrojne Polski Ludowej*; Kajetanowicz, *Polskie wojska lądowe w latach 1945–1960*.
20. CAW, GZPW IV.502.1.247, k. 29. Meldunek specjalny Z-cy D-cy OW Łódź do spraw pol.-wych., b.d.
21. CAW, GZPW III.2 t. 212, k. 45–49. Meldunek specjalny o sprawie repatriacji i osadnictwa wojskowego i związanych z tym nastrojach, n.d.
22. Ogrodowczyk, *Nad Odrą i Bałtykiem*, 170 et al.
23. Osękowski, *Pionierzy w mundurach na Ziemi Lubuskiej*, 39. See also Kersten, "Osadnictwo wojskowe w 1945 roku," 640–59; Styś, *Osadnictwo wojskowe na Dolnym Śląsku w latach 1945—1948*.
24. "O natychmiastową opiekę i pomoc zdemobilizowanym," *Sztandar Ludu*, October 4, 1945.
25. AAN, Ministerstwo Administracji Publicznej (dalej MAP) 121, k. 205. Sprawozdanie miesięczne Wojewody Rzeszowskiego, 12 Nov. 1945.
26. "We do not employ war invalids and demobilized soldiers" was the typical formula conveyed by most employers in Cracow to the employment office in early 1946. Archiwum Państwowe

26. w Krakowie (State Archive in Cracow, henceforth APK), Urząd Zatrudnienia 41.

27. AAN, URM 5/406, k. 1. Pismo prezydenta miasta st. Warszawy do prezesa rady ministrów, February 23, 1946.

28. "Po zwycięskiej kampanii—na warszawski bruk," *Ilustrowany Kurier Polski*, November 5, 1945.

29. Cf. Kersten, "Osadnictwo wojskowe w 1945 roku. Próba charakterystyki," 657.

30. See Bettelheim and Janowitz, "Pozycja społeczna, degradacja społeczna i wrogość wobec mniejszości."

31. AIPN 00835/68, k. 35. Sprawozdanie o stanie moralno-politycznym jednostek Wojska Polskiego za m-c maj 1946.

32. AIPN 835/68, k. 66. Sprawozdanie o nastrojach moralno-politycznych w jednostkach Wojska Polskiego za miesiąc lipiec 1946.

33. Ryszka, *Pamiętnik inteligenta*, 10.

34. AAN, MIiP 591, k. 7. Wyciągi ze sprawozdania Woj. Urzędu Informacji i Propagandy we Wrocławiu z miesiąca III 1946.

35. AIPN, Wolność i Niezawisłość (Freedom and Independence, henceforth WiN) 92, 38, 39. Raport sytuacyjny nr 10, n.d.

36. Ryszka, *Pamiętnik inteligenta*, 276.

37. This sentiment is expressed in a column in *Kurier Popularny*, a Łódź newspaper, describing the imperative of cutting short the soldiers' frolic: "Undisciplined units that abuse the importance and seriousness of the uniform need to be disciplined by the proper authorities, lectured about the Polish soldier's rights and duties, or even put outside the framework of the army so as not to dishonor it with shocking and irresponsible actions" ("Minęły czasy," *Kurier Popularny*, November 16, 1945).

38. MIiP 1004, k. 27. Sprawozdanie sytuacyjne Wojewódzkiego Urzędu Informacji i Propagandy w Lublinie, b.d.

39. More about demobilization in the West in this influential book: Nurek, *Gorycz zwycięstwa*.

40. Borodij et al., *Rok 1946*, 17.

41. Dąmbski, *Egzekutor*, 46.

42. Klukowski, *Zamojszczyzna*, vol. 2: *1944–1959*, 129, 130.

43. Olbrzym i zapluty karzeł reakcji, poster, https://pl.pinterest.com/pin/728246202226905474/.

44. AIPN 835/210, k. 495. Specjalna informacja Szefa GZI WP, n.d.

45. Mandalian, *Czerwona orkiestra*, 122, 123.

46. "Inwalidzi wojenni nie mogą cierpieć biedy. Wywiad *Expressu Wieczornego* z przewodniczącym Związku Inwalidów Wojennych płk. Kielczyńskim," *Express Wieczorny*, January 31, 1947.

47. AAN, URM 5/739, k. 101. Przewodniczący Związku Inwalidów Wojennych RP Franciszek Bazydło do Obywatela Prezesa Rady Ministrów.

48. Wolski, "Problemy inwalidzkie," 312.

49. Borodij et al., *Rok 1946*, 138.

50. "Inwalida nie jest pasożytem. Praca i renta—sprawy do załatwienia," *Dziennik Bałtycki*, June 24, 1945.

51. Mierzwiński, "Akcja zatrudniania inwalidów kuleje," *Inwalida*, 3, 1945.

52. AAN, CUP 430, k. 10. Sprawozdanie Izby Przemysłowo-Handlowej w Krakowie o położeniu gospodarczem okręgu izbowego za czas od 1 IV do 31 VIII 1945.

53. AAN, URM 5/739, Przewodniczący Związku Inwalidów Wojennych RP Franciszek Bazydło do Obywatela Prezesa Rady Ministrów.

54. CAW, GZPW IV.502.1.247, k. 142. *Raport z inspekcji*, n.d.

55. Cała and Datner-Śpiewak, "Sprawozdanie referatu ds. pomocy ludności żydowskiej przy Ministerstwie Pracy i Opieki Społecznej o stanie bezpieczeństwa Żydów, sierpień 1945," 32.

56. CAW, GZPW IV.502.1.247, k. 161. Raport za czas od 1–15 XI 1945, n.d.

57. "Zdemaskowana prowokacja lubelskich naśladowców Hitlera," *Sztandar Ludu*, October 23, 1945.

58. "Inwalida nie może być traktowany jak żebrak," *Sztandar Ludu*, October 25, 1945.

59. Nałkowska, *Dzienniki 1945–1954*, vol. 6, part 1, 78.

60. APK, Urząd Wojewódzki II 2567, k. 3. Wykaz ilościowy inwalidów wojennych i wojskowych przedstawionych Inwalidzkiej Komisji Rewizyjno-Lekarskiej od dnia uruchomienia komisji do dnia 31 X 1945.

61. CAW, II Wiceminsterstwa Obrony Narodowej (dalej: II WON) IV.500.2.56, k. 16. Ppłk. Hajdukiewicz, gen. Więckowski do II Wiceministra Obrony Narodowej.

62. AAN, MAP 787, k. 40. Raport o wystąpieniach antyżydowskich inwalidów W.P. w Rynku Głównym w Krakowie, 21 III 1945.

63. CAW, II WON IV.500.2.56, k. 27, 28. Do KG MO w Warszawie. Wystąpienia antyżydowskie inwalidów WP w Rynku Głównym w Krakowie.

64. Huchlowa et al., "Sprawozdanie informacyjne za kwiecień 1946 r.," in *Zrzeszenie "Wolność i Niezawisłość" w dokumentach. Wrzesień 1945–czerwiec 1946*, 441.

65. AIPN KG MO 35/922, k. 63. Sprawozdanie z pracy polit.-wychow. na terenie województwa wrocławskiego za okres od dnia 1 X do dnia 31 X 1946.

66. Tkaczew, *Organa Informacji Wojska Polskiego 1943–1956*, 332.

67. Kamiński, *Polacy wobec nowej rzeczywistości 1944–1948*, 232.

68. AAN, PPR 295/VII–163, k. 219.

69. Kamiński, *Polacy wobec*, 234, 235.

70. AIPN 3378, k. 65b. Specjalne doniesienie dot. prowokacyjnych pogłosek, May 14, 1945.

71. AIPN 3378, k. 81. Specjalne doniesienie dot. działalności dywersyjnych band.

72. "In the month of December the state of hygiene with the exception of the First Army was critical in all the units, and even catastrophic in some. One of the most important reasons for this state was the shortage of uniforms, underwear, soap, disinfectants and the bad organization of work. All this led to an intensified infestation with lice and illnesses such as colds and scabies. The battle with them was made more difficult by the lack of drugs" (AIPN 00835/126, k. 7. Sprawozdanie Głównego Zarządu Polityczno-Wychowawczego Wojska Polskiego za grudzień 1944–luty 1945).

73. Assorodobraj, *Początki klasy robotniczej*, 67.

74. An example of the fortunes of three deserters: On May 1, 1946, the Military District Court from Poznań held its second session in the common room of the District Security Office in Bydgoszcz. Three deserters were put on trial for

> having formed an armed band, lived by theft, terrorizing the population and attacking Citizens' Militia and Security functionaries. All three are thick individuals of a low level of intelligence.... After they deserted in March of last year from the 11th Infantry Regiment of the Polish Army, all three met in Sypniewo, Sępólno District, where they joined a band under the command of the self-appointed first lieutenant Dula. After the band was smashed, they joined the "Głowiak" group in which, armed, they performed further assaults and robberies. After this band was also smashed, they joined the "Marynarz" group and launched attacks including the KKO bank in Sępólno, where they stole 60,000 zlotys.... The court, assuming their low level of intelligence, gave them relatively short prison sentences.... 5 years,... 5 years,... 4 years ("Banda dezerterów," *Ziemia Pomorska*, May 19, 1946).

75. KR. Zb., "Plaga żebractwa," *Dziennik Polski*, September 29, 1945.

76. AAN, MAP 1697, 12. Do Obywateli Wojewodów i Prezydentów m. st. Warszawy i m. Łodzi.

77. AAN, Ministerstwo Aprowizacji 126, 9. Serwis Informacyjny 4 I 1946 r. Ministerstwo Aprowizacji i Handlu Biura Informacji Gospodarczej. Pomoc dla głodujących powiatów woj. kieleckiego.

78. AAN, Centralny Komitet Opieki Społecznej (henceforth CKOS) 28, k. 96. Sprawozdanie opisowe Wojewódzkiego Komitetu Opieki Społecznej w Kielcach za miesiąc kwiecień 1946.

79. AAN, Centralny Urząd Planowania (Central Planning Office, henceforth CUP) 880, k. 10. Statystyka ludności w zagadnieniach aprowizacji i próba oceny, n.d.

80. AIPN KG MO 35/2038, 53. Raport sytuacyjny nr 11 za czas od 19 XII do 28 XII 1944.

81. "Wśród bezdomnej nędzy Warszawskiej," *Życie Warszawy*, April 5, 1945.

82. Braudel, *Civilization and Capitalism, 15th–18th Century*, vol. I, 75.

83. AAN, CKOS 42, k. 14. Sprawozdanie Opisowe Wojewódzkiego Komitetu Opieki Społecznej z działalności Powiatowych Komitetów Opieki Społecznej Rzeszowie za miesiąc sierpień 1945.

84. KR. Zb., *Plaga żebractwa*.

85. "Inwazja żebraków na stolicę przed świętem Zaduszek," *Express Wieczorny*, October 25, 1946.

86. "Inwazja żebraków na stolicę przed świętem Zaduszek."

87. "Inwazja żebraków na stolicę przed świętem Zaduszek."

88. "Inwazja żebraków na stolicę przed świętem Zaduszek."

89. "Żebrak właścicielem domu," *Express Wieczorny*, August 24, 1946.

90. *Echo Wieczorne*, November 11, 1946.

91. "Szczecin da nam bogactwo," *Dziennik Polski*, August 9, 1945.

92. Ziemian, *Papierosiarze z placu Trzech Krzyży*.

93. Ziemak, "Niedola sierot," *Ziemia Pomorska*, December 20, 1945.

94. See also "Dzieci na ulicy. handel i żebranina zamiast szkoły," *Gazeta Ludowa*, March 13, 1946.

95. "Dzieci czasu wojny," *Robotnik*, July 18, 1945.

96. Wytrążek, "Żebrzące dziecko," *Ziemia Pomorska*, December 8 and 9, 1945.

97. AAN, Ministerstwo Pracy i Opieki Społecznej (Ministry of Wor and Social Services, henceforth MPiOS) 236, k. 31. Notatka dla C.A.R.E w Warszawie na użytek Wydziału Prasowego w Stanach Zjednoczonych Ameryki.

98. Iwaniak, *Służba zdrowia w województwie kieleckim (1944–1974)*, 33.

99. It is noteworthy that in Lvov, groups of this kind sprang up immediately after the Germans' first anti-Jewish extermination operations. This is the product of the school of hatred:

> Bands of children roam the city's outskirts, at the border of the ghetto, and attack passing Jewish women. They snatch their purses, reach into their sleeves and pockets. Mrs Ziemilska has been robbed twice this way. Today, eight children, about 12–13-years-old, assaulted her. One of them was a girl. When Mrs Ziemilska began to tell them that she is not Jewish, they dropped her bag with her documents in it but took her money. On her way back along the same route she saw a band of children preparing an ambush. This is happening on Zamkowa Street. Walking to Zamarstynów by the ghetto a few weeks ago, I too saw a group of children closely observing passersby. One of them said to another: "Let her go, she's not Jewish." A boy began to tug at a passing woman, who shouted at him, and he left. Today Ziemilska saw a boy, about 13, reeling as if he was drunk (Tomaszewski, *Lwów 1940–1944*, 141, 142).

100. Michałowska, "Przestępczość wśród nieletnich," *Gazeta Lubelska*, January 30, 1946.

101. *Ocalony na Wschodzie. Z Julianem Stryjkowskim rozmawia Piotr Szewc*, 173.

102. Babisiak, "Na tropach przestępców i szabrowników," *Ziemia Pomorska*, September 29, 1945.

103. AAN, Krajowa Rada Narodowa (State National Council, henceforth KRN) 457. Notatka dla ob. Wiceprezydenta Szwalbego z posiedzenia Gdańskiej WRN odbytego w dn. 25 I 1946, k. 91.

104. Cf., for example, Sobalkowski, "O wychowaniu chrześcijańskim dzieci i młodzieży," *Współczesna Ambona*, January–February 1946.

105. Mniejszy (B. J. Radwański's penname), *Pod Wawelem*, 6.

106. Gil, "Z rajzerami na etapach PUR-u," *Odrodzenie*, July 7, 1946.

107. Geremek, *Ludzie marginesu w średniowiecznym Paryżu XIV–XV*, 43.

108. AAN, Komisja Specjalna 3156, k. 1,2. Akta dochodzenia przeciwko Anatolowi Wieliczko.

109. "Opuszczą Gdynię łowcy łatwych zarobków," *Dziennik Bałtycki*, June 22, 1945.

110. "Ująć mocno w garść włóczęgów. Zwyrodniałe objawy pionierstwa," *Dziennik Bałtycki*, July 19, 1945.

111. AAN, Komisja Specjalna 3155, k. 7b. Wniosek o skierowanie do obozu pracy.

112. AAN, CKOS 42. Sprawozdanie opisowe Wojewódzkiego Komitetu Opieki Społecznej Rzeszów za miesiąc grudzień 1945 r. k. 56.

113. "Zlikwidować plagę włóczęgostwa," *Kurier Szczeciński*, May 31, 1946.

114. "Zlikwidować plagę włóczęgostwa."

115. "In Słupsk, there is a noticeable inflow of people without an occupation who cannot find work in town. But these people don't want to go to the countryside to work on farms. A group of jobless is forming. But there is still a shortage of specialists, carpenters, ceramicists, metal-worker mechanics and electricians" ("Nie chcą pracować na wsi," *Express Poznański*, April 21, 1947).

116. "Sklepy będą wolne od wizyt żebraków," *Echo Wieczorne*, November 20, 1946.

117. "Reflektorem po Bydgoszczy," *Ziemia Pomorska*, January 28, 1946.

118. AAN, DRnK 202/VIII-4, k. 4a. Nota, n.d.

119. AIPN, MBP 3378, k. 49. Doniesienie specjalne.

120. "Gospodarka materiałem ludzkim," *Dziennik Powszechny*, May 23, 1945.

121. "Blaski i nędze życia robotnika," *Dziennik Powszechny*, June 1, 1945.

122. AAN, CUP 430, k. 11. Sprawozdanie Izby Przemysłowo-Handlowej w Krakowie o położeniu gospodarczem okręgu izbowego za czas od 1 IV do 31 VIII 1945.

123. AIPN, MBP 3378, k. 44. Doniesienie specjalne dot. sytuacji gospodarczej kraju.

124. Szczepański, *Dzienniki z lat 1935–1945*, 244.

125. AAN, CKOS 42, k. 14. Sprawozdanie Opisowe Wojewódzkiego Komitetu Opieki Społecznej z działalności Powiatowych Komitetów Opieki Społecznej Rzeszowie za miesiąc sierpień 45.

126. AAN, MAP 2442, k. 54–57. Sprawozdanie delegata Departamentu Ministerstwa Pracy i Opieki Społecznej jako członka Komisji Międzyministerialnej z podróży służbowej na terenie województwa kieleckiego.

127. AIPN, MBP 3378, k. 44. Doniesienie specjalne dot. sytuacji gospodarczej kraju.

128. "Działalność Biura Pośrednictwa Pracy w Kielcach," *Dziennik Powszechny*, June 7, 1945.

129. AIPN, KG MO 35/793, k. 21. Raport sytuacyjny KW MO w Kielcach od dnia 15 VIII do dnia 31 VIII 1945.

130. AP w Kielcach. Okręgowy Urząd Zatrudnienia w Kielcach (dalej: OUZ), 4, k. 1,5. Ruch ewidencyjny poszukujących pracy w Częstochowie.

131. AP w Kielcach, OUZ 7. Ruch ewidencyjny poszukujących pracy w Kielcach, k. 3–16.

132. It rose from 3,501 registered in September 1945 to 16,049 in July 1946. AP w Kielcach, OUZ 1, k. 2–11. Liczba poszukujących pracy w województwie kieleckim.

133. AIPN, KG MO 35/793, k. 42. Raport sytuacyjny od dnia 15 11 1945 do dnia 1 12 1945 r., Kielce 10 XII 1945.

134. In late February 1945, Kielce Province registered 478 industrial enterprises; in October the number was 1,233. But the number of employed only barely went over 30 percent of the pre-1939 figure. Iwaniak, *Migracje chłopów kieleckich (1945–1949)*, 23.

135. AIPN, MBP 3378, k. 124. Specjalne doniesienie.

136. AAN, CUP 401, k. 3. Sprawozdanie gospodarcze za miesiąc luty 1946, Narodowy Bank Polski Oddział w Kielcach.

137. AAN, CUP 401, k. 16. Sprawozdanie gospodarcze za m-c lipiec 1946 r., Narodowy Bank Polski Oddział w Kielcach.

138. "Wyżywienie Krakowa," *Dziennik Polski*, February 6, 1945.

139. "Na krakowskim Śląsku. Reportaż z dzielnicy fabrycznej," *Dziennik Polski*, February 15, 1945.

140. "Na zew Ojczyzny," *Dziennik Polski*, February 15, 1945.

141. *Dziennik Polski*, February 15, 1945.

142. State Archive in Cracow (Archiwum Państwowe w Krakowie, henceforth AP w Krakowie), Urząd Zatrudnienia Kraków (henceforth UZKr) 2, k. 7. Sprawozdanie z działalności Społecznego Biura Pośrednictwa Pracy Okręgowej Komisji Związków Zawodowych w Krakowie za okres od 1.4.45 do 15.4.45.

143. AP w Krakowie, UZKr 6, k. 11. Ruch ewidencji poszukujących pracy za okres od 1.7.45 do 31.7.45.

144. In January 1946 the Citizens' Militia Provincial Command in Cracow reported, "There is quite a large number of unemployed in our province. This is caused by two fundamental reasons: (1) the majority of existing factories has been devastated and they do not employ the normal number of workers and (2) wages, provisions and supplies are still low, which is why many people avoid work preferring to make a living their own way. Workers' and office workers' wages remain disproportionate to the market prices of necessities" (AIPN KG MO 35/879, k. 101. Raport sprawozdawczy za czas od 10 i 1946 do 10 II 1946).

145. "O mieszkania dla pracujących i wysiedlenie spekulantów. Uchwały Miejskiej Rady Narodowej," *Dziennik Polski*, September 30, 1945.

146. *Sprawozdania z inspekcji powiatu brzeszkiego* (Report on an inspection in Brzesko District) of early December 1946 discusses the nature of this phenomenon: "The population does not have good living conditions here. The countryside is overpopulated. The farms are mostly small. There are no larger towns or industrial centers nearby for people to earn a living. 50% of the people live mostly on what their 1.5– or 2-hectare farm can yield. The little village shops give out basic goods, such as salt or kerosene, in exchange for eggs, which reveals the shortage of cash. I visited several homes and saw the primitive conditions in which people are living here. In dirty houses, shabbily dressed, no standards of hygiene to speak of." AAN, MIiP 80, k. 26.

147. "Wzrost bezrobocia w Poznaniu," *Kurier Kaliski*, October 6, 1946.

148. "Wzrost bezrobocia w Poznaniu."

149. Baryła, *Okręg Mazurski w raportach Jakuba Prawina. Wybór dokumentów 1945 r.*, 134.

150. AIPN, MBP 3378, k. 104. Specjalne doniesienie.

151. Archiwum Państwowe w Białymstoku, Wojewódzki Urząd Informacji i Propagandy w Białymstoku 21, k. 12. Sprawozdanie

z działalności Pow. Oddz. Inf. i Prop. w Augustowie za miesiąc styczeń 1946 r.

152. AAN, MIiP 363, k. 198. Sprawozdanie referenta propagandy masowej za miesiąc marzec 1946.

153. "Ludzie szukają pracy," *Ziemia Pomorska*, May 31, 1946.

154. Babisiak, "Na Zachodzie wciąż brak sił," *Ziemia Pomorska*, June 1, 1946.

155. In late August 1946, 1,878 persons were registered with the employment office in Bydgoszcz. Borodij et al., *Rok 1946*, 122.

156. AIPN, MBP 3378, k. 32. Specjalne doniesienie.

157. *Ziemia Pomorska*, February 9, 1946.

158. "Ludzie szukają pracy," *Ziemia Pomorska*, May 31, 1946.

159. "Nie gardźmy pracą," *Dziennik Bałtycki*, June 3, 1945.

160. "Rynek pracy na Wybrzeżu," *Dziennik Bałtycki*, November 16, 1945.

161. Cf. Ligarski, *W zwierciadle ogłoszeń drobnych. Życie codzienne na Śląsku w latach 1945–1949*, 134.

162. "Polak przyjeżdżający do Szczecina nie może być bezrobotnym," *Kurier Szczeciński*, January 29, 1946.

163. AAN, MPiOS 554, k. 7. Sprawozdanie z działalności Wydziału Zatrudnienia w Ministerstwie Pracy i Opieki Społecznej i terenowych Urzędów Zatrudniania za okres 1 I–30 VI 1946.

164. AAN, MPiOS 571, k. 16. Wyliczenie bezrobotnych względem zawodów w 1946 r.

165. AAN, MAP 649, k. 28. Sprawozdanie delegata MAP z konferencji odbytej w dniu 20 V br. w CUP, 21 V 1947.

166. Ligarski, *W zwierciadle ogłoszeń drobnych*, 138.

167. Gałązka-Petz and Jezierski, "Odbudowa gospodarki narodowej 1944–1946," 212.

168. For example, *Dziennik Powszechny* of August 30, 1945, reported on its front page, "Dramatic rise in unemployment in England"; "London: because of the war's end, the English government sent letters to 45,000 businesses cancelling orders for the army. In the course of 8 weeks over 1 million English workers will be dismissed from factories working for the needs of the war. Women, who were mobilized to work in the armaments industry, will be the first to be dismissed. Statistical data show that over 70 percent of male and female workers worked directly or indirectly for the army."

169. Zagórski, "Żydzi, Polacy i zaminowane dusze," *Tygodnik Powszechny*, September 16, 1945.

170. AIPN, MBP 3378, k. 104. Specjalne doniesienie.

171. "Posady szukają ludzi," *Dziennik Polski*, July 3, 1945.

172. AAN, MIiP 89, k. 55. Sprawozdanie terenowe zaznane przez referenta świetlicowego Powiatowego Urzędu Informacji i Propagandy w Radzyminie, 15.04.1946.

173. Borodij et al., *Rok 1946*, op. cit., 72.

174. AAN, MIiP 227, k. 106. Raport sytuacyjny nr 13 Urzędu Informacji i Propagandy.

175. AIPN, MBP 3378, k. 63b. Specjalne doniesienie dot. Volksdeutschów.

176. AAN, MAP 2466, k. 3. Sprawozdanie pow. instruktora w Gliwicach.

177. "The situation is all the more unhealthy that even some state and self-government offices employ germans [*sic*], because it is cheaper, while for Poles there are no available jobs. Because of this reprehensible policy in Wrocław there is already joblessness" ("Polityka kieszeni," *Trybuna Dolnośląska*, October 15, 1945).

178. Ligarski, *W zwierciadle ogłoszeń drobnych*, 138, 139.

179. List inż. J. Boreckiego opisującego gehennę transportu żydowskich repatriantów nr 282, jaki w kwietniu maju 1946 r. błąkał się po Polsce, wszędzie stykając się z niechęcią Polaków (AAN, MIiP 1000, k. 2).

180. AAN, MAP 788, k. 113. Sprawozdanie z akcji repatriacyjnej Żydów polskich ze Związku Radzieckiego.

181. Allport, *The Nature of Prejudice*, 59–60, 220.

182. "Walkę z pokątnym handlem ulicznym zapowiada Zarząd Miejski," *Dziennik Powszechny*, January 2, 1946.

183. Zelska-Mrozowiecka, "Unormować ceny na artykuły pierwszej potrzeby," *Dziennik Bałtycki*, June 1, 1945.

184. "Obozy pracy dla spekulantów i marnotrawców," *Sztandar Ludu*, September 12, 1945.

185. "Zamiast zniżki—zwyżka cen," *Gazeta Lubelska*, September 29, 1945.

186. Kaliński, *Bitwa o handel 1947–1948*.

187. *Sztandar Ludu* newspaper, September 12, 1945.

188. AAN, Komisja Specjalna do Walki z Nadużyciami i Szkodnictwem Gospodarczym 82, k. 106. Referat Przewodniczącej Delegatury na woj. rzeszowskie, 20 XII 1947. (M. Mazurek showed me this article.)

189. Beginning with the "battle over commerce," "freewheeling" no longer played a role in defining who was a "profiteer" as it expanded to cover all private entrepreneurs: shopkeepers and wholesalers. Now "profiteer" became a synonym for *prywaciarz*, a private entrepreneur.

190. For more see Jastrzębowski, *Gospodarka niemiecka w Polsce 1939–1944*, 355–64; Wyka, *Życie na niby*, especially the chapter on "Gospodarka wyłączona"; Szarota, *Okupowanej Warszawy dzień powszedni*, chapters on "Ludzie marginesu" and "Czarny rynek."

191. AAN, DRnaK 202/VIII–4, k. 77. Sytuacja aprowizacyjna Warszawy, 25 VI 1941.

192. Jastrzębowski, *Gospodarka niemiecka*, 356.

193. Tomaszewski, *Lwów 1940–1944*, 111 and 38, 108.

194. Tomaszewski, 360, 361.

195. Szarota, *Okupowanej Warszawy dzień powszedni*, 220.

196. Jastrzębowski, *Gospodarka niemiecka*, 363.

197. Tomska, "Życie z zyskiem," *Kurier Popularny*, November 8, 1945.

198. AIPN, MBP 3378, k. 49, 49b. Doniesienie specjalne dot. Warszawy.

199. AIPN, MBP 3378, k. 43. Doniesienie specjalne dot. sytuacji gospodarczej kraju.

200. "List A. Szewczyka, Kto szabruje w Słupsku?," *Dziennik Bałtycki*, December 8, 1945.

201. AAN, CUP 432, k. 5. Sprawozdanie z sytuacji gospodarczej okręgu Izby Lubelskiej w IV kwartale 1945 r. z uwzględnieniem przeglądu sytuacji gospodarczej.

202. Konopińska, *Tamten wrocławski rok. Dziennik 1945–1946*, 102.

203. AAN, PPR 295/IX–128, k. 36. Sprawozdanie KW PPR śląsko–dąbrowskiego za miesiąc marzec 1946.
204. Godycka-Ćwirko, *Lata klęski 1944–1973*, 46.
205. Cf. "Przeciwko 'tandecie' w Sukiennicach," *Dziennik Polski*, February 22, 1945; Prawdzicka, "Skończyć z 'tandetą,'" *Dziennik Polski*, April 9, 1945.
206. In December 1946, the militia detained a young swindler who specialized in playing *blaszki*. His next post was outside Cracow's office of the Special Commission to Fight Misappropriations and Economic Abuse. The "request to assign the suspect to forced labor" includes an interesting profile of the boy, as well as a commentary on the "plague" of street gambling that has gripped Cracow and other places:

> The young suspect . . . turned 17 in the course of the investigation. He said himself that he is engaged in trading in the bazaar. According to him, his father is deceased, while according to our agent Łaptaś he is in prison. This casts a light on both the credibility of the suspect's statements and the milieu he comes from. The fact of the suspect's spending time in the bazaar, which he admits, where he must come into contact with thieves and fences and all sorts of swindlers, must have influenced his young soul at least to some degree. Interrogated in the local Branch he gave the impression of having lived through a lot, being bright, but not yet debauched. The 'blaszki' scam designed to exploit naïve people in Cracow is widespread. All of the authorities' attempts, administrative and legal sanctions, have not improved this situation. This game, in various forms of 3 cards or dice is becoming a plague and a form of economic exploitation" (AAN, Komisja specjalna 3155, k. 85).

207. Levi, *The Truce*, 247.
208. "Rynek płocki znowu zalany przez szmuglerów," *Jedność*, June 17, 1945.
209. AAN, KRN 213, k. 57. Komendant Garnizonu m. st. Warszawy Sokólski J. płk. dypl. do Ministra Administracji Publicznej, 26 July 1945.
210. Żelawska, "Parę godzin w Warszawie," *Dziennik Bałtycki*, August 4, 1945.
211. An example from a diary, November 1944, near Warsaw: "Since we weren't familiar with the side roads, we traveled on the path alongside train tracks. A train came. It stopped. It had nowhere to go. The people got off and squatted down on the path under the embankment. A terribly long line. Men with their trousers down, women with their skirts raised, a very embarrassing sight. Just as with animals, but animals couldn't do it in a line. A departure from civilization, a bad sign" (Sebyłowa, *Notatki z prawobrzeżnej Warszawy*, 368).
212. Wyka, *Życie na niby*, 144.
213. Tomska, "Życie z zyskiem," *Kurier Popularny*, November 8, 1945.
214. AIPN, KG/MO 35/921, k. 77. Sprawozdanie z pracy polit.-wychowawczej w MO miasta st. Warszawy za okres od 1 IV do 1 V 1946.
215. AAN, KC PPR 295/IX–91. Sprawozdanie KW PZPR w Bydgoszczy za lipiec 1946, n.d.
216. Sołtysiak, "Komisja Specjalna do Walki," 81–87; Jarosz and Wolsza, *Komisja Specjalna do Walki z Nadużyciami i Szkodnictwem Gospodarczym: wybór dokumentów 1945–1954*; Fiedorczyk, *Komisja Specjalna do Walki z Nadużyciami i Szkodnictwem Gospodarczym*.
217. Osęka, "Spekulancie, nie chowaj twarzy!," *Gazeta Wyborcza*, December 3–4, 2005.
218. Kochański, *Polska 1944–1991*, 139.
219. AIPN, KG/MO 35/921, k. 90. Sprawozdanie z pracy polityczno-wychowawczej w MO miasta st. Warszawy za okres od 1 VI do 1 VII 1946.
220. "Likwidacja handlu na czarnym rynku," *Kurier Szczeciński*, March 19, 1946.
221. "Źle się dzieje na bazarze," *Kurier Szczeciński*, June 9–10, 1946.
222. AŻIH, CKŻP, Komisja Specjalna, 303/XVIII/40. Sprawozdanie Komisji Specjalnej przy Woj. Komitecie Żydowskim w Warszawie od V 1946 do II 1947, n.p.
223. *Dziennik Polski*, July 13, 1945.
224. Two days before the pogrom, the ministry of supplies and trade issued a regulation requiring all merchants to display their prices, which hit the vendors the hardest. But we do not know whether news of this regulation reached the vendors before August 11, 1945. If it did, it would explain their nervousness. Kochański, *Polska 1944–1991*, 93.
225. Zagórski, "Żydzi, Polacy i zaminowane dusze," *Tygodnik Powszechny*, September 16, 1945.
226. Wyka, "Potęga ciemnoty potwierdzona," *Odrodzenie*, September 23, 1945.
227. Osęka, *Spekulancie, nie chowaj twarzy!*
228. Zaremba, "Milicja Oprychów," *Polityka*, November 16–22, 2011.
229. "Za bandytyzm—kara śmierci," *Gazeta Lubelska*, May 14, 1945.
230. Archiwum Państwowe w Ełku, k. 40. Starostwo Powiatowe Ełckie 15, Zarząd Gminy w Wiśniewie do Starosty Powiatowego w Ełku, 23 VII 1947.
231. About the Citizens' Militia in those years, see Jakubowski, *Milicja Obywatelska 1944–1948*; Kochanowski, "Do raportu!," *Polityka*, February 12, 2000.
232. AIPN, 35/897, k. 32. Wyjątek z raportu z-cy Komendanta RKU Ostrów Mazowiecka do spraw pol.-wych., 28 III 1945.
233. AIPN, KG MO 35/793, k. 84. Sprawozdanie z pracy polit.-wych. MO woj. kieleckiego za okres od dnia 1 II 1946 r. do 1 III 1946.
234. AIPN, KG MO 35/785, k. 104. Sprawozdanie z pracy polit.-wychowawczej w MO woj. rzeszowskiego za okres od 10 i do 10 II 1946.
235. AIPN, KG MO 35/764, k. 13. Raport z przeprowadzonej inspekcji w Pow. Kom. MO w Mielcu, 10 Sept. 1945.
236. A report came from the vicinity of Szczecin in August 1945:

> The militia's work leaves a lot to be desired. The men are mostly straight off the street, without clear-set goals, too young, with undeveloped personalities and very low social and political maturity, most have joined the militia for their

own benefit and have almost no training and professional knowledge, are of low moral status, and a high percentage of militia men who have not had military training bring with them the abuse of arms for hooraying-pleasure purposes. The population cannot trust a militia that is and looks like this, and so its intervention in cases of need is largely disregarded, and the officer, who is often mocked, blushing, wraps things up in a hurry and walks away from the people to stop being their laughing stock" (Twardochleb, "Prolegomena do ethosu pioniera," 436).

237. Jakubowski, *Milicja Obywatelska*, 56–124.

238. AIPN, KG MO 35/785, k. 104. Sprawozdanie z pracy polit.-wychowawczej w MO woj. rzeszowskiego za okres od 10 i do 10 II 1946.

239. Wnuk, *Atlas polskiego podziemia niepodległościowego 1944–1956*, XXVIII.

240. AIPN KG MO 35/954. Raport specjalny dot. wrogiej działalności w szeregach MO za miesiąc sierpień 1946 r., k. 3, 4.

241. AAN, DRnK, 202/III–36, k. 62. Raport szczegółowy nr 3. Powiaty: nieszawski, wrocławski i mogileński, n.d.

242. AIPN, KG MO 35/897, k. 32. Wyjątek z raportu z-cy Komendanta RKU Ostrów Mazowiecka do spraw pol.-wych., 28 Mar. 1945 r.

243. Stefan Jędrychowski put it most succinctly at a meeting of the Union of Polish Patriots: "We are émigrés, and for this reason we must especially appreciate the role of the local factor [i.e., the Communists active in Poland–MZ]. Immediately break some of the administration, for example the police, which must be disbanded, organize a citizens' militia taking into account the partisan element, which is politically valuable" (Protokół nr 20/30 z posiedzenia Prezydium Zarządu Głównego ZPP odbytego 24 kwietnia 1944 r., *Archiwum Ruchu Robotniczego*, vol. 2 [Warsaw, 1975], 105).

244. AIPN, KG MO 35/870, k. 24. Raport sytuacyjny [KW MO Gdańsk] od dnia 10 IX 45 do dnia 25 IX 45; AIPN, KG MO 35/879, k. 55. Raport [KW MO w Krakowie] od dnia 1-go do 15 VIII 1945. See also Jakubowski, *Milicja Obywatelska*, 143–53.

245. AIPN, KG MO 35/890, k. 3. *Nadzwyczajny raport sytuacyjny KM MO Poznań*, 14 V 1945.

246. AIPN, KG MO 035/953, k. 12. Sytuacja w woj. warszawskim na podstawie raportów i materiałów poinspekcyjnych, September 8, 1945.

247. IPN, KG MO 35/793, k. 46. Raport sytuacyjny [KW MO w Kielcach] od dnia 15 11 1945 do dnia 1 12 1945.

248. IPN, KG MO 35/793, k. 52. Raport sytuacyjny [KW MO w Kielcach] od dnia 1 12 1945 do dnia 15 12 1945.

249. Archiwum Państwowe w Kielcach, KW PPR 186. Rezolucja Konferencji Partyjnej PPR MO przy Komendzie Wojewódzkiej MO w Kielcach odbytej w dniu 27 III 1946, k. 5.

250. AIPN, KG MO 35/879, k. 85. Raport sprawozdawczy [KW MO w Krakowie] za czas od 25 XI do 10 XII 1945.

251. AIPN, KG MO 35/879, k. 96. Raport sprawozdawczy [KW MO w Krakowie] za czas od 25 XII do 10 i 1946. AIPN, KG MO 35/793, k. 43, 44. Raport sytuacyjny [KW MO w Kielcach] od dnia 15 11 1945 do dnia 1 12 1945.

252. AIPN, KG MO 35/793, k. 21. Raport sytuacyjny [KW MO w Kielcach] od dnia 15 VIII do dnia 31 VIII 1945.

253. AIPN, KG MO 35/793, k. 43, 44. Raport sytuacyjny [KW MO w Kielcach] od dnia 15 XI 1945 do dnia 1 XII 1945.

254. AIPN, KG MO 35/879, k. 119. Sprawozdanie z pracy polit.-wych. w MO woj. krakowskiego za okres od 1 II do 1 III 1946.

255. AIPN, KG MO 35/879, k. 137. Sprawozdanie z pracy polit.-wych. w MO woj. krakowskiego za okres od 1 II do 1 III 1946.

256. In Dzierżoniów alone, nine militia functionaries were arrested for their "anti-Semitic attitude" (AIPN KG MO 35/954, k. 4. Raport specjalny dot. wrogiej działalności w szeregach MO za miesiąc sierpień 1946).

257. AAN, PPR 295/VII–267. Raport J. Biernackiego, n.d. See also Kochanowski, "Do raportu."

258. Kochański, *Protokół obrad KC PPR w maju 1945 roku*, 47.

259. Kochanowski, "Do raportu!"

260. AIPN, KG MO 035/953, k. 14. Sytuacja w woj. warszawskim na podstawie raportów i materiałów poinspekcyjnych, September 8, 1945.

261. AAN, PKWN I/78, k. 4. Sprawozdanie za miesiąc listopad b.r. [1944].

262. AAN, PKWN I/78, k. 4. Sprawozdanie za miesiąc listopad b.r. [1944].

263. Kochanowski, "Do raportu!"

264. AAN, PPR 295/VII-253, k. 13. Raport z podróży do Komendy MO Woj. Warszawskiego z dnia 17 i 18 XI 44.

265. AAN, PPR 295/VII–164, k. 7. Raport por. Łabędzia, October 17, 1944.

266. AIPN 3378, k. 17. Doniesienie specjalne dot. wypowiedzi o treści antypańst.

267. AP w Białymstoku, k. 78. Urząd Wojewódzki Białostocki 531. Protokół.

268. Jakubowski, *Milicja Obywatelska*, 177, passim.

7

LOOTING FEVER

In the summer of 1945, Poland lived by looting.[1] The Poles were either talking about it or doing it. We usually call this kind of collective emotions caused by the promise of quick riches a rush. "I daresay right now," wrote a columnist in the Kielce-Radom daily *Dziennik Powszechny* in July 1945, "that... the huge majority of people in our society have already looted, are looting right now or intend to loot. People who are afraid to do it envy those who have already done it."[2] This postwar excitement to report on it is inversely proportional to what is written about looting today.[3] Even though objects appropriated after the war embellish some homes to this day, people have mentally rejected looting. Its absence in the historical discourse is connected to a tangible shame and embarrassment that so many people took part in looting then. People try to reduce the resultant cognitive dissonance between actual behaviors and an idealized image of the Poles by explaining that looting was a kind of native revenge on the Germans for their crimes. It is true that an anti-German spirit and the wish to take revenge were forces driving the looting mobs in the Regained Territories, but not necessarily the most powerful ones. The most important questions to answer are: What motivated the Poles to loot? What was it like? What were its mental consequences?

A THEORY OF LOOTING AND THE PEASANT WORLDVIEW

All of modern Europe experienced peasant raids on manor houses at times of unrest or servants stealing property left after the master's death. These incidents had in common an instant when the structures of power were suspended, in a state of chaos, or nonexistent, usually following a natural catastrophe, revolution, or war. Social controls were weakened, and the fear of punishment evaporated. At this precise moment, the looters believed that the objects they were taking had no owner, which did not preclude the existence of a distant owner, perhaps an heir, who might one day ask for them. Taking part in plunder also united people who felt deeply deprived materially, such as domestic servants, poorer peasants, or the urban plebs. We may venture that most understood the world according to the peasant worldview where resources are limited, and something, usually food, is always in short supply. This vision was inextricably interwoven with the apprehension that there would not be enough food, with the fear of hunger. The tragedy of life, according to the sociologist George M. Foster, lay in the fact that there was no straightforward way of increasing the quantities of available goods. The only solution was to acquire them to someone else's detriment.[4]

Looting was a sort of folk reaction to crisis, to what at times seemed to be a permanent state of shortages and poverty. Its genesis also includes other elements of the peasant mentality, such as pragmatism and utilitarianism. "Who knows what life will bring? It's best to protect oneself," "It may come in useful," and "Nothing should go to waste" are sentiments expressed by looters for whom, it must be emphasized, looting was not ordinary theft. They would assuage their conscience by saying "found, not stolen." But this does not mean that by breaking the principle of communally protecting private property they were fully rejecting the commandment "do not steal." According to Dariusz Stola, they probably used it in a form they narrowed down to "my people," which would explain why it was easier to loot the master's, the Jew's, the German's, or the state's property than the neighbor's. To the "expendable" people, the huge majority were "others" (and this feeling was mutual), which explains why they would take part in every looting adventure. Marginalized groups (those closer to the center of society) took less part in plunder, as they must have had greater inner barriers.[5] But the lengthy moral erosion brought on by the Second World War may also have weakened these barriers.

There are many other examples in history that shed light on the study of looting. There are obvious elements of it in the Galician massacre of 1846, even though it was provoked by the Austrian government and, as a result of bloody murders, became a crime. Stefan Żeromski's short story "Rozdziobią nas kruki, wrony" (The ravens and crows will peck us to bits) has the best, albeit literary, description of behaviors of this kind. In the story, a peasant comes upon a dead horse with his harness still on, and next to it is the body of a Polish nobleman killed by Cossacks who had earlier carried arms for Poles fighting in the January 1863 Uprising. The peasant takes everything he may be able to use: the harness and the man's shoes. The nobleman, dead or alive, is twice an "other" to him, as a member of a different social class and as a representative of Polishness, which the peasant cannot relate to. Another example, this one nonliterary, can be found in Bolesław Prus's *Kroniki* (Chronicles). In 1874, huge fires burned in villages including Pacanów and Siedlce. Local peasants arrived in their wagons and demanded exorbitant payment for help or appropriated possessions being brought out of the burning buildings, which they then buried (the archetypal burying of loot). The prelate's threats that they would go to hell were of no use. It was the police who finally recovered the stolen items.[6]

In the story, the origins of looting were twofold. First was the pandemonium caused by the fire, the instant when society's control evaporated and no one was keeping an eye on things. Second was the peasants' distance from the townsfolk, probably mostly Jews, which made solidarity unthinkable.[7] The urban equivalent of looting is taking from shops and warehouses during street riots when some of the rioters take advantage of their anonymity and the absence of police on watch. It occurred, for instance, during the January 1905 riots in Warsaw, which lasted several days and were a prelude to revolution.[8] Looting also took place during the fires in the Eastern Borderlands in 1918–20, when there were also mass-scale pogroms of Jews and invasions of deserted manor houses. It also happened during the great flood of 1934, but then the looters were caught and immediately put on trial. Persons who refused to assist the flood victims landed in the Bereza Kartuska internment camp,[9] and so looting did not become a mass phenomenon.

SEPTEMBER 1939 AND THE "THEORY OF SMASHED WINDOWS"

The September 1939 German invasion brought the next "great chaos" accompanied by "great plunder." It did not begin with the war, but over time, as the disintegration of the state structures became evident and the flight of the elites a fact, there were incidents of plunder of abandoned and unguarded homes, shops, and warehouses, as well as military warehouses and barracks; one such place was Pionki, near Radom, home to armaments factories and the apartments of engineers working in them. According to a witness, "They first robbed the wealthier people, later the others, usually at night."[10] After the Soviet invasion of Poland in September 1939, Belorussian peasant bands attacked many manor houses and foresters' houses inhabited by Poles. But research conducted by Marek Wierzbicki shows that these were at least partly organized actions in which the owners were often murdered, and thus looting, which is defined as chaotic, random, and sparing people (let alone murdering them), was not always their primary goal.[11]

Still, there, too, over the several days of the interregnum, there were incidents of classic looting. Zygmunt Klukowski's diaries describe an incident when Polish peasants arrived on horse-drawn wagons at the Zamoyski family's palace in Klemensów. "Bolsheviks" (many Poles' name for anyone working for the Soviet authorities) were summoned to stop the plunder.[12] Not only the masters' but also neighboring Jews' property was looted. Many incidents of this kind took place in early October 1939. When the Ribbentrop-Molotov pact of August 23, 1939, ordered the Red Army to leave a large part of Lublin Province that it was occupying, a majority of the Jews who sympathized with the Communists and all those who wanted to avoid the German occupation went east together with the Soviets. In the time between the departure of the Soviets and the arrival of the Germans, the power vacuum was ideal for plunder. Looting of abandoned property and violence against the remaining Jews took place in over a dozen villages and towns, including Wysokie, Turobin, Biłgoraj, Frampol, Piaski, Izbica, and Żółkiewce.[13]

But looting was not limited to the provinces. It also took place in Warsaw under siege in September 1939, when there was a prominent shortage of police due to evacuations and flights. A citizens' militia could only marginally replace the missing guardians of the law. Sabina Sebyłowa, who was living on Brzeska Street in the Praga district, witnessed mass plunder on September 18, 1939—people stealing from burning warehouses, private homes, and even corpses. "I saw a neighbor wearing shoes he had taken off the feet of a dead pedestrian. He talked about it openly." She did not categorize the perpetrators in sociological terms but described them only as "skunks, scoundrels, animals."[14] It is easy to guess who these "scoundrels" were, since Brzeska Street was home to railroad workers, factory workers, and horse cab drivers.[15] This part of town, to put it euphemistically, was not the best. Sebyłowa's notes also tell about the looters' great determination as they operated under bombardments and gunfire. Robberies were also taking place in other parts of Warsaw, including Powiśle, where many "expendable" people lived, especially in cellars.[16] "The boys" from Czerniaków, Stanisław Grzesiuk's friends, confessed in October 1939, "We're living off what we grabbed in the burning warehouses and factories during the siege. We sell some things, and for this we buy what we need."[17] Ludwik Landau believed that looting was widespread in Warsaw as it was being bombarded.[18]

After the front passed in 1944 and 1945, from September 28 to October 1, in the moment of suspension between Warsaw's capitulation and the institutional establishment of the German invader, looting was widespread. There are numerous accounts about the "lack of discipline" in the population, which manifested itself in stealing and looting. People were coming out of damaged and deserted homes carrying furniture and clothing left by their occupants. "And after the surrender, how they pounced on it, not only the poor people, but even the police!"[19] In the Praga district, people plundered shops, probably in reaction to the enormous problems with supplies in the city under siege. According to Landau, "The scale of the pillaging showed that it was impossible that only 'petty criminals' were involved." The social base must have been broader. "It was the whole population that took advantage of opportunities to loot: neighbors, chance pedestrians, soldiers stationed everywhere in the city and who now completely lacked discipline."[20]

Since most of the people who joined in the looting would not ordinarily take other people's property, this is precisely its nature. Does this mean that these people were no different from others and that out of the blue "the devil got into them"? Sabina Sebyłowa used this metaphor: "Moral, civilized principles chip off some people like the enamel on a pot that was hit."[21] The chipping may have occurred because especially young people had not gone through the full process of socialization, and most looters were young. As for older people, it is possible that their "enamel" was superficial and that they had never internalized the official value system. Dominant among the thieves were individuals from lower social strata, excluded people, the "expendable," all of them unquestionably poor since they risked stealing as bombs dropped. But most important is the fact that people were plunged into circumstances that could hardly be called normal.

Let us pause over the theory of chaos, which is also known as the theory of smashed windows, according to which chaos breeds chaos. In a deteriorating environment (sometimes broken windows are enough), people are less determined to do what is right. When one social norm is violated, we are tempted to ignore all the others. When we see that others are not punished for their bad behavior and when we feel anonymous, we decide that our offense will also go unpunished. According to the psychologist Philip Zimbardo, "Deindividuation facilitates violence, vandalism.... When all members of a group of individuals are in a deindividuated state, their mental functioning changes.... In such a state, the usual cognitive and motivational processes that steer their behavior in socially desirable paths no longer guide people."[22] This mechanism is confirmed by many experiments in social psychology. The war and foreign occupation were a unique laboratory.

PLUNDER IN THE GHETTOS, AND MORE

The next wave of plunder swept the Polish Eastern Borderlands in July 1941, as Germany attacked the Soviet Union, showing that plunder is a child of chaos. Jan Chustecki's memoir published in 1961, *Byłem sołtysem w latach okupacji* (I was a village administrator under the occupation), describes three pillaging behaviors. The first kind was done by the people of Wołkowyska and environs:

> The town is deserted. Now it's the snaking trains' turn as they stand in the station. What a celebration, as if the world was brand new. Soldiers are perishing in the flames and from bullet fire, children are squealing inside the train, dying in the fires started by bombs, human bodies are frying, the wounded are crawling, and a wrenching scream "help, water, mom!" resounds everywhere, as neighboring villages go on the attack. And they bring out wheat, shoes, undergarments, leather, clothing, textiles, wool, crystals, eiderdowns, what marvels! Good Lord, they have it all! Belts, saddles, shotguns, revolvers, furs, silks. Some grabbed tens of thousands of yards because it's so thick and just jumps on the wagon all by itself, oh my. What commotion, din, swearing at the rail cars. There are long lines of wagons loaded to the brim going home, their wheels squealing, as more people take their turn.[23]

This was just like the situation with the 1874 fires: the tragedy of death, people crying for help as local peasants looted. Chustecki also witnessed people taking the shoes off the feet of murdered Soviet soldiers:

> They've begun to stink, they need to be buried. Franek Nikłas is back, pulling off the best shoes. He begins to pull at them, they won't come off, the legs have gone stiff. He persists, while the corpse watches him with his open eyes. His arms are spread out wide, his head bangs on the pavement. Franek drags him down the street. Well! He's got three pairs already. They should last him two winters. But he needs to bury that body. Mr Village Governor has said so. He took the belts off two of them, tied their ends together put them over his neck, and slowly, like a harrow in his garden, he pulled the corpses into the meadow. He piled them straight and threw some soil on them, they're ready! He went home, shoes in his hand, smiling. He threw off his clogs. He tried on a pair, the best ones, just like they'd been made to order. He washed the blood off them. He polished them with lard. Wow! They are as shiny as the master's.[24]

This situation may be difficult for us to understand, but it's a little easier when we remember that in their daily lives people went barefoot in the Polish countryside, especially in the south and east. The poverty that weakened social bonds dictated behaviors, attitudes, and opinions. For this reason, becoming wealthy by looting brought the joy of the miracle that transformed a life—but accompanied by fear. "Quietly, the folks started to count who had grabbed what and how long it would last. There were rumors that the Germans would search villages they were suspicious of.... People had shuddered for their lives as pilots shelled and bombed less than they do now over these riches. What luck that there is a lot of straw. Let's dig trenches in the barns, put straw bales around them, hurl the booty in. But there's more fear: what if the barn catches fire, who cares about the barn, but the trench, it's worth twenty barns! Pity."[25]

Another example of archetypal behaviors. Just as in the wake of the fire in Siedlce, the peasants buried the loot, as if they were following a script on how to act in these circumstances. It is possible that the script also included peasants plundering Jewish property in Jedwabne and nearby towns in the July 1941 wave of pogroms. Here, too, there was the chaos of the first days after the front passed. Historians have argued that at least two related scripts concurred to culminate in these events, the looting and the pogroms.[26] In *Neighbors*, Jan T. Gross writes that in the early morning of July 10 peasants from areas surrounding Jedwabne streamed into the town on foot and on wagons, even though it was not market day.[27] People from villages near Tykocin, Suchowola, and Jasionówka also stole Jewish property. In Wasilków, "the leaders ... shouted during the pogrom: 'Don't break anything, don't tear anything, all this is ours now.'"[28] Perhaps there were two versions of a single scenario: the mild and the bloody. The former, nonviolent, was followed when the looters believed that someone's belongings belonged to no one. In the latter, the owner "was there," and thus for his property to land in "our" hands, he had to be removed by beating, killing, expulsion. The second script was naturally much more difficult to follow, as it required a modicum of organization, a dominant group of young, well-armed men, overcoming potentially greater moral and psychological reservations involved in inflicting pain and suffering, and thus it happened much less often.

It is much easier to draw the limits of behaviors in the extermination of Jews in Szczebrzeszyn in the autumn of 1942. There, the Germans were the principal killers, with "loose" Poles they assigned to assist them. Some Poles took advantage of this opportunity to loot. The Germans launched operation "the window got smashed" to signal that looting was permitted. Zygmunt Klukowski noted in his diaries:

> 22 OCTOBER 1942. Some Jewish homes have been sealed, but the plunder is in full swing.
> 24 OCTOBER. Many of the town's inhabitants shamelessly plundered whatever they could.
> 26 OCTOBER. In the early evening many inhabitants dove into plunder with even greater passion. The gendarmes finally shot a boy and Felka Sawicówna, who lived across from the hospital.[29]

Similar scenes played out in many other towns, especially in those where the ghettos were being liquidated.[30] As soon as the Jews were expelled from their homes, the local Poles robbed, destroyed, and sometimes broke them up for firewood (since they feared another cold winter).[31] In some places, looters literally walked over dead bodies. Golda Ryba remembered Poles in her native Sokołów stepping over murdered corpses, carrying whatever was left in the abandoned and devastated houses.[32] The September 18, 1942, issue of the Home Army's *Biuletyn Informacyjny* wrote that Poles in Otwock, Rembertów, and Miedzeszyn "on that memorable day when the Otwock ghetto was liquidated, a few hours after this barbaric event, they came on trucks in the night and began to ransack whatever Jewish property was left. They took everything they could lay their hands on, tore out doors and windows, shelves, floorboards, not to mention furniture, clothing and undergarments, which were the first to fall victim to the robbery.... We beg you, countrymen, with God's and humans' loftiest words, to refrain from becoming jackals."

The underground noted similar behaviors in the cities, including Warsaw[33] and probably in Lublin, but on a smaller scale than in the smaller localities, partly because there the navy-blue police and the gendarmerie sealed the ghetto more tightly.[34] In Kielce, for instance, the Germans executed Polish looters searching for Jewish property on the spot.[35] There is no question that ransacking Jewish property was a national phenomenon, as it passed over the lands of the General Government like a wave and also happened in eastern Lesser Poland.³⁶ People would also buy possessions from Jews for next to nothing. Father Józef Anczarski's mother wrote to him, "In Złoczów, the Jews are selling everything they own because they are to be taken to the ghetto on the first of December. They are selling all they own for nothing. Our neighbor bought two beds for her daughter and a cupboard and two beds for herself, all of them new, nice-looking. To get them she sold 30 kilograms of white beans, twenty kilograms of wallflowers. All of it just about for free."³⁷

It is difficult to estimate the total value of the looted property. It was probably less than what happened after the war in the Regained Territories, since the Jews had already been robbed by the Germans previously or had sold whatever they still owned to buy food. A peasant memoirist near Kielce discusses this. His testimony is all the more valuable since it points to a continuity of behaviors: those who during the war robbed the Jews (or bought their clothes from them for next to nothing) after the war looted German property. "In my village [in 1948] as for the clothing or attire, if you cast your eye, it is very poor. During the riots and the Jewish catastrophe, when the Germans took them away and took them in an unknown direction, so then some bought their rags from them Jews, and later again started to go West again to get those post-German rags."³⁸

Klukowski's diary does not explain what the social makeup of the looting crowd was. But the text allows us to presume that it did not include town hall clerks. Most were probably young people and the town poor. In Warsaw, this crowd was probably dominated by people from the "worst" parts of town—Czerniaków, Annopol, Wola, Powiśle, or Praga—who, let's not forget, already had some experience in looting from September 1939. The mob in Otwock probably included peasants arriving in horse-drawn wagons.³⁹ Were these people pushed to steal by their poverty and a "view of a world of limited resources" or by their hatred of Jews? This may be the wrong question, since they were probably driven by a combination of the two. But it is important to note that ethnic hatred did not usually play the principal role in the looting. An incident described by the historian Anna Machcewicz shows this.

A Liberator KG-890 1586 bringing supplies from England to the Warsaw Uprising crashed in the hills near Nieszkowice Wielkie, a village near Bochnia in southern Poland, on the night of August 14–15, 1944. The seven-man Polish crew perished. The villagers panicked, and after they learned what had happened, some pounced on the plane to take whatever they could—watches, wedding bands, and money. It was probably impossible to tell in the dark that the airmen were Polish. A nearby Home Army unit discovered the accident at dawn. The Germans arrived, took away some pieces of the wreck as well as its radio, arms, and ammunition. They tore the insignia off the crew's uniforms. They ordered the local village administrator to bury the bodies and left. The peasants, who by then must have known that the airmen were Polish, went back to plundering. They tore the corpses' uniforms off. They took the parachutes, a total of several hundred meters of valuable fabric. They worked away on the wreck like an ant colony. The Home Army organized a recovery unit and ordered a public whipping of the peasants who did not manage to hide their newly acquired treasures. The airmen's funeral was held three days later. "For many years, this was our shame, which we didn't tell outsiders about," villagers told Anna Machcewicz.⁴⁰

In the cases of the towns of Szczebrzeszyn and Nieszkowice, the authorities' behavior was critical. In the former, the Germans were generally not interested in the Poles' robberies, ignored them, and thereby de facto encouraged them. As the liquidation of the ghetto was drawing to a close, the Germans restored order and the looting ended. In Nieszkowice, where the Home Army ruled hearts and minds, its unit would come and go, and not everyone respected it, and so looting resumed. The chaos and the weakening of institutions engendered impunity. Operating in a crowd gives people a feeling of anonymity, and as soon as owners leave property behind, the looting mechanism kicks in. These circumstances became magnified as the front passed. Joy merged with relaxation, freedom with an absence of authority. The property abandoned by the Germans created an opportunity.

LOOTING IN WARSAW

Four big waves of "looting fever" struck Poland in 1944 and 1945. The first one mostly swept the cities and involved mostly their inhabitants, the "expendables" and the urban proletariat, and in the case of Warsaw also peasants. The second wave traveled through the countryside. The third, most likely the largest, passed through the Regained Territories. The fourth one involved soldiers of regular army units, the Internal Security Corps, and the militia, and it was aimed at the property of Ukrainians and Lemkos who were expelled from Poland in 1945–47.

A wave of looting hit Lublin on July 21–24, 1944, as the Germans were fleeing and the Red Army was marching in. A cynic might say that the July 22 holiday, celebrated in People's Poland as the day when the Polish Committee of National Liberation manifesto was published, should actually commemorate looters. An article in *Gazeta Lubelska* read, "The dregs of society, sure of their impunity, openly stole not only public property but often also private possessions. They escaped unpunished."[41] They took the portable parts of the equipment and furniture of the city slaughterhouse at 107 Łęczyńska Street, and the management placed a notice in the newspapers calling on the thieves to return them.[42] Losses in other institutions and factories must have matched these, since Polish Committee of National Liberation staff had nothing to sit on in their offices. Minister of Public Security Stanisław Radkiewicz ordered posting notices in which "the harshest penalties" would be administered to those who did not return the stolen property.

Tadeusz Tomaszewski's diaries recount looting in Lvov. He observed a group of people not taking part, which gradually shrank under the influence of the crowd's behavior. He noted on August 15, 1944:

> Warehouses were looted again on Monday. Whole buckets of marmalade were carried out of the store in Chorążczyzny Street, and the entire Ossolińskich Street was covered in this marmalade. People were carrying sacks, rolling barrels, lugging chairs, sets of bedsprings. Down Łyczakowska Street came strings of people loaded down with empty marmalade cans, looking like a balloon vendors' parade. Those who did not take part in the stealing stood in doorways and looked on, commenting with moral indignation. But every now and again one of them would take off to "get something." A person can resist temptation, but only for a time. My pimply neighbor spent several hours standing outside our building, but in the end she, too, joined in.[43]

In Radom, which was liberated on the night of January 15–16, 1945, people first hurled themselves at the railway ramp hoping to steal something to eat from stores of flour, sugar, and kasha. Someone took the shoes off a dead German soldier's feet on Czachowskiego Street.[44] Next came the local factories, and the tanneries suffered the most. According to *Dziennik Powszechny*, "In the critical days when the Germans were fleeing Radom, the tanneries...suffered the fate of many other enterprises in our city. The local population stole everything they could carry."[45] The use of the term "local population" may serve as the next piece of evidence that it had not only been the dregs of society taking part but also other social groups.

There was more to steal in Cracow, the capital of the General Government. Tens of thousands of Germans had lived in the city, and they were leaving behind flats, albeit most of them no longer furnished. The Germans had also managed a sizeable industry, including warehouses and military storerooms. The people of Cracow attacked these places as the Germans were rushing out, on January 12–13, 1945. An eyewitness saw that the tobacco factories and a cigarette factory at the corner of Dolnych Młynów and Czarnowiejska were the first to be stormed. For several days, crowds of people circulated, carrying backpacks, suitcases, and all kinds of bags stuffed with tobacco and cigarettes.

The wave also swept the Herbewo factory, producer of cigarette paper, and gradually moved into the center of the city. It took one day to empty the textile warehouse located in a multistory building on Mikołajska Street. Because it was fortified with a massive door, small holes were made to go inside, and the wares were thrown out into the street. The crowd also broke into grocery stores, but they were empty. Offices were less attractive. Someone made a hole in the oak doors of the former NSDAP headquarters in the main square, and every so often someone would go inside. The looters were in no hurry, lacking the nervousness generally associated with such situations.[46]

Lublin, Lvov, Radom, and Cracow were not unusual. Plunder also took place right after the liberation of Łódź, home to a one hundred thousand–strong German minority during the war. Because the Łódź ghetto was the last one the Germans liquidated, it, too, was plundered thoroughly. From January to July 1945 or even later, everything and anything that could be taken out of the ghetto—doors, roofs, windows—was dismantled and carried away.[47] The parallel looting of formerly German and formerly Jewish property is noteworthy as it demonstrates that they were part of one and the same social phenomenon.

In January 1945, the Poles' plunder of German warehouses in small towns was the rule. Mills, sugar mills, distilleries, bakeries, and butcheries managed by Germans were also targeted. If one was not looted, it was only because the public was not aware of its existence or because German troops were faster. Plunder occurred spontaneously, without prior organizing, in the chaos that followed the fleeing Germans. The writer Irena Krzywicka took part in looting in Zalesie near Warsaw, with mostly local villagers as her accomplices. She was not shocked by it but on the contrary saw it as society's natural and fully justified reaction to the Germans' mass theft as late as the autumn and winter of 1944. She seemed to consider the plunder of abandoned German stores, whose owners really "no longer existed," as a patriotic deed. Without ignoring her genuine hatred of the Germans, it is likely that Krzywicka, a prewar elite intellectual, many years later wanted to explain her behavior and blamed the occupiers for it. In fact, her reaction was probably spontaneous, unreflected, and instinctive. She remembered:

Marynia and I went out at night [probably on January 16–17] to that warehouse not so much to find and to get something but to rob no one other than the Germans, to take the Germans' property after they had taken everything from us. We went and we dragged out all kinds of odd things. An iron bed with a metal mattress, a can of marmalade. There were quite a few people from the villages there already, stealing whatever they could. I thought that they were absolutely right since everyone had been robbed by the Germans in one way or another.[48]

In Łódź in January and February 1945, looters pursued not only German and Jewish property. Since "it's not a sin to take a German bed or a Jewish bed cover," ethnic otherness was only a marker of sorts for the stolen item, which made it easier to overcome inner barriers. This otherness was not the most important or even the necessary factor in setting the looting mob in motion. Examples of this are Nieszkowice and the burned-down and deserted left bank of the Vistula in Warsaw, which at this time experienced the greatest invasion of looters. The plunder of belongings left behind after the Warsaw Uprising began one day after liberation, on January 17, 1945. It was a two-pronged attack, first from the nearby villages on the left bank of the Vistula. The January 20 issue of *Życie Warszawy* wrote, "Throngs of robbers have popped up to roam through the empty houses. They steal everything: clothing, bedclothes, tableware, pots and pans, even furniture, which they carry away on handcarts and trucks that have come from who knows where."[49] From the right-bank section of Praga, its inhabitants launched the attack as they crossed the frozen Vistula on foot. Immediately, on January 19, the city's military commander issued an order prohibiting anyone from coming to the left bank, under threat of a court-martial. The militia cordoned off the city, but this was of no use.[50] Not only did the population lay siege to it, but some of the militia officers also tried to enrich themselves.[51] An article with a title typical of the time, "We Demand Harsh Punishment for the Thieves," which appeared in *Życie Warszawy*, described the state of affairs in early February: "One can see women loaded down with housewares, children hauling sacks of books, men pulling carts filled with furniture. Soft armchairs are flying out of windows straight into the robbers' waiting arms. Bands of thieves are invading abandoned apartments through broken-down doors, only to reappear an instant later carrying their booty."[52] The reporter conventionally accused "society's scum, filth," but it was not only the social margins that rushed out to loot. Mentioned most often are peasants, who wandered from apartment to apartment with sacks on their backs. They would look in through a window that had lost its panes. When they bumped into an owner, they would mumble, "Oh, you've moved into the apartment, Madam," and continued on their looting way.[53]

Let's stop here and analyze this scene, which says a lot about the nature of looting: there was no violence and no owner, since his absence made property rights fade away. Our moral rules, including "thou shalt not steal," are addressed mainly to people we know, to "us," and when those people are "not there," the rules weaken dramatically. Plunder, writes the historian Dariusz Stola, is a relationship between people and objects and not between people and people, and for this reason inner barriers to it are weaker.[54] In Warsaw, looters acted more quickly than the returning apartment owners. "As I walked into my house, we saw the embodiment of destruction: all the doors had been pried out, the leather furniture had had its leather torn off. Masses of feathers from bedding, since the looters had taken the covers and spilled the down all over the apartment."[55]

The second wave of looting swept the provinces. The looters were mostly peasants, agricultural workers, and "expendable" people who made landed estates their targets. Here again, the role of the authorities, this time the new regime's, was crucial: as it instituted its agricultural reform, it encouraged people to take over land for "historical justice" to triumph. As an estate was being divided up, people stole farming equipment and tools, something the people's power did not want to oppose too much. Initially, the Home Army tried to resist, but the thefts proliferated as its influence in the countryside waned. An example is the looting of an abandoned estate in the village of Morawsko near Jarosław.[56] Franciszek Starowieyski's memoir gives us another example: the rush to find valuables, anonymity guaranteed by the overused "we." The means of transportation were always the same: horse-drawn wagons. The presence of women and children in the manor house disrupted the looting but, remarkably, to the peasants, a woman was a secondary owner. And perhaps from the peasant point of view the owners had already become a "dead class." Starowieyski recalled:

> The first home invasions began when only women and children were present. Several wagons filled with armed people arrived. They were armed sloppily, in half-Polish, half-Russian uniforms. About four or five wagons arrived, and, in the name of the people, they launched a search of the manor. The great plunder began. . . . They stole what they could. Even some toys of ours, they took my paintbrushes. . . . Some things were already gone. They did not steal what to us would have been valuable. They were looking for jewelry, money and furs. . . . It was a nervous search for hiding places, for things to acquire, quickly, quickly before a pal finds a better piece. Later, we also had to sign a paper that this or that had been confiscated in the name of the people. The vocabulary, which we would be fed daily for 40 years, took over immediately. No one was an I, everyone was a we. We, each of them said of himself, we, this vocabulary immediately grabbed people.[57]

THE LOOTERS' UNION

The third wave, the most real and most powerful wave of the "looting fever," gripped the lands that had belonged to the Reich and the Polish lands that were being colonized. It came in the winter of 1944–45 and crested, in terms of numbers of looters, in the summer and autumn of 1945. It is difficult to know who dominated it in terms of age, gender, or social group. "Certainly, looting is not our people's only sin," admitted the Częstochowa newspaper *Głos Narodu* in August 1945, "but there is luckily no other such widespread 'plague' that would affect the totality of citizens, regardless of the age, occupation and social class of the individuals involved. Hundreds of people loot, ranging from the half-blind old men dragging themselves to Silesia all the way to the enterprising youths, who cruise West in their cars weekly."[58]

It is equally difficult to determine the dimensions of this "plague," but it would not be an exaggeration to describe it as mass-scale. Some towns, especially those on the Polish side of the border with the Reich, emptied out almost totally. Thousands of people wanting to take advantage of this opportunity to loot set out for Lower Silesia and the Gdańsk coast. *Dziennik Bałtycki* of June 1, 1945, read, "In recent months, we have seen tens, hundreds and thousands of people, possessed by a frenzy, who plunder homes and farms that belong to someone else, roiling like the locust behind the troops who were the first to invade the towns and settlements abandoned by the Germans—and robbed, destroyed and trampled them."[59] In November, a manhunt was organized at a train station in Poznań, one of many. Reportedly 60 percent of the travelers were looters. Even if the number was half that size, the "people on the roads" were a very important feature in the landscape of the day, and this speaks volumes about the scale of this phenomenon. The majority came from Warsaw, Cracow, and Tarnów.[60] Remember: these were just the plunderers traveling by train when, at least initially, the majority of them must have come on foot or on horse-drawn wagons or got rides from Soviet drivers. The largest "looters' basins" were the Augustów region, northern Mazovia, Kashubia, western Greater Poland, and Lesser Poland, and around Częstochowa. People prowled areas that were nearest to where they were living. Thus, people from Kashubia made Elbląg their gold vein. The writer Edmund Osmańczyk encountered "bands of the worst scum" coming to the Opole region from areas near Kielce, Częstochowa, and the [Dąbrowskie] Basin.[61] Looters from Zakopane went to the Sudeten Mountains, and their booty included telescopes for watching Mount Giewont from Gubałówka Mountain. Stanisław Ziemba, then-editor in chief of *Dziennik Zachodni*, which extensively covered the areas along the Oder River, recalled that his paper sold very well around Rzeszów and in central Poland. He thought that his readers there were mostly "travelers" who regularly went to Silesia for merchandise, and after coming home each time wanted to have the most current news about changes in those areas and the risks of another journey to the West.[62] If this was indeed the case, it would show a degree of professionalism of the looting expeditions. But the beginnings were different.

Looting evolved in several stages.

The first stage closely followed the passing of the front through ethnically mixed areas. It was the most chaotic and haphazard and at times exposed a blind fury. People took everything they could lay their hands on, wreaking mindless devastation. A teacher in the village of Racice, Inowrocław District, Kuyavia-Pomerania Province, remembered the destruction of a school:

> The long occupation has distorted people's characters, something that could best be seen in the first days after the Germans took flight. The people of the village, who had spent the whole occupation at home, decided, if one may say so, to take advantage of the new situation and immediately began to steal, taking everything that could be taken and that had any value whatsoever, or else to destroy. People robbed former German farms, also robbed farms belonging to Poles who had been expelled, and did not even spare the school. A wild mob armed with axes smashed the door, stealing everything inside: furniture, pots, paintings, books, gymnastics equipment, maps, posters, globes (which they immediately smashed in the courtyard), radios, etc. A whole window was stolen, as were grates from the oven, and hooks were pulled out of the walls. They only left the four bare walls and floors strewn with plaster and trash.[63]

Since this is not the only case we know about a village crowd ransacking a school, we can imagine that the first reaction to the interregnum in the border areas was an insane race powered by the idea of who can grab more.[64]

The next stage did not follow immediately. Fighting still continued in Lower Silesia and along the whole

Baltic coast. Red Army units were stationed everywhere. It was very risky to venture far from home, and therefore those who did not need to travel did not go far. As the front moved westward in April 1945, the next wave of looting followed. A rural memoirist from Łódź Province wrote, "Unimaginable joy descended on the village. The people of Bzów took off for nearby Silesia in the wake of the military, many in Soviet cars and on trains that were immediately put on, to find what they had lost, and there was plenty: sewing machines, bicycles, radios, various kitchen equipment, linens, clothing, shoes, acquiring what they had lost under German rule: prosperity."[65]

Encouraged by the mirage of treasures the Germans had left behind, people became bolder and began to come from more and more distant places. But they were still taking mostly small items they could carry themselves or load onto a cart. Initially only the army could afford to loot larger items since only it had the necessary means of transportation. But sometimes a horse-drawn wagon was enough. Elisabeth Kunert, a German teacher in Karkonosze Mountains, recalled, "Early in the morning Polish soldiers would take off on their looting expeditions on horse-drawn wagons, taking anything that had any value whatsoever, from silver spoons to tastefully woven tablecloths and window curtains, knick-knacks, china, paintings and so on. Everything was sorted here and sent on."[66] Over time, looting gangs formed, and they could comb through the land more methodically, house after house; they organized dens and transfer points and bribed officials to obtain the necessary permits. Maria Zientara-Malewska remembered:

> Already in March the first looters appeared in Olsztyn. They loaded what they could onto trucks and took it away. They went from house to house in search of treasures. They took the best furniture, rugs, porcelain, glass and paintings from the houses, everything that landed in their hands. Their appetite was so huge that sometimes they would take things they then abandoned in the street as they looked for more. More and more various pieces of junk and furniture were lying in the streets.... It was only half as bad when those who were fleeing left these things to their fate. But sometimes they took everything from people who were right there. I saw myself how they would bring mountains of sewing machines, carpets and furniture from nearby villages to the house where I was living in Pułaski Square. I must add that the looting took place not only in Olsztyn. Armed gangs would set off to rob villages, where they robbed defenseless rural people. They didn't ask whether something was Polish or German, they just took it.[67]

An apartment on Brata Alberta Street in Wrocław served as a warehouse for looted property that had been set aside to be traded. "The floor of this apartment was covered with rugs piled up one on top of the other in a thick layer. Paintings of various value leaned against walls, there were wall and upright clocks and hand and pocket watches, in the next room stood a few pianos."[68] Looting was gradually professionalized as it became a source—the principal source—of support, a way of life. An oft-repeated trifle said, "We have a new labor union, it has countless members, it's the looters' union."[69]

A division of labor evolved: some looted, some delivered the necessary documents, others moved the merchandise east and south, and still others sold it. The looters' gangs had their people in town offices, in the militia, and on the railroads. Militia and soldiers often also looted. Actually, the first anti-looting roundups in the train stations served as a means for the Citizens' Militia and railroad guards to appropriate items looted by someone else. While on the one hand it seems that there were many demobilized soldiers, jobless, and occupation-era smugglers among the smugglers, on the other hand looting fairly quickly stopped being a peasant phenomenon limited to "expendable" people and became universal. Civil servants were also infected with "looting fever." According to an inspector from the Ministry of Public Administration to Lower Silesia and Opole region, half of the civil servants left work in the middle of the day to plunder and sometimes also to peddle their wares.[70] Higher-ups often used their official

Looting Fever

cars to do it as well as their power to seize apartments, strip them, and then use them in their patron-client relationships. In Lower Silesia, in a few weeks of August and September alone, fourteen lawsuits were filed with the prosecutor's office whose defendants were starosts and mayors.[71] This phenomenon is explained in part by the civil servants' and militia officers' very low salaries. There was no way that anyone, especially people with families, could support themselves on such a salary, and everyone knew it. But equally important was the collective sense that if all kinds of goods were literally lying in the street, they should be taken, since everyone was doing it. A report by Jerzy Zubek, one of the more intelligent inspectors in Lower Silesia, reads, "People who came here with an idealistic predisposition yielded to the psychosis as soon as they found themselves in this 'gold rush' atmosphere."[72] This manifested itself most evidently when Germans were being expelled, as the Poles waited impatiently. The "looting fever" could be seen in some people's excitement and joy when they managed to acquire something and in the brutal behavior toward the Germans when the loot disappointed.

In the so-called Regained Territories, Germans, almost exclusively women, were an important group of looters, as they knew where to find worthy items, which they exchanged for food in a *szaberplac*, a loot square. Joanna Konopińska has written about the all-knowing "old Mrs. Weiss" who brought home a variety of objects to swap for food in Grunwald Square in Wrocław.[73] The situation was similar in other towns and cities. In Bytom, "German women brought various items to the bazaar and spread them out on the ground on towels... while repatriates operated on the principle of buying for less and selling for more. People came home at the end of the day with a small profit, sometimes with unsold goods."[74] Next, "ants" took items people had bought for next to nothing or looted to central Poland, often hiding them on their bodies. An early reportage about the coastal region after the war included this probably somewhat exaggerated picture: "A huge load on the back, a suitcase in each hand, bicycle inner tubes around the neck, some lesser 'looted' booty dangling from the belt. And our citizen can barely breathe under the burden worthy of a pack animal; he has fixed his roving eyes far ahead, as if wanting to bring that Poznań, Łódź or Warsaw closer."[75]

After the war these people packed trains and train stations. When the Orbis travel agency put in a bus line from Warsaw to Wrocław, a distance of over two hundred miles, it quickly acquired the nickname "looting bus."[76] Some people took it back and forth a dozen times, maybe more. Czesław Borek, twenty-eight, a turner's assistant, spent only a brief time working for the militia and moved on to buying up various objects in Jelenia Góra and transporting them to central Poland. According to his testimony before the Special Commission, he visited Jelenia Góra about ten times. He also mailed some of his acquisitions. He himself did not loot but bought some of his wares from Germans and most from Citizens' Militia officers he had known for a long time.[77] In February 1946, two unemployed women were arrested; they traveled regularly between the Regained Territories and Poznań, one since April, the other since July 1945, bringing watches, cameras, and clothes, and sold them to consignment shops. They were arrested carrying three suitcases filled with tablecloths, bed sheets, cloth napkins, two motorcycle wheel rims, and a coil of cable.[78] But they were mere retailers.

VARIETIES OF LOOTING

Apart from the most numerous retailers, the "ants," over time looters took up different specializations. While clothing, shoes, rugs, and household equipment such as sewing machines did not require specialization, moving furniture, not to mention farm equipment, did. Thousands of UNRRA trucks entering Poland from Czechoslovakia and traveling to Warsaw and elsewhere were filled to the brim with furniture and other goods. Espresso machines, coffee grinders, equipment for cafés and restaurants, and plates and tea and coffee cups for Varsovians were most likely specially ordered. Some of the merchants specialized in car parts, others, such as the gang of employees of the Headquarters of the Postal and Telegraph Service in Katowice, in telecommunications equipment. This gang looted the equipment of the telephone exchange in Strzelce Opolskie while driving a postal truck.[79]

There were specialists in entering abandoned pharmacies and moving expensive and rare drugs into central Poland.[80] A subset of looters took over apartments formerly occupied by Germans, stripped them bare, and moved on to the next one. The deputy starost of Kudowa changed his service apartment five times in six months (he lived in one of them less than a day) and brought out their complete furnishings with him each time.[81]

Another specialty was the "cultural looter." According to Stanisław Ziemba, the looting of books appeared last of all cultural goods. "Initially, there were no specialists in this field among looters."[82] But soon book lovers appeared.[83] In early August 1945, dozens of people roamed the ruins of Gdańsk in search of artwork they could sell—although they may have been hungry Germans who knew where to find them.[84] According to the court documents for the case of Stanisław Ziewiec, in the first half of 1946 he had moved four Afghan and Persian rugs, three Dutch paintings, one painting of the Munich School, four Empire paintings, and many small knickknacks out of the Regained Territories.[85] The putti that decorate some intelligentsia flats to this day must have been taken from ruined churches in the wake of the war. The archives of the Special Commission include documents about an individual who in September 1946 in Kłodzko bought a collection of nineteen cases of butterflies and beetles—and served three months in a work camp for it.[86]

There was also the official type of looting, for which most offenders were not sentenced. It began already in the ruins of Warsaw and continued very successfully. Many institutions, including universities, which had been stripped of all equipment, had to operate somehow and so sent out expeditions to "secure" chairs, desks, typewriters, and books.[87] Many schools, libraries, and health centers, especially in the so-called Regained Territories but also in central Poland, could begin to function thanks to such expeditions. At times, they were guided by the genuine civic concern of its people who, wanting to get a school or library going, brought in everything that could be of use, which they had looted.[88] This could hardly be called looting, since it was not motivated by private gain. Still, this "official looting" sent a negative educational message since it showed that elites, too, were allowed to engage in it.

Top military and Security Office officers furnished the new homes they had "captured,"[89] for which they could effortlessly organize transportation and the necessary permits. Some acquired real fortunes this way. Lieutenant Colonel Faustyn Grzybowski, serving as head of the Provincial Office of Public Security in Wrocław, acquired a diadem with twenty-five to thirty diamonds, a twenty-four-karat gold bar, twenty-four gold marks, several gold-and-diamond brooches, and sixty-five other pieces of jewelry. If the Ministry of Public Security defector Józef Światło is to be believed, Grzybowski "was one of the most energetic looters in Wrocław in his time as chief of the Security Office. He collected a whole fortune of antique furniture, clothes, jewelry and furs, things that he had never had nor even seen before. The looted fortune traveled to his apartment in cars. Not only to his, though. As head of the Security Office in Wrocław, he delivered hunting rifles and furnished the homes of [head of secret police Stanisław] Radkiewicz and Second Deputy Minister of Security Mieczysław Mietkowski."[90]

Some behaviors should be placed on the spectrum between looting and an owner's care—for instance, the lawful seizure of formerly German property by settlers cannot be defined as looting. But how does one judge a repatriated person who was given a farm that had been stripped bare and who is looking for the equipment he needs in another, more prosperous farm and, once he finds and takes what he needs, never again goes on such an expedition? No one arrived in the Regained Territories with possessions. After the war everything had a value—a washbasin, a pail, a bicycle, or a window.

The gangster behavior of Polish soldiers and militia officers toward Germans and Ukrainians should not be categorized as looting. They often expelled these minorities without giving them time to pack and limiting the amount of luggage they were allowed to bring with them so that they could loot the "abandoned" possessions. During operation "Vistula," such behavior was virtually the norm.

Looters, especially the young ones, easily turned into thieves or even bandits when they bumped into the owners of a German home that they expected to be abandoned. The surviving image in the collective German imagination of Poles was of a mob taking all it could violently and unthinkingly. In their treatment of Germans and Ukrainians, they would repeatedly cross the line between looting and armed robbery. At times, their aggression also harmed Poles, both locals and those who had only just been resettled. A man who lived near Olsztyn remembered, "We felt totally unsafe. Looters would appear, steal at night or, more often, arrive armed in broad daylight and take whatever they wanted, actually whatever was left: eiderdowns, clocks, bicycles that had survived somehow, clothes, undergarments, sewing machines and so forth. Not a day went by without the looters coming to visit someone in the village. The tragedy was that these were Poles, our brothers, and these brothers of ours came to rob their own brothers."[91]

Looting also resembled digging up cemeteries, which has happened across history. One of the first postwar incidents in Poland happened in Jasło. An article in *Dziennik Polski* in March 1945 reported, "In the wake of such operations, the graveyard looked like a battlefield. Dozens of bodies that had been dragged out of their coffins were strewn all over the ground. The city of the dead came to look like the city of the 'living.'"[92] The author of the article blamed the Germans for desecrating the graves. But since blaming them for all crimes was in fashion then, we cannot reject the possibility that the culprits were Poles or Soviet troops who had liberated the town. We also do not know whether this article inspired Polish specialists in extracting gold teeth, but the practice became widespread—for instance, in distant Cracow. A woman living there, whose family graves were probably in one of the city's cemeteries, wrote in a private letter on May 21, 1945: "The thieves have been robbing graves in the cemetery in search of gold teeth. The tomb where Kazio is buried was also opened and 3 coffins were moved, Kazio's, Wanda's Mother's and sister's. We saw Kazio's coffin, it was turned over on its side. . . . In the night from Saturday to Sunday, 24 graves were opened and robbed, of course it's the fault of the management because they guard it during the day, close up early, but these days even the management can't do much."[93]

Best known is the case of Treblinka, where local peasants developed a specialty in combing through the graves of murdered Jews. In the autumn of 1945, the entire area of the former camp looked like a strip mine, dug through and emptied out, with ditches full of human bones. The smell of rotting corpses was in the air. Some of the "gold diggers" used grenades to bring them up. The gold acquired in this way allowed the nearby villages to recover materially.[94] A report from Treblinka in *Dziennik Ludowy*:

> They are digging in Treblinka: gold! Who? Everyone, children and women. Young and old. Yes. They're extracting gold from death pits, out of rotten rags, from in-between heaps of corpses! They're breaking fingers shrivelled in deathly pain, shattering jaws. This operation has been going on for months. Right at dawn, they come from everywhere: Guty, Wólka Okrąglik, Kosów, Małkinia, that's nothing! They're even coming from Sokołów, Siedlce, Warsawa, Ostrołęka, bringing their own 'work' tools, shovels, hoes and pickaxes. Those few who cannot imagine this kind of riches say that organized group will appear, too. They dig through the grounds faster and more efficiently with mines and grenades. . . . More than one of them has perished on the hands of a competitor. But gold is more powerful. Very few, let me stress, have resisted this mass psychosis, this temptation to make money so effortlessly. The "conquerors" are easy to recognize by their new, spacious houses, sheet-metal roofs, generosity for crowds of drunks and the appraising professional's vocabulary of "standards" and "carats." Other shady, shifty types supply Warsaw (intersection of Ząbkowska and Targowa) by train, going through Siedlce and Małkinia with their precious, oh so precious, merchandise.[95]

Legends about hidden Jewish treasures made the rounds nationally. The papers wrote about them.[96] The team that made the film *Skarb* in 1949 may have been influenced by such stories. The cemetery hyenas searching for gold teeth and wedding bands also destroyed German graveyards in the Regained Territories. The writer Wojciech Żukrowski, who lived in Wrocław after the war, recalled, "I sometimes . . . saw old bourgeois graves with their stones moved to the side, tin coffins with holes cut in them right on the spot where the corpses' folded hands with a wedding band were expected to lie." "They rolled up the tin tops of the coffins like a sardine can and broke out their teeth and bridges."[97] Later, some cemeteries, which included German graves, including in Szczecin, Kołobrzeg, and Gdańsk, were leveled, with slogans about returning what was Polish the official excuse. These dug-up graves and smashed crypts should be added to the panorama of the postwar period.

But these were not the most spectacular examples of "looting fever." On September 28, 1946, while the peasant "diggers" were ploughing through the fields of Treblinka, a train crashed at the Łódź Kaliska station. Twenty-one people were killed and more than forty injured. The mass of people waiting on the platform went at the victims—not to help them but to rob them. But available sources tell us nothing about the victims' ethnic origins.

CAUSES AND CONSEQUENCES

Looting both grew out of wartime demoralization and worsened it. The deputy commander of the Provincial Citizens' Militia in Lower Silesia reported in November 1945:

> A person arriving in Lower Silesia is struck by the moral gangrene which has attacked everyone everywhere. It is there among prosecutors, starosts, in the provincial administration, on all levels of the administrative and court apparatus, and in all social strata. To this is added the wave of people who come here only to steal whatever they can and take it to central Poland. Bribery is a common phenomenon, as everything everywhere can be had for money. Looting, or actually the theft of public property, is virtually an element in the air people breathe here. People have completely lost their basic ethical sense.[98]

Looting became an element of the air, of the postwar lifestyle. Outside official debates among the intelligentsia, few thought of looting as something bad. On the contrary, items acquired this way were a source of pride, and people showed them off to each other.[99] Handing them out in the Regained Territories played a crucial role in building social ties, often of the patron-client kind.[100] Furniture, apartments, horses, and all other needed items were given by the mayor to the Polish Workers' Party secretary, by the Citizens' Militia commander to the mayor, and by the mayor to the very necessary doctors and teachers, and the Soviet commander also got his share. Thus arrangements, constellations, and connections created society. In central Poland, successful escapades to the "Wild West" were viewed as evidence of manly resourcefulness and cleverness. Looting shaped the culture of daily life, its value system, material culture, and free time. A ditty to the tune of a mazurka went, "One more looting today/We'll fill the car/One more fur for Krysia/And on we go so far."[101]

Looting undermined the purpose of work and corrupted people. Now it did not pay to work well or to work at all when it took only minor effort to live in relative affluence. Many civil servants in the Regained Territories walked out of their jobs: who wants to sit behind a desk as "looting fever" rages outside? Breathing the air with its looting element also weakened immunity to other crimes. The obvious question is: were looting not as widespread, would it have been possible for militia officers to barge into the Jewish community building on Planty Street in Kielce—launching a pogrom—with robbery as their focal goal? Were their colleagues in Lower Silesia not looting with impunity?

The "fever" was helped along by the passing front, followed by chaos and weakness of the controlling institutions. Germany's surrender gave many Poles a feeling of victors' impunity. The moment of suspension, relaxation, and interregnum guaranteed almost total anonymity. According to Philip Zimbardo, when all the members of a group cease to function as individuals, "their mental functioning changes: they live in an expanded-present moment that makes past and future distant and irrelevant. Feelings dominate reason, and action dominates reflection."[102] As a result, the situations that were observed during looting may have occurred more easily: people mindlessly wrecked buildings, madly competed for abandoned possessions, and dug up graves. "An amok reigned in those 'Regained Territories.' Even people who are not dumb destroyed everything. Maybe as revenge on the Germans, for the years of the occupation? I could feel myself that if I came upon a pretty German window, I would have to smash it," a National Military Union man serving in the Olsztyn region remembered years later.[103]

The thirst for vengeance on the recent killers, even bordering on destructive madness, fueled looting, especially in its first stage. Jan Chodakowski, a prisoner of the Mauthausen-Gusen concentration camp in Austria, went to the nearby town of Linz with some friends on the day after US troops liberated the camp. "We walk to Linz, we cross a bridge, through the train station, we reach a shop. We look, it's a deli, we immediately smash it, go in, take out the food, all outside, we steal what we can. We picked some, then I look and the Austrians are also coming and taking it.... We simply roamed around. Smashed warehouses, shops."[104]

The spectacle of thousands of Poles clawing at others' property can be explained by the moral downfall that had taken place during the war and occupation. Yet looting predates the Second World War and is born of chaos. It happened in Warsaw in September 1939 prior to the Germans' arrival. It happened in Jedwabne and other small towns of the region and in the Eastern Borderlands in July 1941, before the German occupation could have its demoralizing effect. But on the other hand, we cannot ignore the importance of the five-year-plus education in thieving the Poles received. Its most important lesson was: there is a war, you are living outside the confines of good and evil, so switch off your ethics. The scale of the postwar "looting plague" should be explained with the earlier lessons of the plundering of ghettos in 1942. Red Army troops contributed to the education in looting.[105] The "trophy mood" that Polish soldiers were the first to adopt inevitably also spread to the population. No one could avoid noticing the Soviet transports overflowing with German property heading east. A private letter reported on this in August 1945: "Theft and bribery are thriving from top to bottom.... Over 5 years people have got used to stealing with impunity, so they are stealing from each other, and this is called looting.... They take others' rags en masse.... In the areas taken from the Germans the local Poles and the new settlers are also being harmed."[106]

The wave of plunder would not have become a tsunami had it not been for the resettlement of the German population from the Regained Territories, which left behind what was a fortune to the Poles. Incidents of shoes and even socks being taken off the feet of dead Wehrmacht troops were not very rare in the battlefields of Normandy in the summer of 1944. In France, even "upstanding citizens" took furniture out of homes abandoned by Germans or by French collaborators.[107] And yet the looting in western Europe, where the Germans did not abandon their property, cannot be compared to what happened on the Oder and the Baltic. There, the precondition for looting, ownerless property, did not exist. Looting did happen in the Sudetenland, albeit on a smaller scale, but there, as we know, the Germans were forced out of their homes. Another consideration is that as a whole the populations of France, Belgium, Denmark, and the Czech lands were much more prosperous than the Poles, and they did not want others' used bedding, clothes, or shoes. In other words, they were unfamiliar with the "vision of a world of limited goods."

A woman living in Płońsk wrote on August 23, 1945, "Everyone needs to steal today, since honest wages are not enough even to buy food. That's why those who don't have a conscience and don't care what anyone else thinks have enough to get drunk and for other luxuries, while the honest person is croaking of hunger."[108]

Without a doubt, poverty was one of looting's most important driving forces. Were it not for the shortages of shoes, clothes, sewing machines, bicycles, furniture, and radios, no one would have undertaken these risky expeditions. No one would have ripped handles out of doors, pulled windows out of their frames, or demolished ovens to get at their racks. The wartime and postwar looting was a specific reaction of those who were excluded during the 1930s crisis, condemned to living in dark cellars, and persistently unemployed, and then during the war reduced to the role of *Untermenschen*. And in the postwar economic instability, with unemployment and starvation wages, plunder was the only available means of support for thousands of people. The expression frequently used then and in all the earlier "gold rushes" was that this would be the only time in a person's life when they could get rich quickly, to "catch up" and to "make a deal." Stanisław Łach adds another interpretation, this one in the crowd psychology of irrational behavior, which is sometimes summarized as: you cannot hesitate, because the hungry hounds will catch up with you.[109] The looters seemed to be operating under the motto "don't stop, don't wait, just steal."[110]

The sphere of the imagination was also important, as the legends making the rounds about Poland's "Canada"—that is, the Regained Territories—included stories about swift climbs from homeless to millionaire. The new regime's propaganda also contributed to the myth of the Regained Territories as the land of plenty; it promoted the successful settling of the Regained Territories as a solution to most social problems and to give itself legitimacy. Newspaper stories about abandoned towns filled with a wealth of goods and of farms impatient for new owners acted as a magnet. An inspector noted that the expectations set off by this, which could not come true for everyone, pushed people to steal. He reported in August 1945:

> The propaganda presented Lower Silesia as a land of milk and honey, it shouted that there are fully furnished and equipped luxury villas waiting with open doors for those who will be so kind as to take possession of them, that there is plenty of everything, one need only go and take it. And people went to this Wonderland with this attitude—and they were disappointed. Yes, there are villas, but they are occupied by germans [*sic*], there is food but in cafeterias. They wanted to have everything, straight away, because the press articles were promising it to them, but instead . . . this is why people started to loot, so as not to go home empty-handed, and this is how it started. The germs of looting lie in the bad, unsophisticated propaganda.[111]

Or there is the interpretation inspired by nature. After a fire, according to nature's ancient rhythm, you have to return to life, make things right after the destruction. This is what people said then. Could the rush to loot to some degree come from the rush to life?

The "looting fever" began to come down in the spring and summer of 1946. People continued to loot but much less. The progress of the settlement process was the cure. It became more and more difficult to find living quarters that were not already occupied by Poles. The sources of looting began to dry out. The authorities' roundups at train stations had been effective,[112] as had been the combing through squares and markets, confiscating looted items and punishing arrested looters, which included sending them to work camps. In the autumn of 1945, Wrocław was cordoned off and guards were placed at the city gates to search everyone leaving town. Objects that were not accompanied by "red cards," special government permits, were confiscated, and those carrying them landed in a "concentration camp for looters." The authorities threatened to put drivers carrying the wares in them, too, and to confiscate their drivers' licenses and cars, regardless of who owned them.[113] Since acquiring the necessary documents in corrupt postwar Poland was easy[114] despite these sanctions, in March 1946 Minister for Regained Territories Władysław Gomułka reduced the group of people issuing permits to himself.[115] Clearly, he did not trust even his closest colleagues, at least on this matter. In May 1946, he decided that the stick alone was not enough and produced a carrot, a ruling to reward those who contributed to uncovering possessions illegally exported from the Regained Territories.[116]

Transporting furniture to central Poland became more difficult. Corrupt civil servants were now penalized. To use a metaphor, the government began to put in windows. But the looting tradition did not die out. Justyna Kowalska-Leder is right to argue that the looting that started in 1939 formed the Poles' lack of respect for others' property, especially state property, teaching people to accept wheeling-dealing or laying their hands on hard-to-get goods, which was often ordinary theft, all without burdening their conscience.[117] Taking virtually anything that could be useful or have any value home from work on a mass scale is evidence of the long afterlife of the culture of looting.

NOTES

1. The original version of this chapter appeared as M. Zaremba, "Gorączka szabru."
2. "Jadę na szaber," *Dziennik Powszechny*, July 18, 1945.
3. Writings about it include Urbanek, "Wielki szaber," *Polityka*, April 29, 1995; Cichy, "1945—koniec i początek," *Gazeta Wyborcza*, May 26, 1995; Kowalska-Leder, "Szaber," 334–41.
4. Foster, "Peasant Society and the Image of Limited Good," 293–315. For more on Foster's ideas see Zaremba, "O polskiej banalności zła."
5. D. Stola's remarks during a discussion at the Polish Academy of Sciences Institute of Political Studies, March 22, 2009.
6. Prus, *Kroniki*, vol. 2, 24, 330.
7. E. J. Hobsbawm notes that the majority of the peasants did not necessarily hate city dwellers, but at least distrusted them. Hobsbawm, *Bandits*, 17.
8. Prus, *Kroniki*, vol. 18, 460–63.
9. Kalicki, "Z deszczu pod klucz."
10. Misiuna, "Pionki w latach II wojny światowej—wspomnienia," 184.
11. Wierzbicki, *Polacy i Białorusini w zaborze sowieckim*; Wierzbicki, *Polacy i Żydzi w zaborze sowieckim*.
12. Klukowski, *Zamojszczyzna*, vol. 1: *1918–1943*, 98.
13. Libionka, "Polska ludność chrześcijańska wobec eksterminacji Żydów—dystrykt lubelski," 307.
14. Sebyłowa, *Notatki z prawobrzeżnej Warszawy*, 46.
15. Urbanek, *Lęk i strach warszawiaków wobec zagrożeń Września 1939 r.*, 94.
16. Urbanek, 95.
17. Grzesiuk, *Boso, ale w ostrogach*, 172.
18. Landau, *Kronika lat wojny i okupacji*, vol. 1, 18.
19. Wróblewska, *Listy z Polski*, 105. B. Brzostek told me about this book.
20. Landau, *Kronika lat wojny i okupacji*, 18.
21. Sebyłowa, *Notatki z prawobrzeżnej Warszawy*, 46.
22. Zimbardo, *The Lucifer Effect*, 219.
23. Machcewicz, "Wokół Jedwabnego," 39, 41.
24. Machcewicz, 39, 41.
25. Chustecki, *Byłem sołtysem w latach okupacji*, 66, 70, 73.
26. Machcewicz, "Wokół Jedwabnego," 39, 41.
27. Gross, *Neighbors*, 90.
28. Machcewicz, "Wokół Jedwabnego," 40.
29. Z. Klukowski, *Zamojszczyzna*, op. cit., vol. 1, 304, 305, 307, 310.
30. Libionka, "Biedni AK-owcy opisują Zagładę na prowincji," 118–29.
31. See Panz, "Zagłada sztetl Grice," 32–37.
32. Melchior, *Uciekinierzy z gett po "stronie aryjskiej" na prowincji dystryktu warszawskiego—sposoby przetrwania*, 331.
33. As soon as the buildings in the Warsaw ghetto emptied out, bands of jackals moved in, over those ghastly walls, to steal senselessly belongings covered in blood and soaked in the smell of corpses. The police, of all kinds, which had been the first to reach out their foul and greedy paws for these pitiful scraps, looks on patronizingly as society's scum follows in its footsteps, looting and stealing whatever it can get at.... Nowadays, groups of adolescents, even 12–14-year-old kids, trail in the streets of Warsaw, shamelessly peddling the stolen objects. Most disturbing is the fact that the public at large does not react to this repulsive sight, and all sorts of gentlemen and dames eagerly purchase "for nothing" some unfortunate rags, plates, paintings, etc. It is a pity to see that not only the lowly, people with a low intellectual level, but also individuals with distinctions, or at least those who aspire to the intelligentsia, soil themselves by filching Jewish property. They are all sorts of administrators of Jewish homes, who are "securing" valuable objects, as well as those who with their "passes" for the ghetto don't miss any exceptional opportunities . . . to sully themselves for the rest of their lives. We are getting reports from all over Poland about similar cases of the collective lack or atrophy of honesty and humane feeling. ("Niebezpieczeństwo wewnętrzne," *Agencja Prasowa*, October 7, 1942.)
34. Libionka, "Polska ludność chrześcijańska wobec eksterminacji Żydów—dystrykt lubelski," 310.
35. Młynarczyk, "Bestialstwo z urzędu," 368.
36. Anczarski, *Kronikarskie zapisy z lat cierpień i grozy w Małopolsce Wschodniej*.
37. Anczarski, 256.
38. Kersten and Szarota, *Wieś polska 1939–1948*, 18.
39. I have intentionally omitted the seizures of Jewish property, such as workshops, homes, and land lots, by the "new bourgeoisie." This was done through official channels and had nothing in common with the looting of abandoned property. Similarly, I will not treat the taking over of German farms and homes by Polish repatriates as plunder, strictly speaking.
40. Machcewicz, "Tajemnica liberatora."
41. "Obrazki ulicy," *Gazeta Lubelska*, October 27, 1944.
42. *Gazeta Lubelska*, July 29, 1944.
43. Tomaszewski, *Lwów 1940–1944*, 202.
44. Loth, *Wspomnienia Kochanowskie*, 15.

45. *Dziennik Powszechny*, May 19, 1945.
46. Ziemba, *Czas przełomu*, 129.
47. Sitek and Trębacz, "Życie codzienne w Łodzi w 1945 r.," 173.
48. Krzywicka, *Wyznania gorszycielki*, 397.
49. "Warszawa żyje," *Życie Warszawy*, January 20, 1945.
50. The deputy commander of the Citizens' Militia for Warsaw reported on January 26:

> There is only one way in which the militia are not doing their job: they cannot stop the mass robberies and thefts being carried out by criminal elements from the outskirts of the city and neighboring villages, this symptom exists as a result of the absence of rightful owners of the cellars that have not burned and unexamined nooks and crannies of surviving apartments. These robberies are of a mass nature and because of this the authorities have issued several orders about the prohibition on entering the city of Warsaw, prohibition on new arrivals to settle there, prohibition on transporting things and furniture, etc. (AIPN 01265/379, k. 3.)

51. A report on the activities of operations groups of political-educational officers sent to Warsaw in September 1944: "The citizens' militia, a majority of whom took part in the robberies under various pretexts, was an additional obstacle to fighting civilian marauding" (AAN, PPR 295/IX-353, k. 1).
52. "Żądamy surowych kar dla rabusiów," *Życie Warszawy*, February 8, 1945.
53. Dąbrowska, "Z Bielan do Zalesia," vol. 1, 245.
54. Stola, discussion at the Institute of Political Studies, Polish Academy of Sciences, March 22, 2009.
55. Borycka, "Exodus z Powiśla," 192.
56. Kopecki et al., *Kronika rodzin Kopeckich i Turnauów*.
57. *Franciszka Starowieyskiego opowieść o końcu świata czyli reforma rolna*, 115, 116.
58. "Zaraza," *Głos Narodu*, August 29, 1945.
59. "Skończyć z szabrem," *Dziennik Bałtycki*, June 1, 1945.
60. "Nagonka na szabrowników," *Ilustrowany Kurier Polski*, November 17, 1945.
61. Osmańczyk, "Szabrownicy," *Dziennik Polski*, April 7, 1945.
62. Ziemba, *Czas przełomu*, 213.
63. *Wieś polska 1939–1948*, vol. 1, 157.
64. Chmielinka village, Nowy Tomyśl District:

> In the watershed days of January, when the Germans were leaving in a panic and the Russians hadn't yet arrived, there was a hiatus of less than a day, and anarchy in the village. The Poles, farmhands who hadn't fled with their [German] employers, took advantage of this. They "compensated" for all their pain and scarcities they had had to suffer from the German farm owners all occupation long, now taking what they could of the German things, primarily clothing, shoes, underwear, bicycles and other things, carrying it all to their families nearby. They even "retaliated" against the school, smashing locked doors, desks and cupboards with axes, searching for valuables. (*Wieś polska 1939–1948*, vol. 1, 418.)

65. *Wieś polska 1939–1948*, vol. 1, 647.
66. Weber, *Kobiety wypędzone*, 65, 66.
67. Zientara-Malewska, *Śladami twardej drogi*, 247, 248.
68. Konopińska, *Tamten wrocławski rok*, 148, 149.
69. Konopińska, 73.
70. AAN, MAP 2443. K. Janczewski, Sprawozdanie z lustracji Śląska Opolskiego oraz województwa Dolnośląskiego, 15–25 IX 1945, k. 41.
71. AAN, MAP 2443, k. 40. Ibid.
72. AAN, MAP 2443, k. 31. J. Zubek, Sprawozdanie z przeprowadzonej inspekcji, August 18, 1945.
73. Konopińska, *Tamten wrocławski rok*, 63, 95.
74. Wróbel, *Przystanek Gliwice*, 11.
75. Dróżdż and Milczarek, *Zakochani w Pomorzu*, 24.
76. Urbanek, *Wielki szaber*.
77. AAN, Komisja Specjalna 1079, k. 2. Akta sprawy przeciwko Czesławowi Borkowi.
78. AAN, Komisja Specjalna 1088, k. 1, 18. Akta dochodzenia przeciwko Krzywińskiej Ludwice i Jacek Wiktorii.
79. AAN, Komisja Specjalna 760, k. 8–10. Akta sprawy.
80. Ropelewski, *Pionierskie lato*, 172.
81. Urbanek, *Wielki szaber*.
82. Ziemba, *Czas przełomu*, 215.
83. The reportage *Zakochani w Pomorzu* (*In Love with Pomerania*) offers a very exaggerated picture:

> Now we have a brand-new graduate, a rare book enthusiast, with the face of an ascete, his woodpecker's nose lengthening from a thirst for knowledge. His enormous glasses set in American-made frames conceal a pig's eyes, cunning and sly. At first, he surprises with his speech and his knowledge of the topic, creating the impression that he is a museum curator or an art and culture manager. He rustles the heaps of parchment and 13th-century Bibles, his sticky, alert fingers multiply like a centipede's legs. He grabs, loads, ties up.... You want to laugh and to vomit, then you are tempted to go up to him, spit in his infected little eyes, grab him by the collar and hurl him out of the third-floor window into the trash, so that this vulture will stop soiling the precious tomes grayed over the centuries. (Dróżdż and Milczarek, *Zakochani w Pomorzu*, 25.)

84. "Szabrownicy kultury," *Dziennik Polski*, August 6, 1945.
85. AAN, Komisja Specjalna 3155, k. 66. Akta dochodzeń przeciwko Ziewcowi Stanisławowi.
86. AAN, Komisja Specjalna 1094, k. 1. Akta dochodzenia.
87. See Samsonowicz, *Wspomnienia o Straży Akademickiej Politechniki we Wrocławiu*; Marzecki, *Tym gorzej dla faktów*, 18, 19.
88. Cf. Priebe, "Szkoła szabru," 79–91.
89. Communist leader Bolesław Bierut himself confirmed this. During a meeting of the Politburo of the Central Committee of the Polish Workers' Party, he said, "Abuse is a fact. There is a tendency to treat the security office as a source of personal enrichment." Kochański, *Protokoły posiedzeń Biura Politycznego KC PPR 1944–1945*, 85.
90. Szwagrzyk, "Przestępstwa funkcjonariuszy Urzędów Bezpieczeństwa na Dolnym Śląsku w latach 1945–1953," 196–97.
91. *Wieś polska 1939–1948*, vol. 1, 91.

92. Peters, "Jasło—miasto śmierci," *Dziennik Polski*, March 10, 1945.

93. AIPN, MBP 3378, k. 75 b. Specjalne doniesienie dot. działalności dywersyjnych band.

94. Rusiniak, *Obóz zagłady Treblinka II w pamięci społecznej (1943–1989)*, 29–33.

95. Eglantowicz, "Treblinka—niesamowita kopalnia," *Dziennik Ludowy*, August 30, 1945.

96. "Poszukiwaczy skarbów wystraszyło widmo śmierci," *Echo Wieczorne*, December 23, 1946.

97. Żukrowski, *Zsyp ze śmietnika pamięci*, 85.

98. AIPN, KG MO 35/922, k. 58, 59. Raport sytuacyjny Z-cy Komendanta Wojew. MO do spraw polit.-wych. na Dolnym Śląsku za czas od dn. 25 października 45 r. do dn. 10 listopada 45.

99. "Those who would not stoop to steal a mere zloty coin, shamelessly plunder thousands of zlotys' worth of objects. And they're not embarrassed about their actions, on the contrary, declare proudly that they have managed to loot this or that" ("Zaraza," *Głos Narodu*, August 29, 1945).

100. Cf. Priebe, *Szkoła szabru*.

101. Urbanek, *Wielki szaber*.

102. Zimbardo, *The Lucifer Effect*, 219.

103. Karwowski "'Newada': Ludzie akcji specjalnej," 21.

104. AHM, reminiscences of Jan Chodakowski. Interviewed by T. Gleb.

105. British and US troops also served as models. A daily carried an interesting account of British behavior:

> The British attitude toward the Germans is a very curious thing. They go back and forth between indulging them and beating them, destroying their possessions, burning and sowing panic among them to which they bring along Poles and other foreigners. The way they do it is that in the evening a few soldiers and foreigners drive to nearby villages and farms in convertibles. As they draw close, they suddenly start to shoot at the windows of houses at items they can see, such as mirrors, clocks, chandeliers, hanging paintings, and every now and again throw a grenade into the courtyard (an old one, just to scare people). There is bedlam, noise, chaos, people running around, shouting, and they leave. They encourage us to collect old German grenades because they can be useful next time.... The English keep reminding us that if we want to pay the Germans for our suffering, we have to take something or destroy something, that we must do it now before the administration comes. (Jakubaszek, *Mój ostatni rok wojny*, 454, 455.)

106. AIPN, MBP 3378, k. 104. Specjalne doniesienie.

107. Beevor, *D-Day*, 210, 296, 374.

108. AIPN, MBP 3378, k. 103. Specjalne doniesienie.

109. Łach, *Osadnictwo miejskie na ziemiach odzyskanych w latach 1945–1950*, 219.

110. "Kto pierwszy, ten lepszy," a short item in *Dziennik Polski* on July 26, 1946, discussed resettlement in the Regained Territories but also referred to a more general trend.

111. AAN, MAP 2443, k. 31. J. Zubek, Sprawozdanie z przeprowadzonej inspekcji, August 18, 1945.

112. For an account of one such roundup, see Babisiak, "Na tropach przestępców i szabrowników. Jak pracuje Milicja Obywatelska—Nocna obława," *Ziemia Pomorska*, September 29, 1945.

113. "Wrocław walczy z szabrownictwem, wywiad J. Podolskiego z wiceprezydentem Wrocławia A. Górnym," *Dziennik Polski*, October 3, 1945.

114. "The authorities have declared an unsparing war on the raging looting. During a roundup in a train station it transpired that the passengers were overwhelmingly looters, who unfortunately provided evidence that they were on official work trips. One of them even had a document issued by some starost testifying that he was traveling to Wrocław 'in search of his missing hogs.' The 'plundered' items, which were mostly undergarments and clothing, were confiscated and donated to the District Social Services, and the plunderers were directed to work on fixing roads" ("Nieubłagana walka z szabrownictwem," *Dziennik Polski*, July 11, 1945).

115. Kochański, *Polska 1944–1991*, 139.

116. Kochański, 146.

117. Kowalska-Leder, *Szaber*, 341.

8

OUTLAWS

"THE DISHONORED SOLDIERS' PEASANT WAR"

After the war ended, most Poles feared nothing more than an attack by bandits.[1] One of the most powerful emotions of the time was the fear of a brutal raid, which would often end with murder. Someone might say: but this kind of crime tops the list of fears in Poland today, so what's new?[2] But the important difference between then and now is that in 1945 the likelihood of assault and robbery was very high and the sense of security virtually nil. Excerpts from private letters intercepted by the Wartime Censorship Office reveal the physical dimension of this fear, which people felt "day and night":

Village of Turobin, Biłgoraj District, Lublin Province, June 1, 1945: "Dear husband, if only you knew how much fear I'm living with. Things are not going well here, every week the gang comes and smashes people. They take pigs, horses and grains. They haven't come to me yet, but I expect that they will and take away my cows. Things are going badly here, everyone lives in fear."[3]

Izbica on the Wieprz, June 5, 1945: "Huge gangs of thieves are roaming our area now. As evening approaches, a person starts to tremble like a leaf because he can't be sure that the thieves won't be visiting him. You can't dress nicely, you must wear your worst dress. Life has been like this for 4 months. We will go mad if things go on like this. Janek had such an assault: they robbed him of everything and also beat him, poured cold water on him and beat him again."[4]

A letter from the area of Częstochowa, August 11, 1945: "Thieves stole underwear, clothing and two bicycles from us. We were not in bed yet when they came, we were sitting outside, Michałek and Bronek Kołodziej were still here, so they took the bicycle. There were 6 of them, they chased us into the house and told us all to lie on our beds, so we wouldn't see anything."[5]

Near Okocim, August 20, 1945: "You will hear bad things about this place now, dear son, because thieves roam at night, no longer just to one house but to 4, and they take what they like. They took Serafin, Władek's, horse, they went to Komin's house; they took all they could from Palenko's, Rajkowa Janek's and beat everybody up. Janka is covered in bruises, we're all scared because they won't tell them anything [unclear—MZ]. So now when a person goes to bed he's afraid because it's not enough that they robbed them, they will also thrash them."

A letter from a village in Oleśno District, Silesia (today Opole) Province, August 21, 1945: "I'm reporting that they are plundering here, nearly every night there are all kinds of robberies, we're scared. A week after you left, they came to Konik, Marcin, in the night, took away a cow and a horse. They saw them taking them, began to shout, and the bandits began to shoot terribly, so what could be done? And so we're scared."

A wife to her husband in the army, village of Sztobrów, Brzesko District, August 21, 1945: "Dear Husband, mom was robbed today. They took her last cow. Husband, they came to us, too, and they beat each other a lot. And I was in the house with mom. She is barely alive and very terrified from this fear. This happens all the time."

Letter from Chełm Lubelski, August 26, 1945: "There is no good sleep at night, everyone sleeps in fear that thieves will steal something from the cow barn, a cow or a piglet and, finally, of them coming into the house and stealing everything there, clothing and household goods. This is what's going on here and in our area there are lots of thieves and bandits, roving during the day and at night."[6]

SOCIOLOGICAL THEORIES OF CRIME

Numerous theories analyze the roots of criminality.[7] The classic is Eric Hobsbawm's *Bandits*.[8] Hobsbawm argued that premodern outlaws usually came from the borderline of peasant societies, and as they lived by robbery and theft they became popular heroes. Tales were told that they took from the rich and gave to the poor. Some launched popular uprisings.[9]

Was Poland's postwar banditry also an expression of class ferment? It was not what got Ogień (Fire) the bandit going in Podhale, the Polish highlands; legends were told about him. The peasants did support the destruction of documents about delivery quotas in district offices during the war and after, in which underground units participated—much like tax documents, a symbol of class exploitation, which became a target of peasant aggression during the many *jacqueries* on the eve of the French Revolution. It is also not out of the question that the hatred of landless stable hands, who had been the lowest rung on the social ladder in interwar Poland, was one of the reasons for their attacks on manor houses and on rich peasants. Notable in the postwar militia reports is the bands' special interest in the minor entrepreneurs, most of them shopkeepers, in small towns. This could be interpreted in two ways: as a manifestation of villagers' hostility toward urban dwellers or, more likely, because more was worth stealing in towns. There is therefore no clear evidence that postwar banditry was especially deeply rooted in class hatred. Nonetheless, numerous sources document Robin Hood–style actions. What to make of them? For instance, on September 20, 1946, a group of forty people in uniform, including one woman, stopped two trains in Bąk station, one from Gdynia to Bydgoszcz and the other from Bydgoszcz to Gdynia. Two of their cars were carrying UNRRA parcels. The thieves took some of the parcels and distributed the rest among passengers.[10] There is no denying that incidents of this kind took place, but peasants were still more likely to be bandits' victims than bandits, and thus it was not class revolt that engendered postwar banditry.

The theory of anomie, which finds the roots of criminal behavior in the upsetting of the traditional axiological order, goes further and fits into the situation of the Second World War. Also helpful is the theory of control, which states that the growth of criminality is brought on by a weakening of social and physical control, which otherwise reins in criminal behaviors. The postwar weakness of the state apparatus, a lack of authority figures, and society's overall uprooting entailed, to use Florian Znaniecki's term, "the decay of the active moral control."[11] The pervasive disrespect for human life stemmed from Germany's policies aimed at exterminating the Jewish and Polish populations and from the omnipresent feeling of endangerment. All this led to deep changes in people's thinking, an atrophy of empathy and the destruction of moral connections, which aided criminal behavior. At the same time, fear of punishment evaporated and banditry brought profits.

Postwar banditry had other roots. To rob someone it was necessary to use violence, or at least give the impression of being capable of inflicting violence. A firearm was useful for show, even though the *szmalcowniks*, other than the navy-blue policemen, carried none. Even in late 1944 some burglars were armed with nothing more than sticks.[12] But banditry would not have become a social epidemic had it not been for the enormous numbers of weapons left from operation "Tempest" and the passing of the front.[13] A letter dated August 20, 1945, reported, "There are very many robberies and bandits in Poland because now all those young people have rifles left from the war. They got their Brownings from the army and they go out to rob, and the Polish police are afraid of them."[14]

Throughout history, the invention of a new weapon (such as the multi-chamber Colt) introduced new social behaviors, as owning one in itself tempted a person to use it. But now there also came psychological change and greater aggression in relations among people during the war.

HISTORICAL EXAMPLES OF THE THEORY OF BANDITRY: THE REVOLUTION OF 1905 AND THE POST–WORLD WAR I PERIOD

Banditry emerges out of the chaos of war and the growing power vacuum. Civil war and the weakness of institutions responsible for keeping legal order create excellent conditions for the spread of banditry. Similarly, security worsened in the seventeenth century after the Polish-Lithuanian Commonwealth's nonstop wars with Sweden, Moscow, the Cossacks, Sweden again, Moscow, and Turkey.[15] Other examples include the comparable upsurge of crime during and after the revolution of 1905 and in the wake of the First World War.

The progressive anarchy, chaos, and weakening of the Russian civilian administration during the revolution of 1905 made it easier to disobey the law, regardless of the degree of urbanization.[16] Crime spread in the cities, and there were home invasions, while in the countryside manor houses were robbed and in villages horses were the bounty of choice. Peasant kangaroo courts formed to try captured bandits.[17] In Warsaw there was a workers' pogrom of pimps, human traffickers, and bordello owners.[18] We can interpret these trials and lynchings as a case of social control galvanizing when the state fails to manage society.

Crimes of this kind multiplied during the First World War. Warsaw, occupied by the Germans in 1915 and facing economic ruin, was plunged into food rationing and mass unemployment.[19] Neither the new Polish police nor the German criminal police was able to halt the anarchy, and the situation in the areas where the Russian civil war was being fought looked even worse. The incessantly streaming troops confiscated and stole, adding to the chaos of power changing hands.[20] Banditry both contributed to creating the chaos and was born of it, as all the sides used it as a weapon. It especially grew in central Poland when the new structures of the fledgling Polish state could not be effective as it replaced the partitioning powers' departing administrations. Walenty Górski, a Polish Army deserter who in 1919, together with his three brothers, started a gang, which at its peak had fifty-four members, became well known. The gang roamed on the outskirts of Warsaw and in Łódź Province and was responsible for 140 robberies, while its boss was responsible for 36 murders, some preceded by torture.[21] The crime wave did not begin to recede until a few years after the Polish-Soviet War.[22]

WARTIME ORIGINS OF POSTWAR CRIME

The same scenario followed in the Second World War and in its wake, but it was different in three respects. First, a vast partisan movement survived well into 1945, when some soldiers became bandits. Second, large numbers of Citizens' Militia and Security Office functionaries also became corrupt, in contrast to the civil service, which had maintained its ethos of honesty after the First World War. Third, crime was much more widespread than in 1918–22. To some historians, it should be placed second on the list of threats to the nation's existence, right behind the occupying powers' policy of extermination. Not only did the native criminals physically endanger the Poles but so did their attacks against Germans or German institutions and enterprises, as they led to repressions by the Nazi security apparatus against innocent locals.[23] A mass execution of more than one hundred Poles in Wawer, near Warsaw, in late December 1939 came in retaliation for the murders of two German noncommissioned officers by Poles with criminal records. It was among the first in the Germans' regular use of the principle of collective responsibility. Poles knew what to do when Germans were attacked nearby: flee, since retaliation was inevitable, and the Germans would execute people or burn down a village. Thus, it was not only a representative of the "master race" but at times also the common thief or bandit who personified fear. The fact that fear lived on after the war proved its power. As Zygmunt Klukowski noted after a Soviet soldier was killed by accident in April 1945, "People were naturally terrified because there would certainly be retaliation, as usually happens after such incidents."[24]

The crime curve began to go up after the German invasion of September 1939. The release of hundreds of repeat offenders from prisons that month contributed to it significantly, as did the appearance of large quantities of firearms for sale. Now the most violent kinds of crimes rose markedly. According to Polish police data, twenty-two robberies occurred in a single month in 1940 in Puławy District, and there were thirty-seven in November 1940 in Radzyń District.[25] The wave came down in late 1940–early 1941 but rose again with the German-Soviet war and the resultant slackening of behavior. But the arrival in the forests of many Soviet prisoners of war who had fled Nazi captivity turned out to be the most important factor affecting crime statistics. Desperate, they would attack villagers to obtain food. Often, according to the Home Army's *Biuletyn Informacyjny*, they also raped and murdered.[26] The launch of operation "Reinhardt" in 1942 led Jews, too, to seek help in the forests, and in Lublin region alone they formed dozens of armed units of various sizes.[27] Suffering from hunger and exhaustion, they would also sometimes attack peasants very brutally,[28] making hatred of the Jews escalate, which worsened their already tragic situation. This fear lived on. A memoir by a villager from Fiukówka, near Łuków, Garwolin, and Radzyń Podlaski in Mazovia, was submitted for a March 1948 contest. He recalled:

> Russians and Jews needed the countryside to acquire clothes and food, the partisans also often abused their power and the bandits stole. The countryside literally turned into a Sodom and Gomorrah. Everyone got goose bumps as night fell because it was difficult to know who would visit them in the middle of the night and what rules he would dictate. The situation became such that no one had decent shoes or clothes because if the bandits didn't take them away, the mice would drag them into some hole and eat them, not to mention money, hogs, undergarments, etc. Things became normal again toward the end of the occupation.[29]

We should not rush to conclude from the fear people could remember that most Jews living outside the ghettos were thieves. Across Poland, they would come at night to beg for food (which naturally people did not remember as well), and not as violent bandits.[30]

Some peasants' robbing and murdering of hiding Jews had a far greater impact on the birth of postwar banditry. It became surprisingly easy to steal everything a defenseless Jew owned after the Germans began their mass destruction of the Jewish people in 1942, especially since such robbery was often rewarded by a German gendarme with a bottle of vodka or a kilogram of sugar. The Germans not only created an auspicious atmosphere for this kind of crime but also demonstrated how it was done. We know from Jan Grabowski's work[31] about how the Germans organized hunts for Jews in hiding, *Judenjagd*. It was usually done by a handful or a dozen gendarmes supported by navy-blue Polish policemen, sometimes accompanied by volunteer firemen and peasants thrown together into village guards. The order would come from the top, a village administrator who had been told by the local gendarme or Gestapo man to bring together some "beaters." This request was made legitimate by the presence of men in uniform, who were associated with authority and power and guaranteed a high degree of compliance. According to Barbara Engelking,[32] taking part in this type of hunt, as well as the spontaneous individual murdering of Jews in hiding for profit, wiped out the mental resistance against this type of crime, later also against non-Jews. We may therefore speculate that some of the wartime and postwar bandits had earlier been the Germans' assistants and collaborators in murdering Jews. These lessons yielded immediate results.

The year 1943 was the pinnacle of crime-induced fear. The Government Delegate's Office deemed banditry one of the "most serious and dangerous plagues in the Polish provinces."[33] Everyone, including inhabitants of manor houses, wealthier farm owners, entrepreneurs, and farm and forest administrators, had reason to be apprehensive. According to a representative of the Central Welfare Council, in Serokomla village in Podlaskie Province, "the nervous atmosphere has attained a pathological level [emphasis in the original—MZ], as a woman gave the impression of going insane with fear."[34] The never-ending invasions by bandits, who not only took away all the food and farm animals but often also raped, evoked terror.[35] In the first summer months of 1943, in the majority of districts of the General Government, at least several dozen robberies were recorded weekly.[36] The farther east one went, the greater the chaos brought on in part by bandits. Jan Chustecki, village chief of Prudno near Wołkowyska, remembered over a decade later:

> In 1943 large bands flourished here, they robbed people so much that no one was able to hold onto anything. They took everything people had: children's clothes, shoes, bedding, wool, fat. There were so many of them that when someone bought a pair of trousers or a coat in town today, tonight they would appear at his house and say "hand it over, we know you have it!" If he doesn't give it, they will grab him, beat him. Nothing could be done. It's freezing terribly, there's a blizzard, the children have to sleep in a pile of bedding by the stove, covered with sacks of oat chaff because everything else had to be hidden, saved. Some stole and others, who were closely associated with the gang, traded the stolen things.[37]

The wartime and postwar bandits can be divided into peasant, urban, and forest categories, according to where they lived, where they were active (city or countryside), and their earlier organizational connections, as well as their willingness to identify with the pro-independence underground. The criminals of all three categories had roots in the countryside. The peasant gangs were often led by people who had had military training and had been in the Polish Army, or by partisans and deserters. Chustecki writes about Józek, a onetime stable boy, who for some time fought with the partisans, "He beat up people like an executioner and raped women and girls whenever he got a chance." He killed seventeen people.[38] In 1943, a soldier who had fought against the German invaders in September 1939 and been decorated with the Virtuti Militari medal became a bandit in Węgrów District.[39]

It is noteworthy that young men engaged in all three types of banditry. Because they had no occupation and no education, they were often "freewheeling," had a strong sense of material deprivation, and thought of banditry as an easy way to get rich. Some of them may have viewed banditry as an opportunity to escape patriarchal limitations and to prove their manhood and maturity. Parents warned their son serving in the military service (August 2, 1945), "We are writing to you that there are gangs here. They steal and kill, and now . . . they also killed a young girl in Jaszczynowice, every night they rob and roam, what's going on? It's only because boys, youths stay home and steal, they should put them in the army, then this would never happen."[40]

In another letter, from Wolsztyn, someone knew who was "walking around armed" and robbing: "The thieves steal every night. They stole 5 piglets from Sinkiewiczko, but have stolen nothing from us yet. And every night the dogs bark so loud that they won't let you sleep, and they are all such thieves who walk around armed. Like Bronek Sz. and Piotr Oławka and Edek Sz. There may be more of them."[41]

THE PEASANT WAR

In the countryside during the war, the initially spontaneous and only barely organized gangs gradually became more professional and made banditry a common occupation. "Nowadays, the bands of thieves rule," read a report about Kielce region in the summer of 1945. "These are not strictly speaking gangs, but groups of individuals who live among others in daytime and at night go out for their 'prey.'"[42] In Lublin Province, there were entire "bandit" villages, as the locals called them, in which many of the men worked as robbers.[43] At times, gangs recruited members in nearby villages.[44] But family ties, which had always been strong in the countryside, grew even stronger in the war and became even more important. In this world where cynicism had replaced trust, they gave people a sense of confidence and solidarity, indispensable in the criminal profession. Peasant banditry was usually a family business, in which father and son, brothers, and brothers-in-law set out on the hunt. Someone from the area of Kalisz reported in September 1945, "One more criminal incident has been uncovered. A woman found him killed in the forest, he was from Grodziec, his name was Michał Zbanuszek, and they killed him for money, he had 20 thou. on him, he was on his way to buy a cow. He was killed by the Wieczoreks, father and son killed him."[45]

The criminals usually operated far from their own villages, perhaps out of neighborly solidarity, which would mean that local ties were still alive, and also fearing revenge. But they could not go much more than ten to fifteen kilometers away, since they usually stole farm animals and tools. To avoid being recognized, they often appeared in masks and told the victims to turn their backs or lie flat on the floor. A victim in Kraśnik, most likely a shop owner, associated the thieves' masks with the Wild West:

> I was held up by robbers, the robbery was organized by 5 ruffians wearing masks, at 11 at night. The robbery lasted over an hour. Maj the night guard and Miss Broncia, who kept on fainting when they terrorized them by putting guns to the heads and demanded 100,000, were present during the robbery. After they plundered downstairs and the cash register, we went to my apartment at gunpoint and here a search of everything began, in the bedding, cupboards, closets, attics, etc. They took blankets, my undergarments and Stefan's shirts, various things. . . . They were dressed so wonderfully with red nets on their heads, heavily armed, I thought that I had landed in Mexico at least.[46]

The bandits' victims were usually the wealthier farm owners, and in towns shop owners and merchants—anyone who had some money. It seems that no one was treated leniently, since even priests were not safe.[47] In the countryside it was impossible to keep a secret about who owned a horse, who had gone to market, or who had cash. A villager from Cyców, Lublin Province, wrote on August 14, 1945, "Father is not back from the market yet, and here the night gentlemen are already waiting for their money. They came here, took the pigs, harnesses, cash and many other things."[48]

In 1940–43, before weapons could be found scattered all over former battlefields and before criminal behaviors became established, isolated houses inhabited by solitary or old people were most vulnerable to home invasions. What mattered was not only the defenselessness of the victims but also a smaller chance of retribution. But because home invaders could not always avoid being recognized, in some regions wars raged between villages. The background to these conflicts was revenge, defending one's territory, and the traditional peasant brawls with youths from rival villages. It would start out innocently when potatoes, firewood, or a pig was taken, but over the years the violence and aggression escalated. Beating was the response to beating, violence to violence. When a suspect went into hiding, his family members were punished by whipping, their property was taken, and their buildings were set on fire. Disappointed or infuriated attackers were often capable of killing. In some places the conflict came to resemble what Eric R. Wolf calls a "peasant war."[49] It was most virulent in the Lublin region and in Rzeszów Province. A man from the village of Dębowa Kłoda in Parczew District (Lublin Province) whose farm was burned down knew who had done it: "In the night of the 10th–11th, everything we owned burned down. One building and one horse survived, everything else went up in flames. So we are left with nothing and don't know what to do. And the reason for the fire was that our enemies set fire to us, they pestered us and still do."[50] Since this was August 1945, it is possible that these enemies were Ukrainians.

A letter from Siennica, near Mińsk Mazowiecki, dated June 6, 1945, read, "Maybe they even write to you, [how things are] in our area between neighbors and colleagues. Huge hatred in the daytime... but at night, at every hour you must be prepared to die."[51]

In Pomerania, too, people called the situation war. One aspect of it was the conflict between locals and repatriates from the Eastern Territories. A wife wrote to her husband who was serving in the military, "Yesterday, we had a blessing in disguise, 4 hulks came to us and wanted to rob us. They went from cottage to cottage. They took Kaczmarek's bicycle. There are lots of stories like that here, so for a woman it's impossible to live here alone, because the locals are rebelling against the people from across the Bug River. A civil war is coming."[52]

The animosity between the repatriates coming from various parts of the country, such as Kielce region and the Eastern Territories, and the locals, who for clarity's sake were simply called Germans or Krauts, was beginning to look like a "peasant war" also in Opole region, Lower Silesia, and Masuria. Peasant raids were recorded in Masuria. People from around Grajewo, Szczuczyn, and Suwałki allegedly organized raids using more than twenty wagons each on the nearest Masurian villages, stealing possessions and animals, threshing the grains, and taking them away. One Łutaj was known as the greatest thief.[53]

Political conflicts had already worsened family and village differences during the war. One village would favor the Home Army, another the Communists or the Peasant Battalions. Banditry joined forces with hit-and-run tactics, and every year the mulishness and impetuousness driving revenge grew. The situation began to resemble the peasant countries of southern Europe, Albania, Yugoslavia, and southern Italy, where the responsibility to maintain the vendetta was passed on to all, beginning with the oldest family members. A memoirist noted that in his village more people died in this war than at the front.[54]

Some gangs claimed to belong to the underground movement and robbed villages pretending that they were collecting taxes for their armed struggle, preferably in the form of valuables and clothing. This was first mentioned in 1942.[55] The Home Army warned against such impostors,[56] but farmers continued to be told to make these contributions to the underground even after the war was over. In reality, the soi-disant partisans were thieves. A private letter mailed on August 20, 1945, implies that its author was robbed three times in only three summer months:

> So much trouble with them bandits here because they visit us often. They took our sow and a young hog in June and July when I was visiting you. Others came, ordered a 10,000 contribution from us and Jankowski. They came again, took 3,000 zlotys and 8 kg of butter, the remaining lard and meat, 4 liters of moonshine, a teapot, an electric torch, Janek's shirt, handkerchiefs, everything that had been washed. Hela and Grandma were told to turn to the wall, and he did what he wanted. So I'd be left with nothing. He smashed one of our windows facing the courtyard because we didn't hear him knocking right away.[57]

The commander in chief of the Home Army issued instructions about fighting banditry as it grew in 1943. It ordered the bands' leaders killed and, as far as possible, liquidating them totally. The instructions treated local initiatives of self-defense and a warning service seriously.[58] The Home Army's *Biuletyn Informacyjny* included reports of death sentences issued for captured bandits.[59] The underground continued to sentence criminals even after the military operations had ended. An underground unit captured two men carrying stolen property in early June 1945 near the village of Wyczółki, near Lublin. They gathered the locals and told them to take back what was theirs. The men were executed, and the local militia station was informed about it.[60] In mid-August 1945 in Białystok Province, near Zabłudowo, a unit abducted three men from their homes and executed them, attaching notes to their bodies saying that they had been punished for thefts and robberies.[61] The sources do not mention whether locals watched the executions. Other sentences were issued at the time,[62] but they did not hold back the crime wave. Contributing significantly to its spread was the disintegration of the underground organization as well as the moral self-destruction of some of its soldiers (more about this later in this chapter).

In the postwar chaos, people felt helpless, believing that they had no one to turn to for protection from crime. Some of the letters quoted above, especially those written by women, convey this feeling of powerlessness. They describe fear that led people to faint, the powerlessness and despair even after the war had officially ended. But not all peasants waited passively for the next attack, and some attempted to fight back. The simplest well-tested method was to bury possessions. Chustecki describes how Germans accompanied by dogs often found hiding places with stolen property in them. They would take the most valuable items for themselves and distribute the rest among the villagers. "Oh, those little people loved to lie in wait for such opportunities! Whoever came first took the best things. He filled his wagon and cried that it was too little."[63] The strategy used to stop the stealing of farm animals was to sleep in the stable to protect their greatest treasure, horses, wrote Czesław Miłosz about Żuławy, the delta of the Vistula. In winter people slept inside their houses, but not having an alert and vicious dog was a major handicap.[64] But the settlers luckily did not only have to rely on dogs for protection, since they also had weapons. In some localities rural militias formed spontaneously, in Kielce region a Polish SS (most likely Social Self-Defense Units—MZ),[65] and communities brought back night watchmen. For some farm families, sending a son to serve in the Citizens' Militia or the secret police may have been a strategy used both to reduce the number of mouths to feed at home and to advance on the social ladder. It may also have served as an armed entity to settle local scores and as a cure for the perceived insecurity. Three letters show how people tried to handle the looming threat of banditry.

Krasnystaw, June 1, 1945: "Nowadays, forest bands with various names and nicknames, some very funny, rove around here. You can't keep anything out in your house, clothes or bed linens. Three villages around here went up in smoke recently, and all this comes from disillusionment with life in the countryside."[66]

Near Jarocin, August 19, 1945: "There is thieving all over our Kuchary. They stole both of Józio Kaliszewski's horses, only the one-year-old colt is left because he was in our house then. One day the thieves came to Biegański and killed his two-hundredweight hog, but he was sleeping in the stables guarding the horses and heard them. He jumped out the window in his nightshirt and ran to Skularz, to Popówka, they came running with their weapons from Skularz's and there was shooting because the thieves also had guns, but they had to run away and leave the hogs. This is how things are here."[67]

Near Olsztyn, August 29, 1945: "You can't imagine how they're stealing at night. We keep our hogs in the house and take our cows to Bogmał, to their sty because there is a guard there, even though their horses have been stolen, but they bought more. They stole 4 horses from them. Four families live there, and they stole all their horses."[68]

FORBIDDEN AREAS

The second category of banditry, the urban kind, developed along similar lines. At the beginning of the occupation, the Germans' permanent presence in the streets, their patrols and searches of random pedestrians, and the curfew made it quite difficult to move around the city, especially for large groups carrying weapons. This meant that there were relatively fewer break-ins and murders in bigger towns and cities than in rural areas. Developing crime took three directions. First were very tiresome and minor break-ins, pickpocketing, and trapping people in dark corners and stripping them of valuables. Second was the underground economy: smuggling, doing business with the Germans, and speculation on the black market, which became a source of support for thousands of people, not only and not even primarily for those who had been active in the prewar world of crime. The third direction was: let's go for the Jews!

Preying on Jews, *szmalcownictwo*, was a form of wartime banditry (in criminal slang, *szmalec* meant money, dough). The Jews were dream victims for the *szmalcownicy*. They lacked any support whatsoever and were being hunted, and it was not even necessary to use physical force against them as a *szmalcownik* could merely threaten to turn them in or reveal their hiding place. Furthermore, risking little and with minimal effort, when a person knew where and how to find a Jewish victim and blackmail them, he could make a profit unmatched by any other type of crime. Gangs of *szmalcowniks* appeared, and within them some specialized in intelligence and informing and others in blackmail and coercion. Jan Grabowski's book *Hunt for the Jews: Betrayal and Murder in German-Occupied Poland* describes such gangs operating in Warsaw. It is difficult to know their number, but Gunnar S. Paulsson estimates that there "were perhaps a few hundred or as many as 1,000 gangs, perhaps 3,000–4,000 people all told."[69] But szmalcownictwo, just like the drug trade or prostitution, should not be linked to distance from others. Of course, common people in Warsaw did not like the "Yids," but the finest szmalcownicy harassed Jews in hiding not because they were antisemites but because they saw them as a goldmine to exploit at will. Things were different for the "social denouncers," who were motivated by a mixture of anti-Semitism, conformism, and fear.[70] Historians have also rightly questioned the stereotype, convenient for many Poles, in which szmalcownicy were to be found solely on society's margins.[71] On the other extreme is Grabowski, who treats them as a pars pro toto reflection of Polish society, with its totality of attitudes and opinions.[72] "Professional" szmalcownicy (much like American slave catchers) were not institutions of social order or representatives of socially accepted values but criminals of the same ilk as moonshiners, pickpockets, or pimps. Even though déclassé or even quite prosperous citizens could be found in their ranks, the social genesis of szmalcownictwo should be linked to the people who had been excluded and "expendable" before the war. The largest group of denouncers and informers were ordinary people.[73] Their psychology tended to be rooted in destitution and its correlates—absence of a connection to mainstream social institutions, distrust of strangers, skimpy education or even illiteracy, tendency to commit crimes. The sociological imagination suggests that many szmalcownicy lived in the prewar "bad" neighborhoods, Warsaw's Czerniaków, the homeless barracks in Annopol, or the cellars of Powiśle, Praga, and Wola.

The year 1943 saw a rise in all types of crimes in urban areas, including the most violent ones: murder and robbery. According to estimates made by the Government Delegate's Office, in the first half of August in Warsaw, thirty-two major robberies and thirty-seven murders took place (although some of them may have been committed by people of the underground).[74] The increase in urban crime may seem surprising in view of the curfew and the large numbers of Germans in the streets. The historian Tomasz Szarota explains this with several factors. First, the resistance movement became more active, as measured by the number of armed operations, and this probably reduced the occupation authorities' already limited interest in fighting common crime. In other words, supervision by institutions in charge of maintaining the legal order diminished, much like in the countryside. Weapons became more widely available, as they could be bought in virtually every bazaar. The underground's stepped-up activity made it easier to pretend that one was its soldier.[75] Finally, a factor that has already been discussed was the progressive atrophy of moral connections.

The passing of the frontline in 1944 and 1945 made this the best time for crimes of all kinds. Initially, the absence of institutions of social order outside regions where the underground was weak encouraged criminals to operate virtually unpunished. Even the proximity of a militia station improved security only marginally. Many stations were repeatedly destroyed by underground groups in the Kielce region, Mazovia, and northeast and southeast Poland,[76] and large numbers of militia officers turned out to be unprepared to handle their functions. A militia report admitted that the "reason[s] for the rise in crime are the shortage of trained cadres, insufficient knowledge of investigation services."[77] This was to be eliminated, especially in the cities, by the introduction in mid-November 1945 of martial law, including a curfew.[78] It was instituted again in some districts threatened by banditry or ones in which the pro-independence underground was active in spring and autumn of 1946. From July 11–24, 1945, Augustów and Augustów District saw the introduction of martial law by the Soviet *komendantura*.[79] It was difficult to travel in all these places, and searches and arrests were frequent.

The postwar crime statistics do not paint the true picture of crime because of the dark figure of crime, as sociologists call it—what was never reported to the proper authorities. Even today, the police are aware of fewer than half of all crimes.[80] We can assume with almost absolute certainty that after the war, the dark figure must have been much higher for several reasons: there was no militia station nearby, people did not trust the militia, and the victim of a crime feared retribution and so did not report it.[81] Not a single one of the letter writers mentions reporting what happened to them to the police. This could hardly have been an accident. On the other hand, we should not dismiss all of the statistics from that time. One thing is certain from the figures: security hit rock bottom in 1945 and then began to improve gradually, especially beginning in 1947. According to Citizens' Militia statistics, in 1945, 26,471 burglaries were reported; in 1946, there were 23,987; and in 1947, there were 10,231. In 1945, the militia noted 121,729 thefts (pickpocketing, break-ins), in 1946, a high of 139,594, and in 1947, a drop to 128,310.[82]

It would be difficult to find areas on the postwar map of fear devoid of the fear of banditry. Practically everywhere in Poland, people could expect to have their property taken away by force. But indicators of the feeling of threat were not equally high everywhere. How can it be measured? We could use current studies of fear; they show a high correlation between crime and fear of crime, and the higher the crime rates in a given area, the greater the fear. "Hence," writes Andrzej Siemaszko, "the strong correlation between the scale of crime and fear means that we can treat the feeling of being threatened by crime as a *sui generis* measure of its actual level."[83] But this correlation would not be complete after the war without knowing that fear was transmitted, by letters for example, or be felt more intensely because of previous experiences, such as those of the First World War. Another obstacle to gauging the actual level of banditry in the wake of the Second World War is the fact that it was not only "our" people who were responsible for fear everywhere. Soviet troops played a role in raising fear, especially in western and northern Poland. The fact that the crimes they committed were often ascribed to "unknown assailants" makes it much more difficult to analyze native crime. Any map of fear must include a margin of error. But it is not wrong to assert that the highest level of victimization, and therefore of fear, appeared in Białystok, Lublin, and Rzeszów Provinces and was slightly lower in a part of the northern Mazovia, Świętokrzyskie, and Podkarpacie regions.

Let's look at this issue more carefully. In a single winter month of 1945 (January 22–February 22), 95 murders, 27 armed robberies, and 781 thefts were reported to the militia in a part of Warsaw Province.[84] The report that includes these figures does not mention the perpetrators. Many of these crimes may have been committed by Soviet troops, which just then were moving west behind the front.

A more remote area is Rzeszów Province. Over only twelve days in April, the militia recorded 532 murders, 331 holdups, 79 home invasions and 449 horse thefts.[85] Here, the Polish world of crime looks bleaker thanks not only to Soviet marauders but also to the victims of the Polish-Ukrainian war. This does not alter the fact that from the perspective of these data, Poznań Province was an oasis of calm, since there the monthly figures for murders and armed robberies reached at most a dozen or so.

The lower crime rates in Upper Silesia and Greater Poland can be explained by the fact that the tendency to violate the law was poorly rooted in the Prussian partition, in contrast to the Congress Kingdom. On the other hand, in the lands that had been incorporated into the Reich, the Germans attempted to stamp out criminal activity, while in the General Government they generally left crime fighting to the Polish navy-blue police, despite the fact that it was steadily growing weaker. Also, in Greater Poland and Upper Silesia, there was virtually no underground, so there were no "forest people" who could be transformed into "expendable" people. After the war, fewer repatriates from eastern and central Poland came there, and so life was more ordered, social ties were stronger, and social control was more advanced.

Let's take a look at another area: Kielce Province. In July 1945, 1,532 crimes of all categories were reported, in August only 801.[86] The dramatic drop at this time of year may be explained by the hiring of unemployed men for seasonal harvest work. If this were indeed the case, it would give us an idea about the figures for country folk engaged in crime. But this drop may also have been influenced by other factors. Data may not necessarily have been falsified, since the militia was not held accountable for solving crimes then. What played the greatest role in Kielce Province then was probably the emergence of many people from the underground in the summer and autumn of 1945, which in turn may prove that the underground had been infected with banditry.[87]

And now for the last regional example, the new Lower Silesia Province. In two weeks, late August–early September 1945, reported crimes included 20 murders, 86 robberies, 1,084 thefts and break-ins, 162 cases of disturbing the peace, 440 political crimes, 125 revolts and resisting the authorities, 29 other crimes against the authorities, 92 cases of arson, and 45 sex crimes.[88] This large number of crimes reported in such a short period of time appears to confirm the thesis that people felt more endangered in the "Regained Territories" than, for example, in Kielce Province. But again, we must remember that Red Army units were stationed in many towns in Lower Silesia. The large number of reported cases of arson, of which the Soviets were often suspected, and of rape reveals the Red Army's large role in the victimization indicator. "Things would be nice here if we had some calm, if there were no robberies and no thefts.... Everyone's main problem is lack of safety," reported a militia station in Lower Silesia.[89]

In Warsaw, under the German occupation and until the end of 1944, the number of robberies was many times higher than the number of the underground's operations.[90] There are many indications that this situation persisted after the war. For instance, in the first ten days of August 1946, there were 135 home invasions, including 76 burglaries. The largest number of the latter, 21, took place in Białystok Province. Militia stations were attacked 7 times, train stations and trains 11 times, and cash registers and banks 4 times.[91] In September 1946, Department III of the Ministry of Public Security recorded 1,114 attacks by "bands," of which 751 were classified as robberies, including 466 of private property, 10 of banks, and 165 of "other institutions." In that single month, over 22 million zlotys, an astronomical sum then, was stolen.[92] Incidentally, there were no figures for bank robberies. Without a doubt, at no other time in Polish history were the jobs of bank clerk, cashier, and train ticket vendor as dangerous.

The data are not organized by locality. But the letters quoted here allow us to offer the hypothesis that the universal fear of a bandit attack, break-in, robbery, or physical assault was smaller among people living in the largest towns than in rural areas. If this were indeed the case, it would mean that then crime was a threat in different places from today. Today, the strongest correlation is between crime and the percentage of rural population in a given province: the higher the percentage of villagers the lower the crime rate, and the lesser the fear of crime.[93] But why was fear greater in the countryside than in the towns after the war? There are at least two answers to this question. First, in the wake of the Warsaw Uprising, armed resistance evidently moved to rural areas, where the conflict had many features of a civil war. Second, the military had a presence in the large cities. But this is not to say that towns were islands of safety on the postwar map of fear.

Every town was different, with both safe and "bad" neighborhoods. In Gdańsk, the crime underworld loitered in drinking holes. Warsaw traditionally had its Praga district, and the crime underground in other areas degenerated drastically during the Warsaw Uprising. In Częstochowa, Stradom was the crime nursery. In Cracow, it was not safe to walk around Kazimierz and Podgórze. Everywhere, the most dangerous areas were concentrated around marketplaces, bazaars, and train stations. Travelers, especially Jews, were often assaulted on trains, and anyone could be pushed off a speeding train. The regime's functionaries could be thrown out, as could those who refused to give up their place or please the assailant by handing over their luggage. Red Army troops also engaged in this sport.

In Warsaw, Wrocław, Gdańsk, and Elbląg, the near-absence of street lighting and the omnipresent ruins added to the atmosphere of terror. People were afraid to go out alone in the evening. A description of Warsaw in October 1945 noted that "today, going home from a faraway workplace in the evening involves a sizeable risk. Various types of hooligans, hoodlums and muggers attack pedestrians, beat them up, snatch whatever they are carrying, steal whatever they can. They attack not only solitary women but also men, they're growing increasingly bold, especially since the darkness and the empty streets guarantee them almost total impunity."[94]

The high point of urban crime was the winter of 1945–46. In many towns, people skulked down the dark streets, their hearts in their mouths. A memoirist who was living in Warsaw at the time was once so afraid of being assaulted that when he heard gunshots he hid his watch and money, took off his shoes, and walked home barefoot so as not to make noise.[95] Joanna Konopińska from Wrocław wrote in her diary on December 9, 1945, "I came back from Lena's in the late evening, and father scolded me terribly for being late. He was actually right because it's better not to be out alone after dark. Our neighbor was recently attacked downtown. They stole her purse with money and food ration cards in it, pulled her watch off her wrist, her fur hat off her head and her shoes off her feet. When she reported it to the militia the next morning, they only advised her not to walk alone in the evening. But it was five p.m.!"[96]

THE SOLDIER-OUTLAWS

The third category of banditry, by men living in the forest, was already described in the greatest detail of the three. It is noteworthy that all those who have studied the postwar underground euphemistically describe some of its people turning into bandits as a problem.[97] It would be more appropriate to view it as a fear- and terror-inducing disaster with far-flung consequences, not only social and economic but also political. Raids on trains, train stations, and road transportation damaged Poland's communications network while robberies of banks, cooperatives, shops, wholesalers, and factories made it difficult to amass resources to rebuild the economy. The large numbers of thefts in the countryside prolonged the state of destabilization and may also have played a role in inflating the food prices in the cities. The remaining Jews wanted to emigrate because of anti-Semitic violence. Banditry also contributed to an increase in the numbers of supporters of the new regime, which represented itself as the guarantor of order and safety.

To be honest, it was not only underground fighters who risked turning into bandits. The gangs also included former Polish Army soldiers and deserters avoiding cities. The banditry of the Citizens' Militia and Security Office men is a separate category, but many of their leaders were underground soldiers gone rogue. Their downfall resembled the experiences of German soldiers after the First World War, with their brutalized behavior and radicalized political views of the world in black-and-white Manichean terms, in which Jews and Communists were "black." Both groups also shared powerful feelings of defeat.[98] Zygmunt Klukowski observed how the views of the forest commanders in the Zamość region in mid-1945 were radicalized, becoming outright fanatical. He saw them as overbearing, having had their sensitivity dulled, and accustomed to solving problems by force.[99]

Some Home Army leaders knew that this infection might spread. Andrzej Przemyski, a biographer of the last commander of the Home Army Leopold Okulicki, discusses an order from the commander of Cracow region Home Army, Colonel Przemysław Nakonieczny, dated January 18, 1945, as supporting this knowledge: "Make sure you precisely collect, conserve and conceal arms and equipment. Arms may not remain in the hands of individual Home Army soldiers because of the possibility that soldiers of the Uprising will not be distinguished from bandits."[100] The signatories of a letter of July 1945, who included the Home Army figure Kazimierz Moczarski, warned about the potential consequences of the underground shutting itself off in the equivalent of Catholic obscurantism.[101] Their fears were confirmed. But it would not have been possible to prevent underground fighters from turning to crime without the Soviets' failure to occupy Poland and General Władysław Anders's return from the West. Had that happened, it would have made no sense to remain in the forest, but then there would also not have been the endless layers of disappointed hopes, anger, and hate.

On the other hand, underground activity in itself bore the germs of what in auspicious circumstances may easily have become criminal.[102] Most importantly, prewar norms were redefined during the war. As long as they harmed the occupiers, killing, violence, cheating, and theft not only lost their negative value but, on the contrary, were grounds for glory. Conspiratorial organizations were opaque by definition while the actions of individual soldiers and units were kept secret and were often insufficiently supervised by their commanders.[103] This meant that the bandits' spontaneous actions to satisfy their own needs became easier, all the more so since some soldiers engaged in sabotage were specially trained for such exploits. The underground's expanding structures and units needed money to buy food, clothing, and arms to continue fighting. This meant that the leadership authorized the many expropriation actions targeting offices, banks, and German institutions. But inasmuch as this type of activity was justified and necessary during the war, once the war was over the numbers of attacks on cooperatives, train ticket offices, banks, and forestry offices cannot be explained only with the need to collect resources to fight the Communists. It would have been possible to equip an infantry division with the 22 million zlotys stolen in September 1946 alone. Even though some amateurs may have taken part in it, only professionals would have been capable of robbing Warsaw's District Court of 300,000 zlotys (August 7, 1946),[104] Lublin's Labor company office of 400,000 zlotys (October 26, 1946), and a food cooperative in Białystok of 797,000 zlotys (October 30, 1946).[105] Burglaries of state institutions in smaller towns became a postwar plague.

Some were real raids from village to village with a stop at the train station or cooperative, much like Bonnie and Clyde, with the only difference that these criminals mostly used horse-drawn wagons.[106] They stole everything that had any value. In August 1945 in Barcin, near Poznań, cash registers were taken from the train station and the forestry office. Perhaps the same people robbed a sugar refinery in nearby Żnin. Two letters about it survive.

Żnin, August 13, 1945: "P.S. I forgot to tell you that last night, Sunday, some bandits barged into Barcin station and forced the supervisor at gunpoint to give them money. They stole 5,000 zlotys."[107]

Żnin, August 15, 1945: "Thieves have taken over here, they steal from cash registers, the sugar refinery in Żnin twice. Forestry office and Barcin station and so it goes."[108]

The author of a letter bumped into one such partisan group (place of dispatch unknown, June 7, 1945):

> We had just turned down our road into the forest, two carriages with Polish soldiers arrived, they stopped and shouted hands up, a uniformed miss with a machine gun jumped off the wagon, searched Radomek and Bolek, later they checked our i.d. cards.... This was a band, they robbed the cooperative of 80,000 and went on their way. Two Russki soldiers came, they wanted to take their weapons away, they shot at them so much that they wounded them a lot. They smashed the telephones at the station, disarmed the railway militia and no one knows where they came from or where they went.[109]

At times, larger partisan groups occupied entire small towns, especially in eastern Poland. Almost always at such times the commander would order his men to steal state and private money, but this may have been one of their goals. On March 24, 1945, a unit led by Kazimierz Kamieński (pseudonym "Huzar") occupied Czyżew. It executed twelve people, three Catholic Poles and nine Jews, alleged Security Office collaborators.[110] According to the starost, "the murders had to do with robbery."[111] On August 1, 1945, another unit overran Tykocin, but since its functionaries put up a vicious fight, it did not manage to take the militia station. But they took 24,000 zlotys of government money and personal cash from the home of the village secretary instead, and they also stole goods and cash from the local Agricultural-Trade Cooperative.[112] While many soldiers and officers of the anti-Communist underground fighting for a free and sovereign Poland were no doubt heroes, there is also no doubt that their struggle gradually turned into a vicious caricature of itself.

The fighters would always take a break in distilleries they came upon during their raids. In that period, distilleries far outranked train stations, agricultural cooperatives, and forestry offices on the list of most frequently robbed places. A letter from Krasiczyn dated May 29, 1945, read, "Nasty times. Robberies in the villages and estates at night. The Boniecka distillery has been a victim again and again. They've already taken countless liters of those spirits, now they leave empty-handed because there's nothing left."[113]

On March 16, 1947, a group of thirty led by a commander going by the fighting name Ordon raided a marmalade factory in Milejów, Lublin Province. They disarmed the guards and stole 1,400 kg of sugar and 30 kg of marmalade.[114]

Not only state institutions and factories but also individuals were victims of the underground soldiers' lawless acts, of both those who still belonged to the organization and those acting on their own. At least two issues were relevant in this context. First, the forest people had become detached from mainstream society. Without social norms, they regressed psychologically. Partisans and civilians understood each other less and less. Second, the partisans were condemned to seeking help from villagers. This had not been a problem during the war since there were not as many underground groups regularly active in the countryside. But this changed radically after operation "Tempest" began. From then on, hundreds of units, some of them very large, had to take food from peasants, who gradually became less willing to share their food or clothing. The partisans, on the other hand, often hungry, cold, and living in constant danger, were not choosy with their methods when they encountered resistance. When the peasants saw partisans in the distance, they naturally reacted immediately by hiding their shoes and their slab of pork fat.[115] For example, on August 8, 1945, thirteen men claiming to be Home Army fighters searched the village of Poręba, Kamyk District, in Kielce Province. They calmly asked for a donation in every house. They went inside to search the house only when its owners outright refused, and they took more than they had initially asked for. They took Lucjan Bania's pigs and suit jacket. Bronisław Szulc willingly gave them 100 zlotys, and they took 400 zlotys more out of the cupboard. They entered Józef Kaczmarek's house by force and took 2 suits, 1,700 zlotys, 20 meters of linen, and a revolver. Władysław Młynek tried to resist, and so they took 2,000 zlotys, a leather jacket, a coat, a loaf of bread, 7 bottles of beer, 20 bottles of lemonade, and a kilogram of yeast.[116] But things were usually done more brutally.

The disintegration of the underground organization, which had been a real social network with contacts and norms, proved crucial in the history of the corrupt soldiers and the fear of them. According to the historian Rafał Wnuk, in the areas "liberated" by the Soviets, the Home Army lost more officers to arrest and exile in the summer and autumn of 1944 than throughout the entire German occupation.[117] As Zygmunt Klukowski wrote in his diary in late December 1944, "The organization's authority and importance are clearly diminishing daily." He added that banditry had "become a widespread phenomenon, and there is no evidence that anyone is trying to stop it."[118] Growing numbers of underground fighters spun out of control without an income or hope to settle into civilian life. Many of them, especially the young ones, knew nothing more than how to assemble a machine gun and fight with it. Lacking a useful role, fighters, like those after many other modern wars,[119] took advantage of the state's weakness, formed new groups, and stole. They became more and more violent. They found it easier to polish off someone, sometimes for a minor reason. They also, unlike during the war, increasingly used the principle of collective responsibility. Now, individuals charged with having served as German confidants or with adhering to Communist views were killed together with their families, a father-in-law, children, and a sister-in-law.[120] Stealing usually accompanied execution by members of the underground. There were two schools of thought: either rob and shoot behind the barn or abduct so that the children won't see and the neighbors won't gather, and shoot the guy in a nearby ditch or at the edge of the forest. But don't forget the wagon, which is overflowing with stolen property, pigs. The list of people who died in such circumstances, often because of unverified accusations or only because of opposing political views, is very long. Two examples from a single month in the village of Lipsk, Augustów District:

On 5 April 1945 at 11 p.m. unknown people abducted Jan Sewatianowicz, age 35, from the village of Skieblewo. Together with the abducted, the following was taken: a wagon, two horses, two suits, two pairs of shoes, two hogs, two wool blankets, two sheets and two pieces of linen. On 20 April 1945 at 10, three men in uniform came to forester Stanisław Guzowski in Gruszki. They took a typewriter, cash from the cash register, and destroyed documents. They took Guzowski with them. After going about 400 meters from his house, they shot the forester three times in the head.[121]

Countless murders that merged political revenge and robbery took place in postwar Poland. Their victims could be Polish, Belorussian, German, or Jewish. From our distant perspective, it seems that it made no difference who they were, only what they owned. But looking closer, a rule emerges: bandits killed Jews more often than non-Jewish Poles, which means that the perpetrators' anti-Semitism must have been an additional motivation to rob. The victims themselves could sense it. One of them wrote in a letter sent from Radom on June 17, 1945, "I imagine that you understand the reasons why I left Suchedniów: bandits. But let me stress that it wasn't only a question of robbery, although they took almost everything from us, but that when they returned, they were more interested in liquidating the Jews."[122]

It seems that the two armed men who invaded the home of Aleksander Ułomek, a Pole, in the village of Golcowa, Rzeszów Province, on October 1, 1944, were motivated by anti-Semitism. From Ułomek they took a pair of shoes, but Emil Jammel, a Jew from the same village who was staying with him, had a rope tied around his neck and was led away. The intruders spared the Pole and probably murdered the Jew. Most likely the same people kidnapped a Pole, Mikołaj Piertas, on the same night from the same village and shot him a few times in the forest, luckily only wounding him.[123] There are other examples. On February 18, 1945, in the village of Sokoły (Wysokomazowiecki District), seven Jews, including a four-year-old, were murdered.[124] On March 9, 1946, men of a Freedom and Independence raiding party commanded by Kazimierz Harmida (pseudonym "Lech"), active in Bielsko-Podlaski District, invaded a house in which five Jews and a Polish woman and her child were living. They killed two of the Jews immediately and took the others away on a wagon, shot them, and threw their bodies into the bug River, and robbed the house. To Rafał Wnuk, all evidence points to the fact that the murders were dictated solely by anti-Semitism and profit.[125] This was a component of a spontaneous ethnic cleansing being performed in various places in Poland on the minuscule remains of the Jewish population. Jews were also victims of "ordinary" bandit raids.

In mid-November 1946, the Regional Military Court in Łódź tried Bronisław Misler, Tadeusz Miedzierski, Tadeusz Adamski, and Stanisław Czuma. A little over a year earlier, one Stefan Markowski had been murdered in his own apartment. After killing him with a shot to the head, his killers tied up his corpse with a rope. They plundered the apartment, and 25,000 zlotys in cash and 150 dollars in gold disappeared. The investigation determined that Misler, who lived with the victim's wife's sister, was the culprit. The murder was partly an act of revenge against the Markowski family, who had accused Misler of killing the sister. The second defendant was Tadeusz Miedzierski, an "old, pre-war criminal," who had been tried and sentenced numerous times. In 1939, he had been sentenced by the District Court in Piotrków Trybunalski to life in prison for robbery and murder. He now took part in killing Markowski. On November 8, 1945, the two men again committed murder, this time in Piotrków Trybunalski, at 22 Łąkowa Street, where they robbed and killed Lejzor Melc, Sura Uszerowicz, and Ruchel Rolnik. The investigation showed that Miedzierski was assisted in the killings by Tadeusz Adamski. Taking part in the robbery was also Stanisław Czuma, a first-year secondary school student. The defendants confessed to only some of the charges.[126]

According to historian Julian Kwiek, after liberation, about 1,100 Jews died in Poland in pogroms, the underground's actions, armed robberies, and assassinations.[127] For a conservative estimate, under 10 percent were pure robberies—bandit raids in which the killers did not know that their victims were Jewish, or their victims' ethnicity did not matter to them. But more than half may have had mixed motivations, anti-Semitism and robbery, expressed in the thinking that it is better to rob a Jew than a Pole. In Lublin Province, one of the most dangerous regions for Jews, Adam Kopciowski counted 118 murders from the second half of 1944 to the end of 1946. About 80 percent may have been described as "anti-Semitism and/or robbery."[128] It is also significant that some of the criminals were ordinary repeat offenders.

In conclusion, let us remember that criminal acts (murders, robberies, or beatings) directed at Jews were only part of the phenomenon that, as has been said before, became an epidemic. We need to see them against the broader background of the general surge in crime, brutalization of public life, and increase in aggression.[129] To quote Marek Edelman, "Murdering Jews was pure banditry, and I would not explain it as anti-Semitism."[130]

Incidentally, Jan T. Gross in *Fear* argues that people who had hidden Jews during the war were later afraid of admitting to it in public because they feared that their neighbors would disrespect them or even take revenge on them. To him, this is crucial evidence that anti-Semitism was universal across Polish society.[131] Not to deny Gross's final conclusion, but there may have been another reason why people did not admit to having hidden Jews: fear of a bandit attack. It was enough sometimes for people to know that a person was back from selling something in the market, had cash on him, or was the only one in the area to own a horse—he would be robbed. People who had given shelter to Jews may have been a target for robbers since, according to the common stereotype, Jews had gold, and now the Poles who had saved them in the war would have some, too. Thus, the reason why people may have concealed the truth about their heroism during Hitler's occupation may have been not only fear of their anti-Semitic neighbors but also—or perhaps primarily—of their neighbors who were bandits.

Another consequence of the fear of robbery was the universal exhaustion with chaos; for some, this was also a reason to approve of the new regime, especially when it declared that it would combat banditry mercilessly. "Indeed, these killings, 'liquidations, bumping off' are becoming more and more distasteful," noted Zygmunt Klukowski in March 1945.[132] For a large number of Poles, there was no point in continuing to fight. Few of them cared much about the rogue soldiers' psychological problems, their shortages of supplies, or the conspirators' organizational needs. At the same time, everyone, regardless of their political views, wanted to live free of the fear that someone would visit them in the night and take away their possessions by force. Making this point, indirectly, is a letter intercepted by the censorship office. A woman from Kalwaria Zebrzydowska wrote on August 5, 1945, "Thieves are everywhere, and so is, it's a shame to say, the Home Army. All I'm doing is trying to figure out how to escape from the countryside."[133]

The new regime's functionaries also noticed the leftward turn taking place in many parts of society in the spring of 1946 as a reaction to the prolonged state of terror brought on by banditry.[134] The opposition to the crime wave could be seen in the crowds of as many as thousands at the funerals of murder victims.[135] Does this mean that the activities of the anti-Communist underground, which was increasingly evolving into a criminal underground, were destroying their popular support rather than building it up? To answer in the affirmative would be to generalize. After all, many of the underground's soldiers remained faithful to the conspiratorial ethos, which was expressed, among other things, in killing common criminals. Finally, some of its fighters' postwar banditry was only one piece in a much larger phenomenon characteristic of periods of chaos and disintegration. It had occurred in Poland not only in the wake of the Second World War but also after the 1905 revolution and the First World War, and in post–Civil War in the United States when thieves and bandits, some of them also victims of the war, roamed the Wild West.

NOTES

1. The first version of this chapter appeared as Zaremba, "'Człowiek drży jak liść'—trwoga przed bandytyzmem w okresie powojennym (1945–1947)."
2. People answered questions posed by three research centers (CBOS, DGA PBS, and TNS OBOP) in January 2009: "What are the Poles afraid of?" with, in this order: "careless drivers," "vandals destroying property," "attacks by drunks and drug addicts," "assault, robbery," "home, basement, car break-ins," "harassment by aggressive youths" and "fights and beatings." Zawadka and Nisztor, "Polska lista strachów."
3. AIPN, MBP, 3378, k. 75. Specjalne doniesienie dot. działalności dywersyjnych band.
4. AIPN, MBP, 3378, k. 74b. Specjalne doniesienie dot. działalności dywersyjnych band.
5. AIPN, 01265/752. Specjalne doniesienie dot. bezpieczeństwa w kraju według opisów w listach cywilnej ludności, 10 X 1945, n.p.
6. AIPN, 01265/752.
7. For a bibliography, see Giddens, *Sociology*, chapter 19, "Crime and Deviance."
8. Hobsbawm, *Bandits*; see also Hobsbawm, *Primitive Rebels*.
9. In Poland, native social banditry, apart from the overused case of Jánošík, the Slovak highwayman, has remained practically unanalyzed in academic literature. And yet in the twentieth century alone, at least two bandits, Pistułka and Wiktor Zieliński, fit the model described by Hobsbawm. On Pistułka, see Cisek, *Beztroskie lata 1946–1956*, 41; Dzieszyński, *Ciemna, węsząca, żerująca*, 70.
10. Borodij et al., *Rok 1946*, 128.
11. Thomas and Znaniecki, *The Polish Peasant in Europe and America*, 84.
12. "On 23.10.1944 at about 9 p.m. five unknown individuals armed with wooden clubs entered the home of Gac Rozalia in Krzywcza, Przemyśl District, and after terrorizing the inhabitants took clothing, undergarments and shoes and departed in an unknown direction" (AIPN, KG MO 35/2038, k. 36. Raport sytuacyjny nr 6, Wydział Śledczy MO w Rzeszowie, 13 XI 1944).
13. "The main reason for these anti-social and anti-humanitarian behaviors was, first of all, the abandonment by the fleeing panicked occupants of large numbers of weapons of various types, which are now being kept and carried by individuals who by no means deserve to be trusted by society, which simply tempts and forces them to commit these despicable acts" (APK, Urząd Wojewódzki 1337, k. 166. Sprawozdanie sytuacyjne starosty powiatowego w Opatowie za lipiec 1945).
14. AIPN, 01265/752. Specjalne doniesienie dot. bezpieczeństwa w kraju według opisów w listach cywilnej ludności, 10 X 1945, n.p.
15. Osiński, *Lęk w kulturze społeczeństwa polskiego w XVI–XVII wieku*, 131.
16. The lower number of people sentenced by all kinds of courts in the Russian partition zone in 1906, compared to previous years, may serve as evidence of the lower efficiency of the institutions of control (Konczyński, *Stan moralny społeczeństwa polskiego*, 24, 25).
17. Blobaum, *Rewolucja*, 142, 155.
18. Kalabiński and Tych, *Czwarte powstanie czy pierwsza rewolucja*, 217, 218.
19. See Dunin-Wąsowicz, *Warszawa 1914–1918*, 97, 140–51, et al.
20. Wróbel, "The Seeds of Violence," 125–49.
21. Dzieszyński, *Ciemna, węsząca, żerująca*, 63.
22. But it began to grow again in 1926. Radzinowicz, *Przestępczość w Polsce w latach 1924–1933*.
23. Hempel, *Pogrobowcy klęski*, 277.
24. Klukowski, *Zamojszczyzna*, vol. 2: *1944–1959*, 174.
25. Hempel, *Pogrobowcy klęski*, 280.
26. *Biuletyn Informacyjny* of August 6, 1942, warned:

> We have managed to ascertain that the gangs roaming in Łuków and Siedlce Districts are recruiting members from among escaped Soviet prisoners. These bands have nothing to do with any sabotage actions. Several dozen escaped Soviet prisoners of war were shot during the roundups organized by the Germans in July in the aforementioned areas. Large (often multi-thousand) amounts of money coming from robberies were found on all the dead. The prowlers commit murders on the defenseless in order to force the population to cooperate. There have been a few cases of rapes of women. The disappearance of the self-defense instinct in the population, which passively allows thefts and murders to happen, is striking.

For more, see Kowalczyk, "Obraz partyzantki sowieckiej na terytorium północno-wschodniej Rzeczypospolitej Polskiej w świetle meldunków Delegatury Rządu na Kraj)," 377–99.
27. For more on this topic, see Krakowski, *The War of the Doomed*; Puławski, "Postrzeganie żydowskich," 271–300.
28. Engelking, *Jest taki piękny słoneczny dzień*, 126, 127.
29. Kersten and Szarota, *Wieś polska 1939–1948*, 169.
30. For strategies of survival, see Melchior, *Uciekinierzy z gett po "stronie aryjskiej" na prowincji dystryktu warszawskiego—sposoby przetrwania*, 344; Engelking, *Jest taki piękny słoneczny dzień*.
31. Grabowski, *Hunt for the Jews*.
32. Engelking, *Jest taki piękny słoneczny dzień*.
33. Gmitruk et al., *Pro Memoria (1941–1944)*, 398.
34. AAN, Rada Główna Opiekuńcza 749, k. 167–169. Raport nr 92 z lustracji Delegatury Serokomla w dniach od 30 VII do 2 VIII 1943, as quoted in Bechta, *Rewolucja, mit, bandytyzm*, 95.

35. AAN, Rada Główna Opiekuńcza 749, 96.
36. Gmitruk et al., *Pro Memoria (1941–1944)*, 398, 399.
37. Chustecki, *Byłem sołtysem*, 169, 170.
38. Chustecki, 239, 240.
39. Bechta, *Rewolucja, mit, bandytyzm*, 79.
40. AIPN, 01265/752. Specjalne doniesienie dotyczące bezpieczeństwa w kraju według opisów w listach cywilnej ludności, 10 X 1945, n.p.
41. AIPN, 01265/752.
42. AAN, MIiP 79, k. 24. Sprawozdanie z komisyjnej lustracji powiatów zniszczonych działaniami wojennymi w woj. kieleckim (pow. Kozienice, Stopnica, Opatów, Sandomierz, Iłża), dokonanej przez inspektorów Biura Kontroli Państwa oraz delegata Wojewódzkiej Rady Narodowej w Kielcach w dniach od 24 VIII do 28 VIII 1945.
43. Strzembosz, "Przestępczość i okupacja," 7.
44. Bechta, *Rewolucja, mit, bandytyzm*, 73, 80.
45. AIPN, 01265/752. Specjalne doniesienie dotyczące bezpieczeństwa w kraju według opisów w listach cywilnej ludności, 10 X 1945, n.p.
46. AIPN, MBP 3378, k. 73b. Specjalne doniesienie dotyczące działalności dywersyjnych band, n.d.
47. A report from the Citizens' Militia station in Magnuszew (Kozienice District) read, "On 8 July 1946 at 11 p.m. an armed attack took place . . . in the parish house of Father Gajos Jan in the village of Rozniszew, Kozienice District, by 4 unknown individuals in civilian dress with short weapons, one of them with a bayonet, and they stole from the priest: 1,700 zlotys in cash . . . from voluntary contributions for rebuilding the church" (J. Boniecki, *Napady zbrojne w powiecie kozieckim 1945–1947*, 72).
48. AIPN, 01265/752. Specjalne doniesienie dotyczące bezpieczeństwa w kraju według opisów w listach cywilnej ludności, 10 X 1945, n.p.
49. Wolf, *Peasant Wars of the Twentieth Century*.
50. AIPN, 01265/752. Specjalne doniesienie dotyczące bezpieczeństwa w kraju według opisów w listach cywilnej ludności, 10 X 1945, n.p.
51. AIPN, 01265/752.
52. AIPN, 01265/752.
53. APB, Urząd Wojewódzki [henceforth UW], 285, k. 93. Pismo Zarządu Polskiego Związku Zachodniego w Białymstoku do Białostockiego Urzędu Wojewódzkiego, July 13, 1945.
54. Kersten and Szarota, *Wieś polska 1939–1948*, vol. 3, 142.
55. See, for example, *Biuletyn Informacyjny* of February 26, 1942: "The patriotic bandits are proliferating in various parts of the country horrendously. We mean the bandits pretending to be raiding parties of 'patriotic organizations.' For example, in Włoszczowa District, a single individual armed with a rifle is roaming; he visits the more prosperous inhabitants and demands cash, leaving behind a written receipt which he signs as a member of some 'organization.'"
56. "Manifesto. Here, as across Poland, thieving has spread on a large scale. Various gangs usually pretend to be Home Army people, whom the public trusts and supports and commit simple robberies. The militia does not counteract sufficiently, as it is mostly made up of an untrained element and often cooperates with the thieves" (AAN, KC PPR 295/VII–187, k. 82).
57. AIPN, 01265/752. Specjalne doniesienie dotyczące bezpieczeństwa w kraju według opisów w listach cywilnej ludności, 10 X 1945, n.p.
58. Meldunek organizacyjny nr 220 za czas od 1 III do 31 VIII 43, 92; also Puławski, "Postrzeganie żydowskich," 284.
59. For example, "Wyroki wykonane. . . . Dutkowski Henryk, zam. w Garwolińskiem—za napady bandyckie przeciw ludności polskiej," *Biuletyn Informacyjny*, February 3, 1944.
60. AIPN, KG MO 35/2260, k. 72. Raport sytuacyjny nr 16 za trzecią dekadę VI 1945.
61. APB, UW 285, k. 175. Meldunki o aktach terroru za czas od 4 VII do 1 IX 1945.
62. See Kułak, *Białostocczyzna 1944–1945 w dokumentach podziemia i oficjalnych władz*, 132, 137, 138, 154.
63. Chustecki, *Byłem sołtysem*, 172.
64. Miłosz, "Na Żuławach," *Dziennik Polski*, December 3, 1945.
65. Śmietanka-Kruszelnicki, "Problem 'bandycenia się' podziemia," 64.
66. AIPN, MBP 3378, k. 75. Specjalne doniesienie dotyczące działalności dywersyjnych band, n.d.
67. AIPN, 01265/752. Specjalne doniesienie dotyczące bezpieczeństwa w kraju według opisów w listach cywilnej ludności, 10 X 1945, n.p.
68. AIPN, 01265/752.
69. Paulsson, *Secret City*, 149.
70. Paulsson, 143–44.
71. Żbikowski, "Antysemityzm, szmalcownictwo, współpraca z Niemcami a stosunki polsko-żydowskie pod okupacją niemiecką," 429 et al.
72. Grabowski, *Hunt for the Jews*.
73. See i.a. Skibińska and Petelewicz, "Udział Polaków w zbrodniach na Żydach na prowincji regionu świętokrzyskiego," 123, 124; Engelking, "Szanowny panie gistapo," 62–72.
74. Gmitruk et al., *Pro Memoria (1941–1944)*, 399.
75. Szarota, *Okupowanej Warszawy dzień powszedni*, 185–86.
76. By April 1947, the underground had destroyed about 1,300 Citizens' Militia stations. See Wnuk, *Atlas polskiego podziemia*.
77. AIPN, KG MO 35/888, k. 9. Raport sytuacyjny MO w woj. poznańskim za czas od 16 V–5 VI 1945.
78. Kochański, *Polska 1944–1991*, 115.
79. APB, UW 148, k. 49. Sprawozdanie sytuacyjne starosty powiatowego augustowskiego za lipiec 1945, August 3, 1945.
80. Siemaszko, *Geografia występku i strachu*, 33.
81. Hrubieszów, April 1945: "The population does not report cases of theft committed by the Citizens' Militia, being afraid as there have been cases of threats" (AAN, MIiP 81, k. 56. Sprawozdanie terenowego instruktora ob. Z.a Sulimierskiego z inspekcji Powiatowego Oddziału Informacji i Propagandy w Hrubieszowie w dniach 2–5 IV 1945).
82. *Przestępstwa zameldowane Policji w latach 1924–1938*, 33.
83. Siemaszko, *Geografia występku i strachu*, 111.

84. The districts were Mińsk Mazowiecki, Ostrów Mazowiecki, Garwolin, Ostrołęka, Węgrów, Radzymin, Pułtusk, Sokołów Podlaski, Pruszków, Błonie, and Warsaw. AIPN, KG MO 35/897, k. 20. Raport Wydziału Śledczego Komendy MO m. st. Warszawy i woj. warszawskiego, Otwock, March 5, 1945.

85. AIPN, KG MO 35/785, k. 20. Raport od 18 IV do 1 V 1945.

86. AIPN, KG MO 35/933, k. 17, 21. Raporty sytuacyjne, lipiec–sierpień 1945.

87. Śmietanka-Kruszelnicki, "Problem 'bandycenia się' podziemia," 64.

88. AIPN, KG MO 35/922, k. 37. Sprawozdanie sytuacyjne od 25 VIII–10 IX 1945.

89. AIPN, KG MO 35/922, k. 47. Sprawozdanie sytuacyjne od 25 IX–10 X 1945.

90. Strzembosz, "Przestępczość i okupacja," 7.

91. AAN, KC PPR 295/IX–415, k. 1–8. Raport specjalny o napadach bandyckich i przeprowadzonych operacjach na terenie Rzeczypospolitej Polskiej za okres od 1 VIII do 10 VIII 1946.

92. AAN, KC PPR 295/IX–415, k. 48–71. Raport specjalny o napadach bandyckich i przeprowadzonych operacjach na terenie Rzeczypospolitej Polskiej za okres od 1 IX do 30 IX 1946.

93. Siemaszko, *Geografia występku i strachu*, 23, 24.

94. "Poprawy stanu bezpieczeństwa domaga się ludność Warszawy," *Życie Warszawy*, October 4, 1945.

95. Bednarczyk, *Zgruzowana Warszawa w latach 1945–1947*, 2.

96. Konopińska, *Tamten wrocławski rok. Dziennik 1945–1946*, 108.

97. See Śmietanka-Kruszelnicki, "Problem 'bandycenia się' podziemia"; Wnuk, "Problem bandytyzmu wśród żołnierzy," 67–79; *Problemy bandytyzmu w okupowanej Polsce*.

98. Mosse, *Fallen Soldiers*, 159–81 et al.

99. Klukowski, *Zamojszczyzna 1944–1959*, vol. 2, 192.

100. Przemyski, *Ostatni Komendant*, 194.

101. Memoriał Z. Kapitaniaka, W. Lechowicza i K. Moczarskiego z 18 VII 1945 r., 279–88.

102. For more, see Strzembosz, "Przestępczość i okupacja," 7–24.

103. Wnuk, "Problem bandytyzmu wśród żołnierzy," 72.

104. AAN, KC PPR 295/IX–415, k. 9. Raport specjalny o napadach bandyckich i przeprowadzonych operacjach na terenie Rzeczypospolitej Polskiej za okres od 1 VIII do 10 VIII 1946.

105. AAN, KC PPR 295/VII–184, k. 4. Komunikat nr 142 o sytuacji operacyjnej i działalności jednostek i formacji na terenie RP, celem likwidacji band na dzień 1 i 2 XI 1946.

106. Various sources give numerous examples of attacks by bandits who owned a car or cars. Underground units regularly requisitioned cars. On July 3, 1945, at 12:30 p.m., a car stopped outside Bank Ludowy at 3 Maja Street in Ostrów Mazowiecka, and five soldiers in Polish Army uniforms got out. They terrorized the bank personnel and stole 35,662 zlotys, then drove off in the direction of Warsaw (AIPN, KG MO 35/2260, k. 83. Raport sytuacyjny nr 17 za I i II dekadę VII 1945). Indeed, a Polish Army uniform meant nothing as soldiers of various underground units could practically not be distinguished from soldiers of regular units. Another example is a letter from someone in Majdan village, Kraśnik District, Lublin Province, of June 12, 1945; note the opening sentence of this quote, in which the author compares the current threat with that of the time of war: "The thieves attacked just like under the Germans. Now, too, it'll probably be hard to save a piglet because whatever they grab they take, they're even driving cars now. In Rudnik and Majdanek Starowiejski they say the bandits had 7 cars. What's the world coming to, they take horses, hogs and even cattle from farmers" (AIPN, MBP 3378, k. 74b, 75. Specjalne doniesienie dotyczące działalności dywersyjnych band, n.d.).

107. AIPN, 01265/752. Specjalne doniesienie dotyczące bezpieczeństwa w kraju według opisów w listach cywilnej ludności, 10 X 1945, n.p.

108. AIPN, 01265/752.

109. AIPN, MBP 3378, k. 71b. Specjalne doniesienie dotyczące działalności dywersyjnych band, n.d.

110. Wnuk, *Atlas polskiego podziemia*, 90.

111. APB, UW 285, k. 36. Meldunek starosty czyżewskiego "Donoszę, że w nocy z dnia . . ." [marzec 1945?].

112. APB, UW 285, k. 36. Meldunki o aktach terroru za czas od 4 VII do 1 IX 1945.

113. AIPN, MBP 3378, k. 73b. Specjalne doniesienie dotyczące działalności dywersyjnych band, n.d.

114. AAN, KC PPR 295/IX–415, k. 80. Raport specjalny o napadach bandyckich i przeprowadzonych operacjach na terenie Rzeczypospolitej Polskiej za okres od 1 do 31 III 1947.

115. Strzembosz, "Przestępczość i okupacja," 19.

116. APK, Wojewódzki Urząd Informacji i Propagandy 27, k. 294.

117. Wnuk, "Problem bandytyzmu wśród żołnierzy," 71.

118. Klukowski, *Zamojszczyzna*, vol. 2, 145.

119. Delumeau, *La Peur en Occident*, 158–62.

120. Klukowski, *Zamojszczyzna*, vol. 2, 15, 55, 63, 96, 143.

121. APB, UW 148, k. 29. Sprawozdanie miesięczne za kwiecień 1945.

122. AIPN, MBP 3378, k. 80. Specjalne doniesienie dotyczące działalności dywersyjnych band, n.d.

123. AIPN, KG MO 35/2038, k. 11. Raport sytuacyjny nr 2, Wydział Śledczy MO w Rzeszowie, October 15, 1944.

124. *Jedność Narodowa*, March 4, 1945.

125. Wnuk, "Problem bandytyzmu wśród żołnierzy," 76, 77.

126. Zuchwałe rabunki i mordy, *Echo Wieczorne*, November 16, 1946.

127. Kwiek, *Nie chcemy Żydów u siebie*.

128. Kopciowski, "Zajścia antyżydowskie na Lubelszczyźnie w pierwszych latach po drugiej wojnie światowej," 178–207.

129. Discussions of this include Dariusz, "Nieudana próba Grossa," 269.

130. "Powszechna rzecz zabijanie, rozmowa Joanny Szczęsnej z Markiem Edelmanem," in Gądek, *Wokół Strachu*, 286.

131. Gross, *Fear*, 261.

132. Klukowski, *Zamojszczyzna*, vol. 2, 164.

133. AIPN 01265/752. Specjalne doniesienie dotyczące bezpieczeństwa w kraju według opisów w listach cywilnej ludności, 10 X 1945, n.p.

134. AAN, MIiP 81, k. 73. Sprawozdanie instruktora terenowego Zbigniewa Sulimierskiego z inspekcji Powiatowego Oddziału Informacji i Propagandy w Łukowie, n.d.

135. For instance, after the raid on Czyżew in March 1945 in which nine Jews and three Poles were killed, on March 25 there was a mass, and afterward a rally took place. The starost estimated the crowd at seven thousand locals. This number seems high, since this would have been the total population of Czyżew. At the time, state employees were not forced to demonstrate that they could mobilize the masses. In other words, the starost had no reason to lie and inflate figures. The spontaneous attendance at a mass and a rally should be viewed as public protest against the local tragedy and, because nine of the victims were Jewish, against their murders.

9

IT WAS MORE THAN JUST TRAVEL NERVES

The historian Krystyna Kersten captured the reality of the postwar period in her metaphor of the "people on the roads." Tens of millions were swept across Europe in resettlements, deportations, migrations, and remigrations. Poland became a stage for the great human traffic of Poles, Germans, Ukrainians, Jews, and others. As soon as the fighting ended, they began to go home. Concentration camp inmates, prisoners of war, and forced laborers were on the move. By August 1945, some 8,000 Poles had returned from Germany, and by the end of 1947 their total number was about 1,600,000. Some 285,000 Poles were also traveling back from England, Hungary, Italy, and other countries where the war had tossed them. At the same time, nearly 250,000 Poles and Jews left Soviet Siberia and Kazakhstan, where they had been deported in 1940. The largest group of them, about 200,000, returned in the spring of 1946. The first half of 1946 also saw the most focused expulsions of Germans from Poland.

The end of the war began not only the homecoming of millions but also a new stage in the resettlements dictated by the victors' political decisions. Boundary changes, losses of lands that before the war had belonged to different states (Poland's Eastern Borderlands, which included Vilna and Lvov), and their compensation with lands to the west, the Regained Territories, was a huge impulse to migrate. By the end of 1946, nearly 800,000 Poles had come from lands incorporated into Soviet Ukraine, 274,000 from Belarus and 197,000 from Lithuania.

In 1945–47 the number of repatriates topped two million, then another 1.5 were resettled from the Eastern Borderlands. But there were more than these 3.5 million "people on the roads." Others were moving inside the country: hundreds of thousands who had been expelled by the Third Reich from the prewar Western and Northern Territories to the General Government, and those who had dispersed after the Warsaw Uprising. Poles settled in the Regained Territories and on formerly Ukrainian and German farms in eastern and central Poland. Overall, in a short period of time, several million people were moving within Poland.[1] The State Repatriation Office was formed by a decree of the Polish Committee of National Liberation of October 7, 1944, to direct their movements. But neither expanding its area of responsibility (after initially being charged with repatriating people from and to Poland's post-Yalta areas, it was later also made responsible for returning and resettling those who had been expelled by the Germans to the Regained Territories) nor changing its organizational structure improved the situation. The State Repatriation Office was no Moses; it could not command the sea.

The settlers came as large families, loaded down with suitcases, often with farm animals in tow. Most traveled by rail. Former concentration camp inmates, forced laborers, and prisoners of war usually carried a single bundle. Train stations resembled nomadic encampments. Babies were born, people fell ill, some died. A portrayal of Poznań, a key transition point, in June–July 1945 gives us an idea:

> The train stations are extremely busy. Various military transports are moving through, adding to the already dense passenger traffic. Thousands of people are passing through the Poznań stations (about 25,000 per day in the Main Station). This is a very high number if we take into account the fact that the Main Train Station's building has burned to the ground, that the rolling stock has mostly been destroyed. Every day we see train cars in the station with hundreds of people glued onto them, riding on roofs and steps. The Poles returning from the German Reich and from the other side of the Bug River are adding to this volume of passengers. With all this, the Main Station in Poznań still has no proper waiting room, only two tiny rooms. Thousands of people are spending the night on the platforms, out of doors or in the underground tunnels between the tracks. These discomforts and the shortage of toilets and places to buy food cause many illnesses and death (especially children and old people) in the train stations.[2]

The story of this mass exodus has already been told in studies, memoirs, and symbolic commemorations.[3] What may be missing is an understanding of how much this exodus influenced postwar national emotions. How did this great wandering affect the Poles psychologically and socially? "Our nation resembles a liquid that has been poured into a rubber bag, which is lying flat," explained a postwar analyst. "When it is pressed on one side, the liquid shifts and the shape of the bag changes. But the liquid does not come out of the bag, nor does the bag change its size."[4] This metaphor is only partly accurate. During the exodus, not only did hundreds of thousands of Poles escape from the bag by deciding to remain in the West or the East, but the national minorities also shrank. The liquid was both shaken and stirred.

Everyone came carrying their hopes and fears with them. Definitely more hopes. Some were so powerful that they raised the drained prisoners from their concentration camp bunks and injected them with the energy to head home, even if many died shortly after arriving there. Hopes of starting a new—that is, a better—life pushed peasants from Mazovia and Lesser Poland, who owned no land or only very small plots, to settle down in the Regained Territories. Thousands of people with leftist views, their eyes aglow for the victorious Soviet Union, counted on political change in their countries, an imminent "vault to the kingdom of freedom." In the Polish émigré community, it was especially the workers who had moved to France and Belgium before the war who believed that the new Poland would have no capitalists and be ruled by the left, which would believe in social justice. One of them reported from France, "That bourgeoisie had it good in Poland, and the Polish nation was forced to go abroad to earn a piece of bread, but now it seems that Poland will not belong to the masters, but democratically to the peasants and workers, everyone will go back and work for Poland's good and be treated like a human being, because the Poles here . . . are in favor of the government that is in place in Poland."[5]

But they also carried their fears. These were as different as the lives of the people who had them, so it would be impossible to find a common denominator for them. Also, the fears evolved with this exodus.

Deciding to return was not an obvious choice to everyone. The Poles who had been scattered around the world needed to decide whether returning to their country, which had landed in the Soviet sphere of influence, would not bring on a new kind of oppression. "I'm constantly going back and forth," Jan Maria Jakubaszek, a former forced laborer in the Reich, wrote in his diary on April 18, 1945. "My decision should be easy, since so much bad news is coming this way about what's going on in Poland: supposedly the NKVD is going wild, there will be a russki government, and when we return, they will send us deep into Russia. The Russians themselves confirm this last bit of news and say that they will only go back if they are forced to."[6] The Poles in France had similar apprehensions. One wrote in a letter dated August 1945, "We are asking you, is Poland free or occupied by Russia because we're getting ready to go back, but we're afraid of Russia. Please tell us how things are, should we come right now or await further instructions?"

Another letter written at around the same time reads, "We've thought of going to Poland straight away, but we're a bit scared of the Russkis."

The specter of a Third World War looming over Europe (see chap. 11, "The Phantoms of Transience") implied waiting. Workers who had left Poland to earn a living before the war were not sure now whether they would find work and decent wages there. One wrote in a letter, "Dear Mom, please write about how things are going for you, do you have enough to eat because here people are saying that things are bad in Poland, but others are saying that they're good."[7]

The Western occupation authorities in Germany and Austria built hundreds of displaced persons camps for refugees, former prisoners, prisoners of war, and forced laborers. Although they were to be temporary, the camps gave the displaced east Europeans political and material security as well as a sense of cultural belonging, since schools and theaters operated in them, and newspapers were published. An opinion poll conducted in the three Western occupation zones by UNRRA in May 1946 showed that 80 percent of the Poles living in the camps ruled out repatriation.[8] Both sides sent their emissaries to persuade the residents to return home or to remain in the West. Jan Wojciech Topolewski, who, following the Warsaw Uprising, was imprisoned in Auschwitz and then in Mauthausen-Gusen, landed in a displaced person camp in Indersdorf in Austria after liberation. He reminisced years later, "A liaison officer came from Poland saying that people who did not go back to the motherland by a certain date would lose their Polish citizenship and then would no longer be able to return. On the other hand, men from the Anders army tried to scare us that the transports from Germany are only transiting through Poland and then going straight to Siberia. So we were afraid of going back and discussed with our friends what to do. I decided that since I was the youngest I had nothing to fear and would go back after all."[9]

People who had spent time in German concentration camps tended to be less afraid, as whatever would happen to them now could not be worse than the camps. Soldiers from General Władysław Anders's Second Corps who had survived exile in Siberia were more afraid, and most did not return to Poland. A total of about half a million Poles decided not to go back to their Communist-ruled homeland.[10]

The natives of prewar Poland's Eastern Territories, which were annexed by the USSR following the Yalta Conference, were similarly torn. They had to decide whether to stay and risk being attacked by Ukrainian nationalists, when they also feared the next wave of Soviet collectivization, or to take their families away from their "small homeland" and move somewhere new. "To live in a state of uncertainty is worse than not to live at all, this is what it's like for us," wrote a father from the village of Czabarówka to his son who was away serving in the army.[11] The news about the situation of the resettled people coming from central and western Poland made many wait before deciding. A soldier wrote in a letter sent by field post to her family in Mołodeczno, warning them between the lines not to come, "People who have come here from the other side of the Bug have been wandering for 2 months, and no one has given them allocations or a place to live. They are living together with germans [sic], who are trying to chase them away. There is no order. Many people have gone back across the Bug."

Another woman soldier, this one from the First Sapper Brigade, predicted that a new form of slavery, with Germans as masters, awaited the settlers: "This place looks nothing like Poland, except the red-and-white flags on houses. The repatriates are settling down, but the germans [sic] come back after a while and, with the help of the town boss, throw out the Poles. At best they leave them to work for the germans [sic]."

A soldier of the Second Flamethrower Battalion compared the jobless and poor settlers to Gypsies: "I've seen the people who have come here. They walk like

It Was More Than Just Travel Nerves

sheep. They own nothing. They need to buy everything, but they have no money. People are laughing at them. They sit around train stations like gypsies. Some are going back home."

A soldier told his wife not to move: "If they start to register people to go to Poland, don't do it. Better stay home. Those who come here spend 2 months in the train station hungry and cold. No one cares about them."[12]

The war censorship office intercepted 98 letters of this kind in just one week of July 1945. Their writers were all presumably hesitating. Yet when in the last months of 1944 and the early months of 1945 registration began of people wanting to leave Lvov, Vilna, and Grodno, the drive to migrate proved very powerful, with the fear of remaining in the USSR a crucial consideration. People were torn by conflicting emotions, and discussions raged. Someone wrote, "You know, things are boiling here like a pot of water, everyone is going on about this resettling of Poles across the border to Poland. The Commission made up of two soviets (jews [sic]) was formed on 10 November, and they are signing up people who want to leave, they are even going to places which until now were occupied by the germans [sic]. Many people have signed up. We're staying put, have no intention of leaving for now."[13]

The Soviet authorities put different kinds of pressure on the Poles to make them leave. A Slavic studies professor at Jan Kazimierz University in Lvov wrote on November 11, 1944, "Dear Sir, you probably know that Poles and Jews are being vigorously pressured to move across the San and Bug Rivers as soon as possible. At the university, we feel it in the constant attempts to reduce the numbers of Polish professors, which to some degree has touched me, too. It's even more difficult for the people who would like to move permanently from there to Lvov."[14]

The gentle pressure apparently did not bring the desired results, and in January 1945 the NKVD arrested large numbers of Poles in Lvov, agitating and depressing them, speeding up the repatriation process.[15]

There were other fears. The huge majority of peasants living in prewar eastern Poland had never left their homes. For them, moving to the post-German lands meant a sort of emigration to a different country and different people, which was extremely stressful. A woman writing to her husband, who spent the war in Egypt, reported on August 19, 1945, "We went to an unknown place. We can see that we will be poor and can see hunger. What will happen? I think it will be difficult to wait for you. We are living in State Repatriation Office barracks now. It's difficult to get a place to live. I have no energy left to live."[16]

A man who had been resettled from the east could remember years later, "We were leaving home in fear. Poland is a great word, but we have to live, work somewhere, and we're going into the unknown." People moving from central and southern Poland experienced similar unease. Franciszek Smag, who moved from Rzeszów Province to Lower Silesia, did not manage to convince his parents to leave with him. They were simply afraid. They didn't believe that "these lands will be ours forever.... Go, go ... some said, and you will run away from that west again on foot in tears."[17]

There was anxiety about the journey itself, as it took about a month and was rarely comfortable. They traveled in cattle cars, which were barely adjusted to accommodate humans. People from the east often traveled on flatbed rail cars. A woman who arrived in Słupsk believed that the journey traumatized her more than everything she had lived through in the war. In September 1945 she wrote:

> We were beaten down by rain and dust all through the trip in the flatbed car, so that our clothing and products were soaked and spoiled. We waited for 6 days in Słupsk before they unloaded the car at the ramp. We then hired horses and did not arrive in our apartment till 11.8.45. The journey took a whole month, the conditions were difficult, people were left to their own devices with no help.... Everyone who arrived at their destination had to find a place to live, work by themselves and only then report to the office, to take care of the formalities. I didn't experience such hardship and misery even during the war.[18]

Traveling in such conditions, often without running water, in extreme heat and rain, and often together with farm animals, exhausted people physically and psychologically. Children and old people were especially vulnerable. Many transports carried typhus, and there was even talk of cholera. The repatriates experienced chronic shortages of food. In places where the trains stopped for longer, temporary cemeteries would sprout up along the tracks. The massed inflow of transports from the east created tailbacks of dozens of trains. The settlers would spend weeks camping out in small stations, which were unprepared for so many people, or in open fields.[19] Several letters written in August and September 1945 describe their ordeal. From Bytom: "We spent three weeks outside. Outdoors just like gypsies.... They brought us to Bytom, told us to unload, and do whatever you like. We had spent three weeks standing on the tracks in manure, in the middle of all kinds of disgusting things. It's difficult to find a place to live. We were to go on. We got into the car.... Mirek got the measles on the train, Jędruś diarrhea, Maryś is holding up somehow." And from Gdańsk:

We were on our way to Bytom, where they also didn't stop the train and they were right since thousands of people were just sitting there in the station, awaiting God's mercy. Out of our window we asked a man standing on the platform, and he told us that they were from Równe and surrounds, and they had been waiting there for 3 weeks. We asked where they were going, and they answered "we don't know." We sat there the same way in Strzelec, and they finally threw us out of the cars, Dolek had a stomach ailment. My auntie, who was traveling with us, fainted, and was dead in 15 minutes.

From Wrocław:

We passed through Przemyśl, Katowice all the way to Bytom (our escort ran away in Katowice). In Bytom, our driver, a soviet [sic], says "vygruzhaitsya" ["get out"]. And here are thousands of people who had come from various towns, Stanisławów, Kołomyja, Horodewka, Lvov, Stryj, etc., they are all waiting in the field (they got off the train), out in the open, in the rain. These poor people have made roofs and little houses with planks, and they've been waiting like this for 3–4 weeks, for the Committee to take pity on them, and they're sleeping together with cows, goats, dogs, etc. And the engine driver tells us to unload, and it's raining and it's getting dark.... And he wanted vodka, so we told him that he'll get his vodka but only if he takes us farther. He listened to us. They didn't unload us in Bytom. We went 200 m further (little wood), and we look and there are 7,000 people waiting here, too, they've also built little huts, and a fire is burning in front of every little house. It looks exactly like the Gypsy life. But, so what, we kept going. As we traveled at night, someone was shooting, I don't know where, whether at our car or not. They wanted to rob the last 2 cars, but the people who were in them shouted so loud that they scared them and they ran away. All this happened in the former German lands. We went to the Polish committee to complain, but unfortunately it didn't do anything. There are 10,000 more Poles here, unloaded, cattle together with people. Total despair.[20]

In 1945, repatriation offices couldn't handle the hundreds of thousands of arrivals. The situation improved in 1946, but only slightly. The repatriates came physically and emotionally exhausted and hungry to the places where they were supposed to settle. They were lonely and homeless, getting no assistance from the state administration. They experienced extreme emotions ranging from joy to panic and fear. Fear especially accompanied the pioneers of the settlement process, the first to land in the "new world." "The streets are empty," railway worker Marian Bogusz remembered of his first night in Szczecin. "Far away, somewhere downtown, I heard firing, individual shots. We were feeling low. A woman began to cry. We, the men, are pretending to be carefree but it's only for show. Our hearts are filled with anguish and fear."[21] The difficulties and anxieties didn't end as soon as people found an apartment or a house, as it was only the beginning of the next stage. Forced to feel at home in a new place, a new town, a new house, and new surroundings, people were naturally unsure of themselves. The resettlement destroyed the cultural and group norms and family ties that before had given them stability and security. They managed the feeling of being aliens, the bane of all emigrants, by building new ties, integrating with others who had also been transplanted. The first pioneering period favored cooperation among the settlers, as they tried to band together to face many problems and dangers.[22]

Adding to their anxiety was political insecurity, the mood of impermanence pervading the whole country and the doubt that the western and northern lands really belonged to Poland (see chap. 11, "The Phantoms of Transience"). Those observing this exodus of millions, especially the native populations, were also aware of the chaos and instability. Their anxiety produced conflicts and aggression. The locals viewed the new arrivals, even though they were also Polish, as different and foreign. The way they talked and acted was different, as was their way of dressing, and altogether it represented an economic threat. A letter confiscated by military censorship read: "My little wife! . . . The people here are very strange, stingy, and they don't think of us, Volhynians, as Poles."[23]

A woman from Warsaw, who felt like a stranger in Katowice, had the same complaints about aversions, even animosity: "You have no idea what a bad attitude the people of Katowice have toward us from Warsaw. Wherever we go, they look at us like we're intruders, the relations are really awful here. There are more Germans here than Poles. You hear the German talk and the damn Silesian talk in the streets, which we cannot bear listening to but stay calm."[24]

A rally was held in the main square in Cieszyn on September 1, 1945. The starost, a former military man, said in his speech that "the repatriates should be swept out with an iron broom because they've taken our possessions, which the local population would otherwise have." He also attacked the staff of the State Repatriation Office. He turned directly to the crowd to hear its verdict. People said, "We'll go to their homes, drag them out and kill them."[25]

It was not only spatial migrations that could make people anxious. Hundreds of thousands of people moved from the countryside to the cities (see chap. 11, the section titled "A New Evil: Housing"), and thousands moved up professionally, even vaulting up a few levels in occupation and prestige. The postwar cadre revolution not only carried the "expendable" people but also created opportunities to advance those who, in ordinary times, would have had to wait for a long time to move ahead. As they took on new responsibilities and new positions, they were enthusiastic and eager to work, which is the only attitude that many postwar memoirs mention. But some, especially the uneducated workers and peasants who were placed in positions that far surpassed their skills, felt out of place and dreaded humiliation. Often, they were mocked. The intelligentsia would sarcastically cite the postwar slogan "It's not graduating from high school, but zeal that will make you an officer." Many such "officers" tried to catch up by attending crash courses, which became one of the reasons behind the rush to education. This mixture of limited social acceptance, awareness of one's inadequate skills, and fear explained their obedience to the authorities to whom they owed their careers. Every government office, institution, factory, and armed forces unit employed people like this, who would later become an important driving force of Stalinism.

From the psychosocial point of view, the great migration of peoples had the short-term effect of explosions of aggression, and it augmented collective anxiety and fear, but it also inflicted long-term scars, which left a mark on collective attitudes and behaviors for many years. Krystyna Kersten includes in them social isolation, a mix of passive and arriviste attitudes, personality disorders, neuroses, the slackening of moral norms, and a rise of social pathologies.[26] All this added to the other consequences of the war and the postwar periods.

NOTES

1. For detailed data, see Eberhardt, *Przemieszczenia ludności na terytorium Polski spowodowane II wojną światową*; Sienkiewicz and Hryciuk, *Wysiedlenia, wypędzenia i ucieczki 1939–1945*.

2. AIPN, KG MO 35/888, k. 17–18. Raport sytuacyjny MO w Woj. Poznańskim za czas od 20 VI– 5 VII 1945.

3. It would be impossible to list all the works. The most important ones, which include bibliographies, are Kersten, "Migracje w Polsce," 3–26; Banasiak, *Działalność osadnicza PUR*; Szarota, *Osadnictwo miejskie na Dolnym Śląsku w latach 1945–1948*; Kersten, *Repatriacja ludności*; Ciesielski, *Przesiedlenie ludności polskiej z kresów wschodnich do Polski 1944–1947*; Wróbel, *Na rozdrożu historii*; Piskorski, *Wygnańcy*.

4. Krasocki, "Metamorfozy migracyjne," *Praca i Opieka Społeczna*, January–March 1946, vol. 1, 9.

5. AIPN, MBP 3378, k. 118. Specjalne doniesienie dot. emigracji we Francji.

6. Jakubaszek, *Mój ostatni rok wojny*, 458.

7. AIPN, MBP 3378, k. 116, 117. Specjalne doniesienie dot. emigracji we Francji.

8. Lembeck and Wessels, *Befreit aber nicht in Freiheit*, 146ff.

9. Madoń-Mitzner, *Ocaleni z Mauthausen*, 316.

10. Kersten, *Repatriacja ludności*, 216–25.

11. Okrzesa, "Listy z końca wojny," 109.

12. AIPN 835/137, k. 123. Do Ministra Obrony Narodowej Marszałka Polski M. Żymierskiego, August 22, 1945.

13. AAN, PKWN I/78, k. 14. Doniesienie specjalne dotyczy repatriacji.

14. AAN, PKWN I/78, k. 15. Doniesienie specjalne dotyczy repatriacji.

15. Hryciuk, "'Ciężkie dni Lwowa,'" 21–33.

16. AIPN, MBP 3378, k. 108. Specjalne doniesienie.

17. Bigorajska and Jabłoński, *Nasze nowe życie. Pamiętniki z konkursu na wspomnienia mieszkańców ziem zachodnich i północnych*, 179.

18. AIPN, MBP 3378, k. 108. Specjalne doniesienie.

19. For more see Banasiak, *Działalność osadnicza PUR*, 37–57.

20. AIPN, MBP 3378, k. 108, 109. Specjalne doniesienie.

21. Białecki, *Drogi powrotu*, 15.

22. For more see Magierska, *Ziemie zachodnie i północne w 1945 roku*; Osękowski, *Społeczeństwo Polski zachodniej i północnej w latach 1945–1956*; Kwilecki, "Migracje pionierskie na Ziemiach Odzyskanych," 5–29.

23. AAN, PKWN I/78, k. 3. Sprawozdanie za miesiąc listopad [1944].

24. AIPN, MBP 3378, k. 63b. Specjalne doniesienie dot. volksdeutschów.

25. AAN, MIiP 497, k. 19. Sprawozdanie wiecu Centralnej Komisji Związków Zawodowych.

26. Kersten, "Ruchliwość w Polsce po II wojnie światowej jako element przeobrażeń społecznych i kształtowania postaw," 191.

THE POLITICS OF FEAR

Fear keeps company with social conflict, power, and decision-making—in a word, with politics.[1] People have always feared authority, the kind before which the knees bend on their own, which has always existed in relations between the rulers and the ruled. Those who have power have also always feared losing it, whether to an aristocratic conspiracy or a popular uprising. Observing the omnipresence of fear in politics, Thomas Hobbes believed that fear is a crucial force shaping public space and that sovereign power uses fear to govern.[2] Machiavelli's advice to his prince was different when he argued that "it is far safer to be feared than loved" because "fear is bound by the apprehension of punishment which never relaxes its grasp."[3]

In Hannah Arendt's view, fear is a component of our political tradition. She wrote in *The Origins of Totalitarianism*, "Arbitrary power, unrestricted by law, wielded in the interest of the ruler and hostile to the interests of the governed, on one hand, fear as the principle of action, namely fear of the people by the ruler and fear of the ruler by the people, on the other—these have been the hallmarks of tyranny throughout our tradition."[4] Today's liberal democracies have been known to employ fear in political rivalries. Some sociologists, most prominently Frank Furedi, Anthony Giddens, and Ulrich Beck,[5] go so far as to believe that we are living in a culture that is marked by an exceptional aversion to danger. Their contention is debatable, for how would one fit into it the dictatorship of Lucius Cornelius Sulla, the era of the Ottoman wars, or Stalin's Great Purge? Historians know this much: the association between fear and politics is old and not in the least bit boring. Governing Communists have written an important chapter in the history of fear. Even though they did not discover anything new, in line with Marx's belief that quantity begets quality, they did set countless records. To Michał Heller, the Bolsheviks were the first to produce "a means of transforming human consciousness" out of fear.[6]

Things were supposed to be different. Communist ideologues promised that in the final reckoning, the imminent arrival of universal equality would eliminate fear of the higher-ups in a hierarchy. Lenin's cook governing the state symbolized the beginning of an era of absolute egalitarianism that would put an end to the history of the politics of fear. The "paradox of progress" lay in eliminating "backward social classes" before universal equality could be attained. Therefore, in the Communist countries, political fear became an intrinsic feature of the public space, and the Communists' policies were founded on it. The postwar period can be called revolutionary also from this point of view. To stretch out the title of Krystyna Kersten's book, the establishment of Communist rule in Poland was born of fear.[7] It became a component of the new post–Second World War political culture and was internalized by most Poles and their ruling elites.

Even though political fear has a long history, we feel it rather than comprehend it. Fear of political persecution is the most obvious association, and terror and fear are inseparable. In the long term, eliminating political opponents calms the public down and intimidates anyone who might even think about resisting. Earlier, persecution rarely happened on a mass scale, and it generally affected only a few or a dozen percent of the population. But with show trials, public executions, and other displays of power, the new fear became universal. The Soviet purges of the late 1930s are a classic example of this kind of political fear.

A more sophisticated method employed in the politics of fear to construct an atmosphere of threat is propaganda; rhetoric and political marketing can also serve as tools. The intellectual historian Corey Robin defines political fear as "a people's felt apprehension of some harm to their collective well-being—the fear of terrorism, panic over crime, anxiety about moral decay—or the intimidation wielded over men and women by governments or groups." Robin views fear as a "political tool, an instrument of elite rule or insurgent advance, created and sustained by political leaders or activists who stand to gain something from it."[8] Frank Furedi stresses that politicians "self-consciously manipulate people's anxieties in order to realize their objectives."[9] The tactics of instilling fear may thus be used both to win voters' support and to delegitimize a political opponent.[10] After the Second World War, terror and the rhetoric of fear went hand in hand in Poland.

TERROR AND FEAR

This idea was not new. It was imported from Moscow in late September–early October 1944 by a group of Polish Communists. Stalin was openly displeased about the state of affairs in the territories occupied by the Red Army. He subjected Bolesław Bierut and his comrades to a critique of principles or, to put it bluntly, made them stand at attention, scolded them crudely, and browbeat them. In a tamer version of his words, which survive in two sets of minutes of the October session of the Politburo of the Central Committee of the Polish Workers' Party, Stalin accused them of "softness" and "decadence." He took the Poles to task upon learning that no landowner had been put behind bars: "What sort of Communists are you? You're not only lacking Communism, you're lacking patriotism." He referred to the presence of the Red Army: "You are so powerful now that if you say 2 times 2 is 16, your enemies will agree." During their next visit eight days later, he ordered the Poles in his typically fierce way not to defend the Home Army but to "grab the adversary by the throat."[11]

Władysław Gomułka's memoir includes the blunt version. After the official talks ended around midnight, Stalin invited everyone to his residence outside Moscow. A few hours into the libations, Stalin and Molotov "linked arms with Bierut" and took him aside. Gomułka remembered that "the conversation was very particular. Stalin immediately dropped his jovial tone and brutally attacked Bierut in vulgar language. According to Bierut's report to the Politburo, Stalin began by asking '*Shto ty, yob tvoyu mat, delaesh v Polshe? Kakoi s tebya komunist, ty sukin syn?*' ['What are you, mother f*, doing in Poland? What sort of a Communist are you, you son of a bitch?'] Bierut himself recounted that he had though Stalin, who had drunk a bit, was playing with him, merely joking. He smiled back at Stalin's tirade. Molotov brought him down to earth, attacking him crudely just like Stalin: '*Shto ty, durak, ulybaeshsya? Zdes' nie shutki, a delo seryoznoe*' ['What are you smiling at, you fool? This is not fun and games, but serious work']." Gomułka recognized that this was an attack not just on Bierut but on the entire Polish leadership, "especially over our treatment of the landowners, which according to Stalin (as he repeatedly said later) was liberal, 'Tolstoyan.' Bierut was chosen as the messenger to relay their views and positions to the whole leadership of the Polish Workers' Party."[12]

Stalin was teaching the Polish Communists two lessons. First, he insinuated that he expected them to launch harsh persecution of the "class enemy"—that is, anyone who opposed or might oppose those in power now. He instructed them to use the carrot-and-stick method, with the stick of fear and the carrot of land reform, whose effects interested him as much as the policy of terror. Stalin's method of governing, as Krystyna

Kersten has emphasized, consisted of meting out fear and a feeling of illusory security in such doses as to make people surrender and feel demoralized, in contrast to the Germans' effect during their occupation, which incited universal resistance.[13] Stalin understood the need to fine-tune tools of power according to time and place while believing wholly and without Tolstoy's hesitation in the view presented in *The Prince* that fear never fails, as it makes the ruled dread punishment.

Stalin's second lesson for the Polish Communists was that they, too, should experience fear. This was the next dogma in the art of governance, described so well by Simon Montefiore.[14] Not only the ruled but, perhaps even more importantly, the rulers, too, should be afraid. These two lessons were learned, and beginning in October 1944 the Polish Communists persecuted more dynamically.

Of course, policies of terror and fear were employed earlier. The NKVD and SMERSH (military counter-intelligence) began to arrest and deport people immediately after "liberation." In the summer of 1944 they targeted Home Army soldiers and officers who were coming out of the underground during operation "Tempest." From July to December 1944, in the Vilna district alone, 8,592 people were imprisoned and 1,589 killed.[15] At times they were arrested in the quiet of night; at other times people were surprised by roundups in daytime. Villages and forests were combed, and checks were conducted in city streets and at town gates. Now, fear returned to the first areas liberated from the Germans. Some even believed that the new fear was greater than the fear under German rule because the Soviets tended not to adhere to any laws and could act unpredictably. While the Poles had had time to get used to living under the German occupation, the unfamiliar Soviet regime was stirring up greater fear now. This is evident in a report by Irena Sztachelska about the emotional atmosphere in Vilna in the summer of 1944:

> Fear of oppression and deportation to Kazakhstan was omnipresent. Many people justify this by saying that they are much more frightened of the "soviets" [*sic*] than of the germans [*sic*] because the germans [*sic*] do everything in the "majesty of the law" and when they execute someone or deport them to do forced labor they will always write about it and announce what's going on, while the "soviets" [*sic*] take people "no one knows why, no one knows when and no one knows where to."... So far mobilization has not been announced, individual summons have been handed out, no one wants to go to the *voyenkomat* [military commissariat] for any reason, they're afraid that they will be deported beyond the Urals, and so on. All the more so since unofficially no one is writing or saying that the Poles are to go to the Polish Army but, on the contrary, that agitators and the Polish paper in Vilna *Prawda Wileńska* are agitating for people to join the Red Army.[16]

Beginning in October 1944 the already considerable persecution became mass-scale. In just five days, October 20–25, Soviet operations groups in Lublin and Białystok Provinces arrested 1,051 people.[17] Improvised internment camps were put up to accommodate the detainees, whose numbers began to grow exponentially. One of them sent out a secret message about those inside his camp: "Some 500 people, majors, colonels and 1 general, we were taken into the fenced-in area 4 km from Lubartów, to the Skrobów agricultural school. We are visible because we walk around freely behind the wire, communicate with people across it, and this is how this letter got out."[18]

But the persecution was not limited to those active in underground organizations; it could affect anyone anywhere. Krystyna Kersten interpreted it as touching the group symbolizing national aspirations and values most of the population believed in. Arresting the Home Army leadership and those in Poland working for the office of the representative of the government in exile aimed to isolate them and—more importantly—to infect people with anxiety and make them believe that renouncing their ties to the Home Army, the Polish government in exile, and Western culture would buy them security.[19] In terms of social behaviorism, which Stalin may have been familiar with,[20] the idea was to use the stimulus of fear to prompt the conditioned reaction of giving up at the very thought of resisting. Whatever the theoretical foundations of this school of thought, in practice the wave of persecutions called the "October turnaround"[21] increased tensions, fear, and terror. We read in Zygmunt Klukowski's diary:

> OCTOBER 7, 1944: "All the roads are blocked. Yesterday, even right outside Szczebrzeszyn on our way back from Zamość, we were stopped and asked for ids. The NKVD came to town last night, and we were expecting house searches. Our general situation is becoming more and more difficult."
>
> OCTOBER 10: "On Sunday, 8 October, late at night, the bolsheviks [sic] encircled Tomaszów and after going through all the homes detained about 300 men, most of recruitment age; they took them to the barracks in Zamość."
>
> OCTOBER 26–27: "News has been reaching us of more and more arrests in our region, especially among the so-called inheritors, i.e., landowners or even renters.... These growing numbers of arrests are creating a very heavy atmosphere in the affected areas. People who are known locally don't know what to do with themselves. They have gone into hiding, try to come out as little as possible, work is suffering, everything is falling apart."
>
> OCTOBER 31: "There is a heavy atmosphere among those in town who are of interest to various degrees. No one sleeps in his house. Long before curfew, even though the moonlight is bright, the streets are deserted, not a soul is out. Just as it was under the Germans at times of arrests and roundups."
>
> NOVEMBER 8: "Very badly dressed, shifty, Russian-speaking types are walking around, lying in wait in a place for several hours at a time, on the lookout for new prey. They are the NKVD, undercover. This has an awful impact on the public psyche. People are uncertain, they don't know what to do."
>
> DECEMBER 23: "Several NKVD men came to Szczebrzeszyn yesterday afternoon. They locked themselves in the town office with Secretary Skórzyński. They forced him to show them the population register and read out all the names on it. They went over some lists they had brought with them. The news traveled at lightning speed, and people were terrified because everyone knows what it's all about when the Gestapo or the NKVD looks at population registers in the municipal office. They say that the NKVD will be staying in town longer to bring order and peace."[22]

Klukowski's diary paints a picture of a community whose emotional space is dominated by fear and anxiety. As we try to imagine this atmosphere, we realize immediately how quickly it could become infected with fear. People shared information ("the news traveled at lightning speed"). In those days social communication was mainly oral, and we can surmise that at least the first reactions to fear did not necessarily tear social ties but, on the contrary, may even have strengthened them. The catchphrases "they're arresting" or "the NKVD came to town" played the same role as the historical bugle call from the tower of Saint Mary's Basilica in Cracow alerting people to the danger of a Tatar attack in 1241. The people of Szczebrzeszyn, however, did not leap onto the town walls, as they would have done in a medieval town, but tried to hide instead.

Another finding is that people continued to use wartime survival strategies even though the German occupation was over. A tormenting anxiety entered their lives on the heels of the initial mobilization spurred by fear. Hiding did not make everyone feel secure, as some people experienced a fear-induced depression from a feeling of futility, helplessness, and disorientation. "This state of affairs has a terrible effect on the collective psyche. People are undecided, they don't know what to do." According to psychologists, prolonged exposure to fear and anxiety can erode social ties and undermine the role of tradition.[23] Growing alcoholism was certainly another consequence. Furthermore, living with uncertainty and under threat made life seem transitional and fluid. For some, this released anger, especially because of the stability, order, and security the government was promising. A letter from a village near Szczebrzeszyn reflects this mood: "This russki gestapos are all over the villages and there is no certainty whatsoever day or night. The best people are constantly being arrested and taken away. And when they take someone, you can't even find out where that prisoner is! This didn't use to happen even at the worst of times. People are beginning to lose faith that this government is our own."[24]

This insecurity was practically omnipresent in the areas the Red Army had come into, at times becoming a collective panic. In Lvov in January 1945 (as described in chap. 9), after over seven thousand people, mostly the local intelligentsia, were imprisoned, fear ruled the land. Soviet reports noted that their action had instilled a greater discipline and increased productivity in some enterprises.[25] In Warsaw and environs, too, such harassment marked the collective sense of security.[26] In the winter of 1945–46, rumors traveled about alleged lists being compiled of people to arrest in Warsaw.[27] The underground publication *Alarm* published in the Warsaw district of Praga informed:

> In the town of S. the NKVD visits a citizen. They eat, drink, talk. They ask their host to walk them home, and he is never heard from again. They walk around at night, eavesdrop under windows, peek around. They barge into homes, arresting people for uttering a single careless word at a family gathering. You should whisper, and then only to your people. The network of NKVD agents has grown more in three months than the Gestapo did in five years. Death sentences in Lublin destroy some traitors and wait patiently for others. The number of arrests is growing frightfully. So far, no one has found out what has happened to them.[28]

The terror generated by the NKVD's arrests also governed the lands that were being liberated by the Red Army after its January 1945 offensive. At least 25,000 to 30,000 civilians were deported from Pomerania and Upper Silesia to the USSR; 15,000 of them were miners who were incarcerated in camps in the Donbas and the West Siberian Basin. A total of 34,787 Poles were detained by March 1945 in "operation clearing the rears," and most of them were interned in the USSR.[29] People were seized by different methods, as they walked down the street or at home, ambushed or summoned to the police station under false pretenses. Searches were conducted in public places such as cinemas and ended with arrests, especially of young men. Someone wrote from a locality near Lublin in April, "You know, Staś, what these times are all about. There are roundups, they are rounding up young boys, and no one knows where and why, everyone is hiding as well as they can, we haven't had it here yet, but nearby villages are getting their roundups and they're grabbing people."[30]

Prisons filled up, and NKVD offices emanated terror. The NKVD headquarters at 10 Strzelecka Street in Warsaw had the worst reputation. An inmate wrote, "In Warsaw (Strzelecka 10) people are dying without getting any help."[31] In some localities, including Lvov, the NKVD took over buildings that had previously housed the Gestapo.

Fear was used to break people during interrogations, and pretend executions were one of the most treacherous methods used. The whole operation culminated in the arrest in early March 1945 of sixteen leaders of the Polish Underground State. Subsequent accounts of their trial in Moscow made many people surrender psychologically. The message of these unlawful arrests was all too clear: the Soviets could do whatever they liked, and no one, not even the British and the Americans, would stop them. These accumulated experiences and apprehensions yielded gossip circulating around the country about banishments present and future. There was talk of labor camps in Siberia, of the vast steppes of Kazakhstan. In May 1945, a man from Rembertów near Warsaw wrote, "We've been deluding ourselves for so long, and the oppression is getting worse.... Every few days, trains carrying 3,000 young people each roll east."[32]

News about arrests made people panic, increasing the already heightened fear that accompanied the marching armies, slowed down the restoration of a psychological equilibrium, and, instead of disarming resistance, heightened anti-Soviet hostility. It discouraged people from doing anything and made it difficult for the new government to build structures, all the more so since the pointed knife of terror often struck at the remaining local elites. Landowners, farm managers, and local administration and government employees, such as foresters, railway workers, and teachers, as well as priests were taken into custody. Immediately after liberation, in January 1945 in Kielce, Soviet counterintelligence detained almost all the staff of the local justice system who appeared for a meeting with the deputy minister of justice: judges, prosecutors, lawyers, notaries, and even court ushers. That deputy minister, Leon Chajn, remembered "this generated enormous anxiety in town." Rumors attested to the total distrust of the new authorities, as if they had set a trap on purpose. A large crowd of women gathered outside the mayor's office. Chajn saw "naked terror"[33] in their faces, in the first of the many terrors that would roll through Kielce after the war.[34] A similar mass arrest of lawyers and judges was organized by Soviet counterintelligence in Radom, and sporadically in smaller localities.[35] We can imagine that the popular reaction was similar.

In some regions, especially the northeast and southeast, pacifications that began on a huge scale in April 1945 increased fear of the NKVD, whose troops became the main weapon in the politics of fear in Poland now, their numbers reaching some 35,000 troops and functionaries. The Government Delegate for Poland telegraphed London on April 26, "Pacifications of Garwolin, Łuków, Lubartów and Zamość Districts have begun. The Soviet troops surround a village and transport all the men, with the exception of juveniles and old men, east. The reasons for the arrests of an estimated ten thousand or more, led to a mass escape to the forest and the formation of informal armed units, which, however, are passive and defend themselves only when attacked. The Soviet air force has bombed Czeremieckie Forests."[36]

This three-act pacification scenario—the army encircles the village, manhunt, arrests—was repeated not only in Lublin Province but also in the Podlasie and Rzeszów regions. The anonymous author of a letter dated May 30, 1945, reported on the burning of a village, probably in Lublin Province: "Dear Wacio, 3 Russian [soldiers] were killed in the village of Borówek, 7 km from us, and so our army and the russkis came and burned the village. . . . Some guys came after this tragic burning and wrote about what they saw and what people told them. They took pictures of the burned place and said that someone would be held responsible."[37]

In July 1945, the NKVD arrested several thousand people in the Suwałki region, of whom nearly six hundred were never heard from again. According to a Russian historian, the combat methods were similar to those used in Russia during the civil war: picking out hostages from the civilian population and the families of underground members, and exiling Home Army people to the USSR.[38] Circulating open cars with bodies of those who had been killed and the burning of villages were also used to intimidate, something the Gestapo and the Polish Security Office did, too. No wonder that fear of the Soviet secret police spread like wildfire. "The NKVD legend is coming from Russia and Lublin Province. People are afraid to talk to one another, since the least bit of inattention can lead to arrest," said an officer who spent a few months in Poland after being released from a prisoner-of-war camp and before he left for the West in April 1945.[39] A poem by Tadeusz Borowski written before he returned to Poland from a displaced persons camp also discusses how fear travels:

> And we, one by one, secretively
> across the border illegally down a forbidden road
> to our homeland in our dreams
> home to the graves . . .
> We will seek but not find anyone
> look into strangers' faces
> keep silent, after all everyone knows . . .
> yes . . .
> someone will whisper quietly: the NKVD
> fear . . .[40]

The forces keeping fear alive did not evaporate for the whole year after the war. The NKVD army units were still pacifying towns and villages as late as 1946. Two Soviet officers were murdered in Janów Lubelski in July 1946, and an NKVD army unit retaliated by arresting locals.[41] Actions of this kind had an impact on collective behavior. In Lubaczów, Rzeszów Province, on April 23, 1945, the army and militia fled their barracks, and the next day a panic broke out. Offices ceased functioning, shopkeepers closed their shops, and the local population hid in their homes or dispersed in the countryside. The army's mass desertions and the civilians' panic were caused by the news—true, as it would turn out—that a unit of the NKVD border forces had come to town. They disarmed four soldiers, killed a militia officer, and wounded another.[42] In Białystok Province, a Red Army unit set fire to an area in the village of Olszewo, killing two people, in retaliation for the burning of a few of its trucks. "Fearing more harassment," reported the village head, "the whole population of the village of Olszewo has fled, and currently no one is left."[43]

The fresh memory of the persecutions was the perfect underpinning for outbursts of panic. Silesia experienced one in March 1946. In Bytom, people were talking about how "Red Army soldiers are organizing roundups in the streets, packing people onto trucks and taking them away for forced labor." The terrified Silesians consulted local newspapers to check whether this was true: "They are calling from Zabrze, calling from Gliwice, Sosnowiec, asking directly about the 'roundups' in Bytom."[44] Sometimes a regular army unit, even of the Polish Army, appearing in a small town, especially in eastern Poland, was enough for a panic to start and for people to flee into the fields and forests. In Lublin Province in 1945, "the local population (Janów), swayed by skillful agitation, was living in constant fear that an 'action' was about to take place." In Siedlce and Sokołów Districts, "The civilian population flees the church as a group, even during Mass, at the mere sight of the Army. The soldiers, irritated by the civilians' mass escape from the church, wanting to hold them back, fired in the air several times to make them stop; some did stop, and the troops got along fine with them. The soldiers bought ice cream for the children, candy for the young women and talk with the men to convince them that they were Polish."[45]

But it was not only the Soviets who triggered political fear. In the collective imagination, the Polish Security Office was becoming the new bad guy. Establishing the new regime involved institutionalizing fear. Over time, the Security Office became synonymous with insecurity: "The first institutions of 'people's power' that people came in contact with, remembered Franciszek Ryszka about life in Sokółka in the summer of 1944, were the Military Replenishment Office and the Security Office, working hand-in-hand.... It was soon confirmed that this is an authority that should be feared."[46] Arrest statistics show that the ministry was becoming well established,[47] adding to the collective fear. In 1944, the Security Office arrested just over 11,000 people; in 1945, they arrested 45,000; and in 1946, they arrested 44,500. Only in 1947, when 30,000 people landed in jails and prisons, did the figure drop noticeably.[48] People instinctively compared these arrests with those of the German occupation, often calling them roundups. In early December 1944, someone wrote to a priest friend, "The Reverend Father, I hear that there are many arrests in Lublin Province, and the arrestees are being sent to Majdanek. What a disgrace that people in Polish uniforms but without a Polish soul are tormenting those Poles who worked for Poland's welfare and suffered so much also from the Germans, had to hide. Today, society's scum is also tormenting them. May the Lord make this, too, pass, and may Poland stop being Communist."[49]

Another letter, this one mailed in a village in Lublin Province, reads, "On 12.1.45 there was a mass arrest in our village, they learned how to do it from the Germans and they're doing it, too, this is even more distressing because now it's brother against brother. What for? For getting back a free Motherland?"[50]

In some regions, the Security Service and the Domestic Security Corps joined forces to fight the underground by systematically pacifying villages, some of which they burned, and even entire towns. An example was the town of Leżajsk, where in the night of April 27–28, 1946, an operations group of three hundred Domestic Security Corps and forty Security Service men organized a raid "to arrest the bandits from the 'Wołyniak' gang." A local employee of the Ministry of Information and Propaganda described it:

> The town and its environs were surrounded. Some were arrested already in the night, and others' homes were searched. At about 8 a.m. men were not allowed to walk in the streets, and an announcement went out that all men of 14–50 years of age should register with the Security Office Commission stationed in the municipal office in Leżajsk. All the men were held in the Municipal Office, the remaining 500 people in the courtyard under Citizens' Militia escort. In the meantime, the Security Office authorities arrived and put on a speech for the population, who were brought into the market square and encircled by the army, about combating banditry, the strength of the worker, the power of democracy and so on. It was noteworthy that one of the speakers said that an "action" would take place today in Leżajsk, which gave a great fright to the population, who could remember the Gestapo action in 1943 on 28 May, when 48 of the best Poles were executed. The arrested were interrogated in the municipal offices. At about 15:30, 38 of them, including 22 people from Leżajsk (and all the restaurant bosses), were put in cars and taken to the Security Office in Rzeszów. Most of them were released without interrogations or any interpellation [sic] by the Security Office. It must be stressed that the Security Office criticized the local secondary schools the most, both teachers and pupils, and Scout troops, calling their leader a bandit, which isn't right, since both the schools and Scouting have a good reputation in Rzeszów Province and, as far as learning and upbringing are concerned, are among the top schools according to the School Inspectorate. Furthermore, the people (men) were outraged that they were not allowed to go to church, since the army was standing at all three church entrances, and they were shooing people away and putting them in the market square and in the town office courtyard. . . . The Security Office conducted a search of the monastery during mass, looking for weapons, and they arrested 3 citizens, which even the Gestapo didn't do. They were looking for weapons under the pews and lecterns, and removed the population from the monastery.[51]

The war diary of the Internal Security Corps Rzeszów branch show that similar raids, which involved dragging people out of their homes and searching and arresting some of them, were the security forces' standard operating procedure at this time.[52] Often, operations of this kind were transformed into a battue with weapons.[53] One can only begin to imagine the trauma that stayed with its victims when so much more than capture and arrest was inflicted on them.

In the postwar years, jails and prisons could be recognized not only by their architecture but also by the throngs churning outside their gates, delivering clothing and food to their nearest and dearest. People drew great pride and joy from news about the underground's many forays to free inmates. Similar emotions accompanied the opening of prison gates. An inhabitant of Krasnystaw wrote in a private letter in early June 1945, "As you know, because there will be a new government, prison gates are gradually opening and people are coming out. Crowds gather at prison gates, waiting for their relatives and friends. Those coming out are pale and feeble, but somehow happy and joyous that providence smiled at them and gave them freedom, something that some had not expected. Our people are helping them, giving them money for the road. Maybe Marysia and her youngest brother, our organist's children, will come back, too."[54]

The elation at being released must have come with anguish about future arrests. Lublin Castle prison became exceptionally infamous. An official report from Lublin Province stated that "there is never-ending public conjecture and suspicion of the barbaric treatment of the inmates, which has a negative effect on the authority of Public Security. The locals are saying: there is no difference in the way the Poles and the Germans treat their inmates."[55] Underground publications reported cases of needles being driven into heads, the crushing of testicles with tongs, beatings with sticks, and stripping naked and scalding. Prisoners in Łomża, Białystok, and Wysokie Mazowieckie were said to have been held in cellars with standing water.[56] Janina Godycka-Ćwirko, who was randomly arrested by the Security Office in early 1946, recalled, "They brought a prisoner who had fought for a free Poland, he had belonged to the Home Army, was put in the cell next to mine. We shared a door. We could hear his screams. He was definitely tortured. When his screams stopped, they poured water on him. Bloody water flowed under the door between our two cells. I was shivering as if I had a fever. I was reminded of the beatings of prisoners in the Gestapo courtyard, which I could see out of my window in Horodyszcze."[57]

The constant stream of newspaper reports about death sentences may have sustained the intense collective fear. Special Courts were handing down death sentences to wartime collaborators and German war criminals right and left. Headlines announced, "Traitor sentenced to death." There was no opinion research at the time to tell us how the Poles received headlines of this kind, but is very likely that they did not surprise many of them. News about death sentences for people connected to the underground, who were officially called bandits, probably evoked the opposite reaction, which was based on fear and anxiety. So far, historians have not studied the public's understanding of the legal system. But it is doubtful that people were familiar with the contents of documents such as the Polish Committee of National Liberation's "O ochronie państwa" (About the protection of the state) of October 30, 1944; they must simply have intuited that many acts could result in the death sentence.[58]

On the other hand, the authorities did all they could to educate the public about the new system's oppressive nature. The texts of decrees were displayed in public places, printed in newspapers, and read on the radio. Show trials played a crucial role in educating the public through fear. They were sometimes staged in cinemas and factory halls, usually in provincial capitals, with large numbers of people brought in to watch. At times courts would have guest sessions of trials in towns that did not have them. They would often be held in towns where pacifications were underway. Posters and flyers then notified the public about the sentences. The numbers of show trials and death penalties went up in the second half of 1946. In October 1946, the Regional Military Court in Warsaw tried eleven members of the underground Polish Organization and the National Armed Forces. Three defendants were sentenced to death. Twelve more of the organization's members were tried in late November–early December, and this time six were given the death penalty. Capital punishment was not only a way for "people's power" to penalize or take revenge on the underground but also a warning to anyone who might think of resisting it. In 1944–48, some 2,500 people of the underground were sentenced to death, and most of them were executed.[59]

Public executions were also used to sow fear. The press described them in detail, but only when German war criminals were executed. A soldier of the Ukrainian Insurgent Army was executed on March 28, 1945, in Chełm. The town garrison's prosecutor used posters for official announcements about this "spectacle."[60]

Poles, too, were put to death in public, by firing squad or by hanging. Crowds were usually herded in by force to watch this depressing murder show, often of people they knew well. In June 1945, the public execution of Stanisław Wojciechowski (pseudonym "Miś") was staged in the market square in Zwierzyniec near Zamość.[61] In Sanok in southeastern Poland, public hangings became a virtual fad. On May 24, 1946, two men from Antoni Żubryd's unit, who had been sentenced by a summary court, were put to death in a sports stadium. "The execution made a powerful impression on the local population.... There has been relative calm since the executions in Sanok and Sanok District."[62] They apparently had the desired effect, as eleven days later another person was hanged, this time in the main square.[63] Even local schoolchildren were forced to watch.[64]

Public executions also took place elsewhere in Poland. On December 27, 1946, four executions had the goal of cleansing two districts of Białystok Province. Put to death publicly were Mieczysław Wyrozębski in the village of Grodzisk for "belonging to Sikora's band," Władysław Ratyński in the village of Dzierzby for giving shelter to members of "Bartosz's gang," and Lucjan Marchel and Zygmunt Marchel in the village of Wojtkowice Glinne for "belonging to Sikora's band." On December 31, 1946, Stanisław Wojstkowski was hanged in the main square in Ciechanów, reportedly before an audience of several thousand.[65]

A public execution on January 8, 1947, was probably one of the last. A Citizens' Militia platoon stumbled upon a group of armed men in the home of "Citizen Mróz" in the village of Piaski near Radzymin outside Warsaw. One of the men was shot in the fight while the others escaped. A militia officer was grievously wounded. It turned out that the house owner's sons belonged to a "gang." The commander of the military unit arriving as reinforcements ordered the woman and her twenty-year-old son executed. Her other son, age five, was spared, but may have watched the killings. The soldiers burned down the house and the farm buildings and threw the corpses into the burning barn. All farm tools, household equipment, and threshed cereals were handed over to the village administrator to hold temporarily, and the army walked away with the livestock. The whole village witnessed the execution.[66]

In the modern era, the body of a hanged man was traditionally left on the gallows as a deterrent to others. The Germans did this during their occupation of Poland, and it also occasionally happened after the war. In Sanok, a body was left hanging all day while elsewhere they were taken away sooner. One thing is certain: public executions should be analyzed on two levels, of the wartime savagery and toxicity of death and of the postwar politics of fear, which was based on the belief that nothing could crush the spirit of resistance better than an execution squad and a crowd watching the execution.

But the politics of terror and fear was a double-edged sword. One side's brutality exacerbated the other side's. Murdering or raping family members of people linked to the regime was not rare. About six hundred women were killed in that period,[67] and often their only crime was having a husband or a brother who worked for the Polish Workers' Party or the militia. Fans of the new regime often received threats in the mail; this is an example of one sent to a person in Białystok: "[Home Army]. Your sentence has been set. If you don't stop your criminal work, in one week we will kill you, like we did many of your colleagues. For those you've betrayed and judged. Home Army executive department."[68]

Those working for the militia were also afraid. Łapy, Białystok Province, June 3, 1945: "It's very dangerous here still because there are bands, partisans in the forest, and we mostly fight them. In just one day, 3 of us were killed, 5 wounded, you can't always be sure about your life, when you're walking from town, you have to watch that someone doesn't shoot you in the head, you can't be sure of your life, so you say, what will be will be."[69]

Security Office functionaries were also afraid. Letter of May 16, 1945: "Here, the bands are roaming everywhere, attacking militia stations and beating up our people. They have killed Stefan P. and other colleagues. Dear brother, I'm home, also scared, this is how things are now, and when the germans [sic] were here people hid in the forest, now we have to hide in holes. Maybe you can come on your vacation here because maybe we won't see each other later because now every day is like a bubble in water."[70]

They were afraid as they faced the execution squad:

> I'm in the militia now, and I will tell you in a minute why. A month ago eleven Home Army types dropped by my place and Edek Lutomski's place and they walked us out and also all our underwear and clothes, the horse and cart.... They took us to Nowe Załucze to try us. After they read out our sentences, that we're condemned to death, that we belonged to the People's Army, they told us to get down and walk toward the woods, but I thought to myself, this is death, so I started to run from their bullets of 2 automatics and 2 rifles, and somehow the Lord helped me and I made it out in one piece, but they killed Lutomski in the place where I escaped.[71]

Zygmunt Klukowski wrote in his diary on January 1, 1946, "Another difficult year has passed, and we are entering a new, the eighth, year of the war."[72] For many Poles, the war did not end with the capture of Berlin. A regular conflict continued, and in some respects it was a civil war, with fanaticism and growing cold-bloodedness, especially in Białystok region, northern Mazovia, and Lublin Province.[73] The underground, too, was responsible for armed invasions of villages and even small towns as well as robberies and murders of Jews, members of the Polish Workers' Party, militia and Security Office functionaries, and even Red Army officers. People called southern Poland, especially those areas where there was fighting with Ukrainians, a "new Mexico."[74] Poland's western and northern regions were dubbed the Wild West. The behavior of some Security Office and militia officers, especially in small towns, could be compared to the rule of the sheriff of Nottingham. They were arrogant, certain of their impunity, brutal and infected by the war. The head of the District Office of Public Security in Jasło "treats the population cruelly, using any excuse to strike them."[75] Security Office and Citizens' Militia people in Oleśnica in Lower Silesia "treated the Polish people worse than the Red Army troops did."[76] Even a civil servant reported that "I'm afraid to go to [the Provincial Office of Public Security in Radom] by myself because I don't know if the person I report on won't come over at night and shoot me."[77] A citizen's complaint quoted in an official report stated that in Kielce Province the Citizens' Militia and the Security Office "rounded up men of recruitment age at county fairs in the German way" just so they could release them for a bribe.[78]

There is some validity in a comparison to the Middle Ages, since then, too, people reacted to the evil brought by Satan, but also by Jews or Turks, with mockery, satire, and the grotesque.[79] Now Poles relieved the stressful fear of the Security Office (SO) or the NKVD with laughter:

> I like everything, but the SO,
> When I see the SO, I feel doomed,
> But you have to consider,
> As you do big business,
> That you'll always bump into the SO,
> Dangerous and useless, our beloved SO!
> I've gone through my ordeals with them,
> When I smell it I'd like to flee to Cuba,
> And though I brag and boast,
> That I don't get easily lost,
> I'm helpless when I smell the SO...[80]

THE LANGUAGE OF FEAR

In January 1946, the *Kurier Szczeciński* daily ran an ironic "Handbook for Orators" ("Poradnik dla mówców"):

> In view of the fact that speeches are made in Poland on every possible occasion, we have decided to issue this handbook for beginning speakers, with only those words and terms that will yield the desired result when they are used together.
>
> Festive occasions in the west of Poland: forebears, pillars, pioneers, millennial mission, Slavs, Germanic aggression, barrage, Nazi, historic mission.
>
> Political debates: violet, crimson, brown, gray, extremist reactionaries, drive a wedge, thugs, elements, interwar intelligence agent, *Sanacja* Fascists, from around the corner, retrograde clericalism.
>
> Publicity for one's own views: we were the first (author's reminder: may begin every sentence with it), tirelessly, before anyone else, thanks to us.[81]

The handbook pinned down the essence of the political discourse of the day, which was supported by two pillars. The first was to legitimize the new government by using national terminology.[82] The second was to construct an atmosphere of the menace coming from the "lowliest reactionaries,"[83] *Sanacja* Fascists" or Teutons. Ideally, the two would be merged in a single speech. Another theme, which came from the political culture freshly imported from the Soviet Union, is also often present: ordering the total destruction of the adversary. No one had used terms such as "finish off" or "destroy" in prewar Poland, in even the most vicious parliamentary debates.

Polish Workers' Party leader Władysław Gomułka said at a congress of enterprise-level labor union council representatives, "We also need to finish off the reactionary Hydra, which is strangling us."[84] Józef Cyrankiewicz, secretary general of the Executive Committee of the Polish Socialist Party, argued, "We must destroy all organizations that want to make Poland into a tool of international rivalries."[85]

These were terrifying words.[86] They may easily have made people think that Poland was embarking on a new phase of political terror. After Gomułka's speech at the Polish Workers' Party congress in December 1945, someone from the "merchant milieu" allegedly said on a tram in Łódź, "The [Polish Workers' Party] is beginning to go after us a bit. [It] is beginning to play first violin." A person from the "intelligentsia milieu" responded, "Gomułka's speech is the prelude to red terror in Poland."[87] A woman in Lublin, likely after hearing the same speech, burst into tears[88] and said, "This will bring on a civil war.... Those [Polish Workers' Party] people, they're calling on the nation to start a civil war, but the time will come when they, too, will be finished off."[89]

This language terrified some, while others—those in power and those who supported the regime—used it nonstop to describe the world and to attempt to change it. Thus, police terror was powered by the terror of propaganda. Posters with the caption "[Home Army], drooling reactionary dwarfs" were displayed in 1944–45, the peak of the arrests. In the same way, signs of "[Polish People's Party] to the gallows," which appeared on walls and sidewalks in September 1946, paved the way for the political murders by Security Office execution squads of opposition Polish People's Party members on the eve of the Sejm elections of 1947.

All this gives the impression that the new government thrived in a climate of threat. It manipulated public anxiety and exploited it to legitimize its rule. There were two other sources of this threat: profiteers and Germans. In both cases, those in power represented themselves as being the sole force capable of sympathizing with the population's fears and of countering and wiping out the threat. According to psychologists, propaganda based on fear distracts us from carefully examining a problem and making plans to free ourselves of it.[90] It was infinitely easier to blame blood-sucking profiteers for economic problems than to explain the complexity of the postwar economic situation and to beat one's chest in repentance for inept agricultural and supply policies. It was not an accident that profiteers were loudly attacked every time prices rose drastically and supplies of ration-card goods disappeared.

The surrender of the Third Reich changed little in the continuing anti-German campaign. Jakub Berman, member of the Politburo, said at a conference of press control officers in late May 1945, "With the war over, should we relent in our hatred and evoke pity? There is no reason to do this.... We have not settled accounts with the Germans. We must preach to the international and to our own domestic public opinion, strengthen vigilance of the German threat."[91] The government emphasized the possibility that the German monster would be reborn and presented Poland's alliance with the Soviet Union as the only guarantor of the Oder-Neisse border. Its propaganda boosted the nationalist legitimacy of the ruling Communist party for the long term, at least about the western border. It delegitimized the Polish People's Party by representing it as an ally of the British and Americans and as allegedly promoting an overhaul of Poland's borders. In the short term, it was ineffective, intensifying apprehension of a new war, leading to market panic. It, too, reinforced political fear.

"PUBLIC LIFE IS SIMPLY HORRENDOUS"

The government's politics of fear produced political fear. The most important questions are: How widespread was it? What were its long-term effects on public behavior? Today, a sociologist would find it difficult to describe current mass perceptions and emotions. The historian is almost equally helpless. But it would seem that political fear, as measured by popular knowledge of the words *NKVD*, *UB* [Security Office], *exile*, and *Siberia*, must have been universal in postwar Poland. In areas where harassment was most intense, it turned into a psychosis and brought on outbursts of panic. Elsewhere, especially in the larger cities, not everyone went to bed fearing that they would be arrested or exiled that night, which is not to say that people were totally unfamiliar with being unable to sleep because of worry. For example, according to a government report, in Pabianice near Łódź, there was "great fear among those who continually compare the security authorities to the Gestapo."⁹² In Cracow, too, where a demonstration was brutally suppressed on May 3, 1946, and also in many other localities where people had protested in the streets, political fear must have been in the air. Thousands of soldiers of the underground tried to conceal their identities in the cities, and especially in the "Recovered Territories" where they were intent on starting a new life. They, too, feared being tracked down and seized by the security police. Filling out any kind of personal forms made them nervous. In April 1946 the underground Freedom and Independence publication *Wolność* wrote about "living in an atmosphere of terror":

> They can't intimidate the whole nation and at the same time expect that nation to be creatively innovative. They can't create artificial work systems in which the individual is designed to function like a soulless automaton. This method of government will not yield good results. We are seeing its effects in all the areas of our lives. There is an airless atmosphere of terror and expectancy. A centralized bureaucratic system, which very much resembles the dull, automated Bolshevik bureaucracy, will not change this. The tensions need to be "relieved." A sense of personal security is a basic precondition in a person's job. And what's it like here? Very many people are arrested for no reason, and many disappear without a trace. Fear of NKVD agents is a universal phenomenon in Poland. We have witnessed it in every office and factory. Everyone is trying to hide their past. Boxes in personnel forms asking about occupation, military rank, underground activity and pre-war service usually go unfilled. Very many people still live with phony documents, avoid housing registration offices or do not disclose their address.⁹³

Analyzing this mood from a class perspective, it would appear that workers were the least afraid. They did not need to deliver compulsory quotas, they had not been pacified, and they did not have to feed bandits on the run. But this would be true as long as People's Poland existed: workers continued to speak more freely and were not as afraid, which explains their greater tendency to rebel than other social groups. But not all groups. For example, the relatively small number of strikes in Upper Silesia is usually explained by its population's attachment to legal norms, higher wages, and better access to consumer goods. But we should not forget that three uprisings had taken place in Upper Silesia after the First World War, and thus the spirit of challenge and rebellion was not foreign to its people. The mass arrests and deportations of miners to the collieries of the Donbas in the spring of 1945 must have been an important factor in inclining the Silesians to conform. Virtually all native Silesians knew about them and were probably afraid, if only subliminally. It takes much courage to go out in the streets and strike carrying such a burden.

Krystyna Kersten wrote, "The terror of these dozen or, in some parts of the country, several months, which was mostly implemented directly by the NKVD, largely exhausted the society's ability to oppose and resist. It injected a new fear into the society, which after years of living under incessant threat longed for nothing more than security, calm, stability a normal existence."⁹⁴ The terror immediately helped to disarm the population and encourage surrender. It also had long-term effects. Most importantly, it launched the lengthy process of producing conformists. Of the many theories explaining the sources of the stability of Communist systems,⁹⁵ this one, which identifies the merger of fear and conformity, seems most accurate. In the population as a whole, only a very small minority was capable of resisting, and the majority adjusted to the imposed rules, or at least pretended to. A report of the commander of a "protection-propaganda group" that dispersed across Poland on the eve of the 1947 elections to persuade and intimidate shows what this looked like in practice:⁹⁶

> As for the teacher body, I must conclude that there is here [Okuniew, near Warsaw] the school director, Citiz. L., who recently returned from Anders's Army and was using German tactics and wore a beret with an eagle, and neither the population nor we liked his feats. For this reason, I arrested Mr. L., who became a democrat under the influence of fists and black eyes and confessed that he had been a [Polish

Socialist Party] supporter but that now he is no activist because he hadn't known earlier what democracy is capable of. I must conclude presently that Mr. L. has become an activist in Okuniew, participated in a meeting, addressed the population at a rally and encouraged people to vote for list no. 3."[97]

Coming into contact with brute force, in order to survive and avoid going to prison, people had to display their submission and at times excessive zeal and hide what they were thinking. A woman would say to her husband, a father to his son, "Don't stick your neck out" and "Keep quiet," and ask, "What good will it do you?" A letter writer in August 1945 noted, "We have many people here who think differently, like in Russia, so everyone else must keep quiet because otherwise they will take them away and they will never be heard from again."[98]

Practically all groups and circles, even intellectuals and academics who may have seemed to be living in a different world, used the strategy of keeping quiet. The eminent art historian Karol Estreicher wrote in his diary on November 5, 1946, "You can sense fear in many people. It makes them overzealous. Joining them are ambitious youths, many of whom have connections to the most secret party organs. We must keep quiet and be active in such a way as not to endanger anyone in the neutral spheres. Seemingly neutral. Here, we must create bastions of Polish culture, which don't make the party activists vigilant."[99]

But it was the rural folks, especially in the east and south, who were affected most harshly by political fear. It was here that a civil war raged and the bloodiest acts of revenge were perpetrated and here that both sides descended into fanaticism and cruelty. For this reason, the peasants tended to conform, and already during election campaigns they would avoid discussing political subjects, believing that once their views became public they would be arrested. Men aged twenty to thirty, fearing mass arrests, would not show up at campaign meetings.[100] The political persecution led people to shut themselves off from the outside world, friendly ties to weaken, apathy to grow (people in the countryside would say, "This is none of my business, pal" or "I don't get involved in that stuff"). A peasant diarist wrote in 1948, "The public life is simply horrendous, no one will utter a word to anyone else because they don't know what party the other guy belongs to, whether what I tell my neighbor . . . whether I won't be arrested for it and put in prison, maybe my neighbor will report some untruth about me. . . . This is what public, political life is like, nondescript."[101]

This feeling contrasted sharply with the time before the war, when rural communities bubbled with politics, and the peasant strikes of 1937 demonstrated the rural population's ability to mobilize and fight for its rights. But the experiences of 1944–47 discouraged the peasantry from becoming involved in politics.[102] In January 1947, the head of the District Public Security Office in Czarnków wrote about what had happened to the local Polish Peasant Party chapter, which once had eighty-four members: "After the harassment of [Polish Peasant Party] members in the pre-election period, some members left and entire cells dissolved, where most became unaffiliated, not deciding to join any other political party, fearing similar oppression in the future."[103] This fear traveled not only in space but also in time and was reproduced in subsequent generations. Unexpressed, it continued to hover over public life in People's Poland.

But these were not all the consequences of fear's omnipresence in the postwar years. David Engel points out the relationship between periods of intensified persecution targeting political opposition and the increase in the numbers of the underground's killings of regime associates.[104] It more or less overlaps (among the exceptions were the relatively few people killed during the October 1956 unrest) with the sine wave of political fear. The sociology of emotions would explain this with the anger brought on in reaction to the fear caused by oppression. Anger thwarts fear and diminishes empathy.[105] A mix of these emotions combined with fanaticism, nationalism, and the ways people had lived during the war into a sort of time bomb that exploded often at this time. This may be the only explanation for the February 1946 raid on the Poznań-Katowice train and the execution of at least eight Red Army soldiers and officers and two Polish Army officers aboard by a unit of the National Armed Forces unit.[106] Even though the underground did not target Soviet soldiers and often released them after capturing them, at least 650 were killed.[107] The Enemy No. 1 were soldiers of the Internal Security Corps, Security Office functionaries, and members of the Polish Workers' Party. Once caught, most were killed, sometimes after being tortured. There were also lynchings. In August 1946, a fight broke out at the harvest festival in the village of Kaczyce (Pińczów District). A District Office of Public Security functionary called on the crowd to disperse and began to fire in the air. Someone hit him on the head. He managed to shoot three others and tried to flee, but he was captured and stoned to death.[108]

When Security Office people, militia officers, and Communists were not on hand, anger could stay bottled up. Then, the aggression might shift to Jews, commonly believed to be a pillar of the new regime—regardless whether this was a fact or an opinion based on the persecution stereotype. Only some cases of postwar violence against Jews can be explained by aggression shifted onto scapegoats. It would seem that it was primarily the cases in which the attackers belonged to an armed underground group and felt hatred and anger toward the "institutions of fear." The most typical situations were those in which, in the absence of someone believed to be a Communist, preferably a secret policeman or a member of the workers' party, the mob would kill a Jew. In other words, the Jew was not a target as such but an ersatz who needed to be "liquidated" in order to execute an order, from a military point of view, and, from a psychological point of view, to release frustration, anger, aggression, and fear that had accumulated over a long stay underground.

The first corroboration of this hypothesis was the chronological concurrence between the westward shift of millions of Red Army troops in January and February 1945 and the wave of aggression toward Jews in March, within two months of the beginning of the anti-German winter offensive.[109] The fury brought on by the mounting persecution beginning in October 1944, which was contained for several months by the overwhelming presence of Soviet troops, may in some cases have turned against innocent and defenseless Jews. In Lublin Province, the relocation of the institutions of the Provisional Government from Lublin to Warsaw in January 1945 may have been a similar correlation of this wave. According to a military report:

> From the very first days of moving the central organs to Warsaw, the reaction became more active. In the first phase, it was characterized by increased agitation and propaganda: flyers, provocative graffiti on walls, false rumors, etc. But the [Home Army] and [National Armed Forces] bands, reinforced by deserters and other shady elements . . . moved to an organized and premeditated individual and social terror in the entire province, including [Lublin]. It was expressed in the murders of political-educational officers of the Polish Army, officers of Jewish nationality [emphasis added], militia officers, activists of the democratic parties and non-party activists, but also of the more active individuals.[110]

The second factor, which to some extent supports the hypothesis about the transfer of aggression, may be the usually different numbers of people killed in attacks on trains or small localities: either large numbers of Jews and at most a handful of representatives of the regime or vice versa.[111] Of course, in the second scenario, there may have been no Jews in the attacked train or town. Or, it may have happened that plans were made to murder a Jew and no one else. Or, someone died not because their name was Mosze or Miriam but because they happened to be in the wrong place at the wrong time during the civil war.[112] There have been many instances in history when collective fear, usually brought on by a plague or hunger (back to the Middle Ages again), made Jews into scapegoats.

Thus, the postwar period brought us the Great Terror. Because it was widespread and carried social consequences, political fear was its *basic fear*.

NOTES

1. This chapter initially appeared as Zaremba, "Polityka strachu i jej konsekwencje," 113–40.
2. For more on Hobbes's views, see Robin, *Fear*.

3. Machiavelli, *Of Cruelty and Clemency*, 84, 85.

4. Arendt, *The Origins of Totalitarianism* part I, 461.

5. Beck, *Risk Society*; Giddens, *Modernity and Self-Identity*; Mack, "Fear"; Robin, *Fear*; Furedi, *Politics of Fear*.

6. Heller, *Maszyna i śrubki*, 95.

7. Krystyna Kersten was the first historian to view the postwar fear more broadly, and her book extends an earlier focus. Kersten, *The Establishment of Communist Rule in Poland*, especially chapter 5, "Society"; and her "Terror na przełomie wojny i pokoju." For a general discussion of the politics of terror, see Kostewicz, "Terror i represje," 121–78; Paczkowski, "Poland."

8. Robin, *Fear*, 2, 16.

9. Furedi, *Politics of Fear*, 123.

10. The politics of fear is one of the most dynamically developing areas of contemporary sociology. For a representative example, see Czech, "Polityka strachu."

11. *Protokoły posiedzeń Biura Politycznego KC PPR 1944–1945*, 18, 19, 22, 23, 36.

12. Gomułka, *Pamiętniki*, vol. 2, 308–309.

13. Kersten, "Terror na przełomie wojny i pokoju," 107.

14. Montefiore, *Stalin*.

15. Cariewskaja et al., *Teczka specjalna*, 154.

16. AAN, Zespół Krajowa Rada Narodowa (hereafter KRN) 143, k. 1–6. Raport o sytuacji w Wilnie kpt. Sztachelskiej Ireny (na podstawie wyjazdu służbowego w dniach, 18 VII–3 IX 44.

17. Materski and Paczkowski, *NKWD o Polsce i Polakach. Rekonesans archiwalny*, 37.

18. AAN, PKWN I/78, k. 6. Sprawozdanie za miesiąc listopad b.r. (1944).

19. Kersten, "Terror na przełomie wojny i pokoju," 106.

20. Ivan Pavlov was the darling of the Soviet rulers, and his theories were a compulsory part of Soviet physiology and psychology.

21. For more on the "October turnaround," see Skrzypek, *Mechanizmy uzależnienia*, 55–75.

22. Klukowski, *Zamojszczyzna*, vol. 2, 113, 114–15, 118, 120, 124, 144.

23. Wilkinson, *Anxiety in a Risk Society*, 15–40.

24. AAN, PKWN I/78, k. 12. Doniesienie specjalne, 27 XII 1944.

25. Kulczyńska, *Lwów—Donbas 1945*; Hryciuk, "'Ciężkie dni Lwowa,'" 21–33.

26. Kalbarczyk, "Sowieckie represje wobec polskiego podziemia niepodległościowego w Warszawie i okolicach na przełomie 1944 i 1945 roku," 139–55.

27. AIPN 01265/379. Raport Kierownika Urzędu Bep. Publ. Warszawa—Miasto por. Grzegorza Łanina, styczeń 1945, n.p.

28. *Alarm*, November 12 1944, Biblioteka Narodowa [National Library], Warsaw, microfilm dept., 71280.

29. Cariewskaja et al., *Teczka specjalna*, 226.

30. AIPN, MBP 3378, k. 63. Specjalne doniesienie dot. prowokacyjnych pogłosek.

31. *Raport Witolda Bieńkowskiego "Kalskiego,"* 85.

32. AIPN, MBP 3378, k. 68. Specjalne doniesienie dot. prowokacyjnych pogłosek.

33. Chajn, *Kiedy Lublin był Warszawą*, 78.

34. The detained court employees were deported to the USSR on February 13. At least one of them, the prosecutor Jerzy Marcinkowski, was taken to camp no. 280/18 in Stalino, where he still remained in late August 1945 (*List żony Władysławy Marcinkowskiej do Prezydenta RP*, Kielce August 26, 1945, AAN, KRN 816, k. 91).

35. Chajn, *Kiedy Lublin był Warszawą*, 84.

36. "S. Korboński do centrali: Depesza," in Pełczyński et al., *Armia Krajowa w dokumentach 1939–1945*, vol. 5, 382.

37. AIPN, MBP 3378, k. 70. Specjalne doniesienie dotyczące działalności dywersyjnych band.

38. Aptekar, "Walka wojsk wewnętrznych NKWD z polskim," 58, 59.

39. Kersten, "Społeczeństwo polskie," 14.

40. Excerpt of the poem "Powroty" in Borowski, *Utwory wybrane*, 55–57.

41. AAN, MIiP 1004, k. 13. Wyciąg ze sprawozdania nadesłanego z Urzędu Informacji i Propagandy woj. lubelskiego z dnia 6 lipca 1946.

42. AP w Rzeszowie, KW PPR 28, k. 4. Sprawozdanie sytuacyjne z terenu województwa rzeszowskiego za czas od 1 do 31 maja 1945.

43. AP w Białymstoku, Urząd Wojewódzki Białostocki 285, k. 80.

44. *Echo Krakowa*, March 19, 1946.

45. CAW III.2.204, k. 349. Meldunek specjalny o sytuacji w terenie Zarządu Pol.-Wych. WP, 16 VI 1945.

46. F. Ryszka, *Pamiętnik inteligenta. Dojrzewanie* (Warsaw: BGW, 1994), 244.

47. Dominiczak, *Organy bezpieczeństwa PRL 1944–1990*; Paczkowski, *Od sfałszowanego zwycięstwa do prawdziwej klęski*, 33–75.

48. These figures do not convey the scale of the phenomenon. It is notable that especially in 1944 and 1945, smaller localities did not even record many of their arrests. Also, because Military Information and, mostly, the Citizens' Militia also arrested people. For example, from November 6 to December 28, 1944, the militia arrested 4,002 people for all categories of crimes in all the areas liberated by the Red Army, and handed only some of them over to the Security Office. To extrapolate, in 1945 the total number of people arrested by the Security Office, including for criminal offenses, may have topped 200,000 (AIPN, 0887/73. Zestawienie statystyczne osób aresztowanych przez Służbę Bezpieczeństwa w latach 1944–1956, n.p.; AIPN, KG MO 35/20033, k. 14. Raport sytuacyjny nr 2 za okres od 6 listopada do 28 grudnia 1944).

49. AAN, PKWN I/78, k. 11. Doniesienie specjalne.

50. AIPN, MBP 3378, k. 57. Doniesienie specjalne dot. wypowiedzi o treści antypaństw., April 23, 1945.

51. AAN, MIiP 437, k. 35. Wojewódzki Urząd Informacji i Propagandy w Rzeszowie do Ministerstwa Informacji i Propagandy w Warszawie.

52. AIPN 578/353, k. 30, 35, 44.

53. Another operation was described thus:
    On the night of 20–21.8.1946 at 23:00 hours, a car arrived, and immediately after coming out of their cars [*sic*] soldiers began to shoot all over town. It only turned out later that this

is a special expedition, which came to check the documents of the inhabitants of the town of Łańcut.... Citizens of the town of Łańcut in some cases were unfamiliar with these individuals and did not want to unlock their doors at night, on the basis of the directive that no one should be let in at night, all the more so since in some places they said they were the police, when there is no such thing in Poland. The whole action was very poorly organized, and for this reason several individuals were killed and wounded, and unable to orient themselves they shot at each other, not knowing that both were Security organs. (AAN, MIiP 439, k. 74. Raport Powiatowego Oddziału Informacji I Propagandy w Łańcucie.)

54. AIPN, MBP 3378, k. 76. Specjalne doniesienie dot. działalności dywersyjnych band.

55. AAN, MIiP 182, k. 25. Wyciągi sprawozdań poszczególnych województw za miesiąc październik 1945.

56. AIPN, WiN 92, k. 118. Sprawozdanie informacyjne za miesiąc VII 46.

57. Godycka-Cwirko, *Lata klęski 1944–1973*, 63.

58. (Dz. U. 1945, nr 53, poz. 300). For more information about the list of actions punishable by death, see Kładoczny, "Kara śmierci jako wykładnik polityki karnej państwa w latach 1944–1956," 67–81.

59. Socha, "Te pokolenia żałobami czarne," 119, 130–31, 312, passim; Borowiec, *Aparat bezpieczeństwa a wojskowy wymiar sprawiedliwości*.

60. AIPN, MBP XI 13A.

61. Klukowski, *Zamojszczyzna*, vol. 2, 189.

62. AAN, MIiP 437, k. 55. Powiatowy Oddział Informacji i Propagandy w Sanoku donosi.

63. AAN, MIiP 591, k. 38. Powiatowy Oddział Informacji i Propagandy donosi.

64. Romaniak, "Publiczne egzekucje w Sanoku," 73–86; Romaniak, "Powstanie, działalność i likwidacja antykomunistycznego," 349, 363–66.

65. Dominiczak, *Organy bezpieczeństwa PRL 1944–1990*, 79, 80.

66. AIPN 0206/384, k. 1–2. Meldunek Komendanta Powiatowego MO w Radzyminie do WUBP w Warszawie. (T. Rutkowski alerted me to the existence of this document.)

67. Not all these women were killed to settle scores. Some may have been killed by accident. See Brzeziński et al., *Polegli w walce o władzę ludową*, 23.

68. AIPN 3378, k. 79. Specjalne doniesienie dot. działalności dywersyjnych band.

69. AIPN 3378, k. 79. Specjalne doniesienie dot. działalności dywersyjnych band.

70. AIPN, MBP 3378, k. 81. Specjalne doniesienie dot. działalności dywersyjnych band.

71. AAN, PKWN I/78, k. 4. Sprawozdanie za miesiąc br., listopad 1944.

72. Klukowski, *Zamojszczyzna*, vol. 2, 213.

73. I am aware that the discussion about the nature of the postwar conflict has been going on for a long time. To generalize, the opinion that it was either an insurrection or an "internal war" has won. Not making light of the arguments used to support these terms, I believe that two issues have not been sufficiently considered. First, analysts forget that the majority of public opinion then, the popular voice, treated the conflict as fratricidal. Second, the conflict has some features of a civil war, including its characteristic fanaticism and cruelty. Furthermore, unlike a national war, the conflict deeply fragmented society. For these reasons, I believe that the most appropriate term is "a conflict with some features of a civil war." For more, see Ajnenkiel, *Wojna domowa czy nowa okupacja? Polska po roku 1944*.

74. "The security unit's operation in Rzeszów that was recently conducted in this district [Jarosław–MZ] brought some calm. But the method of conducting the operation eminently resembled Mexican conditions: machine guns were fired at fleeing individuals in a crowd, inflicting wounds and injuries on many citizens" (AAN, MAP 122, k. 1,2. Sprawozdanie miesięczne Wojewody Rzeszowskiego, December 13, 1945).

75. AIPN, KG MO 35/764, k. 17. Raport z przeprowadzonej inspekcji w Pow. Kom. MO w Jaśle, 11 IX 1945.

76. AAN, MIiP 550, k. 27. Sytuacja polityczna, February 6, 1946.

77. AAN, MIiP 79, k. 18. Sprawozdanie z wyjazdu służbowego do Radomia instruktora terenowego ob. Krogulca Czesława w dniu 8 sierpnia 1945.

78. AAN, MIiP 79, k. 22. Raport Czesława Dragana, September 3, 1945.

79. Cf. Gutowski, *Komizm w polskiej sztuce gotyckiej*; Guriewicz, *Problemy średniowiecznej kultury ludowej*, chapter on "'Góra' i 'dół': średniowieczna groteska."

80. Excerpt from a satirical piece probably written by Kazimierz Rudzki, "Wgląd w rząd," in Janta-Połczyński, *Wracam z Polski*, 62.

81. *Kurier Szczeciński*, January 20, 1946.

82. See Zaremba, *Komunizm, legitymizacja, nacjonalizm*.

83. For more, see Kersten, "Polityczny i propagandowy obraz zbrojnego," 162–71.

84. *Sztandar Ludu*, September 16, 1945.

85. *Sztandar Ludu*, July 9, 1946.

86. They were all the more terrifying since people could easily see that these were not empty words. The people's government wanted to coordinate their words and deeds. Jakub Berman discussed this at a conference of the CC of the Polish Workers' Party Propaganda Department in April 1945: "We must move on the offensive vis-à-vis the aggressive elements, but alongside the moment of persecution we absolutely need a broad political-propaganda action, which must be developed because of the 1st and 3rd of May" (AAN, KC PPR 295/X–2, k. 16. Protokół konferencji).

87. AIPN 01206/112, k. 27. Do MBP Departamentu V z UBP Łódź, 12 Dec. 1945.

88. It is not out of the question that this was the excerpt of the speech that brought out the tears: "The great social changes cannot happen without a struggle, and therefore without victims. A new life is always born in pain and blood, and our new life is being created thus." Gomułka, Przemówienie wygłoszone na otwarciu I Zjazdu Polskiej Partii Robotniczej, 426 (emphasis in the original).

89. AIPN 01206/112. Agenturalne doniesienie "Józi," December 11, 1945, n.p.

90. Pratkanis and Aronson, *Age of Propaganda*, especially chapter 24, "The Fear Appeal," 161–66.

91. Nałęcz, *Główny Urząd Kontroli Prasy 1945–1949*, 37.

92. AAN, MIiP 82, k. 9. Sprawozdanie z wyjazdu służbowego do Łodzi Instr. ter. ob. Poczmańskiego Witolda i ob. dyr. Bahracha w dniu 14.9 i 15.9.1945.

93. "Atmosfera trwogi," *Wolność* [Jelenia Góra], WiN, April 15, 1946, BN, mf .70387.

94. Kersten, "Społeczeństwo polskie," 14.

95. For more on the sources of stabilization of Communist systems, see Zaremba, *Komunizm, legitymizacja, nacjonalizm*, 81–118.

96. For more, see Wtorkiewicz, *Wojsko Polskie w akcji propagandowej*; Skoczylas, *Wybory do Sejmu Ustawodawczego z 19 stycznia 1947 r. w świetle skarg do ludności*.

97. AAN, KC PPR 295/VII–223, k. 121. Meldunek z pracy grup ochronno-propagandowych.

98. AIPN, MBP 3378, k. 109. Specjalne doniesienie, October 13, 1945.

99. Estreicher Jr., *Dziennik wypadków 1946–1960*, vol. 2, 5.

100. Wtorkiewicz, *Wojsko Polskie w akcji propagandowej*, 49.

101. T. Szarota showed me memoir no. 293 from the Wieś Polska collection.

102. Young people's migration to the cities, in keeping with modernization, played a very important role in weakening the potential for rebellion in the countryside. The statement that the countryside was extremely overpopulated before the war is trite.

103. AIPN w Poznaniu 06/119 t. 12 z 21, k. 135. Raport okresowy Kierownika Referatu V Pow. Urz. Bezp. Publ. w Czarnkowie, 26 I 1947.

104. Engel, "Patterns of Anti-Jewish Violence in Poland, 1944–1946," 64, 65.

105. Oatley and Jenkins, *Understanding Emotions*.

106. AIPN 835/168, k. 1. Raport specjalny o walce z bandytyzmem na miesiąc luty 1946.

107. There were numerous causes of death: murder, fighting, being shot by a militia officer or a Polish Army soldier, car accident under the influence of alcohol, et al. (Brzeziński et al., *Polegli w walce*, 567–600).

108. AAN, MIiP 924, k. 123. Protokół Powiatowego Oddziału Informacji i Propagandy w Pińczowie.

109. AAN, MAP 786, k. 17–18. Pismo Naczelnika Wydziału Społ.-Politycznego MAP do MBP, September 29, 1945.

110. CAW III.2.212, k. 1. Meldunek specjalny o sytuacji w terenie, 22 VI 1945.

111. Two examples: The first, banditry, which has already been mentioned in this context, was the invasion of Czyżew, Białystok Province, in the night of March 24–25, 1945. The first target was probably the militia station, fought off without militia losses. But (in revenge?) thirteen people (nine Jews, three locals, and one Red Army officer) were murdered. Second example: attack on Parczew, Lublin Province, on February 5, 1946. The available document shows that Jews may not have been the principal target: "The attackers stop pedestrians, ask for their identity documents and tell them to put their hands up." The shooting in different places in town lasted several hours, but no government representatives were killed. But four Jews were killed by the attackers. Others' property was stolen. AAN, MAP 786, 41.

112. For more on the various motivations of anti-Jewish aggression, see Engel, *Patterns of Anti-Jewish Violence*; Gross, *Fear*.

11

THE PHANTOMS OF TRANSIENCE

Transience has mostly negative associations: with instability and insecurity and anxiety. Living in a state of impermanence means dealing with constant change, without the support of permanent structures, with constant uncertainty about what tomorrow will bring. The human being yearns for life in an ordered world whose origins, rules, and goals he or she can grasp, and which is not anyone's historically relative passing whim but a lasting part of the human condition, noted Leszek Kołakowski.[1] According to sociologists, these days, because of the fluidity of modernity, this yearning is rarely satisfied. To Zygmunt Bauman, "Fear is arguably the most sinister of the demons nesting in the open societies of our time."[2]

Historians are unanimous: in Poland, the demon of anxiety revealed its most terrifying persona during the Second World War. It accompanied people like a shadow, not leaving them even for an instant. It lurked even at times of leisure. They tried to drown it in vodka, but every time it invariably floated up like a cork. A week after the Third Reich surrendered, *Gazeta Lubelska* wrote:

> We no longer look around vigilantly like hunted animals to see if a German police vehicle is approaching, we no longer stare our eyes out to see if from far away, around a corner or in a crowd a machine gun won't bare its horrific teeth and we won't hear the ominous and eloquent words, "Papiere, Ausweis." ... We lived with the feeling of provisionality, and every morning we would tell ourselves that we had another night behind us, and every evening that we had managed to snatch another day from fate. Contempt for death, but also what horrible contempt for life. It created a psychosis inside us of surviving from one day to the next, from one hour to the next, it taught us to see everything as provisory and trivial.[3]

Because the psychosis of impermanence did not end with the war, the article appealed for an end to the wartime lifestyle, the provisionality. The moment called for looking to the future and rebuilding. Otherwise, the consequences would be disastrous.

Let's be honest: such appeals did not help much. Not only did the well-established wartime anxiety live on, but the new reality brought plenty of new reasons to feel uncertain. Most Poles experienced those feelings of impermanence, suspension, and anxiety, if only briefly, in the first postwar years. Elation that their country had been liberated and the war had ended not only did not soar to the West's heights of enthusiasm, but it quickly fizzled. For all the different difficulties and postwar poverty, to the British, French, or Italians the future seemed predictable, while for the peoples of east-central Europe it served up a stubborn question mark. In late May 1945, the journalist Edmund Osmańczyk wrote to Polish Workers' Party activist Jerzy Borejsza about the state of ongoing impermanence that was numbing the Poles: "Society is paralyzed by a fear of the abyss."[4] This view was by no means isolated. In the November 1, 1945, issue of the underground Freedom and Independence publication *Wolność* we read, "The spirit of passive resistance looms permanently over our entire ruined life. The fatalism of impermanence weighs on the entire nation's psyche. We get lost and waste huge national energy in never-ending suspense."[5] In March 1946, Bolesław Piasecki made a similar diagnosis of the national psyche: "The Poles' collective unconscious is living in a state of unease."[6] Minding censorship, the author could not list all the reasons for this state, of which he saw many. They included the Red Army, native banditry, migrations, "the security apparatus," and others, most of which had to do with the political, social, and economic consequences of Poland becoming a Soviet satellite.

POLAND, BUT WHAT SORT OF A POLAND?!

Perhaps it's this uncertainty that's the worst, strangling the whole world like a phantom. What will emerge, what new forms? Will they be better? Will the chaos last long? Will the sun come out for humanity, peace, joyful work, a sense of oneself and one's nearest and dearest living safely? We miss this so much. I know, I really know that evil cannot last forever because it would make the world perish, but how long can this era of uncertainty, of evolution last? This is the darkest transitional era, and yet we're living in it, and individually and collectively divided, full of hesitation, uncertainty. . . . The burden of uncertainty is crushing everything.[7]

This excerpt from a letter sent in March 1948 by Warsaw teacher Jadwiga Wróblewska to her son in England sets the tone perfectly for this section. The era of uncertainty was already nine years old. Its new phase was marked by liberation by the Red Army and the resultant installation of Communist power. The uncertainty it brought about the future crushed virtually everyone. A person living in Poznań Province wrote immediately after liberation, "Even though we were waiting for it, i.e., freedom, and looked forward to this day, and it came, everyone is even more depressed than before, everyone is afraid of something and spouting different stuff about it."[8]

People were "spouting." It would not be an overstatement to say that never in Poland's recent history had it happened that people did not know the answers to so many crucial questions. For starters, those about the new regime: Should we expect a Communist revolution and regime change? Will the Soviet political culture, with its brash indoctrination and one-party rule, be imposed on Poland? Will they implement collectivization? Will the Polish frontier run along the Bug and San Rivers or will it stay the same?[9] And then there were the questions about the Great Powers' intentions: What is Stalin after? What plans do the Anglo-Saxons have? How far will the native Communists go? The calculations also aimed to determine whether the Polish army under Anders's command would return from the West. There were also purely practical questions. If we're going to treat the rulers as new occupiers, should we take part in the reconstruction movement they are pursuing? Where does acting for the common good end and collaboration begin? Krystyna Kersten noted that the Poles' postwar thinking formed around issues such as this one.[10] The underground elite's and government-in-exile's failure to propose clear answers compounded the problem. They agreed in principle that rebuilding the country, getting the economy going, and launching educational and cultural institutions was the order of the day. And yet wanting to cooperate politically with the new regime and working in its institutions of fear meant going over to the enemy's side. But, as is often the case, not everything could be resolved with easy prescriptions: What were judges, journalists, and municipal civil servants to do? Or those soldiers who had not deserted? Did militia officers who had not left their posts automatically become traitors to the nation? In January 1945, the authors of a report of the Government Delegate's Office admitted that "because of a lack of clear directions and news from abroad, a general depression has set in in this patriotic and sovereignty-oriented society."[11]

To put it differently, two points of view emerged: a fatalistic one predicting that Poland would be Sovietized and an optimistic one (that augmented the sense of impermanence) that things could not possibly end up this way, that something would make the Communists fail.[12] More than a handful of people believed that Poland would be occupied again. In early March 1945, a man living in Bydgoszcz assessed the situation thus:

> We have one difficult phase behind us, we're living under a Soviet occupation, which is covered with the fig leaf of [the provisional government of] Lublin. We have the difficult phase of the departure of the Soviets ahead of us, which will involve a civil war.... Sovereign Poland's international situation is worse that defeated Germany's or Japan's. Terror, robbery... bleeding out, getting rid of people, especially of the intelligentsia, depleting various currencies through thieving conversions, stopping train and postal communications, these are all routes to chaos and the beginnings of Communism, which will weaken Poland for generations to come.[13]

Still, after the period of the "first chaos," the world did not look uniformly negative, and it had nothing in common with the Soviet Union during the Great Purge. The dynamic culture growing right after the war was not yet being strangled by ideology. There were still articles in the papers about the anniversaries of the Battle of Monte Cassino or about the death of General Władysław Sikorski. Relations with the West continued to appear very strong. Double-decker buses, a gift from the City of London, transported people around Warsaw. A few US politicians visited Poland in a short period: in September 1945 General Dwight Eisenhower, in March 1946 former president Herbert Hoover, and in August 1946 the head of UNRRA and former mayor of New York City Fiorello La Guardia.

The governing Polish Workers' Party was also not behaving anything like Bolshevik hoi polloi during the war of 1920. The Polish Communists' national camouflage, their declarations and reassurances that things would be different here, that there would be a "Polish way," fogged up the picture, made it difficult to answer questions about Poland's future. The July 1944 Polish Committee of National Liberation Manifesto promised five-point electoral law and solemnly declared that all democratic freedoms would be restored. Later, until mid-1947 and the announcement of the "battle over commerce," the ruling Polish Workers' Party did not present its ideas about what Poland would look like ten years later, beyond Władysław Gomułka's statement that "we want the strong hand to govern"[14] and declarations that "reaction" must be destroyed. Let us not forget that Poland B, people who were conservative, traditional, less educated, attached to the Catholic Church, and rural, were still suspended. Some of them were torn between accepting the new regime's populist promises and remaining attached to traditional values. Aware of their doubts, the government attempted to dispel them. Gomułka denied that revolution was necessary and stressed that "in the conditions of people's democracy... evolution is absolutely possible to institute social change and to make the transition to a socialist regime."[15]

"But in 1945," as Czesław Miłosz noted years later, "there were no facts that would justify emigration as a political act unless one did not wish to understand the situation soberly."[16] He was wrong. Terror policies, in place from the word *go*, and an understanding the true nature of how people were living in the USSR prescribed caution, which Miłosz lacked. The portraits of Stalin and his marshals, the red flags that decorated every Soviet military commandant's office[17] and sometimes also town squares and parks, added to the atmosphere of temporariness. Anyone who read the Polish Workers' Party newspapers could easily find references to the necessity of conducting "class warfare all the way to total victory."[18] But no one really knew whether this alleged "soft revolution," as Jerzy Borejsza[19] defined it, would not harden or if, as the Communist Party of Poland had proclaimed before the war, Poland would become the seventeenth Soviet republic or people would take bloody revenge on the Communists, which many steadfast Home Army and National Armed Forces soldiers dreamed about. Hence, the Poles continued to live in a state of collective suspension, a momentary state between war and occupation: and then what? A Poland, but what sort of a Poland?

A man living in Wesoła, near Warsaw, voiced his quandaries in a letter posted on September 13, 1945: "We have a sovereign Poland, but there is a lot of the foreign element here, whose baton we must allow to conduct us. And we were promised that there would be no interference in our domestic system. But strange times and strange customs have come, when people say one thing and do another, and in the end we don't know whether we're an independent country or not."[20]

In a seemingly unintelligible situation, instinct dictates caution. It is better to lie in wait, linger, and see what others are doing, to gather information before taking a stand. This is how the Poles tended to act in their new postwar reality. An attitude of waiting prevailed, especially in the first year following liberation. People gathered information, discussed it with their closest family and friends, often over the omnipresent moonshine. They also observed their cultural and academic elites and political leaders. The public watched closely for signals from the Communists and then decided whether they were dealing with the "Bolshevik plague" or a sort of hostile takeover, or perhaps the fulfillment of prewar dreams about social justice. Some people were unable to interpret any of these signals, felt lost, and hesitated about what to do. There was an objective reason for this uncertainty, an absence of Lenin's instruction on "*shto delat?*" coming from local opinion leaders, who had been decimated during the war and now continued to be hunted. And the London émigrés' voices were growing weaker not only because they had no influence on events in Poland but also because they were not right there. For all these reasons, the majority of Poles decided spontaneously that the best strategy was to wait and to remain uninvolved. This was more or less the message in a letter from a mother to her son serving in the army written in early April 1945: "Oh, Lord, there is no reason to live in poverty, to spill blood, fathers and sons and orphans are left here and there because we're not home and our only motherland is Communist Poland. But what can we do, we must suffer and wait."[21]

A man from the prewar elite, perhaps a landowner, wrote in a similar vein; believing that the situation might change, he decided to wait: "The Provisional National Government has instructed the breaking-up of estates, and the peasant is now to be the young master. But I hope that after the war ends a lot will still change on this question, so we must 'wait it out.' I buy the newspapers to stay informed as such instructions develop."[22]

The intelligentsia waited. Leon Chajn, deputy minister of justice, talked with many lawyers in Lublin, but none wanted to work for the Polish Committee of National Liberation. "The situation looked almost hopeless," Chajn recalled. The two attorneys he did finally hire told him that "since they began to work for the [Polish Committee of National Liberation], everyone has turned away from them, no one wants to talk to them, no one wants to say hello, and friends and acquaintances are boycotting them socially. One of them even confessed that his wife would not stop crying because her friends and acquaintances do not want to know her, and her family doesn't let her into their house."[23] The creation in December 1944 of the Provisional Government as a replacement for the Polish Committee of National Liberation confirmed the state of impermanence.

The peasants were also waiting, in character with their traditional diffidence. Many feared the consequences of future political changes and refused to take the land offered them under the land reform. An underground report from Pomerania typified their thinking: "The current government is temporary, so all its rulings are temporary. When the right government comes it will take this land away from us, and all our farm work will be wasted."[24] Łukasz Kamiński's research shows that in some parts of the country large numbers of peasants returned the land they had only just been given. In Greater Poland by October 1, 1945, 47.2 percent of the documents granting them plots of land were returned or not accepted, while in some districts in Pomerania the figure was 80 percent.[25] Do these figures illustrate the feeling of impermanence? Not totally, as another factor in resisting land reform may have been loyalty to the former landowners. Elsewhere, peasants eagerly took the land offered them as they wanted to have it more than they feared taking it. At the time, no one was conducting opinion polls about political preferences or about public moods and apprehensions, but had someone had the courage to do it, a majority of interviewees would probably have agreed with what "a woman of the people" was overheard saying by a Security Office informer in February 1945: "Let there be some congresses and conferences [Yalta—MZ] but no one will agree with this government."[26]

The issue of regime legitimacy seems tangential, but only at first glance. As Andrzej Rychard has noted, the fact that the public considers the government legitimate to some extent describes its frame of mind, its moods, and therefore its identity.[27] There is no point in explaining the significance of legitimation to the rulers themselves. In the postwar period, it was illustrated, for instance, by the authorities' nervousness or irritation at the public reserve toward the emerging new order, especially the intelligentsia's. Their irritation is easy to find in numerous publications of the period. Konstanty Ildefons Gałczyński wrote about the Polish intelligentsia's dilemmas and indecisions and the mood of uncertainty and waiting in the satirical poem "Śmierć inteligenta" (The death of a man of the intelligentsia):

Cold-ridden. Apolitical.
Aching. Nostalgic.
He paces in circles. Annihilation.
He would like to. He would aspire. He could. If only.
He rubs his eyes. Looks out through the windowpane.
A white horse? No, it's only the snow.[28]

Maria Hirszowicz showed in her *Pułapki zaangażowania* (The traps of engagement) what joining the Communists meant for Polish intellectuals: a life of self-delusion.[29] Yet those who decided after the war to wait without becoming involved also fell into a trap, perhaps not an equally dangerous trap but still the trap of disengagement. To remain in it meant to learn about the feeling of impermanence through and through, to live with an expectation of change, with the increasingly desperate hope that the usurpatory Communist rule would end one day, that General Anders would be back, and that the West, or perhaps the Virgin Mary herself, would rescue Poland. This waiting was accompanied by a feeling of growing helplessness, which to Zygmunt Bauman was fear's most terrifying effect,[30] that nothing can be done, that all decisions are being made higher up. As a memoirist remembered, "Even worse than this whole nightmare was the feeling of powerlessness and hopelessness vis-à-vis the lawlessness being legalized by every new ruling of every local petty chieftain and by every new 'decree' of the traitorous Lublin 'State National Council.'"[31] For some, the powerlessness led to despair that we, the heroes of Monte Cassino, had been sold out. And to fury at the West, even though at the same time the Poles continued to count on England, on America. Others became bitter, complained that things had been different, better, before the war. Finding meaning in daily routines, closing oneself off inside one's professional life, and pragmatically adjusting to the new reality were a method to escape this noose and to cure this impermanence. The writer Karol Estreicher's diaries discuss the traps of the postwar thinking. For example, on July 27, 1945: "Everyone here (in Poland) is counting on England's and America's intervention with our regime. But nothing of the kind is going to happen! Our affairs, our sovereignty, were lost as soon as Germany declared war on Russia in 1941. I can see it clearly now. But the locals can't. The pre-war intelligentsia still thinks that Communism is temporary in Poland."[32]

The Communists put in motion a range of strategies to convince cultural and academic elites, indeed even the church, to create a movement supporting their rule. Since they had no opinion-making elites of their own, they were correct to realize that winning over the prewar elites was the only way to overcome the public's resistance and to change its attitudes. Playing a key role in convincing groups of Polish writers to support the new reality was Jerzy Borejsza, a charismatic leftist intellectual. He appealed to some with his vision of a social-democratic Poland, the Poland of the revered poet Adam Mickiewicz, classless and united as a nation, similar to the visions of the prewar left-wing and liberal intelligentsia. He ensnared the intelligentsia with apartments, publishing contracts, and generous royalties, which in those days meant a lot.[33] Another strategy was to denigrate the views of those who steadfastly resisted the regime by labeling them "reactionaries" or "lords from London." Those who could not be pigeonholed, such as Socialists, underground Freedom—Equality—Independence Socialist leaders, or centrist Christian

Democrats, were deprived of a chance to influence public opinion by being forbidden to create political associations or publish their own newspapers and periodicals. Yet another strategy was to shatter groups and milieux with surveillance, creating false divisions and fictional political representations, such as the People's Party or the Polish Socialist Party, which served, on the one hand, to display alleged political pluralism and, on the other, to exhibit a broad front supporting the new order. Their existence also served to draw supporters of the old parties to the new ones—for example, the opposition Polish People's Party's to the People's Party.[34] But these efforts turned out to be only marginally successful.

Already in February 1945, government in exile delegate Jan Stanisław Jankowski sent news to London that the intelligentsia was "not holding up" any longer and was beginning to cooperate with the new regime, to accept jobs.[35] The camp with the red flag, which initially had only a handful of supporters, was growing. Indeed, the Polish Workers' Party topped three hundred thousand members in the spring of 1945.[36] One could call them sellouts, Communists, or taking the bait, but this would oversimplify the motivations of individuals, who included realists, those who became fascinated by the "victorious Red Army," and those who had strong beliefs linked to their social class, whether prewar stable boys and the poorest of peasants, hordes of "expendables," or the numerous industrial workers. Letters captured by the censorship office demonstrate the new regime's genuine social base.[37] In September 1945, someone wrote in a letter from Dąbrowa Tarnowska to France, "We have a National Unity government, which is purely of the workers and democratic. It divided up estates and gave land to the poor people, chased out the masters and gave the land to the servants and the poor from the countryside, and this government is real, for the workers."[38]

But few Poles were captivated by the social revolution. Those with high self-esteem, deep connections to their social group, and personal achievements tended to hold on to their old ideals and beliefs. For them, cooperation with the Communists was limited almost exclusively to culture, education, the health service and rebuilding their devastated country. A national legitimation of political leaders, alliances, long-range plans, and methods of government lay far outside the ruling group's reach. These people answered the referendum of June 1946 with an "I'm still checking it out." Its 25 to 30 percent support,[39] impressive compared to the interwar period, certainly did not fulfill the Polish Workers' Party ambitions of rebuilding the country from the ground up. Thus, teachers, the largest share of the intelligentsia at that time, were one of the groups that remained unconvinced, and documents frequently mention their opposition.[40] Mass strikes at the very least revealed the workers' lack of trust and support. Before political fear closed all mouths, the daily manifestations of aversion to the Communists were widespread, feeding the general feeling of impermanence.

PEOPLE ON A SEESAW

Impermanence was not uniformly vexing. After days or weeks of increased anxiety and expectation, there would be periods of relaxation, of carnival. One person's optimism was mixed with another's nervous tension. For some, such as the concentration camp survivors, the war syndrome revealed itself in shutting themselves off from the world, and in others overstimulation and nervousness, often accompanied by aggression. "The atmosphere in which we are constantly living is loaded with electricity. The storm around us is over but, what is worse, it is still roaring inside us," wrote a *Dziennik Bałtycki* reporter. "We complain that our nerves' 'endurance' is 'at its end' after these 6 nightmarish years and that 'we can't do it any longer!' Someone might think that a jaundice epidemic or hyperacidity of the stomach is raging as powerfully as the memorable Spanish flu that followed the previous great war."[41] The "illness" of some translated into group behaviors.

The seesaw of moods was one of the most important emotional experiences of the time. It could be compared to an electrocardiogram chart, which goes up and down. Periods of greater public optimism and hope brought on by good news were interwoven with weeks of collective depression, emotional nosedives.

This mechanism first began to operate in 1939, when on September 3 England and France declared war on Germany. Then, in the autumn came the shock of defeat. The rising optimism of the spring of 1940 was linked to hopes for a quick end to the war in the west.

But let's not go back that far. More recently, optimism, outright euphoria, arrived at the beginning of the Warsaw Uprising. Its defeat and the destruction of the city came as a huge shock. For five years leading up to it, the Poles were kept alive by hopes of victory. Their total collective effort focused on the expected defeat of Germany and rebuilding a sovereign and just state. They believed that the nightmare of the occupation, with its hunger, fear, and mistreatment would one day end. They also had faith in their British and American allies. With the defeat of the Warsaw Uprising and the Red Army's cynical stand, and the establishment of the new Communist authorities in Lublin, hopes were lost, and an awareness of Poland's absurd position and national tragedy won. As General Leopold Okulicki telegraphed to London in December 1944, "a mood of defeat has been spreading among the public, and it has not spared the ranks of the Home Army."[42] In Lublin-governed Poland, fear of terror, which was growing in the "October turnaround," was mounting. The people of Grodno were said to be suffering from a powerful depression brought on by the prospect of the region being taken away from Poland. "We hear despair. People are having nervous breakdowns. Depression is even creeping into our ranks."[43]

But the Poles greeted 1945 with hope, as the war would soon be over, and men were returning home and beginning to rebuild their lives. The rapid Soviet offensive and the liberation of Łódź, Cracow, and Poznań confirmed these hopes. Yet the currency exchange and hunger during preharvest, as well as news about the decisions made at the Yalta Conference, spoiled the mood. A letter written in April 1945 read, "So maybe you think that the spring we've been waiting for has arrived? Unfortunately, it will be long before we welcome the real Polish Republic. The current government is made up of Stalin's puppets."[44]

The people of the Eastern Borderlands who identified with the Home Army took the news about the decisions made at Yalta especially badly. "The mood of the Polish people after the Crimean Conference," reads a Home Army Białystok region report, "is depressed because of the unfavorable resolution of the Polish question. People expected this conference to resolve the Polish question conclusively, and that the legal London government would return to Poland. But the public has been disappointed, the soldiers and the public cannot believe that the Home Army has been disbanded and they believe that this has happened for political reasons and they continue to take jobs eagerly."[45]

The closer to the center of the country and the lower a person's social rank, the greater was their indifference and occasional lack of understanding. Indeed, huge difficulties in daily life would often overshadow any interest in public affairs. The decisions made at Yalta seemed very distant to the person in Warsaw living in a burned-out building or the peasant whose farm had been reduced to ashes by the Germans and whose field was dotted with land mines instead of potatoes. But some people did not see these decisions as final, continuing to believe that help would come from the British and the Americans. A street vendor in Targowa Street in Warsaw's Praga district told a secret police informer, "There was a meeting in Crimea, it ended with nothing, but now England won't be giving the Soviets any weapons or food. There will be hunger here, but not for long, since we and the English will be chasing out the Soviets."[46]

The elation at liberation was followed by a few months of waiting, which was interrupted by a brief period of euphoria as the war ended. A large part of the population believed that the new regime would not last long, which meant that the government could not always count on the people working for it.[47] It seems that everyone, including the Communists, was waiting for a political resolution. According to a Poznań Province militia report, "One clearly senses a mood of expectation, which reflects the international situation, among the population, as people talk insistently about the looming third [world] war in Europe."[48] At first it seemed that the negotiations taking place on June 17–21 in Moscow about forming a Polish government that would be recognized by Britain and the United States would be a breakthrough. The talks led to the creation of the Provisional Government of National Unity, whose deputy premier and minister of agriculture and agricultural reforms was Stanisław Mikołajczyk. "The petit-bourgeois–civil servant circles awaited this agreement as an absolution," read an underground report.[49] The more than one-and-a-half-year period of suspension and conditionality seemed to be drawing to a close.

Mikołajczyk was welcomed as a national hero. On the day he arrived back from Moscow, June 28, Warsaw literally went wild. What people had been anticipating for many months, in vain, suddenly seemed within reach. The multitudes that gathered spontaneously at the airport and the Żwirki i Wigury Avenue leading from it, were so huge that the capital's entire population seemed to have come out to welcome its prime minister. In the words of a witness, "A single huge shout came out of tens, no, hundreds of thousands of mouths: 'An-ders, Ma-czek, Mi-ko-łaj-czyk, An-ders, Ma-czek, Mi-ko-łaj-czyk!'"[50] The welcomes he got in Cracow and Poznań were similar. The Poles yearned for a living hero (they had a surfeit of dead ones) who would be theirs, not Moscow's, who would shoo away anxieties and restore a feeling of security. Mikołajczyk personified the nation's heroic past, the London government in exile, the Polish army, the Home Army, and Western values. He also embodied hopes that Poland would not become Soviet. He was the icon of Polish dreams about freedom, much like Gomułka would be eleven years later. As it turned out, Mikołajczyk was not allowed to fulfill the hopes vested in him while Gomułka would not really want to.

A private letter written in August 1945, whose author linked Mikołajczyk to the restoration of Poland's prewar territory, shows the enormity of the expectations: "After all this, those whom our nation has been awaiting with such impatience are coming from England. When Mikołajczyk arrived in Warsaw, what joy the nation welcomed him with. How many flowers it threw to him. The people shouted: 'We want Mikołajczyk.' The borders will be the same as before the war of 1939."[51]

The lack of documentation about public anxieties over the political situation in the summer of 1945 allows us to guess that this was the beginning of the era of difficult stabilization.[52] But already in the autumn, the level of public anxiety rose again, and this time it was only slightly connected to the weather at that time of year. Inflation and shortages of goods were more important. More and more people were also beginning to realize that nothing had changed since Mikołajczyk's return, that he was only the feather in the cap of the governing Polish Workers' Party. Someone wrote as early as August 1945, "The Soviets are still ruling Poland. Brother in law, you shouldn't think that things in the Soviet Union are the way the French papers wrote about them from '28 to '34. I myself was a Communist until 1944. Poland will only be free when the soviets [sic] leave."[53]

"The year 1946," wrote a memoirist, "was not only 'eventful' but also 'bursting with hope.'"[54] Taking into account the numerous social tensions, the accumulation of various anxieties, and the overload of the feeling of impermanence put the first half of this year at the top of the postwar years. According to Krystyna Kersten, "People continued to wait, deluding themselves with hopes for change, and thus were unusually susceptible to various rumors. They expressed common feelings of uncertainty, fear, and hope."[55] Public irritation, anger, and, at times, raw loathing of the ruling Communists continued to grow. And, what is worst for any politician, they made people laugh. A report from the Provincial Citizens' Militia Headquarters in Cracow in early January read, "The complaining, whining and criticizing the Government everywhere in public places, trams, trains, waiting rooms, may serve as a measure the mood in our province. Quite a few whispered sendups, jokes ridiculing our Government are circulating among the people here."[56]

Support for Mikołajczyk and the hopes he stirred up by returning to Poland peaked in the spring of 1946, in the time leading up to the referendum. It can be measured by the increase in Polish Peasant Party membership, which reached the colossal figure of over eight hundred thousand.[57] The mood also heated up after Winston Churchill's speech at Westminster College in Fulton, Missouri, in which he criticized Soviet policies leading to the establishment of the Iron Curtain.

There was new hope just as people were worn out by the present, again waiting for a break after which order and safety would govern. The Office of Information and Propaganda in Kielce reported, "A mood of dissatisfaction with the current state of affairs is dominant among the masses. People do not believe or feel certain that the current state of affairs won't be changed by a return of the pre-'39 situation or else by a further turn to the left toward the system that exists in the USSR. There is also fear of domestic tremors in socio-economic issues as a consequence of opposing currents in the ideological struggle. In case the reaction wins, there'll be enough bread, and order and security will rule."[58]

As soon as the date for the referendum was announced, tensions began to grow again—a state of collective mobilization also experienced elsewhere in crucial voting, when the public typically focuses on them. A song was often heard on trains:

Take the machine gun in your hand,
To crush the Workers' Party.[59]

Rallies and demonstrations of thousands in support of the Polish People's Party were held in April in Katowice, Szczecin,[60] and Gdańsk.[61] "We haven't had such a demonstration in a long time," read a letter from Katowice. "'Mikołajczyk, save Poland,'" people shouted.[62] The postwar period's largest numbers of strikes also took place in April and May.[63] On May 3 demonstrations of thousands, as well as clashes with the militia and the military, took place in Cracow and in dozens of other towns. But it was not political fear alone that governed them.

The events of May 3 and subsequent days, as well as later protests known by the months in which they occurred—October '56, March '68, December '70, and August '80—all presented a mix of national (less often purely anti-Semitic) and religious elements. Many of the demonstrations, including the one in Cracow, began with a mass. Later, the gatherings often sang patriotic and religious songs ("Rota," "Boże, coś Polskę"). They shouted, "Mikołajczyk," "Long live the PSL [Polish Peasant Party]," "Down with Bierut," "Out with the PPR [Polish Workers' Party]," "Down with propaganda," "We demand Vilna and Lvov," and "Out with the Soviet occupation." Apart from these and similar slogans ("Long live Anders," "Long live the AK [Home Army]," "Go away, terror," or "Down with the UB [Security Office],"), people also habitually shouted, "Down with Jewish Communism" (Katowice, Gliwice) and "Jews, go away" (Gliwice). In subsequent days, protests and strikes at universities (Cracow, Gliwice, Poznań, Gdańsk, Łódź, Toruń, Warsaw) and at least a few dozen secondary schools in various places took place in solidarity with those arrested by the secret police. Things calmed down only somewhat in early June.[64] Missing were national and religious issues, an economic dimension, and meaningful participation by workers and peasants; the protest was not transformed into a revolutionary movement. But its geographic spread to dozens of cities and towns, violence (numerous arrests), and duration and the participation of thousands of mostly young people made this a youth rebellion comparable to what was to come in 1956–57 and 1968. A rebellion that revealed yet another symptom of public distress, agitation, and tension.

Even without more protests or strikes in June, this mood escalated daily in the time leading up to the referendum. People waited for the results of the June 30 vote with concern and hope. The rigging of the vote finished off hopes for a political breakthrough and made people feel even more abandoned and defeated. This mood may have played a role in creating the atmosphere that led to the anti-Jewish pogrom in Kielce and efforts to start others elsewhere. There is another hypothesis: had the authorities published the real results of the referendum, perhaps the mechanism of taking revenge on the losers would have kicked in—we will let you, Jews, have it now. One thing is certain: the Kielce pogrom distracted Polish and international attention from purely political issues. But it would be wrong to draw the hurried conclusion drawn by many then, that the pogrom was a government provocation to create this distraction.

The autumn was as hot as the summer. It began with disquiet brought on by the threat of war and then moved on to a lengthy and violent parliamentary campaign. Was something in the air again? The literary critic Kazimierz

Wyka gauged the emotional situation as even more tense than a year earlier. He feared an anti-Communist "tempest" whose outcome would resemble the routing of the Warsaw Uprising.[65] Others made similar predictions; most of them expected bloody retaliation or an anti-Communist revolution.[66] In Warsaw, people mentioned November 11, the anniversary of the restoration of sovereignty in 1918, as a potential date for it to start.[67] Predictions and panic were linked to the fear of the Communists and hopes that the opposition would take revenge. This connection was similar to the tension felt by the people of Warsaw in July 1944 on the eve of the Warsaw Uprising, but naturally not by all social groups and not across the whole country. In the rumors, optimistic prognoses battled fatalistic ones. In Myślenice, for example, people were saying, "Everything will change, the war is not over yet. Anders will free us, he will leave the Polish Workers' Party people hanging."[68] In early December in Warsaw, there was hearsay about the impending "bloody settling of accounts with the Polish Workers' Party."[69] People said that US and British troops, two thousand of whom had already been seen in Poland, would come as election observers.[70] The United States would force the USSR to leave Poland. In Włocławek people said that "a new government will come from the West, and we will wallow in riches."[71]

The value of fear went up on the opinion exchange. People mostly feared where the Red Army would march and be stationed to pacify the public mood before the approaching elections.[72] In Namysłów, "In recent days [second half of October—MZ], the news has spread that 6,000 Red Army troops will arrive and be quartered here, while civilians will be forced to leave the quarters they inhabit now. This completely unjustified piece of news appears to be gossip intended to sow confusion and uncertainty."[73] Pre-election harassment, arrests of members of the Polish People's Party, and mass expulsions to Siberia were also expected. "The results will be rigged," people repeated, especially in December in Poznań, Szczecin, Gdańsk, Lublin, and Warsaw.[74] Were the Communists to win, the plagues of nationalization, collectivization, and hunger would descend on Poland.

We do not know the emotional context of the rumors nor the circumstances in which they were transmitted. People probably repeated them during ordinary interactions, at the hairdresser's, in a train compartment, in a queue, or after Mass. There is no doubt that they were proliferating. This allows us to imagine that the level of collective anxiety must have been exceptionally high and that it rose to its highest level on the eve of the elections, January 19, 1947. The writer Maria Dąbrowska recorded the next day:

> Yesterday was the annoying election day. The government proved it had great diplomatic skills of using blackmail and intimidation as it organized the "electoral victory." They organized pre-election meetings in all government offices and institutions, and even in private homes at which those present were to promise to sign the declaration of the Democratic Bloc [controlled by the Polish Workers' Party]. At work, people heard openly that they would lose their jobs if they voted differently. The blackmail was less subtle in the provinces: people were threatened with "further consequences," including "Siberia." The intimidation was so great that people came to us almost crying from despair and humiliation. Everybody felt a murky and exhausting threat around them.... And the intimidation was so great that people were afraid that, as they walked into the voting station, their ballots would be checked or that they might not even... be searched.[75]

Remarkably, following the election things calmed down again for a month or two. In Żagań, for instance, "the atmosphere of waiting and uncertainty eased."[76] The impermanence had been exhausting the Poles. This is how we can interpret the note in Dąbrowska's diary soon after the election: "Mulling over everything that has happened with the elections, I think that all in all it wasn't bad. A single government, no matter what it's like, is better than constantly changing governments."[77] People's political emotions calmed down in the spring of 1947. But not for long. In the autumn, the creation of the Cominform to coordinate the activities of Communist parties gave rise to a new wave of speculation. A man wrote to his daughter, "Beloved child, very difficult and stormy times lie ahead. I'm even beginning to doubt whether this may evaporate, especially after

The Phantoms of Transience

the Communist Information Bureau was created with headquarters in Belgrade adding fuel to the fire, but then he who worries suffers twice. Big kisses, Daddy."[78]

JUST LIKE BEFORE MUNICH

Hopes and worries associated with a third world war had a heavy impact on the collective electrocardiogram in this period. Nothing else fed the specter of impermanence as well. "In the meantime, you know, there may be another war," Polish officers in the West would say to one another as they temporized on whether to return to Poland.[79] Peasants said similar things as they delayed work in the fields. The war psychosis led to a panic that made the public strip shops of everything there was to buy and the shopkeepers to raise prices by as much as several hundred percent. Stories that Anders was to land and that Soviet armored divisions were being relocated in preparation for war allegedly strengthened the expectation syndrome, made the public more nervous, and prevented mental stability from taking root. Witold Bieńkowski noted this and, with the March 1946 panic in mind, wrote in the periodical *Dziś i Jutro*, "The specter of impermanence lurks behind the war psychosis, paralyzing resolve and wiping out the will to work. Because in the war psychosis, everything is good and brings salvation except constructive work. Because the war psychosis excuses crimes, spreading chaos and makes it necessary for Poles to rise up against other Poles. Because the war psychosis controls nerves, leads to nervous actions and nervous contractions."[80]

The mix of hopes and anxieties stemming from the belief that there might be another war exposed the Poles' collective neurosis, their trauma, their postwar disorientation, and the despair at defeat. Some people, but there is no way of knowing how many, hoped that a war was inevitable, with the British and the Americans joining forces against the Soviets, which would lead to the expulsion of the Soviets from Poland. These were probably people who were better informed in international affairs, usually middle-class and definitely opposed to the new regime.

Among those fearing another war were probably some who had lost their closest family and friends in the last one. Hanna Świda-Zięba's analysis, based on the private correspondence of intelligentsia youth after the war, gives more examples of such hopes in letters written by boys than by girls. It is therefore possible that adult and elderly women feared war more than men. But, according to Świda-Zięba, most people were ambivalent. She quoted a letter written in 1945:

> People say that there will be war, and I should wish for one because (they say) this would be the only deliverance for Poland. But I'm very afraid . . . not only for myself but also for mom, for Andrzej. . . . We've already lost Jurek. Maybe this is why I'm afraid? It's so horrible that we would have to attach hopes to something as horrific as war. . . . Is this the way one should think? Because, you know, I think sometimes: Whatever will be will be, as long as we live in peace. Study, have fun, fall in love . . . isn't this what's most important? Does my thinking this way mean that I'm a traitor and a coward? Tell me what you think.[81]

We know less about people's fear of nuclear annihilation, which reached its high point a few years later during the Korean War. For now, public knowledge about the A-bomb was only beginning to take shape. And no one thought that its allies would use it on Poland.

Firing up the panic was the universal belief that whether there is war or not, we have to eat, which came from the experiences of the German occupation. The memory was so alive that the same people who were counting on a third world war jumped into queues for potatoes or wicks for oil lamps as soon as a rumor appeared that one was looming. The Poles were schizophrenic in both wanting war and fearing one.

Zygmunt Woźniczka described the wait for a third world war.[82] Long before the Second World War ended, the underground came up with the idea that the world might have another war, this time pitting the British and Americans against the Soviets. The Home Army's *Biuletyn Informacyjny* wrote in March 1944, "Poland's sovereignty is the threshold at which the Soviets' fate will be decided. Either they will temper their appetites and retreat, and then the appeased world will cooperate with them peacefully, or they will want to cross that threshold and then the Anglo-Saxon vs. Soviet conflict will become inevitable."[83] Woźniczka explained the circulating belief that a new war would break out. First, there was the underground's lack of access to credible information that both the elites and populations of the English-speaking countries were averse to a potential armed conflict with the USSR. Second, he pointed to the Poles' megalomania: they were so important to the West that it would go on a crusade against the East to save their country. Third was the kind of wishful thinking that prospered in the postwar atmosphere of despair and disaster. In February 1941 in Soviet-occupied Lvov, Kazimierz Ajdukiewicz expressed his conviction that "the English will attack the Soviet Union out of their sense of honor, since they have moral obligations toward Poland."[84] If a philosopher, one of the most eminent minds of the era, could take this kind of hope seriously, no wonder that there were others who did, too. An underground fighter wrote in June 1945, "We're sitting in a hide-out near the border with the Reich.... There are only 60 of us now, with 25 submachine guns, the others have left. Let me finish these few words, cheers, Witek. And I hope you survive the [new—MZ] war because the Russians are getting ready in their west."[85]

The belief that another war would be necessary had enormous therapeutic value. It restored the meaning of the past fight against the Germans, legitimizing Poland's alliance with the Western democracies. It also gave people enormous hope. It was a balm for post-defeat depression and a powerful mobilizing force for resistance. To the underground fighters, honor and homeland were important, of course, but they paled in comparison with the pointlessness of continuing to fight. The appeal from the Government Delegate's Office titled "Soldier, Citizen," which was distributed in Rzeszów in October 1944, was to comfort and sustain the spirit of resistance: "very soon, our army will enter the Polish lands together with the allied armies, and we will be able to start rebuilding the State ourselves, not short of one single square centimeter."[86] In September 1945, the underground Freedom and Independence organization published propaganda instructions to "spread tales ... about the unavoidable conflict between Russia and the Anglo-Saxons ... about the atomic bomb, etc."[87]

The underground leadership should not be lightly accused of egging on their people cynically in order to keep them in the forest. The belief that a third world war was unavoidable was motivated rationally by the ideological and cultural differences between the USSR and Poland's recent Western allies, which was crystal clear to the Poles. It was not very long since similar calculations had come true. After the defeat of France, almost everyone expected Hitler to turn his attention eastward. And, according to conventional wisdom, history likes to repeat itself. Indeed, reality continued to deliver new, apparently reliable evidence that a military clash would come any day now. Supporting this were the Red Army's permanent presence in Poland, its mobility, and its obscure movements. Soviet soldiers would often tell Poles in private conversations that they would soon be moving on to "capitalist England." There were various decrees and rulings that kept people guessing, including one in early June 1945 in Bydgoszcz that ordered people to take flammable materials out of their attics, to bring up sand and water instead, and to neaten up the air-raid shelters.[88] Finally, all this speculation came somewhat true: a war did come, albeit a cold one.

But the question of why so many Poles were expecting a third world war is different from the question of why a majority was so prone to panic. The fresh memories of the Second World War were decisive. People had already panicked during the war, which is only a superficial paradox. There was panic in March 1941 in Lvov, when people swarmed into shops as they tried to buy sugar, flour, and kasha, certain that the Soviets would be going to war with someone immediately.[89] They had conditioned people so powerfully that only a minor stimulus was enough to make them behave as if there were a war. Next came particular mental habits. Jerzy Borejsza wrote about them: "It's a question of the war surviving in people's psyches in the form of catastrophic complexes, faith in some magical changes and 'Polish atom bombs.'"[90] He was quite right. During the occupation, especially in 1943, catastrophic predictions of the kind "after the Jews, we'll be next" circulated with great force. The faith in miracles also thrived, but more about this later. It is enough to read Ludwik Landau's diaries to see how many outrageous hope- or terror-filled tales rolled over Poland beginning in September 1939. The Poles were capable of believing almost anything after experiencing the war, with everything that beforehand had seemed implausible actually happening: the gas chambers, crematorium ovens, and pseudo-medical experiments on humans. People also easily acted like a herd, both as an aggressive mob lynching or killing in pogroms and in neutral situations, such as scares about the currency exchange or war.

In the end, the sentence "a war will break out between England and the Soviet Union" was also a sort of code that defined the political identity of the person saying it as someone who opposed the regime, also in the practical dimension of fighting against it. A person's attitude toward a new war did not come from political views dominant in Polish society but also resulted from psychological, cultural, and ideological factors, and a shortage of some information and a surplus of other.

It is difficult to say when the belief in a new war spread. Probably at the time when the defeat of the Third Reich became inevitable and the Poles began to intensely discuss the postwar order. The impulse may also have come from the outside. It is possible that the war psychosis was strengthened by a decree of March 30, 1945, mobilizing women for auxiliary military service (Dz.U. 1945, nr 11, poz. 57). During the occupation, people had learned the fine art of reading between the lines, interpreting all signs on earth and in heaven. When the Germans confiscated coats and furs, people concluded that their soldiers were suffering in the harsh Russian winter. When someone saw trucks arrive, there would certainly be a roundup. A similar process of collective deduction took place in the spring of 1945: why register women if the war is drawing to a close? They are clearly preparing for another one. In late May–early June in Przemyśl, the "obligatory registration of women for the army in 5-year groups for the army is causing quite a sensation. This puzzling official order is surprising everyone: why a women's army when the war has ended?"[91]

Someone wrote from Lublin, "Because when the war with the Germans ends, there is to be another one right away with Russia because some Poles can't agree with other Poles, and when the two sides finish each other off things will be good, but the western side has more and better weapons."

And from Gdynia: "Who knows what will happen to us, because we have a long way to go, the war is not over, and we will have to live through another one."

Someone else prophesied, "Turkey, Egypt and Syria have declared war, and Sweden and others will declare it any day now, too. Russia is preparing for a war with England, it will pull along the Germany it defeated, which it will first try to Communize. I wonder what will come of it."[92]

Maria Dąbrowska noted on June 6, "The people in the streets of Warsaw all together repeated the rumor... that the curfew has been moved to eight and a blackout would be instituted."[93] This was heard elsewhere.[94] Rumors about a new war arrived in waves. In 1945, the largest one came in August and September. It is difficult to understand the meanders of collective thinking, all the more so that there is so little data, but it seems that this one was brought on by the news about the nuclear bombs being dropped on Hiroshima and Nagasaki. We do not know how the Poles reacted to it, but it is likely that its significance did reach them. The Americans now have these weapons, people said, from which Stalin will have to hide. Some did not conceal their enthusiasm. A secondary-school student wrote, "Some hope is opening up for us thanks to the discovery of the atom bomb. Too bad that Churchul [sic] and Roswelds [sic] are not there, or we would have a war for sure! But even so, I'm jumping for joy at this advantage. When I heard about this invention, I danced for joy. I'm trying to be optimistic. Maybe a light will shine in the tunnel for us, too?"[95]

In the autumn of 1945, people everywhere were saying that the Yalta order would collapse, that it was only a matter of time.[96] People repeated:

Truman, Truman, drop this bomb
'Coz we can stand it no longer.

Even though we do not know when it was composed,[97] this ditty clearly encapsulates the public mood immediately after the war. Rumors of war may have grown in August–September 1945, influenced by Churchill's sterner tone in his Fulton speech, as well as by a decree of August 10 about registering health service employees and newspaper news that bicycles and horse-drawn wagons were to be registered by September 1.[98] A second interpretation is based on the later date. Some people seemed to attach magical powers to dates. For instance, since the currency exchange was conducted in January 1945, the next one would also happen in January. Since the last war had started on September 1, the next one would also begin on that day, perhaps a few days later, but definitely in September. When September was over, rumors changed its projected start to October 15.[99]

Already in July, a man wrote, "But, dear wife, this is not all because I'm expecting another war."

A letter dated August 22 from Suwałki: "Clouds are coming from the east and a big rain is coming."

September 2, Upper Silesia: "They're talking here about how on 15 September the Americans will start to chase the Russki rabble out."

September 2, Września near Poznań: "There is a lot of talk here that we may get a war yet."[100]

The author of another letter who lived near Czarnków in Greater Poland searched for signs of war by folk methods, seeking them out in abnormalities in nature. He prophesied the extermination of the nation, out of which 25 percent of Poles would come out alive. His letter posted on September 19, 1945, read, "It's clouding over and thundering amazingly, and the crows are flying, sometimes 100 of them. Wet weather is coming, not a drizzle but a downpour. Only a quarter of the nation will survive. Over there, our Poles are being killed by the germans [sic] and the russkis [sic]. There is still war in Szczecin. When war comes again, maybe one of us will perish, and if we don't see each other it'll be hard to die."[101]

The news about the nuclear bomb may easily have reawakened the old belief that the world would end soon. But we know nothing about how widespread these apocalyptic moods were. Hope still outweighed them, as gossip continued to circulate about Americans landing and General Anders returning soon. The newspapers tried to bring people down to earth with titles such as "No Miraculous Landings in Sight."[102] We will also never know how far the food price rises in September and October (see chap. 12) were caused by shortages of supplies and how much by precisely such rumors.[103]

The next major war scare came in the wake of Churchill's Fulton speech on March 5, 1946.[104] But even earlier, in February, Polish papers wrote about panic in the streets of Paris.[105] This is worth tracking since it shows how unconfirmed reports, panic behaviors, and postwar anxieties were not exclusive to Poland but at this time were quite common across Europe.

On the evening of February 4, without announcing that its news broadcast *Ce Soir en France* was over, Radio France continued with a program featuring an alleged academic specializing in nuclear issues. He discussed the Manhattan Project and warned that pressing a small button could annihilate the planet. He also talked about tests on the effects of radiation, of which there had already been victims in Canada and Siberia. He reassured his listeners that scientists from all over the world were keeping in touch with each other but also warned about underground explosions, light flashes in the sky, and malfunctioning of electric equipment as well as psychosomatic reactions in people, such as excitement and temporary loss of balance. For the next half hour, listeners were bombarded with dramatic announcements about equipment breaking down, fatal accidents, a giant wave crossing the Atlantic to Europe, and earthquakes and fires threatening Paris. In the end, Radio France, too, experienced a disaster, as sounds of fire and shouting were heard from the studio. Silence. After a pause, the "professor" announced that this had been a joke. But some in the audience had not understood the joke and took the program seriously. Some theaters interrupted their shows, children cried in front of radios, women suffered miscarriages, and men had heart attacks, and Catholics raced to confession. Some people went mad; others committed suicide. These consequences were so severe that doctors in Paris hospitals protested. During the broadcast police stations and newspapers were inundated with calls for help.[106]

The Poles lived through a similar panic, but there is no evidence of suicide attempts, miscarriages, or heart attacks. The difference between the two scares is that the Polish one lasted a few days or a couple of weeks, and not a few hours. The spark came from BBC programs, popular in Poland, which amply quoted and commented on Churchill's speech of March 5. In Warsaw, a panic under the slogan "It's war!" began on March 8. Something must have happened in the meantime, such as a Red Army unit marching, an ordinary occurrence, since rumors had it that "enormous Soviet units are in Otwock! Wawer is occupied by huge forces! Great numbers of Soviet artillery and tanks are headed for Germany!"[107] Next day, a Saturday, in Warsaw, masses of people rushed out to shop for potatoes, flour, sugar, salt, and lard. Early the following week, prices of basic foods rose by 50 to 100 percent in Warsaw.[108] People also bought up clothes, kerosene lamps, matches, and kerosene. The panic was so great that "on Saturday, every last item was sold out" in Szembek Square, one of the largest bazaars of the era.[109] Maria Dąbrowska wrote in her journal on March 12, "This morning's news from London is alarming. When you listen to London and then to Warsaw (or Moscow), it is clear that these are not allies talking, but mortal enemies. The atmosphere is probably heavier than during Munich. Oh, Lord, no one wants to live through a third war."[110]

Other parts of the country panicked, too. A new armed conflict was to break out *cito, bene cito ac valde breviter* (soon, very soon and indeed shortly).[111] Some said that it would all start in three days, and others in a month. In Cracow people argued that the outbreak of a war would mean the end of the world by atomic bomb. According to a newspaper article, "The city's inhabitants believed fully in what the whispered propaganda was spreading. Confessionals in churches were under siege; as they faced the enormous catastrophe that threatened everyone, they all wanted to put their conscience in order so that if they died they would stand purified before God."[112] There is no confirmation that queues formed in Cracow's churches for confession. There also came a rumor that the USSR had been waging war against Turkey for three weeks.[113] People repeated that Warsaw had been surrounded by Soviet troops, but other versions had them occupying Cracow or Poznań.

In Częstochowa, people talked about the coming of a universal mobilization. The local paper *Głos Narodu* claimed that this was "trumped up" but admitted that in fact men of draft age were being registered regularly.[114] "Of course, rumors about mobilization had the right impact on the mood of the working people who would have to abandon their work, their home, wives and children and go to war maybe tomorrow or the day after tomorrow at the latest, never to return."[115]

"In Kielce there was also talk of 'imminent war.'" In Radom rumor had it that "the Soviets have placed their artillery on the frontier and occupied Polish airfields for a war with England."[116]

Near Szczecin some people claimed that the Americans had already taken over airfields in Turkey. Diplomatic relations had been severed between Britain and the United States and the USSR. And the nuclear bombs had left their bases.[117]

In Pomerania, the dominant opinion was that the first line of defense would be built right there because of the location, and therefore people predicted the arrival of additional Red Army units. They expected war to come any day, and so the people of Pomerania were also stocking up.[118]

People said that trenches were being built in Gdynia. Gdańsk would be transformed into a fortress. *Gazeta Kujawska* wrote, "From time to time, waves of various gossip and the most 'authentic' rumors that preoccupy everyone and bring together people who fearfully repeat them to one another travel through Poland like convulsions. As they go from one part of town to another, then from town to town, they take on a specific weight, they grow and become horrific."[119]

This is probably how things happened. People shared news in markets, streets, and queues. The great mobility meant that what people said was then carried to other urban areas and excited others and brought clients to merchants. "The psychosis of fear and uncertainty has swept up weak and cowardly individuals," wrote the weekly *Ziemia Lubuska* about another phenomenon of the time: in the Regained Territories, settlers were fleeing from the imaginary returning Germans.[120] There is no way of knowing how many people left the places they had only just moved into in fear of war and its consequences for Poland's territory. In some districts a dozen people daily applied to leave.[121] Evidently, it was people living in the western and northern areas who felt the war threat and the resultant impermanence most acutely. In Sławno, between Koszalin and Słupsk, there were reports that "many panicking individuals have taken their things and left for the central provinces."[122] The evolution of a panic in the village of Piaski Wielkie, five kilometers from Wolin in Western Pomerania, has been recorded. A local resident spread the word—he was "very agitated, all across the village"—that he had heard on Polish Radio that a war had begun and that all the Poles in this area were in grave danger. He tried to persuade the people he discussed it with to sell their property and move to central Poland. "Because of this rumor, a panic broke out among the people."[123]

Things calmed down somewhat in late March. But actually tensions persisted through 1946. According to the governor of Pomerania, "Rumors about a coming war disappear and explode, overcoming a part of the population with a war psychosis."[124] It continued to return after symptoms of the disintegration of the Allied coalition. Historians agree that 1946 was a sort of prelude to the Cold War.[125] Indeed, this was the time when Stalin was testing Turkey to see how far he could push his demands vis-à-vis the West, now hoping to gain access to the straits to the Black Sea. "The USSR is demanding control of the Dardanelles," "Peace in the Balkans under threat" reported Polish newspapers.[126] The situation in Iran was equally laden with conflict. On March 13, 1946, the *New York Times* ran this headline: "RED ARMY POURS IN; Believed 25 Miles from Teheran as 3 Columns Fan Out in Force TENSION NEAR CLIMAX Byrnes Awaits Moscow Reply to His Inquiry Sent on Friday Encircling Move Possible Pressure on Turkey RUSSIAN COLUMNS MOVE WEST IN IRAN."[127] The first nuclear test took place on the Bikini Atoll in July, and Polish newspapers covered it. All this news about a cold war taking shape kept the flames under the cauldron going and did not allow the Poles to forget the threat of war.

The satirical weekly *Kocynder* commented on the returning waves of war rumors:

> "See that man over there under the painting? He's got a terrible memory for dates!"
> "How d'you know?"
> "He gave the date for the start of the third world war five times, and he was always wrong!"[128]

Anxiety disorders increased again in September and October 1946. There were many reasons for this. First, there was the conference of foreign ministers in Paris from July to October. A report from Białystok: "The people of our province are following the peace conference closely, a mood of expectation is rising."[129] Second, a Communist insurrection broke out in Greece. From Toruń came the news that "there is whispering about Greece, that this unrest can lead to war."[130] Third and most important was a speech by US Secretary of State James Byrnes on September 6 in Stuttgart, where he announced that US troops would remain in Europe and described the Oder-Neisse line as temporary.[131] A speech by British Foreign Secretary Ernest Bevin in early October only added oil to the fire.

Virtually all the state institutions charged with tracking public opinion reported that panic was growing. Yet these reports are exceptionally inscrutable, since they merely note opinions and do not answer sociological questions. Their authors often use the impersonal form, such as "it is being said." Who is saying it? In what circumstances? How many people are saying it? What social groups do these people come from? Reports that in Katowice people were talking about war in shops, during miners' meetings, in local government offices, and even at dances and in social clubs is an exception.[132] There is only one thing about which we can be certain: the war scare emerged across the country. To repeat the impersonal style, in Łódź soldiers were accosted and questioned: "Is war inevitable?" and "Which side will the Polish Army be on?"[133] In Sosnowiec: "General psychosis in the city. War is inevitable."[134] And in Lublin: "War psychosis in a society with impaired nerves is catching on despite its lack of reality. It is enough to say 'war' to excited people and they panic."[135] People were trapped in conjecture. It was said in Lublin Province that ten thousand soldiers led by General Władysław Anders had landed in Radom.[136] In the Dąbrowski Basin, people speculated that the USSR would be defeated by a US-China alliance.[137] Since people could remember well that a mobilization precedes a war, there were rumors about this, too. In Żywiec claims were made that ten age cohorts would be drafted, since war may come at any moment.[138] People keenly observed the movements of Soviet armies in order to learn something. An employee of the Ministry of Information and Propaganda in Bielsko-Biała reported that "I saw myself pedestrians nodding their heads meaningfully after passing a pair of Soviet officers, what are they looking for here now?"[139] In Gubin increased activity at the Soviet air base added to the Poles' disquiet.[140] In many places, especially in central and western Poland, people expected Soviet troops to move through and to requisition. At the western border, people feared resettlements.[141] This news, too, returned like a boomerang. Tales were told about the Red Army putting up fortifications, digging trenches, and amassing gas, ammunition, and equipment. In this case, Polish railroad workers were the "carriers of fear."[142] In Upper and Lower Silesia, people agitatedly told tales about preparing living quarters for Soviet officers. These were based, reasonably, on a story from Legnica, where some residents had been forced to leave their homes, so they could be taken over by the commanders of the Northern Group of Forces. In November, news broke out that ferries crossing the Oder were being destroyed.[143] In Namysłów, an outbreak of war was being foretold for the following summer "since the atomic bomb works best then."[144]

Available data about attitudes and behaviors stimulated by the war scare is chaotic and at times contradictory. For example, in Inowrocław there was no reaction to stories about a new war.[145] In Białystok, "The population was gripped by some panic," and people were buying up salt, sugar, and flour.[146] The price of potatoes at the market in Ostrołęka jumped up 52 percent. In other parts of the country, people explained shortages of potatoes with requisitions by the Red Army as it prepared for war. Salt, too, proved priceless as people expected war, and at the market in Ostrołęka it sold out. Lard also evaporated from shop and markets, and Kazimierz Wyka wrote that already during the war it had taken on the preciousness of a mimosa, and sold out over any pretext.[147] In Bielsko-Biała, people spent their entire savings on hoarded food.[148] News came from western and northern areas about a renewed feeling of impermanence and the settlers' conviction that they would soon be forced to leave. Peasants talked about interrupting their work in the fields because of the threat of war.[149] It is difficult to say how much the good feeling toward Britain and the United States cooled down as a result of James Byrnes's speech,[150] in a place like Sosnowiec in Upper Silesia, for example. The barely camouflaged joy of some of the indigenous population (their enthusiasm to learn Polish reportedly diminished) and the Germans after the speech worried the Poles, especially those who were dreaming about returning to Lvov. The war psychosis, even though it waned, survived until the election.

The next spate of collective fear came in March 1947, when President Truman asked the US Congress for funding for Greece and Turkey, which were threatened by Communism. Then in 1948, the largest wave of war panic swept Poland, even before the Korean War, as the border strip was being cleared and the first Berlin crisis came. Some days people predicted an armed conflict within the next twenty-four hours. Parents in a village kept their children home from school, since "there is no point, there will be a war anyway."[151] These were not isolated reactions; someone, most probably a railroad employee, wrote, "So we are again living with incredible tension, and I'm afraid to leave my child at home even for three days."[152] Again, people were expecting war on September 1.[153] Virtually all of Poland experienced a panic—as government reports called it, "a run on the shops." People were stripping shops of food, candles, kerosene, and paper for covering windows.[154] History repeated itself only a tad less intensively in November 1949, after Konstantin Rokossovsky was appointed minister of national defense.[155]

Stalinist acceleration in the summer of 1948 led some social groups again to hope desperately for another armed conflict would begin. It would free Poland from the "bolsheviks" and especially stop collectivization and finish the "battle over commerce." A letter from Łódź remarked on the crowds in church praying for a new war: "The Communists are ruling here. We can't wait for better times. In 1939 every polish [sic] man and woman feared war powerfully, and today everyone is asking God for war because there is no life for us anymore. If this goes on, these damned bolsheviks [sic] will murder all of us poles [sic]. You have no idea how the whole nation is praying. Churches are overflowing and every day 10 masses are said and it's still full. This is how the nation is asking for war."[156]

It seems, however, that as the situation stabilized, hopes for a new war slowly died down and were replaced with various shades of fear. Was this process accompanied by a receding feeling of impermanence? This would be confirmed by this excerpt of the memoir of the philosopher Stefan Swieżawski, who remembered from 1946, "I was listening to the radio somewhere . . . and I happened to hear information from some very authoritative place in the West. I remember the impact on the words that the United States would need fifteen years to catch up with Russia's armaments had on me. So we must wait fifteen years for some change or improvement! I thought. This radio program was a turning point for me. I said to myself: there will be no landing, no war; we cannot live 'as if' and in constant impermanence, we cannot just wait and just endure."[157]

This could lead to the conclusion that the phantom of impermanence weakened as hopes died out. They were replaced by reflection about the absurdity of continuing to wait. Now was a hard time to come to terms with the unwanted reality of getting used to the system, which for some meant political engagement and for others a flight into the private sphere. The process that Swieżawski describes was what some Poles, though certainly not all of them, did then, as the letter from Łódź indicates. The war scare persisted and reared its head during renewed explosions of war panic.[158] Fear of an atomic explosion and destruction, which was fed by propaganda and education, grew. The mimosa-like lard was still pricey.

POLAND, BUT WHERE?!

In everyday conversations in 1945–46, Poland's future borders were one of the most frequently discussed subjects. No one knew not only what the new Poland would be like but where it would actually be. Even though people expected the lands to the east of the Bug River to be conceded to the Soviet Union, they continued to hope that not everything was lost and that in a month or a year "we will be going back to Vilna and Lvov." The uncertainty increased the feeling of impermanence and swayed public moods. Man is a territorial animal and has an instinctive need to mark his territory. We do not feel safe when its lines are fluid, broken, or crossed.[159] After the war, people living in the areas along the borders did not feel safe.

Initially the greatest uncertainty involved the future of Vilna and Lvov. People could literally not grasp that both these outposts of Polishness in the northeastern and southeastern borderlands had been lost. This inability to come to terms with their loss can be explained with nationalism. In November 1944, a family letter expressed a touch of superiority vis-à-vis the Lithuanians: "My dearest, the saddest thing is to have to leave our beloved native Vilna, home to ardent and true Poles. How will the Lithuanians feel without their Polish national majority?"[160]

But this was something more than nationalism: every person with even a little bit of education could close their eyes and see their country's map and think about the geographic shape of their motherland. This map had "always" included Gdynia, Poznań, Cracow, Warsaw, Vilna, and Lvov, and the Vistula and Niemen Rivers. They were spatial points of reference that joined into a network plotting Poland's territory and the Polish safe space. They were also hugely symbolic as sacred places. Certainly none matched Warsaw's and Cracow's wealth of cultural references, but Vilna and Lvov came in a respectable third. The post–First World War fighting for Lvov was carved not only on the Tomb of the Unknown

Soldier in Warsaw but also into living memory. The story of the Lvov Eaglets, the Polish children who took part in the battle, became one of the founding myths of interwar Poland. It was thus not surprising that it was difficult to take leave of Lvov. The Polish Workers' Party's decision to abandon the city was seen as treason, a key argument delegitimizing the Polish Communists—which they were fully aware of. Władysław Gomułka wrote to Moscow in March 1944, "In Poland, even if the Brothers of Saint Anthony supported a revision of Poland's eastern border, the reactionaries, too, would have called them Moscow's agents working for Moscow's money to put the Polish nation in Stalin's bondage."[161]

Clearly, the populations of Lvov and of elsewhere in the Eastern Borderlands, some two million Poles, experienced some of the most powerful sense of temporariness and faced the quandary of whether to stay or to go. But disquiet and hopes kept people awake at night elsewhere, too. On February 15, 1945, Anna Kowalska wrote in her diary, "Yesterday, Mr. Kowalczyk confirmed the news that Anielka told us. Poland is to be in the English sphere of influence. The Lvov, Tarnopol and Stanisławów Provinces will be Poland's. I couldn't sleep all night. I said 'Te Deum laudamus' all night long. Lvov, poor and martyred, sunk in hopelessness."[162]

Even after the decisions of the Yalta Conference became known, uncertainty about which country Lvov would end up in continued. "The owner of a few large pieces of real estate" in Warsaw confided in a secret police informer, "The conference took place in Yalta, they talked about Poland's borders. Brest-Litovsk and Lvov will belong to Poland, and Vilna region to Lithuania. In the west up to the Oder. The war will be over very soon."[163]

The combination of a shortage of information and a surplus of hope influenced individual decision-making. People living in the Eastern Borderlands did not know what to do. Those who believed that Communist Poland was a temporary creature hesitated, and the atmosphere of war strengthened their resolve. There was a saying, "One A-bomb and we'll land back home." Absolutely fantastical views about the eastern border circulated—for example, that after Poland won a war with the USSR, it would acquire the lands all the way to the Dniepr River.[164] Letters read by the censorship office demonstrated this state of transience:

> Warsaw, April 1945: "Something new will happen here on 25 April, maybe they'll move the frontier to its old spot, they say."
>
> Zakopane, April 1945: "We're told that they're evacuating Lvov, and yesterday they said that the evacuation has stopped, Lvov belongs to Poland. You don't know whom to believe, which version is true."
>
> Jarosław, April 1945: "Now they're saying that the borders will definitely be moved all the way to Złota Lipa. Few people are going west from Sambor because there they don't doubt that that area will still be ours, especially Lvov and the Borysławski Basin."[165]

In the second half of 1944, people around Białystok had a similar feeling of transience, remembering that during the first period of Soviet rule in 1939–41 their region had been annexed by the USSR. This justified their fear that history might repeat itself. Now, the fear was doubled by the very sizeable presence of Red Army units and the pacifications they conducted, as well as the local authorities' symbolic gestures. Immediately after the Soviet troops occupied Białystok, posters appeared on walls announcing that the city would be incorporated into the USSR. In September, "for lack of the Supreme Leader [Michał Rola-Żymierski's] portraits," a portrait of Stalin was displayed in a city park. Some public announcements were decorated with five-pointed red stars.[166] Because of the very long-lasting transportation problems between Białystok and the rest of the country, people felt cut off. A civil servant visiting the city declared, "The population does not know precisely whether the city is Polish or Soviet."[167]

Farmers reacted idiosyncratically: in August 1945, fearing the USSR's annexation of the Białystok region, they stopped working in their fields.[168]

People in the Suwałki region also lived in fear of what the Red Army troops would do as they liberated the Polish lands.[169] Their nervousness came not only from the area's geographic location, farthest to the northeast, which would be easy to cut off, but also from their historical experience. Despite the provisions of the Ribbentrop-Molotov Pact, in September 1939 the Red Army occupied the Suwałki region for a few weeks and retreated. People no doubt remembered this.

Also in the north, people worried about the lack of clarity of the border, not because of the past but because of the present. In September 1945, the Soviet authorities in Königsberg pushed the frontier twelve to fourteen kilometers deeper into Polish territory, occupying Bartoszyce, Gierdawy, and Darkiejmy Districts, while the town of Malbork was taken over by the Soviet administration.[170] Government Plenipotentiary for Mazury Region Jakub Prawin reported, "The violation of the border has brought chaos into the organization of the local administration and has had a terrible impact on the local mood. This insecurity in border relations has paralyzed the movement of settlers to the region's northern districts, and has even led to population flight from this area, even though the good soil and total depopulation should make it attractive."[171]

Exactly a year later in the Lublin region, persistent rumors made the rounds about the frontier being shifted in Poland's disfavor. Three districts were to have been the USSR's booty, and their people were to be resettled in the west. It was reported that "these stories brought on panic and damaging commentaries." The Provincial Office of Information and Propaganda attempted to refute the rumors by distributing flyers signed by the provincial governor. But the Cassandra prophecy proved partly true. In early September 1946, the Red Army moved some of the population, including villagers from Hrebenne,[172] but most likely as an element of the operation to combat the Ukrainian underground.

People living along the border with Czechoslovakia were also afraid of frontier changes. Their fear exploded for the first time in June 1945, on the occasion of the border dispute about the future of formerly German lands, including the Kłodzka Dales and the area of Głubczyce and Racibórz, which the Potsdam Agreement had awarded to Poland.[173] Czechoslovakia occupied a part of this area, and the Polish government responded by preparing for "military operations."[174] At the same time, the media demanded that Zaolzie be given to Poland.[175] The appearance and disappearance of Czechoslovak administrative centers and the propaganda war gave the incoming Polish settlers an impression of instability. The uneasiness lasted at least until the summer of 1946. In Bystrzyca, located between Złotoryja and Jelenia Góra, "The country people are convinced that they will be forced to leave the western area, which will go to Czechoslovakia." Repatriates from beyond the Bug River were conducting "hostile agitation." Allegedly because of this, and because of the frequent attacks and robberies by Soviet troops, as many as half of the people of nearby Lwówek Śląski moved to central Poland.[176]

It was also in the formerly German areas that the deepest feelings of provisionality persisted. The Poles who were settling there now often had no idea where exactly they were going, what conditions they would find, or whether they would be able to put their lives together again. One of them remembered:

> I noticed a painted-over but still legible German name of the town on the train station building. I quickly climb off the platform, jump over a few tracks and run to the guard with a machine gun on his shoulder. "Mister! Where are we?" I call out to him. "In the Regained Territories!" I was no wiser than before because I hadn't heard about such a country, and until that moment none of us had thought to ask about our final destination. We all knew that we were going to Poland, and that was all. "Do you know by any chance where we're going?" "To the Regained Territories," he said, smiling. So I went back to the platform and because the name Regained Territories meant nothing to me, I announced out loud that they're taking us to Germany.[177]

There, impermanence was most widespread and lasted the longest. The Polish settlers from Szczecin and Kołobrzeg in the north to Jelenia Góra and Opole in the south lived with deep stress, not knowing whether to expect a new war and with it a shifted border and returning Germans. The hundreds of reports and accounts from the so-called Regained Territories carry a variety of types of fear: disquiet, anxiety, dread, and

The Phantoms of Transience

uncertainty. Fear also made an imprint on the collective memory of the people of western and northern Poland, an open secret to everyone even if not everyone experienced it. The Communist authorities constructed their legitimacy there as the sole defenders of the historic Piast lands and at the same time fed the fear.

There was panic, expressed in flight behaviors, especially in the first years after the war. A letter written in the autumn of 1948 by a woman living in Nysa in Upper Silesia to her mother illustrates this well: "Here in Nysa there is a lot of action. People are moving out, I hope we can stay through winter because by spring we'll have to run with our bundles and leave the furniture, which we've paid for already, to the Germans. Yes, Mother, my love, we're here today, but tomorrow we'll have to leave Nysa, but where to? But maybe things will clear up in Silesia and there'll also be room for us here."[178]

People sitting in a waiting room on their bundles, living in fear of expulsion: this is a metaphor for the emotional state of some of the settlers in the Regained Territories.[179] Most likely for all those who had come from the Eastern Territories, the poorly educated, rootless, and lost Polish peasants who did not understand the world's complexities. They knew what to fear because they had experienced the tragedy of exile at least once before. But in mid-1945, Poland's western border remained fluid to boot. The case of Szczecin, which changed hands twice (it was Polish, then from May to July German and then again Polish) illustrated this fluidity.[180] Rumors persisted that the same would happen to Zgorzelec (Görlitz).[181] In April 1945, there was talk in Gliwice about "some secret German agreement . . . that the area around Opole would not go to Poland, and here there will be a Red Germany."[182] Edward Ochab, at the time a member of the Central Committee of the Polish Workers' Party and minister of public administration, expressed concern that "there are already rumors about Wrocław."[183] In October 1946, the view circulated in villages around Strzelce Opolskie that "everything . . . is provisional now." People predicted that Poland would disintegrate on October 30 as a result of the peace conference going on then, which would fail to sort out Poland's western frontier.[184] Shattered nerves and the phantom of temporariness lived on. The Soviet military authorities' positive attitude toward the German population, which stunned Polish observers, also fed their uncertainty. "What are they plotting with those Germans? Maybe they want to let them stay?" was the question on many lips. The Soviet troops themselves, who passed on unconfirmed information about the allegedly set change of frontiers, could also be a source of disquiet.[185] A person writing a private letter to France on September 8, 1945, described the atmosphere of impermanence in the Regained Territories: "Now they've gone somewhere west to get a farm. They're giving farms to people for free. They don't want to go. They're living on top of each other, quarrelling, fighting, but they don't want to be there because now there is the Provisional Government, so they say that when a new Government comes, the Germans may get everything because the Germans are getting more and more rights."[186]

The threat of war became the most powerful impulse to leap up from one's bundle. The years 1946–53 and 1960–62 (the shooting down of the American U-2 over the USSR, the construction of the Berlin Wall, the Cuban Missile Crisis) were among the most anguish-filled. When there was nowhere to flee to, people stopped working in their fields and did not invest in the houses and farms they had taken over from the Germans. A peasant memoirist from Olsztyn region wrote, probably with the autumn of 1946 in mind:

> Last year my neighbor did not plow a single inch of his land. So I asked him why because I knew that he had the time and the means to do it because he owned a pair of horses, and he says, "There may be war." Another neighbor sowed only 100 kg of rye even though he could have sown more, I ask why and he says: "I'll tire myself out and tire out my horses and I don't know if I'll be able to use it." There are thousands of examples of various kinds like this, especially in the Regained Territories where a man's life is hardly different from a hare's in the field.[187]

Settlers in Rzepin, east of Frankfurt and der Oder, had the same sense of impermanence and fear to keep them awake at night. In 1948, one of them diagnosed the destructive anxiety in as many as 90 percent of his neighbors. He noted in his diary, "The worst experience for our health is not knowing what tomorrow will bring. What does this mean? It means that people are afraid of their future in these lands. Ninety percent of the people in the village, in this area and also in town are simply vegetating after collapsing psychologically. People are saying 'Maybe we won't be here long,' 'Things may change,' 'These lands are Polish, but the farms are German' and 'Lord, don't let there be war because we will be lost here.'"[188]

There is no question that the fear of changing frontiers and the feeling of temporariness accompanying it were crucial in shaping the postwar reality, influencing such behaviors and phenomena as learned helplessness, apathy, social disintegration, and legitimation of authority, which was stronger in the Regained Territories,[189] a great distance from the Germans and economic decay of the formerly German lands.

TRADING MONEY FOR FEAR

The currency exchange of January–February 1945 was an important chapter in Poland's postwar emotional history. It has been covered in this book in the context of economic chaos, a halt to the circulation of money, and the persistence of wartime habits of financial speculation. But it also helped to perpetuate fear and distrust of the rulers for many years to come.

The first currency panic exploded in late July–early August 1944. For several days or even weeks it was impossible to buy anything in practically the whole area occupied by the Red Army. Farmers stopped deliveries to the cities. Shopkeepers and artisans did not open their shops and workshops. All were tormented by uncertainty about money. The answer to the question why this was so sat inside people's wallets. In central Poland the wallets were filled mostly with General Government bills, which had been introduced in 1940. People living in the Białystok and Łódź regions, Silesia, and Pomerania continued to use reichsmarks, which had been the currency in the areas incorporated into the Reich. Rubles entered into circulation together with the Red Army. The most farsighted individuals had long been amassing US dollars. Commerce stopped because of anxiety. In Sandomierz, merchants and artisans met with representatives of the new government and asked about guarantees for the "Cracow" zlotys to remain in circulation, their value, and whether to accept money owed them in rubles, but they did not know what their exchange rate would be.[190] The state of suspension caused by these questions continued because the Polish Committee of National Liberation, notes Zbigniew Landau, was largely improvised, and so it had not prepared the indispensable attributes of power, such as its own currency.[191] The committee's Department of the National Economy and Finances began to operate with a delay. It was only a decree of August 24 (Dz.U. 1944, nr 3, poz. 11) that regulated currency, ruling that General Government bills were to remain in use. It introduced new treasury bills (subsequently, of the National Bank of Poland). Because of the presence of the multimillion-man Red Army in the liberated territories, the ruble was temporarily sanctioned at the rate of one ruble to one zloty.[192] Newspapers attempted to calm people down with assurances that the "Cracow zloty" was still valid and that people should not believe vicious rumors spread by "German spies." They argued that there was no way that a person holding these notes would be harmed in any way.[193] Whoever believed these assurances lost. Even though one could imagine in late 1944 that soon the General Government currency would be withdrawn, no one could have expected it to happen so soon, without warning, and, in the popular perception, at a thieving exchange rate.

News about the currency exchange struck the Poles like a bolt of lightning. The decree of January 6, 1945, on the deposit and exchange of bills (Dz.U. 1945, nr 1, poz. 2) announced that on January 10 "Cracow zlotys" would lose their value, and by February 28 anyone who had them should report to the treasury department or selected bank branches. Every person over the age of eighteen who was not an entrepreneur would be able to exchange five hundred–zloty bills at the rate of one to one, up to five hundred of the new zlotys.[194] Thus, a mother of five would be left virtually penniless to take

The Phantoms of Transience

care of her family. But there were other flaws in the currency exchange.

To exchange the old money for the new, a person needed to have a wartime *Kennkarte*, a German ID card, which was to be punched like a bus ticket. But people who had been resettled, whose houses had burned down, or who had served time in prison had no documents. In these cases, a Provincial Command of the Citizens' Militia issued the proper documents. Yet to obtain them in winter, with colossal transportation difficulties and during the Red Army's offensive, was absolutely impossible for many people, especially the elderly. So people did what they could. First of all, black market operators began to sell forged *Kennkarten*. A man living in Warsaw's Praga district wrote, "I don't know whether you've already exchanged money for your id cards and what profit the bank made on them. If they didn't cut out the 'crows' and 'eagles' on them, in Praga you can get 50–100 zlotys for an 'eagle' and get 500 zlotys back. New procedures. If you have the old Polish id cards, yours and mom's, you can exchange them, too, tell them you never had German ones."[195]

An overdue money exchange operation was undertaken in the lands to the west of the Vistula that had been liberated in the January offensive. For ordinary people, the rules of the exchange remained the same, but institutions and enterprises were not allowed to do it (Dz.U. 1945, nr 5, poz. 18). This meant that during preharvest, homes for the elderly, orphanages, and all other social welfare institutions could not function. Entrepreneurs could not pay their employees. People living in the lands of the prewar Province of Silesia suffered the most as they could receive only up to 250 zlotys per person for their reichsmarks.[196] There was no money exchange in the Regained Territories, including parts of Silesia, and so the circulation of money remained unregulated there longer than anywhere else.

What were the economic consequences of the exchange? In the spring of 1945, trade returned to the era of bartering with animal skins or amber. Now it was dollars, whose value grew exorbitantly (see the section of this chapter titled "Liquid Fear"). Yeast and moonshine, which were in high demand, were also used as ersatz money. "There is no question that the shortage of National Bank-issued money on the market puts brakes on the economy," assessed the mayor of bydgoszcz.[197] A private letter from Sieradz written in early March 1945 describes the situation there: "Trade using money does not exist here, only barter, for example textiles for tobacco, for vodka and so on."[198]

This situation persisted in some smaller towns, for example in Western Pomerania, until the second half of 1945. As Germans were not covered by the currency exchange, many died of starvation. But this was not the Poles' concern.

There were no plans to accompany the exchange with an information campaign. Newspapers did not list the documents required to take advantage of it or provide the addresses of exchange offices. No wonder people panicked.

Scenes straight out of the inferno could be seen outside the treasury office in Warsaw's Praga district, and the militia was often forced to intervene. There were victims: an inebriated officer wounded one person seriously, two lightly.[199] At first, this was the only exchange office for all of Warsaw, and so the queues were endless, even by that era's standards.[200] According to the *Życie Warszawy* daily, "Sketchy figures mingle with the people of Praga, purposely sowing chaos and panic. They start all kinds of troubling rumors in order to make an already difficult operation even harder. One of these rumors told people to exchange as quickly as possible because tomorrow would be too late."[201] These worries were prophetic.

Many places quickly ran out of bills, especially ones with smaller denominations. For example, none were delivered to Cracow or Lublin. In late February in Rzeszów, of the 39 million zlotys set aside for exchanges, 90 percent came as 500-zloty bills.[202] "There are terrible problems with the money exchange here, they hand out 500 zlotys and they have no change," wrote someone from Radom.[203] According to one estimate, about 30,000 entitled individuals could not exchange their cash for technical reasons.[204] By mid-April in Zakopane, only a handful of people were able to take advantage of the "Lublin currency." In Myślenice District, with about

110,000 inhabitants, the exchange was available for only two days, and in Nowy Sącz it was five days with an estimated 20 percent of the town and surrounding area benefiting from it.

The positive public feelings about liberation were abruptly crushed by the currency exchange. A letter from Łódź reported on March 5, 1945, "We can only pay the doctor with food because he doesn't want money, and he charges a lot for a visit."[205]

People complained and pleaded with the authorities to extend the deadline for exchanging money. Despite the regime's populist slogans, it was the poorest who suffered the most, including blue-collar workers whose wartime savings were lost. Many of them, in Cracow for instance, fearing expulsions by the Germans, had sold their belongings to have cash. The more prosperous, who owned objects, dollars, and gold, even if they lost their 500-zloty bills, could still instantly transform what they had into cash.[206] A lucky owner of dollars described his problems and solutions to them:

> As a result of this speculation of mine I got stuck already on 15 January with 3,000 Cracow [500-zloty bills] I held for Katowice and 5,000 of mine. I also knew that my landlady won't be able to accept them and will not take devalued currency, so when the Lublin zlotys first appeared on the black market, I bought 3,000 of them for exactly 20 paper dollars and my wife paid the rent for 2 months. By 1 April, so as not to get caught a second time, what with the rumors about an even newer government and a third currency to be issued in Poland.[207]

Some historians view the exchange as a "dramatic but necessary solution to that era's economic situation," which preempted hyperinflation.[208] But, even without delving into economic analysis and its critique, there are obvious reasons why the exchange should not have happened. It is possible that had the government waited for two to four months and prepared for it better, there would not have been such dramatic inflation. Economic disruptions and social panic would probably have been less abrupt had the period of transition been half a year instead of six weeks and the February 28 deadline more flexible (it was pushed back only in Greater Poland and Łódź Province). The authorities' incompetence and lack of preparedness were obvious every step of the way. The freezing of monetary transactions prolonged the chaos of the first days, extending it into months. A letter from Żyrardów near Warsaw said, "No one knows what's next, prices are going wild, and this is because of the new currency has no value or Minister Dąbrowski's signature. Unluckily the town and central authorities have failed to contain all the chaos that comes from the change of the central authorities at a time without all the things people need to keep living calmly."[209]

The sociologist Stanisław Ossowski wrote to his wife, Maria, on February 12: "Spend whatever money you can as quickly as possible." In a second letter he wrote on the same day he argued, "Officially [General Government 100-zloty bills] are valid until the end of March, but it is unlikely that you will be able to get anything for them (apart from 500 for a *Kennkarte*). The optimists are counting on 25%, and others are treating the [General Government 100-zloty bills] like wallpaper."[210] It seems that allowing the two currencies to operate in parallel would have calmed people down. As the exchange reduced the amount of money in circulation, the population's purchasing power was reduced in leaps and bounds. A private letter from Poznań discussed this: "Everything would be fine if money was worth anything or if it was possible to sell something on one's own, but there is no money or materials turnover."[211]

The situation was similar in Ostrowiec Świętokrzyski (letter of March 4, 1945): "People are poor here because this money is worthless, and now they're exchanging 500 zlotys per person, no more for now, and the prices are extremely high."[212]

It is likely that had the pauperization brought on by the exchange not grown, in the first half of 1945 there would have been less hunger, and it would have been easier to discover and to control. Also, even the greatest fear of hyperinflation should not excuse the decision not to allow children and adolescents the money exchange quota.

There was also the psychological price, more difficult to quantify but longer-lasting and more difficult to surmount. "People are afraid of this new money," read a letter from Krotoszyn in early March 1945.[213] The money exchange allowed anxiety to take root and was seen as the first instance of the new government's arrogance, and it would take a long time to rebuild the public's shattered trust in its monetary policies. No economy can operate steadily without a foundation of social trust in the government's adherence to fiscal rules. The Communists violated this basic principle, which was evident in the next currency panic, which came soon enough, in April 1945.

The second panic began with a rumor that swept the whole country, that 500-zloty bills of the AA series had lost their value. As a newspaper reported, "The gullible rural population has begun to get rid of these bills in a panic, buying up various goods."[214] Private letters discuss the situation in the vicinity of Warsaw (both posted on April 7, 1945): "They're constantly releasing gossip about currency changes, and that's why they're hiding and locking up everything so that we can't get at anything. There is bedlam and uncertainty at every step." And: "Imagine, people have gone absolutely mad here, releasing rumors that money will be changed, and things have become terribly expensive."[215]

Distrust of the new money and fear of the next change again froze trade. An informer complained to the governor of Cracow Province about a shop owner by name, alleging that he had stopped accepting the new bills: "J.M. lives in Brody near Kalwaria Zebrzydowska and manages a shop.... He now has entire warehouses loaded with artificial fertilizers and he gives them to rich farmers without taking money because he says that this money can go to hell because this is Bolshevik money and the government from London will come and there will be new money."[216]

The *Życie Warszawy* daily called this phenomenon "endemic faintheartedness of the market"[217] and linked it to public distrust in the government's monetary policy, which continued in this period. The introduction of every new bill, including the 1,000-zloty bill in September 1945 and the 500-zloty bill in July 1946, fed the disquiet on the market and undermined faith in the zloty—instead of contributing to stability.[218] Waves of gossip traveled across the whole country every few months with "confirmed," "surefire" news about an exchange of this or that bill or about the invalidation of a particular series of bills.[219]

The largest panic of this kind erupted on the first anniversary of the January exchange. Those who yielded to the psychosis of the rumor, fearing the next total or partial exchange, depleted their savings and invested in gold or in foreign currencies. Newspapers across Poland reported on the panic and accused the "wheeler-dealer and profiteer mafia" of bringing it about.[220] Actually, the accelerated transmission of the rumor and the ease with which it made people panic stemmed from earlier anxieties, the population's up-and-down emotions, and negligible trust in the new government. The events in Kielce are a good example.

Panic broke out in Kielce on January 14, 1946. It could not be subdued for a week, despite articles in local and national newspapers. Prices in independent trade climbed by tens of percent, for some items even more (in Ełk, for instance, prices reportedly went up by 300 percent[221]). Some merchants stopped selling altogether, and peasants stopped delivering food. The town's dramatic shortages of bread and other ration-card items worsened the situation, and the mayor described it as catastrophic. If we add the rumors about grains being transported to the USSR, thefts of UNRRA Christmas packages, and interruptions in electricity and gas deliveries (allegedly also intercepted by the Soviet Union), it is easier to understand that the public became more susceptible to panic and frustration in winter and spring of 1946.[222]

TWO PLAGUES: COLLECTIVIZATION AND NATIONALIZATION

For the Polish peasants, collectivization was the worst plague. This fear turned into absolute terror after the Polish Workers' Party plenum in July 1948 at which Communist official Hilary Minc announced that the efforts to push out "capitalist elements will not only not die out, but on the contrary grow fiercer."[223] A genuine psychosis gripped the countryside, persisting virtually until Stalin's death in March 1953. Expecting the worst, farmers reached out for the "weapons of the weak,"[224] slaughtering their animals en masse, selling off the crops they had only just harvested, or delaying work in the fields. Gossip and speculation seized Poland: "Now all small farms up to 5 morgens in size are to stay, above that they are to be divided up into kolkhozes, but will it happen? Please, Lord, don't let it happen!" Or, "People say that peasants will only own one set of clothes in the kolkhozes, they will get their soup from a cauldron, and that it's better to go into the forest and spill blood than to give in to this serfdom."[225] These were not empty threats.

The terror experienced in the countryside resembled the early modern peasant riots in western Europe. Someone left a note in a cooperative in Radom after it was plundered: "Cheers, red masters, today I'm starting to pacify your kolkhozes."[226] Incidents of sabotage and destruction of crops and tools proliferated. Union of Polish Youth activists who came to agitate had to run away from furious peasants. There was fighting, and some people were killed. People were genuinely afraid, some even more than of war. In the autumn of 1948, someone wrote in a private letter, "People are talking here about war and about kolkhozes, that people will be forced into them, and the people are very afraid because there is plenty to be afraid of. War is terrible but these kolhozes are even more terrible because in war the person who is killed will perish, but here we will all perish."[227]

Dariusz Jarosz's pivotal study of the Stalinist period includes an analysis of peasant opposition to and fear of collectivization.[228] The state of collective emotions brought on by the fear of collectivization immediately after the war had been moderate, which is not to say that this issue was indifferent or of little importance to the peasants.

The fear of collectivization was born in the 1930s. It subsequently grew in Poland with the experience of the first Soviet occupation of 1939–41 and the German propaganda in operation "Berta" targeting the population of the General Government.[229] The Home Army's Office of Information and Propaganda and other underground organizations also focused on the threat of collectivization. The underground not only feared the Soviets itself but also attempted to sow fear of them among the public. Instruction materials suggested:

> Inform as often as possible about the Communists' attacks (People's Guard, Stalin's Children, Kuba's Children etc.) [Kuba the Ripper, most likely—MZ] on poor teachers, doctors on their way to seen poor patients, soldiers' widows, orphans, poor peasants and laborers. The news should include details of cruelty (burning, rapes, cutting off women's breasts, smashing children's heads, etc.) and descriptions of the ragged belongings they stole (a suit, almost new shoes, the last cow, a tired old horse, a piglet, goat, two rabbits, three hens, five eggs, a small sack of flour, kasha—people's very last belongings). Such news should be relayed on the basis of existing materials in the largest quantities possible, not fearing exaggeration since the roaming Communist bands are not picky in their methods of taking booty nor in the kinds of things they take.

Other scare tactics should also be used. The most important ones were collectivization and hunger. The document continued, "Point out Russia's economic bankruptcy, its fantastic debt vis-à-vis America, its total dependence on imports, hunger, the increasingly frequent unrest among peasants being murdered by the NKVD in the kolkhozes, the 18-hour workdays in factories and collectives under threat of execution and so on."[230]

With the Red Army marching into Poland, Polish peasants had every right to be afraid. They associated the kolkhoz with having their land taken away, collective living in crowded conditions in barracks, the Soviet *uravnilovka* with everyone wearing identical clothing and eating from a single large cauldron. Cynics added that even "wives would be shared." But the worst effect of collectivization would be the hunger that would hit the people in the countryside. Hence, the peasants thought of it as the worst of the potential plagues.

"The creator of the kolkhoz regime,"[231] Stalin, was aware of this fear. By ordering the Polish Workers' Party to implement land reform in Poland, he wanted to reduce this fear and at the same time attempted to create an informal populist arrangement: land in exchange for support for the new government.[232] This plan worked only in part. The reform not only failed to crush the fear but actually fed it. As for its broader emotional background, the revolution from the top[233] imposed by the land reform deepened the chaos and confusion. The ancient peasant order was collapsing under its pressure, even though the peasants did not always view it positively but felt that it gave them continuity and stability.[234] On the other hand, the rural population as a whole definitely accepted the decree about land reform enthusiastically, even though a closer look reveals that it was mostly the landless and the smallholders who accepted it, and wealthier farmers were more reserved. But all of them remained somewhat aloof, first of all because they tended to believe that the Polish Committee of National Liberation would not last long and neither would their parceling out of estates. The peasants were afraid that when the masters returned, they would have to pay for the land they were now getting for free. Flyers were passed around in the countryside: "Peasants, don't grab others' property because you'll lose yours." On the day after an estate in Radom District was split up, one of the families found a coffin on its field with the sign "Death to those who will till this land."[235] Peasants feared the overly energetic "boys from the forest," who knew how to punish those who wanted others' property, by whipping, even with murder. Peasants also feared collectivization.

People also believed that because land was being measured, land reform would lead to the creation of kolkhozes. In the autumn of 1944 in the Białystok region, this fear took on near-apocalyptic dimensions. There was talk of exile to Siberia for those for whom there would not be enough land and about collectivization, which would happen shortly after the land reform. Some peasants reportedly feared being exiled and refused to take the land.[236] This shows that this unique image of hell, with a first circle of collectivization and a second circle of Siberia, sprouted in some minds. People also suspected that the government, with its long-term goal of collectivizing, was aiming to break up the ownership structure in the countryside by creating thousands of two- to three-hectare farms. This way, in the future the new landowners who could not manage on their own would be more easily convinced about the economic benefits of farming collectively. Thus, the various types of cooperatives (machinery or milling partnerships, breweries) created with what remained of the divided-up landed estates (buildings, factories, orchards, apiaries, fish ponds, etc.) were thought to be the vanguard of the kolkhozes.[237] They grew dynamically in 1945–46,[238] worrying some of the rural population that they would be used as the core of future kolkhozes. The underground's frequent destruction of these cooperatives' property was probably motivated by this fear.

Indeed, the landowners whose estates were divided up through the land reform, the underground press, and rural leaders aligned with the underground fired up the fear. To calm them down, the authorities sent propaganda teams and agricultural instructors to the countryside to convince the fearful peasants that they were in no danger of collectivization. The many congresses, conferences, briefings and village meetings also served to deny the rumors about kolkhozes. Newspapers argued against it, too, with headlines such as "There Will Be No Collectivization."[239] The stakes were high, as Bolesław Bierut noted in May 1945, over undermining the "masses' trust in the Provisional Government."[240]

In the battle in which one side was feeding the fear of danger and the other was attempting to diminish it, the "reactionary camp" unexpectedly won a surprise ally in the "old Communists" who already in 1944 had proposed quickly transforming farmland into cooperatives. The party in power tried to shush such voices by calling them sectarian, and yet some of them reached the public. Indeed, the new agrarian civil servants did not always perform well, sometimes limiting the peasants' rights to the crops from land they had been given in the first year they were farming it, shifting the right to harvest to the cooperative. The intention was to level the ground between farmers who had received unsown land and those who could take advantage of the winter corn. Yet the peasants saw this not as justice but as a limitation of their property rights.²⁴¹ In the Regained Territories, placing several families on one farm was an additional source of worry, as they suspected that they "were living in a kolkhoz."²⁴² Despite the land reform, the fear persisted also because people who had been given land did not also receive the documents to assure them of their ownership. This fear lay directly behind the decision to put off fieldwork, renovations, and investments. A woman repatriated to the village of Radzicz near Bydgoszcz wrote in her diary in 1948, "There is one more, very important, the most important, reason why the people from our village do not want to put all their profits into the renovation of buildings. This reason is that so far not all farmers have been given the [property] title, and the annoying word 'user' takes away one's desire to work and the self-assurance of even the most determined who were given land because they owned no land earlier."²⁴³

It was only in the autumn of 1946 that the government announced it would begin to issue property titles, which we can interpret as the next move in the game to win support, this time ahead of the approaching parliamentary elections. Still, many peasants became more confident and came to believe that the existing situation would last.²⁴⁴

The fear of collectivization, much like the other fears, came in waves. It peaked in the autumn of 1944 and spring of 1945 as the land reform was being implemented. "Polish peasants are very afraid of kolkhozes, they don't want kolkhozes," Władysław Gomułka reported to Moscow in May 1945. "We should not even think about Polish kolkhozes, we will just say to our peasantry that our party is opposed to kolkhozes, that our party will not go against the nation's will."²⁴⁵ There were reports from Greater Poland in June 1945 about the "psychosis that is eating away at the peasants' minds" as they live in fear of collectivization.²⁴⁶ Emotions were similar elsewhere.

Fear diminished in the summer. After all, the Peasant Party's Stanisław Mikołajczyk had been named minister of agriculture. The peasants were also preoccupied with other matters at this time of year—fieldwork and compulsory deliveries—which meant that, to use the words of a farmer from Kielce, "you never know what's coming." Their private correspondence illustrates well the problems they were tackling.

A woman farmer from Trzcianka, near Piła in Pomerania, wrote on September 5, 1945: "I can describe our harvest, that we had to harness ourselves to the wagon and pull the wagon and we did this all harvest long because we didn't have one bit of a horse."

Chełmża, near Toruń, August 20, 1945: "We now have to deliver grains, potatoes. The amount is very high and the rye is very poor, the soil is very sandy, nothing but sand. A horse is 30 thou."

Radomsko, September 3, 1945: "We have taxes imposed on us. We have to give very large deliveries, my dear brother. If this continues like now, it'll be hard to bear. Hundreds of hectares are lying fallow in the masters' estates."

Starogard, August 31, 1945: "But I want to give up my plot because they're constantly sending papers, to pay taxes, to make deliveries, and where am I supposed to get it from and this is all too much for me."²⁴⁷

Peasants again came in close contact with collectivization in the autumn of 1945 and the following spring. A mouse plague and drought in the summer of 1946 again distracted them from the kolkhozes, which returned as a topic of discussion in the autumn and winter. In April 1947 in Ostrowiec District, Kielce Province, there was hearsay that the land given out in the land reform would be taken away. The peasants reportedly were outraged and stopped working.²⁴⁸ In July the Sejm allegedly debated forming kolkhozes, and half of the deputies favored them and half opposed them.²⁴⁹ The ebb and flow of the feeling of threat coming from potential collectivization seems to have been strongly correlated with other anxieties, primarily political ones. Fear of the kolkhozes thus appeared in a packet with overall nervousness, as did the agricultural seasons. In autumn and winter, with more free time, a farmer could sit and chat with a neighbor. One typical meeting of this kind was described by a peasant memoirist:

> One Sunday I stopped by a certain home and found several farmers who came by for a chat as is the custom, and they again got into the subject of kolkhozes

in Russia and the subject of this conversation were the words of re-émigrés who came from Russia last year and who worked either in a vegetable kolkhoz or in a vineyard kolkhoz and still others in farming kolkhozes. The question came up: why are the workers who came back from France, from England or from Germany all very well dressed, each one of them brought with him apart from personal items something for their brothers and sisters and relatives, while those returning from Russia are mostly poor and badly dressed, where does this big difference come from? Didn't both of them stay and work for foreigners? We couldn't answer this question and we also can't find an explanation in the newspapers."[250]

We may risk the hypothesis that the announcement of collectivization in the summer of 1948, which evoked terror, would not have been so violent had the peasants not discussed the subject earlier, in 1944–47.

Less is known about the public fear of nationalization. The people's government did not particularly care for entrepreneurs. It did not care about the views of merchants or producers, and at this time it did not monitor their moods as much as it did peasants' or workers' views. But we know enough that "uncertainty about tomorrow" (an expression from that era) constituted a component of the psychological state of private entrepreneurs long before the "battle over commerce," which influenced the frequent explosions of market panic.

In early autumn 1944 and spring 1945, feelings of uncertainty, transience, and anxiety must have been especially prominent. Will they put us out in the street? Disenfranchise us like they did the landowners? These questions nagged many groups of entrepreneurs, both the leftovers of the prewar middle class and the "new bourgeoisie." No one knew what the new regime's economic policies would be, although its initial decisions did not seem too bad. In January 1945, "government operations groups" moved right behind the front with the mission of taking over factories on behalf of the people's government to start them again and keep away looters. The government's support in individual factories were the Factory Committees, whose main task was to prevent former owners or their agents from taking them over after the Germans had abandoned them.[251] The January 1945 currency exchange appeared to confirm pessimistic scenarios. It launched the new rulers' unfortunate manner of imposing economic decisions without consulting the public and without prior notice. The Communists were thus not only failing to build an atmosphere of trust but also causing anxiety about new, unannounced moves (later, for instance, price rises). Also in January, a decree adding a 50 percent war supplement to the existing income tax came into force (Dz.U. 1945, nr 3, poz. 8). This meant in practice that the highest earners were to pay an 80 percent income tax on their income. On April 13, two new decrees came into force, the first about tax on wartime enrichment (Dz.U. 1945, nr 13, poz. 72) and the second a military tax (Dz.U. 1945, nr 13, poz. 74). At that time, many governments were implementing restrictive fiscal policies, using the war to justify them. Yet in Poland the levels of various types of fiscal burdens had become so high that people had reason to question their intentions. The interpretation was not far-fetched that this was motivated not only by the need to finance the war effort and to rebuild the country but by a crawling revolution aimed at gradually "finishing off the class enemy" with taxes.

This universal uncertainty shaped attitudes and made people wait and watch developments. Businesspeople delayed starting businesses, did not open shops, and did not launch production or hire staff. This passivity is reflected very accurately in a report by the Government Plenipotentiary for Economic Issues, who inspected Włocławek in February 1945: "At the time of our arrival, the economic lifelessness in both the town and the district was total."[252] In Greater Poland, a region known for its thrift, the torpor lasted until the end of May.[253]

For a time, Mikołajczyk's arrival blew away the "specter of Communism" in the economy. Everywhere, prewar Polish owners attempted to reprivatize their property that had been taken away by the Germans. Private enterprises took off. But, according to a report by the Chamber of Industry and Trade in Cracow, the mood sank again in the second half of 1945, as people did not know where the Communist policies were going. Entrepreneurs were most afraid of having their businesses confiscated by the government, then called the "Bolshevization of economic relations." Evidence was forthcoming. It came as the so-called Bierut decree about nationalizing land in Warsaw (Dz.U. 1945, nr 50, poz. 279). It is not out of the question that this deepened the general anxiety in the autumn. An article by Communist official Edward Ochab, which stated that the current "people's democracy" in Poland would serve as a transitional phase to "proletarian democracy" as it existed in the USSR,[254] further heightened unease among businesspeople.

Again without warning, the State National Council voted in favor of nationalization on January 3, 1946, which was what entrepreneurs feared the most. It largely endorsed the expropriations that had taken place earlier, during the occupation and immediately after the war. The state was taking over the key branches of the economy, medium and large enterprises, which employed more than fifty people per shift. Enterprises and institutions that had belonged to the Third Reich and the Free City of Gdańsk, and their citizens (non-Poles), were nationalized without compensation, as was the property of Polish citizens who were shown to have collaborated with the German occupying power.[255] Hilary Minc, the architect of the new economic policy, was well aware of how much fear the word *nationalization* evoked. In his speech to the State National Council, he promised that compensation would be paid out, wanting to calm down the mood not only in Poland but also abroad. He said that "confiscating enterprises without compensation would mean starting on the road to a socialist revolution. We are not going down this road, and this is why we will conduct the taking over of enterprises by the State with compensations, just as is happening in Czechoslovakia, France or England, and unlike in Soviet Russia."

At this time, a bill regulating new businesses and supporting private enterprise was put up for a vote. It was to confirm officially that change was heading in a non-Communist direction, in Minc's words, serving as a safe-conduct for merchants and industrialists to guarantee their right to own property. Minister Minc argued in a speech to "support healthy private enterprise by creating a suitable atmosphere for it, a suitable climate, a suitable framework for their activities and the greatest feeling of safety."[256] A little over a year later, this safe conduct was worth the same as the guarantees given Jan Hus.

It is normal that when something we have been fearing actually happens, our fear evaporates. But the announcement of nationalization did not dispel anxieties. The Polish Workers' Party newspapers published caricatures and texts declaring its victory over the capitalists.[257] A rumor was repeated all over Poland in January that UNRRA assistance would be halted, allegedly as England's and America's retribution for the expropriations.[258] According to the National Economy Bank, the "general mood of uncertainty" in private industry did not change. No one knew which enterprises would be nationalized. Trying to prepare for change, some owners divided up their businesses into two independent halves and reduced their personnel—in vain, as it would turn out. The anxiety among business owners came into view during the First Congress of Private Industry, which was held in Łódź on February 20–21, 1946. One of the assembly's most important demands was to "stabilize the current structural forms," which would be significantly influenced by the executive orders on the new nationalization. The National Economy Bank analysts noted that a large part of the entrepreneurial class were only just emerging from the underground and not registering their businesses with the Chambers of Industry and Trade. We know they were clearly fleeing the state's tightening fiscal noose, distrusting the state. The analysts also observed most private entrepreneurs' lack of interest in investment credits.[259]

There were other factors contributing to the uncertain situation. The pioneers of prewar private entrepreneurship struggled with numerous obstacles, primarily extensive corruption, local authorities' arbitrariness, difficulties with finding space, and excessive fiscalism— not to mention the high taxes or compulsory charitable contributions to schools, winter assistance, and loans to the fund to rebuild Poland. Reporting on the economic situation in Lower Silesia, the Chamber of Industry and Trade in Wrocław noted that "the unsatisfactory state of security, frequent thefts of merchandise in the daytime and at night, incessant inspections and 'verifications' of industrial certificates and space allocations, the legal authorities' illegal expropriations or shutting down of enterprises, complete the panorama of the uncertain and impermanent atmosphere in which even the most dynamic entrepreneur will frequently collapse."[260]

Fear of the "Bolshevization of the economy" deepened in the autumn of 1946. It was most likely more than just the collective rise in nervousness preceding the elections that had a bearing on it. In the previous early spring, authorities had already introduced licensed restaurants—one restaurant, bar, or café per one thousand or eight hundred inhabitants—explaining this with the difficulties with supplies (see chap. 12). The newspapers printed populist arguments that favored shutting down all kinds of small cafés, hole-in-the-wall restaurants, and bars, which incidentally were booming then, as they only "use up gas, electricity and heating, just the things that the working man needs." In the spirit of the socialist welfare state, they demanded that the space thus saved be used for day care centers and cafeterias.[261] In July people began to talk about plans to "nationalize the printing industry totally," even those enterprises that had not been declared critical to the national economy earlier, and in violation of the ruling that only enterprises with a staff of over fifty were to be nationalized. But the delegates of the Association of the Graphic Industry who met with officials at the Ministry of Information and Propaganda to discuss this were told that this was a "political matter" and that the decision had been made already.[262] Then, in September, the Ministry of Industry decided provisionally to nationalize paper wholesalers, which businesspeople learned by word of mouth,[263] and presumably not only those in the printing and paper industries. In June newspapers were forced to refute hearsay about the introduction of state control over the grain trade.[264] In autumn, rumors made the rounds about the nationalization of entire trade and also, for instance, of law offices, and were repeated by even "the most serious merchants."[265]

This kind of fear must also have hidden behind the price rises since the news about a transformation of the economic regime seeping into business circles led to the sudden rise of profit margins in privately owned shops and wholesalers.[266]

But much worse times lay ahead. During the May Day celebrations of 1947, Hilary Minc gave a speech in Katowice in which he said, 'We have won the battle over production, now we will try to win the battle over commerce."[267] The Sejm voted on the bills that were the legal foundation of the "battle over commerce" in early June. They included strict price controls, increased fiscal pressure on the private sector by imposing higher tax rates, and, most importantly, expanding the system of supertaxes.[268] From this moment on, to the owners of private companies, supertaxes became synonymous with supreme fear, as they forced mass bankruptcies. The weapons used in this revolution from the top were the Treasury Office flying patrols, whose searches included orders to line up against a wall with raised arms,[269] something naturally associated with the German occupation. The owner of a small weaving workshop remembered fear most of all:

> Inspectors from the Treasury Office could burst into workshops at any time, and here we have five or six people instead of the one who is registered. We women lived in constant fear. We devised a warning system. We wrote next to our doorbell "Please ring twice," and we told all our friends to ring three times. At the sound of two rings, everyone would jump off their looms and spinning wheels, sit down at the tables as if they had just dropped by "for a chat".... I also had to pay taxes. I never knew how they would be calculated. Every expedition to the Treasury Office was terrifying to me. Vicious and inept officials, dingy offices. I can still remember a chilling event. I was standing in line in a dark hallway in the office, and suddenly the man standing before me fell over, died on the spot. There was great nervousness and fear of potential harassment, supertaxes.... In a word, running a business was living under constant threat. I literally couldn't sleep from fear.[270]

The uncertainty was over in the autumn of 1948 as Stalinist fear took over. Excerpts of letters the censors read testify to the fear of private businesspeople.

From Katowice: "You complain that you had to pay 600,000 zlotys, but I believe that you will pay more after the latest regulations. Here, quite a few of us have turned gray for this reason. I'm now working in a new, united cooperative and every day we get offers from various producers and little factories to take them over because their owners cannot support themselves."

From Łódź: "Tadzio has been working terribly hard and he is worried about the factory because there is less and less of the raw materials. The Tax Office adds on such surtaxes without recording them in the books that you can see the harsh course coming against private entrepreneurs in every line of business. Here there are masses of shops that are closing, with signs reading 'stocktaking,' and from 1 January it will definitely be 90%."[271]

A NEW EVIL: HOUSING

"Whenever a journalist from Warsaw arrives and asks 'and what problems do you citizens have in your famous burg?' the citizens of every revered and ancient town in the Polish lands always and everywhere answer as one, recklessly thinking of effects as causes: 'housing.'"[272] In the aftermath of the war, housing had an exceptionally bad name. The startling news that "those guys from the housing office have been going from apartment to apartment" did not let people sleep and made them panic. It was not enough that the procedures involved in getting anything done in housing offices required overcoming numerous bureaucratic obstacles, which in any case often ended with a bribe; there was also the real threat of being expelled virtually overnight or of having strangers added to the people already living in their homes. There were two factual reasons and one political one for this. First was the great migration to the cities, which in Kazimierz Piesowicz's estimate was 1.4 million people in 1944–45, the greatest increase in the urban population in such a short period in the history of Poland. Several smaller migrations followed. Many young people originally from the countryside, who were returning from forced labor in Germany, headed for the cities. A large share of the migrants from the Eastern Borderlands settled in urban centers in the so-called Regained Territories. In 1946–50, an average of 250,000 people migrated to urban areas annually.[273]

The second reason why housing was maligned was its shortage, a result of wartime destruction. Warsaw suffered from the most difficult, actually catastrophic situation, with an average of 2.2 people per room. Lublin and Częstochowa had similar densities, Kielce, Cracow, and Poznań slightly lower ones. In Cracow in 1945, an average of 3.87 persons lived in an apartment, and the highest density was in studios, which housed four, five, or more people.[274] In cities such as bombed-out Wrocław, Gdańsk, and especially Warsaw, people slept in ruins, partly burned-out or partly bombed-out buildings.

A woman living on Jagiellońska Street in Warsaw wrote on March 20, 1945, "The housing situation is very difficult, you need tens of thousands [of zlotys], and those who haven't got it sleep in the street in rubble, the drinking water is awful, everything is impossibly expensive, but everything is available."[275]

The population density was difficult to imagine. *Daily Herald* correspondent Charles Lambert reported from Warsaw, "People are living in Warsaw's ruins 10 people to a room. They bring water, perhaps contaminated, in buckets. They live by candlelight. Not every apartment has a heater. Many of the apartments are in cellars. People are sleeping several to a bed, some on tables or under tables."[276]

Fear of the housing office did not affect those living in cellars or crumbling houses, however. It was felt by the relatively wealthier people, owners of houses or of two or more rooms in a building. And now for the political third reason for the sense of endangerment, which was the result of the Communists' revolutionary method of solving problems. Looking at the sequence of events—October 1945, nationalization of land in Warsaw; December, first housing decrees (more on these shortly); January 1946, nationalization of industry—the images move before our eyes like a film in slow motion, like stages of "vaulting to the kingdom of freedom," in which property rights, the

Marxists' source of all evil, have ceased to exist. To Dariusz Jarosz, this may have been a sort of punishment. After the referendum, in Cracow and other urban areas including Łódź, and strikes in those places, the authorities wanted to punish the "reactionary element" by expelling it and hence changing these cities' ideological identities.[277] It was also a question of rewarding "our" people or buying support of groups considered most important, especially workers and the intelligentsia. In Łódź, in March–April 1945, the Workers' Housing Action handed out 8,500 flats to labor union members, Polish Workers' Party and Polish Socialist Party activists, and cadres of the most important factories.[278] The reason it is difficult to interpret the regime's intentions is that the new housing policy, unlike the Soviet Union's in the 1920s, did not come with a mass ideological campaign, which on the one hand was directed against class privileges ("war against the palaces!") and on the other promoting a more collective lifestyle. In Poland, the revolution was moving ahead, although it had clearly been decided that it would be better for the "cause" to spread it out over time and to do it quietly.[279] But there was also authentic pressure coming from the housing desperation of thousands of people who had been living in extremely difficult conditions since the war.

There is no question that their desperation was enormous. It is visible in the letters intercepted by the Wartime Censorship Office. The frustration of people who could sense their relative handicap in being assigned places to live—which was expressed as "others got them, so we deserve them, too" or "we fought for Poland and what did it get us?"—magnified the pressure. A woman living in Sosnowiec wrote to her husband in the army on September 17, 1945:

I haven't got an apartment yet, when you were here on leave they told you that you would get an apartment, also furnished, in a week. Since you left . . . it's been 2 months already and I go there every day, ask and shed bitter tears that winter is coming, that they give me a place to have shelter with my child. None of this helps. There is nothing for the wives of soldiers who fought on the front. Dear Janek, this is how you won freedom, prosperity, not for your wife and your child but for those looters and scoundrels who are sitting in their high places today. . . . We have nowhere to live and nothing to eat, and those scoundrels have beautiful apartments and they have, if I may say so, what to wolf down."

And a similar letter, from the Regained Territories: "I'm living like the lowliest beggar because you lost your health in the field of glory for the Motherland, and here those who didn't serve in the army or who went and ran away, lay about, and now they got first-class apartments, and I would like to get a better place to live than the one I have now."[280]

These letters express more than anger and frustration. They also show that the end of military operations was a signal for a new war to start, the war over living space. The chaos and the weakness of the local administration made people want to operate on the cusp of legality or outside the law altogether. In other words, there were two fronts in this new war, northwest and central. People were hurriedly looking for places to live and often did literally everything to get them. When they found empty houses, including those abandoned by the Germans, they simply moved in without asking questions. In Bytom this was a common practice, which we can see from the mayor's special regulation threatening to "send people to work camps."[281] "Shocking disputes, even battles . . . are being waged in Wrocław about assigning houses and apartments to institutions and Polish citizens," someone complained to Bolesław Bierut in September 1945.[282] In 1945, in Poznań and other towns in Greater Poland, in Pomerania, and on the coast from which the Germans had expelled hundreds of thousands of people at the beginning of the war, these homes were often taken over by Poles who had signed the *Volksliste* or by those who had simply landed in them first come, first served. Now, the prewar owners' return led to disagreements. A private letter described the situation in Gdynia in May 1945: "The inflow of people is increasing, as is poverty, lack of food. All the expelled people are coming back and tragedies are playing out, everything has been stolen, the new people are living in their homes, finding germans [*sic*] . . . who have turned into Poles. They've given them greater rights than us, who have spent time drifting."[283]

People attempted to intimidate, to write denunciations to the authorities. We know little about this aspect of the housing wars. Someone remembered how it played out in Katowice: "There was the fighting over shops and workshops. Denunciations became a popular weapon in this war. It was enough, after all, to write to the executive power that the counter-candidate is a crypto-German or that he acted inappropriately toward Poles. Often denunciations were mutual."[284] They were not innocent correspondence. Treason of the Polish nation led to jail and a court appearance—not too harsh a consequence. Others ended up with their whole families in a work camp for Germans in Łambinowice, Jaworzno, or Potulice, and hundreds of them remained there.

In central Poland, properties previously owned by Jews were plum housing.[285] Here, too, attempts by previous owners to take back property led to conflicts and tensions. According to a report from a Security Office functionary in Kielce in October 1945, "The fact that Jews are taking over their pre-war real estate is creating a certain kind of resentment in the population."[286] Cracow's Jewish community grew to 6,637 in 1945–46, and most of them probably wanted to go back to their old places, which had been taken over by Poles during the war. Jan T. Gross described the "new" owners' bitterness, disillusionment, and feeling of having been wronged as they faced the returning Jewish owners. Thus, a woman in Ożarów, Ludwika Chrapczyńska, refused to return two eiderdowns and four pillows to a Jewish neighbor, Jochweta Rozenstein, who had entrusted her with them. "Why did 'her' Jew have to come back from the dead while all the others, most of the others in any case, had disappeared and wouldn't bother the neighbors who also stocked up on Jewish stuff."[287] In small towns, the bitterness and anger at destiny that "our Jew survived" served as the psychological motivation of the murders for hire. Indeed the direct reason was not an eiderdown and pillows but an apartment, house, or workshop that had belonged to a Jew.

On the northwestern front of the housing wars, people did not kill to get housing, as there was none there that had once belonged to Jews. If we use "beastly anti-Semitism" as a sort of control group, we can see that it was not necessarily the fuel for the postwar conflicts over real estate and other possessions. Otherwise this would not have happened in the Polish lands that had been annexed by the Reich, since there the issue of restitution of formerly Jewish property did not exist. So what drove this war? Gordon W. Allport notes that a realistic confluence of interests lies at the source of all ethnic conflicts. "It is often said that Negroes constitute a realistic threat to the lower classes of white people, since both are competing for lower class jobs. Strictly speaking, of course, the rivalry is not between group and group, but between individuals." They become frustrated and angry when they feel insecure and fearful. The situation was the same in post-Second World War Poland, as Allport notes, with the exception that impoverished Jews and Poles, for whom the return of previous owners represented a threat to their economic existence, replaced the "impoverished blacks" and "impoverished whites."[288] Sociobiology also offers answers, as it seeks out reasons for the postwar housing wars in the animal fight over the nest, favored by an institutional vacuum and a feeling of chaos. But there is also no doubt, as both Allport and Gross posit, that the fear of losing one's home, the threat of returning previous owners, lengthened the interethnic distance, not only to all Jews but also to all Germans. The anti-German and anti-Semitic sentiments that grew in this way were unanticipated mental consequences of the Poles' wartime gains.

After the pogroms in Cracow and Kielce, emigrating Jews sold their homes to Poles. In families where no one had survived the Holocaust, local authorities, which were frequently ruled by cliques, took over their properties and handed them out to their families and clients. There were also gangs made up of a Polish investor, a Jew who was allegedly related to the deceased owners, and their chum the lawyer or notary. Such a group would appear in court to take over the inheritance, which would then immediately be sold to third parties who suspected nothing. In this way, some people acquired two or more apartments. One such combat zone was Łódź, where at least several thousand apartments had been left by Germans and Jews. According to private letters:

August 5, 1945: "The apartment won't be ready on Sunday, and that's when we'll move in. It is quite expensive, 6 thou. The people who came earlier have taken several apartments and are selling them now."

August 29, 1945: "The housing conditions are very difficult, but that's only because of the locals' egotism. Some have several apartments and they speculate with them, the prices range from 5 to 20 thou., which here, too, is quite a lot."

Things were also difficult in, for example Toruń, as a letter of August 29, 1945, shows: "It's difficult for ordinary mortals to find a place to live, although you can get a room for a fee for 1,000 zlotys."[289]

But as in every war, force was decisive: Polish Army officers, Security Office functionaries, and the militia often took over homes by sending over uniformed members of their staff who did not care about the law or about what would happen to the people living in them now. Without talking directly about such situations, these letters convey this very modus operandi:

Sulęcin, September 11, 1945: "Even though we have moved into the house don't know how long we will stay here because when I went to get the document the lieutenant told me that we have no right to stay here, and if I do he will send his soldiers and they'll throw us out in the street."

Lublin, September 27, 1945:

They're removing us from the apartment on Saturday. A clerk from the office and two military men came and told us to empty the apartment, and on Monday they came with the militia to throw out our things. When I gave Mister lieutenant a certificate that we have a son serving in the army, he said, I won't be reading this and turned his back to me. It's always the same with the allocation and registration. Mister administrator doesn't want to change the date from the 7th to the 6th [unclear—MZ] because we haven't received an allocation and they don't want to give us one because they've supposedly stopped and it's the same again and again. When I or father apply, it's always the same answer that the allocations have been suspended, and when you prove to them that a given person has received one, they say that they give them in sudden cases, and I've already written to you sometime what our case looks like: it looks like [a 500-złoty bill], and we don't have any.[290]

Such practices occurred daily in the period immediate after the war. Kazimierz Rusinek, then-chair of the Extraordinary Housing Commission, even spoke about them publicly.[291]

In 1944 and 1945, it was common for Red Army officers and noncommissioned officers to be quartered with Polish families. People took in these "guests" without complaining while military operations were still underway, sometimes even treated it as a distinction. But when the Red Army went back to the USSR, distaste and hostility replaced openness and hospitality. Most of the towns on their route, including Kielce, were told to prepare housing for the troops.[292] It is easy to understand why people feared being made to put up soldiers after learning how they left their quarters. Wacław Kubacki noted in his diary, "The flat [in Częstochowa—MZ] after the military's stay looks deplorable. Missing door handles. All internal doors have been taken. The kitchen floor has been hacked up. There are marks on the bathtub from the little pig, which stayed here as a subtenant. The last whiff of the war passed through our home."[293]

The housing situation was dramatically difficult indeed, requiring quick action, setting things straight, and putting an end to irregularities. But this only partly explains the solutions that were adopted. The authorities could have promoted housing construction by reducing the fear factor and giving people housing credits. Immediately after liberation, people rebuilt spontaneously, but this slowed down in Warsaw after land was nationalized. Also, many buildings were only partly damaged and could be renovated. To finance this, investors needed guarantees from the state that it would not seize a just-repaired piece of real estate. But the authorities, claiming to promote social justice, broke the law with the goal of "increasing density." As early as spring of 1945, housing offices, guided by the need to find housing for thousands of refugees, introduced measures to forcibly add tenants, strangers, to homes occupied by families, to divide up larger apartments or houses "in the Soviet way."[294] In August, the Cracow daily *Dziennik Polski* announced that "special supervisory teams" would be inspecting homes across the city to check how many people were living in each one. When the number was too low, additional "citizens" were moved in.[295] We can only guess how the population of Cracow reacted to this. But in this context—not in direct connection— five days later an anti-Jewish pogrom took place there.

The government introduced the legal foundations for these actions in three steps. First was the decree in September 1944 about housing commissions (Dz.U. 1944, nr 4, poz. 18). The second was a decree of December 21, 1945, which covered the public management of spaces and rent control (Dz.U. 1946, nr 4, poz. 27). National Councils would be responsible for establishing norms of occupation for apartments, establishing minimum numbers of occupants per room. When the number of people living in space was higher than the set norm, the housing commissions had the right to enforce moving in additional residents. Third, the decree about the Extraordinary Housing Commissions (Dz.U. 1946, nr 37, poz. 229) was made into law on August 8, 1946. It gave the commissions the right to remove those who refused to work or who engaged in profiteering, with their families, from the entire or a part of the living quarters.

Thus, on April 1, 1946, the Starogard city government established on the basis of the December decree that a family with one or two children would be allowed to get an apartment of one room and a kitchen, a family with three to five children two rooms and a kitchen, and with more than five children three rooms and a kitchen. An extra room would be assigned to municipal and social workers; people whose occupations required an additional room, such as artisans, drafting technicians, teachers, or painters; families with a child who was ten or older; tenants who were supporting a parent or another relative; and persons whose health required a separate room.

This regulation required owners to reach the prescribed number of residents within a month by finding someone to live with them. After the deadline, the authorities would assign someone themselves.

The standards set for Lublin were slightly different: two persons per room. The maximum surface was nine square meters per person, including the kitchen but not auxiliary rooms, such as a hallway, toilet, bathroom, or pantry.

In Warsaw, the space per person was to be at least five square meters; this included the kitchen but not hallways, toilets, bathrooms, pantries, and, in apartments that could not be split up, the common area shared by several people.[296]

Owners of larger apartments or houses were afraid that strangers would suddenly be moved into "their" space, that they would lose their property, and, probably most important, that they would be socially downgraded in a situation where a home was the last remaining symbol of prestige and social status.

The announcement of the housing standards led to frantic calculations of square meters. *Kurier Kaliski* reported from Warsaw in an article about "The general battle over 'housing space'" that "no inhabitant of the undamaged provinces will be able to understand how in Warsaw now people are taking measurements of their apartments, with a beating heart await top-level inspection which may appear any day and . . . move in God knows who."[297]

When it turned out that fewer people than the norm were living in an apartment, they would frantically look for a relative or an acquaintance who could move in with them. The deadline for finding someone was August 31, 1946.[298] "Flying commissions," who had the right to enter every home, including its attics and cellars, scattered across every town and city.[299] Their task was to check their area and number of registered residents. Some owners fictitiously registered relatives who actually lived elsewhere. The vigilant housing offices sent out patrols to find such "dead souls." The National Council in Włocławek hired "two additional intelligence agents for its housing office and award 300-zloty bonuses for the one who finds an unoccupied or an illegally occupied apartment."[300]

When there were no relatives or friends available to move in, the housing office divided up large prewar apartments into smaller ones, usually lodging one family per room. This way some obtained a room with a bathroom and others with a kitchen. Some used the elegant stairway, others the old service entrance.[301] Such divided apartments were called, from the Russian, "komunalki" or even kolkhozes.[302]

But this was not the end of worrying about apartments, or by now individual rooms. It happened that a person was traveling for a longer period for work and the housing office learned about their absence but not the reasons for it and forced the rest of the family out.

All this imposing of density from the top greatly increased the postwar anxiety. According to Irena Paczyńska, "Let's hypothesize that the political campaign aimed at addressing the housing situation of the working class, and the working people in general, and then introducing extraordinary regulations and functions of the [National Housing Commission], was a set of methods calculated to manipulate public opinion, to influence the public mood, boost anxieties, tensions and differences between people, and to win over some and intimidate others."[303] Regardless of the goals behind these policies, from now on the words *housing assignment* occupied one of the top places on the list of Polish fears.[304]

MINES AT EVERY STEP

Land mines were an important feature of the postwar landscape, one that not only deepened the feeling of impermanence but, of course, also killed or injured. The sign "Checked. No mines," or, in Russian, "*Min nyet*," left by Polish or Soviet sappers, became a license to resume living. The progress in mining techniques made by the Soviet defenders in the Battle of Kursk turned postwar Poland into a minefield. The most heavily mined were areas along the German line of defense from Suwałki along the Rospuda, Biebrza, Narwia, Vistula, and Wisłoka Rivers, around Pułtusk, and at the Warka–Magnuszew, Puławy, and Sandomierz Bridgeheads, as well as towns and cities that had been transformed into fortresses, including Warsaw, Kołobrzeg, Wrocław, Głogów, and Piła, and transportation routes. An inhabitant of the village of Stara Jakać, near Łomża, shared his fears (July 3, 1945): "Dear Miecio, Łomża has been terribly smashed, and mines have been put down so it's very dangerous. The river banks are mined the most, so you can't even go down to the river, the bridges were burned."[305]

In Warsaw alone between January 18 and March 1, 1945, sappers found 33 minefields and removed 10,231 mines of various types. By the end of June 1945, one sapper battalion (several of them were operating in Warsaw) neutralized 49,775 antipersonnel land mines, 16,478 anti-tank mines, 24,019 mortar shells, and 2,082 aerial bombs. In view of the possibility that German sappers may have left behind delay-action bombs, Warsaw was quarantined. The commander of the Red Army's engineering units ordered buildings in Szucha Avenue, previously occupied by the Gestapo, quarantined for sixty days and the rest of the city for thirty-five days after its liberation. But the spontaneous inflow of people meant that these regulations were not fully respected.[306]

In 1945 alone, across Poland, 10,240,327 mines were defused; in 1946, a total of 2,954,413 were defused, and in 1947, a total of 1,197,806 were defused. By 1956, sappers had removed over fourteen million mines. Strewn around in areas where fighting had taken place, there were still duds, shells, abandoned weapons, and various kinds of grenades. In 1945–47, more than thirty million pieces of ammunition were destroyed. During the defusing operations, 613 sappers were killed. Civilian losses were even greater. It has been estimated that between the end of the war and 1994 about five thousand people died and about nine thousand were injured, most of them in the years immediately after the war.[307]

The ubiquity of unexploded ordnance made people delay their fieldwork, which may have added to the fear of hunger, which was already significant with the postwar shortages. "The danger of being outside, sometimes even going into one's own field was so great that no one could be sure if they would come back alive," remembered the starost of Opatów.[308] By the end of April 1945, approximately 1,000 people had been injured (severed limbs, burns, blindness) in his district, about 2,000 in Kozienice District, and 263 in Stopnica District.[309] A special hospital was built. Because children playing outside were in the gravest danger, fear for their well-being increased, as children playing with unexploded ordnance were killed or injured. Indeed, of the human losses, about 81 percent were children. There were families in which two or three or even four people died this way. A villager near Suwałki made this list in a letter dated June 15, 1945: "Here in Sambras many people were killed by mines. Dyć went to his hamlet and stepped on mines and they killed him. . . . There were four Czartulińskis killed by mines: Czartuliński, Czartulińska, Radzia and Franek and also Gandziaług Franek, Karwel, Burzyński killed by mines. In our family trouble, too, Janek crossed the road to get firewood, pulled out a piece and a mine exploded, it cut him up and broke his leg."[310]

Some mothers panicked. One of them remembered, "There has been an immense number of deathly accidents. I ran home whenever I heard a louder shot or detonation to see if my children are there. If I didn't find them, I searched through the whole village, going out of my mind."[311]

Letters seized by the War Censorship Office in the Augustów and Łomża regions show this fear and the omnipresence of death. There are indications that things were much the same in other parts of Poland, especially in places where the Wehrmacht had had time to dig in.

A letter from someone in the village of Bronowo, Łomża District, to a brother in the labor camp in Potulice, dated June 26, 1945, read, "Dear Edmund, We've been having very many accidents with mines. Józef Mocarski is dead, he was ripped up by a landmine . . . and many other accidents which you may not have heard about yet."

A man wrote from Augustów on June 26, 1945, "Dear ones, I feel fine and things aren't too bad, but there are the places where there are very many mine accidents because whole fields are mined, and you can walk on them sometimes by accident."

A sender from the village of Brzozówka, Augustów District, June 22, 1945, wrote, "Dear Family, A person's life is uncertain here at every step. Our hospitals are full of invalids and so many have died from mines. . . . Because here the roads and fields are mined, you walk somewhere and straight away they tear you to pieces."[312]

THE SPECTER OF GODLESSNESS

The most difficult thing to document with sources is the presence of anxiety, which can be called eschatological. We conjecture that it was present, and yet we cannot use the research methods we know to grasp it. It is not possible to make general observations about the contents of this anxiety, its transmission, and society's reception of it without having access to church archives with the texts of sermons; those that appeared in print in *Współczesna Ambona* have been edited, not to mention the security authorities' lack of interest in the church and the faithful at this time. The population's religiosity and popular culture during the war and immediately afterward are a giant gap in research. There has been no study of the religiosity of simple people similar to that conducted by Bartłomiej Gapiński, who used the letters sent to Kalwaria Zebrzydowska monastery from the late 1960s–late 1970s to study the religiosity of simple people.[313] As a result, we paradoxically know much less about the mentality and spirituality of especially the lowest social groups in the mid-twentieth century than about the eschatological fears of Hieronymus Bosch's contemporaries.

There are three irrefutable facts. First, at that time, Poland was a country of traditional religiousness, of regular patron saints' festivals and pilgrimages in which thousands took part, and of women's rosary gatherings, which lasted many hours, in almost every village. Second, the war made many people much more religious (something that was already discussed in chap. 3). Crowds would welcome every traveling church official ostentatiously. There were many religious processions through the streets of cities and villages for the blessings of new churches or flags, of the Polish Peasant Party, for example. All larger ceremonies, even state-sponsored ones, began with a mass, and immediately after Poland's liberation Soviet officers also attended. In First of May parades, especially in small towns and villages, some of the marchers carried religious symbols. The harvest festival in Kielce in 1945 typifies that, as it was described sarcastically in the leftist-peasant newspaper *Dziennik Ludowy*:

> This town is a village that has spread out on the outskirts, with a few dozen tenements downtown, 12 churches, a monastery and army barracks in the nearby forests, this is Kielce. All of it lies on hills among twisty little streets. Henryk Sienkiewicz alone has a splendid street, an impressive 1,500 meters long, named after him. . . .
>
> On this, like on other similar occasions, the Wici military association, from an impressive nine districts, arrived at the cathedral with wreaths, listened to the sermon and set off down the street toward the stadium.
>
> There, the young people had been arranged in rows and the miracle play began. The Wici club from Łączna came forward to stand 100 meters from the bench singing "Beloved Mother" and moving their listeners to tears, letting loose the march toward Provincial Governor Wiślicz, Chairman of the Peasant Party Podrygałło and finally Deputy Minister Wycech. This took a solid 5 minutes.
>
> The second club advanced on their knees with prayers requiring Scholastic interpretation on their lips . . . and I saw the priest behind me clapping passionately and crying for an encore. At that instant I understood that some Wici clubs are clubs of Catholic Action. And that was why the bishop can fit in the cab together with Wici chairman perfectly well. The messages of the little anti-Semitic plays put on by Wici are just the perfect stuff for this crowd.[314]

According to some estimates, more than four million people took part in pilgrimages in 1946,[315] and this can be used as the measuring stick for the Poles' spiritual condition at that time. The third question regards the direction this religiousness was headed, and especially its focus on the Passion of Christ, the issue of suffering, and the symbolism of blood. Examples of it can be found, first of all, during the war in the lowbrow booklets of religious poetry in vogue at the time. Many of the popular symbolic representations compare the nation's suffering with Christ's Passion. Indeed, in their narrative scheme, heroism, suffering, and sacrifice are followed by rising from the knees, resurrection, and victory, and this could even subconsciously be used to tell the nation's history. It is at the core of the Christian message, on which the national self-stereotype was built. To use Krystyna Kersten's words, it "merged martyrdom, suffering, tragedy united with bravery, love of freedom, patriotism, Catholic faith, national tradition."[316]

People frequently compared war to the Apocalypse, but more in its common understanding as a turbulence or a time of destruction than in its universal definition as the end of the world ordained by God. Millenarianist thinking, which had been so widespread in the Middle Ages, did not gain in popularity, but war was viewed as a type of catastrophe like the one that Job had experienced. A horrific catastrophe that had no analogies in the past, but a catastrophe nonetheless, which the Polish nation would overcome with the help of God and the British.

It is noteworthy, especially in the context of the myth of ritual murder (which will be discussed in chap. 13), that already during the war and after it ended, especially in public discourse, people overused the word *blood*. This word has a long history, and many myths, meanings, and contexts have been attached to it.[317] It reemerged now and shaped the postwar time's thinking. It can be found in underground newspapers and flyers as well as in official newspapers. The term *spilled blood* especially came into fashion then, in various contexts, such as "the spilled blood demands vengeance" or "the blood they spilled together" (about Red Army troops). There was also the "tribute extracted in blood," which can be found, for example, in the decree about a war tax. As the government tried to justify why people should contribute, it argued that "the Polish Army is paying the tribute extracted in blood." An order from the Polish Army's Main Command published on the first anniversary of Warsaw's liberation touched on mysticism: "Your blood has given life to Poland's heart, Warsaw."[318] A popular song could be heard in streets, on trains, and in restaurants sung by begging children and invalids: "The red poppies on Monte Cassino / Which drank Polish blood instead of dew."

Blood also popped up in daily conversation: "People are constantly talking about the awful spilling of blood," read a private letter.[319] Blood symbolized suffering, and its presence in the postwar discourse played along with the nation's self-stereotype of suffering. And there was another interdependence. The horrors of the war and the spilled blood awakened ancient narratives about blood as in a thriller, the myth of Jews murdering Christian children. The poem below was handwritten as a flyer and copied by the Citizens' Militia District Command in Starachowice-Iłża in June 1945.

> TO CITIZENS' MILITIA OFFICERS
> Is it the Polish peasant's blood
> That scares you so, brother of mine,
> That upon the jew's lowly call,
> On Polish blood you pour manure?
> Come to your senses, you madman,
> Stop listening to the jew's counsel,
> Be a pure knight,
> And not a bandit, a lowly reptile,
> For the avenger from Polish blood will arise
> To restore its honor,
> And to you an order
> To sweep the scum off this blood with your maw.
> Lt. Sokół[320]

A deep critical analysis of this poem would require a whole chapter, and so a few comments must suffice. The poem is a folksy interpretation of the militia's customary abuse of power at this time. People viewed them as brothers, which is not surprising since most militia functionaries came from the countryside. In the poem, if they leave the road they have chosen and come to their senses, they will have a chance of becoming "pure knights." Real evil lurks elsewhere; it emanates from the Jews. It seems that the idea that evil could come from "us," the Polish peasants (as in the familiar "scum"), but also more broadly from the Manichean folk mentality was inconceivable to the poem's rural author. The world is ordered, and evil is "them," not "us." Jan T. Gross is right to write about the Polish intelligentsia's self-definition of serving to "carry on the intelligentsia's most important mission rooted in the traditional ethos of the gentry and honed by the great Polish romantic literature. He or she was supposed 'to be a repository of supreme values, the idea of Poland, and "the spirit of idealism."'" Killing Jews did not fit into this.[321] In this poem, "they" are most likely secret police functionaries, who in the folktales of that time were mostly Jewish. The text uses outdated words from the mythology of the Old Testament, such as *reptile* or *Jew*. The use of the adjective *Polish* three times implies that the author was familiar with modern structures of nationalist thinking. All three times it is associated with the noun *blood*, which appears four times. It is tempting to treat this poem as an example of the broad phenomenon, the popular reaction to the crisis of the postwar period.

Should the belief in miracles also be linked to the crisis? Yes, as it had spread during the war, and the Poles told hundreds of stories about miraculous rescues or people digging their way out of mass graves, which fired up the imagination. Also, we know that the more uncertain a situation, the greater our tendency to adopt magical behavior. In September 1940, the windows of a militia station in Lvov were washed. But rainbow-like spots remained, which someone interpreted as an image of the Virgin Mary. The Soviet militia could not manage the crowds that came to see it.[322] The growing faith in miracles is an important indicator of growing anxiety. After the war, it was also built up by Poland's hopeless situation under Soviet tutelage and the oppression from which only divine intervention could rescue Poland. The Miracle on the Vistula was readily brought up. A flyer passed out by an "old man" in the streets of Kielce on August 22, 1945, treats the miracle rationally as a positive twist of fate, which people may assist, for example, by spreading the news about the threat. Remarkably, it copies from prewar Roman Catholic propaganda, or perhaps German wartime propaganda, the "Jewish Bolshevism" flooding "our soil, and fields, villages and towns."

> Again, the same horrible danger threatens us from the east, from the same enemy. Again, the red danger is attacking our frontiers and flooding our soil and our fields, towns and villages. Misery and poverty, persecution and exile, murder and fire are the bloody marks in the Polish lands, which have been taken over by the red hordes. How are we Poles to fight this threat? Do we even realize how vast it is? Or do we believe in miracles today, too, as we did in 1920? If we do, what are we doing to bring on the miracle of once again freeing our nation from the threat of destruction by Jewish Bolshevism?[323]

The document does not tell us how many of these flyers the "old man" handed out in the streets of Kielce. But it would not be wrong to think that it was an item on the long list of reasons for the Kielce pogrom, which took place eleven months later.

Let's return to the belief in miracles for a moment. It exploded after the so-called Lublin miracle in the summer of 1949, but its first harbingers came earlier. In late April 1947, in the village of Górka, Kielce District, a four-year-old girl was said to have seen the Virgin Mary in an attic. The news made the rounds in a flash. On April 28, a Sunday, crowds from neighboring villages came to see the attic, which was decorated with devotional articles.[324]

But it was not only the belief in miracles that should be seen as a manifestation of popular religiosity, and its rise as an expression of the public reaction to crisis and threat. All sorts of circulating prophecies also showed that a collective sense of uncertainty and thirst for hope that fate would change were widespread. Apart from the wartime prophecies discussed earlier, after the war people also favored prophesies with an eschatological anxiety. On April 16, 1947, the *Express Poznański* daily printed a letter "circulating in Białystok," which predicted that many plagues would descend on humanity to punish it for its sins:

> Whoever finds this letter should pass it on, and he will be saved. You, beloved brothers and sisters, the more you take of the Holy sacrament the better because there will be thunder and lightning, believe in everything. On 6 May in the night the southern king will come, on 28 May there will be an earthquake. On 4 June there will be unbearable heat, the sun. On 18 June there will be a water surprise. The provincial governor will come forth with his armies. On 22 June blood will be spilled, on 28 June only half of the people in God's World will survive. For four days, blood will flow in the streams. On 20 July the war will end. Remember, Jesus Christ himself wrote this letter. Expect a huge punishment for your sins. Whoever has this letter with him will be saved at any moment and at any hour, remember that Jesus and the Virgin Mary protected us. Read it, pass it on. Let these God's teachings spread because judgment is near, let's pray humbly. Oh, Jesus, bless us, let's pray for you. Please give this to others in the whole world. Amen.

This letter is a classic prediction of the Last Judgment, to be preceded by the Apocalypse, earthquake, drought, and flooding. It forecasts the spilling of blood but also promises salvation. It was probably written in 1947, as the precise dates of horrific events in it, instead of the usual ten, thirty, or one hundred years, would indicate. The date of June 22 is also noteworthy as the beginning of a war during which "blood will flow in the streams." The people of Białystok region were familiar with this date, since six year earlier the Third Reich had invaded the Soviet Union on that day. Also, the fact that war is the greatest catastrophe in the text appears to indicate the last war was most prominent in the author's memory. The editors added a brief commentary: "These are the letters circulating in Białystok. Who wrote them? No doubt a madman. Some people, nonetheless, are very nervous. The spinsters and bigots in Białystok and the area are hysterical."[325]

A similar mood persisted elsewhere. A copy of this newspaper found its way to Jędrzejów in Kielce Province, where the letter was copied and reportedly distributed widely. According to the Ministry of Public

Security, it brought on a war psychosis there and nearby. People swarmed into shops, and the shopkeepers raised their prices.[326] Within two weeks, this prediction was also reported in Warsaw and Szczecin Provinces.

Other prophecies also made the rounds. In Złotów District in Szczecin Province, the Security Office found copies of the two-hundred-year-old "Wernyhora's Prophecies" (Proroctwa Wernyhory) and the nineteenth-century "Przepowiednia z Tęgoborza" (Tęgoborze Prophecy).[327] "Wernyhora's Prophecies" stated that "the Muscovites will twice be beaten to a pulp.... From then on Poland will thrive from the Black to the White Sea and will last forever and ever." The Tęgoborze Prophecy said, "The barbarian into eternity/Will flee in fear to Asia."

The two texts came alive again during the war. Could it be that someone still had copies from that time, or were they copied out again after the war? We do not know the answer, but other facts further confirm the belief in prophecies of various kinds and miracles. In August 1948, the population of Gniezno and its area was swept by terror from an eschatological prophecy. Sand would fall from the sky instead of rain, "and people will die from fear."[328] A private letter written in late October 1948 also contained chiliastic prophecies: "We must patiently await Christ's Reign. I heard recently that this will happen in 1950, and after that we will have 10 very happy and good years until 8 May 1960, and then something so horrible will happen in Europe that whoever can should flee to the other hemisphere. There will be revolution everywhere on earth. Our Holy Mother continues to warn humanity of God's looming punishment and is repeating her apparitions in Italy, Belgium, etc."[329]

Although the "epidemic of miracles" that engulfed Poland in the following few years[330] came from a current sense of endangerment from collectivization and the state's battle with the church, it was also the latest manifestation of the popular religiosity that became stronger during the war and took on a new dynamic after the war as Catholics felt themselves to be in increasing danger. In Italy after the Second World War, similar manifestations of popular religiosity were also due to the growing power of the Italian Communist Party.

This brings us to the crucial question of how Catholic priests reacted to the Communist takeover, and together with the faithful, especially the poorest and least educated following suit.[331] This group should be differentiated by age, gender, and location. Even then, however, it was not made up solely of submissive believers. Even before the war, the peasant movement had followed powerful anticlerical trends. Still, most villages or small towns had groups of older people, mostly women, who were close to their parish and to "their" curate, and who were convinced that the phantom of godlessness loomed. A peasant memoirist portrayed one such rural community: "Conversations ... among the women bigots who have no idea about the issues of today's economic and social policies and often also don't understand contemporary Poland's regime, were humorous. Nodding their heads, they talked about those 'kolkhozes,' about how they will chase God out of the faithful people's hearts, about the 'anti-Christ,' and if she hears someone praising the system of cooperative economy she goes running to the priest to complain that they are against the church and religion and so on, and the priest blasted them from the pulpit, coming close to naming them."[332]

The anti-Christ, the devil, is dangerous to a Christian in many forms. Every era imagines the devil in its own way. After the war, he wore the outfit of the Communist who did not go to church, pulling young people away from it, depraving them, wanting kolkhozes to form, and, worse, plotted against the church, wanting people to become atheists, which may lead to the nation's spiritual degeneration, the loss of its inner ability to steer itself. It is not enough to say that these were fantastical delusions that usually form at times of upheaval and chaos.

The postwar folk imagination formed its own representations of evil on the basis of its memory of two revolutions, the Bolshevik and the Mexican. Chapter 2 of this book discussed the terror the former evoked while the latter was covered extensively by the right-wing press in the 1920s.[333] It would not be until much later, the 1960s, when the term *Saigon's victory* came into use, that the phrase *What a Mexico!* was used to mean

The Phantoms of Transience

frightening chaos and disorder. The two revolutions nearly stamped out the institutional Catholic Church, and thus fear of the "red devil" was to some degree realistic, even though its growth after 1945 was due to an open conflict.

Indeed, confrontations between the church and the Communist regime were unavoidable in the long term. But in these first postwar years, nothing happened. The Communists avoided all irritations like the devil and, actually, did everything to please the church. In January 1945, Edward Ochab handed over half a million zlotys for the renovation of the monastery on Jasna Góra, on behalf of the provisional government.[334] There were more such gestures. "The future adversary," wrote the historian Marek Łatyński, "did not reveal his intentions, did not show his cards."[335] A *Tygodnik Powszechny* reporter asked parish priests in Lower Silesia the same question: "Have you experienced any unpleasantness or difficulties from the government or the party, Father?" The answer was always the same: "There are no difficulties. We are living in harmony."[336] But the question itself had a whiff of the anxiety that Catholics were feeling. After all, it had been stated clearly that change was coming. In September 1945, the state authorities annulled Poland's concordat with the Vatican, which may have been seen as the first step on the road to reproducing the Mexican or Bolshevik model. Because it took away the legal status of several decrees closely linked to the concordat, religious instruction in schools became an elective subject. More important from the point of view of the church was the new marriage law, which validated secular marriage and simplified divorce.[337] The Episcopate wrote to the government stating that "forced lay marriages are unacceptable to Catholics,"[338] and a bishops' gathering at Jasna Góra called on the faithful to protect "the sanctity and honor of the Polish family, which must not fall victim to any revolution."[339] Some bishops, including the bishop of Rzeszów, whose special letter on this subject was read out in all the parishes of his diocese, spoke up. News about the new law brought mayhem among lower-level priests. A man from Piotrków Trybunalski complained in a private letter, "The priests are rebelling very much and trying to convince people to rebel. It's just as well that they're not allowed to fight because they would probably beat up this Government."[340] And, "Some of the faithful reacted in outrage, accusing the 'democracy' of godlessness: I learned yesterday that lay marriages will be valid. My Lord, what godlessness, whose business is it what God has decided. This democracy is to blame for everything. We know a thing or two about it here."[341]

In the village of Nieszawa, in Aleksandrów Kujawski District, there was even a group protest. The local priest was reportedly arrested for opposing civil marriages. But the local people disarmed the militia (who may actually have been other uniformed services). "And the venerable Mr. Starost was smashed in the mug so hard that he almost came to in the Vistula, and women have kept the hair that was ripped off his head as a souvenir," someone wrote in a letter with some satisfaction. Children punched holes in the tires of the starost's car.[342] This story may illustrate the postwar ties between the faithful and the church, and it also shows how the rebellion was spreading to lay Catholics. In the aura of the postwar years, some priests began to define the situation with the help of the topos of an invasion happening under the banner of atheism.

The Europeans had known this kind of anxiety about the barbarian/Muslim/heretical danger for thousands of years. The Nazis also used it to construct their propaganda. It is also visible in Government Delegate Jankowski's telegram to London. In mid-February 1945, he wrote about the Red Army, "The troops' appearance alone with their rags, Kalmyk faces, uniforms and behavior has had the impact of an invasion of Asian savages in towns and villages. By someone incomparably lower than us. People wondered how such hordes could have defeated the Germans."[343] Zygmunt Zaremba had a similar impression: "I thought that it was a Tatar army, brought out of somewhere in the steppes of distant Asia, flooding my country."[344] Even though both opinions of these prewar left-liberal intellectuals were widespread, they verged on racism and did not include the belief that these hordes threatened religion. There were probably two clichés that, when they overlapped, created the specter of eschatological terror, worry about secularization and godlessness endangering the nation. This dread was fed by priests and disseminated in their sermons. Because of censorship, it cannot be found in the Catholic press of the day or even in various types of printed matter issued by the church.

A piece of evidence about this anxiety is dated July 21, 1946, and was prepared by a Security Office employee in Gdynia after a mass he attended in the Church of the Virgin Mary on Świętojańska Street. In his sermon, Father Józef Miszewski reportedly said that "we are living in uncertain times, in times where there is a push to infect people with the rot of distrust so that if we don't rebuild the church ourselves no one will rebuild it for us." He went on, "You can see yourselves that this God's House cannot accommodate all of you, but there are so very many of you flocking to God, come to your senses, beloved brothers, don't let the horror that is stretching its arms toward you kill your spirit, swallow you up." The preacher criticized the abrogation of the concordat and finished by calling on the people to pray for the persecuted.[345]

On September 8, 1946, the parish priest of the church in Daleszyce, near Kielce, also preached about the dangerous spate of godlessness. An instructor from the local Office of Information and Propaganda saved the sermon. The priest began by referring to the "Miracle on the Vistula": "In 1920 when our whole country was flooded by the enemy and there was no hope, the Polish people were lying side by side at the Virgin Mary's feet, and she made a miracle and on ascension day the enemy left Poland." This suggested a parallel to Poland's current situation: "And now 1945 is here and the wave of godlessness is so big that no one has heard of it and for centuries the wave covered Catholic countries one after the other and today it is flowing scot-free across Poland." The priest did not say directly that the Communists were the source of this danger: "And today those grand personalities who want to be popular here start by declaring war on God, religion and the priesthood." Godlessness must be combatted. The priest challenged it, as well as the propaganda of progress, in the name of the entire priesthood: "We, the Catholic clergy, are declaring war on it and will fight against the hostile propaganda which wants to destroy faith in God in Catholic souls and to introduce progress in its place calling us backward and retrograde, after all it was the clergy that was the first to engage in farming, and the nobility's sons abandoned their manors and palaces and went into the desert to live alone and they taught people." In this battle, much like in 1920, the Virgin Mary's intercession would help: "And today Catholic cardinals are gathered on Jasna Góra to hold council and ask the Holy Mother for help and strength to fight godlessness."

According to the person who summarized it, the locals, astonished by the sermon, gathered outside the church after mass to discuss the priest's words.[346] Was this really out of the ordinary? Or was it an example of the broader feeling of endangerment rising among Catholics? The timing of the two sermons does not put them at the roots of the Kielce pogrom. But it is highly likely that this anxiety about "the destruction of faith in God in the Catholic souls" did not make an appearance suddenly in the second half of 1946 but had been growing slowly to explode more powerfully for the first time in September 1945, after the announcement that the concordat had been terminated and lay marriages were introduced.

Who apart from the Communists was accused of bringing this threat? A historian must be cautious, even though it is clear that in these social groups the Jews were traditionally considered to be its carriers. There are examples of such thinking a little later. In April 1949, in the church in the village of Dobra, near Szczecin, a Father Walczak reportedly said in his sermon, "Those who govern our country now are throwing religion out of schools. The Jews crucified Christ, and now the Jews are forbidding us to learn religion. We must be prepared for the greatest torment." At this, women and children inside the church began to wail.[347] The traditional stereotype of the Jews as Christ's killers is less shocking than the priest's use of the fear that the world's religious dimension will be disrupted, creating an atmosphere immersed in eschatology. The priest was predicting a national ordeal.

A similar concurrence of prophecies, belief in miracles, and anti-Semitism occurred in France in the last quarter of the nineteenth century and at the beginning of the twentieth. Its defeat in the Franco-Prussian War, the explosion of violence during the Paris Commune, the secularization of education, the new divorce law, and the severance of the concordat brought a feeling of threat and oppression. Numerous manifestations of faith in miracles and in the circulating predictions, as well as other manifestations of popular religiosity, reflected the population's fears and hopes. Anti-Semitism thrived there, even though the real sources of social problems and conflicts lay elsewhere.[348]

From a psychological point of view, the origins of religious fundamentalism in postwar Poland were complex. They were a reaction to the threat coming from the "Communist godlessness," which at that time was more imaginary than real, but had been internalized already in the 1920s. The feeling of living under siege in reaction to the presence of the Red Army and the behavior of some of its troops added to the religious tension. On January 13, 1945, immediately after "liberation," inebriated Soviet tank crews set the Gniezno cathedral on fire, and everyone in town knew who had done it.[349] Hearsay that made the rounds in Częstochowa may testify to the fears about the future of the church in Poland. In the second half of July 1946, shortly after the series of anti-Semitic pogroms, people were terrified by the report that Saint James Church was to be transformed into an Orthodox church.[350] Religious fundamentalism, much like in France and Italy in the second half of the twentieth century, also came from general premonition as well as fear of change and of the destruction of the old order by modernization. In the conservative and traditional Polish society, all radical social projects, indeed even the idea of them, naturally made people very anxious. Hence the appearance of rumors, such as the one in January 1946 in Białystok Province, that the Gate of Dawn in Vilna, a very important holy site for Poles, would be torn down.[351] At around this time, Witold Bieńkowski wrote in in the Catholic weekly *Dziś i Jutro*, "If we look at the process of searching for solutions to social issues outside Catholicism, which the Catholics are watching, a rightful and justified anxiety appears."[352] It especially struck fundamentalist groups, which some priests egged on to resist. The Episcopate certainly sensed these moods and encouraged them. A pastoral letter of September 10, 1946, analyzed, "Stressed out by the difficulties of social and economic life, the nation is still consumed by disquiet and is painfully living through obstacles set up by hostile and unfavorable factors."[353]

Also aware of the anxieties of Polish Catholics was Bolesław Bierut, who, in an interview he gave Ksawery Pruszyński, which made the rounds, discussed the church's "distrustful or disbelieving" attitude toward the new regime. Despite Bierut's conciliatory tone and his admission that "the Catholic Church is one of the factors that are shaping the psyches of wide strata of our citizens,"[354] this anxiety survived for a long time and was most intense in the Stalinist period.

LIQUID FEAR

To summarize, in 1945–48 the feeling of transience and anxiety was like a balloon, by turns filling up and deflating. The postwar reality was fluid, insecure, and not yet stabilized. Furthermore, the fledgling system of power encouraged emerging threats instead of spreading an umbrella of security over them and calming down the inevitable postwar social tensions. It did poorly with managing anxiety. Or maybe, like with the politics of fear, it 'intentionally fabricated uncertainty'? "The totalitarian state was feared as the *source of the unknown and the unpredictable*: as the perpetual, irremovable element of uncertainty in the existential condition of its subjects."[355]

Panic was an indicator of anxiety. Its frequent appearances show that people felt insufficiently secure. Anxiety also appeared in rumors and prophecies. But it may be that the fluctuations in the dollar exchange rate, which were to last as long as the Polish People's Republic, say the most about the index of fear. Its sources are worth examining.

In winter of 1944–45 and spring of 1945, a dollar was worth 350 "new" zlotys.[356] Its value went up with the uncertainty linked to the passage of the front and the installation of the new regime. But the complexities of the currency exchange of January 1945, in which a person was allowed to receive 500 zlotys, played a major role in adding uncertainty, too. In some occupational groups this amount remained the basic income for a few months. The atmosphere improved, and the collective sense of impermanence after Mikołajczyk's return meant that at midyear one dollar could be bought for 130 zlotys. But by December 1945, its price rose to 560 zlotys. According to a report by the Chamber of Industry and Commerce in Cracow, the zloty's rise in late summer was due primarily to large industrial imports. But soon, again, "psychological moments" returned to front stage. They included a lack of confidence in the zloty, which was not based on the gold standard, and the secrecy attached to issuing bills; the absence of trustworthy data about the state's financial situation; fear of inflation; fear of an official devaluation, similar to those in France, Hungary, and Finland; uncertainty about the future direction of the state's economic policy, especially the next steps in nationalization; investors' fears of investing in areas such as construction; and fear of the state gradually eliminating individual commerce.[357] All these concerns and uncertainties drove the flight from the zloty and the widespread tendency to stock up on dollars bought with unneeded and distrusted zlotys.

In the summer of 1946 one dollar cost about 500 zlotys, and this drop in value should probably explain the short-lived calm following the referendum. But its price again began to rise quickly in August, and in September it reached 750 zlotys, in October 1,000 zlotys, and in early November 1,100 zlotys. In January, the dollar's black-market exchange rate fluctuated around 1,020 to 1,050 zlotys. This shows clearly that the variations in Polish collective fears translated into the price of the dollar.

Zygmunt Bauman wrote in *Liquid Fear*, "If the volume of local fears grows too large for comfort, there are so many other localities to move away to, letting the natives stew and burn alone in the cauldrons of panic and nightmares."[358] The question remains: what happens when it is impossible to leave and anxiety becomes unbearable? Bauman answered this question in his review of Jan T. Gross's *Fear* as he described the months preceding the Kielce pogrom: "The growing sense of insecurity and barely realized mass anxieties created a favorable climate to persecute, and who was better suited for this than the Jews, scapegoats permanently on call."[359] There is no agreement on one question. Observers at the time were aware of the phantom of impermanence and anxiety, which is another piece of evidence of how much it had increased.

NOTES

1. Kołakowski, *Metaphysical Horror*, 41.
2. Z. Bauman, *Liquid Times: Living in an Age of Uncertainty* (Cambridge: Polity Press, 2007), 26.
3. "Skończone życie z dnia na dzień," *Gazeta Lubelska*, May 18, 1945.
4. Kersten, *The Establishment of Communist Rule in Poland*, 163.
5. "Głos polskiego podziemia," *Wolność*, WiN, November 1, 1945.
6. Piasecki, "Kierunki," *Dziś i Jutro*, March 17, 1946.
7. Wróblewska, *Listy z Polski*, 130, 131. (B. Brzostek told me about this book.)
8. AIPN, MBP 3378, k. 57. Doniesienie specjalne dot. wypowiedzi o treści antypaństwowej.
9. Cf. Burda, *Przymrozki i odwilże*, 17.
10. Pobóg-Malinowski, *Najnowsza historia polityczna Polski 1864–1945*, vol. 3, 391; Kersten, *Między wyzwoleniem a zniewoleniem*, 46.
11. AAN, DRnK 202/III-26, k. 35. Sprawozdanie z kraju za okres od 21.XII. 1944 do 21.II.1945 i uzupełnienia za okres poprzedni.
12. For more on the Poles' postwar choices and orientations, see Kersten, *Między wyzwoleniem a zniewoleniem*.
13. AIPN, MBP 3378, k. 57. Doniesienie specjalne dot. wypowiedzi o treści antypaństwowej.
14. Gomułka, "Przemówienie końcowe po dyskusji," 525.
15. Gomułka, 515.
16. Miłosz, *A Year of the Hunter*, 143.
17. Hytrek-Hryciuk, "Rosjanie nadchodzą," 108–109.
18. "Walka klasowa w demokratycznej Polsce," *Trybuna Dolnośląska*, August 27, 1945.
19. Borejsza, "Rewolucja łagodna," *Odrodzenie*, January 15, 1945.
20. AIPN, MBP 3378, k. 111. Specjalne doniesienie.
21. AIPN, MBP 3378, k. 60. Doniesienie specjalne dot. prowokacyjnych pogłosek.
22. AIPN, MBP 3378, k. 65.
23. Chajn, *Kiedy Lublin był Warszawą*, 40, 45.
24. AAN, DRnK 202/III–36, k. 143. Sytuacja na Pomorzu (do 10 VI 1945).
25. Kamiński, *Polacy wobec*, 204.
26. AIPN 1572/1192, k. 3. Wypowiedzenie się ludności w sprawie konferencji Trzech w Jałcie, 14 II 1945.
27. A. Rychard, *Komu potrzebna jest legitymizacja? Legitymacja klasyczne teorie i polskie doświadczenia*, eds. A. Rychard and A. Sułek (Warsaw: PTS, IS UW, 1988), 302.
28. Gałczyński, *Wiersze*.

29. Cf. Hirszowicz, *Pułapki zaangażowania*.
30. Bauman, *Liquid Fear*, 40.
31. Marzecki, *Tym gorzej dla faktów*, 22.
32. Estreicher Jr., *Dziennik wypadków 1939–1945*, vol. 1, 791.
33. For more, see Krasucki, *Międzynarodowy komunista*.
34. For the opposition of the 1940s, see Łatyński, *Nie paść na kolana*; Friszke, *Opozycja polityczna w PRL 1945–1980*, 7–66.
35. *Armia Krajowa w dokumentach 1939–1945*, vol. 5, 282.
36. Kersten, *The Establishment of Communist Rule in Poland*, 171.
37. Letter posted in Lublin dated December 21, 1944:

> Lenia! . . . We are indeed building a New Poland, and I can assure you that it will be a happy country with happy people. We still have many problems to overcome, but you can feel the fraternal helpful hand of our great ally the Soviet Union everywhere, in uniforming and equipping the soldier and in sending flour to the people of [Warsaw's] Praga district, which our ally has deprived himself of. And all this shows that things would be different for us if we had had this alliance before the unfortunate year '39. Yes, this is the important truth: "You learn who your friends are when times get tough." (AAN, PKWN I/78, k. 17. Doniesienie specjalne.) Another letter, this one from Łódź, dated February 8, 1945, shows that not only exhilaration with the "victorious Red Army" was at the root of support for the new regime but also (an outmoded term) class hatred: "Today, our Silesian, Piast old lands are free thanks to the Soviet armies, praise to the leader Stalin and his heroic troops. There will be no more *Sanacja* and nobility warts in Poland, to hell with them once and for all." (AIPN, MBP 3378, k. 45. Doniesienie specjalne dot. wypowiedzi o marszałku Stalinie i o Armii Czerwonej.)

38. AIPN, MBP 3378, k. 124. Specjalne doniesienie dotyczące korespondencji idącej za granicę.
39. These are the real, unofficial results of the referendum. For more, see Paczkowski, *Referendum z 30 VI 1946 r. Przebieg i wyniki*.
40. For example, "Petit-bourgeois groups and the intelligentsia, including teachers, have adopted a shaky, indecisive position. Alongside serious influences of declaring themselves on our side, there is some reserve and waiting" (AAN, PPR 295/X–19, k. 2. Minister oświaty S. Skrzeszewski podczas konferencji nauczycieli, członków PPR, May 14, 1945).
41. Zelska-Mrozowiecka, "Nie bądźmy tacy surowi," *Dziennik Bałtycki*, June 15, 1945.
42. Gen. Okulicki do Prezydenta RP, 9 XII 1944 r. in *Armia Krajowa w dokumentach 1939–1945*, vol. 5, 173.
43. Załącznik nr 11 do raportu sytuacyjnego Komendy Okręgu AK Białystok z 5 XI 1944 r., 69.
44. AIPN, MBP 3378, k. 57. Doniesienie specjalne dot. wypowiedzi o treści antypaństwowej.
45. Raport sytuacyjny Obwodu AKO Zambrów z 1 III 1945 r., 116.
46. AIPN BU 1572/1192, k. 1. *Wypowiedzenie się ludności w sprawie konferencji Trzech w Jałcie*.
47. The deputy commander of the Citizens' Militia for the Kielce-Radom region reported in April 1945, "The public mood is unclear, expectant, especially in Sandomierz, Opatów, Iłża and Pińczów Districts, partly in Jędrzejów and Kielce, even hostile. To summarize, especially since the militia can't be relied on too much, the moment is very serious and calls for vigilance" (AIPN, KG MO 35/793, k. 5). The deputy commander in Warsaw made a similar observation: "There is a feeling among the more ignorant part of the population in the city of Warsaw of some expectation of events that could introduce various changes" (AIPN, KG MO 35/921, k. 11).
48. AIPN, KGMO 35/888, k. 11, 12. Raport sytuacyjny MO w województwie poznańskim za czas od 6 VI do 20 VI 1945.
49. AIPN, MBP 2506, k. 20. *Meldunek*, n.d.
50. Marzecki, *Tym gorzej dla faktów*, 72, 73.
51. AIPN, MBP 3378, k. 92, 93. Specjalne doniesienie.
52. There is plenty of information, such as this item from Chodzież, located between Bydgoszczą and Poznań: "People's mood: Things have calmed down for now, but nervousness is increasing because of the Russian looter army's operations in this district, when they take pigs and horses, machines, tractors, etc. by force" (AIPN Po 06/118/9, k. 11. Raport sytuacyjny za czas od 21 VII do 31 VII 1945, Powiatowa Komenda MO w Chodzieży).
53. AIPN, MBP 3378, k. 111. Specjalne doniesienie.
54. Marzecki, *Tym gorzej dla faktów*, 72.
55. Kersten, *The Establishment of Communist Rule in Poland*, 252.
56. AIPN, KG MO 35/879, k. 95. Raport sprawozdawczy za czas od 25 XII do 10 I 1946.
57. Friszke, *Losy państwa i narodu 1939–1989*, 119. R. Turkowski believes that already in December 1945 the Polish People's Party had six hundred thousand members, and by June 1946 over one million (Turkowski, "Polskie Stronnictwo Ludowe," 12; see also Turkowski, *Polskie Stronnictwo Ludowe w obronie demokracji 1945–1949*).
58. AP w Kielcach, Wojewódzki Urząd Informacji i Propagandy w Kielcach 20, k. 103. Sprawozdanie za miesiąc styczeń 1946.
59. Burda, *Przymrozki i odwilże*, 92.
60. A private letter read by the censors reported:

> Dear Friends, I just spent those three days, 12–14 April, in Szczecin at the city's celebrations. . . . At 10 a.m. an assembly of all organizations and the army in Jasne Błonia Square for mass. . . . So much to look at, but mostly to listen to. As the standard bearers came in, our Boy Scouts observed keenly and reacted appropriately, for example when the [Polish Workers' Party] standards were brought in, and even those "from our people" who had been fortunate not to die by Hitler's hand, you could hear awful whistling and howling. The same when these banners were carried out. But, when the green flags with the letters [PSL—Polish People's Party] were coming and going, there was no end to cheering, and 10,000 caps went flying in the air like a flock of swallows. (AIPN BU MBP 445, k. 20.)

61. Letter from Gdańsk: "In Gdańsk on Sunday there was a ceremony for regaining [access to] the sea, and of course a parade. I hadn't seen such a parade ever before. Like a funeral. People marched in silence. The masses did not react at all either to the military or to other groups. Only a small [Polish People's Party] group got a storm of applause. Only they did. So the mood is the same everywhere." (AIPN BU MBP 445, k. 21.)

62. Private letter from Chorzów: "My dear ones, . . . You probably don't know that yesterday, Sunday, Mikołajczyk came to Katowice. On Thursday, there are a few posters around the city about the blessing of the [Polish Workers' Party] banner and that Mikołajczyk would be taking part, you should know that everyone is going, but suddenly on Saturday we get the poster at the office and a Great Labor Union Demonstration on the same Sunday and also in Katowice and of course everyone must be present. The mines and steelworks are giving their cars and trams if you show your labor union id card, special trains to Katowice for free, and the cinemas are free that evening. What a rumpus. The guys were boiling with righteous outrage, but if something is free, you have to take advantage of it, so everyone went for free, and instead of the rally and the demonstration, they went to see Mikołajczyk. There hadn't been such a demonstration in a long time, great masses of people, they were carrying him and howling as well as anyone can, the Gliwice polytechnic appeared in full force with banners, and everyone chanting 'Mikołajczyk, save Poland.' Then he gave a speech. . . . Imagine, what enthusiasm that several thousand people stood in a field from 8 a.m. to 3.40 p.m. And no one came to the Labor Union demonstration, a handful of people from each mine, so there was a total of maybe 500 people or maybe not even that many from everywhere in Silesia. But to see Mikołajczyk there were uncountable masses, machine guns in the streets, they say light cannon too, and a militia patrol every few steps, but the militia screamed like madmen, 'Mikołajczyk, save Poland.'" AIPN BU MBP 445, k. 18.

63. Górecki, "Strajki robotnicze w Łodzi w latach 1945–1947," 93–121; Kamiński, *Strajki robotnicze w Polsce w latach 1945–1948*; Kamiński, *Polacy wobec*, 89–93.

64. For more, see Brzoza, *3 V 1946 w Krakowie*; Mazowiecki, *Pierwsze starcie*; Kamiński, *Polacy wobec*, 160–98.

65. Miłosz, *Zaraz po wojnie*, 117.

66. For example, in Bydgoszcz in early November, a rumor spread that a revolution would break out as soon as elections were scheduled (AAN, MIiP 184, k. 4. Propaganda szeptana. Do Biuletynu nr 4).

67. *Biuletyny Informacyjne Ministerstwa Bezpieczeństwa Publicznego 1946*, 61.

68. AAN, MIiP 184, k. 7. Propaganda szeptana. Do Biuletynu nr 6.

69. AAN, MIiP 184, k. 11. Propaganda szeptana. Do Biuletynu nr 8.

70. AAN, MIiP 184, k. 2. Propaganda szeptana. Do Biuletynu nr 2.

71. AAN, MIiP 96, k. 94. Informacje z terenu.

72. *Biuletyny Informacyjne Ministerstwa Bezpieczeństwa Publicznego 1946*, 98.

73. AAN, MIiP 591, k. 66. Do Wojewódzkiego Urzędu Informacji i Propagandy.

74. AAN, MIiP 184, k. 13. Propaganda szeptana. Do Biuletynu nr 9.

75. Dąbrowska, *Dzienniki*, vol. 5, 202.

76. AAN, MIiP 591, k. 87. Sytuacja polityczna powiatu.

77. Dąbrowska, *Dzienniki*, 203.

78. AIPN, MBP 3380, k. 5. Załącznik do listu dyrektora Biura "B" MBP do dyrektora V departamentu MBP, October 13, 1947.

79. Tadeusz Juliusz Kroński's letter to Czesław Miłosz in Miłosz, *Zaraz po wojnie*, 292.

80. Bieńkowski, "Polskie biedy," *Dziś i Jutro*, May 26, 1946.

81. Świda-Ziemba, *Urwany lot*, 82.

82. Woźniczka, *Trzecia wojna światowa*. See also Łatyński, *Nie paść na kolana*, 76.

83. "Na co liczymy?," *Biuletyn Informacyjny*, March 16, 1944.

84. Tomaszewski, *Lwów 1940–1944*, 47.

85. AIPN, MBP 3378, k. 70. Specjalne doniesienie dot. działalności band.

86. Woźniczka, *Trzecia wojna światowa*, 41.

87. Huchlowa et al., *Zrzeszenie "Wolność i Niezawisłość" w dokumentach*, 135.

88. AAN, DRnK 202/III-36, k. 149. Sytuacja na Pomorzu (do 10 VI 1945).

89. Tomaszewski, *Lwów 1940–1944*, 53.

90. Borejsza, "Ostrożnie z bombą atomową," *Odrodzenie*, October 14, 1945.

91. AIPN Rz-0057/22 t. 2, k. 42. Raport sytuacyjny Komendy Powiatowej MO w Przemyślu Nr 11 za czas od dnia 26 V do dnia 5 VI 1945.

92. AIPN, MBP 3378, k. 60. Doniesienie specjalne dot. prowokacyjnych pogłosek.

93. Dąbrowska, *Dzienniki*, 146.

94. AAN, Delegatura Rządu 202/III-36, k. 222. Kronika Tygodniowa PAT'A z Ziem Zachodnich, 16.6.45.

95. Świda-Ziemba, *Urwany lot*, 82.

96. Cf. "W sprawie bomby atomowej," *Trybuna Dolnośląska*, November 19, 1945.

97. Czesław Miłosz wrote that it first appeared on a wall in a Silesian factory. Miłosz, "Kto to był Truman?," *Tygodnik Powszechny*, August 17, 2003.

98. "Rejestracja rowerów i wozów," *Rzeczpospolita*, August 26, 1945.

99. Kamiński, *Polacy wobec*, 14.

100. AIPN, MBP 3378, k. 109. Specjalne doniesienie.

101. AIPN, MBP 3378, k. 110. Specjalne doniesienie.

102. People both in the countryside and in the city must finally understand that the war is over and with it the expectation, whether with hope or fear, of something out of the ordinary, some "miraculous landings." Things are calm now, and relations have stabilized. There won't be, cannot be, any fundamental changes. . . . Here and there people are convinced that we are living through a passing, temporary period. This is the propaganda of evil. It distracts people from working, it makes them wait for God only knows what, introduces a constant state of expectation and nerves, often also leads to trouble, a situation with no way out. (*Dziennik Ludowy*, August 30, 1945)

103. The Political-Educational Department of the Łódź Military Command assessed, "In Ostrowiec rumors about impending war between the USSR and England and America have resulted in significant price rises of necessities" (CAW IV.502.1.247, k. 101. Raport za miesiąc X 1945).

104. I have found no evidence that Stalin's words put Poles in a similar panic. A month earlier, on February 9, Stalin had made a speech in which he said that "Communism and capitalism cannot coexist" and announced a plan of "in five years preparing the USSR for every eventuality." The West took this as a declaration of a third world war. "Speech Delivered by Stalin at a Meeting of Voters of the Stalin Electoral District, Moscow," February 9, 1946, History and Public Policy Program Digital Archive, Gospolitizdat, Moscow, 1946, http://digitalarchive.wilsoncenter.org/document/116179.

105. "Paniczna noc w Paryżu. Tragiczne sceny wywołane przez słuchowisko 'Wiek atomowy,'" *Gazeta Ludowa*, February 6, 1946; "'Nastąpił rozkład atomu.' Świat czeka . . . zagłada, Paryż oszalał!," *Rzeczpospolita*, February 6, 1946; "Strach ma wielkie oczy," *Kurier Szczeciński*, February 15, 1946; "Panika w Paryżu wskutek imaginacyjnego słuchowiska," *Dziennik Powszechny*, February 8, 1946.

106. For a more detailed account of the panic and the general atmosphere, see Pace, "'Voilà les atomes qui arrivent,'" 157–77.

107. "Niedorzeczności i kłamstwa," *Rzeczpospolita*, March 14, 1946.

108. "'Trzecia wojna' a słonina," *Rzeczpospolita*, March 13, 1946.

109. "Niedorzeczności i kłamstwa."

110. Dąbrowska, *Dzienniki*, 185.

111. This is how the time of Judgment Day was called in the fifteenth century. See Delumeau, *La Peur en Occident (XIVe–XVIIIe siècles)*, 199ff.

112. "Plotka . . . Plotka . . . Plotka," *Gazeta Kujawska*, March 19, 1946.

113. "Upaństwowić plotkę," *Echo Krakowa*, March 20, 1946.

114. "Dementujemy plotki," *Głos Narodu*, March 15, 1946.

115. "Plotka . . . Plotka . . . Plotka."

116. AIPN 1572/321, k. 9. Raport dekadowy WUBP—Kielce za okres od dnia 20 III–31 III 46.

117. AIPN 1572/734, k. 21. Raport dekadowy WUBP—Szczecin za okres od dnia 10–20 III 46.

118. Sprawozdanie wojewody pomorskiego za marzec 1946 r. in Borodij et al., *Rok 1946*, 38.

119. "Plotka . . . Plotka . . . Plotka."

120. "Niezdrowy objaw," *Ziemia Lubuska. Ilustrowany Tygodnik Informacyjny*, March 24, 1946.

121. Łach, *Pomorze zachodnie w latach 1945–1949*, 57.

122. AAN, MIiP 227, k. 20. Sprawozdanie ogólne Oddziału Sławno, April 4, 1946.

123. AIPN 1572/734, k. 24. Raport dekadowy WUBP—Szczecin za okres od 1 do 10 IV 1946.

124. Sprawozdanie wojewody pomorskiego za marzec 1946 r., 117, 118.

125. Mark, "The War Scare of 1946 and Its Consequences," 384.

126. *Rzeczpospolita*, August 13, 1946; *Kurier Popularny*, September 8, 1946.

127. "Kaczki dziennikarskie w marszu na Teheran, czyli jak się fabrykuje sensacje i łowi ryby w mętnej wodzie," *Robotnik*, May 3, 1946.

128. *Kocynder*, July 7, 1946.

129. AAN, MIiP 77, k. 20. Sprawozdanie z inspekcji Wojewódzkiego Urzędu Informacji i Propagandy w Białymstoku, przeprowadzonej w dn. od 7 IX br. do 12 IX [1946] przez inspektora Makowskiego Stefana.

130. AAN, MIiP 365, k. 10. Sprawozdanie z krążącej propagandy szeptanej na terenie woj. pomorskiego.

131. For more on this, see Borodziej, *Od Poczdamu do Szklarskiej Poręby*.

132. AAN, MIiP 523, k. 73. Propaganda szeptana, October 15, 1946.

133. CAW IV.502.1.248, k. 321. Sprawozdanie miesięczne za miesiąc wrzesień 1946.

134. AAN, MIiP 523, k. 61. Doniesienie Miejskiego Urzędu Informacji i Propagandy w Sosnowcu, September 24, 1946.

135. AAN, MIiP 1004, k. 2. Sprawozdanie za m-c wrzesień z sytuacji politycznej na terenie województwa lubelskiego.

136. AAN, MIiP 1004, k. 46. Sprawozdanie z województwa lubelskiego za okres od 6 do 13 [października 1946].

137. AAN, MIiP 523, k. 61. Doniesienie Miejskiego Urzędu Informacji i Propagandy w Sosnowcu, September 24, 1946.

138. AAN, MIiP 1000, k. 79. Wyciąg z telefonogramu.

139. AAN, MIiP 523, k. 1. Doniesienie Powiatowego Oddziału Informacji i Propagandy w Bielsku, October 11, 1946.

140. AAN, MIiP 1008, k. 4. Notatka dot. nastrojów ludności.

141. AAN, MIiP 184, k. 1. Dane o szeptanej propagandzie. Do biuletynu nr 1.

142. AAN, MIiP 1000, k. 77. Telefonogram.

143. "Szkodliwa psychoza," *Kurier Szczeciński*, December 1–2, 1946.

144. AAN, MIiP 571, k. 5. Działalność reakcji.

145. AAN, MIiP 365, k. 13. Sprawozdanie z krążącej propagandy szeptanej na terenie woj. pomorskiego.

146. AAN, MIiP 77, k. 20. Sprawozdanie z inspekcji Wojewódzkiego Urzędu Informacji i Propagandy w Białymstoku, przeprowadzonej w dn. od 7 IX br. do 12 IX [1946] przez inspektora Makowskiego Stefana.

147. Wyka, *Życie na niby*, 166, 167.

148. AAN, MIiP 523, k. 1. Doniesienie Powiatowego Oddziału Informacji i Propagandy w Bielsku, October 11, 1946.

149. For example, AAN, MIiP 1008, k. 4. Notatka dot. nastrojów ludności.

150. AAN, MIiP 523, k. 61. Doniesienie Miejskiego Urzędu Informacji i Propagandy w Sosnowcu.

151. AAN, PPR 295/IX-411, k. 283, 288. Biuletyn Informacyjny nr 19 za miesiąc luty 1948, Zarząd Pol.-Wych. WP.

152. AIPN, MBP 285, Referat sprawozdawczy od 1 do 31 VII 1948 na podstawie sprawozdań z WUBP, n.p.

153. Miernik, *Opór chłopów*, 30.

154. AIPN, MBP 383, Sprawozdanie miesięczne za wrzesień UBP na miasto st. Warszawę, n.p.

155. M. Zaremba, "Jest marszałek, wyszedł cukier," *Gazeta Wyborcza*, November 9, 2009.

156. AIPN 1572/1183, k. 7. Biuletyn Informacyjny nr 72/48.

157. Świeżawski, *W nowej rzeczywistości 1945–1956*, 54.

158. Jarosz, "Kriegsgerüchte in Polen, 1946–1956," 310–21; Jarosz and Pasztor, *W krzywym zwierciadle*; Zaremba, "Smalec strategiczny," *Polityka*, November 2, 2002.

159. There is a rich anthropological, political science, and sociological literature about borders. To mention two books: Hall, *The Hidden Dimension*; and Donnan and Wilson, *Border Identities*.
160. AAN, PKWN I/78, k. 14. Doniesienie specjalne dotyczy repatriacji.
161. List KC PPR "do tow. D," 189.
162. Kowalska, *Dzienniki 1927–1969*, 94
163. APN 1572/1192, Wypowiedzenie się ludności w sprawie konferencji Trzech w Jałcie, k. 1.
164. AAN, MIiP 1004, k. 25. Sprawozdanie polityczne z wydarzeń w województwie lubelskim za okres od 1 VIII do 9 VIII 1946.
165. AIPN, MBP 3378, k. 60. Doniesienie specjalne dot. prowokacyjnych pogłosek.
166. For more, see Kułak, *Pierwszy rok sowieckiej okupacji*.
167. AAN, PKWN I/73, k. 11. Dane z inspekcji inspektora Wydz. Organizacyjnego—o stanie moralnym, politycznym i organizacyjnym propagandy w m. Białymstoku.
168. AP w Białymstoku, Urząd Wojewódzki 523, k. 9.
169. Majcki, Sprawozdania delegatów PKWN z pobytu na Białostocczyźnie w pierwszych dniach po wyzwoleniu spod okupacji hitlerowskiej, 381.
170. AAN, MZO 60, k. 60. Przewinienia jednostek Wojsk Polskich stacjonujących na terenach Ziem Odzyskanych w oświetleniu Pełnomocników Okręgowych i Obwodowych Międzyministerialnej Komisji Granicznej, Komitetów Międzypartyjnych Stronnictw Demokratycznych itp.
171. *Okręg Mazurski w raportach Jakuba Prawina*, 160.
172. AAN, MIiP 926, k. 51. Odpis pisma nadesłanego przez Urząd Informacji i Propagandy w Lublinie z dnia 6.9.46 r.; AAN, MIiP 1004, k. 42. Sprawozdanie za miesiąc sierpień z sytuacji na terenie województwa lubelskiego w ogólnym streszczonym ujęciu.
173. For more on this, see Kamiński, *Polsko-czechosłowackie stosunki polityczne 1945–1948*, 74–124, passim; Pałys, *Kłodzko, Racibórz i Głubczyce w stosunkach polsko-czechosłowackich w latach 1945–1947*.
174. *Naczelne Dowództwo Wojsk Polskich*, Polityka, August 23, 1997.
175. Zaremba, *Komunizm, legitymizacja, nacjonalizm*, 155.
176. AAN, MIiP 550, k. 25. Sytuacja polityczna, Wrocław, February 6, 1946.
177. Sobków, "Do innego kraju," 57, 58, 59.
178. AIPN 1572/1183, k. 7. Biuletyn Informacyjny nr 72/48, November 9, 1948.
179. Sociologist and social anthropologist Z. Mach: "It was no accident that the first generation was said to be living out of their suitcases. They would never feel sure and safe here. They did not think that they were the true owners and hosts of these lands. This only changed a little in the early '70s, after Willy Brandt's symbolic gesture. But it came too late to change the mentality of the resettled people, which had solidified over 25 years." (Marcinkowski interview with Z. Mach, "Kresowe życie na walizkach," *Gazeta Wyborcza*, December 24–26, 2010.)
180. More in, for example, Łach, *Pomorze Zachodnie w latach 1945–1949*, 14, 15.
181. AIPN, KG MO 35/922, k. 245. Sprawozdanie z pracy aparatu polit.-wych. województwa wrocławskiego za okres od 1.1.1948 do 1.2.1948.
182. Tracz, *Rok ostatni—rok pierwszy*, 88.
183. Kochański, *Protokół obrad KC PPR w maju 1945 roku*, 50.
184. AAN, MIiP 523, k. 71. Powiatowy Oddział Informacji i Propagandy w Strzelcach Opolskich. Raport.
185. On 14.8.45 . . . Junior lieutenant of the Guard Aleksandr Vasilevich Suvorov, commander of kolkhoz no. 80318 in Bryśnica declared in the presence of the commander in Bryśnica and District Commander of the Citizens' Militia in Żagań that all Russians and Poles must leave the lands west of the Oder. He gave his officer's word that he was telling the truth. It is notable that the Russian workers who are in charge of grain equipment are spreading the same news among the German population, which creates a mood of excitement and expectation among them. They gave 25 August as their time of departure. These tales are having a very negative impact on the settlement operation since they are making the Polish population nervous. (AIPN, KG MO 35/920, k. 18. Komenda Powiatowa MO w Żaganiu. Meldunek nadzwyczajny.)
186. AIPN, MBP 3378, k. 111. Specjalne doniesienie.
187. Kersten and Szarota, *Wieś polska 1939–1948*, vol. 1, 99.
188. Kersten and Szarota, 457.
189. Kiwerska, "Niemcy w polityce PPR/PZPR," 93; Zaremba, *Komunizm, legitymizacja, nacjonalizm*.
190. Bełczewski, "Przyczółek," 512.
191. Landau, *Gospodarka Polski Ludowej*, 50.
192. This went on for nearly half a year; only on February 15, 1945, by a decree of January 13, did the ruble stop being used in Poland.
193. "Złoty pozostaje w obiegu," *Gazeta Lubelska*, August 8, 1944.
194. "Banknoty 'krakowskie' wycofane z obiegu," *Życie Warszawy*, January 12, 1945.
195. AIPN, MBP 3378, k. 42. Doniesienie specjalne dot. sytuacji gospodarczej kraju.
196. Jezierski and Leszczyńska, *Pierwsze lata*, 52.
197. "Dzisiejsze i jutrzejsze problemy Bydgoszczy. Wywiad z Prezydentem miasta ob. Witoldem Szuksztą przeprowadzony przez Stanisława Babisiaka," *Ziemia Pomorska*, 4 Mar. 1945.
198. AIPN, MBP 3378, k. 43. Doniesienie specjalne dot. sytuacji gospodarczej kraju.
199. AIPN, KG/MO 35/921, k. 1. Raport za czas od 7 do 15 I 1945 Zastępcy Komendanta MO Praga do Spraw Polit.-Wychowawczych m. st. Warszawy, January 16, 1945.
200. "Przy wymianie," *Życie Warszawy*, January 19, 1945.
201. "Pierwszy dzień wymiany," *Życie Warszawy*, January 13, 1945.
202. Jezierski and Leszczyńska, *Pierwsze lata*, 51.
203. AIPN, MBP 3378, k. 42. Doniesienie specjalne dot. sytuacji gospodarczej kraju.
204. Jezierski and Leszczyńska, *Pierwsze lata*, 51.
205. AIPN, MBP 3378, k. 42. Doniesienie specjalne dot. sytuacji gospodarczej kraju.

206. AP w Krakowie, Urząd Wojewódzki Krakowski II 29, k. 1–9. Opinia dotycząca pism Starostwa Powiatowego w Miechowie, N. Sączu, Brzesku na temat wymiany banknotów "krakowskich," Cracow April 12, 1945.

207. AIPN, MBP 3378, k. 42. Doniesienie specjalne dot. sytuacji gospodarczej kraju.

208. Landau, *Gospodarka Polski Ludowej*, 51; Jezierski and Petz, *Historia gospodarcza Polski*, 128.

209. AIPN, MBP 3378, k. 44. Doniesienie specjalne dot. sytuacji gospodarczej kraju.

210. Neyman, *Intymny portret uczonych. Korespondencja Marii i Stanisława Ossowskich*, 400, 401.

211. AIPN, MBP 3378, k. 43. Doniesienie specjalne dot. sytuacji gospodarczej kraju.

212. AIPN, MBP 3378, k. 43.

213. AIPN, MBP 3378, k. 42. Doniesienie specjalne dot. sytuacji gospodarczej kraju.

214. "Nie słuchać plotek," *Gazeta Lubelska*, April 13, 1945; "Panika walutowa przetoczyła się również przez Kraków: Spekulacyjne plotki o zmianie pieniądza," *Dziennik Polski*, April 17, 1945.

215. AIPN, MBP 3378, k. 61b. Doniesienie specjalne dot. prowokacyjnych pogłosek.

216. AIPN, MBP 3378, k. 61b.

217. "Sprawa zwyżki cen," *Życie Warszawy*, November 21, 1945.

218. Cf. AAN, MIiP 1004, k. 52. Sprawozdanie Wojewódzkiego Urzędu Informacji i Propagandy w Lublinie za okres od 13 do 23 IX 1946.

219. "Minister piętnuje kłamstwa i plotki o rzekomej wymianie banknotów. Pogłoski nie mają żadnych podstaw (Inflacji nie będzie!)," *Express Poznański*, April 19, 1947.

220. For example, "Plotki o ponownej wymianie pieniędzy," *Życie Warszawy*, January 10, 1946; "Plotka hula—naiwni płacą," *Życie Warszawy*, January 11, 1946; "Plotka hula—naiwni płacą," *Dziennik Powszechny*, January 13, 1946; "Nie będzie wymiany pieniędzy," *Kurier Szczeciński*, January 14, 1946.

221. AP w Białymstoku, Wojewódzki Urząd Informacji i Propagandy w Białymstoku 6, k. 7. Ocena sytuacji w województwie w miesiącu styczniu 1946.

222. AAN, MIiP 924, k. 2, 3. Urząd Informacji i Propagandy Województwa Kieleckiego w Kielcach, January 22, 1946.

223. Minc, "Wytyczne w sprawie naszego ustroju gospodarczego i społecznego," 103.

224. Cf. Scott, *Weapons of the Weak*.

225. AIPN, MBP 285, k. 30. Referat sprawozdawczy od 1 do 31 VIII 1948 na podstawie sprawozdań z WUBP.

226. AIPN, MBP 285, k. 30.

227. AIPN 1572/1183, k. 4. Biuletyn Informacyjny 72/48.

228. Jarosz, *Polityka władz komunistycznych w Polsce w latach 1948–1956 a chłopi*; Jarosz, *Polacy a stalinizm 1948–1956*, 11–60; Dobieszewski, *Kolektywizacja wsi polskiej 1948–1956*; Miernik, *Opór chłopów*; Kamiński et al., *Opór społeczny w Europie Środkowej w latach 1948–1953 na przykładzie Polski*.

229. For more see Król, *Polska i Polacy w propagandzie narodowego socjalizmu w Niemczech 1919–1945*.

230. AAN, DRnK 202/III-31, k. 29, 31. Przyczyny wzrostu komunizmu na terenie kraju.

231. One of the titles the Polish media gave Stalin in the Stalinist period. See Kupiecki, "*Natchnienie milionów*," 240.

232. Marshal Stalin said, "The Polish peasants will appreciate their government after they receive land" (emphasis in original). "Delegacja Warszawy u Marszałka Stalina," *Głos Ludu*, November 21, 1944.

233. "Our agrarian revolution is taking place in special conditions, land reform. It is happening from the top, but as it passes from top to bottom it also satisfies the long years of the peasant masses' yearnings, resolving the issue for which the peasant masses in Poland fought many times with revolutionary methods" (Referat Romana Zambrowskiego wygłoszony na rozszerzonym plenum KC PPR dotyczącym reformy rolnej, 7 II 1945, 92).

234. For more on land reform, see, for example, Słabek, *Dzieje polskiej reformy rolnej 1944–1948*; Iwaniak, *Reforma rolna*.

235. Iwaniak, *Reforma rolna*, 135.

236. Góra et al., *Reforma rolna PKWN*, 34.

237. Rak, *Reforma rolna w Polsce*, 33, 34, passim.

238. Up to January 1, 1947, 10,311 cooperatives operated in Poland, including 5,619 in trade (2,166,511 members) and 1,503 of the Union of Peasant Self-Help (232,423 members). Jędruszczak, *Upaństwowienie i odbudowa*, vol. 2, 244.

239. For example, *Sztandar Ludu*, May 13, 1945.

240. Kochanowski, *Protokoły posiedzenia Prezydium Krajowej Rady Narodowej 1944–1947*, 59, 60.

241. Kochanowski.

242. *Biuletyny Informacyjne Ministerstwa Bezpieczeństwa Publicznego 1946*, 25.

243. Kersten and Szarota, *Wieś polska 1939–1948*, vol. 1, 319.

244. Kersten, "Początki stabilizacji życia społecznego," 6.

245. Stenogram wystąpienia sekretarza KC PPR, wicepremiera Rządu Tymczasowego RP Władysława Gomułki "Wiesława" o sytuacji w Polsce przedstawionej na spotkaniu z pracownikami Wydziału Informacji Międzynarodowej KC WKP(b) w Moskwie, 10 V 1945, 115.

246. AIPN, KGMO 35/888, k. 11, 12. Raport sytuacyjny MO w województwie poznańskim za czas od 6 VI do 20 VI 1945.

247. AIPN, MBP 3378, k. 105. Specjalne doniesienie.

248. *Biuletyn Informacyjny Ministerstwa Bezpieczeństwa Publicznego 1947*, 39.

249. Biuletyn Informacyjny Ministerstwa Bezpieczeństwa Publicznego 1947, 122.

250. Kersten and Szarota, *Wieś polska 1939–1948*, vol. 2, 221, 222.

251. Gołębiowski, *Nacjonalizacja przemysłu w Polsce*, 103.

252. Quoted by Kamosiński, "Przyczynek do badań nad postrzeganiem nowej rzeczywistości," 156, 157.

253. "Just like every political breakthrough of a fundamental nature, removing Germans from Greater Poland and eliminating the economic system introduced by the occupying power have caused a temporary stoppage in the work of industry and crafts, commerce and agriculture" ("Zacznijmy produkować!," *Głos Wielkopolski*, May 24, 1945).

254. AAN, CUP 430, k. 58. Sprawozdanie Izby Przemysłowo-Handlowej w Krakowie o sytuacji gospodarczej za czas od 1 IX do 31 XII 1945.

255. For a more detailed discussion, see, for example, Topiński, "Nacjonalizacja przemysłu w Polsce," 99–110.
256. *Wyzwolenie gospodarki z niewoli karteli i obcego kapitału. Referat Ministra Przemysłu tow. Hilarego Minca*, *Głos Ludu*, January 3, 1946.
257. For example, "Radomski 'Ericsson' poradził sobie bez kapitalistów," *Głos Ludu*, March 14, 1946.
258. "Przeciw plotce," *Dziennik Bałtycki*, January 26, 1946.
259. AAN, CUP 417, k. 61, 62. *Położenie gospodarcze w Polsce w lutym 1946*.
260. Jędruszczak, *Upaństwowienie i odbudowa*, 91.
261. "Za dużo knajp—za mało mieszkań," *Ziemia Pomorska*, February 9, 1946.
262. Jędruszczak, *Upaństwowienie i odbudowa*, 130–33.
263. Jędruszczak, 148.
264. "Pogłoski o wprowadzeniu monopolu zbożowego nie odpowiadają prawdzie," *Kurier Szczeciński*, June 25, 1946.
265. AAN MIiP 523, k. 3. Raport Informacyjny, Miejski Oddział Informacji i Propagandy w Bytomiu; AAN, MIiP 1008, k. 1. Dot. plotek obiegających Poznań.
266. Kaliński, *Bitwa o handel 1947–1948*, 70.
267. Minc, "Będą zwalczani ci, którzy próbują obedrzeć ludzi pracy," *Głos Ludu*, May 2, 1947.
268. For more, see Kaliński, *Bitwa o handel*.
269. Zaniewicki, *Na pobojowisku 1945–1950*, 93.
270. Knyt and Wancerz-Gluza, *Prywaciarze 1945–1989*, 36.
271. AIPN 1572/1183, k. 14. Biuletyn Informacyjny 73/48.
272. "Powszednie kłopoty prowincjonalnego miasta," *Życie Warszawy*, January 21, 1946.
273. Piesowicz, "Demograficzne skutki II wojny światowej," 127–29.
274. Jasieński, *Problemy mieszkalnictwa Krakowa*, 38.
275. AIPN, MBP 3378, k. 49. Doniesienie specjalne dotyczy Warszawy.
276. As quoted in "Warszawa w oczach Zachodu," *Kurier Popularny*, December 1, 1945.
277. Jarosz, *Mieszkanie się należy*, 28–36, 152–76.
278. Przybył-Stalski, "Robotnicza Akcja Mieszkaniowa," 475–83.
279. "O socjalizm walczymy po cichu, a o demokrację głośno," 33.
280. AIPN, MBP 3378, k. 106. Specjalne doniesienie.
281. "Nie wolno samowolnie zajmować mieszkań po wyjeżdżających niemcach," *Dziennik Zachodni*, July 18, 1945.
282. AAN, KRN 797, k. 49. *List Antoniego Plater Zyberka do Ob. Bolesława Bieruta*.
283. IPN, MBP 3378, k. 79. *Specjalne doniesienie dot. volksdeutschów*.
284. Drabienko, *Jedno życie. Wspomnienia z lat 1942–1951*, 88.
285. Miernik, "Losy Żydów i nieruchomości pożydowskich w Szydłowcu po II wojnie światowej," 166.
286. AP w Kielcach, UW II, 1524, k. 41. Pismo Kierownika I-ego Wydziału Wojewódzkiego Urzędu Bezpieczeństwa Publicznego w Kielcach por. Srokowskiego do Wojewody Kieleckiego, 9 X 1945.
287. Gross, *Fear*, 42–43.
288. Allport, *The Nature of Prejudice*, 223.
289. IPN, MBP 3378, k. 104, 105. Specjalne doniesienie.
290. IPN, MBP 3378, k. 105, 107. Specjalne doniesienie.
291. He said in a press conference, "I am somewhat concerned that some authorities are interfering in housing issues without possessing a legal [right], such as the army, security offices and the militia. We must firmly disallow some functionaries of these offices and authorities to occupy apartments illegally on their own initiative. In Cracow there have been such incidents" (*Echo Wieczorne*, November 10, 1946).
292. "Kwatery dla oficerów radzieckich," *Dziennik Powszechny*, July 11, 1945.
293. Kubacki, *Dziennik (1944–1958)*, 65, 66.
294. AAN DRnK 202/III-36, k. 106. *Postępująca sowietyzacja Polski*, March 27, 1945.
295. "Kontrola liczby lokatorów w mieszkaniach," *Dziennik Polski*, August 6, 1945.
296. Jarosz, *Mieszkanie się należy*, 152–55.
297. *Kurier Kaliski*, September 5, 1946.
298. "Zagęszczenie," *Express Wieczorny*, August 10, 1946.
299. "Kontrola mieszkań rozpoczęta," *Kurier Szczeciński*, November 1, 1946.
300. "Powszednie kłopoty."
301. More in Klich-Kluczewska, *Przez dziurkę od klucza*, 194–98.
302. Jarosińska, *Było i tak*, 14.
303. Paczyńska, "Dekret o Nadzwyczajnej Komisji Mieszkaniowej i jego realizacja w Krakowie (1946–1947)," 333.
304. Cf. Piwońska, "Dokwaterowanie jako temat listów do władz w latach 1945–1956 (komunikat z badań)," 123–33.
305. AP w Białymstoku, UWB 71, k. 74. Wyciąg z listu.
306. Lechowski, *W służbie stolicy*, 41, 74, 75.
307. Quoted after Barszczewski, *Przywrócone życiu*; Kałużny, *Wielka operacja rozminowania*; Ząbek, *Dzieje Makowa Mazowieckiego*.
308. Kaczor, *Wspomnienia ludowego starosty*, 91.
309. AAN, MPiOS 267, k. 10. *Sprawozdanie z inspekcji w zniszczonych powiatach województwa kieleckiego*, 1 V 1945.
310. AP w Białymstoku, UWB, k. 71. Wyciąg z listu.
311. Pilak, "Kocham w nim wszystko, nawet gruzy," 151.
312. AP w Białymstoku, UWB 71, k. 68, 70, 76. Wyciągi z listów.
313. Gapiński, *Sacrum i codzienność*.
314. "Całopalenie myśli wiciowej," *Dziennik Ludowy*, September 15, 1945.
315. Łatyński, *Nie paść na kolana*, 377.
316. Kersten, *Między wyzwoleniem a zniewoleniem*, 43.
317. Tokarska-Bakir, *Legendy o krwi*.
318. *Dziennik Łódzki*, January 18, 1946.
319. AIPN, MBP 3378, k. 92. Specjalne doniesienie.
320. AIPN, KG MO 35/898, k. 7. Ulotka.
321. Gross, *Fear*, 187, 185ff.
322. Tomaszewski, *Lwów 1940–1944*, 24.
323. AIPN, KG MO 35/898, k. 12. Ulotka.
324. *Biuletyny Informacyjne Ministerstwa Bezpieczeństwa Publicznego 1947*, 52.
325. "Za 70 dni koniec świata prorokują w Białymstoku," *Express Poznański*, April 16, 1947.

326. *Biuletyny Informacyjne Ministerstwa Bezpieczeństwa Publicznego 1947*, 61.

327. *Biuletyny Informacyjne Ministerstwa Bezpieczeństwa Publicznego 1947*, 70.

328. AIPN w Poznaniu, PO 06/68 5 z 22, k. 62. Raport specjalny WUBP w Poznaniu, August 12, 1948.

329. AIPN 1572/1183, k. 7. Biuletyn Informacyjny nr 72/48.

330. See, for example, Jarosz, *Polityka władz komunistycznych*, chapter titled "Epidemia cudów"; Jastrząb, "Cuda podwarszawskie," 147–57; Rudnicki, *Cuda i objawienia w Polsce 1949–1986*; Turkowski, "Władza komunistyczna wobec przejawów religijności w Polsce w schyłku lat 40-tych XX wieku," 75–91.

331. For more on church-state relations, see Dudek, *Państwo i Kościół w Polsce*; Żaryn, *Kościół a władza w Polsce (1945–1950)*; Dudek and Gryz, *Komuniści i Kościół w Polsce (1945–1989)*.

332. Kersten and Szarota, *Wieś polska 1939–1948*, vol. 1, 228.

333. See, for example, Wańkowicz, *W kościołach Meksyku*; *O męczeńskim Meksyku*; Kula and Smolana, "Echa meksykańskiego konfliktu religijnego w lat 1926–1929 w Polsce," 21–33.

334. Bełczyński, "Przyczółek," 526.

335. Łatyński, *Nie paść na kolana*, 375

336. Jedlicz, "Bez uproszczeń i bez retuszu," *Tygodnik Powszechny*, July 7, 1946.

337. See Żaryn, *Kościół a władza w Polsce*, 74–76.

338. Werfel, "Prawo małżeńskie w Polsce," *Głos Ludu*, July 11, 1945; "Doniosłe reformy Ministerstwa Sprawiedliwości" *Życie Warszawy*, July 16, 1945.

339. *Komunikaty Konferencji Episkopatu Polski 1945–2000*, ed. J. Żaryn (Poznań: Pallottinum, 2006), 49.

340. The author of the letter also noted the reactions of young people, both men and women. He wrote earlier, "There are to be lay marriages here. Our girls said that none of them will go for such a marriage because then the priest at the pulpit will yell at them and won't want to christen their child. We like this because you can dump such a 'lay hag' faster" (AIPN, MBP 3378, k. 109. Specjalne doniesienie).

341. AIPN, MBP 3378, k. 109. Specjalne doniesienie.

342. AIPN, MBP 3378, k. 109.

343. *Armia Krajowa w dokumentach 1939–1945*, vol. 5, 281.

344. Zaremba, *Wojna i konspiracja*, 297.

345. CAW IV 500.1/17.132. Miejski Urząd Bezpieczeństwa w Gdyni, k. 624. Raport, August 2, 1946.

346. AAN, MIiP 1000, k. 55. Odpis pisma nadesłanego przez Urząd Informacji i Propagandy w Kielcach z dnia 23 IX 46.

347. AAN, KC PZPR, 237/VII-117, k. 99. Meldunek z terenu, April 22, 1949.

348. Kselman, *Miracles and Prophecies in Nineteenth-Century France*.

349. Bojarski, "Czołgi strzelają do katedry, Julian fotografuje," *Gazeta Wyborcza*, January 21, 2011.

350. "Bezczelna plotka," *Głos Narodu*, July 21–22, 1946.

351. AP w Białymstoku, Wojewódzki Urząd Informacji i Propagandy w Białymstoku, k. 7. Ocena sytuacji w województwie w miesiącu styczniu 1946.

352. Bieńkowski, "Katolicyzm głodnych," *Dziś i Jutro*, March 24, 1946.

353. Komunikat Konferencji Plenarnej Episkopatu Polski, Jasna Góra 10 IX 1946 r., 52.

354. *Rzeczpospolita*, November 20, 1946.

355. Bauman, *Liquid Fear*, 156. Emphasis in the original.

356. For a discussion of dollar exchange rates during the war and after 1948, see Kochanowski, "'Niepewne czasy, pewny dolar,'" 29–46.

357. AAN, CUP 430, Sprawozdanie Izby Przemysłowo-Handlowej w Krakowie o sytuacji gospodarczej za czas od 1 IX do 31 XII 1945, k. 58.

358. Bauman, *Liquid Fear*, 159.

359. Bauman, "Wytłumaczyć niewytłumaczalne," 209.

12

THE THREE HORSEMEN OF THE APOCALYPSE

HUNGER, HIGH PRICES, AND INFECTIOUS DISEASES

Humans have always feared hunger.[1] Hunger lurks even at times of prosperity, when people gorge themselves at feasts and festivals. At times of crisis it can lead to panic, revolt, or protest. Hunger lay at the roots of the *Grande Peur* on the eve of the French Revolution. It often fired up wild accusations directed at suspected profiteers.[2] In the Second World War, it proved to be an extermination tool as efficient as the gas chambers. In occupied Poland, the Germans starved hundreds of thousands of Soviet prisoners of war to death.[3] Jews confined to ghettos suffered from deathly hunger, especially in Warsaw, where many simply dropped dead in the street. On the "Aryan side" the situation was critical, too, especially in the winter and spring of 1941 and 1942. The historian Witold Kula noted in his diary in May 1941, "Yesterday for lunch at the Capital Committee for Social Self-Assistance I got a little sweet pancake with a bit of swede. Even with this amazing mix of flavors, how could it tide me over from breakfast to supper? I wandered the streets hungry and livid . . . and hated everyone, not just those who had eaten their fill. I wanted to spite everyone, disagree with everyone and protest whatever anyone said ironically, with disdain and contempt."[4] In 1942, Hunger and his brother Fear ruled the vast lands from Siberia and Kazakhstan, Ukraine, Belarus, and central Poland all the way to Greece, where some three hundred thousand people died of malnutrition and disease. You could hear everywhere: the children are dropping like flies.

People threatened by hunger used all sorts of strategies: they worked on the black market, came together as families, and changed their diets.[5] In Warsaw, potato peels were put on menus and horsemeat had to do instead of beef and pork. The German occupation of eastern Europe could be compared to the medieval and early modern hunger wars in which the destruction of the enemy's food supplies was wielded as a weapon.[6] But this time it was not just a question of weakening the enemy's life forces and redistributing the calories to Germany. The Hunger Plan developed in May 1941 for Ukraine, Belarus, and western Russia aimed for the total "liquidation" of the conquered peoples with starvation.[7]

Hunger is also a player in the history of the Communist-ruled countries, where it was used as a political tool. In 1932–33, it killed about six million in the USSR (in Ukraine, the Volga region, Kuban, western Siberia, and Kazakhstan). In China during the Great Leap Forward, about forty million people died. Collectivization, which aimed to destroy private ownership in the countryside, made sense and had the noble goal of defeating the forces of nature to eliminate food shortages. But here, it became exceptionally counterproductive.

The Communist project also wanted to eliminate the second horseman, the risk of high prices. They were the most obvious sign that class injustice existed, dividing society into those who could afford expensive goods and those who had to settle for hungering after them as they stood outside store windows. Across history, unexpected rises in the price of grain—and therefore bread—which reduced consumption, at best worsened the public mood and at worst brought on panic buying and even riots. To Jean Delumeau, such unrest was most often brought on by a rise in bread prices. A panic would break out among women and then spread, turning into anxiety, inflated fears, and violent behaviors.[8]

And now for the third horseman of the Apocalypse: infectious diseases. Throughout history they have provoked even greater dread than hunger. During the Second World War, Nazi propaganda warned people about the plague-carrying Jews and Soviet prisoners of war, *Seuchenträger*.[9] Wherever an epidemic would break out, the Germans posted signs reading *Fleckfieber—Anhalt verboten* (Typhus fever—no stopping). We do not know the number of casualties of the 1941–42 epidemic, but we do know that in some parts of occupied Poland more people died of infectious diseases than in military operations. For instance, between June 1941 and the spring of 1942, in a district in Podlasie Province, at least 796 people had typhus fever, and 130 of them died.[10] After the war, too, both fear of hunger and anxiety about high prices and about infectious diseases swayed public moods, helping to build up this era's terror.

FEAR OF HUNGER

"We go hungry these days," wrote a woman from Gryfino in Pomerania in September 1945. "There is no flour. We've baked our last bread and I don't know what will happen now. The children are constantly sick and there are no doctors."[11] Analyses of the postwar situation rarely take into account hunger and fear of hunger—and they are wrong.[12] At least in some areas, the scarcity of food and the fears linked to it consumed people, influencing their perception of reality and their actions, more than they did the District Security Offices. Nothing mattered as much as satisfying existential needs such as having a roof over one's head, provisions, basic security, a job, and access to a doctor. The fear of hunger magnified the overall sense of insecurity, which was released in elevated aggression. This fear therefore lay at the roots of not only protests, hunger strikes, and accusations against alleged profiteers but also of acts of collective hatred. Nothing fires up a pogrom like the threatening joblessness or hunger.

Even though this book primarily analyzes human experiences and psychological reactions, some discussion of economic conditions needs to be included as background. In a word, the economy was in a state of absolute collapse. Poland's great material losses had dramatically pauperized its people. There was no clothing or shoes and, most important, no food. A study by the Ministry of Provisions and Trade, which compared the production of basic foods per capita in 1938 and 1945–46, shows a twofold or even threefold drop in production (see table 12.1).

Thus, in 1945–46 a rural inhabitant took in 1,396 calories per day. For the nonfarming population, the figure was even lower: 1,121 calories. Foreign aid was estimated at 280 calories per person, which meant that the average Pole ate 1,400 to 1,700 calories per day.[13] If this estimate is accurate, the amount was only a little higher than during the war. But because this calculation was intended for foreign eyes, it is possible that the figures were lowered somewhat to encourage the West to donate more. According to the Central Planning Office, in 1945 the average daily calorie intake was below 2,000.[14] Also, because these are averaged data, some people must have vegetated undernourished.

Food supplies or, to put it differently, the geography of hunger depended on many factors, but most important was the wartime destruction.

The areas closest to the front line, which stopped in August 1944 and did not move again until January

Table 12.1 Per capita food production in 1938 and 1945–1946 (kg)

	1938	1945–1946
Grains	313	173
Potatoes	1,002	605
Meat	20.5	6.6
Fats	8.9	2.3
Milk	266	111
Sugar	14	7.4

1945, were worst hit. The landscape left by the front literally resembled a desert, not just because of the fighting but also because of the stealing by the two armies that faced each other in place. In the north, the devastation affected Augustów, Łomża, Suwałki, and the western part of Białystok Districts.[15] Farther south, it was the areas around Pułtusk, Przasnysz, Maków Mazowiecki, and Ostrów Mazowiecka. In September 1944, a government report from Ostrów Mazowiecka read:

> According to the districts along the front, what is happening there is beyond your wildest dreams. People who have been evacuated from their homes gather in nearby villages and small towns. The worst of it all is that the Red Army sometimes takes apart houses and farm buildings for their own needs. They dig up potatoes from clamps, and if the farmers buried any belongings, they dig them up as well and trade them for moonshine. Then, in a state of inebriation, the Red Army people simply steal. All this is done in order to acquire *samogonka* or after drinking it. Huge orgies take place in the areas along the front. According to the account of one of the lieutenants who were there to confiscate horses, he says that he has fought in the war in 1918 and even then did not come across such human despair any other time or place in his life. Typhus is making an appearance there, but all the doctors are still taken by the army.[16]

The postwar accounts by government officials being sent out into the countryside reveal the scale of destruction. "In the Maków and Pułtusk Districts, the landscape often resembles a prairie: the fields are covered with grasses, there are no houses, only scrappy sheds here and there, and in the places where villages used to be, instead of houses are hovels with people living in them." The number of people requiring emergency food aid in this part of Poland was estimated at half a million.[17] About 250,000 to 300,000 people lived in similar conditions in the Sandomierz bridgehead, a wedge encompassing Kielce Province, and those districts of Kielce Province that had been totally wiped out by the many wartime pacifications. There, too, people were living in cellars, shanties, and holes they had dug, without food or livestock.[18] In August 1945, "these districts' catastrophic economic situation did not improve at all after this year's harvest. The slim outcomes of the harvest due to a plague of mice unprecedented in years and the cattle drive did not finish off the specter of hunger. The people continue to live like cavemen, which insults human dignity. Walking skeletons in rags, covered with lice, dirty, insufficiently fed, completely dulled to any sociopolitical events, receptive to reactionary whispers, they are susceptible to stormy speeches and demonstrations, to desperate reactions which a hungry mob is capable of at times of total despair."[19]

In the spring and summer of 1945, the nonagricultural population of Kielce Province was unable to use its food ration cards to buy not only meat or fats (pork fat, lard, or butter) but even flour and kasha. In some towns in the province, for two months there was no bread to be had with the cards.[20] In nearby Radom in May, a category I card, which only a few were entitled to, gave 1 kg of wheat flour, 0.75 kg of millet, and 0.25 kg of sugar.[21] The urban population across Poland faced similar problems with necessities. The rural population's food supplies varied by region, with Lublin, for instance, being better off than Kielce. In 1948, a peasant memoirist from a village in Kielce Province noted that people would eat a chicken only on important occasions and, he stressed, only if it died by itself because it would be a "loss and a sin" to kill a healthy one.[22]

In Pomerania, which lay in the way of the Soviet armies as they broke through the Pomeranian Wall, Warmia and Masuria, Upper Silesia, and the Opole region, where the front stopped for three months in

The Three Horsemen of the Apocalypse

January 1945, the situation was equally dramatic. At preharvest, endemic hunger appeared everywhere in northern, western, and southwestern Poland, including the cities of Szczecin, Gdańsk, Elbląg, Katowice, Gliwice, and Olsztyn. In November, in Olsztyn District alone, five thousand people lined up to receive food assistance.[23] In the Masuria region, a Provincial Committee for Winter Help was created to collect food and drugs.

In the spring of 1945, Silesia was ruled by the Red Army and by hunger. Some towns had enough supplies to last a few days while in others thieves had stripped warehouses. The situation must have been truly hopeless in March 1945 in Upper Silesia-Dąbrowa Basin Province for its governor, General Aleksander Zawadzki, to appeal: "Not a single Polish family should go without a communal garden or a small field."[24] This was not a new idea, as the action to start communal gardens had been promoted in the General Government during the war. After military operations were over, local authorities across Poland called for the communal gardens campaign to restart, seeing it as a wonderful way to mitigate want and hunger for workers' families.

Some private letters intercepted by the Office of Wartime Censorship illustrate the dramatic situation and the scale of suffering in Silesia. They reported hunger:

From Katowice on February 20, 1945: "We've had hunger here for nearly 4 weeks, and we've been given nothing yet. The clever ones stole and have enough to eat, and those who didn't are going hungry."

From Siemianowice Śląskie, February 19:

As long as I live, I have not been this hungry and, I don't know, if the Lord doesn't help us, we will perish. We have the [ration] cards, but the shops are locked and there is nothing to be had, those who have anything save it for themselves. I haven't the connections to help me, and my little son doesn't have the strength to walk, and I could eat a horse. We haven't had any potatoes in two weeks. I got a bit of flour and farina, so we ate it because there was no bread and no potatoes.[25]

From January to March in the Silesian towns along the front line, all trade and deliveries stopped. First, shops, bakeries, and butcheries stopped operating, and when they were reopened, it was the Soviet military authorities who operated them. A woman from Gliwice recalled the shortages of February 1945: "To get a bit of food since we were hungry, my mom would go to the school at Hindenburgstr. where there was a Soviet hospital, and she would collect all sorts of waste and peelings that had been thrown out by the kitchen. She once found a large cow bone, and we made broth out of it. Because the bakeries weren't open, we would go to a burned mill where there was a lot of spilled grain. We collected it and ground it in a coffee mill. Mommy baked bread from this flour."[26]

In the preharvest, people also experienced hunger in other places, including Łódź Province, and even more so in Rzeszów Province. Things were not much better in Skierniewice, as can be seen from a letter written in February 1945: "There is terrible hunger here in Skierniewice, there is no bread whatsoever, they don't exchange money, there is literally destitution."

And in Włocławek, a letter dated February 28, 1945: "Food is the worst problem. There are no deliveries, there are no shops, money is in short supply, and even if you have it there is nothing to buy. Trade is non-existent, people are going hungry. Some people have put away a bit, some go to the countryside and grab what they can, but in general the situation is hopeless."[27]

We do not know how many people suffered from hunger then. Using incomplete data, we can estimate that there were at least 2.5 million people needing food assistance in 1945–46 (not counting the German population) (see table 12.2).

The food shortages were brought on not only by the loss of cattle and the destruction of crop and food warehouses in military operations. In the first half of 1945, in many places on the left bank of the Vistula, there was no comprehensive system of supplying food and necessities. The currency exchange of 1944–45 meant that shops and food enterprises (such as bakeries, butcheries, or cakeshops) were not operating. A

Table 12.2 Number of people needing emergency food assistance by province

Province	Number of people needing assistance
Białystok	220,000
Kielce	300,000
Cracow	120,000
Lublin	550,000
Rzeszów	450,000
Warsaw (excluding the city of Warsaw)	500,000

Note: There are no data for the other provinces. Numbers are rounded to the nearest thousand.

man from Krotoszyn wrote on March 1, 1945, "Everything has died down in the town, there is no normal trade, there is no money, only bartering. There is a huge shortage of matches and cigarettes. Prices haven't been set yet."[28]

Until the front approached Berlin in April 1945, military quartermasters governed most of the food trade, and they were often unwilling to share their stores with civilians. The supplies of food also depended on the scale of the theft by the Red Army, which had made Szczecin and Elbląg Provinces into granaries for its troops stationed in Western Pomerania and in Malbork and Königsberg.[29] Already during the battle for *Festung Posen*, the army requisitioned most food warehouses. Theft, with which people compensated for the food shortages, had an enormous impact on the supplies in Elbląg and Masuria and in other parts of the Regained Territories. The scale of the threat of hunger also depended on distance to a food distribution center, which would explain the shortages in Szczecin and Białystok.[30] Piotr Zaremba, mayor of Szczecin, wrote in his diary in July 1945, "There is nothing to eat. . . . Thrashing about with no end in sight, for what good are the promised 600 tons of flour when there is not a single kilo in the warehouse?"[31]

The inhabitants of some of the larger cities were in a marginally better situation than those living in hard-to-reach places where the roads had been destroyed and no transportation existed. Thus, in Warsaw and Łódź, rationed bread was handed out more often than elsewhere, and more kinds of food were available, albeit at higher prices. But this rule did not apply to, for example, Poznań, where the situation in March 1945 was "outright catastrophic,"[32] or in Kalisz, from where someone wrote that "there is an awful situation in terms of the availability of food. God forbid this lasts a long time, this hunger and indigence, but we always hope that it won't last too long."[33]

The situation in many towns in central and southern Poland was similar. Things were a little bit better in Lublin Province, but not enough to stop the Provincial National Council in May 1945 from issuing a ban on transporting food to neighboring provinces. In Greater Poland, a ban on "exporting" food was also in force. The residents of mountain districts, such as Nowy Sącz, Limanowa, Nowy Targ, and Żywiec, suffered from undernourishment because of a combination of the destroyed road infrastructure and unavailability of transportation. On the other hand, people living in towns along travel routes had to feed the incessant stream of military units and hordes of migrants passing through, whether they liked it or not. The dynamism of gangs of robbers and the scale of the civil war affected shortages of food available for sale and its prices in areas including Białystok, Lublin, and Rzeszów Provinces.

Not everyone experienced the same hunger, of course. Those who did not move around much and were not enterprising or did not have family support, such as older people, single women with children, and people whose houses had burned down or who had been resettled, were in the worst situation. Former concentration camp inmates, who were chronically hungry, were a separate category. In the spring of 1945, it also happened that even healthy young recruits complained about being hungry. They wrote letters home:

From Łódź, May 17, 1945: "We don't have our uniforms yet, everything is in chaos, life is lousy, you could croak, breakfast is water with a touch of color, lunch is a splash of soup, everything is even worse than in the volunteer youth work brigades. I don't know how to survive, there isn't even bread, and now the real hunger will come."[34]

From Warsaw, May 20, 1945: "Life is very pathetic, so how do you survive, what poverty, hunger and inflation, typhus is king and the boys are dying. If there is anyone from home or a friend, tell them to send bread and money. We're in Warsaw, precise address: Fifth Company, First Battalion, Twelfth Regiment, Second Platoon."[35]

A clerical worker with the Regional Management of State Railroads also went around hungry in Warsaw. On March 19, 1945, he wrote in a letter, "I am hungry so much of the time! I eat a little soup at work (it's almost all water), then I buy soup at the market for 20 zlotys, I can't live on this, but I can't afford more, things are so expensive, what insane prices."[36]

Our map of hunger does not necessarily overlap with the map of the fear of hunger. Fear is a projection of future threats. But when something that once scared us persists, our fear of it diminishes, and we get used to it. Things were similar in the spring of 1945, all the more so since those who had lived in the General Government had more than five years to get used to living on an empty stomach. Thus, those who suffered from lengthy undernourishment probably feared hunger less. But what terrified people the most was death from starvation.

Fear of death by starvation appears only in private correspondence. Because of high child mortality, parents felt it the most. In the families of repatriates, infant mortality went up to 40 to 50 percent, when the national average was 20 to 25 percent, or about 100,000 deaths per year.[37] It allegedly even approached 90 percent in some villages near Kielce.[38] In Bydgoszcz, from February 5 to July 25, 554 children under the age of two died, the highest mortality ever recorded there. Between February 1 and July 15, 1,097 babies were born, and half of them died. "It is enough to look at the children the mothers bring to the [Mother and Child] Center. They are little skeletons," wrote the daily *Ziemia Pomorska*.[39]

The causes of such high mortality rates were the horrific, at times tragic, unsanitary conditions in which they were born, in transports of repatriates, train stations, clinics, and hospitals. "The epitome of misery and despair" is how staff and patients described the state of hospitals and assistance centers in the spring and summer of 1945. Letters were intercepted by the War Censorship Office:

From Gdynia, April 29, 1945: "Working conditions in the hospital are tough, there aren't enough drugs and bandages. Equipment has been destroyed, epidemics loom. There are shortages of food. They feed us just enough to keep us from starving to death."

Warsaw, May 5, 1945: "There is an insane absence of organization, a mess, shortages of the simplest of things: linens, diapers, clothing; the children are in rags, and on top of it all the director, Dr. Kokoszko, is absolutely abominable. . . . In Warsaw the situation is the same in all such institutions. The clinic at 7 Targowa Street is so horrendous that I had to turn around and run away as soon as I stepped over the threshold."

Busko-Zdrój, April 12, 1945: "I work in a hospital, I have lots of work, the conditions are difficult because there aren't enough drugs or sheets for the patients. It's all unimaginably pitiful."

Kielce, April 12, 1945: "I want you to know that in our shelter people are dying of hunger because there are no fats and no milk, only soup with salt, there's only black salt, and coffee without sugar."[40]

Now the birthweights of children born in hospitals were 30 percent below prewar levels, and the mothers' frailty from undernourishment also played a role in infant mortality.[41] A horrified mother wrote on March 2, 1945: "In our Kalisz region, children are sick a lot and many die because hunger is staring into their eyes, for example for 7 weeks now we've had no fats, we only got 1 kg of bread per person. . . . I'm terrified to look at my emaciated children."[42]

Kraśnik, April 28, 1945: "We are dirt-poor and hungry, the children and I have been going hungry for entire days, we don't even have a piece of bread. Lord, take pity on me because we will die of hunger."[43]

The fear of starvation reached a high point in the early summer of 1945. It stood out on the map of Polish apprehensions and worries not only because of the objective situation with supplies. The memories of hunger from the First World War and the time after may have reinforced this sense of peril. But its roots went much deeper, into the peasant culture, where fear of hunger, of the forces of nature, is a component of the culture of fatalism.[44] According to numerous prophecies, hunger would come in the spring of 1945. Hugo Steinhaus, who was living in southern Poland at that time, predicted, "There is no way that we will come out of this chaos anytime soon! There is no money, there is no transportation, there are no supplies, there is no flour and no fats, and it looks like in the spring there will be horrendous food shortages."[45] Fear of hunger was a major force in the Poles' emotional space and an important topic in private correspondence, which Wartime Censorship scrupulously recorded.[46]

We do not know how many people starved to death. There were not enough doctors to go around. With dead bodies everywhere, the fledgling administration was preoccupied with more burning matters than keeping death statistics. But in the spring of 1945, the number of deaths surpassed the number of births.[47] In the second half of 1945, the mortality coefficient in big cities remained one and a half to two times higher than before the war.[48] The only available estimates put the number of deaths nationally at 30 percent higher than births.[49] Private letters frequently conveyed assertions such as "many people die here because, as you know, many people are desperately poor." In a single village in Opatów District in the preharvest, by April 30, 1945, 180 people were said to have died "of exhaustion and disease."[50] Funeral processions, sometimes of thousands of people, were a major feature in the landscape of that era. People exhumed the bodies of those who had been murdered during the occupation and fighters in the Warsaw Uprising and collected corpses on battlefields. The new dead were joining the old dead. While fallen militia, soldiers, and Security Service functionaries were buried in state-church ceremonies, those who had starved to death were usually interred on the sly. Extreme malnutrition flung doors open to epidemics. In the words of Maria Zientara-Malewska, a poet, teacher, and local activist in Warmia, who was living in Olsztyn then, "Typhus has spread dreadfully. Every day several people died. I often passed Sisters of Saint Catherine in the streets, taking the dead to the cemetery on handcarts. They were buried without coffins, placed in their graves on planks, Franciscan fathers would sprinkle holy water on them and say a prayer, and friends and relatives covered the graves with soil."[51]

In the summer of 1945, food supplies improved markedly. For example in Olsztyn, "you could buy anything you wanted. The stalls were full of bread, rolls, meat and pork fat, fruit and vegetables."[52] Private cafés, bars, and restaurants were opening everywhere. But because of their high prices, like the high prices of what was being sold in the shops, they remained beyond the reach of large numbers of Poles. At the same time, in August 1945 in Olsztyn, food vouchers could not be traded in for anything, as sugar, salt, meat, potatoes, clothing, and shoes were in short supply.[53] The situation in central Poland was similar: food was available, but at very high prices, and the vouchers would not bring their price down. As a result, the frustration and feeling of material deprivation of millions of people grew. *Dziennik Powszechny*, a paper published in Kielce and Radom, allowed its readers to read between the lines: "Everyone always said that the preharvest would be critical, that there might not be enough of this and that—but only for a time, was added to calm people down. Still, the working people, most of whom have no food or cash stored up, are watching the situation on the 'supplies front' with worry. There is the fact: the card rations have shrunk a lot recently, and in July we got almost nothing. Who knows how things will be in August and later, better or worse? If, like everyone expects, better, then when, finally? And what's with that UNRRA?"[54] That summer, people would say: what's with that UNRRA?

Historians have not yet devised methods to measure levels of collective fear. They must rely on scattered information, which seldom allows them to construct a cohesive image of the public's emotions. But it seems that if we did have such a measuring tool, in the spring of 1945 its arrow would have remained in the red field, the fear of hunger, and by the summer, for all the continuing shortages, it would have moved to the field of "hopes and expectations." People were still miserable

The Three Horsemen of the Apocalypse

and hungry, but the war had ended and the harvest was beginning, and so hopes that living conditions would improve grew as pantries were being at least partly restocked. On the other hand, the gap between society's expectations and their satisfaction sustained bad, if not outright rebellious, public moods. They worsened dramatically in October 1945, and the arrow again moved into the red field. The growing collective insecurity then and in the following months stemmed less from fear of the approaching winter than from the drastic price rises (more about this later) and the collapse of the distribution system of food ration cards. The public mood must have been very low and the level of collective fear and anxiety high, since virtually all the newspapers, which would ordinarily attempt to quash critical voices, ran alarmist articles.

Thus, on October 18, 1945, the Radom-Kielce daily *Dziennik Powszechny* informed its readers in an article titled "Why Is There No Bread in Radom?" that "the people of Radom are extremely concerned that there is no bread in our town. Even though ration-card bread has not been available for some time, more expensive bread was available without cards. But suddenly, that bread is gone, too."

A day later, the daily titled an article "Preharvest in October": "People in Poland are familiar with preharvest. Especially in central Poland and farther east. . . . This year, the first year after the war, Radom is experiencing 'preharvest' in . . . October. There is no bread. Not only to be had for September ration cards, but even without cards, illegally. The mills in Radom have no grain, the bakeries have no flour, and so bakery shelves are bare. You can find a loaf of white bread early in the morning here and there, but at slightly higher prices."

A women's bread riot took place in October in Płock as a reaction to the bread shortages. The newspaper *Jedność* reported on October 24, in an article titled "Magic with Rationed Bread": "Last Saturday everyone knew that the rationed bread is gone. There was a great uproar because not everyone can afford to buy white bread, whose price actually immediately went up. Some energetic Płock womenfolk went straight to the mayor. The mayor allegedly set his office work aside and joined these womenfolk on a tour of bakeries."

Szczecin, too, ran out of bread, even with prices rising tens of percent. *Kurier Szczeciński* reported on October 19, "In the last few days, we have observed an—inexplicably—abrupt rise in the price of white bread. A kilo loaf of white bread, which until recently cost 20 zlotys, today costs 30 zlotys, and the bakers are expecting another price increase."

The next wave of the fear of hunger arrived in the winter and during preharvest of 1946.[55] Polish papers bombarded their readers almost daily with news about the specter of hunger looming over Europe and Asia, which must have fed the fear of hunger in Poland itself, as the specter was not imported but grew out of the local supply situation.

In December 1945, the governor of Gdańsk Province pleaded for emergency food aid because "the population is in danger of going hungry."[56]

The shortages were similar in central Poland, in the Świętokrzyskie Mountain region as well as in the south, especially in areas of armed conflicts with the Ukrainian underground. In February 1946, the Provincial Committee of Social Assistance in Rzeszów reported, "The preharvest crisis is becoming severe, food rations have been reduced so drastically that this month even those who work and receive ration cards of the first category obtained no bread. The very high prices everywhere in the province rise daily, so that destitution and hunger are knocking on poor people's doors."[57]

Hunger ruled in Warmia and Masuria, areas being relentlessly plundered by Soviet soldiers and Polish bandits. Their populations often could not go outside to search for food because their shoes had been stolen. In March 1946, a reporter for *Ziemia Pomorska* saw people in Jonkowo whose bodies were bloated from hunger. There were eighteen cases of death by starvation in the village of Bartołty Wielkie.[58] In Königsberg, which was occupied by the Red Army, cases of cannibalism were reported, and the bodies of children who had died were eaten.[59] In Poland, too, for instance in Gniezno in February 1946, after a pause of a few months, stories began to make the rounds about children being abducted "to make sausage." The people of Kielce also succumbed to such talk, and an anti-Jewish pogrom took place there in July 1946 (see chap. 13). The connection between these stories and the omnipresent hunger is obvious.

The population of the bridgehead areas in Kielce region experienced a second harsh winter in a row. Thousands of people continued to live in provisional dugouts. "I managed to reach one of them by wading through a sea of mud," wrote a Życia Warszawy reporter in his piece on "The peasants are coming above ground."

> A wasted woman is breathing heavily as she lies on a pile of straw in a narrow and dark ditch. A boy who doesn't look any better is scratching his puny shoulders, another one is collecting the water that incessantly trickles down the wet walls into a corner. A cow takes up the rest of the space. But since there is no room for it to turn around, I don't know how it can go outside. All winter long they ate nothing but frozen potatoes. In the spring they sowed the seed they had carefully saved up in the fields. But because large areas were mined and therefore could not be plowed, the seed went to waste. At most 80 kg could be harvested from every square meter, the mice ate the rest. Then a disease struck the potatoes. They went hungry a second winter in a row.[60]

The "operation to help the starved population" of Kielce Province launched in late 1945–early 1946 helped 180,000 people. Children were temporarily moved from these districts to towns that were better supplied.[61] But the project was only partly successful since parents did not want to let their children go.

We know from both accounts from the countryside of that era, as well as today's reports about starving populations in Africa, that children are the first victims of undernourishment. First in line to be given the limited food are male manual workers. The appearance of underfed children predicts looming trouble. In Piaseczno, near Warsaw, 60 percent of children had nothing to eat but potatoes, and so nearly all of them were anemic. In some families, children were reportedly fed "nothing but potato peels"—just like during the war.[62] In a soup kitchen on Betonowa Street in Lublin,

> apart from the children, you can see older people in worn-out, tattered clothing, with emaciated faces. "This is supposed to be a center for feeding children, do adults get soup, too?" we ask the manager. "No, these are parents who have come with plates to fill with lunch, since their children could not come themselves as they have no shoes or are sick," she answers. "And how many children do you feed?" "About three hundred. We used to give them bread with their soup every day, but now with the flour shortages, we can only give them one slice every few days," said the manager.[63]

The government was also afraid of hunger. In February 1946, it introduced restrictions on meat sales. Meat was not to be served in cafeterias and restaurants or sold anywhere on Tuesdays through Thursdays. Because of the shortage of wheat flour, the government also introduced "cake-free" days. Appeals reappeared: "Community gardeners! Do not neglect your gardens. Everyone should join the battle against the supply crisis." They urged people to keep rabbits: "With the spring approaching, and it will be difficult in terms of problems with food, people should think about keeping rabbits."[64]

The Cracow magazine *Przekrój* ran a cartoon conveying the mood of the era. A servant says to Queen Marie Antoinette, "Your Majesty! The people are rebelling because they have no bread!" Marie Antoinette: "So why aren't they eating cakes?" The servant: "But, Your Majesty, today is a cake-free day!"[65]

In April 1946, the mayor of Częstochowa argued that the critical supply situation and rising food prices in the free market were making public morale deteriorate.[66] In the "hunger" regions near Kielce and Kozienice, UNRRA staff interpreted the phenomenon of children carrying cooking pots as evidence that schools were providing meals and also reported about people on the verge of the hunger disease with their characteristic pasty complexions and puffed-up faces.[67] Things were similar near Jasło. In July 1946, the starost estimated that food assistance reaching the district did not meet its needs. He wrote:

> This assistance, albeit absolutely efficient, has eased the misery of the malnourished minimally and enabled them not to live, but to vegetate. It is enough to look at our charges, who come to the Social Assistance center in order to share their sorrows, with their yellowed sunken cheeks, stooped, barefoot, in rags. The children resemble wax dolls, and their mortality is high. Everyone in the neverending line of suppliants asks for at least a few zlotys for bread, fats or milk. Hunger stares out of their faces, their eyes beg for a crumb. Many families have no clothes, no shoes, some have a single pair per family. There are 62,000 people who are totally wasted, hungry and without clothes, having been expelled from their villages and towns. About 10,000 charges must be added to this figure, those from the communes who have not been expelled, those who, whether their houses burned down or who lost their only breadwinners as a result of military operations or those who are old and ailing, are extremely impoverished.[68]

In terms of meeting the population's food needs, 1946 was a year in which the situation at the "supplies front" improved. Consumption in the countryside went up to 2,232 calories per person per day and slightly increased in the towns and cities to 2,059 calories per person per day.[69] UNRRA transports were arriving more regularly. US food rations, whether orange juice, a can of condensed milk, or a chocolate bar, could be found in the pantry of nearly every Polish home. The situation in remote areas, such as Szczecin, improved thanks to upgraded transportation and a reduced threat of bandits. The numbers of kitchens and cafeterias, run by organizations such as Caritas, the Ministry of Labor and Social Welfare, or the Ministry of Work and Social Welfare or the State Repatriation Office, grew. In the Regained Territories reportedly 30 to 40 percent of the population took advantage of them while 12 to 14 percent received food packages and monetary assistance, and 20 percent clothing.[70] Increased agricultural production was the crucial factor in improving the supplies situation. Still, it came nowhere near meeting the food needs, which is clear from the low per capita consumption in 1946. For protein it was 55.7 percent of the 1938 figure, for fats 58 percent, and for carbohydrates 55.9 percent.[71] Nationally, hunger was reduced, but islands of persistent hunger survived.

Riding a tram in Łódź, Cracow, or Warsaw, anyone could see winding queues everywhere. People queued for everything: rationed bread, UNRRA products, cigarettes sold in a kiosk by an invalid or, clothing ration cards in hand, outside clothes shops. "That's the street. But let's go into a government office, train station, post office or any box office, and there, too, we will see long, winding lines."[72] A *Sztandar Ludu* reporter confessed about her life in queues in July 1946: "I spent two hours in line in one shop, to get juice. In the meantime, I reserved a place in a different line, to a canned-food shop. I lost that place, I waited two more hours. Sweets and cocoa were luckily sold together, so they cost me two hours instead of four. No one said anything when I got back to the office, since everyone regularly stood in lines in various shops."[73]

In the second half of 1946, as it became clear that the drought would diminish the harvest, people began to worry more about food supplies. The rumors about increased food prices that began in the autumn were quickly confirmed by reality. "In Włocławek they are predicting a hunger disaster, which we can already see in the price rise."[74] The announced suspension of UNRRA assistance also amplified concerns. "After the UNRRA deliveries are suspended, terrible hunger will descend on Poland, and the Government of National Unity will not be able to rise to the challenge of feeding the whole population."[75] People associated the arrival of the "horrible hunger" to the alleged exports of food to the Soviet Union[76] as well as to the Communists' electoral victory.[77] In many rural areas in various regions, a mouse plague made the anxiety worse, something that appears prominently in peasant memoirs. One of these memoirists wrote, "The huge numbers of mice was the second disaster. They have devoured wheat, rape, clover, they have shredded the cereals in the barns and, to top it all, some disease has killed off the cats."[78]

After the harsh winter and flooding, there was another drought in 1947, which in some areas destroyed more than half of the harvest. The deteriorating situation with supplies again heightened social anxiety, maybe even fear. Already in the spring, there were rumors of price increases,[79] and they did indeed happen. There were more shortages. According to the provincial governor of Łódź, "The supplies situation is worse than in March. In many cases, people could not obtain bread with their cards, even with the small bread allowances, and hunger came to many workers' families. These families' earnings were extremely low compared to the free-market prices."[80] As was the tradition, the government introduced limitations on restaurants to begin on March 15: at most one piece of bread and 10 g of butter could accompany a main course.[81] Following the same scenario as with every previous instance of price rises, the newspapers launched a witch hunt with the motto "catch a swindler!" This time, however, the authorities announced a great "battle over commerce," which is commonly interpreted as the next key stage in implementing the Soviet economic model. But the hatchet to be used against independent merchants, shopkeepers, and wholesalers was dug up not only because of the nature of this regime. It was also worried that the dissatisfied public would rebel and wanted to shift the blame for the inflated prices onto "swindlers and profiteers." Beginning in the second half of 1946, the people of nearby Ukraine suffered widespread hunger, which by 1947 became a catastrophe. An estimated million to a million and a half people died there.[82] There is no way the Polish authorities did not know about what was going on in the "victorious workers' and peasants' republic" next door. Indeed, because of the grain crisis, hunger was being prophesied around the world.[83] Informing the public about the arrival of every ship loaded with grain probably aimed to reduce inflationary pressures and to calm people down; the fact that these were Soviet ships was beside the point.[84] The transports of people being resettled from the Eastern Borderlands also influenced the up-and-down moods. Their stories about hunger in the USSR also brought fear,[85] and their destitute appearance alone could strengthen the impression that hunger really was just around the corner. The surviving underground movement fed the anxieties.

Positive change arrived only in 1948, following a harvest that turned out to be exceptionally good. But then came the next source of fear: collectivization.

THE HIGH PRICES ARE FEARSOME

After the war, the words *high prices* were magical. They smacked of a curse but at the same time confirmed reality and expressed people's emotional take on that reality. The Płock newspaper *Jedność* admonished its readers in August 1945, "Widespread complaining about high prices has turned into a regular habit. This horrible term is now the right answer to the customary question 'How are things?' High prices are a conversation topic in drawing rooms, streets and markets, magical words that make those female citizens who 'run households' and who are responsible for kitchens and 'making ends meet' with 800 zlotys per month, which is the salary of the head of the household, spend many sleepless nights. No wonder then that one hears more or less justified complaints and grumbling among the working masses."[86]

There is no question that the public sense of security was shaped by high prices, which can be defined as the difference between free-market prices and average wages, and by inflation, defined as rising prices. All kinds of reports coming in from the provinces to the capital in this period repeat complaints about high prices like a mantra. Beginning in the summer of 1945, the public tended to believe that the problem was not the actual shortages of food in the shops but their prices, which made it impossible for people to buy. People earning an average salary (around 1,000 zlotys) were able to buy very little. Right after the war, employees either received no salary or were paid in kind with flour, potatoes, and other groceries. As late as mid-1946, payments in kind made up 40 to 50 percent of wages.[87] People constantly complained about high prices, also in letters read by the Office of Wartime Censorship:

From Warsaw in February 1945: "Sky-high prices are widespread here because huge numbers of people have descended on us, and food deliveries are difficult. This is why conditions are harsh because we are both destroyed and there is no money."[88]

On March 17, 1945: "If the Lord [doesn't] take pity on us, I don't know how long we'll last. High prices, no regulations to get rid of them, what they give us for our ration cards is absolutely not enough."

On March 24, 1945: "The food situation is bad, because of the high prices. Everything you could dream of is available, but it's expensive because people aren't making money. My work isn't going well even though I work in the city hall, so I get 24 zlotys a day, and one kg of black bread costs 25 zlotys, and forget about pork fat because it now costs 350 zlotys a kg."[89]

From Kielce in March 1945: "I'm annoyed with myself because I thought that there would be some rations because bread is hardest to get, but the trash doesn't have it, and these 500 zlotys per week aren't enough, let alone a month. Here, pork fat costs 400 zlotys, butter 500 zlotys, eggs are 7 zlotys each, milk 30 zlotys, white bread 85, black bread 60 zlotys, and how can you live like that, staring at all kinds of delicacies, hams etc. in shop windows."[90]

From Radom in April 1945: "Living conditions are very harsh here, enormously high prices, 1 kg pork fat for 400 zlotys, butter for 380 zlotys, eggs for 9 zlotys, 1 kg of meat for 120 zlotys, flour for 90 zlotys, 1 kg of bread for 40 zlotys, milk for 25 zlotys, the prices are horrific and people don't earn anything because they are working for free. My sister has no income since the army takes what they produce and there is nothing left for the civilian population."

From Lublin on April 5, 1945: "Imagine, nowadays with such wild high prices they paid us 100 zlotys each. It is laughable that after working all month long 12 hours a day, you get enough to buy a toothbrush or a bread roll, which will last 3–4 days, probably no more."[91]

This dissatisfaction with the high prices was most often voiced by workers in state enterprises, civil servants and functionaries of services such as the militia. A railroad worker's daughter from Radom wrote in April 1945, "But this is nothing compared to the high prices during the war, where all prices rose on average a hundred or even 300 times, and Daddy's earnings on the railroad are the same, or even lower than before the war."[92]

The skimpy earnings and the failure to pay salaries on time added up to a major source of frustration, at times compelling people to seek alternative sources of income. Settlers who arrived after harvest were in an exceptionally difficult situation. Most brought no household effects or food supplies with them. Settlers from the east, who often had no possessions other than the clothes on their backs, were especially poverty-stricken.

According to studies conducted by the Institute of National Economy, prices began to decrease gradually in the spring of 1945; for instance, in Warsaw over five months, the drop was 27.5 percent.[93] But food became more expensive again in the autumn, and in Warsaw bread rose by 15 percent and dairy products by 13 percent. If we take their April 1945 level as 100, the overall indicator of retail prices (calculated as an average of fourteen cities in all the provinces on the basis of free-market prices of thirteen products) in May 1946 reached 128.5, and in June 120.3.[94] On the eve of the June 1946 referendum, prices dropped a little (by 2.5 percent).[95] They rose significantly in September and October 1946 and stopped in December. Rent, urban transportation, and natural gas went up again in the spring of 1947. In October, the price index in Warsaw reached 152.5.

Yet these figures tell us nothing about the universal, very powerful postwar fear of inflation. The Poles had much to be afraid of. Middle-aged and older people could remember the hyperinflation of the early '20s, and everyone else remembered the wartime price increases of basic foods that reached hundreds of percent. But one did not need to remember the previous increases to worry about an uncontrollable repetition. People felt the market instability, did not trust the new government, and took the most minor sign as an alert about inflation. *Dziennik Powszechny* reported on this postwar nervousness in its coverage of Radom in October 1945:

> As we know, the temporary shortage of bread in Radom, which was brought on by certain transportation difficulties, with the concurrent rise of the prices of pork fat caused by the temporary rise in the price of livestock associated with it being bought up by the west, caused a general price rise in Radom, as well as alarm and panic. This tendency to be alarmed and panicked, which we observed last week must be explained by the fact that this society, exhausted by its wartime experiences, has not yet regained its full equilibrium; nonetheless, we must prevent such a mood from appearing. The public itself must, first of all, understand this and not allow itself to be gripped by mindless panic, since when one looks at it logically it is impossible for bread to be exhausted immediately after the harvest, and at a time when there is no shortage of swine in the countryside for the cities to be deprived of fat.[96]

But at the same time as it was asking people to think rationally, the press was adding oil to the fire, worrying people even more as it delighted in reporting every drop on the New York stock market. News in June 1946 about the Hungarian National Bank issuing 10-billion-forint bills may have had a similar effect on the public mood.[97] "The market's customary skittishness," mentioned at the time of the money exchange, manifested itself as constant rumors and market panic. For instance, in May 1946, gossip about a rise in the price of sugar made the rounds in Kielce.[98] Fear of the inflation spiral often appeared in tandem with other doomsday prophecies, such as the coming of a third world war or the return of a million Red Army soldiers. Prices rose each time, with the overall level of anxiety rising simultaneously. In the spring of 1947, the inflation spiral was brought on by the earlier price increase of textiles (10 to 50 percent) and of vodka (30 percent). As a consequence, flour and potatoes became more expensive. In many areas, the emotional climate, strengthened by the preharvest atmosphere, turned into a psychosis of anxiety. In Gdańsk, for example, "there has been a characteristic growth of rumors. There is talk of a new National Tribute, which allegedly is to cover 50 percent of the three-month takings and incomes. There is talk of a currency exchange, about the stamping [of additional zeros onto] bills. People are beginning to get rid of cash, investing in articles. Intensified news about rising tensions between the USA and the Soviet Union. Intensified rumor about the impending ban on listening to foreign radio programs and confiscations of multi-tube radios."[99]

There may have been more than a dozen instances of local price rises and resultant panic in this period, and at least several nationwide ones, some tied to the fear of war and fear of a money exchange. They show that much of the Poles' "psychic space" was taken up by fear of hunger, high prices, and inflation.

THE THIRD HORSEMAN, INFECTIOUS DISEASES

It is difficult to say how much of the "psychic space" was occupied by fear of infectious diseases. People were ill and died quietly, their families knew about it, but little of the information about their moans, pain, and fear became public knowledge. We get some idea from private letters. In the spring of 1945, the people of Warsaw feared a cholera epidemic. A woman living in Hoża Street in Warsaw wrote, "Try to come as soon as you can because I want to take my child away because of the epidemic in Warsaw, and you know how many dead bodies are still lying under the rubble."

A man living in Żelazna Street: "It's getting warmer, and there is an awful smell of corpses, and there are even fears that there will be cholera."[100]

The public was physically and psychologically exhausted, tired out by the war, hungry. A study conducted by the State Hygiene Institute in 1946–47 of 8,749 persons working in Łódź revealed very low levels of hemoglobin in their blood, about 25 percent below a healthy person's, which is determined primarily by nutrition, stress of work, and living conditions.[101]

Lowered resistance led to susceptibility to infectious diseases, with tuberculosis the most dangerous of them.

The Ministry of Health used fragmentary studies to estimate the number of people suffering from tuberculosis at 1,200,000, or 5 percent of the population.[102] In the second half of 1945, reportedly 2,053 people died of tuberculosis in larger towns.[103] But this figure does not reveal the scale of the phenomenon nationally. In Łódź alone in February and March 1945, 274 persons (158 men, 99 women, 17 children) died of it, amounting to 17 percent of all deaths.[104]

The situation in the provinces must have been even worse. In a village on the Toruń-Brodnica route, doctors diagnosed tuberculosis in 96 percent of schoolchildren; 5 percent suffered from scabies, 33 percent pediculosis, and 54 percent early stages of tuberculosis.[105] "According to x-rays," 40 percent of students in a school in Piaseczno near Warsaw were reportedly in danger of contracting tuberculosis.[106] Similar tests in School No. 9 in Kielce revealed that 215 of its 611 pupils had tuberculosis, and 25 of them were contagious. Tuberculosis is a sign of poverty, as it often strikes those deprived of nourishing food who live in unsanitary and crowded conditions.[107] Many students of School No. 9 were also underfed.[108] Tuberculosis was no surprise to the poor, since they were used to living with it cheek by jowl, and yet it is difficult to imagine that news that nearly one-third of the children were in danger of contracting tuberculosis would not have made parents panic.

Typhoid thrives in poverty and poor sanitary conditions. In Poland in the late 1930s, 3,000 to 4,000 people a year contracted it, and around 6 percent of them died of it.[109] According to the Extraordinary Commission for Fighting Epidemics, between January and December 1945 alone, about 100,000 cases of the various types of typhus were recorded. Also, 6,690 people had dysentery, 12,785 scarlet fever, and 21,705 diphtheria, which affected mostly children.[110] These figures are not nationally representative if only because data from Szczecin, Masuria, and Lower Silesia only began to be collected in the third quarter of 1945. The data was usually collected from statistics kept by hospitals, epidemiological offices, and selected doctors. The records of the District Hospital in Ełk show that between September 22 and December 31, 1945, the infectious diseases department took in 118 persons with typhoid fever and typhus, and 10 percent of them died.[111] The problem was that only the insured, who worked for state institutions or the army, and the well-off were able to pay for treatment and could count on a hospital bed. Therefore, the majority of the rural population could not. Germans, who in 1945 were not covered by health insurance, were also not always taken. Hence, the actual number of people infected with typhus must have been at least double.

Concentrations of typhus appeared in virtually all regions of Poland, but the situation was worst in the so-called bridgehead areas, where entire villages became infected. A man from Piórkowo, a village near Opatów in southeastern Poland, recalled, "As I walked down an empty, deserted road in my village, pain gripped my heart. A terrible desolation and horror emanated from everywhere. The neighbors and acquaintances I bumped into looked atrocious. Their bodies were emaciated, their faces skeletal, their eyes vacant. I found four persons sick with typhus lying on the floor in the Jagiełłos' house."[112]

The largest outbreak of the epidemic, 75 percent of those who were infected, was in regions that had previously belonged to the Reich. The people living in these lands, both Poles and Germans, had not had a chance to be immunized during the war, when typhus had been present in the General Government since 1940.[113] According to a doctor in the hospital in Trzebnica, "It was mostly Germans and villagers who had it, many died of it. At those times when the epidemic grew stronger, there was a shortage of hospital beds, and the patients were placed on mattresses in rooms that were converted into isolation rooms and large sick rooms.... Mortality was as high as 10 percent, and the dead were buried in sacks in the monastery's orchard, and when they ran out of planks, they were buried in mass graves in canvas or paper sacks."[114]

The large town of Słupsk also experienced the epidemic. In the spring of 1946, it had a population of 36,421, of whom 18,793 were Germans (3,102 men, 9,913 women, 6,778 children). The two types of typhus fever attacked the town in the spring but peaked in the autumn of 1945. It moved from one neighborhood to the next, infecting as many as 400 people a day. The situation in the hospitals resembled Trzebnica. Between April 12 and December 28, 1945, there were 2,068 Germans who succumbed to it.[115] Because several Red Army units were stationed in the town, large numbers of women had syphilis. "It's like Mexico!" a *Ziemia Pomorska* reporter concluded his article about Słupsk. "I've never come across such devastation in the sphere of health."[116]

Gdańsk and its outskirts also suffered from an epidemic. There are some indications that it was spread by former prisoners of the Stutthof concentration camp, and that the German population was most seriously affected by it.[117] The main cause were the catastrophic living conditions, according to Mayor Franciszek Kotus-Jankowski: "The population is about 130,000. The insufficient provisions meant that there is hunger in the town.... Because of the flight of German men, the German population consists mostly of women, old people and children.... Mortality is rising despite medical care and procedures. In some houses in the center of town the mortality is 6 people per week."[118] Jails, prisons, and labor camps experienced the highest mortality rates, up to tens of percent. In the Kurkowa Street prison in Gdańsk, about 1,100 prisoners died, mostly Germans. Over a thousand people died of it in the labor camp in Świętochłowice near Chorzów.[119] In the camps in Śląsk Opolski, deaths brought on by epidemics reached about 70 to 80 percent of all deaths. A witness who saw the camp in Łambinowice testified many years later, "On the grounds of the camp, in the back, there was a cemetery, in my opinion, quite large if you take into account the number of people in the camp. I saw one grave, with several corpses in it covered with a thin layer of soil, from under which you could see body parts."[120]

The Szczecin city authorities tightened sanitation checks in train stations and issued regulations about the sweeping of streets, staircases, and cellars to prevent the spread of typhus.[121] Despite this, in 1945 nearly seven thousand people died there, most of them probably of typhus.[122]

A German man wrote on July 31, 1945, "Thousands of people stand in line all day long to buy bread, some go home crying. People are dropping like flies. Women give birth to 1.5-pound babies, people are dying in massive numbers."

Another German correspondent wrote on August 18, 1945, "So many people die of typhus every day here that they cannot be buried in time."[123]

Some districts (e.g., Jarocin, Gostyń) set up quarantines, and in Elbląg there was an "outright" order to vaccinate anyone coming to town.[124] Special cemeteries were marked out for those who had died of the epidemic. The numbers of the dead can only be estimated, as those who died in rural areas in 1945 and those who died in resettlement transports were often not taken into account in any statistics. In Lesko alone (Rzeszów Province) in the course of six days in May 1945, reportedly 271 people fell ill with typhus, and 111 of them died.[125] It is unlikely that the cemetery or hospital management recorded all the deaths or causes of death among the Germans. According to 1945 official data, 6,758 people died of typhus, 644 of dysentery, and 1,464 of diphtheria.[126] Assuming that the number of people infected with typhus in 1945 really did top 200,000, with 10 percent mortality, the figure of 20,000 dead does not seem exaggerated.

In 1946, the official figure for typhus deaths was 2,641.[127] The drop can be attributed to the Ministry of Health's vaccination campaign, which in 1945 covered about two million people.[128] In Gdańsk alone, eleven epidemic centers were opened, where the personnel identified infected people, transported them to hospitals, and disinfected their homes and clothing.[129] According to a doctor working then for the Extraordinary Commission to Combat Epidemics, "Time pressed on, infectious diseases were turning into an epidemic, and typhus spread by lice was most dangerous. We began to comb through the district. The Medical Department ... checked villages and settlements daily, imposing a rigorous system in cases of louse infestation, of haircutting, pest control and steam disinfection, as well as baths. The arrival of a column of cars and the setting up of baths made an impression. The mostly

German population submitted to the checks without protest."[130] It is difficult to tell whether such columns instilled fear or gave hope. A man who lived in Białystok Province remembered:

> In 1944, immediately after the war, bloody dysentery arrived in our indigence. People were like shadows of themselves because they were forced to work, and only those who were no longer able to get up because they were so ill stayed in bed. Then, in 1945 typhoid fever arrived. There was a shortage of doctors and, on top of it, in this hardship the people were living in barns, in temporary housing, which had been built hurriedly, so for this reason it took its victims, mothers from their children, young boys, etc. I almost became a victim, too, the deathbed candle was already lit. But I recovered, thanks to the Lord's mercy. When I remember those instants, I shiver, I get goosebumps.[131]

The press disseminated the fear of typhus, much like today the media make people afraid of sepsis or swine flu. A local paper in Suwałki instructed its readers:

> The second very important and pertinent issue in this autumnal time is the issue of the spreading epidemic of contagious diseases, especially typhoid fever. Here, all the members of the Village National Councils should serve as controllers of hidden cases of typhoid fever, understanding that a single case of typhoid fever that is concealed will directly infect a whole village or even several villages. Every case of typhoid fever or dysentery should be reported to the district, then be sent to the hospital by the district so as not to spread the contagion. As a consequence of this and in order to prevent an epidemic of typhoid fever, protective vaccinations are being administered in our district. Everyone who understands the importance of this initiative should contribute by enlightening others in order to fight typhus.[132]

In 1945, some 121,000 flyers titled "Beware dysentery," "Vaccinations protect people from contagious diseases" and "What everyone should know about typhoid fever" were printed and distributed. The public was aware of the threat of typhus. Private letters also carried information about the epidemic and fear of it, revealing the drama of postwar life and death:

A letter written on April 25, 1945: "Here in Bydgoszcz there is terrible typhus. It hasn't reached our area yet, maybe the Lord will protect us."

April 4, 1945: "Things are bad here now because of typhus, many people have died."

From the area of Jarocin on May 1, 1945: "Everyone has typhus here, 20 per day are being taken to the hospital, 3 dead a day, they take the old people away, and the children don't survive this thing and die like flies, and some of the young survive and Paweł D.'s little daughter died."[133]

A German from Wrocław wrote on August 14, 1945: "Here, children, adults are dying of hunger and typhus, hundreds every day. You can't get any drugs."

In a letter from Krasnopol of August 16, 1945: "Here people are dying of typhus very much, it's all from hunger and poverty."[134]

In 1945, precisely 1,599 cases of malaria were recorded. Poles who had spent time in Africa during the war may have brought it. In Kielce Province, it was allegedly carried by soldiers of the Afrika Korps who had served along the Mediterranean. "Malaria in Poland," *Rzeczpospolita* reported in September 1946 and appealed to people to watch out for mosquitoes.[135] But this was not Poland's fear number one.

HUNGER BEHAVIORS

The question the historian needs to ask is: was there a connection between the collective fear of hunger, panic over inflation, and widespread death by contagious diseases, and the population's behaviors and convictions at this time? How did the fear manifest itself? Psychologists distinguish two basic reactions: aggression and escape, or fight and flight. Escapism is most obvious in the drive to leave areas threatened by hunger. It is easy to forget that the "internal migration" of the time was dictated not only by the desire to improve one's existence but also by wanting to escape poverty, hunger, and hopelessness. This is why hundreds of thousands of people left their homes in central Poland. It is noteworthy that it was also hunger, especially in Pomerania, that represented a real obstacle, which slowed down the arrival of new settlers or forced those who had already arrived to go back. Someone wrote from Orłowo near Gdynia on April 18, 1945, "Those who came here from Warsaw or Cracow are now fleeing on freight trains because houses are shabby, there are no government offices and there is horrific hunger on top of it, you can't buy anything, for more than 3 weeks they gave us no bread, and other food is out of the question."[136]

Hunger was also a reason why some men deserted from the army, which soldiers' letters confirm: "And if you could, please bring bread because otherwise I'll run away because many Łódź people are running away because of hunger. We were in Majdanek [concentration camp], and you know what it was like there. There are over 100 deserters from our transport already, since hunger forced whomever came with an empty suitcase to do it."[137]

A document about the situation in Kielce Province includes this description: "Walking skeletons covered in rags, lice, dirt, insufficiently fed, completely inured to any social or political norms, who are easily swayed by reactionary whispers—they are susceptible to stormy speeches and demonstrations, desperate reactions that a hungry throng can give in to at times of utter despair."[138] Difficult living conditions (undernourishment, low wages, inability to buy enough with ration cards) generated a growing irritation, frustration, and rage. Mass unrest and disturbances were expected especially in the spring of 1945.[139] The city government in Gliwice noted that "hunger, if it becomes more widespread, may cause unrest and the spread of epidemics."[140]

Fear, frustration, and anger appeared in many different ways: people most often complained to family members (letters) but often also in public during meetings with representatives of the authorities (appointments, rallies). Outside shops and UNRRA distribution centers, it often came to shoving and tumults brought on by hunger. Women dominated most of these protests, just like in the early modern era. In April 1945 at the train station in Śniadowo (near Łomża), the populace tried to plunder warehouses as seed was being handed out for sowing. The crowd threw stones at warehouse employees and the militia.[141] According to a report by the Government Delegate's Office, in May and a June 1945 outside the Military Department of the Municipal National Council in Poznań, "demonstrations by women, military wives and widows," demanding the allowances owed them, took place daily.[142] The much-reduced supplies of products officially available for ration cards brought on a wave of protests in queues all across the country in September 1945. A *Dziennik Ludowy* reporter described the scene in the Warsaw district of Praga when American pork fat and canned food were "dropped": "An unimaginably long line of people holding cooking pots, plates and other vessels. Urban folklore: womenfolk, old people, children. Elbows rule. . . . From two a.m. the folks have been lying in wait for these delicacies. Obstinately. Obviously, it's fat. American fat. The soldiers in the convoy can't manage the pressing crowd, they shoot to scare it. Cries, whistles, lament and all the damns and all the 'your mothers' that are usually unfit to print."[143]

Also in September 1945, this time in Jarosław, about fifty women from military families demonstrated outside the starost's office, demanding their benefits.[144] In Kościerzyna, for two days in September 1945, a group of women demonstrated outside the municipal offices, demanding bread owed them for their ration cards.[145] There were also the already mentioned events in Płock in October 1945. In Chełm in March 1946, "a crowd lay siege to" the starost's office demanding UNRRA packages.[146] In December 1946, a group of about fifty women, wives of miners from the Modrzejów mine in Niwka, dissatisfied with their food rations, stopped their husbands from going to work.[147]

Workers expressed their impatience and dissatisfaction with protests and strikes. One of them wrote in desperation in April 1945:

> The workers at the Renard mine, and in the whole Dąbrowski Basin . . . appeal to our government and call out: save us because we and our children are drying out, we have no potatoes or salt, and very little

bread, some days we only eat once, and we have nothing left to sell, our children don't get a drop of milk, but the thieves are buying it in the milk store, there are no potatoes, our children wait at the threshold watch out for us returning from work, to see if we're bringing bread, and when they see it they jump for joy, it's worse when there is no bread because then there is a general sadness and you start thinking differently and it would be best if the newspapers didn't feed us promises when these are not being fulfilled.... We are calling out: save us.

A miner from Sosnowiec prophesied, "Also, there will probably be a strike in the mine, since they are not giving us food or money, last time they gave us 100 zlotys. But no one took it because it's enough to buy one loaf of bread and not to live on for two weeks."[148]

The many government institutions charged with managing public disaffection with living conditions—Provincial Commands of the Citizens' Militia, branches of the Ministry of Information and Propaganda, local Polish Workers' Party committees—recorded its growth since May 1945. Its roots lay in psychological perceptions: fear of hunger and a feeling of relative deprivation. Certainly the struggle for agency vis-à-vis Communist domination, defense of the national community or the interests of small groups were secondary.

There was a collective aversion in at least some social groups to "profiteers," defined by some people as all types of vendors, by others also as merchants and shopkeepers. At first, this feeling was not an expression of a false consciousness imposed by propaganda but an authentic outcome of resentment expressed in the thinking that "they have stuff, and we're going hungry." A town office clerk who earned six hundred zlotys per month complained in a private letter, "Yes, there are things in the store windows, but not everyone can buy them at these prices. White bread, cold cuts, butter, milk, sugar and meat are not for the people who work honestly, but for profiteers and skilled thieves."[149]

The authorities eagerly captured complaints and moods of this kind, which were usually shared by workers,[150] and took advantage of them in their legitimation process. The papers branded profiteers, who "are living off us." It was in this time of "righteous outrage" in November 1945 that the Special Commission for Fighting Economic Abuses and Sabotage was created. Fear of hunger also mobilized the authorities to bring in more compulsory deliveries from the countryside. But the appearance in the countryside of the teams in charge of collecting them, especially early on, threatened the rural population even more, closing the circle of fear.

The disaffection brought on by fear also turned against other ethnic groups. It would be impossible to present a statistical interdependence between the supplies situation and various manifestations of aversion and aggression against the German and Jewish minorities because of insufficient data. Price fluctuations are too narrow a premise to draw any serious conclusions. Still, the price of potatoes, the basic food at the time, rose by 40 percent on the eve of the Kielce pogrom.[151] What is more important is the overall mechanism: chronic terror, which can also be caused by the fear of hunger, prepares people to view all stimuli as threats. The historian Witold Kula has written about it. At such times people treat foreigners as a distinctive threat, if only because they will reduce the already limited supply of food. The anxiety about the Great Depression had already made people fear the Jews more. After the war, the economic situation was much worse, and fear—however difficult it is to compare it in the two periods—was probably even greater. Public dissatisfaction stemming from people's inability to satisfy the most basic food needs turned against strangers. In August 1945, when an anti-Semitic pogrom exploded in Cracow, acquiring anything with ration cards bordered on the miraculous. "The difficult economic situation is at the core of these [anti-Semitic] sentiments," Roman Zambrowski diagnosed the situation in September 1945.[152] The pogrom in Kielce occurred in the main city of a starving region. Similarly, hateful acts against Germans took place in areas of food shortages, such as Olsztyn, where they were herded into a ghetto. To repeat this chapter's introductory thesis:

nothing makes the likelihood of a pogrom or ethnic unrest more likely than the threat of unemployment or hunger.

NOTES

1. Cf. Zaremba, "Trzej jeźdźcy," 182–206; Zaremba "Oni mają, a my głodujemy," *Polityka*, October 11, 2008
2. Delumeau, *La Peur en Occident*, 178–79.
3. Snyder, *Bloodlands*, 175ff.
4. Kula, *Dziennik czasu okupacji*, 24, 25.
5. Cf. Voglis, "Surviving Hunger," 16–41.
6. Samsonowicz, "Głód i władza w Polsce w XIV–XVI w.," 74.
7. Snyder, *Bloodlands*, 162ff.
8. Delumeau, *La Peur en Occident*, 162–67.
9. "There have been many cases of typhus fever recently in Łowicz. It has been determined that jews [sic] carry it. I recommend that, in order to stop the disease from spreading, every loitering jew [sic] be handed over to the nearest police station" ("Odezwa starosty powiatu Łowicz," 434).
10. Kisielewski and Nowak, *Chleb i krew*, 41.
11. AIPN, MBP 3378, k. 107, 107a. Specjalne doniesienie.
12. See, for example, Kersten, *The Establishment of Communist Rule in Poland 1943–1948*; Jankowski, "Warunki bytu ludności"; Jarosz, "Bieda polska 1944–1956," 15–31.
13. AAN, Zespół Ministerstwo Aprowizacji i Handlu (henceforth MAiH) 197, k. 3–7. Przewidywania sytuacji żywnościowej w Polsce w roku 1946/47.
14. Jezierski and Petz, *Historia gospodarcza Polski Ludowej 1944–1985*, 75.
15. AAN, URM 5/786, k. 9–16. Sprawozdanie delegacji w sprawie zbadania na miejscu ciężkiej sytuacji życiowej ludności wojew. białostockiego, styczeń 1946.
16. AAN, PKWN VII/12, k. 59. Szef Wydziału Ogólno-Organizacyjnego Głównego Zarządu Polityczno-Wychowawczego do Zastępcy Kierownika Resortu Administracji Publicznej, September 23, 1944.
17. AAN, MPiOS 273, k. 56, 69. Memoriał w sprawie pomocy powiatom: grójeckim, makowskiemu, ostrołęckiemu, przasnyskiemu, pułtuskiemu i radzymińskiemu województwa warszawskiego.
18. AAN, URM 5/784, k. 21, 22. Dyrektor Biura Prezydialnego KRN do Obywatela Premiera w sprawie sytuacji na tzw. ziemiach przyczółkowych.
19. AAN, MIiP 79, k. 27. Sprawozdanie z komisyjnej lustracji powiatów zniszczonych działaniami wojennymi w woj. kieleckim w dniach od 24 VIII do 28 VIII 1945.
20. AAN, MAiH 509, k. 12. Wojewoda Kielecki do Obywatela Ministra Aprowizacji i Handlu w Warszawie, July 30, 1945.
21. *Dziennik Powszechny*, May 16, 1945.
22. Kersten and Szarota, *Wieś polska 1939–1948*, 18.
23. Pełnomocnik Rządu na Okręg Mazurski płk. Dr Jakub Prawin do Ministerstwa Administracji Publicznej i Generalnego Pełnomocnika Rządu RP dla Ziem Odzyskanych. Sprawozdanie za listopad, 17 XII 1945 r., 190.
24. "Przemówienie gen. dyw. Aleksandra Zawadzkiego w dnia 11 III 1945," *Dziennik Zachodni*, March 13, 1945.
25. AIPN, MBP 3378, k. 40. Doniesienie specjalne dot. sytuacji gospodarczej kraju.
26. Tracz, *Rok ostatni*, 71.
27. AIPN, MBP 3378, k. 41. Doniesienie specjalne dot. sytuacji gospodarczej kraju.
28. AIPN, MBP 3378, k. 42. Doniesienie specjalne dot. sytuacji gospodarczej kraju.
29. "The settlers literally have no potatoes or bread. Entire Red Army units come from Królewiec [Königsberg], dig up all the potatoes and carry them away. They don't allow the Poles to harvest the cereals in the field, and they don't do it themselves either, and so the cereals rot uselessly in the field, and so because of the above the matter of supplies for the approaching winter is desperate" (AAN, MAP 51, k. 121. Raport z przebiegu akcji osiedleńczej na terenie Powiatu Elbląg za czas od 15 IX do 30 IX 45).
30. In Białystok:

> The issue of supplies is appalling. The prices of food being sold on the free market are 20% higher than in Warsaw. The reasons for this situation are bad transportation and a general lack of food in these areas. The population obtains almost nothing with their ration cards. The bread that is handed out from time to time leaves a lot to be desired, as it is made out of barley flour, bitter, crumbling and not fully baked, like clay. There is almost no public transportation in Białystok Province. The reasons for this are a shortage of petrol and wide rail tracks. Everything that is going west, such as coal, needs to be reloaded in Warsaw. The effects are visible quickly. The electric power stations come to a halt because of the shortage of coal. . . . There is no sugar and no matches in the countryside. The peasant in the countryside doesn't have money even to buy a newspaper. A universal indigence is appearing. (AAN, MIiP 77, k. 10. Sprawozdanie z wyjazdu służbowego do Białegostoku instr. ter. Cichockiego Ryszarda w dniach od 1.8–4.8 br. [1945].)

31. Zaremba, *Dziennik 1945*, 83.
32. AAN, DRnK 202/III–36, k. 72. Raport sytuacyjny za okres I–III 1945.
33. AIPN, MBP 3378, k. 40. Doniesienie specjalne dot. sytuacji gospodarczej kraju.
34. CAW, III. 2.200, k. 51. Specjalne doniesienie dot. skargi żołnierzy na złe warunki materialne w jednostce w Łodzi.
35. CAW, III. 2.200, k. 52a. Specjalne doniesienie dot. skargi rekrutów z Warszawy na złe warunki w wojsku.
36. AIPN, MBP 3378, k. 49b. Doniesienie specjalne dotyczy Warszawy.
37. AAN, Ministerstwo Zdrowia 8, k. 6. Bilans działalności i osiągnięć Ministerstwa Zdrowia 1945.

38. AAN, CKOS 28, k. 47. Sprawozdanie opisowe Wojewódzkiego Komitetu Opieki Społecznej w Kielcach za miesiąc grudzień 1945.

39. "Wielka śmiertelność dzieci w Bydgoszczy," *Ziemia Pomorska*, August 7, 1945.

40. AIPN, MBP 3378, k. 68b, 69. Specjalne doniesienie dot. ciężkich warunków materialnych ludności.

41. These data can be found in a March 1946 world food report published by the US Department of Agriculture (*Robotnik*, April 1, 1946). Częstochowa-based *Głos Narodu* addressed the inadequate supplies in maternity hospitals:

> The shortage of milk can be felt most acutely; the hospital has received none in a year. Mothers who do not receive milk from home are unable to feed their babies. The hospital recently bought a goat, but this does not solve the problem. Black ration-card bread, peas, kasha, beans and potatoes are given to the mothers after they give birth. Not very nutritious! The ill women should be given 80 g of fats, but they get 20, and this only for the past month because before that they got 3–4 g. Vegetables do not reach them at all. ("Troska o dziecko prawdziwym wyrazem kultury miasta," *Głos Narodu*, June 30, 1946.)

42. AIPN, MBP 3378, k. 42. Doniesienie specjalne dot. sytuacji gospodarczej kraju.

43. AIPN, MBP 3378, k. 66b. Doniesienie specjalne dot. ciężkich warunków materialnych ludności.

44. Kochanowicz, "Gospodarcze dzieje strachu," 34.

45. Steinhaus, *Wspomnienia i zapiski*, 307.

46. In Kielce Province, of the 54,763 letters intercepted in ten days, 961 discussed hunger, high prices, and epidemics; of the 47,736 intercepted letters from Bydgoszcz, 270 mentioned hunger; of the 4,183 letters from Gdańsk, 200 did. Of the 14,899 letters from Katowice read by the censors in the first ten days of March, 1,020 included news about hunger (AIPN, MBP 3378, k. 40. Doniesienie specjalne dot. sytuacji gospodarczej kraju; AIPN, MBP 3378, k. 66. Doniesienie specjalne dot. ciężkich warunków materialnych ludności).

47. "Ubytek naturalny ludności w Lublinie," *Gazeta Lubelska*, April 20, 1945.

48. *Rocznik statystyczny 1947* (Warsaw: GUS, 1947), 32

49. AAN, URM 5/784, k. 21. Dyrektor Biura Prezydialnego KRN do Obywatela Premiera w sprawie sytuacji na tzw. ziemiach przyczółkowych.

50. AAN, MPiOS 267, k. 10. Sprawozdanie z inspekcji w zniszczonych powiatach województwa kieleckiego (stopnickim, opatowskim, sandomierskim, iłżeckim, kozienickim), May 1, 1945.

51. Zientara-Malewska, *Śladami twardej drogi*, 253.

52. Zientara-Malewska, 273.

53. Łach, *Osadnictwo miejskie na ziemiach odzyskanych w latach 1945–1950*, 231.

54. "Troski aprowizacyjne," *Dziennik Powszechny*, August 14, 1945.

55. Sprawozdanie wojewody pomorskiego za styczeń 1946 r., 17.

56. AAN, MAP 53, k. 3. Sprawozdanie sytuacyjne listopad 1945.

57. AAN, CKOS 42, k. 73. Sprawozdanie opisowe Wojewódzkiego Komitetu Opieki Społecznej Rzeszów za miesiąc luty 1946.

58. Ziemak, "Tragedia Mazurów," *Ziemia Pomorska*, March 20, 1946.

59. MacDonogh, *After the Reich*, 167.

60. Fedorowicz, "Chłopi wychodzą spod ziemi," *Życie Warszawy*, March 20, 1946.

61. AAN, MAiH 126, k. 9. Serwis Informacyjny Ministerstwa Aprowizacji i Handlu, January 4, 1946.

62. "Gruźlica dzieci i świadczenia rzeczowe," *Życie Warszawy*, January 31, 1946.

63. "Tam, gdzie dożywia się dzieci," *Gazeta Lubelska*, February 25, 1946.

64. "Hodujmy króliki," *Dziennik Powszechny*, March 18, 1946.

65. *Przekrój*, August 14–20, 1946.

66. AP w Kielcach, Urząd Wojewódzki II 1346, k. 107. Sytuacyjne sprawozdanie miesięczne za miesiąc kwiecień 1946.

67. AAN, PPR 295/IX–19, k. 21. Sprawozdanie z podróży z przedstawicielami UNRRA na tereny "głodowe" w powiatach Stopnica-Busko i Kozienice, May 4, 1946.

68. AAN, MPiOS 267, k. 61. Starosta Powiatowy Jasielski do Wojewódzkiego Wydziału Pracy i Opieki Społecznej, Jasło July 18, 1946.

69. Gałązka-Petz and Jezierski, "Odbudowa gospodarki narodowej 1944–1946," 210.

70. *Dziennik Gospodarczy*, December 16, 1946.

71. Quoted from Chumiński, *Ruch zawodowy*, 129.

72. "Ogonki . . .," *Ilustrowany Kurier Polski*, July 22, 1946.

73. "Niemowlę w kołysce," *Sztandar Ludu*, July 6, 1946.

74. AAN, MIiP 96, Informacje z terenu, k. 94.

75. *Biuletyny Informacyjne Ministerstwa Bezpieczeństwa Publicznego 1946*, 61.

76. AAN, MIiP 184, k. 3. Szeptana propaganda, October 30, 1946.

77. AAN, MIiP 184, k. 24. Dane o propagandzie szeptanej do biuletynu nr 15, 14 I 1947.

78. Kersten and Szarota, *Wieś polska 1939–1948*, vol. 1, 649.

79. Kaliński, "Bitwa o handel," 174.

80. AAN, MAP 101, k. 3, 4. Sprawozdanie sytuacyjne wojewody łódzkiego za miesiąc kwiecień 1947.

81. *Express Wieczorny*, March 13, 1947.

82. Ellman, "The 1947 Soviet Famine and the Entitlement Approach to Famines," 603–30.

83. Cf. *Światowy kryzys żywnościowy przedłuża się*, Serwis Informacyjny Ministerstwa Aprowizacji, September 16, 1947, 3.

84. Cf. Serwis Informacyjny Ministerstwa Aprowizacji, August 6, September 16, September 18, 1947.

85. H. Steinhaus's notes. August 1, 1945: "Lasko is telling people that in Russia you never see a smiling face. Destitution, hunger, there are no properly fed children, pork fat is 700 rubles a kilo, and a worker earns 180–200 rubles." July 28, 1946: "but in many [Soviet] districts, there is hunger, deathly hunger. This is why many Russian workers leaving Germany stop here and pretend

to be repatriated Poles, so they don't have to go back" (Steinhaus, *Wspomnienia i zapiski*, 344, 362).

86. "Normalizacja życia gospodarczego," *Jedność*, August 5, 1945.

87. Jankowski, "Warunki bytu ludności," 454.

88. AIPN, MBP 3378, k. 41. Doniesienie specjalne dot. sytuacji gospodarczej kraju.

89. AIPN, MBP 3378, k. 49. Doniesienie specjalne dotyczy Warszawy.

90. AIPN, MBP 3378, k. 41. Doniesienie specjalne dot. sytuacji gospodarczej kraju.

91. AIPN, MBP 3378, k. 67, 67a. Specjalne doniesienie dot. ciężkich warunków materialnych ludności.

92. AIPN, MBP 3378, k. 67. Specjalne doniesienie dot. ciężkich warunków materialnych ludności.

93. AAN, URM 5/671, k. 2. Sprawozdanie Instytutu Gospodarstwa Narodowego o ruchu cen w okresie od marca do sierpnia r.b.

94. AAN, MAiH 219, k. 2. Zagadnienie zwyżki cen artykułów rolnych w miesiącu wrześniu 1946.

95. AAN, URM 5/671, k. 23. Tygodniowy Komunikat Informacyjny Instytutu Gospodarstwa Narodowego nr 17, July 11, 1946.

96. "Zarząd Miejski nie dopuści do zwyżki cen," *Dziennik Powszechny*, October 28, 1945.

97. "10-billion Hungarian banknotes," *Express Wieczorny*, June 9, 1946; "Katastrofalna inflacja na Węgrzech," *Głos Narodu*, June 29, 1946.

98. "Fałszywe pogłoski," *Dziennik Powszechny*, May 17, 1946.

99. AAN, MIiP 227, k. 101. Raport sytuacyjny nr 11 Urzędu Informacji i Propagandy w Gdańsku, February 25, 1947.

100. AIPN 3378, k. 49. Doniesienie specjalne dotyczy Warszawy, April 10, 1945.

101. Quoted from Chumiński, *Ruch zawodowy*, 126.

102. AAN, Ministerstwo Zdrowia 8, k. 5. Bilans działalności i osiągnięć Ministerstwa Zdrowia 1945.

103. *Rocznik statystyczny 1947*, 146.

104. "Dane o rozpowszechnieniu gruźlicy w Polsce," *Gazeta Lubelska*, October 21, 1945.

105. "96 proc. dzieci chorych," *Ziemia Pomorska*, February 9, 1946.

106. "Gruźlica dzieci i świadczenia rzeczowe," *Życie Warszawy*, January 31, 1946.

107. Humphreys, "Tuberculosis," 136–41.

108. "SOS dzieci Kielecczyzny," *Express Wieczorny*, June 19, 1946.

109. "Dur plamisty w Europie w 1937 r.," 1–6.

110. Sprawozdanie z działalności Nadzwyczajnego Komisariatu do Walki z Epidemiami w latach 1944–1945, 13.

111. AP w Ełku, Księga inwentarza Szpitala Powiatowego w Ełku.

112. Kaczor, *Wspomnienia ludowego starosty*, 109.

113. It was estimated that the epidemics of the two world wars immunized about 50 percent of the population to typhus (Sprawozdanie z działalności, 7).

114. Kos, "Chronić zdrowie," 77, 78.

115. Quoted from Hejger, *Polityka narodowościowa władz polskich*, 103.

116. Babisiak, "Nędze miasta Słupska," *Ziemia Pomorska*, April 10, 1946.

117. "The infectious section is most crowded right now. In the halls and rooms with 5–8 beds with people with typhus, mostly germans [*sic*] being cared for by german [*sic*] nurses" ("Szpitalnictwo gdańskie ośrodkiem lecznictwa w Polsce," *Dziennik Bałtycki*, July 14, 1945).

118. Hejger, *Polityka narodowościowa władz polskich*, 54.

119. Borodziej and Lemberg, *Niemcy w Polsce 1945–1950*, vol. 1, 87.

120. Nowak, *Cień Łambinowic*; Nowak, *Obozy na Śląsku Opolskim*, 123.

121. *Kurier Szczeciński*, October 15, 1945.

122. Statystyki Urzędu Stanu Cywilnego w Szczecinie.

123. AIPN, MBP 3378, k. 89a. Specjalne doniesienie, September 13, 1945.

124. "Elbląg ostrzega przed durem brzusznym," *Dziennik Bałtycki*, June 16, 1945.

125. AP w Rzeszowie, Urząd Wojewódzki 1720, k. 4.

126. Sprawozdanie z działalności, 17.

127. *Rocznik Statystyczny 1948*, 187.

128. AAN, Ministerstwo Zdrowia 8, k. 6, Bilans działalności i osiągnięć Ministerstwa Zdrowia 1945.

129. Żelawska, "Wszyscy do walki z epidemią," August 13, 1945.

130. Żak, "Drugie narodziny Elbląga w oczach lekarza," 170.

131. Kersten and Szarota, *Wieś polska 1939–1948*, vol. 4, 21.

132. *Jednodniówka*, October 1, 1945.

133. AIPN, MBP 3378, k. 27, 68. Specjalne doniesienie dot. ciężkich warunków materialnych ludności.

134. AIPN, MBP 3378, k. 108a. Specjalne doniesienie, October 13, 1945.

135. "Malaria w Polsce," *Rzeczpospolita*, September 22, 1946.

136. AIPN, MBP 3378, k. 67. Doniesienie specjalne dot. ciężkich warunków materialnych ludności.

137. CAW, III. 2.200, k. 49a, 50a. Specjalne doniesienie dot. złych warunków w wojsku.

138. AAN, MIiP 79, k. 27. Sprawozdanie z komisyjnej lustracji powiatów zniszczonych działaniami wojennymi w woj. kieleckim w dniach od 24 VIII do 28 VIII 1945.

139. A person from Chojno, near Szamotuły, wrote in April 1945, "There is no work. . . . They haven't given us old people any food tickets yet, and second, 2 pounds of bread per person per week. . . . There will be hunger and hardship, and people will kill each other in the streets" (AIPN, MBP 3378, k. 61. Doniesienie specjalne dot. prowokacyjnych pogłosek).

140. *Sprawozdanie Zarządu Miejskiego m. Gliwice z 30 kwietnia 1945*, quoted from Tracz, *Rok ostatni*, 101.

141. AIPN 035/953, k. 4. Sytuacja w województwie białostockim na 12 maja 1945.

142. AAN, Delegatura Rządu 202/III-36, k. 162. Raport o sytuacji na Ziemiach Zachodnich (od 15 V–15 VI 1945).

143. "Co się dzieje na tej Pradze?! Dantejskie sceny w kolejce po amerykański szmelc," *Dziennik Ludowy*, September 5, 1945.

144. AAN, MAP 121, k. 132. Sprawozdanie miesięczne Wojewody Rzeszowskiego, October 10, 1945.

145. AAN, MIiP 229, k. 32.

146. AAN, MIiP 926, k. 6. Sprawozdanie w trybie przyśpieszonym.

147. AAN, PPR 295/IX–411, k. 109. Meldunek nr 5 o pracy grup w terenie (na podstawie meldunków Szefów Sztabów Kierownictw Wojewódzkich), December 11, 1946.

148. AIPN, MBP 3378, k. 66b, 66. Specjalne doniesienie dot. ciężkich warunków materialnych ludności.

149. AIPN 3378, k. 104. Specjalne doniesienie Wydziału Cenzury Wojennej, October 13, 1945.

150. For more about the moods and workers' strikes, see Kenney, *Rebuilding Poland*; Kamiński, *Strajki robotnicze w Polsce w latach 1945–1948*; Kamiński, *Polacy wobec nowej rzeczywistości 1944–1948*, 64–150; Chumiński, *Ruch zawodowy*.

151. AAN, MAiH 574, k. 67. Zestawienie cen detalicznych wolnego rynku artykułów żywnościowych i powszechnego użytku wg danych nadesłanych z Urzędów Wojewódzkich za czas od 20 VI do 1 VII 1946.

152. Kochański, *Protokoły posiedzeń Sekretariatu KC PPR 1945–1946*, 115.

13

ETHNIC PHOBIAS AND VIOLENCE

"*La guerre n'est pas finie*,"[1] a Polish lawyer he came across told Primo Levi in March 1945 in a liberated area of Poland. Indeed, the war had left in its wake a cauldron of national phobias and neuroses, hatred and desire for revenge. At the bottom of this cauldron festered a thick layer of anti-Semitism that predated the war. The postwar emotional atmosphere of political fear, a profound sentiment of defeat and multidimensional temporariness, and insurmountable problems in daily life did not make it easy to regain psychological stability. As this atmosphere pushed the different ethnic groups further apart, it, too, fed the fire under the cauldron. Amplified aggression also had its roots in the war. The long-lasting era of fear made people revert to primeval behaviors and fortified their magical thinking. Tales about German bands, called Werwolf, promoted by the regime's media, and the myth of ritual murder were passed around, building up some of the postwar "psychological *Lebensraum*."

Strictly speaking, ethnic phobias can be defined as persistent and usually long-lasting fears of the Other. They surface as exaggerated reactions of unease and terror, and in extreme cases lead to panic attacks. The greater the sense of endangerment, the bigger the chances that ethnocentrism will surface.[2] According to sociologist Antonina Kłoskowska, the Poles' collective psyche resembles the psyches of ethnic minorities in that after numerous long-term experiences, the public continues to feel anxious vis-à-vis its more powerful neighbors and cannot forget past injuries.[3] After the Second World War, this cauldron exploded and scorched the "others"—Belorussians, Germans, Ukrainians, and Jews.

In her study of the history of the anti-Semitic phobia, historian Joanna Michlic wrote, "The increasing intolerance of minorities, manifested in open hostilities toward Jews and also Slavic groups, was one of the chief features of early postwar social life. Despite the various political and ideological declarations, the [Polish Workers' Party] not only failed to alleviate interethnic tensions, but in fact contributed to sustaining ethnic tensions."[4]

The idea of the one-nation state propagated by the Communists and their policies of ethnic purges of Germans and Ukrainians mandated by the Allies (resettling the Germans) and supported by the majority of the Poles accompanied this explosion of nationalism. Yet this book's focus is on the spontaneous grassroots ethnic purges and not on what the state organized, however much it was supported by the public.[5]

The Poles were not the only nation experiencing the powerful emotions of fear and hatred as well as hope. The defeated Germans also suffered deep trauma: humiliation and expulsions. This can be seen clearly in letters written by Germans living in Łódź and the surrounding area on the eve of the Red Army's arrival.

January 14, 1945: "Germany is large, and the Bolsheviks will not get here. We've dug deep ditches, so they won't get here too quickly."

Sieradz, January 16, 1945: "Our victory is certain as long as the Führer is alive."

Litzmannstadt (Łódź), January 17, 1945: "We got the news last night that we are to surrender this morning at 7. Nothing scares me more than falling into the hands of the Bolsheviks alive."

Litzmannstadt, January 18, 1945: "I received the devastating news today that we are to leave our fatherland."

Litzmannstadt, January 17, 1945: "Things are going badly for us. I'm only waiting for the office to tell me whether I'm free. I fear that the Bolsheviks are almost here. We're probably done for. I'm afraid of the Bolsheviks."[6]

The fear of the "Bolshevik beasts," which had been fed by Nazi propaganda for years, reached its zenith and turned into a collective psychosis in the days prior to the arrival of the Red Army in Olsztyn and Elbląg, Gdańsk, Kołobrzeg, and Lower Silesia. Edmund Dmitrów, the author of a study of the stereotype of the Russians in Nazi propaganda, recapped its "achievements": "At least Goebbels had no reason to worry about the level of fear of the Russians: it was high."[7] Indicators of this "high fear" among the Germans were typical. There were fantastical rumors, both optimistic and pessimistic, about a *Wunderwaffe*, a miracle weapon, and about Russian cruelty. Delays in decisions to evacuate often made people panic, which could be difficult to control. The chaos and abruptly rising fear weakened the population's mechanisms of self-control. Some went into a stupor while others panicked and tried to escape. When all other routes to the west were cut off, as many as several thousand old people, women, and children may have perished in the icy waters of the Vistula Lagoon. One of the most powerful emotional experiences for the Germans in East Prussia and Silesia, who until then had barely felt the effects of the war, was the dramatic flight in freezing temperatures and often under bombardment.[8]

Fear motivated both those who managed to flee and those who wanted or had to stay. People became more pious in the months prior to the capitulation of Wrocław. But there were also diametrically opposed behaviors, similar to those in cities under siege, for instance in the Middle Ages: abandoning faith, drinking heavily, loosening sexual mores. Tens of thousands of Germans, unable to deal with the suffocating fear and humiliation and rape, committed suicide. From January 23 to February 10, 1945, alone, Breslau (Wrocław) municipal registers recorded 49 suicides.[9] In Berlin, 7,057 people, sometimes entire families, killed themselves. According to Christian Goeschel, "The Third Reich culminated in a massive wave of suicides." Only some of the suicides, top military officers or state and party officials, were Hitler's fanatical supporters. There were civilians who for many months had been fed visions of the "Bolshevik-Mongol hordes" and who, anticipating the Red Army's abominable behavior, chose to slit their veins or to swallow a cyanide pill.[10] Many women who could not bear the hell of rape killed themselves after the front had passed. In the first two weeks after the arrival of the Soviets in Zielona Góra, more than 500 people reportedly killed themselves. In Wałbrzych, 300 suicides were recorded.[11] Suicides continued in the spring and early summer of 1945 when the Polish administration began to take over lands formerly belonging to the Reich, but then tapered off.[12] The earlier fear was tamed and became more commonplace, but now new dangers loomed: hunger and the typhus epidemic, the terrors of resettlements and of plundering Poles. As they were being forced to leave their homes, many Germans heard the farewell "all Germans out!"

The indigenous population of Warmia and Masuria were also living in terror. The region's chronicler, Erwin Kruk, wrote years later:

> One can find many forgotten examples of how the native populations were treated in the so-called western territories—much like the Jews. There were virtually no Jews in our area. But if you use a tad of imagination, you can compare the situation of the Jews in areas in which they were a visible minority to what people from Kurpie and Mazovia inflicted on the Masurians. . . . I know that post-war fear in

Masuria and Warmia. Even today no one wants to talk about what happened in some districts. And the audiences won't believe these stories. After all, the Poles are noble. This is the prevailing view.[13]

Almost exactly two years before the fall of Berlin, on May 8, 1943, as the insurrection in the Warsaw ghetto was dying down, about eighty Jews, many of them members of the Jewish Fighting Organization hiding in a bunker at 18 Miła Street, killed themselves. In the countryside, some psychologically and physically drained Jews who got no help from the terrified Polish peasantry surrendered to the Germans, which was equivalent to suicide, to saying "let it all be over." Henryk Wejsberger, a doctor in Dąbrowa Tarnowska, committed suicide with his whole family.[14] A bottomless feeling of insecurity, which could become physical pain, could lead to thoughts of suicide. Simone Weil wrote about this kind of fear becoming a deathly poison for the soul. Aleksandra Sołowiejczyk-Guter, who lived in hiding with "Aryan" identity documents in a village near Warsaw, learned its bitter taste and noted in her diary:

> I sometimes think that I'm headed for insanity, without cessation, without a moment's rest, regardless of what I'm doing, I think that I can see the police coming out from behind the fence, and this brings a deathly fear over me, makes me break out in a cold sweat. I lie at night unable to sleep staring into the darkness, my ears listening out for every rustle, constantly on the lookout, with my nerves constantly tensed to breaking point, to the point where this psychological nervousness becomes physical pain. In reality, this seemingly peaceful, quiet, comfortable life is actually inexpressible torture. This is not ordinary human fear, it's an illness, an obsession, something that a psychology textbook calls "obsessive-compulsive," which reportedly leads people to commit suicide. Thinking about suicide is increasingly persistent. But the inertia is too great to make one act by walking over to the train tracks or to a bridge over the Vistula. If only I had poison, a revolver, something that would not require such a huge amount of energy to take a trip to the other world! What a strange paradox, I don't understand it. I dream about death as liberation from my torment, and at the same time my fear of death is the reason for this torment.[15]

Jews who survived the Holocaust were left alone with their fear and their profound sadness. The occupation was over, but its mental consequences lingered.[16] And liberation brought new fears, of Polish bands and of anti-Semitic lynching.

A late March 1946 memorandum of the Provincial Committee of Polish Jews in Lublin read, "A panic is spreading among Polish Jews, but unfortunately it is largely justified. So far, the crushing of German Fascism has not brought the Polish Jewry the peace they had been longing for. Many Jews who have come out of bunkers or forests, Jews who have come back from camps, from exile, from emigration have encountered a hostile attitude from a segment of Polish society."[17]

"The fear appeared after the Kielce pogrom," remembered Michał Głowiński.[18] In opinion polls of Polish Jews in 1947–50, Irena Hurwic-Nowakowska diagnosed the syndrome of what she called flight from the group, severing ties to other Jews, and concealing one's Jewishness from the anti-Semitic Polish majority.[19] The writer Agata Tuszyńska wrote in her *W rodzinnej historii lęku* (A family history of fear), "In Poland after the war, many of the Jewish survivors preferred to keep quiet about their roots. They survived and decided that they would never again be Jews. It's better not to own up to it, you never know when they will hunt you next. They didn't want to feel like tracked animals. They wanted to spare their children this fear of humiliation. Anything was better than contempt."[20]

Fleeing one's own group because of anxiety was an important experience not only for Jews but also for Germans[21] and for Ukrainians who were resettled in Poland's north and west. Some would continue to hide their ethnicity for years, fearing "Polish anger," losing a job, or being identified or degraded. The origins of these discriminatory behaviors include the nature of Communism itself, which rejects all otherness and tries

Ethnic Phobias and Violence

to homogenize everything, as well as the absence of the kind of tolerance training present in a democracy. Some came from the war and the immediate postwar period, and from Polish emotions and traumas specific to that time. It is not this book's intention to make excuses for anyone but rather to understand the Poles' behaviors vis-à-vis the Jews. After all, the anti-Semitic pogroms were the quintessence of the Great Terror.

THE GERMANS: THE VICTIMS TAKE REVENGE

Primo Levi got another piece of advice from three different Poles he bumped into after leaving Auschwitz: don't speak German. This time it came from a Polish gendarme. "I asked why: he answered with an eloquent gesture, passing his index and middle fingers, like a knife, between chin and larynx, and adding cheerfully, 'Tonight all Germans kaput.'"[22]

Throughout the previous six years, Poles never stopped asking God to punish the Germans. "Crimes take place daily," Father Józef Anczarski wrote in his diary after the murder of all the Jews in Podhajce and Buczacz in eastern Lesser Poland where he lived. "But God is just and he can see the streams of Jewish blood, God can hear the moaning of despair and terror. The day of Lord's justice and the Lord's judgment will come to this criminal German nation."[23] Generalizations such as "all Poles," "all the people in Warsaw," and "all Jews" are driven by the same emotions and are characteristic of stereotypical and un-sociological thinking. But there is an exception: in 1945, virtually all Poles really did hate the Germans.

The changes in postwar moods came in waves. The German problem gradually receded. The initially intense hostility toward the Germans softened a little as Poles being resettled into areas that had belonged to the Reich were exposed to German civilians. "He was very well disposed toward the Germans," said Lucia Müller, who lived near Braniewo, remembering her boss.[24] As Poles and Germans began to live together, positive emotions such as empathy or willingness to help appeared. At the same time people did mention unacceptable fraternization with the recent enemy, and emotions located somewhere between dislike, hostility, and hatred were still dominant. The belief that Poland should get rid of the Germans, preferably by resettling them, grew on a foundation of such feelings. "Expelling the Germans," wrote the sociologist Edmund Dmitrów, "became a universal, mass demand of the people of liberated Poland."[25] It is not necessary here to list the German transgressions. While people had encountered "good Germans" during the war, and some even owed their lives to them, most Poles still believed that the German nation must be punished.

German language and culture seemed repulsive to the Poles, and some of them experienced panic attacks when they heard German spoken in the street. In the early postwar years, Polish radio broadcasts of classical Russian music, whether Borodin, Tchaikovsky, or Mussorgsky, represented not only Soviet cultural imperialism but also opposition to German music.[26] Writing the noun *German* or *Germany* with a lower-case *g* in violation of spelling rules, in both private and official correspondence and in newspapers, was a routine symbolic expression of this hatred. At a national sports conference in Bydgoszcz in March 1946, activists demanded that Germans be banned from sports.[27] Articles appeared arguing that the only "obviously correct solution" was to create labor camps for the Germans.[28] Many Poles treated them as a much needed free-of-charge workforce. Affirmations of a new version of slavery were published without commentary: "[The Germans] are indeed here. They are sitting with us and working. They are still working as if this was their country, they don't even need to be told how to do things. They do everything, and we can relax. Except that everything is ours now, and they're working for us."[29]

The Germans were closely supervised, they were not allowed to travel freely outside their places of residence, and they were given work orders, especially clearing rubble. They were often moved into separate closed-off sections of towns. They could be arrested for little nothings, such as speaking German in public or traveling without a permit. Some towns ordered them to wear white armbands. The Poznań municipal authorities, for example, argued that "this way it may be possible to prevent, make difficult for the Germans to engage in anti-state activity, establish commercial relations with Poles or use state transportation."[30] Germans were expelled from their homes, could not freely go to the theater or cinema, and were given reduced food allowances. They could not take part in the currency exchange and, indeed, were often not paid for working, while some shops displayed signs saying "not for Germans." Looting and attacking them has already been discussed.

The journalist Helga Hirsch calls the Poles' postwar behavior toward the Germans "victims' revenge."[31] The Poles were indeed yearning for revenge, and they did not hide their feelings. This was evident in the letters they wrote. Hanna Świda-Ziemba's book *Urwany lot* (Interrupted flight) discusses two letters that seem to represent a general trend.

A secondary-school student wrote in 1945, "After our victory, we needed to deal with the Germans with our own hands. And with sufficient cruelty, by hanging them on posts, poking out their eyes. So they would be afraid and suffer in proportion to the evil they have inflicted. Only this could bring us satisfaction."

Another student wrote in a similar vein in 1946:

There are Germans crawling all over Wrocław, carrying bundles, trying to butter us up, they work for us. I look and feel gratified. It serves them right. They're all criticizing Hitler now, but mostly they are reproaching him for losing the war. We've been treating them with kid gloves too much, anyway. They should experience destitution, humiliation so that they can be slaves at least for some time, just like they wanted others to be. Or maybe we should set an example by executing entire neighborhoods, families, just like they executed Jews, Poles, others? They deserve it, and they deserve to get it from us.[32]

There was something primeval and savage in this desire for revenge. But also something natural in that evil deserves to be punished. The public reacted with outrage to suggestions that German civilians, especially the *Volksdeutsche*, be treated leniently, and readers wrote letters of protest to newspaper editors. They did not want forbearance, opposed the "atmosphere of compromise," demanded revenge. The War Censorship Office intercepted such letters.

From Łódź, March 17, 1945: "The krauts did not put us Poles into categories. To them, a Pole was a mortal enemy, and the terms 'damned Pole' and 'Polish pig' were in daily use. There was no defense, no lawyer for a Pole accused of something. We suffered for 5½ years. There were no mitigating circumstances for us, so let there be none for them. The thugs kept on shouting that in 5 years there would be no Poles left."[33]

From Wieluń, March 7, 1945: "We believe in the idea that when someone throws the first stone at you, you throw bread at them; fine, it's all very wonderful, but who's going to pay for those thousands of victims of Treblinka, Majdanek, Oświęcim, Gross-Rosen, Dachau and so many others? For those TB sufferers, for those rags of human beings–who will compensate us, what culture and civilization is capable of covering up all those thousands of our brothers' graves? The heart turns into shreds at the thought of this bleeding Poland of ours, and we want to be lenient? And for what?"[34]

And Katowice, April 29, 1945:

We may not forget. It's not about revenge the way the Nazis believed in it.... It's about our peace, safety and rebuilding our social and personal lives. Just as for 6 years we fought against death every step of the way, now we must fight for life and happiness every step of the way for ourselves and for future generations. We must fight the mood of compromise, which will sow the seeds of a new war. The nations that suffered the greatest blood victims in this war must not forget their losses. They must present a bill that will secure peace, prosperity and development for many years to come.[35]

It is easy from today's vantage point to criticize such sentiments for adhering to the concept of collective responsibility, of punishing a whole nation for the crimes of individuals. These emotions were real, and they partly translated into behaviors toward the German population. They should be treated as yet another remnant of the war, since the Germans applied the principle of collective responsibility very broadly from the very beginning of their occupation. Yet "victims' revenge" does not explain all behaviors. As has already been discussed, the war was also a six-year course in killing, which taught aggression, stigmatization, and humiliation.

Many studies discuss various facets of the Polish-German relationship.[36] But this history of fear also needs to discuss the Poles' emotions toward the Germans. The letters intercepted by the Office of War Censorship in November and December 1944 reveal hatred and a thirst for revenge. Some commented on a trial underway in Lublin, of camp functionaries from Majdanek, where some seventy-eight thousand people were killed. "Dear Parents. . . . I looked at and visited the death factory in Majdanek. Looking at it, a person is crushed by horror and revenge. The Poles captured the Majdanek executioners. Today is the first hearing, tomorrow the second. There are 6 of them. The crowd is demanding death for these killers." And, "Dear Gusti! . . . I visited Majdanek, and what I saw there is simply incomprehensible, the scale of the crime. On top of it is the trial of 6 Nazis from that camp, which is going on here now, and witness testimony."

The crowd wanted to lynch the SS functionaries being escorted down the streets of Lublin. The fact that they were made to walk from Lublin Castle prison to the Soldier's House, where the trial was held, seems to suggest that the authorities wanted to exploit the spectacle for their own ends, perhaps to distract the public from the "October turnaround," when Moscow was putting pressure on the Polish Communist leadership to step up their actions against Home Army fighters and against those suspected of sympathizing with the government in exile. This was also the time of the NKVD's increased persecution in the areas being "liberated" by the Red Army in the autumn of 1944. And yet, it did not take much to lead a crowd into a pogrom mentality. "Dear Jaś, I went into town today and I saw 6 germans [sic] being led from the castle to the court, the same Germans who murdered people in Majdanek. You won't believe how many people were watching, spitting into their faces, shouting, whistling, threatening. The Polish police were escorting them and shooting the whole time." And another: "Dear Mommy. . . . The trial of 6 germans [sic], the butchers of Majdanek, is taking place here now. I saw them being led down Krakowskie [Przedmieście] Avenue, their noggins down and their glances cowardly. They were being taken to be tried in the Soldier's House. I have the impression that they'll be hanged in public. I wouldn't hang them by their heads but by their tongues, so they could suffer longer."

If the new regime really did want to redirect the public hatred onto the Germans, it certainly succeeded. Another letter reveals the public mood in Lublin: "Dear Friend. . . . The mood among the people and the hate of Fascism were clearly visible today. The nation is demanding pure revenge on the bandits, it is demanding that they be hanged in the streets, so that everyone can see the punishment they deserve. A large crowd has gathered in the main streets of Lublin, where they talked about these bandits very excitedly and nervously."

On December 23, 1944, five of the defendants were publicly hanged in the grounds of Majdanek. The trucks that brought them were used as the trapdoors. After the execution, they drove off with their engines roaring, leaving the bodies hanging. Over ten thousand people watched the execution. According to a letter, the crowd wanted to lynch them: "Good day, dear Semen, yesterday the trial ended and they hanged 5 'Fritzes,' who used to be the leaders in Majdanek and to kill people. They hanged them at 2 p.m. You can just imagine what went on there. Ten thousand people, the shouting, crying of people whose families had been killed, people were just trying to pounce on them and wanted to tear them to pieces. Of course this was not permitted."[37]

The writer Zbigniew Załuski had a different memory of the executions. The onlookers did not try to lynch.

The same mob, which nearly tore to pieces the defendants with their meager escort in the street a few days ago, the mob against whose ire and in the name of justice and order it was necessary to send the tanks out into the street, was now silent, surely unaware of why its yearning for revenge was not properly sated by this execution. There was certainly a discrepancy between the crime and the punishment. But certainly also the unrealized knowledge that something morally irreversible happened in the war years . . . that the previous state of affairs could not be brought back and that there was no stepping back over the moral threshold that humanity crossed then.[38]

This was the first public execution in liberated Poland, not counting the frequent executions of deserters that preceded the arrival of the front. The second one, the hanging of SS-Unterscharführer Paul Hoffmann, who had supervised the camp crematorium, was staged on December 23, 1945, also in Majdanek. About twenty thousand people watched it.[39]

The most spectacular was the execution of eleven functionaries of the Stutthof concentration camp, including five women, a camp in which some sixty-five thousand people had died. It took place on July 4, 1946, on Stolzenberg Hill in Gdańsk. The *Dziennik Bałtycki* daily ran a front-page note that it would be taking place the next day.[40] Offices and factories cut short their work hours, and some organized transportation for their employees. The estimate of fifty thousand spectators seems exaggerated, but there were definitely women and children in the crowd.

The gathering began in a picnic atmosphere. It was warm, and beer was sold. At 5:00 p.m., eleven trucks arrived at the scene of the execution, accompanied by a convoy and executioners dressed in striped camp uniforms with numbers, including one woman. The multitude began to undulate and drone. The hanging technology copied Majdanek's. The trucks, whose beds would be used as trapdoors, stopped under the gallows. After the prosecutor read the sentence, he gestured for them to move. "The crowd surged. Here and there, women held out their arms: for our husbands, for our children," wrote *Dziennik Bałtycki*. Some whistled. The soldiers fired in the air. *Ilustrowany Kurier Polski* and *Express Wieczorny* were among the papers that described the executions in detail. *Przekrój* carried a reportage illustrated with photographs.[41] But they failed to mention that the show did not end with the hanging. The mob rushed to take the shoes off the feet of the dead and then cut the bodies down. Some believed that a noose taken off a hanged person's neck brings luck.[42]

Ten days later, on July 14, 1946, in Poznań, Warthegau Gauleiter NSDAP Arthur Greiser was hanged. "Tomorrow at 7 a.m. Greiser will hang. The sentence will be carried out publicly on the slope of the Cytadela," *Głos Wielkopolski* reported in a special edition. People got up very early to secure a good place. Again, over ten thousand watched the spectacle. Just as in Gdańsk, the mood was picnic-like: children were present, and ice cream, drinks, and sweets were sold. Here, too, people fought over the noose. This was Poland's last public execution of a German war criminal.

We do not know the behind-the-scenes politics of the public hangings in Gdańsk and Poznań. Such an important decision could not have been made by local prosecutors without the minister of justice being consulted and he, in turn, without someone in the Polish Workers' Party leadership, most likely security chief Jakub Berman. Was the government playing a game, like in Majdanek, of wanting to distract the public from current problems, to show that the regime was responding to the people's desire for revenge? We can only guess. It is not out of the question that the Polish spate of public hangings was influenced by news from abroad. In Prague in June 1946, the Nazi ruler of the Protectorate of Bohemia and Moravia Karl Hermann Frank was executed in public, and public executions of German war criminals also took place in the USSR. These hangings, like other pathologies of postwar public life, expressed the degeneracy present everywhere in Europe.

In Poland, intellectuals, including Adam Kryński writing in *Tygodnik Powszechny*, the sociologist Professor Stanisław Ossowski, and the writer Ewa Szelburg-Zarembina, protested these spectacles.[43] The theatrologist Jan Kott admitted in the weekly *Przekrój*, "Hating Germans is a precious social value." He saw the punishment of crimes as a moral value and believed that people should be allowed to feel righteous anger and righteous contempt, righteous outrage and righteous hatred. But he also noted that a public execution was governed by the sociological laws of a folk spectacle, commercialization, and theatricalization. He wrote, "I am convinced that of the thousands of people who watched the execution at Stutthof, the majority came to satisfy their thirst for cruelty, which we must censure, and not their desire for vengeance, which we must respect." In the public execution he also saw the influence of "mass mystiques," which were a characteristic feature of Fascism, the horror of appealing to irrational urges. He exclaimed, "Careful with the mystiques!"[44]

A couple of weeks later, Premier Edward Osóbka-Morawski wrote in a note to the minister of justice, "I have my doubts about the public executions to which tickets are allegedly being sold to the population."[45] The September 13, 1946, hanging of Amon Göth, commander of the Płaszów camp near Cracow, as well as the April 1947 hanging of Auschwitz commander Rudolf Höss, were conducted more "privately," with the latter watched by only about one hundred people who carried special passes.

Today, too, a similar "reality show" would likely attract thousands of people eager to watch an execution, but the behavior of the audiences at the time says something about the unique emotional climate of the postwar years, which was governed by the universal conviction that revenge was necessary as well as the familiarity with death acquired in the course of the war. During the occupation, Poles and Germans staged hundreds of public executions in Poland. They shot and hanged, and gathered crowds to teach them fear. There are many indications that these experiences taught the Poles to want revenge. The war also promoted magical thinking, which manifested itself in the jostling over the noose and the desire to lynch. On the very same day that the war criminals were being hanged on Stolzenberg Hill in Gdańsk, an anti-Semitic pogrom erupted in Kielce, instigated by the belief in Jewish cannibalism.

But people manifested their need for revenge and the aggression they had learned not only and not primarily by partaking in spectacles of criminals being hanged. The propensity to be violent often found a release especially in ethnically mixed areas and in the first weeks and months after liberation. Its abruptness and abandon resembled what the Germans were subjected to by Czechs in the Sudetenland and French collaborators by their own countrymen at home. Acting similarly in the chaos after the passing of the front were young men, usually third-tier underground activists or those who had had nothing to do with the underground, who now became self-appointed leaders, the only "guys with guns," and the militia.[46] Some wanted their hyperactivity to mask their wartime sins, including collaboration with the Gestapo. In small towns, where they were posted to guard Polishness and order, unsupervised, they organized ghettos and mini work camps for "our Germans." They beat them, tortured them, deprived them of food, and raped them. A German from Kołobrzeg wrote in a letter to his family about his experience (August 7, 1945): "As we were going home, we suffered so much nastiness. We were stopped by Poles on the open road. They first asked about valuables, then raped the young women and girls, and even children, and then robbed us. You could hear nothing but cries and weeping, they were terrifying to hear. They stole everything from us. A Soviet soldier took our last suitcase away from us on the road between [probably—MZ] Stargard and Nowogard.... We are living in terrible conditions, you just can't imagine."[47]

There were also anti-German pogroms. We have the most horrific description of one that took place in Aleksandrów Kujawski and Nieszawa (in today's Kuyavia-Pomerania Province). Immediately after the Soviet winter offensive had gone through Aleksandrów, a militia group formed with Mateusz Pawlak as its commander. The majority of the Germans, civil servants and NSDAP functionaries, had fled with the retreating Wehrmacht. Left behind were old, sick people and women with children. Already in early February 1945, Pawlak had shot to death Edmund Weber, who declared that he was a Pole albeit from a German family, as his wife and little daughter watched. A pogrom took place in nearby Nieszawa, near Aleksandrów. All the local Germans were herded to one location. As they marched off to work, they were forced to chant loudly, "We, Germans, murdered Poles." In the night of February 4–5, several militiamen, drunk, as was often the case, took some of the Germans to the bank of the Vistula and drowned between ten and fifteen of them.[48]

It is likely that more such lynchings took place. After the war, it was very easy to kill a German, especially if it could be claimed that he had offered resistance, and no one was persecuted or punished for it. The final victim count should also include those Germans who died of disease, hunger, and psychological and physical mistreatment in labor camps, hundreds of which dotted the so-called Regained Territories. The number of anti-German kangaroo courts in Poland was actually low compared to the Czech Sudetenland, where in the spring and summer of 1945 murders and pogroms proliferated. But this difference cannot be explained by the Poles' greater empathy for the defenseless and defeated Germans or by the Czechs' greater desire for revenge. Instead, it can be ascribed to the presence of many thousands of Red Army troops in Pomerania, East Prussia, and Lower and Upper Silesia, where soldiers with red stars on their helmets could be seen everywhere. In the Sudentenland, by contrast, virtually no one except a handful of Soviet units was present, only Czechs and Germans coming face to face.

In Poland on many occasions, after they captured a town or village, especially one that had been well-defended by the Wehrmacht, Red Army troops would fly into a destructive, vengeful rage, which could include executing women and children. For example in Przyszowice in Upper Silesia, after a battle in which they suffered heavy losses, the Red Army murdered over one hundred civilians.[49] Germans were still being executed in June 1945, according to a letter posted in Brzeg, a small town in Lower Silesia. A Pole who continued to fear the Germans wrote, "This is what happened here this week: civilian germans [sic] attacked in the town, murdered 15 russki soldiers and 5 Polish girls. The town was surrounded by the russki army. 150 germans [sic; certainly an inflated figure—MZ] were executed at a wall. There are still many germans [sic] here, we're sitting in dungeons, it's scary to go out at night because someone may suddenly shoot, run away and hide in a hole."[50]

The fury of battle and frontline behaviors gradually gave way to the mechanisms of governing. The Supreme Command Headquarters ordered Red Army troops to adopt a "more humanitarian" approach toward German civilians already on April 20, 1945. Poles repeatedly suggested that they did not understand why the Soviet military, who had earlier been focused *protiv Germantsom* (against the Germans) now began to side with their recent enemies, spreading a protective umbrella over them to protect them from Polish aggression. Some German memoirs and accounts also mention the Russians as "protecting us from the Poles."[51]

The violence also ran on fear, which is difficult to quantify. Fear breeds hatred, hostility, and prejudice. Even after liberation, fear lived on in people's minds, bringing on panic, the drive to hunt Germans, and escapist behaviors. Kazimierz Pużak, Polish Socialist Party—Freedom, Equality, Independence activist and chairman of the underground Council of National Unity, passed through the train station in Zagłębie in March 1945. The monotony of waiting for his train was often interrupted by alarms "raised, usually by women, who can detect Germans hiding everywhere. So they make a ruckus and drag in militia officers, who do not like to intervene, since it never leads to anything, and to the outrage of those hysterical creatures."[52] This fear was expressed in rumors circulating in the spring of 1945 that the retreating Wehrmacht was poisoning wells and food warehouses and leaving behind methyl alcohol to blind and poison the arriving Slavs.[53] A letter posted on April 13, 1945, related, "There are rumors that they brought 16 rail cars from Prussia with poisoned people, but who knows whether this is possible."

There was similar gossip in Rzeszów Province: "Again, people are talking about how the Germans have poisoned everything, sugar, sweets even well water, we are afraid to buy sugar because many people have died in Sandomierz, and you, too, should be careful."[54]

A wave of rumors about the post-Nazi underground, Werwolf, traveled across Poland in the second half of 1945. As Hugo Steinhaus noted in his diary, "People are returning from Lower Silesia because they're afraid of German raiding parties."[55] Many factors shaped the appearance of this proliferation of hearsay and returns, most importantly the general atmosphere of insecurity. Teeming crime, especially in the post-German lands, also played a role. Another likely factor was the transfer of thinking about experiences of occupation-era underground activity to the postwar era along the lines that since "we" conspired, "they" will too. Also important may have been the panic about a fifth column, which in September 1939 had made people see every German one-dimensionally as a potential enemy. Furthermore, there indeed were some sporadic attacks or acts of self-defense by Germans,[56] which in the collective imagination grew to armed resistance, if not something even bigger. Someone wrote on August 21, 1945, "It's dangerous to go to Prussia . . . because there are many germans [sic] there and they're killing Poles." A woman living in distant Hrubieszów in the southeast wrote about her fear of the Germans: "I'd like to go to the German lands, but I'm afraid to because people are coming back from there and talking about holdups by German bands."[57]

The Communist authorities quickly learned how to exploit this fear. The alleged threat from the Germans helped to legitimize the new regime as the defender of the national interest, made it possible to shift the blame for the Soviet marauders' misbehavior onto the no longer existing Werwolf bands, and was used to argue for speeding up the forced expulsions. *Głos Wielkopolski* reported in September 1946, "The Germans are murdering Poles. German bandits are roaming Polish forests."[58] But anti-German phobias intensified the most over the expected return of the Germans to the so-called Regained Territories, as, people believed, what the Poles had taken in accordance with the Potsdam Agreement and what they had looted afterward would be taken away from them. This fear survived until the end of People's Poland in 1989.

UKRAINIANS AND BELORUSSIANS: THE SLAVS' PEASANT WAR

The postwar ethnic violence against the Ukrainians was also driven by fear. The events of 1918–21 were an early stage of this conflict, as were the battles for Lvov and the Ukrainians' disappointed hopes of living in their own sovereign state. The interwar period had also not been emotionally neutral. The terror inflicted by the Ukrainian underground on the one hand and the vengeful policies of the Polish state on the other did nothing to help bring the two nations close. The conflict took on a new dynamic after the German-Soviet war broke out in June 1941. Mutual perceptions, which had earlier ranged from positive to negative, came to be dominated by hostility and hatred, in part thanks to the German policies of setting the two nationalities against each other.[59] The war cast the Ukrainians and the Poles on the opposite sides of the barricade. Now, the Ukrainians attached hopes of national sovereignty to the war while the Poles at first were relieved that the Soviet occupation had ended, but soon learned that the Ukrainian-German cooperation represented a deathly threat to them.

A top-down political decision of the Ukrainian underground led to the mass murders of the Polish population in Volhynia. They began in the spring of 1943 and carried on until the spring of 1945, leaving some one hundred thousand dead. They followed the German example of the recent "modern" extermination of the Jews, but the slaughter, which the historian Grzegorz Motyka calls "genocidal ethnic purges," most often followed the peasant tradition of using primitive methods, wielding axes, pitchforks, and singletrees. "Ax-men" were probably the most terrifying.[60] Adding to the fright was also the fact that the killers spared no one, not even women, children, or the elderly.

In describing the conflict, all memoirs from Volhynia feature the total fear brought on by the slaughter.[61] Some people panicked, running as far as possible from the burning buildings and the screams of those being murdered. Others were paralyzed by fear and surrendered to their fate, followed orders to lie down on the ground or stand over a ditch, and waited for the shot or the ax to strike. Someone remembered that "when they start killing us, we must sing [the religious hymn] 'Pod Twą obronę' out loud. Granny's advice inflated the anxiety to the verge of panic."[62] Even those who attempted to defend themselves were terrified. Father Anczarski wrote in late July 1943 that "the people are terrified. Almost no one sleeps at night. They have pitchforks, axes and scythes at the ready. Fear is suffocating the poor folks. The day goes by somehow. But not the night, what horrific nights. Anxiety and terror come crawling out of every hole."[63] The universal presence of these emotions allows us to define the Poles' psychological condition as a collective psychosis of fear resembling the German terror in the winter of 1944–45 and spring of 1945.

A maximum dose of negative emotions, fear and hatred, was stored in nightmares, which would recur for years, as did insomnia and neuroses. It would infect Polish perceptions of Ukrainians for many years, even though reminiscences often included statements like this one: "There were very noble people among the Ukrainians, who opposed this criminal activity, often risking their lives."[64] The anti-Polish ethnic purge nonetheless strengthened the stereotype of the Ruthenian slaughterer, which for many Poles meant that the Ukrainians personified fear. It injected them with resistance to rational arguments, which during and after the war led to outbursts of mass panic, which spread with great ease thanks to the "trauma of Volhynia." The largest such outburst went through the towns and villages of eastern Lesser Poland in the spring of 1944. The anxiety that accompanied the approaching front further magnified the hysteria. The panic—as usual—began with a rumor. Father Anczarski noted:

> First 48 hours of terror. The Soviet army is attacking with all its forces. The Germans are running away.... There is deathly dread in town. I don't know where the story came from that before the Red Army comes, the Ukrainians will organize a bloody massacre of the Poles. They're getting ready, masses of them will come, they're armed. No one will come out of this butchery alive.... People's nerves are magnifying the terror of the situation. The town is totally panicked. Bloody slaughter is coming. People are wandering around like lunatics and thinking of ways to save themselves. The day passes in nervous excitement. The night is worse. This pogrom will definitely happen tonight. Dull sounds of war can be heard from a distance.... The band did not attack the town, there was no slaughter. But the dread was horrific.[65]

People also reacted to fright with flight. Villagers would move to larger towns, but because they often still did not feel safe there, they migrated farther west, and so the prewar Poland's southeastern territories emptied out.

The next part of this story took place in 1945–47, when the Ukrainian-Polish war shifted to Lublin Province, to the areas around Chełm and Hrubieszów, and to Rzeszów Province, near Przemyśl and Ustrzyki. The two sides burned each other's villages and ruthlessly murdered civilians. The laws of revenge and fear ruled in the midst of chaos. This state of affairs is often described in letters intercepted by the War Censorship Office as their principal topic. Members of both nationalities wrote about the anxiety that tormented them day and night, the horror at the news of bloodshed, the escapes and the panic. In their private correspondence, virtually all the Poles wrote the word *Ukrainians* with a lowercase *u*.

A man living in the village of Gozdów, Hrubieszów District, wrote on May 6, 1945:

> We are not safe because Ukrainian bands attack villages and burn them, they also kill people, so on 18–19 May a Ukrainian band came to a village 2 km away from us and burned the whole village and killed many civilians and also wounded many. They also came to our village. The drove their car through the whole village and didn't bother anyone, so people went into a terrible panic and we fled to another village where there is a police station and a village office. We only came back home yesterday. There are awfully many such incidents since the ukrainians [*sic*] threaten the Poles terribly.[66]

The authors of the letters often referred to the Volhynia experience, fearing a repeat of 1943. In a letter of May 23, 1945: "There are more and more fires in the

Ethnic Phobias and Violence

area. The Ukrainians are on the move again . . . things are just awful."[67]

On May 31 (Hrubieszów District): "And so we live from day to day, in fear. We are on the lookout every night because about a hundred Bandera people are nearby."[68]

And on September 2: "Yes, Stach, we're in danger now. There are masses of Bandera's people in our forests. No one can sleep at night, everyone is on guard. All the young people are in the forests, making bands and so on. So we're scared of this, hope that it doesn't end up like in the east. Our lives aren't safe."[69]

Thousands of people were murdered with axes, sawed through with saws, and drowned in wells. The ruthlessness attributed to the Ukrainians seemed savage, inhuman, and primitive, and it evoked supreme fear. No wonder, then, that it featured prominently in the correspondence. Several letters include descriptions of bodies that were tortured before they were killed: ripped-out tongues, poked-out eyes, cut-off breasts. A letter posted in Łaszczów, Tomaszów District, in southeastern Poland on May 22, 1945, reads:

> Things are very bad here, we're always ready to run, our life hangs by a thread because we're thinking about this only. On 18 May we had a huge disaster, some people went to Rzeplin and Łachowiec [villages near the border with Ukraine] to work in the field, the ukrainians [sic] attacked them and murdered 35 people. Ten have been found, murdered in such a way that you can't bear to look at them. They beat them with sticks, broke their arms and legs, stabbed their eyes out, twisted their heads and burned their flesh here and there, they're burned, with peeled-off skin, noses, lips and tongues [ripped out], they cut off a woman's breasts and knocked out her teeth. You can only imagine how they suffered. These people were brought to our cemetery, so I saw everything with my own eyes.[70]

Village of Borów, Krasnystaw District, June 10, 1945: "On 26 May a very important accident happened here: some Poles came to do a roundup in the next village, the forest army surrounded [us] and they killed everyone. They poked out eyes, sliced off ears, noses, broke out arms. They didn't kill them dead, those who before they finished their lives dug out holes a meter deep under themselves. Very ghastly things are happening here, whenever a military person shows up, he won't be back. The forests are full of them, just like in our Volhynia."[71]

A letter written in June 1945: "We're thinking of going to East Prussia because there is no hope of going home. Taras Bulba's people are still patrolling the villages. They come from the stations in Sokal, Bełżec, Uhnów. Any Pole they catch, they murder him dishonorably. They poke out eyes, cut out tongues, noses, ears, they knock out teeth, poke them through with bayonets and throw them into ditches covered with straw and burn them. So that if you see this person, you can't bear to take a bite for a week."[72]

In these accounts, an ethnographer would probably see a traditional society's interest in what death looks like. Indeed, it was a Polish village custom to take photographs of the living next to the dead lying in a coffin. A psychologist would note the witnesses' natural need to talk about a trauma they experienced, to share it in order to protect their mental health. They wrote about their dread, their perpetual fear, their thoughts of fleeing from the areas immersed in war. "It's all going up in smoke, fear after fear." Experiences and fear paralyzed people: "I will write more in my next letter because right now my nerves are torn up so I can't focus." A hermeneutist would interpret the descriptions of the massacred bodies not in terms of what the letters' authors meant but in terms of the meaning that would be assigned them by the addressees. He or she would note that the descriptions of poked-out eyes on the one hand emphasized the Ukrainians' savage nature and on the other elevated their Polish victims and fired up the mechanism of Polish hostility. Thus was created the topos of the horrific tale of the murdered Poles, of "Polish innocence," of the nation that was being harmed and betrayed by all while it remained pure.

Letters also told about corpses floating down the San River, on May 31, 1945: "There are terrible attacks by Bandera's people against Russkis and Poles. On Friday the 25th and Sunday the 27th of May, drowned people were floating down the San. There were men, women and children, their hands tied back, no one knows who drowned them."[73]

And the burning of a village described to an addressee in Poznań and posted in June 1945: "We're living now in fear of Ukrainian attacks. In Borownica they shot 70 people and burned the whole village; the same happened to the village of Dolna Tyrawa near Mrzygłód.... And the corpses are lying everywhere. People are dropping like flies."[74]

A statement to the police from a father whose daughter allegedly "traipsed around with a Ukrainian" is an interesting example of the growing distance between the ethnic groups and the anti-Ukrainian phobia. Women who "collaborated vertically" with Germans received similar warnings and threats. The harshest penalty such women suffered was head-shaving. A letter dated June 1, 1945, reads:

> I would like to draw your attention to the fact, Sir, that your daughter has been a tramp, hanging around with a soldier who is a Ukrainian. She brings him home and spends a week at a time in the area of Cracow and traipses around like the basest of harlots with a ukrainian [sic], who is an enemy of the Polish nation, and your daughter is betraying the Home Army organization. I am giving you this warning because you housed him from 22 May 1945 to 30 May 1945. You must admonish your daughter that she may meet the same fate as those misses who waited on the germans [sic] and traipsed around with germans [sic]. I am sending this notice with the assistance of witnesses Garczewski, Woźniak, Bystry.[75]

Psychological corruption, mental leftovers of war, can also be seen in the actions of some soldiers of the Polish underground. The idea of forcing Ukrainian boys and girls to dance naked before they were executed brings to mind the "games" the Nazis invented for Jews. A Polish unit invaded the village of Świerże on the Bug River, in which many Ukrainians lived. It was probably Polish villagers who described what happened:

> Some [Stanisław Mikołaczyk's backers] came to our village, Świerże and put on dancing and then they locked the doors so that no one could get out and forced the russki girls to strip naked and dance like that with the boys, who were also naked. After the dancing was over, they cut off the girls' hair and also killed three people in the room and drove off. It's very difficult for us to bear living through such times when at any moment these damned vipers may appear. As long as the armies were here things were calm, but as soon as they left, those guys started up again.[76]

And: "There are awful bands here in Świerże. They killed 4 boys. There was a dance, which some military guys organized, and the young people went. More of them came late in the night, they surrounded it and told both the lasses and youths to take off their clothes and dance. And this is how the Home Army does things here. We don't sleep at home, if you come you'll see what's going on here."[77]

In the spring and summer of 1945, Polish underground units (National Armed Forces, Armed Forces, National Military Organization, Freedom and Independence) pacified over a dozen Ukrainian villages, murdering the majority of their inhabitants. In the village of Pawłokoma, Home Army soldiers commanded by First Lieutenant Józef Biss (pseudonym "Wacław") killed close to the whole population, 365 people including women and children,[78] and on April 17, 1945, in the village of Piskorowice, a unit of the National Military Organization killed over 400 Ukrainians. Smaller liquidation actions that killed a dozen or a few dozen people were carried out almost daily. According to Grzegorz Motyka, there was a significant asymmetry between the numbers of the victims on the two sides. He argues that while the Ukrainian partisans generally carried out mass murders of civilians, the Poles also murdered, at times also ruthlessly, but this was an exception and not the rule.[79] The Polish authorities also attempted to push the Ukrainians out of Poland, harassing those who resisted. Up to November 1945, terror by the underground and government security organizations forced 123,000 Ukrainians to leave Poland. In revenge, the Ukrainian Insurgent Army burned down Polish villages. Both sides were afraid, and cruelty and violence diffused the fear. The governor of Rzeszów Province wrote in a report,

"The Polish population is living in constant fear of raids by Bandera's and other bands. And the Ukrainian population is living in fear of Polish Army actions, which in their pacification actions use persecution against them."[80]

The Polish-Ukrainian conflict became an ordinary ethnic purge, in which the goal of defeating enemy troops was outweighed by forcing the other side's civilian population to leave the disputed territory with continual raids, rapes, and burning of villages. Letters written by ordinary Poles reveal their authors' belief that ridding Poland of their Ukrainian neighbors was essential, which seems to have been a widespread belief in Polish society. A letter mailed from Przemyśl on August 18, 1945, reads:

> There is no one who can force the Ruthenians to leave, even though they are being robbed very much at night, their possessions are being taken away, clothing, and on top of that they kill them as much as they want, all this week not a night passed without a robbery. They also came to our farmer's wife, but she hid her cows in the orchard. They only asked me where the farmer is, but I said that everyone has run away, so they left. There were 4 of them, so they took 13 pieces of cattle. The ukrainians [*sic*] here are saying that this didn't happen when there were no Poles from the east. They won't even let people go out in the fields, they only kill and will take away the poor farm, but they say that they took everything away and they won't leave.[81]

From Sielce near Chełm, June 1945: "Father's brother Andrzej came to stay with us so they [the Polish partisans—MZ] took his uniform, and if he'd resisted they would have killed him. They don't kill Polish military men, they only took all his clothes off till he was barefoot, burned the airplane in the airfield, killed two russki airmen, the day before yesterday they killed all the Ukrainians who didn't want to go to Russia in the village next to ours."[82]

In 1947, the Communist authorities issued a decree about operation "Vistula," the resettlement of the entire Ukrainian population from southeastern Poland mostly to the north and west. Motyka believes that this resettlement was unnecessary and that by implementing it the government was adopting the principle of collective responsibility and that its only real goal was to create an ethnically homogeneous Polish state.[83] But again: there are many indications that this operation had the support of the Polish people, who remained under pressure from their powerful fear and their desire for revenge for the Ukrainians' slaughter of Poles in Volhynia, something that the Communist government was well aware of, if only from the correspondence quoted here.

Ethnic phobias also influenced postwar Polish-Belorussian relations. The several hundred thousand Belorussians living in Poland, mostly in districts of Białystok Province along the new Polish border, were Orthodox and mostly peasants, and had none of their own organizations. These relations had worsened already in 1939. After the arrival of the Red Army, Communist raiding parties made up mostly of Belorussians robbed Polish landed estates and often brutally murdered their owners, attacked Polish soldiers who were attempting to evade capture. Subsequently, the Poles blamed the Belorussians for collaborating with the NKVD, organizing and joining Soviet government organizations, reporting to the authorities, and creating lists of Poles to exile into the far reaches of the USSR. After Poland's 1944 "liberation" by the Red Army, it remained unclear which state the region would become a part of. No one knew whether Stalin would incorporate it into the USSR, something a majority of the Belorussians were hoping for. These hopes worried the Poles (see chap. 11's section titled "Poland, but Where?!"), and their anxiety, or maybe actual fear, influenced their relations. "There is great antagonism between the Belorussian and the Polish populations," reads a report by the official Eugeniusz Szyr, who visited Białystok in September 1944.[84]

According to the historian Eugeniusz Mironowicz, the Polish Committee of National Liberation authorities' justified fears about which state the Białystok region would be incorporated into made them develop a strategy of including the Belorussians in the construction of the Polish Communist power apparatus. Many Belorussians, sometimes a majority, were employed in local Polish Workers' Party committees, as well as in local village offices, National Councils, and the Security Office and Citizens' Militia. In early 1945, the Polish Workers' Party in Białystok District had 228 members, of whom 175 were Belorussian, 52 were Polish, and 1 was Jewish.[85] But there were reasons for this makeup other than the government's political strategy to acquire broad support among the population. In prewar Poland, ruled by the "lords," the Belorussians who had been discriminated against for being Orthodox and "russkis," hoped that "people's" Poland would be a country where they would have a shot at social and national advancement, something they had in common with some Jews. But the Polish underground viewed this stance differently, as disloyalty and support for an alien regime. The pacifications conducted in the Białystok region by the Germans and later the Red Army showed how such "sins" should be punished. Their ideological motivation was the prewar National Democratic slogan "Poland for the Poles," whose fulfillment appeared to the underground's supremely patriotic fighters as the order of the moment. To force it to leave Poland, the Belorussian population was thus intimidated, beaten, and robbed, and its villages were burned.[86]

Fear and uncertainty vis-à-vis the Poles and the Polish state dominated the Belorussian state of mind.[87] "Here, Polish bandits are going after the Belorussians . . . and none of us is sleeping at home," reads a private letter.[88] The aggression that grew during the war, combined with a radicalized nationalism, ended with the murders of civilians. A letter from the village of Kleszczele in Białystok Province read, "We led a calm life until the Polish partisans appeared. They burned us to ashes, the whole village was burned, all the buildings and all people. Our building was burned with all the building and inhabitants . . . In our building they burned 7 sheep, a cow and a colt, and they took the mare with them."[89]

The "Polish bandits," said the Belorussian people, would murder for a trivial reason—for example, for allegedly having a negative attitude toward the forest army. In late January–early February 1946, the Third Brigade of the National Military Union commanded by Captain Romuald Rajs (pseudonym "Bury") burned the villages of Zaleszczany, Zanie, Szpaki, and Końcowizna. Eighty-seven people, including women and children, died in the flames or by gunfire, and dozens were seriously injured. Some were spared by declaring themselves Catholic—just like during religious wars. Some Poles accepted the violence against their Belorussian neighbors while some, maybe out of great fear, pointed out the houses inhabited by Belorussians. But the majority of Poles could not believe that it was Poles who burned the villages.[90] People accepted the goal of creating a one-nation state but not the methods used by Captain "Bury."

THE JEWS, THEY'RE MURDERING OUR CHILDREN!

"The Jews' situation is strained, people are assaulting and robbing them. In Radom 4 jews [sic] were killed. In the evening the jews [sic] go out till 9, they're afraid of the night, this is the second time they are living like this. There are still Fascist bands, which are immersed the Nazi spirit, in the forest. There are pogroms all over Poland. They want to murder all the others. Don't come."[91]

This letter was sent from Radom on August 14, 1945. It reveals the dramatic situation and the tragedy of the Jews who have survived the Holocaust, the terror and fear they must have felt at the news coming from everywhere about Jews being murdered. The victims were coming out of hiding, sometimes whole families, returning from the camps; some were Jewish militia officers and Security Service functionaries. Between the time the Germans fled and the end of 1946, more than a dozen pogroms, lynchings, and anti-Semitic disturbances occurred across Poland. According to the latest research, about 1,100 Jews were murdered.[92] On the one hand, if we take into account the fact that there were times in the Polish-Ukrainian conflict when as many as several hundred civilians were killed in a single skirmish, this number of Jews murdered after the war may seem low. But, on the other hand, the tragedy of killing people who had only just survived the Holocaust is staggering. And it begs the question: why would anyone kill Jews in Poland after the Second World War?

Jan T. Gross's widely discussed study *Fear: Antisemitism in Poland after Auschwitz* is constructed around this and related questions. Gross argues that an unwritten social agreement existed in Poland that allowed people to suspend the norm "thou shalt not kill" in the context of Jews. He explains the murders of Jews with fear and guilt—fear of responsibility for shared involvement in the Holocaust and the Jews' potential claims on their homes and other property taken over by their Polish neighbors, and guilt about it.[93]

Gross is right to point out the prevalence of anti-Semitic views and to treat them as an important clue to understanding that era's collective behaviors in Polish-Jewish relations. But it is not the only clue. Also, apart from the pogroms, violence against the Jews was not much different from other ruthlessness and wrongdoing in wartime and after the war. True, it was not motivated by "victims' revenge," as was the case with violence against the Germans, nor by a desire to avenge earlier massacres, as was the case with the Ukrainians. But the Belorussians were also not murdered "in retaliation" for harm they had inflicted during the occupation. The fact that a Belorussian woman may have been killed for putting up a religious icon in her home of course does not make this crime any easier to explain than the murders of Jewish survivors. But it does not make Gross's questions any less important: How was it possible that Jews were killed after the war in Poland, where the crime of the Holocaust had taken place? Why did the anti-Semitic pogroms occur in August 1945 in Cracow and in 1946 in Kielce? Let's add three more questions: In the middle of the twentieth century, how could anyone believe in ritual murder? What is the connection between the belief that Jews drink human blood and the roots of these pogroms? Ethnologists and anthropologists emphasize that the meaning of a myth lies in its function. What were the social functions of the myth of ritual murder then, and how did the postwar condition of the Poles influence its eruption? To quote Jan T. Gross again, "That Jews were Communist, or that Jews were vampires, could not have been the reason they were perceived as a threat by their neighbors—because they were neither."[94]

Some hints and some answers to these questions are strewn around this book. The last part of this chapter, which summarizes the Jewish issue, brings them together and adds others. First, the myth of ritual murder was present in the postwar collective imagination, as were fears associated with it.[95] Much like archeologists do with the artifacts they study, this book will discuss all the known sites where this myth surfaced in 1945–47. A rumor about ritual murder preceded each one of the postwar pogroms.[96] We have a rough idea about how they progressed,[97] and therefore the focus here will be on the role of myth in these pogroms and its ability not only to inspire and shape attitudes but also to muster people to be violent. The story of this myth is the story of the Great Terror in a capsule.

THE PRESENCE OF MYTH

One of the first mentions of ritual murder appeared in the spring of 1945 in a report from Major Szlomo Herszenhorn, the head of the Office of Assistance to the Jewish Population, a government office, listing assaults on Jews in March of that year. Herszenhorn wrote, "In Chełm Lubelski rumors spread recently that Jews had killed a Christian boy and used his blood to make matzo. Responding to a request from anti-Semitic activists of the Home Army persuasion, the local militia arrested some Chełm Jews and only released them in response to a strict order issued by the town's Soviet commander."[98] Herszenhorn did not specify what he meant by "recently"—mid-March or early April? (His report is dated April 4, 1945.) Throughout history, anti-Jewish unrest would usually occur close to Easter, which in 1945 was on April 1. The myth of ritual murder, which Christians had believed in for centuries, was linked to Passover, when Jews allegedly used the blood of an innocent Christian child to produce matzo. Blood was also allegedly needed to cure circumcision cuts or to remove the odor allegedly emitted by Jews. Another version of the accusations was to replicate the Passion of Christ: the victims were allegedly first tortured and then crucified.⁹⁹ Passover usually coincides with the Christian Good Friday, and so the rumors about the Jews killing the boy, if they were told then, may have had a deeper religious basis. We do not know who started them, but for the purpose of this analysis, we need to note that they mentioned militia officers. We also do not know the broader background to the events that took place in Chełm. According to earlier reports from the Office of Assistance to the Jewish Population, between October 1944 and February 1945 relations between the Polish and Jewish communities worsened noticeably.¹⁰⁰ This coincided with the wave of assaults on Jews that crossed Poland in March and April 1945. The fact that the Soviet military commander needed to issue a "strict order" may mean that it was a major incident, and everyone knew about it locally. But there is no evidence that it went any further.

Rzeszów

The next chapter of the mythology of ritual murder was written in Rzeszów. But our knowledge about what happened in that town in June 1945 is based on scraps of information and still remains very unclear. We do know that on June 7, nine-year-old Bronisława Mendoń, daughter of a horse carriage driver, went missing. According to the report written by an investigator at the District Command of the Citizens' Militia in Rzeszów who was on duty at the time, her book bag was found on June 11 in a cellar of the house at 12 Tannenbaum Street (today Okrzei) by Kazimierz Woźniak, son of the teacher who tutored the girl. He reported his finding to the district commander of the Citizens' Militia, First Lieutenant Jan Grzeszek, who, along with seven of his colleagues, went to the cellar and found the girl's body. Its decay indicated that she had been dead for a few days. The murder was sexually motivated, and the killer had torn the skin off her face and cut out her thigh muscles.¹⁰¹ The militia officers summoned the Citizens' Militia operations battalion and announced that she had been murdered by Jews.

The ground and first floors of the building were occupied by Polish families. The second-floor apartment served as a sort of hostel for over a dozen men, Holocaust survivors.

Jonas Landesmann, a thirty-seven-year-old merchant who lived on the second floor and who was later accused of killing the girl, recounted the subsequent course of events of the night of June 11–12 after the girl's body was found: "About 200 militiamen surrounded the house at about midnight; about 20 militiamen entered our apartment. They were violent, they were shouting, 'Sons of bitches, you wanted Poland, you felt like murdering.'" They conducted a search and found some women's hair in an unused furnace. One of the officers declared that it was evidence that a corpse had been incinerated in it. Another one, probably in a fit of rage, began to shoot at the walls. 'They found the blood of some chickens the shochet had slaughtered together with the shirt of one of the Jews living there, which was bloody from a pustule on his body which had burst."¹⁰² The case documents also mention a page from the girl's notebook.¹⁰³ The Jewish residents of the second floor were taken down to the cellar and shown the girl's corpse. It was then that the militia reportedly declared that "the blood was drawn for ritual purposes and the apartment's previous owner, Rabbi Dr J. Leib Thorn, currently the Army Rabbi in Warsaw, is involved in this case."¹⁰⁴

The myth of ritual murder was reactivated. The militia officers did not create it, but each one of them most likely knew it from birth. When they discovered the girl's body and learned that there were Jews living in the house, they instinctively manufactured a falsehood: the Jews did it. They now only needed evidence, which they found during their search of Landesmann's quarters. The earlier suspicions became truth, which led to the persecution of Jews in Rzeszów, as a case of using the mechanism of a self-fulfilling prophecy with ritual murder as its flywheel. Given nothing more than a superficial makeover, adjusted according to whatever could be of use as evidence, it plotted the logic of subsequent events.

The officers in Rzeszów were likely country boys who, like the majority of those who joined the Citizens' Militia, got their jobs straight after coming out of the forest and received no training. They had no idea about how a murder investigation should be conducted, including confidentiality "for the benefit of the investigation." There is no doubt that as they became very agitated at discovering the corpse of the abused child, they wanted to boast that they already knew the perpetrator. This would explain why they spread the word that they had found a girl who had been killed by the Jews. It is unlikely that they wanted to use this as a provocation, which was noted already in 1945.[105] While conspiracy theories had their heyday in that time of conspiracy, secret services, and informers, today we should not believe in them. There is no evidence whatsoever that Polish or Soviet secret police were involved in any of the postwar pogroms. The documents that landed on Stalin's desk also do not justify believing that the Soviet authorities at that time even considered using an anti-Semitic provocation.[106]

What did the prosecution's investigation in the summer and autumn 1945 find? It came up with three items. First, the crime was most probably committed in the cellar of the house in Tannenbaum Street, and it was near there that the girl had last been seen. Second, the blood found in Rabbi Thorn's flat was not animal blood, as Landesmann claimed. But there was no evidence either that it was the blood of the murder victim or that it was not. Third, a graphologist determined "with likelihood bordering on certainty" that the writing on the notebook page found in the apartment "was in the same hand as the writing in 7 notebooks signed by Bronisława Mendoń." The investigation was dropped in December 1945 for lack of evidence.[107] Its materials do not include the testimony of key witness Kazimierz Woźniak, the boy who found the book bag. No one seemed to notice that the boy's family shortly moved away from Rzeszów.

Now let's look at the investigation from the point of view of the myth of ritual murder. There are many indications that the militia functionaries believed in the myth and that they used the girl's body and the material evidence to confirm it. First Lieutenant Grzeszek played a crucial role throughout the incident, but after the arrest he, and the other militiamen, reportedly disappeared.[108] It is noteworthy that similar circumstances led to both the Kielce pogrom and the attempts to start unrest in Kalisz. There, too, militia functionaries were important actors and there, too, they were the ones talking about ritual murder. In Rzeszów they created public hysteria, fury, and aggression, which were directed at the local Jews.

In the morning of June 12, all the Jews living in Rzeszów were taken to the militia station. They were beaten and insulted by the militia who had escorted them. The crowd, electrified by the news of a ritual murder, jumped to rob and plunder Jewish homes and workshops (including Józef Landau's small sweets factory). According to a report by the Jewish Religious Association, twenty-two homes and fifty-seven families were stripped.[109] People called the Jews being led to the militia station "criminals and murderers of Catholic children."[110] Stones and fists were put into use, and many people were beaten up. The Intelligence Brigades of the underground Armed Forces Delegation for Poland reported that taking part in the beating were not only the militia and civilians but "partly" also Security Office functionaries and Polish Army men.[111] Officers and men of the 104th Border Regiment of the sixty-fourth division of the NKVD Internal Security Forces put an end to the unrest.[112] It was probably "Soviet factors" that issued the order to release all the Jews immediately without questioning. The Provincial Command of the Citizens' Militia in Rzeszów declared the investigation of the District Command of the Citizens' Militia to have been baseless and the whole operation of charging Jews with ritual murder to have been a political provocation.

The girl's murder became the story of the day. Even though there was no mention of it in the morning papers, paperboys cried out, "The Jews murdered Catholic children." According to a Rzeszów Jew, who wrote down what happened after moving to Cracow on June 16, "The news of the murder of a dozen or so children spread through the city like wildfire. . . . The Catholic population gathered in the streets into the evening hours, commenting on the above-mentioned incident, and it even accompanied the ambulance carrying the corpse of the murdered child."[113] A Security Office functionary eavesdropped on some women chatting in

Rzeszów's market square: "See, says a woman in a group, they are murdering our children to repay us for feeding them and hiding them. Another one says: 'Here's a Katyn for our poor children, who already spent five years being tormented. Tut-tut, if it was my child who died like this, I would scratch out those jewlings' eyes, so that even the militia couldn't save them." This conversation reveals the power of the collective agitation that gripped the town's people, which was so great that lynching loomed. "They are praising the Nazis' deeds of stamping out Jews and the Poles who kept Jews." There were different versions of the story, including ones that as many as thirty children had been killed. There were predictions that a bloody revenge would take place.[114] In effect, the majority of Rzeszów's Jews left the town, fearing for their safety. The girl was buried in secret on the morning of June 13. This prevented the funeral from turning into a demonstration, an opportunity to start another pogrom.

The local daily *Dziennik Rzeszowski* attempted to convince its readers on June 12 and 13 that the murder had been sexually motivated and that only one girl's body—not over a dozen bodies—had been found, as rumor had it. The murderer would be found and punished. The paper suggested that it had been a "deceitfully invented provocation."[115] The historian Krzysztof Kaczmarski believes that instead of calming people down, the article only increased the anti-Jewish feeling, as it answered none of the questions the horror-struck people of Rzeszów had been asking, and only intimated, unconvincingly, that it had been a provocation.[116]

New speculation emerged, as people stubbornly believed that Jews were murdering Catholic children.[117] The persistent social disquiet gave rise to mythical thinking. The collective imagination fed on increasingly fantastical stories about sausage that was being made out of the flesh of Polish children. On June 14, a Security Office functionary summarized what the people in the street were thinking: "Where did the stories come from about human skulls, clothing, shoes with feet still in them. No one will be able to cover up this horrific massacre of Polish children and the making of sausage, of which kilograms and kilograms were found in a chimney." The culprits were the Jews, who were "most respected and valued" by the government, and at the same time who had "forever been exploiters, capitalists, persecutors of Christ's faith, murderers of the Polish people."[118]

We do not know whether it was the same individuals who spoke up about the Communist authorities' exceptionally favorable attitude toward the Jews and about Jewish vampires. Still, the anti-Semitic chimera was present in Rzeszów.

Landesmann, who was initially released with all the other Jews and subsequently rearrested on charges of murder, became the scapegoat. He stayed in a Rzeszów jail, where he was beaten and humiliated as a "cannibal and murderer of Polish children," until October 1945, then released for lack of evidence.

The story of this "unfinished pogrom" in Rzeszów shows how myth takes root in the collective imagination, and the ease with which it can mobilize people to engage in ethnic violence. We regrettably do not know the initial form of the myth, but it probably did not differ much from the version remembered by Landesmann, which he heard from the militia. Many authors who wrote about the Rzeszów events[119] cite the version that was already circulating in Rzeszów about a militia patrol who "came upon a rabbi in a blood-covered kittel standing next to the hanging dead girl, Bronisława Mendoń. Furthermore, pieces of human bodies belonging to 16 children were also found."[120] In fact, this version comes from an underground booklet published after the Cracow pogrom of August 11, 1945. And so it is not out of the question that the original story was built up over the two months and was therefore different from the one being told in the streets of Rzeszów. The figure of sixteen children seems to have appeared later, since in June there had been talk of eight or even thirty victims. The hanging girl was also probably added later. But the rabbi may have featured in the Rzeszów version already, since "Rabbi Thorn" appears in the documents of the case. It is also possible that in the version that was passed around orally the rabbi's clothes were covered in blood since, as we know, the evidence included bloodied clothing.

Polish anti-Semitism was not born in Rzeszów, and the myth of ritual murder existed in the public imagination earlier. But the context in which it erupted now is important to know. Beginning in March 1945, especially in the east and south of the country, Jews were increasingly attacked, mostly robbed. The motivation was usually to prevent them from taking back the property they had lost during the war. Rzeszów Province also saw robberies and murders.[121] The "unfinished pogrom" gave a new impulse to the existing wave of anti-Jewish violence. From a symbolic point of view, it boosted the stereotype of the Polish victim, which the Poles had constructed themselves. It morally justified aggression against the Jews: since they are murdering "our children," we must defend ourselves. In some circles, also those that usually came nowhere near mythical thinking, news of the murder of a child allowed people to say, "There must be something to it." Because the newspapers quickly forgot about the girl's murder and the murderer was not found, people could suspect that "they" were hiding something from "us," which stoked the atmosphere of suspicion, which helped myths to spread. All the more so since alleged new facts materialized. The underground booklet about it confirmed the "Rzeszów myth" with "when pressed, the rabbi broke down and confessed to everything."[122] The significance of the Rzeszów events also lay in the fact that they launched the myth's triumphant march, which was accompanied by escalating collective violence against the Jews.

The Jews left Rzeszów, but the myth went ahead of them. Likely with the militia in mind, Landesmann wrote that as early as June 12, "calls were made to different towns to stop traveling Jews and shoot them."[123] In this area of Poland, few places other than state institutions, including the militia, owned telephones. Could it therefore have been the militia who were responsible for spreading the myth by calling from station to station? If so, this would explain the spread of the news at lightning speed. However it happened, it must certainly have reached Przemyśl. The report of the Central Committee of Polish Jews by its members who were sent to inspect the situation in Rzeszów and Przemyśl reads, "During the conference, one Gruenbaum appeared in the Committee and declared that a woman, who had a child with her and who did not take him for a Jew, told him that she had miraculously extracted her daughter from the hands of a Jewish woman, who had kidnapped her and begun to flee with her." The myth was also recorded in Gorlice District, Cracow Province.[124] Hugo Steinhaus wrote in his diary on June 22 that in Tarnów people had invaded a house in which Jews were taking shelter, allegedly because little girls were disappearing. "It turns out that the ritual murder of Jews did not stop the myth, which will outlive the Jews."[125]

Cracow

In Cracow, people believed in the myth even before the Rzeszów events happened. The fact that it surfaced suddenly before Easter would support the hypothesis about the religious inspiration of the belief in the collective imagination that ritual murder was real. Jacek Kuroń, who was living in Creacow then, remembered:

> One day Mom asked grandfather to take [younger brother] Felek for a walk. Granddad took him by the hand and was pulling him along, as tearful Felek tried to escape. There was a bazaar right next to our house, which, with Easter coming, was very crowded. I was playing in the courtyard. Suddenly, a mob dragging granddad and Felek, who was wailing appallingly, invaded the courtyard. Note that Felek was a light-skinned blond, granddad an old worn-out man in a cap. Someone shouted: Where is that mother, let's see if it's her child. Felek, surprisingly, kept on crying, even though Mom took him into her arms as the crowd, ready to grab him, watched her carefully. 'If she was his mother, the child would not be crying,' they shouted. It turned out that the people had decided that granddad was a Jew, who was dragging the child for ritual slaughter, to make matzo. When the situation was cleared up, people in the crowd said that they had wanted to keep children safe.[126]

Kuroń does not write where in Cracow they were living then, but it is noteworthy that an old man with a crying child created such a sensation in the bazaar. The subsequent pogrom in Cracow, like the unrest in Lublin and Warsaw, started in market squares.

The security services were probably informed about this incident. Head of Cracow Security Office Jan Frey-Bielecki said in mid-August, "The story about murders allegedly committed by Jews of Polish children had been promoted in Cracow for several weeks."[127] The "sensational" news that thirteen bodies of Christian children had been found dashed through squares, bazaars, and junkyards in Cracow.[128] It likely came from Rzeszów and resurfaced on July 27, 1945, with the arrest of a woman suspected of abducting a child. In fact, the child had been left with the woman by its mother. But the rumor that a Jewish woman had kidnapped the child for ritual reasons, spread like wildfire.[129] "The throngs shouted anti-Jewish slogans, and a crowd, egged on by reactionary elements, attempted to demolish a shop owned by a jew [sic]," reported the militia.[130] Even without a pogrom, the hostility swelled.[131]

On Saturday, August 11, during a Sabbath service in the Kupa synagogue, dozens of hooligans began to throw rocks at the synagogue. Someone came out and grabbed one of the youths. He escaped, shouting as he ran toward the nearby bazaar, "Help, the Jews wanted to kill me!" This was the signal for an anti-Semitic riot to begin. A special Citizens' Militia report reads, "The rumor spread instantaneously in the so-called Tandeta square that two Polish children had already been murdered for ritual purposes, and the crowd began to lynch the Jews in the square."[132] The women vendors in a nearby square began to tell macabre stories. Some began to cry and wail. Some were talking about two murdered children, others eighteen or even eighty.[133] At the same time, three soldiers entered the synagogue and, coming out, announced to the throng that they had found the murdered child's body. People began to grab and beat Jews, including women and children. The crowd has been estimated at as many as one thousand people and "in the teens of thousands of observers."[134] Much like in Rzeszów and later Kielce, the militia played a key role here, actively taking part in the pogrom.[135] Five people were probably killed, and many more were injured.[136]

The myth of ritual murder gripped the popular imagination. By preempting interpretations and freeing people from having to think for themselves, it eliminated the need for critical analysis. It also shut out all doubt and defined the situation clearly: "The Jews killed the child." It imposed a normative order of behaviors, compelling people to act, to "beat up the Jews" in order to defend "our children." Asked in court "What made you act so bestially?" an active participant in the pogrom, a janitor in the Jewish shelter, testified, "Everyone here said that the Jews were murdering children. I also knew that soldiers were arresting mostly Jews, and so the old hatred of the Jews was reborn and I just got it off my chest."[137] As he beat a Jewish woman during the pogrom, he shouted, "You old whores, Hitler couldn't finish you off, we will finish you all off. You're living on Polish land, and you're murdering Polish children on top of it?"[138] One of the many militia officers taking part in the pogrom threatened, "You lousy kike woman, you killed two Polish children, you'll die in prison."[139]

The myth's rule of the popular imagination did not die out with the unrest. Its life after the pogrom is a separate chapter in its history. The number of witnesses who allegedly had proof of ritual murder suddenly began to grow, and the story of the myth lengthened, was enriched with new details. The story's background did not change much, only the props changed, as did the numbers of allegedly killed children. The absence of the children's corpses was explained variously—for instance, they had been burned. The day after the fight, a soldier who had been in the synagogue said that "he found children's corpses right there where he is standing. Some woman probably recognized one of the children and took it with her, and there was blood in the cellar on the left, and she was taken away by the authorities. Children's corpses were probably burned in the ruined oven."[140] According to the *Informacji o przebiegu zajść antysemickich w Krakowie* (Information about the course of the anti-Semitic incidents in Cracow), a "Soviet doctor" had seen the children's corpses and "in a conversation with Soviet soldiers had said that there were children's corpses, but they were not allowed to say it because the NKVD bosses are Jews!"[141] The myth condensed into a rumor during the pogrom did not explain directly why Jews would want to kill Christian children. This, too, was added afterward. Direct statements about vampirism appeared. In Niepołomice, railway guards told two Jews, "If you're going to drink Catholic blood, you must be swept out of this world."[142]

The myth of ritual murder was not a pretext or a smokescreen for violence against Jews. It had nothing to do with imagination, exaggeration, or insignificant gossip. As the historian of religion Mircea Eliade wrote, "To tell a myth is to proclaim what happened ab origine. Once told, that is revealed, the myth becomes apodictic truth; it establishes a truth that is absolute."[143] For some people in Cracow, the story of Jews killing Christian children revealed a definitive truth.

Private letters intercepted by the Office of Wartime Censorship in August 1945 confirm this:

Letter number one, from Cracow:

Unrest with jews [sic] is taking place here because, can you imagine, the jews [sic] have gone so far as to kill Polish children for their blood and they have been taking them by ruse, asking them to bring their suitcases to the synagogue. They paid them 100 zł each, and you know how children crave money, especially boys. One of them turned out to be cool, he heard children crying as he came close to the synagogue and without waiting for the rest of the five, he ran and let the militia know. The militia found a few corpses in the synagogue cellar. The news spread instantly across the whole city, and the Poles beat every Jew they saw and smashed the stalls at the bazaar. There was even a terrible shoot-out and there were some dead I don't know who exactly."

Letter number two, from Brzesk:

Let me tell you about one more incident in Cracow, which played out in the part of the city where I'm living now. Children have been missing for some time now, until on 11.8 a 14-year-old boy, whose arm veins had been cut, escaped from the clutches of the jews [sic]. The Jews were draining blood from the arms and legs of Catholic children, why? We will know soon. There have been incidents like this in Rzeszów, but the press explained that this was impossible. So now it has turns out to be the gospel truth. The population hurled itself and demolished the synagogue, and they made lynchings of jews [sic] they met in the street. The armed Jews defended themselves, but the army got involved and there was some brawling. Now no one can deny that the *yevrey* didn't do these things, not even the papers."

Letter number three, from Kralka in Niedźwiedź District: "What's new now in Cracow, the jews [sic] have murdered a dozen or so Polish children. Barrels of blood have been found. The Polish and Soviet armies are focusing on it now."

Letter number four, from Cracow: "There is unrest with the jews [sic] in Cracow now, that jews [sic] are catching small children and draining their blood for the jews [sic] who are coming back from the camps."

Letter number five, from Cracow: "You may have read in the newspapers about what was happening in Cracow on 11.8.45. What the Nazi jews [sic] wanted to do and what they did. They have been captured and there is no trace of them."

Letter number six, from Okocim: "I'm bringing you news from Cracow, the jews [sic] have tortured 17 Polish children, all this came out because a 12-year-old girl escaped with broken arms and lips and there was terrible noise and chaos. The Jewry began to shoot at Polish soldiers out of windows, and you couldn't walk in the streets. Several Polish soldiers were killed."

Letter number seven (only the soldier's family name and unit were given): "In Cracow the jews [sic] killed many Polish children again and drank their blood. Polish soldiers killed many jews [sic] and the NKVD shielded them."[144]

The letters quoted here reveal the background of the anti-Jewish terror. Who spread the stories about ritual murder? We will analyze their sociological characteristics and their typology later. It is clear from the letters that the authors' written Polish was poor or very poor, which means that they had completed only a few years of elementary school. They included at least one woman (letter number one) and two men, but the absence of first names makes it impossible to determine the others' gender. It is difficult to reconstruct their thinking, and therefore the conceptual origins of the pogrom, from these excerpts of letters, which report on events and do not try to analyze them. Furthermore, none of the people who relayed the myth took part in a pogrom, and all of them only reported what they had heard. In wanting to interest the "myth's recipients," they wrote "imagine" or "what's new now in Cracow" and called "adventures" they reported "news." Only one author appears to be a deviant anti-Semite, as can be seen in the epithet he uses of "Nazi jews" (letter number five). Nothing is evident about the other authors' views of the Jews, apart from one observation: all of them believed without an ounce of doubt that the Jews were killing Polish children. None of the authors used terms such as *reportedly*, *allegedly*, or *people are saying that*; in other words, none of them questioned the information he or she was relaying. The author of the second letter, the only one who read the newspapers, had come across someone questioning the authenticity of ritual murder, which can be seen in the phrase "now no one can deny," but even this would not change his views. Thus, all the letter writers were convinced that Jews were murdering children, but only one person had a vague notion of the motives for the alleged murders. For that person, the sense of the killing was not ritual but, so to speak, health-improving, as children's blood was allegedly being set aside to be drunk by Jews weakened by captivity in the Nazi camps. The question remains: if all these people really believed that children were being abducted and murdered, what was the pogrom to them? It was probably an act of revenge, but perhaps also a natural reaction to guarantee the safety of the youngest, who were in danger of being killed by bloodthirsty Jews. In other words, society's tolerance of violence against Jews may have originated from the social fact that people believed that Jews carried the danger of suffering and death. Paradoxically, concern for children would combine with ethnic hatred of the Jews to make the uncontrolled aggression targeting the Jews so powerful. Certainly, the hypothesis that primeval maternal instincts to protect one's children surfaced in the postwar pogroms is risky and needs to be further analyzed, which it will be later in this chapter. Anna Cichopek is mostly right when she writes about the Cracow pogrom that "an analysis of sources allows us to conclude that the main cause of these events was neither political ('Jewish Communism') nor economic prejudice (gains from taking over Jewish property), but a medieval stereotype of the image of the Jew as killer, which was deeply rooted in the public's thinking."[145]

The letters quoted here tell how the "Gospel truth" of the myth was transferred. Traveling by mail and orally, it quickly almost became a national truth. Thousands camped out in train stations, and trains were bursting at the seams. People also interacted profusely in the highly frequented market squares and halls in Cracow, Grunwald Square in Wrocław, Lublin's bazaars, and Warsaw's halls. In these conditions, "infection" by this myth could be instantaneous.

Incidentally, the social mandate legitimizing the use of violence against Jews came not only from some Poles' belief that Jews were murdering Polish children. The militia's and army's participation is key to understanding the genesis and evolution of all the postwar pogroms. The letters' authors also mention it. To social psychologists, people usually consider the use of violence by officially licensed formations and institutions lawful.[146] Approval for the army to "settle scores with the Jews" may have been all the greater since at this time the army enjoyed great public trust. During the war, everyone had someone who was close to them in the military, and it was "ours," "longed-for" and "a pearl among all the armies."[147] This is why the participation in a pogrom by people in uniform encouraged people to join in, too, and their most repulsive acts of violence in the Cracow and Kielce pogroms gained society's acceptance and even applause. Fleeing from the Kielce pogrom on July 4, 1946, Rachela Grunglas heard passengers on her train "praising the soldiers' deeds," since "the Jews were murdering children not only in Kielce but also Cracow."[148] Government authorities, too, turned the other way when violence was occurring and tried to cover up the army's and the militia's involvement. The letters also mentioned that "the armed Jews defended themselves" and there was some brawling, "but the army got involved" (letter number two) and "Polish soldiers killed many jews [sic]" (letter number seven), which the "recipients of the myth" could read as an obvious suggestion of which side in the Cracow troubles to be on.

It is likely that individual militia officers also played a role in the pogrom. Immediately afterward, "there were attempts to bring on unrest" in Dębica, Miechów, Słomniki, Wieliczka, Nowy Targ, Tarnów, and Zakopane.[149] Virtually all of Galicia was "infected." In Rabka, probably as revenge for the alleged murder of Polish children, someone threw grenades in the direction of the Jewish orphanage. In early September 1945, on a truck carrying people from Katowice to Sosnowiec, a thirty-five-year-old woman said loudly that "the Jews are not working, but sucking out the nation's blood, they should be put back in Majdanek and Oświęcim, like the germans [sic] did, they murdered children in Cracow, and in Katowice they've also killed a few children already. Interrogated by Security Office officers, she said 'I would rip the jews [sic] to shreds.'"[150] The myth also made its way to Silesia, but there is no information that it caused any social unrest there like it did in Olkusz, located between Cracow and Sosnowiec. The district starost reported that "one could notice great agitation and a lively reaction among the population in response to the Cracow events. Our local population is deeply convinced that the events are true, which is why one could observe a deepened niggling hatred of the jews [sic]."[151] There were similar reports from northern Mazovia, specifically from Płock. There, an attempted abduction of a child heated up the mood. Things came close to exploding in Częstochowa and Lublin. In Częstochowa already in August 1945, "a woman's child went missing. A version spread that jews [sic] had murdered it." Even though the child was found after a few hours, the pogrom hung in the air for the next few days.[152] The Częstochowa *Głos Narodu* wrote about it without giving all the details.[153] Equally little is known about the attempts to stir up unrest in Lublin. It would seem that it began along the same scenario as in Cracow, and the actors and the setting were also similar.

The disappearance of fourteen-year-old Zofia Niemczyńska on October 17, 1945, was the prologue. The girl's father reported her disappearance to the militia. The next day people began to gossip in Lublin's flea market on Lubartowska Street that "the Jews have abducted the girl to murder her for ritual purposes." A crowd, which was probably made up of vendors and invalids, gathered and tried to break into apartments inhabited by Jews. The sources do not tell us when the crowd was brought under control. *Sztandar Ludu* did not report on the events until five days later in language typical of that era's propaganda: "the struggle with the reaction's provocation." It also reported that the girl had run away from home afraid of her father, who was not pleased with her grades. The paper continued, "The Niemczyńska case showed that the poison of Nazi ideology, which was trickled into Polish brains for several long years has left traces in some circles, as a result of which all kinds of provocations, even those based on medieval prejudice, find a following. These lies have now been nailed."[154] Unfortunately, the attempt to "nail" the myth failed. Everything points to the fact that it lived on, although all the signals about its presence that we know come from five months later.[155] It is noteworthy that they came from Greater Poland, which had earlier manifested no symptoms of the "infection."

On March 22, 1946, *Dziennik Powszechny*, a regional Radom-Kielce paper, carried a story titled "Plotki o kiełbasach z mięsa ludzkiego" (Gossip about human-flesh sausage):

Warsaw. Reports from Gniezno: Sordid rumors have been traveling in Gniezno about the murders of children by unknown perpetrators and the making of meat, sausages, out of them, and selling it at very high prices to boot. This humorous rumor has seemingly been confirmed by the fact that several girls have disappeared in recent days, and have not been found. When the rumors caused an enormous panic and people began to point to K. the butcher as the perpetrator of the cannibalism and some parents did not let their children out, the authorities turned to this matter. The security office investigation revealed that one miss had gone to Gniezno for an operation without telling her parents about it, another miss went on an excursion with her fiancé without telling her parents. No one was hurt, and this put an end to the gossip about cannibalism.

Indeed, in November 1945 two girls went missing near Poznań, and they were probably kidnapped by a pedophiliac Soviet soldier. In January 1946, a schoolgirl was murdered. The socioeconomic situation in February and March 1946, a time of increased fear of hunger, may also have greatly influenced the growing panic. Beginning in February 1946, meat sales were limited. Butcher K. may have been thought guilty also, and, perhaps above all, for this reason. But we do not know whether this news from Kielce was noticed much, and how it was interpreted.

Włocławek

The myth's presence in Włocławek was also connected to meat. According to the local Security Office, on June 6, 1946, someone, likely a butcher or a shopkeeper, spread gossip that their competitors were selling "Polish human meat." The competition was the Cedwicka cooperative network run by people with Jewish roots, and their meat products cost less than the Polish butchers'. It is difficult to imagine that this was a coincidence, but on the same day two girls allegedly disappeared in Włocławek. One of them, eleven-year-old Halina Pastusiak, did not come home from school. The father of the second one reported her disappearance to the militia on June 7, after she had gone out to buy cigarettes the day before and not come back. "The rumor went all over town all the faster because of these incidents," said a telephonogram from the Provincial Office of Public Security in Bydgoszcz to Minister Stanisław Radkiewicz.

On 7 June '46 a few boys gathered outside the Jewish Committee at 4 p.m. at Królewiecka Street, shouting that the Jews were killing children. The passing population began to stop near these dozens of people. The Jewish Committee informed the District Public Security Office about it. The District Public Security Office sent several heads of departments to the location and called the Citizens' Militia for help. When the authorities ordered them to do so, the people dispersed immediately. There were no incidents between the Polish and Jewish populations. Patrols near the Jewish Committee and in the area inhabited by Jews were doubled for better security.[156]

This is all we know. Were the two girls found? Was this really an operation, which today we would call negative PR? Did anyone other than Minister Radkiewicz read the account of the events in Włocławek?

Częstochowa

In mid-June 1946 in Częstochowa, "dissatisfaction of an anti-Semitic nature" associated with the appointments of persons with Jewish roots to state office was said to be accompanied by gossip about "the murdering of children" in Wrocław.[157] Even though it is often impossible to decipher the meanders of collective thinking, it should be mentioned that the first issue of the Catholic periodical *Niedziela* published in June in Częstochowa ran a note on "Śląsk Dolny terenem kolonizacji żydowskiej" (Lower Silesia is a territory of Jewish colonization).[158] It seems that Częstochowa quickly began to delve into the local murder of a child. The mayor reported that "the fact of the finding on 18 June of this year in the pits of Hellman's brickyard in Kościelna Street of the body of 15-year-old Krystyna Woźniak, who has been strangled and thrown into a clay pit, is a certain tangible point of reference. Chil Teper, a tailor residing at 16 Wolności Avenue, who has been arrested and charged with committing the murder on the person of this girl, was handed over to the prosecutor's office and imprisoned. The autopsy did not determine deflowering or any other injuries to the body, other than the signs of strangling."[159] Several local girls pointed out Teper as the suspect. They testified that he had tried to convince them to commit depraved acts and to bribe them with sweets. But the defendant did not admit to murdering Krystyna Woźniak. Apart from the fact that he was said to have a soft spot for underage girls (one document described him as a "sexualist," another as "mentally abnormal"), the prosecutors found no evidence against him in the course of the investigation. He was held in jail, however, "in view of the special circumstances related to the Kielce events and the risk of similar events in Częstochowa."[160]

The milk was already spilled. Despite the authorities' news blackout, the rumor about Teper's crime and arrest reached the local population (we can only imagine the reaction of the girls' parents when they later said it had been a Jew who had killed their friend) and came close to bringing on a pogrom, which will be discussed later. It had likely already reached nearby Kielce, and certainly the Kielce militia.

Kielce

"Outright fantastical rumors" circulated in Kielce in early July 1946. "Soviet soldiers were allegedly sticking girls walking to their First Communion onto their bayonets."[161] This was evidence of the mounting anxiety disorder, and collective unease about children's safety, perhaps fed by the news from Częstochowa, was one of its manifestations.

The postwar animosity toward the Jews did not grow solely out of the delusion that they were abducting and murdering Christian children; rather, it was added to other collective beliefs to create an image of the Jewish threat. To be more precise, it was a whole complex of biases and occurrences. Lieutenant Srokowski, a functionary of the Provincial Security Office in Kielce, summarized this well. He reported in October 1945 that "in general, people's attitude toward the Jewish population is characterized by dislike.... This dislike and the negative attitude are expressed in complaints and emphasizing that Jews occupy top positions in the State administration. The rumors that Jews are allegedly receiving huge subsidies from the State are widespread among the Polish population. Furthermore, the fact that Jews are taking over their pre-war real estate creates a sort of dislike among the population."[162] In June 1946, a four-year-old girl went missing.[163] According to Father Roman Zelek, a priest in the Kielce cathedral, there were other abductions. He wrote:

For several weeks now, the people in Kielce have been talking about the quite frequent cases of missing children, parents were asking parish priests in Kielce to announce this, and also private notices about missing children, which included their age, clothing, description and appeals to bring the child to the given address in case of finding them, could be seen on the walls of buildings and on telephone poles. One case: a child (girl) from the Dominican Sisters' preschool in Karczowska Avenue was missing. According to news circulating in the city, two mothers who reported the disappearance of their children to the security authorities after the tragic day of 4 July were arrested, and as a result it is almost impossible to establish facts.[164]

The information he gave about the "frequent cases of missing children" is confirmed by testimony of Citizens' Militia functionary Antoni Kręglicki, according to whom three children had disappeared in the two months since July.[165] With this in mind, the reporting militiaman treated the next report with utmost seriousness, which then lay at the roots of the Kielce pogrom.

On July 1, 1946, nine-year-old Henryk Błaszczyk, son of the cobbler Walenty, went to visit friends in the countryside without telling anyone. His parents started a search, pasting three posters on walls and announcing in church that their son had disappeared.[166] More and more people learned about the boy's disappearance. The boy unexpectedly returned after two days. In the evening of July 3, his father appeared at the Citizens' Militia station in Sienkiewicz Street and claimed that Jews had been holding his boy for three days, but he managed to flee. He instructed his son, "Remember, son, if anyone asks you, you must say that you were with Jews, that you were in a cellar and a Jewish child freed you, opened a window and freed you."[167]

On the morning of July 4, father and son went to the militia station together, and then, accompanied by fourteen militia officers, visited a house inhabited by Jews at 7/9 Planty Street, where the Jewish Committee also had its offices. People, initially mostly women, had been gathering outside the building since morning. As the officers told the mob that they were on their way to look for the murdered children, it swelled and became more excited and aggressive. The mood became even more inflamed by stories of Jews "murdering Polish children." There was talk of a dozen or so victims. Antonina Biskupska, who was charged and eventually sentenced to ten years in prison for inciting murder, testified that on that day she had met a woman who told her that "the children murdered by the Jews [were found] and that their arms and legs are broken. She said that four Polish children were killed 'for their blood' and that their bodies were lying in Planty. The woman continued down the street, wringing her hands and crying 'Oh, no! Oh, no! Our Polish children have been murdered.'" Then, Biskupska and a neighbor went to Planty to "look at those children." There is no reason not to believe her account, as these women were clearly convinced that the killers were Jewish. It should therefore not surprise us that when Biskupska heard that "one of the children is still warm and that the murdered children are in the cellar, later that they were in the square, and later that they had been covered with lime to leave no traces," she began to shout, "Out with the Jews! They're murdering our children! We don't need them!"[168] Belief in a myth confirmed by reports of an alleged mass murder of children created an ontological compulsion and mobilized people to kill.

The psychological barrier between verbal aggression and physical violence snapped when Internal Security Corps and militia units arrived. The soldiers were the first to enter the house in Planty Street. They launched a pogrom, using a "division of labor." The military and militia operated inside the house, stealing, and beating and shooting at its defenseless residents. Dr. Seweryn Kahane, chairman of the Jewish Committee, was killed with a shot to the back. They took the other residents outside, into the throng, whose civilian and uniformed components are uncertain and probably changed. Some of the victims, including women, were thrown out of windows onto the sidewalk. A dozen or so people were killed in half an hour—many of them bestially. The wounded were finished off with whatever was on hand, planks or stones.

Three factors—the army's and militia's involvement, the robbery, and the myth of ritual murder—determined the outbreak of the pogrom and the scale of the violence targeting the Jews. Additional troops and noncommissioned officers dispatched to pacify the crowd either mixed in with it, adding to the mass of onlookers, or joined the attackers. The uniformed men had been trained to beat and kill, and their attitude vouched for impunity and provoked others to join in the pogrom. While the injured and dead were robbed outside, the true orgy of stealing exploded inside the building at 7/9 Planty. First of all, $10,000 that had been sent to help the Jews of Kielce was probably stolen.[169] The militia and soldiers grabbed literally everything they could. A militia functionary took a suit jacket, others a dress, shoes, undergarments, a watch, and money.[170] The second incentive for the pogrom was the myth. Throughout the pogrom, the cry "the Jews murdered Polish children" continued to fire up the mob to beat and murder, and the myth flooded the whole town. Rachela Grunglas, a witness, recalled, "The soldiers who encircled the building, not identifying me as a Jew, told us to go to the patisserie next door to wait it out, and so I made my way to the patisserie, where they answered my question by saying that the Jews had killed 12 Polish children, which is what a boy who was the only one out of the cellar to survive said. Furthermore, the Jews killed an officer and his child, who was found in the cellar and that's why the army is also looking for Jews and shooting."[171] The pogrom wave also reached the Kielce train station, and there, too, people were killed in revenge for alleged ritual murders. A witness remembered, "The mob was incredibly enraged and cried out hysterically: 'The Jews murdered our innocent Polish children in the cellars and took their blood to make matzo.'"[172] The pogrom began to die down, but it was fired up again when several hundred workers, armed with sticks, crowbars, and monkey wrenches, arrived from the Ludwików Steelworks. At this point, under five hundred people made up the crowd.[173] According to a functionary of the District Office of Public Security in Kielce, "As the Ludwików Steelworks workers arrived, murder and robbery flared up again. As a result, about 15 people were killed."[174] Much like in Cracow, the wounded Jews were still being robbed and beaten on their way to the hospital. A total of forty-two people were killed, including three non-Jews.

The Kielce pogrom was the greatest triumph of the myth of ritual murder in Poland's history. The story traveled at lightning speed and was accompanied by mass terror. "The pogrom enthusiasm went outside the town limits," wrote the sociologist Stanisław Ossowski.[175] On the very same day, it reached the village of Piekoszów, a few kilometers away, by train. "Word spread on the train that the Jews had murdered 10 children, and people were shouting: throw the Jews out of the cars, murder them because in Kielce they're murdering Jews."[176] People also passed the news by telephone, mostly on the militia's emergency lines. How else to explain the appearance of the myth in Kalisz, about two hundred kilometers northwest of Kielce, on the same day? The other evidence pointing to the "militia connection" is the purge conducted a short time afterward in the Kalisz Citizens' Militia. It affected 110 officers suspected of anti-Semitism; some were fired, and others were transferred to other posts.[177] Little is known about the events in Kalisz. We can guess that after hearing from their colleagues in Kielce that they were beating up Jews, they did the same. They repeated the rumor that a boy had gone missing. Just like in the game of telephone, the story began to transform itself. New versions of the myth appeared, and the numbers of victims increased. There was even talk of twenty-four. But allegedly, "thanks to the crowd's calm attitude and thanks to the arguments presented by respectable citizens, no disturbances occurred," reported Polish Workers' Party instructors sent there.[178]

The rumor about ritual murder spread across Poland, but the people of Kielce Province became especially excited by it, and there was a high chance of a pogrom happening there. In Ostrowiec Świętokrzyski, which got the news about the Kielce pogrom already on July 4, it was the militia and members of the new bourgeoisie, a restaurant owner and an ice cream merchant, who transferred the myth.[179] There were reports from Pińczów that the myth had spread at "lightning speed."[180] In Sandomierz, "people" were reportedly saying that "the jews [sic] have really murdered several Polish children, and so they deserve the murders that took place in Kielce." They emphasized that "in general this propaganda ends with empty words. No desire for revenge on the Jews has been observed anywhere."[181] The situation was different in Jędrzejów, where the news from Kielce engendered outspoken indignation. Another rumor, that several thousand Jews from the USSR would be arriving soon, appeared on July 12. The public reaction was hysterical: "bitterness, pandemonium, excitement, nervousness, inflammation."[182]

There were also forceful manifestations of the collective fear psychosis in Częstochowa, where the anti-Jewish sentiment had been growing since the Cracow pogrom. It was probably fueled by the rumors about Krystyna Woźniak's murder by Chil Teper in the second half of June 1946. This sufficed for the charges of murdering Christian children being made against Jews to pour out into the town's streets, mostly in poor areas. On July 6 in the Stradom district, a crowd of about four hundred people gathered, incensed by the alleged murder of a child by Jews. The militia searched the place where the corpse had reportedly been found and forced the mob to disperse. A day later in the poor area of Zacisze, some locals went out into the streets enraged by a rumor that the girl's body had been found in a field. The crowd came close to lynching a man walking to his factory job, "who looked like a jew [sic]." Militia and Security Office functionaries, who had searched the field and found nothing, broke up the crowd. On the same day, this time in the center of town, a man walking with a child and giving it sweets attracted a congregation. Probably realizing that the situation was becoming dangerous, he fled. Again, the militia dispersed the mob. Next, gossip had it that eight children with slit throats had been found in trash pits.[183] A week later, on July 15, the story repeated itself. Kazimierz Śpiewak took his brother's son for a walk on Złota Street in the Zawodzie district, which was inhabited largely by people from the social margins. An official document described how "he was attacked by civilians and accused of being a jew [sic] abducting a Polish child."[184] Another document reported that "people took him for a jew [sic] because he was dressed intelligently and wore glasses." After the militia inspected his documents, "the baffled crowd dispersed."[185] As the pogrom atmosphere appeared to be surging, the authorities dispatched military patrols.

In July 1946 in Janów, near Częstochowa, people panicked after hearing that Jews had set up an ambush for children in a nearby forest and were allegedly shooting at them. Some soldiers had come to their defense and allegedly managed to shoot a Jew. District department officials "calmed the excited population and returned it to a normal state."[186]

In Radom, "many groups in our community have morally approved the fact of the pogrom of Jews in Kielce. The general opinion was that ritual murder had indeed taken place. This conviction was widespread not only among people who were not party members, but even some members of the workers' parties allowed themselves to be gripped by the mass psychosis. Still, there was no threat of any unrest related to this."[187]

The anti-Jewish terror also reached Mazovia, with incidents reported in Ciechanów, Siedlce, Ostrowia Mazowiecka, Świder, and Warsaw. The absence of any further information makes it impossible to know whether the myth again served as the spark for the incidents. The unrest in Warsaw was caused by gossip passed around in a bazaar across from Szembek Square that a Jew had murdered a Polish railroad employee.[188] Probably the most highly charged atmosphere seized Otwock. A few days after the Kielce pogrom, a rumor spread that a Polish child was missing. An intervention by the head of the Provincial Security Office prevented collective hatred from exploding. Reportedly, the reason for the child's disappearance was also explained,[189] but it is not clear whether this was an accident or someone had intentionally hidden the child. A report written for the Central Committee of Polish Jews lists attempts to bring on unrest using the "Kielce method" of hiding children and then searching for them in houses inhabited by Jews. This happened in Cracow (four instances), Bytom, Łódź, Skierniewice, Tomaszów, Białystok, Szczecin, Bielawa, and Otwock.[190] A woman searching for a missing child in a building inhabited by Jews at 43 Słowacki Street was arrested in Cracow and charged with "provocative invention." Another woman in Cracow, who was allegedly looking for her child on August 14, was also arrested.[191] A similar case was recorded in September in Tarnów, where a woman charged Jews with kidnapping her child, which "turned out, as usual, to be an invented lie."[192] In some places these were likely cases of sending out women as bait to give the authorities an opportunity to search Jewish homes. But this does not change the overall meaning of the events of July and August 1946: anti-Jewish fear joined hands with various forms of violence against the Jews.

Documentary evidence that large numbers of people believed in the myth began to fade in the autumn of 1946. But whenever a child's body was found somewhere, charges of ritual murder would resurface. This was the case in Legnica in October 1946, where the Soviet troops stationed there and the District Security Office preempted a pogrom.[193] One of the last postwar pieces of evidence for the presence of the myth in popular thinking comes from March 1948. Julia Brystygierowa, director of Department Five of the Ministry of Public Security, sent instructions to all province-level Offices of Public Security, in which she wrote, "In view of the Easter holidays, hostile elements are attempting to create chaos in Polish society and about 'ritual murders.' This fact recently took place in Kielce Province, in Włoszczowo. In order to thwart all attempts at bringing on anti-Semitic trouble, we must: 1. Focus intelligence on signaling all manifestations of anti-Jewish propaganda and statements; 2. React instantly to all anti-Jewish developments, charge the culprits; 3. Report all anti-Semitic occurrences to the Ministry of Public Security immediately."[194] But throughout 1948 the ministry was not flooded with reports about "troubles" brought on by tales of ritual murder. The next known reports are from 1949, from Częstochowa and Cracow.[195]

From March 1945 to March 1948, several versions of the myth appeared. Some had rich plots while others only a terse message: "Jews killed." It is not surprising that the stories of ritual murder differed. Anthropologists of religion note that there is never a single orthodox version of a myth. Here, the greatest disparities lay in the motives for the murders. With this as the sole criterion, we can distinguish three main forms of the myth.

The classic first version, probably the most widespread, was motivated by the Jewish desire to draw Christian blood to use as an ingredient in Passover matzo.

In the second version, the modern one, blood was needed for transfusions. It was most popular in Cracow, as can be seen in letter number four above and in entries in Hugo Steinhaus's diary. Even some of the Cracow intelligentsia allegedly believed in this "improved ritual murder." It is not out of the question that in some minds blood transfusions and the motive of murdering "Polish children" were linked by the name of Ludwik Hirszfeld, an eminent hematologist, which only educated people could have been familiar with. The drawing of children's blood would allegedly help exhausted Jews returning from the USSR.[196] An underground document written after the Cracow pogrom reported, "On 11.6. of this year in Rzeszów, where at 12 Tannenbaum Street the body of 9-year-old Bronisława Mendoń who died as a result of the drawing of blood for transfusions was found."[197]

In the cannibalistic third version of the myth, the children were eaten whole. According to a Citizens' Militia report of late August 1946, in Przemyśl, a three-year-old girl went over to her neighbors' house. Her brother reported her disappearance, claiming that "the jews [sic] had kidnapped her for meat, and he would murder the jews [sic] for this."[198] The public imagination reveled in macabre details during an attempt to start a pogrom in Kalisz. "A boy disappeared who was later allegedly found alive in Ostrów Wielkopolski," read a report from Kalisz. "A ukrainian [sic] had allegedly murdered this boy and taken his flesh away to make sausage out of it. The rumors became more and more preposterous, that there were 4, 8 or even 24 such boys. An uncaptured and unverified woman said that she had seen 14 children's heads and that ukrainians [sic] or soviets [sic] had taken the meat to make sausage, and Jews were drinking their blood."[199] This story is a metaphor for the fate of the nation being "devoured" by its three enemies: Jews, Ukrainians, and Russians. The presence in it of "ukrainians" and "soviets" shows that, to the public, not only Jews were a threat.

INSECURITAS HUMANA

The War Censorship Office report that quoted the abovementioned Polish comments in the wake of the Cracow pogrom also included fragments of letters written by Polish Jews. They all expressed fear after learning about violence against the Jewish population. Some described having sympathetic reactions of trembling or sleeplessness.

Radom, letter dated August 18, 1945:

> Imagine, Sir, last week in the night of Saturday–Sunday a fact occurred here in Radom that did not happen even in Cracow. Imagine that 4 people (jews [sic]) were murdered in a house next to a militia station, they were not shot but slaughtered. Their throats were cut and their chests stabbed, including a Soviet major, also a jew [sic]. Furthermore, already a second warning was sent to the Jewish Committee to remove themselves by the 15th of this month, otherwise all of them would be murdered. The majority left already, of course. Only individuals remain who are trembling. It's impossible to sleep at home, and a person shudders at every step.[200]

The author of another letter, fearing persecution, had fled from a small Subcarpathian town to the larger town of Tarnów. But Jews did not feel safe there either. A letter dated August 16, 1945, relates, "I, too, am in Tarnów because there is not a single jew [sic] in Pilzno because they're still attacking jews [sic] and slaughtering them, and all the jews [sic] from the small towns have come to Tarnów and are living there on one street. Everyone in this town is afraid. . . . All the jews [sic] are thinking about going to Palestine and to America."[201]

The majority of the letter writers were thinking about emigrating, and the only reason they expressed was a feeling of great danger. In a letter dated August 31, 1945, someone wrote that "I have also decided to emigrate from Poland. I will go to America, but there is no possibility of going to America from Poland yet, so for now to Palestine, but to go without papers you may have to wander from camp to camp with one's things. A jew [*sic*] cannot go to the countryside, there are also no jews [*sic*] at all in small towns, many jews [*sic*] from small towns have been killed, so they are all concentrating in individual cities, Cracow, Kielce, Łódź, Radom, etc."[202]

A letter from Bielsko to an addressee in New York dated August 16, 1945: "I now have one favor to ask you, to help me and my family leave for America. The Jews are still in danger. Bandits are attacking Jewish families here and taking [probably killing—MZ] them. Life is not safe yet."[203]

To recap, in 1944–47, Poland experienced two waves of anti-Jewish violence. The first one was a series of murders, which peaked in the spring and summer of 1945, mostly in small towns and villages. Then came the double wave of pogroms, in the summer of 1945 and a year later. The two waves had in common hostility toward Jews and similar origins, but their direct causes (the myth of ritual murder) and forms of aggression (urban tumult) differed. To understand what they had in common, we need to go back to the beginning, the trauma of the war. Then, to try to answer questions about the dual hatred of Jews as Communists and vampires.

There is no doubt that all postwar violence—and not only anti-Jewish violence—had its roots in the war. People became more aggressive toward each other and grew indifferent to death. Both the German and Soviet occupying forces showed that anything could be inflicted on a human being—mistreatment, humiliation, death. These experiences profoundly changed Polish society's morality, and at times moral ties atrophied, which meant atrophied duties toward others and indifference to others' suffering. Grueling living conditions, destitution, and hunger pushed people to seek extraordinary solutions, whether in looting or banditry. Alcohol turned into an important catalyst of group violence, and its consumption reached unheard of levels. The war left behind tendencies to anomie and deviant behaviors. Crime levels rose to the twentieth century's highest, and the Jews were by no means its only victims. In some communities, the wartime plague of informing undermined, or even destroyed, the feeling of community. Deep transformations, disruption (or in some cases annihilation) of many social, state, or family institutions meant a weakening of social control, which brought chaos and anarchy. When the law is binding and there is a system to enforce it, even the most powerful -isms will not dare go out in the street with their slogans if a policeman is on patrol.

But nationalism conquered many Poles' thinking. The war had simplified national identities and pushed ethnic groups apart, and as a result a xenophobic national community continued to take shape. Polishness towered over all other identifications and identities. It dictated a readiness to sacrifice, it demanded idealizing the national past, and it made people proud, while at the same time making them feel that they were living under siege, closed off and endangered. This image of the world filled with national phobias was further strengthened by what many saw as defeat in the Second World War, even though Poland was—paradoxically—on the winning side. Psychologically, the situation resembled Italy's after the First World War, when vivid national emotions went hand in hand with the powerful frustration of having won nothing in the victory. Nationalism feeds on the authentic experience of defeat and suffering. The Poles had been feeling betrayed and abandoned since the Warsaw Uprising, and the capture of Berlin did little to improve this feeling. The outcomes of the nearly six-year conflict, which included the loss of Poland's eastern territories, the destruction of its capital, and the looming threat of a new Soviet occupation crushed people, made them feel depressed, their sacrifices useless. The disappointed hopes and the despair of defeat made people act violently, radicalized their political views, and imposed a Manichean view of the world, black-and-white, where the black was Jews and Communists. The post-defeat feelings and psychological problems must have been overwhelming, especially among those who had spilled blood, the veterans. Filled with the patriotism they had been fed during the war, after leaving the army they encountered many obstacles they could not overcome. They unloaded their aggression and anger on Jews, and where there were no Jews on Germans or Ukrainians.

The veteran syndrome can best be identified by intolerance and the tendency to use violence as much as by military decorations. The enormous political fear of this period kicked off the mechanism of displaced aggression. Hounded by the NKVD and the Security Office, the underground soldiers shook off their anxiety and fear by murdering "Polish traitors" and Jews and Belorussians, nations they considered to be Communism's emissaries. Now, wartime nationalism, the syndrome of defeat, and the veteran syndrome combined to spark off the murders of Jews.

The Jews continued to be targeted by Polish collaborators who, during the war, had assisted the Germans with the Holocaust. The works of Jan Grabowski and Barbara Engelking document the sizeable groups of Poles who informed and killed, especially in small towns and villages.[204] In Jedwabne they burned their Jewish neighbors in a barn, and elsewhere they would catch them and hand them over to the Germans. Sometimes they murdered the Jews they had "hunted" themselves, with a fence post, an ax, or a spade. They were motivated by fear, prewar anti-Semitism, and material incentives. After liberation, the occupation-era collaborators saw the Jews coming out of hiding as shadows returning from the netherworld, as reminders of their crimes as fear that their crimes would be revealed. In the postwar chaos and lawlessness, after millions of Jews had died, nothing was easier than killing one more Jew. We can also interpret the postwar wave of murders of Jews as the last stage of the Holocaust, a continuation of wartime behaviors.

But the effects of the era of mass murder went beyond this group of collaborators. The lesson of hatred the Germans had given also left traces in the minds of many Polish witnesses of the Holocaust. The message was all-out negative: Jews were living corpses psychologically associated with fear. Remembering that they had stood by and not helped their neighbors may have disturbed some Poles' peace of mind. The majority of known cases of Poles turning in Jews or killing them themselves come from the General Government. It is also there that the majority of locations where the ritual murder myth was recorded and all the postwar pogroms took place in 1945–48. Jan T. Gross is right to say that guilt lay at the roots of these and other forms of violence aimed at the Jews. This guilt is especially uncomfortable when it clashes with a crucial element of the national identity embedded already during the Partitions: the heroic Pole suffering for others. The myth of ritual murder turned out to be a convenient solution: it removed the feeling of guilt, restored the national self-stereotype, and restored a moral order,[205] simply by showing that the Jews were guilty and that Polish children were the real victims.

The experience of mass resettlements, both the wartime ones enforced by the two occupying powers and the postwar ones sanctioned at Potsdam, legitimized the thinking that ethnic problems could be solved with purges. The logic of both Stalinism and Nazism was guided by eliminating the enemy—the former for class and the latter for racial reasons. Both systems viewed tolerance as a sign of, respectively, reduced proletarian vigilance or weakness unworthy of representatives of the master race. These experiences and clichés overlapped with Polish prewar anti-Semitism and were reflected in postwar attitudes and collective behaviors. A Polish Jew who had served in the Polish Army wrote on August 11, 1945, "I visited several houses in the village where we are now. In every house the ruling anti-Semitism makes my hairs stand on end. Since they did not take me for a Jew, they told me things that are terrifying to hear."[206]

The few remaining Jews were surrounded by hostility from some Poles, which led to spontaneous ethnic purges in numerous towns and cities with some Holocaust survivors. According to a report from the Government Delegate's Office sent to London in 1945, "And when one or two families return to a town that was once 90 percent Jewish, they find themselves in foreign, hostile territory."[207]

Officially, the Jewish population had it better than the other national minorities. It enjoyed full civil rights and the new government's acclaim. The agreements signed by the Polish Committee of National Liberation and the Lithuanian, Belorussian and Ukrainian Soviet republics included resettling Jews who had lived in eastern Poland prior to 1939, as well as those who had taken shelter in the USSR, in Poland. In August 1944 a Department for

Assistance to the Jewish Population was created within the Polish Committee of National Liberation and a few months later the Central Committee of Polish Jews came into being. The other national minorities could only dream about similar representation. But there was a vast chasm on the Jewish question between the new regime's policies and the public mood.

The conviction that the Jews should leave Poland was almost universal. People would say in everyday interactions: "He's a Jew! Why is he still here?" The national political struggle that became radical in 1946 had a huge impact on the rise of anti-Semitism. The call to rid Poland of the Jews gradually moved up to the top of the list of the demands and slogans present in underground flyers and brochures. After the Kielce events, someone in Wałbrzych produced a flyer on a German typewriter:

"Long live Anders and his men!
Glory to the heroes of the Kielce forests.
Down with the Jews! Poland for the Poles.
The Home Army is vigilant and fighting!"[208]

In Kalisz, "the working youth" wrote an appeal to the local Jewish committee, threatening that, "if you abuse the law in Poland, we will slaughter you all." It continued: "Poland is for the Poles, not for the Jews or another nationality. The Jews must get out of Poland, out with Communism." They promised a pogrom. The letter was reportedly signed by 1,500 people from Kalisz, and, since it is teeming with linguistic and logical mistakes, its authors must have been young and poorly educated.

The Jews who were returned to Poland after years in the Berling Army were unable to understand the behaviors of the Polish majority. The omnipresent anti-Semitism made them, especially those who had "spilled their blood for Poland" bitter, and made many of them want to leave. A soldier wrote in a letter dated 16 August 1945: "There is no room for us here. The reason for this is the antiSemitism of the Polish reactionaries, who still influence the ignorant masses. This is why, as the Polish newspapers are writing, disturbances happen. The Polish government, which has friendly relations with the Soviet Union, opposes anti-Semitism. For this reason, there are emigration moods in the Jewish population."

Another soldier wrote: "It's no secret that anti-Semitism has advanced far in Poland, that open pogroms are happening in some towns. Also, not a day goes by without anyone killed and injured. The handful of jews [sic] who survived the Nazi bands are now dying on every street, in different towns. I'm embarrassed to write that I fought for a free Poland, where people could live in peace."[209]

The origins of the postwar murders of Jews and the anti-Semitic pogroms and disturbances cannot be explained by the impact of the war, pre-war anti-Semitism and surviving wartime guilty feelings alone. The postwar political situation and the ongoing civil war also played a role. Krystyna Kersten wrote about the disjoint between the two "truths," the Polish and the Jewish.[210] The different experiences, perspectives, and evaluations pushed them apart, fortified the antagonisms. To use a personal example, my grandmother Olga Kopecka, the wife of an officer murdered by the NKVD in 1940 in Kharkov, had no doubt that he had been killed by the Bolsheviks. Janina Bauman for a long time could not believe that her father, a Polish Army officer, had been murdered at Katyn by the same people who would later liberate her.[211] The two women never met. With the enormous differences in their political views and experiences, would they have been able to speak the same language? Kopecka lost her home and landed estate to a revolution from the top and to agricultural reform. In the Stalinist period, fearing persecution, she burned her husband's letters. Bauman spent the occupation in hiding in Warsaw, and liberation was a blinding miracle of salvation so powerful that she refused to believe that Stalin had ordered her father's killing. The Poles, focused on themselves, did not understand the Jews' trauma, their joy at seeing the Red Army, their feelings of having been wronged, abandoned, alone, and imperiled by anti-Semitism in Poland.[212] But the Jews who remained in Poland did not see that the Red Army also made people fear marauders and rapists, and that the postwar reality had little to do with the freedom they had been dreaming about.[213] Indeed, for the huge majority of Poles, "liberation" meant the beginning of new captivity and terror, most tangible in arrests, forced exiles, and executions of the Home Army fighters. Both sides had the same attribution bias, overvaluing the other side's conscious explanations and national characteristics and undervaluing situational influences and the current political and social contexts.

Jewish memoirs and letters of the time, as well as declarations by the Central Committee of Polish Jews, often accept the stereotypes of "Polish Fascists," "Home Army bands," "reactionaries," and "National Armed Forces and Home Army criminals" as sufficient diagnosis of Polish attitudes. Communist propaganda hurled the same epithets at the pro-independence underground, accusing it uniformly of anti-Semitism. A newspaper article stated, "For the Polish Jews, with only 80,000 surviving of the tree million, the two letters AK [Armia Krajowa, the Home Army] have the same horrific meaning today as the two letters SS [!]."[214] Poles could not and did not want to agree with opinions of this sort. Rhetoric that considered the other side an enemy virtually equal to the Nazis precluded a dialogue and deepened divisions, including ethnic ones. The writer Maria Dąbrowska noted this on June 1: "How can anyone spit and tread on the Warsaw Uprising at the same time as pasting posters all over Warsaw that read 'Glory to the Warsaw ghetto fighters.' The constant insults directed at the *Sanacja* regime resemble the newspapers from the German occupation, which did nothing other than abuse the *Sanacja*.... To find nothing good in our time of sovereignty and only insult those years is a serious affront to the nation and its autonomous value."[215]

The Poles, too, had an attribution bias as they employed the stereotype of Jewish Communism in evaluating Jews; tried to uncover tendencies to betray, leftist leanings, and hostility to Christian values in the "Jewish soul"; and made no effort to understand the motivations behind some Jewish choices. We know that this stereotype was already imprinted in people's minds before the war. After the war, the belief that Jewish Communists played first fiddle, that "the Jews are in power," became one of the most often repeated folk wisdoms, a common diagnosis of the postwar reality.[216] Jan T. Gross believes that it was completely false. In his *Fear*, Polish Jews did not view Communism favorably in postwar Poland, despite the stereotype that "the Communist party was not interested in the Jews, nor were the Jews interested in Communism."

The problem is that had there not been a grain of truth in these stereotypes, not as many people would have believed in them. The presence of some persons of Jewish origin in the top positions of the new government, foremost among them Hilary Minc, and also Jerzy Borejsza, Jakub Berman, Roman Zambrowski, Józef Różański, Roman Werfel, and hundreds of Jews in the Polish Army officer cadre and in the ranks of Security Office, appeared to confirm the prewar Polish and Nazi scenarios. "The top government offices would have been empty had all the functionaries with Jewish roots left their jobs at the same time," wrote the historian Andrzej Paczkowski.[217] Hugo Steinhaus noted in his diary in August 1945, "It is interesting how the climate of the east has followed the occupation. Because at night you can hear shots, there is nowhere to live, even fewer textiles, freedom is 'ordered'. . . . The Jews are upstairs, and downstairs despises them."[218] The "Jewish landing" in the most important state positions upset people when the majority was boycotting the new regime. Even Maria Dąbrowska, whose views were leftist and not in the least anti-Semitic, could not hide her irritation when she wrote about the minister of education: "This minister Skrzeszewski is a flabby jew [sic] with a fat ass and a cigar in his jaws. He doesn't know Polish. He says 'London is dringking [sic] in your ears.' A Russian jew [sic], Igor [?] Litwak."[219]

The Polish Jews who joined in the process of building a new Poland were rarely motivated by faith in Marx's and Engels's ideals.[220] The majority of the Jewish population indeed expressed their lack of this faith by leaving Poland. The government, on the other hand, cast a wide net for cadres, was not motivated by philo-Semitism, and, for lack of its own elites, hired just about anyone. It gave those Jews who decided to stay in Poland an opportunity to start a new life, to join in the reconstruction. Some of them could cultivate their identity in the approved Jewish schools and cultural centers, and others got rid of the Jewish stigma by assimilating. Non-Jewish Poles, too, were tempted by jobs and perks. Those who became politically engaged, worked for the security services, or joined the Polish Workers' Party were aware of the price they would pay: being excluded from their circle of friends and acquaintances. Because of their ethnic foreignness, those who had Jewish roots suffered even more. Jan T. Gross is right to say that the Jews were not interested in Communism. But he forgets that at that time, no one in government was saying openly that Poland would be Communist, while those Polish Jews who decided to stay supported the new regime in large numbers, not to say ostentatiously. One source where this is evident are the official reports about the January 1947 elections and the figures for Jews living in Lower Silesia. Nearly all of the dozen or so thousand living in Wałbrzych, Wrocław, Bielawa, Legnica, and other towns of the region voted for the Democratic Bloc. In Dzierżoniów one teacher, whom the document labeled as an "assimilator Jew," voted for the Polish People's Party and wrote on his ballot, "Without the PPP, with Lvov and Vilna."[221]

The Polish and Jewish "truths" tragically parted ways after the war. This is all understandable from today's perspective, as we are able to interpret the motivations and sources of frustration, and the two sides' thinking. But at the time, few thought in sociological terms as most people in the shattered society, deprived of its elites, were carrying their wartime anxieties and the habit of making simple diagnoses.

The fear of Jewish vampirism is more difficult to explain, as it seems to come straight out of a distant past. Its roots were archaic, long predating the stereotype of Jewish Communism—medieval. We can easily trace the process of formation and buildup of the forms of the anti-Jewish phobia described so far, but the myth of ritual murder is different. It exploded in 1945, without warning, like a volcano. Before we attempt to find out why it came alive again after a period of sleep, let's recap what we already know.

First, there is no question that some of the postwar pogroms and anti-Semitic disturbances did not erupt by accident. There were groups of people, militia officers in Kielce and Kalisz, butchers and merchants in Włocławek, profiteers and invalids wanting to cause trouble so they could rob the Jews in Lublin or, in Włocławek, make it difficult for Jews to run a business. The "child-as-bait method" used in Rzeszów turned out to be the model that people tried to copy elsewhere. In this sense, at the roots of the Kielce pogrom (and the attempts to bring on pogroms in Kalisz, Włocławek, and perhaps also Lublin and Warsaw) lay attempts to provoke, not as was most often suspected politically, but in business and robbery.

Second, we can be certain that after the war, many Poles believed in the myth of ritual murder and genuinely feared Jews as the killers of "our children." Not all of them were open about this, but many still acted aggressively toward Jews. The numbers of public disturbances started by a rumor of ritual murder make it seem that it was a mainstream phenomenon.

Third, there is also no doubt that while the "child-as-bait method" was effective everywhere, anti-Semitic unrest did not always follow it. Why? Which social groups believed in the myth? In which regions were they dominant? Answers to these questions will allow us to draw a two-dimensional social and territorial map of the myth in the collective imagination. Without such a map, it would be difficult to get to the bottom of the Poles' belief in Jewish vampirism.

The network of variables on this map can come from the analyses made by Hadley Cantril's team as they attempted to establish the genesis of the mass panic that burst forth in the United States in the wake of the broadcast of H. G. Wells's radio play *War of the Worlds* on Halloween night 1938.[222] The belief in ritual murder is, of course, not the same as the conviction that Martians are attacking us, and yet both come from the same irrationality. Since a panic is often born of a flawed assessment of a situation, Cantril et al. set out to find the factors that made some of the listeners believe, correctly, that the broadcast was just a radio play. They did it because they had been taught critical thinking. A poll showed that as the listeners' educational level rose, the number of those who believed that they were listening to news dropped.[223]

There is no reason to suppose that anything was different with those who believed in the myth of ritual

Ethnic Phobias and Violence

murder in Poland. They lacked not only the ability to distinguish truth from falsehood but also a general knowledge that people obtain through formal education and by reading books and newspapers. The majority likely belonged to a group with little or very little education, which is obvious from the letters quoted here and from some information we have about the characteristics of those who were arrested in the wake of the Cracow and Kielce pogroms. Walenty Błaszczyk was semi-literate and asked a cousin to write the notices about his missing son. Antonina Biskupska, who was charged with encouraging the pogrom, had completed one year of elementary school. Three other defendants in the Kielce trial had gone to elementary school for three years and two others for four. The mob in Włocławek was made up of schoolchildren. The militia as a whole, as was mentioned before, could hardly be considered well educated. But the mass of people who believed in the myth was not completely illiterate. The words of the writer Kazimierz Wyka, who must have come across the intelligentsia's anti-Semitism in Cracow, are worth remembering: "the masses' dense ignorance turns into a residue of ignorance in people who, it would seem, should be immune to it."[224] Hugo Steinhaus also noted the presence of the myth among Cracow's intelligentsia. One of the arrested was a judge's wife who had a secondary education. Some noncommissioned officers, as well as militia and army officers, men who had at least started secondary school before the war, probably also gave in to the charms of this myth.[225] But while the absence of an education should be considered the most important variable defining the group of believers in the myth, it was not the only one.

Poverty was another. In the United States, more low-income people believed that Wells's play was a newscast than did people with higher incomes.[226] Again, we can only speculate that the majority of those who believed in the myth, as well as those who took part in pogroms and anti-Semitic disturbances in Poland, came from the group of people of low or very low material status, which was large in the wake of the war. This author has found no documents to prove that any people of means took part in pogroms—those who, confirming Jan T. Gross's thesis, had made money during the war by taking advantage of Jews and now lived in fear that those Jews would return. Descriptions of the eight defendants in the Kielce pogrom trial included the term "lacking assets."[227] Henryk Błaszczyk mentioned that his family of four would divide every potato into four parts.[228] The pogrom in Cracow and the unrest in Lublin and Warsaw started in bazaars, where the urban poor gathered. In Częstochowa, in areas of destitution. At least a dozen Jews outside the big cities were probably murdered by killers hired by those who had acquired their real estate during the war.[229] Still, as is usually the case with such incidents, the majority of those who took part in pogroms and anti-Semitic violence felt extremely deprived materially and had no property to fear losing. In Częstochowa people said that, upon leaving the camps, Jews were given allowances of as much as forty thousand zlotys, Poles only a few hundred.[230] Similar stories about the enormous sums coming to Polish Jews from America made the rounds. While deprivation leads to frustration and anger, there may have been other links between poverty and myth. Seymour Martin Lipset noted the correlation between low social status and fundamentalist religion,[231] to which mythical thinking is connected. Can the belief in ritual murder therefore be seen as a peculiar religion of the disinherited? But the whole Polish society was touched by pauperization, and so poverty should again be treated as only one of many correlates of the "carrying" of the myth. Still, the fact that millions were living in a tragic situation in terms of supplies and existential issues no doubt played a role in determining the numbers of this category of people.

The gender and age of the people in this category are also significant. Cantril noted that younger people and women were less good at telling the difference between a radio play and a newscast.[232] The available sources tell us nothing about the ages of those who believed in the myth of ritual murder, but it appears indirectly that the majority of pogrom participants were men, both young and middle-aged—something that is linked to the elevated level of aggression characteristic of these age groups. But the role of women was also important. The multitudes in Rzeszów, Cracow, and Kielce included both sexes, and there are numerous indications that this was also the case in Lublin, Częstochowa, and Warsaw. Women played the dual role of communicators and mobilizers. First, they were the greatly agitated "carriers" of the myth, forming a unique information network, passing it by word of mouth, exaggerating the story every step of the way. During the unrest in Cracow, a woman who was later arrested reportedly shouted, "The Jews murdered 18 children, people saw their hair and bones."[233] Those who believed in the myth included the already-mentioned judge's wife, who allegedly cried out, "We did not nurture our children just so the Jews could murder them now."[234] Shouting and sobbing, the women mobilized the men, excited them to want bloody revenge. Some joined in the beating. We do not know whether the violence would have been as great had they not participated. It was women who hounded Ida Gerstman several times. She spent two nights and a day hiding in a field near Kielce, fearing a pogrom. On the morning of July 6, after she came out of hiding and went to the train station, she heard a woman say, "I'm on my way, I'm taking a knife, if I catch a Jewish man or woman, I'll cut pieces of meat out of them and salt them." When Gerstman got on a train, a woman pointed to her and said, "This is a lousy Jewess, throw her under the train!" Another woman replied, "At the next station we'll hand her over to the militia, let them shoot her!" At the next station, the women grabbed her head and legs and dragged her onto the tracks, wanting to throw her under the train.[235] This behavior is difficult to explain, perhaps with the women's lower educational level than the men's, since in patriarchal prewar Poland girls tended to leave school sooner than boys, especially in poor families. But the reason may be mostly the contents of the myth: the images of murdered children may have had an especially powerful effect on the female imagination.

The enormous changes in the social structure also lay at the sources of all violence against Jews. In prewar Poland, the intelligentsia guarded cultural models, a canon of attitudes and values. This model was shattered by the extermination of the intelligentsia, and major structural cracks appeared as a result of both the war and the postwar social revolution, which was happening quietly. New groups and strata replaced the old ones. The "loose" population group, from which most of the pogrom participants and provincial killers hailed, grew. This has already been discussed: Poland was a country of immense mobility, both spatial and vertical. Millions relocated from east to west and millions from west to east. In 1944–45, the urban population grew by nearly 1.5 million. The war left behind thousands of "human shreds" who continued to live exactly as they had during the war. They were various types of traders, smugglers, bootleggers, all people who vegetated and were able to think only one day at a time, to live "as if." We have already mentioned that some of the pogroms took place in squares and bazaars. In August 1946, it was "peddlers" who allegedly brought the myth of ritual murder to Lublin Province. "Peddlers are releasing tales that they've seen Polish children who have been murdered by Jews. Some people believe this. This gossip is being spread only by the peddlers."[236] In the battlefield that was Poland then, the leftover "demobilized"— soldiers, deserters, and invalids—were often frustrated and angry. And they were responsible for some of the anti-Semitic disturbances. Vagrants, beggars, profiteers, repatriates, and "loose" people filled the streets of Rzeszów in the spring and Cracow in the summer of 1945. The unemployed, who were omnipresent, especially in central and southern Poland, where the largest number of anti-Semitic pogroms and disturbances took place, were "flammable material." In the spring of 1945, in five districts of Kielce Province alone, the number of rural inhabitants who were defined as "economically expendable" was estimated at 250,000. In Kielce itself, the number of people without a steady occupation may even have reached several thousand. Militia functionaries were an especially important category of the "expendables serving violence." When they rose to the occasion in Włocławek and Warsaw, the pogrom did not happen. In Rzeszów, Kielce, and Kalisz, "bad militia" started the pogrom and later served as its flywheel and led the killings. Let us hypothesize that the pogroms would not have happened had it not been for the postwar instability and the presence of large numbers of human ruins.

In *Golden Harvest*, Irena Grudzińska-Gross and Jan T. Gross write that during the war, "the murders of Jews were done openly, were well attended, and were widely discussed public events—and given the fact that the people involved were regular people, including members of local elites."[237] But this is debatable. In Warsaw, it was mostly people living in the "bad" parts of town who engaged in szmalcownictwo. In the countryside, apart from the local administrators who were following German orders, those who murdered or sold out Jews generally did not belong to the village elites, which stood apart with their power, prosperity, and prestige. There are few examples of foresters, teachers, priests, organists, landowners, millers, prewar political leaders, and members of the "Wici" youth organization, or leaders of prewar peasant strikes, who delivered Jews to the Germans or murdered them. Illiterates or people with only bits of education or at most the six years of elementary school dominated the groups of killers. The trial documents make this clear. Many of those who were charged with collaborating or murdering Jews signed their names with difficulty and used restricted code in their testimony. They were neither people from the social margins nor a peasant elite but simply the peasant middle in central and eastern Poland: poor, uneducated, and often primitive.

Many postwar phenomena can be explained with "expendability" and a disrupted social structure, and yet not all those who believed that Jews were murdering Christian children can be put in the single category of "expendables." Members of the Polish Workers' Party in Radom or workers in the Ludwików Steelworks in Kielce or employees of the textile mills in Łódź, who struck in support of the Kielce pogrom participants who were put on trial, were certainly not "expendable." It is also worth remembering that during the war, Jews in need of help often got it from people who were desperately poor and felt excluded, living both spatially and symbolically on the outskirts of villages. Let's try to locate geographically those who believed in the myth.

As we sketch out the territorial reach of the myth, we should travel through Płock and Włocławek in the north, through Międzyrzecz and Legnica in the west. In the east and south, the line would basically overlap with Poland's border. Even though many anti-Semitic incidents occurred in other regions, in cities such as Szczecin, Wrocław, and Gniezno, the myth generally did not spread in Greater Poland, Pomerania, Warmia, and Masuria or Silesia. In other words, the myth "ruled" in the areas that had been within the Russian partition and in Galicia, some of the most civilizationally backward, as shown by their prewar 20 percent illiteracy rate.[238] Apart from the Ukrainians in the south, the Jews were the only ethnic minority there. In the summer of 1945, in southern Poland, the deepening Polish-Ukrainian conflict made people feel less threatened by the Jews. Therefore, let's venture the hypothesis that Polish-Jewish tensions diminished as relations with another minority group worsened. This would be confirmed by the fact that anti-Semitism manifested itself relatively less often among the Polish population relocating from the Kielce region and Galicia to Lower Silesia, which was one of the regions most heavily populated by Polish Jews. But it was not they but the Germans who, as we know, made people most fearful. This may explain why the myth of ritual murder was weaker there, while the story of the Werwolf was more prominent. There is also another hypothesis. According to Jolanta Żydul, belief in the myth was endemic, which can be seen in the centuries-old accusations that Jews engaged in ritual murder in the same areas.[239] The myth was ancient.

The myth of ritual murder arrived in Poland in the thirteenth century. The first to mention it was the chronicler Jan Długosz, who described how the Jews of Cracow allegedly killed a Christian child in 1407. The first public charge of ritual murder was made in Rawa Mazowiecka in 1547. Trials for ritual murder were most frequent at the turn of the seventeenth and eighteenth centuries. A painting of "ritual murder" by Karol de Prevôt, which hangs in Sandomierz cathedral to this day, comes from this period. It represents children being bought and their blood being drawn, body parts and torture instruments. A similar painting hung until

1946 in the Jesuit church in Łęczyca. It reportedly represented "a group of Jews with beards, wearing tallitot and sitting next to a table, knives in hand. On the table covered with a white tablecloth stands a tub with a child immersed in blood. One of the Jews at the table is drawing the child's blood into a glass." Next to the painting stood a glass coffin with a child's body in it. The caption read that the child had been abducted in 1639 and found with a hundred stab wounds.[240]

In the Polish lands at the turn of the nineteenth and twentieth centuries, dozens of accusations were made, and the newspapers wrote about them, while local communities, according to Jolanta Żyndul, remembered them. In the interwar period, the myth appeared rarely. The most serious unrest took place in the Rzeszów region in the spring of 1919, following a rumor that Jews had attempted to commit ritual murder. Events in Wągrowiec (1922), Dobrzyń (1926), Sochaczew (1934), Zduńska Wola (1935), and Dąbrowa, near Białystok (1938), were local.[241] Nationalist parties did not exploit this myth in the 1930s, most likely considering it non-modern; hence the myth did not reach a wider public, as we can see in an event in Silesia. In May 1934, Edward Chowański, editor in chief of the Fascist-leaning *Błyskawica*, appeared as the defendant before a district court in Katowice. He was charged by the Jewish religious community in Katowice in a civil lawsuit and by the prosecutor's office with insulting the Jewish religion. His paper had reportedly run three articles about the Talmud and alleged suggestions about ritual murder in them. But readers never saw the articles, since the censorship office confiscated them. Three expert witnesses, including a priest-professor, testified that there were absolutely no grounds to claim that Jews committed so-called ritual murder. Chowański was given a nine-month suspended sentence and ordered to pay two hundred zlotys to the Jewish community. *Ilustrowany Kurier Codzienny* covered the trial in the article "Czy wierzy kto jeszcze w mord rytualny?" (Does anyone still believe in ritual murder?)[242]

The Catholic Church did not answer the question clearly. In the 1920s, Father Ignacy Charszewski propagated the "truth" about ritual murder in *Słowo Pomorskie*.[243]

In 1936, Father Franciszek Konieczny published a booklet titled *Żydzi i ich wrogi stosunek do Narodu* (The Jews and their hostile attitude toward the Nation), in which he wrote, "The jews [*sic*], influenced by the baseness that pours forth plentifully out of the Talmud, have reached such degeneracy that they elevate this common, or rather refined, crime to a religious ritual."[244]

Not all church people shared the views of Częstochowa diocesan Bishop Teodor Kubina, who, in a joint statement with the local authorities, pronounced after the Kielce pogrom that "all claims that ritual murders exist are a lie."[245] In August 1946, Lower Silesia diocesan Bishop Juliusz Bieniek tried to persuade the British ambassador to Poland of evidence that Jews had mistreated a child prior to the Kielce pogrom.[246] Also quoted on this subject was reportedly then-bishop of Lublin, Stefan Wyszyński, about the well-known trial of Mendel Beilis (Russia, 1911), who was accused of ritual murder: "in Beilis's trial, many old and new Jewish books were collected, in which the question of blood has not been resolved."[247] Some lower-ranking priests[248] and monks also believed in the myth.[249] They, trusted by the faithful like no one else, repeated the anti-Semitic biases that had been circulating in folk culture for generations. According to the historian Alina Cała, the myth was an integral part of the image of the Jew.[250] It survives in some parts of Poland even today.[251]

But the long life of the myth does not explain its postwar explosion. So where to search for the reasons of the sudden spread of Jewish vampirism in the spring of 1945? Note that there is no evidence that the group of "believers" grew during the German occupation. Nazi propaganda aimed at the Poles basically did not use the argument that Jews kidnap children, or at least it was not an important component of it.[252] So what was it that revived the myth?

The wartime trauma and postwar terror were one component. Let us return to the analyses by Cantril et al. They did not find one psychological factor responsible for panic behaviors. After interviewing people who panicked after listening to *The War of the Worlds*, they concluded that it would be more accurate to talk about a complex of psychological layers. These included insecurity, phobias, anxieties, insecurities, fatalism, religiosity, and frequent church attendance.[253] There was no such study of those people who believed in ritual murder in Poland after the war. The published materials from the interrogations of people detained after the Cracow and Kielce pogroms do not contain sufficient data to re-create what characterized the "believers." But two factors are certain: immeasurable layers of anxiety and growing religiosity.

The war played a huge role in shaping thinking and creating anxieties. "The period of the occupation has left us with a range of traumas, which continue to reappear even with the nightmare gone," the daily *Dziennik Łódzki* wrote, diagnosing the state of public emotions. "When we hear energetic steps on the stairs late at night, we still catch ourselves with an unpleasant shiver going through us. Living one day at a time in constant uncertainty produced an atmosphere of permanent emergency."[254] The Cracow pogrom happened three days after this article appeared.

The war brought with it a civilizational regression. Social communications went back to the pre-Gutenberg era. People learned to believe in word of mouth, gossip, and rumors. The atrophy of critical thinking, which is usually learned by reading, made society's image of the world flatten, and people observed it without reflecting on it. The sources of the instantaneous dissemination of the myth of ritual murder should be sought right here, in the practice of believing oral accounts without analyzing them. An official report from Kielce in January 1946 observed that "the form of gossip and whispered propaganda has become popular, convenient, since it requires no effort to analyze the source, seek the truth, compare, read the newspaper or listen to people who know something about the subject. Underlying this phenomenon are typical lazy thinking, ignorance and a mean spirit."[255] Continuing with the psychological explanations, we should note that in terms of collective reactions and attitudes, people submitted to herd behaviors with extreme ease, both when a crowd was aggressive, as in lynchings and pogroms, and during the currency and war panics.

But their wartime experiences were not the only reason why the Poles believed in Jewish vampirism after the war. Now, the new social situation and new anxieties were decisive. Let's go back one more time to the United States in the late 1930s. When *The War of the Worlds* was broadcast, many social norms had been changing dramatically for some time. People were living with unease and confusion. The Great Depression had brought uncertainty. News from Europe and Asia brought a war scare.[256] American sociologists believe that this atmosphere lay at the roots of the panic.

The situation in Poland was incomparably worse. According to Leszek Kołakowski, fleeing into a myth is connected to "the world's indifference."[257] We may call it the Great Terror in the postwar reality, a state of especially powerful anxious tension, which appeared after the war and which manifested itself in gossip, panic, pogroms and lynchings, hunger protests, and strikes. It is not necessary to list all the dangers in the postwar reality yet again, only to say that there was no area of human activity devoid of specters and fears, whether domestic politics, the international situation, economics, social structure, or health. They occupied a sizable area of the Poles' "psychological life space," and it was there that the myth of ritual murder was reborn.

Let's recall the findings from the first theoretical chapter, chapter 1: enduring fear and anxiety can take people back to primeval behaviors and revive the latent tendency to engage in outdated and magical thinking. At restless times, magical thinking takes over, and the significance of tangential factors is exaggerated. It is then that legends and myths blossom about the "others" who are responsible for the disasters at hand. In psychoanalysis, this is called a decreased level of consciousness. In the postwar period, this post-trauma condition was present on an almost unprecedented scale. Consciousness decreased, and mythical, tribal, and anachronistic contents occupied the empty space, the space normally ruled by reason.

The Poles reacted to the horrors of the occupation by becoming more devout. The wartime horrors and spilled blood awakened ancient narratives about blood.

The Red Army's occupation added to the eschatological anxiety about the specter of godlessness blowing in from the East. What was its connection to the myth of ritual murder? First, mythical and magical thinking are a manifestation of specific religious thinking. Second, as medievalists know, accusations about ritual murder culminated twice, after the fourteenth-century plague and on the eve of the Reformation. Both times the proliferating accusations against the Jews were due to the rise of the people's piety, which manifested itself in the popularity of pilgrimages and millenarian expectations.[258] During the Second World War, too, magical thinking, divinations, and predictions were widespread. As we know, this thinking did not end with the war. Thus, the belief that Jews kidnapped and sacrificed children was not an isolated fact but a piece of a whole.

The Poles were struck by the destructive power of *insecuritas humana*, as Peter Wust, a German existentialist philosopher, would say. How can we disagree? "The eighteenth- and nineteenth-century feeling of security underwent such an abrupt upheaval, and in such a way, that it seemed that humanity had gone back to the beginning of the second millennium of our era, roughly to the times when Abbot Joachim de Fiore's eschatological visions preoccupied the human mind."[259] In this context, it is not the myth of ritual murder that should be called medieval but the nature of the times that allowed it to be reborn. Society's fears were embodied in and channeled by the myth. Pointing out the threat made it easier to combat it. It was a form of articulating anxiety and hostility. Now it seemed that it would be enough to remove the Jews to stop being afraid. This was the social role of the myth of ritual murder.

There are two different schools of thought interpreting the myth. The first, discussed above, is functional and believes that myth plays an important role in eliminating psychological tension and bringing law and order. The second asks about the truth of the myth. It would be an aberration to treat the myth of ritual murder as an ordinary statement about the world, to admit that there is a grain of truth in the sentence "the Jews are murdering children to make matzo." The problem with this was that children really did indeed disappear, even though they were not being kidnapped by Jews who wanted to kill them.[260] In this sense, the myth says something about women's fears.

On June 12, 1945, the day of the incident in Rzeszów, the local newspaper published a notice searching for a missing boy of thirteen, "medium height, blue eyes, round face, dark-blond hair." Newspapers ran many such classifieds after the war, and there was a daily radio program called "Family Search Box." The Kielce and Radom daily *Dziennik Powszechny* also printed such ads.[261] Bronisława Mendoń was murdered. Henryk Błaszczyk did not come home for two days. Large numbers of children died as they played with weapons and unexploded ordnance. Women's memories of that time reveal their panic at the sound of any explosion. Children's mortality due to hunger and infectious diseases amplified their postwar psychosis.

Throughout the history of Europe, accusations of ritual murder often appeared in the wake of plagues, whose first victims were children. It may thus not have been a question of deep-rooted hatred and fear of the Jews but also of reducing the stress from the fear of a child going missing or dying, and perhaps cutting down the guilt of women whose children died. By eliminating the Jews, "our children's murderers," people wanted to remove a real threat. Following Bruno Bettelheim's analysis, one can see the myth as a mother's externalized primeval fear of losing her child.[262] The myth of ritual murder may have been an archetypal projection of the unconscious, an expression of a woman's anxieties not only about her children but simply about her and her family's future. In the wake of the war, there was a peculiar psychosis, an oversensitivity and a specific public focus on the fate of the children. Primeval maternal instincts to protect one's offspring came to the fore in the postwar pogroms. Mojżesz Cukier, a witness to the Kielce pogrom, remembered that people in the mob shouted, "The Jews have murdered 14 of our children, all mothers and fathers should come forth and kill all the Jews."[263] Antonina Biskupska also talked about "the solidarity of mothers" who should defend children.

Biskupska's neighbor Mrs. Mucha told her, "Let's go home because I'm nervous, and let's not, her and me, get into a misfortune." "I didn't listen to her," Biskupska continued, "I went with some women I didn't know, who said that Mucha couldn't be a mother if she is saying this, that there are very few women like us, that we should find the children."[264]

Women had all the more reason to be afraid since children really were being kidnapped by, for example, corrupt Soviet soldiers. In November 1945, "a man in a Russian soldier's uniform" who roamed the area around Poznań probably raped two girls, and locals became involved in searching for one of them.[265] Rapes took place everywhere, also in Rzeszów Province. In October 1945, twelve Soviet soldiers abducted two girls in Przeworsk and took them to Przemyśl, but despite a search of the soldiers' car, the girls were not found.[266] The murders of a female student from Łódź in December 1945 and a schoolgirl in Poznań a month later were widely discussed. When a schoolgirl was murdered in Stargard in January 1947, parents organized teams of three to patrol the streets in the evenings.[267]

Even though, as has already been discussed, the core of the belief in Jewish vampirism lies in magical thinking and Christian anti-Semitism, in the context of what people were hearing, the story of Jews murdering "our children" may have seemed rational and, unfortunately, likely. Again, the Poles were capable of believing in just about anything after all they had seen and experienced in the Second World War, when all kinds of things that would have seemed impossible before did indeed happen—street roundups, gas chambers, crematoria, pseudo-medical experiments on humans—and also justified believing that a third world war would happen. In early June 1945, a few days before the unrest in Rzeszów, *Dziennik Polski* published an article about the "horrific death factory of a 'German cannibal' in Cracow." One Franc Tham, a fifty-three-year-old German, allegedly brought young girls and "even children" home and murdered them. A German court sentenced him to death in 1943. According to the testimony of a Polish woman who was later sentenced with him, "He ate the lard from his victims and their fried livers." The newspaper wrote that the "murderous pair" put on libations with Germans living on Saint Thomas Street in Cracow (all of whom fled before liberation) and Poles who, as we can deduce from the article, remained in the city. Tham likely did commit a few sexually motivated murders. But it is unlikely that he actually was a cannibal and that he quartered and burned his victims' bodies to remove evidence, something that *Dziennik Polski*'s editors did not question. They published the article just as tabloids do today: without a commentary, backing the "truth" with information that the article was based on case documents the paper had obtained from the court.[268] We know nothing about how the article was received in Cracow, but we may guess that people commented on it in the bazaar by its profiteers, market women, and random vendors—all simple people unused to critical thinking. Should we therefore be surprised that the news that Bronisława Mendoń's massacred body had been found, which also came from newspapers, electrified Cracow's bazaar society, which interpreted it as yet another case of cannibalism? If one German could be a cannibal and other Germans made saddles out of human skin (the newspapers also reported this)[269] and soap out of fat, was it not likely that Jews drank children's blood "to fortify themselves" or made sausage out of them in times of hunger? Should we therefore not explain the belief in the myth of ritual murder and its stunning spread in the postwar period in part with this apparent rationality of the information that was reaching people?

Polish antisemitism was not born in Rzeszów, but newspaper reports about the "German cannibal" and the real information about the murdered children gave it a new boost. It was indispensable, it honed in on the guilty party, and it eased the transmission of the myth. But it in turn drew power from the alleged ritual murder. Thus, the belief in the myth of ritual murder grew not only out of antisemitism but also from the Rzeszów events, which brought in a new wave of hostility against the Jews. In other words, were it not for the coincidence of events, foremost among them the killings of Bronisława Mendoń in Rzeszów and of Krystyna Woźniak in Częstochowa, the postwar antisemitic tsunami might not have come.

Actual abductions of children for ransom also helped the outbreak of belief in Jewish vampirism. Three children went missing in early September 1945 in Płock. A female suspect was arrested. A few days later, a fifty-eight-year-old Polish woman tried to kidnap a five-year-old boy in Płock. The two events set a mass hysteria in motion.[270] A year later in Międzyrzecze, home to a hundred Jews, a six-year-old boy went missing. The immediate investigation preempted a pogrom and revealed that the culprit was a Polish woman who was plotting to be paid after she handed the boy over to the Jewish community in Łódź; she said that she had kept him throughout the war.[271] The woman in Płock probably had a similar idea. According to hearsay, Polish children were being taken to Palestine, "since every Jew that goes there must have two children." People told stories about the Polish Jews' riches. The June 1945 decision by the Presidium of the Central Committee of Polish Jews to pay "Aryans" who had taken care of Jewish children one-thousand-zloty rewards also adds context to the kidnappings.[272] Everything points to the fact that news about the rewards spread, and there were those who saw kidnapping as an easy way to make money. On the other hand, we do not know enough stories about the Jewish community or relatives taking Jewish children back from Poles who had cared for them during the war.

The prewar Jewish population of Poland numbered about 3.3 million, and fewer than a million of them were children under fourteen. According to the Central Committee for Polish Jews, fewer than twenty-eight thousand of these children survived the war in Poland. During the occupation, many Jewish parents or guardians, usually in exceptionally dramatic circumstances, handed over their children to Polish families or dropped them off at orphanages, from which some were adopted, especially in Warsaw and the area around it, where the Home Army's Żegota helped to find people to take care of them. When the war was over, the process of taking the children back began.[273] In cases when their parents or closest relatives had not survived, three Jewish organizations became involved. The Central Committee of Polish Jews was the first. The second was the Jewish Congregation, which paid for Jewish children living in Polish homes, especially on behalf of their religious relatives in the West. The third organization, which was founded by the Zionist movement, was Coordination. Its agents traveled through Poland, found Jewish children, and persuaded their Polish caretakers to hand them over, sometimes compensating them with money.[274] Many Polish families had become attached to the children entrusted to them, some had no idea that the children were Jewish, and many had not taken into account the possibility that the adoption was temporary and loved them as their own. Very close ties had frequently built up between the caretakers and the children as they faced the horrors of the war together. Taking the children away was often a great tragedy, especially for women. Many were therefore not disposed to hand the children over to people, especially when they were not even family. The one thousand zlotys was intended to help overcome their dilemmas.

There were conflicts. *Express Wieczorny* wrote about one such situation on July 4, 1946. It reported on a trial in which a Jewish mother, who had left her infant in an orphanage in Warsaw in 1941 and who survived the war, wanted to take the child back from the Polish family who had adopted it. "But the adoptive parents vehemently refused, believing that after six years the demand came too late, since the alleged mother had not made the demand or given a sign of life for such a long period of time." They also claimed that the woman could not prove that she really was the child's mother and only wanted to receive financial assistance from an American charitable institution. The paper was obviously on "our" side. The article could not have influenced the events in Kielce since the paper came out on the afternoon of that day, but it illustrated the dramas of that day and the buried hostility toward Jews.[275]

Echo Wieczorne wrote about a similar trial before a court in Łódź. Waleria Januszewska, an illiterate repatriate from Vilna, took in a one-and-a-half-year-old girl, daughter of Vilna jeweler Samuel Rajdeberd. She had her baptized and officially changed her first name to Teresa, as well as her family name. After the war they moved to Łódź, where the girl's uncle allegedly offered Januszewska ten thousand zlotys. She refused. Because the man left town, the Jewish community took up his case and offered her compensation. Teresa landed in a Jewish orphanage, and Januszewska visited her there. "When she saw her old guardian, Teresa threw herself at her crying and announced that she did not want to remain in the school. Januszewska did not hesitate and brought the girl home."[276] The Jewish community took her to court.

Some Poles, convinced that they would receive heaps of money for taking care of a Jewish child, treated Jewish children as a sort of insurance policy. In November 1945, President of the State National Council Bolesław Bierut received a complaint from a woman from Warsaw who had taken care of a Jewish boy since December 1942. They were deported to Germany after the Warsaw Uprising, and after they returned she took the boy to the Jewish community and received 1,500 zlotys. But after some time she decided that this was insufficient, and she went back to the community, where she was given another 1,500 zlotys. She then demanded 87,000 zlotys, scrupulously calculated, for the twenty-nine months she had taken care of the boy.[277] We do not know how many such conflicts and cases there were, but people knew about them. We can only guess. It is possible that stories of this kind may have helped the myth grow. The sentence "the Jews are taking children away" was true. The collective imagination of the era of the Great Terror may have added to the story about ritual murder. And if, in fact, the process of taking children out of the hands of "righteous Poles" did influence the development of the pogroms, it would be one of the greatest paradoxes in the history of modern Poland.

Let's go back to the most important question about the causes of the dual hatred of the Jews—as Communists and as vampires. There are very many answers to it, and to highlight only one or two oversimplifies the picture of the past. A combination of factors, as well as accidents, was at play. One thing is certain: just as we should not look for the causes of the sudden explosion of the belief in ritual murder and the anti-Jewish pogroms that were its consequence in "hereditary Polish anti-Semitism," we should also not see it as a secret police conspiracy. The key to understanding it lies in the Poles' psychosocial condition, their anxieties and terrors.

NOTES

1. Primo Levi, "The Truce," 254.
2. Kurcz, *Zmienność i nieuchronność stereotypów*, 50. See also Nelson, *The Psychology of Prejudice*.
3. Kłoskowska, *Kultury narodowe u korzeni*, 295.
4. Michlic, *Poland's Threatening Other*, 208–9.
5. For an analysis of ethnic purges, see Madajczyk, *Czystki etniczne i klasowe w Europie XX wieku*.
6. AIPN 3378, k. 47, 47b. Doniesienie specjalne.
7. Dmitrów, *Obraz Rosji i Rosjan w propagandzie narodowych socjalistów 1933–1945*, 281.
8. Sakson, *Stosunki narodowościowe na Warmii i Mazurach 1945–1997*, 16–22, passim; Piskorski, *Wygnańcy*, 145; Hytrek-Hryciuk, "Rosjanie nadchodzą," 34–62.
9. K. Jońca, A. Konieczny, *Upadek Festung Breslau* (Wrocław: Ossolineum, 1963), 31.
10. Goeschel, "Suicide at the End of the Third Reich," 153–73. See also Bessel, "Hatred after War," 199–203.
11. Hytrek-Hryciuk, "Rosjanie nadchodzą," 78, 79.
12. "A German in Bystrzyca District murdered his children by slitting their veins. These children died. The Citizens' Militia station in Bystryca was notified about the above. The chief arrested the criminal and handed him over to the War Command [of the Red Army], which released the German" (AIPN, KG MO 35/922, Sprawozdanie [KW MO w Legnicy] od dnia 10.6.45 r. do 10.7.45 r., illegible page numbers).
13. Kruk, *Spadek*, 114.
14. Bikont, "Puścić Żyda na zajączka," *Gazeta Wyborcza. Duży Format*, February 17, 2011.
15. Engelking, *Jest taki piękny słoneczny dzień*, 93.
16. Ead, *Zagłada i pamięć* is an important book on this subject.
17. AAN, MAP 787, k. 116–118. Memoriał w sprawie bezpieczeństwa życia i mienia żydostwa lubelskiego.
18. Torańska, *Śmierć spóźnia się o minutę*, 118.
19. Hurwic-Nowakowska, *Żydzi polscy (1947–1950)*.
20. Tuszyńska, *Rodzinna historia lęku*, 31.
21. A German woman living in Łabędy wrote a letter in the autumn of 1948, which was intercepted by the censor's office: "When a person reads German books or listens to the radio, the heart tightens and she asks God subconsciously to be German once again at least. . . . You can imagine how we're filled with hatred. But we have to shut up and survive" (AAN, KC PZPR 2807, k. 220. Specjalne doniesienie dot. Niemców).
22. Levi, *The Truce*, 254.
23. Anczarski, *Kronikarskie zapisy*, 254.
24. Karp and Traba, *Codzienność zapamiętana*, 42.
25. Dmitrów, *Niemcy i okupacja hitlerowska w oczach Polaków*.
26. Gios, "Niemieckie wpływy w muzyce," *Ziemia Pomorska*, January 1, 1946.

27. "Zabronić Niemcom uprawiania sportu," *Echo Krakowa*, March 11, 1946.
28. Wirszyłło, "Oczyścimy Dolny Śląsk," *Dziennik Polski*, July 2, 1945.
29. Kragen, "Wieś jedzie," *Dziennik Polski*, October 7, 1945.
30. AAN, MAP 757, k. 10. Pismo Prezydium Wojewódzkiej Rady Narodowej w Poznaniu do Prezydium Krajowej Rady Narodowej, January 14, 1946.
31. Hirsch, *Zemsta ofiar*. See also de Zayas, *A Terrible Revenge*.
32. Świda-Ziemba, *Urwany lot*, 284–85.
33. AIPN 3378, k. 63. Specjalne doniesienie dot. volksdeutschów.
34. AIPN 3378, k. 54. Specjalne doniesienie.
35. AIPN 3378, k. 63. Specjalne doniesienie dot. volksdeutschów.
36. More in Wolff-Powęska, *Polacy wobec Niemców*; Borodziej and Hajnicz, *Kompleks wypędzenia*; Madajczyk, *Niemcy polscy 1944–1989*, et al.
37. AAN, PKWN I/78, k. 7–10. Doniesienie specjalne dotyczy procesu zbrodniarzy z Majdanka.
38. Załuski, *Czterdziesty czwarty*, 501.
39. "Kat Majdanka zawisł na szubienicy," *Gazeta Lubelska*, December 25, 1945.
40. "Zbrodniarze stutthofscy zostaną publicznie powieszeni w Gdańsku," *Dziennik Bałtycki*, July 3, 1946.
41. *Dziennik Bałtycki*, July 6, 1946; *Express Wieczorny*, July 9, 1946; *Ilustrowany Kurier Polski*, July 12, 1946; *Przekrój*, July 14–20, 1946.
42. Rabij, "Sprawiedliwość czy hańba."
43. Kryński's article about the public execution in Prague appeared already in June 1946 (Kryński, "Egzekucje publiczne").
44. Kott, "Kropka nad I," *Przekrój*, July 21–27, 1946.
45. AAN, URM, 5/755, k. 1. Prezes Rady Ministrów do Ministra Sprawiedliwości, August 8, 1946.
46. Cf. Madajczyk, *Czystki etniczne*, 275.
47. AIPN, MBP 3378, k. 89. Specjalne doniesienie, September 13, 1945.
48. Pytlakowski, "Jak na Kujawach zabijano Niemców," *Polityka*, February 24, 2001.
49. Krzyk, "Uderzeni palcem Stalina," *Gazeta Wyborcza*, April 13, 2011.
50. AIPN 3378, k. 80b. Specjalne doniesienie dot. działalności dywersyjnych band.
51. Hytrek-Hryciuk, "Rosjanie nadchodzą," 114–16, 133–42.
52. Pużak, "Wspomnienia 1939–1945," 135.
53. There indeed were cases of poisoning with methylated spirit, but one could hardly say that the Germans were to blame. Polish and Soviet soldiers pounced on every bit of alcohol they saw, also of the industrial kind. Letters read, "Adaś died in the hospital. He drank some poisoned vodka left behind by the Germans." And, "We were on the offensive. We found some German spirits, drank them and went on the attack. What sort of an attack could it be when you can't see anything and many of our guys went deaf and blind" (AAN, PKWN I/78, k. 3. Sprawozdanie za miesiąc listopad [1944]).
54. AIPN 3378, Specjalne doniesienie dot. prowokacyjnych pogłosek, errors in page numbering.
55. Steinhaus, *Wspomnienia i zapiski*, 330.
56. A woman wrote a letter, which was posted in Wrocław on September 1, 1945: "I'm telling you now that we have no peace, I'm constantly thinking about having a sentinel day and night because there are raids. German SS-men beat up Strocki, no one knows why. Two of them came and beat him up very much. Our life is as hard now as when we lived in Przebraże." A letter posted in Opole read, "There are still plenty of German bands around here, who murder both Polish and Russki soldiers" (AIPN mf. 01265/752, k. 5, 5b. Specjalne doniesienie dot. bezpieczeństwa w kraju według opisów w listach cywilnej ludności).
57. AIPN 01265/752. Specjalne doniesienie dot. bezpieczeństwa w kraju według opisów w listach cywilnej ludności, n.p.
58. *Głos Wielkopolski*, September 21, 1946.
59. Protokół posiedzenia rządu GG—Fragment wypowiedzi H. Franka, 438.
60. Motyka, *Od rzezi wołyńskiej do Akcji "Wisła,"* 127, 456; see also Siemaszko and Siemaszko, *Ludobójstwo dokonane przez nacjonalistów ukraińskich na ludności polskiej Wołynia 1939–1944*; Filar, *Wydarzenia wołyńskie 1939–1944*.
61. Sources include Biskupski, *Świadkowie mówią*; Budzisz, *Z ziemi cmentarnej*.
62. Budzisz, *Z ziemi cmentarnej*, 83.
63. Anczarski, *Kronikarskie zapisy*, 293.
64. Justyna, "Ucieczka z piekła," 121.
65. Anczarski, *Kronikarskie zapisy*, 329.
66. AIPN 3378, k. 73. Specjalne doniesienie dot. działalności dywersyjnych band.
67. AIPN 3378, k. 72b. Specjalne doniesienie dot. działalności dywersyjnych band.
68. AIPN 3378, k. 72b. Specjalne doniesienie dot. działalności dywersyjnych band.
69. AIPN mf. 01265/752, k. 7b. Specjalne doniesienie dot. bezpieczeństwa w kraju według opisów w listach cywilnej ludności.
70. AIPN 3378, k. 73b. Specjalne doniesienie dot. działalności dywersyjnych band.
71. AIPN 3378, k. 71. Specjalne doniesienie dot. działalności dywersyjnych band.
72. AIPN 3378, k. 73. Specjalne doniesienie dot. działalności dywersyjnych band.
73. AIPN 3378, k. 80b. Specjalne doniesienie dot. działalności dywersyjnych band.
74. AIPN 3378, k. 78. Specjalne doniesienie dot. działalności dywersyjnych band.
75. AIPN 3378, k. 81b. Specjalne doniesienie dot. działalności dywersyjnych band.
76. AIPN 3378, k. 72b. Specjalne doniesienie dot. działalności dywersyjnych band.
77. AIPN 3378, k. 76. Specjalne doniesienie dot. działalności dywersyjnych band.
78. Misiło, *Pawłokoma 3 III 1945 r.*
79. Motyka, *Od rzezi*, 452.
80. AAN, MAP 123, k. 4.

81. AIPN mf. 01265/752, k. 2b. Specjalne doniesienie dot. bezpieczeństwa w kraju według opisów w listach cywilnej ludności.

82. AIPN 3378, k. 73. Specjalne doniesienie dot. działalności dywersyjnych band.

83. G. Motyka, *Od rzezi*, 457–62.

84. AAN, PKWN I/73, k. 11. Dane z inspekcji inspektora Wydz. Organizacyjnego—o stanie moralnym, politycznym i organizacyjnym propagandy w m. Białymstoku.

85. Mironowicz, *Polityka narodowościowa PRL*, 38, 40.

86. Kułak, *Rozstrzelany oddział*, 77, passim.

87. Mironowicz, *Białorusini w Polsce 1944–1949*, 147.

88. AIPN mf. 01265/752, k. 9. Specjalne doniesienie dot. bezpieczeństwa w kraju według opisów w listach cywilnej ludności.

89. AIPN 3378, k. 78b. Specjalne doniesienie dot. działalności dywersyjnych band.

90. Mironowicz, *Białorusini w Polsce 1944–1949*, 141; Kułak, *Rozstrzelany oddział*, 231–59.

91. AIPN, MBP 3378, k. 87. Specjalne doniesienie dot. zajść antyżydowskich w Krakowie, September 12, 1945.

92. J. Adelson estimated the number of all Jews murdered in 1944–47 at 1,500 to 2,000. (Adelson, "W Polsce zwanej ludową," 401). David estimated the number of Jews killed at 500–600 (Engel, "Patterns of Anti-Jewish Violence in Poland, 1944–1946," 43–85). J. T. Gross believes that Engels's figures are too low because he believes that the ministry often did not register murders. Gross considers calculations by Adelson and others as more accurate (Gross, *Fear*, 35).

The author of the newest and most reliable calculations is Julian Kwiek, who claims that over 1,100 Jews died after the war. Kwiek, Nie chcemy Żydów u siebie; Adelson, "W Polsce zwanej ludową," 401; Engel, "Patterns of Anti-Jewish Violence in Poland, 1944–1946," 43–85; Gross, *Fear*.

93. Gross, *Fear*, 39ff.

94. Gross, 245ff.

95. There are five forms of the story about ritual murder in literature: accusation, gossip, superstition, legend, and myth. For an explanation of why the last word is used here and for its definition, see Zaremba, "Mit mordu rytualnego w powojennej Polsce. Archeologia i hipotezy," 91–135. This article also appeared in abbreviated form as "Oni mordują nasze dzieci! Mit mordu rytualnego w powojennej Polsce," part 1: *Archeologia*, Więź, October 2007, 90–109; part 2: *Hipotezy*, Więź, November–December 2007, 96–112.

96. The events in Parczewo are an exception, an armed assault and not a pogrom.

97. The following discuss the postwar anti-Jewish pogroms: Cichopek, *Pogrom Żydów*; Szaynok, *Pogrom Żydów w Kielcach 4 lipca 1946*; Kersten, *Polacy, Żydzi, komunizm*; Kamiński and Żaryn, *Wokół pogromu kieleckiego*; Gross, *Fear*. There are also collections of documents, including Szaynok and Wrona, "Pogrom kielecki w dokumentach," 75–117; Meducki and Wrona, *Antyżydowskie wydarzenia*; Kaczmarski, *Pogrom, którego nie było*; Joanna Tokarska-Bakir, *Pod klątwą. Społeczny portret pogromu kieleckiego*, Warsaw: Wydawnictwo Czarna Owca, 2018.

98. AAN, MIiP 753, k. 5. Dziewiąte sprawozdanie z działalności za miesiąc marzec 1945.

99. For more, see Węgrzynek, "mord rytualny," 355, 356; and Żyndul, *Kłamstwo krwi*; Węgrzynek, *"Czarna legenda" Żydów*; Guldon and Wijaczka, *Procesy o mordy rytualne w Polsce w XVI–XVIII wieku*.

100. Cf. "Trzecie sprawozdanie z działalności Referatu dla Spraw Pomocy Ludności Żydowskiej przy Prezydium Polskiego Komitetu Wyzwolenia Narodowego (za okres od 18.09. do 10.10.1944 r.)," 20; AAN, MPiOS 335, k. 56. Ósme sprawozdanie z działalności za miesiąc luty 1945.

101. Archiwum Instytutu Pamięci Narodowej w Rzeszowie (henceforth AIPN-Rz) 062/5, k. 3. Meldunek Kaprala MO Jana Łukasza do Kierownika Referatu Śledczego MO, Rzeszów 12 VI 1945. Akta sprawy Bronisławy Mendoń, n.p.

102. AŻIH 301/1581, k. 1–6. Rozruchy w Rzeszowie. Relacja Jonasa Landesmanna. This and other documents are included in Kaczmarski, *Pogrom, którego nie było*, 151–55.

103. See AIPN-Rz 062/5. Akta sprawy Bronisławy Mendoń, no page numbers.

104. AŻIH 301/1581, k. 1–6. Rozruchy w Rzeszowie. Relacja Jonasa Landesmanna.

105. According to the authors of an underground booklet, *Dosyć krętactw sowieckich* (Enough of Soviet poppycock), the criminals were captured. They were allegedly four Jewish NKVD informers, who were released after a few days on NKVD request. According to this booklet, "If the murder had not been committed with the NKVD's knowledge, the NKVD certainly approved of it" (AAN, KC PPR, 295/VII-203, k. 57).

106. Sources include Materski and Paczkowski, *NKWD o Polsce i Polakach*; Cariewskaja et al., *Teczka specjalna J.W. Stalina*. Prosecutor K. Falkiewicz also indicated the lack of evidence of a conspiracy in his decision to dismiss the investigation about the Kielce pogrom (Kamiński and Żaryn, *Wokół pogromu kieleckiego*, 471, 472).

107. Do Pana Prokuratora Sądu Apelacyjnego w Krakowie [rękopis pisma prokuratora Bronisława Gnatowskiego], September 26, 1945, in Kaczmarski, *Pogrom, którego nie było*, 147–50.

108. Kersten, *Polacy, Żydzi, komunizm*, 110.

109. Kaczmarski, *Pogrom, którego nie było*, 25.

110. AŻIH, 301/1320. Sprawozdanie w sprawie wypadków zaszłych w dniu 12 czerwca 1945, n.p.

111. Kaczmarski, *Pogrom, którego nie było*, 25.

112. CAW, GZP, III.2.204, k. 389, 390. Meldunek specjalny o sytuacji w terenie Głównego Zarządu Pol.-Wych. WP, 22 VI 1945.

113. AŻIH, 301/1320. Sprawozdanie w sprawie wypadków zaszłych w dniu 12 czerwca 1945, n.p.

114. "Meldunek specjalny kierownika Sekcji VII Wojewódzkiego Urzędu Bezpieczeństwa Publicznego w Rzeszowie o eskalacji nastrojów antysemickich w tym mieście, 12 VI 1945 r.," 600.

115. *Dziennik Rzeszowski*, June 13, 1945.

116. Kaczmarski, *Pogrom, którego nie było*, 38.

117. AŻIH, 301/1320, Sprawozdanie w sprawie wypadków zaszłych w dniu 12 czerwca 1945, n.p.

118. "Raport sytuacyjny por. Michała Kołacza, kierownika Sekcji VII WUBP w Rzeszowie . . . dotyczący nastrojów społecznych po odkryciu morderstwa dziewczynki, 14 VI 1945 r.," 81, 82.

119. Kersten, *Polacy, Żydzi, komunizm*, and also Cichopek, *Pogrom Żydów*.
120. AAN, PPR, 295/VII-255, k. 6. Polityka narodowościowa PPR.
121. See "Sprawozdanie przedstawiciela CKŻP z podróży inspekcyjnej w dn. 5–18 kwietnia 1945 r. w województwach rzeszowskim i tarnowskim," 24–26.
122. AAN, PPR, 295/VII-255, k. 6. Polityka narodowościowa PPR.
123. AŻIH 301/1581, k. 1–6. Rozruchy w Rzeszowie. Relacja Jonasa Landesmanna.
124. AŻIH 3003/24, Prezydium Centralnego Komitetu Żydów Polskich.
125. Steinhaus, *Wspomnienia i zapiski*, 324.
126. Kuroń, *Wiara i wina*, 23.
127. "Źródła i podłości zajść sobotnich w Krakowie," *Dziennik Polski*, August 16, 1945, quoted by Kwiek, 'Wydarzenia antyżydowskie 11 sierpnia 1945 r. w Krakowie. Dokumenty," 89.
128. "Aneksy. Akt oskarżenia," 202.
129. "Aneksy. Akt oskarżenia," 67.
130. AIPN, KG MO 35/879, k. 46. Raport Komendy Wojewódzkiej MO w Krakowie od dnia 15 VII do 1 VIII 1945.
131. For more on this, see Cichopek, *Pogrom Żydów*, 53–66.
132. AIPN, KG MO 35/878, k. 1. Meldunek specjalny Zastępcy Wojewódzkiego Komendanta MO do Spraw Polityczno-Wychowawczych, Kraków, August 15, 1945.
133. Cichopek, *Pogrom Żydów*, 70.
134. "Sprawozdanie KW PZPR w Krakowie dotyczące oceny sytuacji na terenie województwa krakowskiego," 86.
135. "II Komisariat MO zaalarmowany ekscesami nie dopisał w zupełności. Część milicjantów nie zareagowała natychmiast, lecz wprost przeciwnie wzięli udział w ekscesach" (Meldunek specjalny . . .).
136. For more on the pogrom, see Cichopek, *Pogrom Żydów*. See also documents nos. 108 and 113 in Cariewskaja et al., *Teczka specjalna J.W. Stalina*.
137. "Protokół przesłuchania podejrzanego Franciszka Bandysa w WUBP," 163.
138. "Aneksy. Akt oskarżenia," 206.
139. "Aneksy. Akt oskarżenia," 208.
140. "Sprawozdanie Centralnego Komitetu Żydów w Polsce dotyczące zajść antyżydowskich," 78.
141. *Informacja o przebiegu zajść antysemickich w Krakowie*, 1945; *Informacja o przebiegu zajść antysemickich w Krakowie*, 83.
142. "Sprawozdanie Centralnego Komitetu Żydów w Polsce dotyczące zajść antyżydowskich," 79.
143. Eliade, *The Sacred and the Profane*, 95.
144. AIPN, MBP 3378, k. 87, 88. Specjalne doniesienie dot. zajść antyżydowskich w Krakowie, September 12, 1945.
145. Cichopek, *Pogrom Żydów*, 124.
146. Archer and Gartner, "Peacetime Casualties," 329–40.
147. "Wojsko polskie perłą wśród innych wojsk!," 10.
148. "Protokół zeznania świadka pogromu w Kielcach," 46.
149. AIPN, KG MO 35/878, k. 3. Meldunek specjalny Zastępcy Wojewódzkiego Komendanta MO do Spraw Polityczno-Wychowawczych, Kraków, August 15, 1945.

150. AIPN, MBP 311, k. 11. Sprawozdanie dekadowe za czas od 11 IX do 20 IX 1945 r., Wojewódzki Urząd Bezpieczeństwa w Katowicach.
151. AP w Kielcach, Urząd Wojewódzki II 1338, Sprawozdanie sytuacyjne miesięczne starosty powiatowego w Olkuszu, 7 IX 1945, k. 82.
152. AAN, MIiP79, k. 57. Sprawozdanie z wyjazdu służbowego ob. W. Śliwińskiego do woj. Kieleckiego dla przeprowadzenia akcji informacyjno-propagandowej, mającej na celu zapobieżenie ekscesom antyżydowskim.
153. "The gossip that is repeated by stupid people in ill faith create a base that is exceptionally susceptible to all kinds of violence and street disturbances" (*Głos Narodu*, August 18, 1945).
154. "Zdemaskowana prowokacja lubelskich naśladowców Hitlera," *Sztandar Ludu*, October 23, 1945.
155. It is noteworthy that the myth was transmitted with exceptional intensity in the summer. This must have been due to the increased mobility in street markets and fairs. Most anti-Black lynching in the United States happened in hot periods, and the pogroms in Cracow and Kielce also took place on exceptionally hot days.
156. AIPN, MBP 733, k. 7. Telefonogram z WUBP Bydgoszcz do Ministra Radkiewicza, Warszawa 10 VI 1946.
157. AP w Kielcach, Wojewódzki Urząd Informacji i Propagandy (henceforth WUIP), 4, Protokół XV Konferencji Kierowników Oddziałów Informacji i Propagandy, 18 VI 1946, k. 5.
158. "The government of Poland has directed Jews who engage not only in commerce but also in agriculture and mining to Lower Silesia. Wrocław, where a Jewish theater has opened, has the largest concentration of Polish Jews after Łódź" (*Niedziela. Tygodnik Katolicki*, June 2–8, 1946, 179).
159. AP w Kielcach, Urząd Wojewódzki w Kielcach II (dalej UW II) 1242, k. 3. Odruchy społeczeństwa częstochowskiego w związku z zajściami kieleckimi, July 9, 1946.
160. AIPN, MBP 733, k. 13, 14. Do wiceministra Bezpieczeństwa Publicznego płk. Romkowskiego. Raport w sprawie oskarżonego o zamordowanie dziewczynki w Częstochowie, July 15, 1946.
161. AAN, MIiP 79, k. 50. Uwagi do sprawozdania z dnia 4 VII 1946.
162. AP w Kielcach, UW II 1524, k. 41. Pismo Kierownika I-ego Wydziału Wojewódzkiego Urzędu Bezpieczeństwa Publicznego w Kielcach por. Srokowskiego do Wojewody Kieleckiego, October 9, 1945.
163. Wiślicz-Iwańczyk, "Wspomnienia," 83.
164. "Raport księdza kanonika Romana Zelka, proboszcza parafii katedralnej w Kielcach dla Kurii Diecezjalnej, dotyczący pogromu w dn. 4 lipca 1946 r.," *Dzieje Żydów w Polsce . . .*, op. cit., 53, 54.
165. "Protokół przesłuchania świadka Antoniego Kręglickiego," 300.
166. "Protokół przesłuchania świadka Walentego Błaszczyka," 106, 108.
167. "Ja byłem dziecko niewinne," *Gazeta Wyborcza*, July 4, 1997.

168. "Protokół przesłuchania Antoniny Biskupskiej," 129, 130.
169. See "Zeznanie Morrisa Kwaśniewskiego," 352.
170. CAW, GZPW IV.502.1.13, k. 49–58. Szef Wydziału Karnego Departamentu Sprawiedliwości MON i Prokuratury WP do Naczelnego Prokuratora WP, July 19, 1946.
171. "Protokół zeznania świadka pogromu w Kielcach, Racheli Grunglas," 46, 47.
172. "Relacja świadka wydarzeń pogromowych w Kielcach," 50, 51.
173. According to prosecutor K. Falkiewicz, "This number is determined not only by evidence, but also by the objective gauge of the size of the site of the event measured during its inspection" ("Postanowienie o umorzeniu śledztwa w sprawie pogromu kieleckiego," 480).
174. AIPN, MBP 731, k. 8. Albert Grynbaum. Sprawozdanie z przebiegu zajść antysemickich w Kielcach.
175. Ossowski, "Na tle wydarzeń kieleckich."
176. "Protokół przesłuchania Józefa Sztarkmana," 135.
177. AIPN, KG MO 35/897, k. 47. Sprawozdanie z pracy polityczno-wychowawczej w MO województwa poznańskiego za okres od 9 VII do 8 VIII 1946.
178. "But," as was noted later, "people began to swear at the Jews, graffiti with anti-Semitic content appeared on walls. There were cases of Polish children throwing pebbles at Jewish children in the park. Next, the rumor was started that they are going to empty out all Poles from Łódzka Street, and thousands of Jews will replace them" (AAN, Bolesław Bierut—archiwum, 254/III-6, k. 77. Sprawozdanie grupy trzech towarzyszy wysłanych przez Komitet Wojewódzki w Poznaniu do Kalisza 10 VII dla przeciwdziałania ewentualnym wystąpieniom antysemickim).
179. AAN, PPR, 295/IX-408, k. 44–46. Sprawozdanie CKŻP, oddział w Ostrowcu Świętokrzyskim.
180. See Meducki and Wrona, *Antyżydowskie wydarzenia*, vol. 2, 147–51.
181. "Sprawozdanie Powiatowego Oddziału Informacji i Propagandy w Sandomierzu" in Meducki and Wrona, 144.
182. "Pismo Kierownika Powiatowego Oddziału Informacji i Propagandy" in Meducki and Wrona, 146.
183. Archiwum IPN w Katowicach, ka 011/38. Raport dekadowy za okres od 30 VII do 10 VII 1946, k. 190; see also AIPN MBP 733, k. 9–12. Raport z odbytej podróży do Częstochowy z zadaniem niedopuszczenia do zajść antyżydowskich i postawienia miasta w stan pogotowia.
184. AIPN, MBP 731, k. 15. Telefonogram z WUBP—Kielce, July 17, 1946.
185. AIPN, ka 011/38, k. 202. Raport dekadowy za okres od 7 VII do 17 VII 1946.
186. AIPN, ka 011/38, k. 197. Raport dekadowy za okres od 7 VII do 17 VII 1946.
187. "Sprawozdanie miesięczne Miejskiego Oddziału Informacji i Propagandy w Radomiu za miesiąc lipiec 1946 r.," 151–52.
188. AŻIH, CKŻP, Komisja Specjalna (dalej KS) 303/XVIII/40, Sprawozdanie Komisji Specjalnej przy Woj. Komitecie Żydowskim w Warszawie od maja 1946 do lutego 1947, n.p.
189. AŻIH, CKŻP, Komisja Specjalna.
190. Żyndul, *Kłamstwo krwi*, 226.
191. AŻIH, KS 303/XVIII-41, Sprawozdanie z pracy Komisji Specjalnej przy Wojewódzkim Komitecie Żydowskim w Krakowie za okres 1 VIII do 1 X 1946, n.p.
192. AŻIH, CKŻP, KS 303/XVIII/41. Sprawozdanie Komisji Specjalnej, Tarnów 13 X 1946, brak paginacji.
193. AŻIH, CKŻP, KS 303/XVIII/40. Sprawozdanie z działalności Centralnej Komisji Specjalnej przy Centralnym Komitecie Żydów w Polsce, 30 maja 1947, n.p.
194. AIPN, 1206/75, t. 1. Instrukcja nr 15, 11 Mar. 1948, n.p. (K. Persak told me about this document).
195. "On 16.4 [1949] attempts were recorded in Częstochowa of people trying to provoke anti-Jewish incidents. A taxi driver picked up a 4-year-old girl standing outside a house, and a few minutes later brought her back. Meanwhile, about 150 people gathered in the street, and people shouted from the crowd that Jews had taken the child. The gathering was dispersed. The girl's father, a railroad employee with reactionary views who was the first to share the gossip about the Jews kidnapping the child, and the driver who explained himself that he had taken the child to 'intimidate' her parents, were arrested"; "on 17.9 in Cracow an anti-Semitic incident. The release of the child allegedly kidnapped by Jews was demanded. 1 person was arrested in connection with the above"; "On 21.9 in Cracow in Nowy Square, an inhabitant attempted to bring about an anti-Semitic incident, shouting that Jews had kidnapped her child" (*Biuletyny dzienne Ministerstwa Bezpieczeństwa Publicznego 1949–1950*, 197, 397, 403).
196. Steinhaus, *Wspomnienia i zapiski*, 335, 365.
197. AAN, PPR 295/VII–203, k. 57. Dosyć krętactw sowieckich.
198. AIPN, KG MO 35/895, k. 178. Odpis meldunków nadzwyczajnych, Rzeszów 24 VIII 1946.
199. AAN, Bolesław Bierut—archiwum, 254/III-6, Sprawozdanie grupy trzech towarzyszy wysłanych przez Komitet Wojewódzki w Poznaniu do Kalisza 10 VII dla przeciwdziałania ewentualnym wystąpieniom antysemickim.
200. AIPN, MBP 3378, k. 87–89. Specjalne doniesienie dot. zajść antyżydowskich w Krakowie, September 12, 1945.
201. AIPN, MBP 3378, k. 87–89.
202. AIPN, MBP 3378, k. 87–89.
203. AIPN, MBP 3378, k. 87–89.
204. Engelking, *"Szanowny panie gistapo"*; Engelking, *Jest taki piękny słoneczny dzień*; Grabowski, *Hunt for the Jews*; Grabowski, *Judenjagd*; Żbikowski, "Antysemityzm, szmalcownictwo," 429–505; Engelking and Grabowski, *Zarys krajobrazu*.
205. "Sytuacyjne sprawozdanie miesięczne za miesiąc lipiec 1945 r.," written by the Częstochowa starost, suggested that the Poles may not have liked the Jewish nation's sacrifice. "Because of this, I note as a fact that the Poles are incapable of understanding the Jewish minority when it undertakes efforts to increase its material possessions, and thus mostly does not take into account the facts that occurred in the period beginning in 1939 and when this minority stresses that it was alone in suffering in the war years" (emphasis added—MZ; Archiwum Państwowe w Kielcach, k. 329. Urząd Wojewódzki II 1337).
206. AIPN, MBP 3378, k. 89. Specjalne doniesienie dot. zajść antyżydowskich w Krakowie, 12 września 1945.

207. Quoted in Kersten, *Polacy, Żydzi . . .*, op. cit., 108.
208. IPN KG MO 35/967, k. 3. Do komendy wojewódzkiej MO we Wrocławiu.
209. AIPN, MBP 3378, k. 89. Specjalne doniesienie dot. zajść antyżydowskich w Krakowie, 12 Sept. 1945.
210. Kersten, *Polacy, Żydzi, komunizm*, 76–88.
211. Bauman, *Nigdzie na ziemi*, 20.
212. Cf. Engelking, *Jest taki piękny słoneczny dzień*, 137.
213. An example of the disparity between the Polish and Jewish "truths" and of differences in diagnoses of the postwar reality is a comment dated May 12, 1945, in the diary of Marceli Najder, a Jewish survivor: "I'm *incognito* here, a Pole, so I yield to their influence. They're not satisfied with this Poland, that's fine, but why not be happy that the Germans have been finished off? The Poles want another war. With Russia? Funny: who'll do the fighting? They don't want to because they also didn't want to with the Germans. Maybe England and America would fight for a 'different' Poland" (Najder, "Dziennik z bunkra," 85).
214. Podkowiński, "Żydzi na niemieckim szlaku" (Podkowiński was quoting the English journalist W. Forrest). Exclamation mark in the original.
215. Dąbrowska, *Dzienniki*, vol. 5, 145.
216. Kersten, *Polacy, Żydzi, komunizm*, 78–79.
217. Paczkowski, *Trzy twarze Józefa Światły*, 103; Paczkowski, *Żydzi w UB. Próba weryfikacji stereotypu*, 192–204.
218. Steinhaus, *Wspomnienia i zapiski*, 345.
219. Dąbrowska, *Dzienniki*, 145.
220. More on the Jews' postwar political beliefs in Szaynok, "Społeczeństwo żydowskie w Polasce wobec referendum 30 VI 1946 r. o wyborów do Sejmu 19 I 1947 r.," 137–38; Grabski, "Żydzi a polskie życie polityczne (1944–1949)," 157–88.
221. AAN, KC PPR 295/IX-407, k. 194–199. Telefoniczne sprawozdanie z akcji wyborczej i wyniki wyborów wśród społeczeństwa żydowskiego na Dolny Śląsk.
222. Cantril, et al., *The Invasion from Mars*.
223. Cantril, et al., 113.
224. Wyka, "Potęga ciemnoty potwierdzona."
225. This assessment, even though it does not affirm the myth, needs to be cited. According to the deputy commander for political-educational matters of the nineth infantry division, "It must be stressed that while the majority of soldiers condemn the anti-Jewish incidents [in Cracow], many officers, and even some political-educational officers, on the contrary spoke in a hostile way about the jews [sic]. They say that many jews [sic] now occupy high positions in Poland and that they don't care about the collective welfare; and that as long as jews [sic] are living in Poland, it will not be peaceful" (CAW, GZPW, III.2.192, k. 87).
226. Cantril et al., *The Invasion from Mars*, 113, 114.
227. "Akt oskarżenia Biskupskiej," 150–52.
228. "Ja byłem dziecko."
229. "In Sowina near Jasło, a returning Jewish family who wanted to take back their land from peasants, was killed" (Steinhaus, *Wspomnienia i zapiski*, 333).
230. It is not out of the question that the rumors about Jewish gold were made to seem real by a statement by Gen. Morgan, head of a regional UNRRA office in occupied Germany. He was quoted by *Kurier Szczeciński* as saying that "thousands of Polish Jews are seeping into the US occupation zone from the east with a 'well thought-out plan of getting out of Europe.' These people are excellently dressed and have masses of money. According to Morgan, a secret Jewish organization is behind the Jews' infiltration. Their mass inflow into Germany is not inspired by the Polish government nor by East European governments" ("Gen. Morgan o wędrówkach Żydów," *Kurier Szczeciński*, January 9, 1946).
231. Lipset, *Political Man*, 97ff.
232. Cantril et al., *The Invasion from Mars*, 148.
233. Cichopek, *Pogrom Żydów*, 214.
234. Cichopek, 212.
235. "Relacja świadka wydarzeń, Idy Gerstman, spisana w CKŻP, 11 lipca 1946 r.," 48.
236. *Sprawozdanie Urzędu Informacji i Propagandy w Lublinie za okres 17–23 sierpnia 1946 r.*, AAN, MIP, 1004, k. 17.
237. Gross and Grudzińska-Gross, *Golden Harvest*, 59.
238. According to the 1931 census. See, for example, Bartkowski, *Tradycja i polityka*, 224–25.
239. Discussion during doctoral seminar of Profs. W. Borodziej, J. Kochanowski, and M. Kula, Institute of History of the University of Warsaw, October 16, 2006.
240. Statement by Zielonka, *Karta*, 120.
241. Żyndul, *Kłamstwo krwi*.
242. *Ilustrowany Kurier Codzienny*, May 26, 1934.
243. Żydul, *Kłamstwo krwi*, 191–211.
244. Konieczny, *Żydzi w Polsce i ich wrogi stosunek do narodu*, 6.
245. "Odezwa biskupa Teodora Kubiny oraz władz miejskich i powiatowych do społeczeństwa miasta Częstochowy," 112.
246. Kochavi, "The Catholic Church and Antisemitism in Poland," 123.
247. "Odpis sprawozdania z audiencji biskupa Stefana Wyszyńskiego," 116, 117.
248. See *Raport księdza kanonika Romana Zelka*, 53, 54.
249. AIPN, ka 011/38, k. 203. Raport dekadowy za okres od 7 VII do 17 VII 1946.
250. Cała, *Wizerunek Żyda w Polskiej kulturze ludowej*, 91.
251. See Tokarska-Bakir, "Obrazy sandomierskie," 18–63; Tokarska-Bakir, *Legendy o krwi*.
252. Materials intercepted by the Security Office included two orange cards. One has the prayer "Kto z Bogiem—Bóg z nim" printed on it, and the second one begins with the sentence "In 1939 jews [sic] made up 13% of our country's population . . . but do you know that . . ." which was followed by a typical antisemitic list, which ended with the phrase "jews [sic] practiced 100% of the trade in women and children." The cards were not signed, but the quality of the print makes it seem that they came from an official printer controlled by the Germans (AIPN, WiN 92, k. 237).
253. Cantril et al., *The Invasion from Mars*, 128–39.
254. "Mój dom—moja twierdza," *Dziennik Łódzki*, August 6, 1945.
255. AP w Kielcach, Wojewódzki Urząd Informacji i Propagandy w Kielcach 20, k. 103. Sprawozdanie za miesiąc styczeń 1946.

256. Cantril et al., *The Invasion from Mars*, 153–64.
257. Kołakowski, *Obecność mitu*, 69ff.
258. Po-chia Hsia, *The Myth of Ritual Murder*.
259. Wust, *Niepewność i ryzyko*, 49.
260. More on the situation of children after the war and children's abductions: Ł. Krzyżanowski, M. Zaremba, *"Bić ich za nasze dzieci!" Panika moralna i przemoc zbiorowa wobec Żydów w Polsce w latach 1945–1946)*, in *Pogromy Żydów na ziemiach polskich w XIX i XX wieku*, vol. 4: Holokaust i powojnie (1939–1946), ed. August Grabski, Wydawnictwo IH PAN, Warszawa 2019; A. Bikont, *Cena: W poszukiwaniu żydowskich dzieci po wojnie*, ZNAK, Kraków 2022.
261. For example, *Dziennik Powszechny*, July 22, 1945, classifieds: "Markiewicz J., Kielce District, Słupia Nowa commune, village of Jeziórko: seeking 10-year-old son Stanisław, amputated left arm. He was in the hospital in Arrswald, picked up by an unknown woman. Anyone who knows anything about the boy, please get in touch."
262. Bettelheim, *The Uses of Enchantment*, 206.
263. "Protokół przesłuchania świadka Mojżesza Cukiera," 113.
264. *Antyżydowskie wydarzenia*, vol. 1, 130.
265. AIPN Poznań, Po 06/140/8/1, k. 20. Raport sprawozdawczy powiatowego UBP w Poznaniu, 27 XI 1945.
266. AIPN, MBP, 362, k. 7. Telefonogram z WUBP—Rzeszów, 6 Oct. 1945.
267. *Stargard moje miasto*, 64.
268. "Palił w piecu—głowy kobiece. Potworne zbrodnie niemieckiego wampira w Krakowie," *Dziennik Polski*, June 2, 1945
269. See "Wstrząsające zeznanie świadka w Norymberdze," *Dziennik Łódzki*, January 12, 1946.
270. AIPN, KG MO 35/897, k. 307, 312.
271. Kochavi, "The Catholic Church," 120.
272. AŻIH, 3031/1a, k. 73, 74. Protokół 17 posiedzenia Prezydium CKŻP odbytego dnia 9 czerwca 1945.
273. On picking up children from Polish hands right after the war, see Anna Bikont, *W poszukiwaniu żydowskich dzieci po wojnie*. Wołowiec: Czarne, 2022.
274. More on the postwar stories of Jewish children and the organizations that took care of them in Bogner, *At the Mercy of Strangers*; Datner, "Dziecko żydowskie (1944–1968)," 245–81.
275. "Sąd przed Salomonową próbą. Spór o dziecko z przytułku dla podrzutków," *Express Wieczorny*, July 4, 1946.
276. "Dramatyczny spór o dziecko wychowane w czasie wojny.—Niecodzienna sprawa w Sądzie dla Nieletnich," *Echo Wieczorne*, January 1, 1947. "Gazeta sygnalizowała problem już wcześniej: Dzieci nie chcą wracać do matek," *Echo Wieczorne*, December 7, 1946.
277. AAN, KRN 148, k. 16–18. Do ob. Prezydenta Krajowej Rady Narodowej Bolesława Bieruta.

CONCLUSION

"THE BOOGEYMAN"

Fear can spread at lightning speed like an infectious disease. The infected has difficulty sleeping, panics, and becomes aggressive. It leaves an imprint on the mind. When a threat reappears, it hits a person twice as hard. The Poles experienced this again and again during the Second World War, and then again after it ended.

The Second World War left a mark on the Polish psyche, as a sort of permanent matrix of fear. We have heard of "facsimiles": a war panic that leads people to hoard food, clothing, gas, matches, petrol lamps, and other necessities. The first wave of postwar fear rolled over Poland already in 1945–46. Subsequent ones came during the Berlin Blockade in 1948, during the Korean War, after an American U-2 was shot down over the Soviet Union in 1960, during the second Berlin Crisis as the Wall was being erected, and in 1962 during the Cuban Missile Crisis. In 1967, at the news that an Arab-Israeli war had broken out, the Poles queued up yet again to buy supplies, lest the conflict turn global. The hoarding of food in People's Poland stemmed from both the deep-rooted peasant mentality of stocking up and from the fear of hunger people remembered from the war. The first reactions to the imposition of martial law in 1981 showed that the memory of the war was still alive, with new anxieties of the postwar generations. Communist propaganda, busy disseminating the fear of war, added to them.

The memory of war survives to this day, something that sociological interviews and surveys confirm. The most recent study of the image of war in Polish society conducted in 2009 showed that 43.5 percent of the respondents lived in families that continued to talk about the war era. They defined the daily experience of war as poverty, hunger, shortages (9.3 percent); bombardments and air raids (8.8 percent); forced resettlements, expulsions from one's home (8.2 percent); flight, going into hiding, taking cover, hiding possessions (7.7 percent); the Red Army's invasion of 1944–45 (7.1 percent); executions, genocide (6 percent); and forced labor in Germany (5.5 percent).[1] This study, which was conducted sixty-four years after the end of the war, also shows the still-powerful memories of chaos and the collapse of the legal, social, and moral orders. The interviewees often mentioned robberies by people pretending to be partisans and "roving bands stealing from people."[2]

No comparable data exist to teach us about the Poles' memories of the time immediately after the war, and yet we may hazard a hypothesis that such a study would resemble the general picture of the war. Brighter memories, such as rejoicing about liberation, rebuilding one's life, or being reunited with one's family, are likely accompanied by fear of bandits, rape, hunger, infectious diseases, and difficulties with finding a place to live. Krystyna Kersten wrote in 1993, "It is astounding how the mass oppression that immediately followed Poland's liberation from the Germans disappeared for a long time from collective memory, as well as from historiography."[3] But it did not disappear: even with the subsequent traumatic experiences of the Stalinist period deposited on top of it, people continued to remember the political fear of the immediate postwar years.

We know that fears such as those of a currency devaluation, which appeared as hearsay, were strengthened by yet another "thieving" currency exchange in October 1950, and survived into the late 1970s–early 1980s.[4] Despite the government's departure from that goal at the Third Polish United Workers' Party Congress in 1959 by none other than Politburo member Edward Ochab, peasants continued to fear forced collectivization well into the 1980s. Distrust of the state for wanting to confiscate small businesses and to impose draconian taxes endured until the end of Communism. As Adam Podgórecki, wrote, "Fear could have many faces, private or communal."[5] A 1966 nationwide study shows that 76 percent of the urban population and 69.7 percent of the rural population felt insecure. Jacek Kurczewski analyzed these findings and concluded that "they may be interpreted as a manifestation of the link between low social status and a feeling of endangerment, and a high position in society and an absence of this feeling."[6] Lasting fear and anxiety became the people's reaction to the experiences of the twentieth century. Equally long-lasting was the bazaar culture that had been omnipresent throughout the war and in the immediate postwar years,[7] as was the lack of respect for others' property, a residue of the looting fever. Not very long ago, it was still possible to see, on the maps of Polish cities, areas that had been settled in an improvised fashion during the great postwar rush in search of a home. Poland continues to suffer from the consequences of land reform, the splitting up of land. As a joke in old Cracow would have it, members of the new intelligentsia created by the social revolution initially could not tell Bach from Mozart and were intimidated by this. But over time it became sovereign, both intellectually and in its dealings with the Communist authorities.

The Poles continue to fear Russia and its military to this day. Their fear hit the highest points in 1956, when they could imagine a Soviet intervention, and in the 1980–81 Solidarity years, when the question "will they invade or not?" was on everyone's lips. Through the years, their fear grew when the Soviets intervened militarily in Hungary, Czechoslovakia, and Afghanistan. Even in 1991, as the Red Army pulled out of the former German Democratic Republic, fear of the "grand army" marching across Poland was revived as a memory of 1944–45.

Also surviving practically until the end of Communist rule were fears of Jews and Germans who might reclaim property the Poles had taken from them. Fear of national borders being changed and the resultant feeling of impermanence were a crucial factor shaping the postwar reality. In an anecdote overheard in Lower Silesia, a man waited for the signing of the Polish-German border treaty in 1991 before he grabbed a brush and painted his fence. In other words, the Great Terror did not end in 1947 but was stamped in the national memory, fortified the Poles' religiosity, and pushed roots in habits and customs in the daily life of People's Poland.

NOTES

1. Szacka, "II wojna światowa w pamięci rodzinnej," 119, 121, 122.

2. Kwiatkowski, "II wojna światowa jako doświadczenie narodowe," 199; see also "Świadków ubywa, pamięć słabnie, rozmowa W. Szackiego z P.T. Kwiatkowskim," *Gazeta Wyborcza*, September 1, 2009 (Pentor conducted this study on a representative sample of 1,200 people).

3. Kersten, "Między wyzwoleniem a zniewoleniem. Polska 1944–1956," 14.

4. Kochanowski, "Dziesięć dni, które wstrząsnęły portfelem," *Polityka*, October 30, 2010.

5. Podgórecki, *Polish Society*, 56

6. Podgórecki et al., *Poglądy społeczeństwa polskiego na prawo i moralność*, 207.

7. See Kurczewski et al., *Wielkie bazary warszawskie*.

BIBLIOGRAPHY

ARCHIVES

Archiwum Akt Nowych w Warszawie [Central Archives of Modern Records, Warsaw]
Bolesław Bierut—Archive
Centralny Komitet Opieki Społecznej [Central Committee for Social Welfare]
Centralny Urząd Planowania [Central Planning Office]
Delegatura Rządu na Kraj [Government Delegate's Office]
Delegatura rządu RP przy PGWAR [Government Delegate's Office, Northern Group of Forces]
Jakub Berman—Legacy
Komisja Specjalna do Walki z Nadużyciami i Szkodnictwem Gospodarczym [Special Commission for Fighting Economic Abuses and Sabotage]
Krajowa Rada Narodowa [State National Council]
Ministerstwo Administracji Publicznej [Ministry of Public Administration]
Ministerstwo Aprowizacji i Handlu [Ministry of Supplies and Trade]
Ministerstwo Informacji i Propagandy [Ministry of Information and Propaganda]
Ministerstwo Pracy i Opieki Społecznej [Ministry of Labor and Social Welfare]
Ministerstwo Zdrowia [Ministry of Health]
Ministerstwo Ziem Odzyskanych [Ministry of the Regained Territories]
Polska Partia Robotnicza [Polish Workers' Party]
Rada Główna Opiekuńcza [Central Welfare Council]
Urząd Rady Ministrów [Office of the Council of Ministers]

Archiwum Państwowe w Białymstoku [State Archive in Białystok]
Wojewódzki Urząd Informacji i Propagandy w Białymstoku [Provincial Office of Information and Propaganda]
Urząd Wojewódzki Białostocki [Provincial Office in Białystok]

Archiwum Państwowe w Ełku [State Archive in Ełk]
Starostwo Powiatowe Ełckie [District Starost Office in Ełk]
Księga inwentarza Szpitala Powiatowego w Ełku [Inventory of the District Hospital in Ełk]

Archiwum Państwowe w Kielcach [State Archive in Kielce]
KW PPR [Provincial Committee of the Polish Workers' Party]
Okręgowy Urząd Zatrudnienia w Kielcach [Local Employment Office in Kielce]
Urząd Wojewódzki II w Kielcach [Provincial Office II in Kielce]
Wojewódzki Urząd Informacji i Propagandy w Kielcach [Provincial Office of Information and Propaganda]

Archiwum Państwowe w Krakowie [State Archive in Cracow]
Urząd Zatrudnienia Kraków [Employment Office, Cracow]
Urząd Wojewódzki II Krakowski [Cracow Provincial Office II]

Archiwum Państwowe w Rzeszowie [State Archive in Rzeszów]
KW PPR [Provincial Committee of the Polish Workers' Party]

Archiwum Żydowskiego Instytutu Historycznego [Archive of the Jewish Historical Institute]
Centralny Komitet Żydów Polskich [Central Committee of Jews in Poland]

Archiwum Instytutu Pamięci Narodowej w Warszawie [Archive of the Institute of National Remembrance in Warsaw]
Komenda Główna Milicji Obywatelskiej [Headquarters of the Citizens' Militia]
Ministerstwo Bezpieczeństwa Publicznego [Ministry of Public Security]
Polski Komitet Wyzwolenia Narodowego [Polish Committee of National Liberation]
Wolność i Niezawisłość [Freedom and Independence]

Archiwum Instytutu Pamięci Narodowej w Rzeszowie [Archive of the Institute of National Remembrance in Rzeszów]

Archiwum Instytutu Pamięci Narodowej w Poznaniu [Archive of the Institute of National Remembrance in Poznań]

Archiwum Historii Mówionej w Warszawie [Oral History Archive in Warsaw]

Centralne Archiwum Wojskowe w Rembertowie [Central Military Archive in Rembertów]
Główny Zarząd Polityczno-Wychowawczy z lat 1945–1949 [Main Political-Educational Office of 1945–1949]
Główny Zarząd Polityczny Wojska [Main Political Office of the Army]
II Wiceministerstwo Obrony Narodowej z lat 1945–1947 [II Deputy Ministry of National Defense, 1945–1947]
Sztab Główny WP [Polish Army General Staff]

PRINTED SOURCES

Compilations and Selections of Documents

Baryła, Tadeusz, ed. *Okręg Mazurski w raportach Jakuba Prawina: Wybór dokumentów 1945 r.* Olsztyn: Ośrodek Badań Naukowych im. Wojciecha Kętrzyńskiego w Olsztynie, 1996.

Biuletyny Informacyjne Ministerstwa Bezpieczeństwa Publicznego 1946. Warsaw: MSW, 1996.

Boniecki, J. *Napady zbrojne w powiecie kozieckim 1945–1947 (meldunki milicyjne).* Warsaw: Archiwum Dokumentacji Mechanicznej, 1995.

Bordiugow, Giennadij A. et al., eds. *Polska—ZSRR: Struktury podległości. Dokumenty WKP(b) 1944–1949.* Warsaw: ISP PAN, 1995.

Borkowski, Jan, ed. *Rok 1920: Wojna polsko-radziecka we wspomnieniach i innych dokumentach.* Warsaw: PIW, 1990.

Borodij, Eugeniusz et al., eds. *Rok 1945: Województwo Pomorskie. Sprawozdania pełnomocników rządu i wojewody.* Warsaw: Naczelna Dyrekcja Archiwów Państwowych, 1997.

Borodij, Eugeniusz et al., eds. *Rok 1946: Województwo Pomorskie. Sprawozdania sytuacyjne wojewody oraz protokoły ze zjazdów starostów i prezydentów miast wydzielonych.* Warsaw: Naczelna Dyrekcja Archiwów Państwowych, 1998.

Cała, Alina, and Helena Datner-Śpiewak, eds. *Dzieje Żydów w Polsce 1944–1968: Teksty źródłowe.* Warsaw: ŻIH, 1997.

Cariewskaja, Tatiana et al., eds. *Teczka specjalna J.W. Stalina. Raporty NKWD z Polski 1944–1946.* Warsaw: ISP PAN, 1998.

Cieplewicz, Marian, ed. *Obrona Warszawy w 1939 r: Wybór dokumentów wojskowych.* Warsaw: MON, 1968.

Ewakuacja 1945. Doniesienia z etapów. Introduction by Jerzy Kochanowski. *Karta* 24 (1998).

Gmitruk, Janusz et al., eds. *Pro memoria (1941–1944): Raporty Departamentu Informacji Delegatury Rządu RP na Kraj o zbrodniach na narodzie polskim.* Warsaw—Pułtusk: Muzeum Historii Polskiego Ruchu Ludowego w Warszawie, Wyższa Szkoła Humanistyczna im. Aleksandra Gieysztora, 2004–2005.

Góra, Władysław et al., eds. *Reforma rolna PKWN. Materiały i dokumenty.* Warsaw: PWRiL, 1959.

Gronek, Bernadetta, and Irena Marczak, eds. *Biuletyny Informacyjne Ministerstwa Bezpieczeństwa Publicznego*, vol. 1: *1947*. Warsaw: Książka i Wiedza, 1993.

Huchlowa, Józefa et al., eds. *Zrzeszenie "Wolność i Niezawisłość" w dokumentach: Wrzesień 1945–czerwiec 1946*, vol. 1. Wrocław: Zarząd Główny WiN, 1997.

Iwaneczko, Dariusz, and Zbigniew Nawrocki, ed. *Rok pierwszy, Powstanie i działalność aparatu bezpieczeństwa publicznego na Rzeszowszczyźnie (sierpień 1944–lipiec 1945).* Rzeszów: IPN, 2005.

Jarosz, Dariusz, and Tadeusz Wolsza, eds. *Komisja Specjalna do Walki z Nadużyciami i Szkodnictwem Gospodarczym: wybór dokumentów 1945–1954.* Warsaw: Główna Komisja Badania Zbrodni przeciwko Narodowi Polskiemu, IPN, 1995.

Jędruszczak, Hanna, ed. *Upaństwowienie i odbudowa przemysłu w Polsce (1944–1948): Materiały źródłowe*, vol. 2. Warsaw: PWN, 1969.

Kamiński, Łukasz, ed. *Biuletyny dzienne Ministerstwa Bezpieczeństwa Publicznego 1949–1950.* Warsaw: IPN, 2004.

Kisielewski, Tadeusz, and Jan Nowak, eds. *Chleb i krew. Moja wieś w czasie okupacji. Wspomnienia.* Warsaw: LSW, 1968.

Knyt, Agnieszka, and Alicja Wancerz-Gluza, eds. *Prywaciarze 1945–1989.* Warsaw: Fundacja Bankowa im. Leopolda Kronenberga, Karta, 2001.

Kochanowski, Jerzy, ed. *Protokoły posiedzenia Prezydium Krajowej Rady Narodowej 1944–1947.* Warsaw: Wydawnictwo Sejmowe, 1995.

Kochański, Aleksander, ed. *Protokół obrad KC PPR w maju 1945 roku.* Warsaw: ISP PAN, 1992.

———. *Protokoły posiedzeń Biura Politycznego KC PPR 1944–1945.* Warsaw: ISP PAN, 1992.

———. *Protokoły posiedzeń Sekretariatu KC PPR 1945–1946.* Warsaw: ISP PAN, Wyższa Szkoła Humanistyczna w Pułtusku, 2001.

Kułak, Jerzy, ed. *Białostocczyzna 1944–1945 w dokumentach podziemia i oficjalnych władz.* Warsaw: ISP PAN, 1998.

Kunert, Andrzej K., ed. *Kazimierz Moczarski. Zapiski.* Warsaw: PIW, 1990.

Kwiek, Julian. "Wydarzenia antyżydowskie 11 sierpnia 1945 r. w Krakowie. Dokumenty." *Biuletyn Żydowskiego Instytutu Historycznego* 1 (March 2000): 77–89.

List KC PPR "do tow. D," March 7, 1944. *Zeszyty Historyczne* (Paris) 26 (1973).

Majecki, H. "Sprawozdania delegatów PKWN z pobytu na Białostocczyźnie w pierwszych dniach po wyzwoleniu spod okupacji hitlerowskiej." *Rocznik Białostocki* 9 (1968–69), 1970.

Materski, Wojciech, and Andrzej Paczkowski, eds. *NKWD o Polsce i Polakach: Rekonesans archiwalny.* Warsaw: ISP PAN, 1996.

Meducki, Stanisław, and Zenon Wrona, eds. *Antyżydowskie wydarzenia kieleckie 4 VII 1946 roku. Dokumenty i materiały*, vols. 1 and 2. Kielce: Urząd Miasta Kielce, Kieleckie Towarzystwo Naukowe, 1992, 1994.

Nałęcz, Daria, ed. *Główny Urząd Kontroli Prasy 1945–1949.* Warsaw: ISP PAN, 1994.

Niemcy w Polsce 1945–1950. Wybór dokumentów, 4 vols. Edited by Włodzimierz Borodziej and Hans Lemberg, introduction by Jerzy Kochanowski. Warsaw: Neriton, 2000.

Okupacja i ruch oporu w dzienniku Hansa Franka 1939–1945, vol. 1. Warsaw: KiW, 1970.

Paczkowski, Andrzej, ed. *Referendum z 30 VI 1946 r. Przebieg i wyniki.* Warsaw: ISP PAN, 1993.

Pełczyński, Tadeusz et al., eds. *Armia Krajowa w dokumentach 1939–1945*, vols. 3 and 5. Wrocław—Warsaw—Cracow: Ossolineum, 1990, 1991.

Protokół nr 20/30 z posiedzenia Prezydium Zarządu Głównego ZPP odbytego 24 kwietnia 1944 r: Archiwum Ruchu Robotniczego, vol. 2. Warsaw: IPN, 1975.

Raport Witolda Bieńkowskiego "Kalskiego." *Dokumenty i Materiały. Archiwum Polski Podziemnej* 1 (1993).

Wojtaszek, Andrzej, ed. *Źródła do dziejów Pomorza Zachodniego: Administracja polska a Armia Czerwona na Pomorzu Zachodnim w latach 1945–1948.* Szczecin: n.p., 2001.

Zaremba, Marcin. "Naczelne Dowództwo Wojsk Polskich, Sztab Główny do Dowódcy 1-go Korpusu Pancernego, 16 VI 1945 [Nieznany rozkaz Roli-Żymierskiego. Na Zaolzie!]." *Polityka*, August 23, 1997.

Żaryn, Jan, eds. *Komunikaty Konferencji Episkopatu Polski 1945–2000*. Poznań: Pallottinum, 2006.

Memoirs, Diaries, Letters, Literature

Anczarski, Józef. *Kronikarskie zapisy z lat cierpień i grozy w Małopolsce Wschodniej*. Edited by Kazimierz Załuski. Cracow: n.p., 1996.

Bauman, Janina. *Nigdzie na ziemi*. Warsaw: ŻIH, 2000.

Beck, Józef. *Ostatni raport*. Warsaw: PIW, 1987.

Bednarczyk, Adam. *Zgruzowana Warszawa w latach 1945–1947*. Iłża: n.p., 1982.

Beevor, Antony, and Luba Vinogradova, eds. *A Writer at War: Vasily Grossman with the Red Army 1941–1945*. New York: Pantheon Books, 2005.

Berezowska, Małgorzata et al., eds. *Exodus Warszawy: Ludzie i miasto po powstaniu 1944. Pamiętniki i relacje*, vol. 1. Warsaw: PIW, 1992.

Białecki, Tadeusz, ed. *Drogi powrotu: Wspomnienia mieszkańców Pomorza Szczecińskiego*. Poznań: Wydawnictwo Poznańskie, 1981.

Bień, Adam. *Listy z wojny 1920*. Edited by Hanna Bień-Bielska. Warsaw: Muzeum Historii Polskiego Ruchu Ludowego, 2000.

Bigorajska, Zofia, and Eugeniusz Jabłoński, eds. *Nasze nowe życie: Pamiętniki z konkursu na wspomnienia mieszkańców ziem zachodnich i północnych*. Warsaw: LSW, 1978.

Biskupski, Stanisław. *Świadkowie mówią*. Warsaw: Światowy Związek Żołnierzy AK Okręg Wołyń, 1996.

Borowski, Tadeusz. *Utwory wybrane*. Edited by A. Werner. Wrocław—Warsaw—Cracow: Ossolineum, 1991.

Borycka, F. "Exodus z Powiśla." In *Exodus Warszawy: Ludzie i miasto po powstaniu 1944. Pamiętniki i relacje*, vol. 1., edited by M. Berezowska et al., 186–95 Warsaw: PIW, 1992.

Budzisz, Feliks. *Z ziemi cmentarnej*. Gdańsk: Skryptor, 1998.

Burda, Andrzej. *Przymrozki i odwilże: Wspomnienia z lat 1945–1957*. Lublin: Wydawnictwo Lubelskie, 1987.

Chajn, Leon. *Kiedy Lublin był Warszawą*. Warsaw: Czytelnik, 1964.

Chustecki, Jan. *Byłem sołtysem w latach okupacji*. Warsaw: KiW, 1960.

Cisek, Andrzej. *Beztroskie lata 1946–1956*. Pelplin: Bernardinum, 2002.

Dąbrowska, Maria. *Dzienniki 1914–1965 w 13 tomach*, vol. V. Warsaw: PAN, 2009.

Dąmbski, Stefan. *Egzekutor*. Warsaw: Ośrodek Karta, 2010.

Djilas, Milovan. *Conversations with Stalin*. New York: Harcourt Brace & Company, 1962.

Drabienko, Edward. *Jedno życie. Wspomnienia z lat 1942–1951*. London: Polska Fundacja Kulturalna, 1987.

Dulczewski, Zygmunt, and Andrzej Kwilecki, eds. *Pamiętniki osadników ziem odzyskanych*. Poznań: Wydawnictwo Poznańskie, 1970.

Estreicher, Karol Jr. *Dziennik wypadków 1946–1960*, vol. 2. Cracow: Towarzystwo Przyjaciół Sztuk Pięknych w Krakowie, 2002.

Godycka-Cwirko, Janina, *Lata klęski 1944–1973*. Tomyśl: Biblioteka Publiczna Miasta i Gminy Tomyśl, n.d.

Gomułka, Władysław. *Pamiętniki*, vol. 2. Warsaw: BGW, 1994.

Góra, Władysław et al., eds. *Takie były początki*. Warsaw: KiW, 1965.

Gross, Jan T., and Irena Grudzińska-Gross, eds. *"W czterdziestym nas matko na Sybir zesłali…" Polska a Rosja 1939–42*. Wrocław: Spółdzielnia Wydawnicza Profil, 1989.

Grzesiuk, Stanisław. *Boso, ale w ostrogach*. Warsaw: KiW, 1999.

Herbert, Zbigniew. *The Barbarian in the Garden*. New York: Harcourt Brace & Company, 1985.

Iwaszkiewicz, Jarosław. *Dzienniki 1911–1955*. Warsaw: Czytelnik, 2007.

———. *Notatki 1939–1945*. Wrocław: Wydawnictwo Dolnośląskie, 1991.

"Ja byłem dziecko niewinne." *Gazeta Wyborcza*, July 4, 1997.

Jakubaszek, Jan M. *Mój ostatni rok wojny*. N.p.: Lulu, Inc., 2006.

"Jak 'uwalniano' Polskę, wspomnienia generała-porucznika N.K. Popiela." *Zeszyty Historyczne* 5 (1964): 194–239.

Janta-Połczyński, Aleksander. *Wracam z Polski*. Paris: Société Nouvelle d'Imprimerie et d'Edition, 1949.

Jasienica, Paweł. *Pamiętniki*. Warsaw: Prószyński, 2007.

Jezierski, Edmund. *A gdy komunizm zapanuje*. Warsaw: Biblioteka Nowości, 1927.

Kaczor, Jan. *Wspomnienia ludowego starosty*. Warsaw: LSW, 1961.

Kamińska, Maria. *Ścieżkami wspomnień*. Warsaw: KiW, 1960.

Kamiński, Adam. *Diariusz podręczny 1939–1945*. Warsaw: IPN, 2001.

Karp, Hans-Jürgen, and Robert Traba, eds. *Codzienność zapamiętana: Warmia i Mazury we wspomnieniach*. Olsztyn—Warsaw: Wspólnota Kulturowa Borussia, ISP PAN 2004.

Karwowski, Jerzy. "'Newada.' Ludzie akcji specjalnej." *Karta* 14 (1994): 15–79.

Kersten, Krystyna, and Tomasz Szarota, eds. *Wieś polska 1939–1948. Materiały konkursowe*, vol. 1, 1967; vol. 2, 1968; vol. 3, 1970; vol. 4, 1971. Warsaw: PWN, 1968.

Klukowski, Zygmunt. *Zamojszczyna 1918–1943*, vol. 1. Warsaw: Ośrodek Karta, 2007.

———. *Zamojszczyna 1944–1959*, vol. 2. Warsaw: Ośrodek Karta, 2007.

Konopińska, Joanna, *Tamten wrocławski rok. Dziennik 1945–1946*. Wrocław: Wydawnictwo Dolnośląskie, 1987.

Kopecki, Kazimierz, Anna Bogdańska-Zarembina, and Elżbieta Sawicka, eds. *Kronika rodzin Kopeckich i Turnauów*. Warsaw: n.p., 2001.

Kowalska, Anna. *Dzienniki 1927–1969*. Warsaw: Iskry, 2008.

Krasiński, Zygmunt. *Nie-Boska komedia*. Warsaw: PIW, 1981.

Krawczyńska, Jadwiga. *Zapiski dziennikarki warszawskiej 1939–1947*. Warsaw: PIW, 1971.

Krzywicka, Irena. *Wyznania gorszycielki*. Warsaw: Czytelnik, 1995.

Kubacki, Wacław. *Dziennik (1944–1958)*. Warsaw: Czytelnik, 1971.

Kula, Witold. *Dziennik czasu okupacji*. Warsaw: PIW, 1994.

Kuroń, Jacek. *Wiara i wina: Do i od komunizmu*. London: Niezależna Oficyna Wydawnicza, 1989.

Lanckorońska, Karolina. *Wspomnienia wojenne*. Cracow: Znak, 2003.

Landau, Ludwik. *Kronika lat wojny i okupacji*, vol. 1. Warsaw: PIW, 1962.

Levi, Primo. "The Truce." In *The Complete Works of Primo Levi*, edited by Ann Goldstein, 207–398. New York: Liveright, 2015.

Ligocka, Roma. *The Girl in the Red Coat*. New York: St. Martin's, 2002.

Loth, Roman. *Wspomnienia Kochanowskie, czyli Radom sprzed półwiecza*. Radom: Społeczny Komitet Ratowania Zabytków Radomia, 2007.

Madoń-Mitzner, Katarzyna, ed. *Ocaleni z Mauthausen*. Warsaw: Dom Spotkań z Historią, Ośrodek Karta, 2010.

Mandalian, Andrzej. *Czerwona orkiestra*. Warsaw: Sic!, 2009.

Marzecki, Andrzej. *Tym gorzej dla faktów*. London: Polska Fundacja Kulturalna, 1979.

Michnik, Adam, Józef Tischner, and Jacek Żakowski. *Między Panem a Plebanem*. Cracow: Znak, 1995.

Miłosz, Czesław. *A Year of the Hunter*. New York: Farrar, Straus and Giroux, 1994.

———. "Kto to był Truman?" *Tygodnik Powszechny*, August 17, 2003.

———. *Native Realm: A Search for Self-Definition*. New York: Farrar, Straus and Giroux, 1968.

———. *Zaraz po wojnie:. Korespondencja z pisarzami 1945–1950*. Cracow: Znak, 2007.

Misuna, Adolf. "Pionki w latach II wojny światowej—wspomnienia." In *Szkice z dziejów Pionek*, edited by Marek Wierzbicki, 179–203. Pionki: n.p., 2000.

Mniejszy, Piotr (B. J. Radwański). *Pod Wawelem*. N.p.: n.p., 1999.

"Mówi generał, z generałem Wojciechem Jaruzelskim rozmawia Teresa Torańska." *Gazeta Wyborcza Duży Format*, December 13, 2004.

Najder, Marceli. "Dziennik z bunkra." *Karta* 68 (2011): 54–87.

Nałkowska, Zofia. *Dzienniki 1945–1954*, vol. 6, part 1. Warsaw: Czytelnik, 2000.

Neyman, Elżbieta, ed. *Intymny portret uczonych: Korespondencja Marii i Stanisława Ossowskich*. Warsaw: Sic!, 2002.

Nowak, Stefan. "System wartości społeczeństwa polskiego." *Studia Socjologiczne* 4 (1979): 155–73.

Ocalony na Wschodzie. Z Julianem Stryjkowskim rozmawia Piotr Szewc. Montricher: Noir Sur Blanc, 1991.

Okrzesa, Jerzy. "Listy z końca wojny." *Karta* 21 (1997): 106–18.

Osińska, Janina. "Warszawa, maj 1945." *Tygodnik Powszechny*, July 1, 1945.

Pacho, Aleksander. *Życie silniejsze*. Warsaw: Czytelnik,1966.

Pamiętniki bezrobotnych. Warsaw: Instytut Gospodarstwa Społecznego, 1933.

Panufnik, Andrzej. *O sobie*. Warsaw: Nowa, 1990.

Parandowski, Jan. *Luźne kartki*. Wrocław: Ossolineum, 1967.

Półtawska, Wanda. *I boję się snów . . .* Warsaw: Czytelnik, 1962.

Priebe, Cyryl. "Szkoła szabru." *Karta* 14 (1994): 79–91.

Pużak, Kazimierz. "Wspomnienia 1939–1945." *Zeszyty Historyczne* 41 (1977): 3–196.

Ropelewski, Andrzej. *Pionierskie lato*. Warsaw: Czytelnik, 1972.

Ryszka, Franciszek. *Pamiętnik inteligenta: Dojrzewanie*. Warsaw: BGW, 1994.

———. *Pamiętnik inteligenta: Samo życie*. Łódź: Dom Wydawniczy ARS, 1996.

Samsonowicz, Zdzisław. *Wspomnienia o Straży Akademickiej Politechniki we Wrocławiu*. Wrocław: Oficyna Wydawnicza Politechniki Wrocławskiej, 2002.

Scholz, Franz. "Dziennik niemieckiego księdza; Bronisław Kowacz, Miejsce przechodnie." *Karta* 21 (1997): 71–82.

Sebyłowa, Sabina. *Notatki z prawobrzeżnej Warszawy*. Warsaw: Czytelnik, 1985.

Sobków, Michał. "Do innego kraju." *Karta* 14 (1994): 57–68.

Stargard moje miasto. Wspomnienia polskich i niemieckich stargardzian z przełomu 1945 roku. Stargard: Towarzystwo Przyjaciół Stargardu, 2005.

Steinhaus, Hugo. *Wspomnienia i zapiski*. Wrocław: Oficyna Wydawnicza Atut, 2002.

Swieżawski, Stefan. *W nowej rzeczywistości 1945–1956*. Lublin: KUL, 1991.

Szczepański, Jan Józef. *Dzienniki 1945–1956*, vol. 1. Cracow: WL, 2009.

Szczepański, Jan Józef. *Dzienniki z lat 1935–1945*. Edited by Daniel Kadłubiec. Ustroń: Na Gojach, 2009.

Świda-Ziemba, Hanna. *Urwany lot*. Cracow: WL, 2003.

Tomaszewski, Tadeusz. *Lwów 1940–1944. Pejzaż psychologiczny*. Warsaw: WIP, 1996.

Tomczyk, Ryszard, ed. *Ocalić od zapomnienia: Półwiecze Elbląga (1945–1995) w pamiętnikach, notatkach i materiałach wspomnieniowych ludzi Elbląga*. Elbląg: Urząd Miejski w Elblągu, 1997.

Trzebnica w pierwszych latach powojennych. Trzebnica: Towarzystwo Miłośników Ziemi Trzebnickiej, 2005.

Uniechowska, Krystyna. *Franciszka Starowieyskiego opowieść o końcu świata, czyli reforma rolna*. Warsaw: Czytelnik, 1994.

Vogler, Henryk. *Wstęp do fizjologii strachu*. Cracow: WL, 1990.

Wat, Aleksander. *My Century*. New York: NYRB, 2003.

Weber, Marianne. *Kobiety wypędzone. Opowieść o zemście zwycięzców*. Zakrzewo: Replika, 2008.

Wróbel, Tadeusz. *Przystanek Gliwice: Dalsze losy chłopca z Borysławia*. Warsaw: n.p., 2004.

Wróblewska, Jadwiga. *Listy z Polski*. London: B. Świderski, 1960.

Wrzos, Konrad. *Oko w oko z kryzysem: Reportaż z podróży po Polsce*. Warsaw: Nakładem Księgarni F. Hoesicka, 1933.

Wspomnienia Stanisława Jarmieńczuka. In *Stargard moje miasto. Wspomnienia polskich i niemieckich stargardzian z przełomu 1945 roku*, 31–35. Stargard: n.p., 2005.

"Wspomnienia Stefana Lipickiego, prezydenta miasta Kołobrzeg w okresie 1 VI – 31 VIII 1945." In Kroczyński, Hieronim. *Powojenny Kołobrzeg 1945–1950: Wybór źródeł*. Kołobrzeg: n.p., 2004.

Załuski, Zbigniew. *Czterdziesty czwarty*. Warsaw: Czytelnik, 1969.

Zaniewicki, Zbigniew. *Na pobojowisku 1945–1950*. London: Polska Fundacja Kulturalna, 1988.

Zaremba, Piotr. *Dziennik 1945*. Szczecin: Wydawnictwo AP w Szczecinie, 1996.

Zaremba, Zygmunt. *Wojna i konspiracja*. London: B. Świderski, 1957.

Ziemba, Stanisław. *Czas przełomu: Wspomnienia dziennikarza z lat 1944–1946*. Cracow: WL 1975.

Ziemian, Józef. *Papierosiarze z placu Trzech Krzyży*. Warsaw: Nowa, 1989.

Zientara-Malewska, Maria. *Śladami twardej drogi*. Warsaw: PAX, 1966.

Żukrowski, Wojciech. *Zsyp ze śmietnika pamięci*. Warsaw: Bellona, 2002.

Newspapers and Periodicals

Agencja Prasowa, 1942.
Alarm, 1944.
Biuletyn Informacyjny, 1942, 1944.
Dziennik Bałtycki, 1945, 1946.
Dziennik Gospodarczy, 1946.
Dziennik Ludowy, 1945.
Dziennik Łódzki, 1946.
Dziennik Polski, 1945.
Dziennik Powszechny, 1945, 1946.
Dziennik Rzeszowski, 1945.
Dziennik Zachodni, 1945.
Dziś i Jutro, 1946.
Echo Krakowa, 1946.
Echo Wieczorne, 1946, 1947.
Express Poznański, 1947.
Express Wieczorny, 1946, 1947.
Falanga, 1937.
Front. Żołnierskie Pismo Codzienne, 1920.
Gazeta Kujawska, 1946.
Gazeta Lubelska, 1944–1946.
Gazeta Ludowa, 1946.
Głos Ludu, 1944–1947.
Głos Narodu, 1945, 1946.
Głos Wielkopolski, 1945, 1946.
Ilustrowany Kurier Codzienny, 1931, 1934.
Ilustrowany Kurier Polski, 1945, 1946.
Inwalida, 1945.
Jedność Narodowa, 1945.
Jedność, 1945.
Kocynder, 1946.
Kurier Kaliski, 1946.
Kurier Popularny, 1945, 1946.
Kurier Szczeciński, 1946.
Kuźnica, 1946.
Niedziela. Tygodnik Katolicki, 1946.
Nowy Kurier Warszawski, 1944, 1945.
Odrodzenie, 1945, 1946.
Polska Zbrojna, 1945.
Praca i Opieka Społeczna, 1946, 1947.
Prosto z Mostu, 1936, 1937.
Przegląd Epidemiologiczny, 1947.
Przekrój, 1945, 1946.
Robotnik, 1945, 1946.
Rycerz Niepokalanej, 1946.
Rzeczpospolita, 1946.
Serwis Informacyjny Ministerstwa Aprowizacji, 1947.
Szpilki, 1945, 1946.
Sztandar Ludu, 1945, 1946.
Trybuna Dolnośląska. 1945.
Tygodnik Ilustrowany, 1921.
Tygodnik Powszechny, 1945, 1946.
Warszawskie Czasopismo Lekarskie, 1938.
Wiadomości diecezjalne—organ urzędowy Częstochowskiej Kurii Diecezjalnej, 1946
Wiadomości Literackie, 1936.
Wolność, 1946.
Współczesna Ambona, 1946.
Zdrowie Publiczne, 1946.
Ziemia Lubuska. Ilustrowany Tygodnik Informacyjny, 1946.
Ziemia Pomorska, 1945, 1946.
Życie Warszawy, 1945, 1946.

Secondary Literature and Articles

Abrams, Bradley E. "The Second World War and the East European Revolution." *East European Politics and Societies* 3 (2002): 623–64.

Adelson, Józef. "W Polsce zwanej ludową." In *Najnowsze dzieje Żydów w Polsce*, edited by Jerzy Tomaszewski, 387–477. Warsaw: PWN, 1993.

Ajnenkiel, Andrzej, ed. *Wojna domowa czy nowa okupacja? Polska po roku 1944*. Warsaw: Światowy Związek Żołnierzy AK, Rytm, 2001.

Aleksiun-Mądrzak, Natalia. "Sytuacja Żydów w Europie Wschodniej w latach 1945–1947 w świetle raportów przedstawicieli dyplomatycznych Wielkiej Brytanii." *Biuletyn Żydowskiego Instytutu Historycznego* 1 (1997): 65–75.

Allport, Gordon W. *The Nature of Prejudice*. Garden City, NY: Doubleday Anchor Books, 1958.

Allport, Gordon W., and Leo Postman. *The Psychology of Rumor*. New York: Henry Holt, 1947.

Antyżydowskie wydarzenia kieleckie 4 VII 1946 roku. Dokumenty i materiały. Vol. 1, edited by Stanisław Meducki and Z. Wrona; vol. 2, edited by S. Meducki. Kielce: Urząd Miasta Kielce, Kieleckie Towarzystwo Naukowe, 1992, 1994.

Aptekar, Paweł. "Walka wojsk wewnętrznych NKWD z polskim podziemiem zbrojnym I deportowanie jego członków do ZSRR przez wojska konwojowe (na podstawie dokumentów z Rosyjskiego Państwowego Archiwum Wojskowego)" In *NKWD o Polsce i Polakach. Rekonesans archiwalny*, edited by Wojciech Materski and Andrzej Paczkowski. Warsaw: ISP PAN, 1996.

Archer, Dane, and Rosemary Gartner, "Peacetime Casualties: The Effects of War on the Violent Behavior of Noncombatants." In *Readings About the Social Animal*, 11th ed., edited by Elliot Aronson. New York: Worth Publishers, 2012.

Arendt, Hannah. *The Origins of Totalitarianism*. Part I. San Diego—New York—London: Harcourt, 1968.

Assorodobraj, Nina. *Początki klasy robotniczej*. Warsaw: PWN, 1966.
Baley, Stefan. "O pewnej metodzie badań wpływów na psychikę młodzieży." *Rocznik Psychiatryczny* 37 (1949): 33–46.
———. "Psychiczne wpływy drugiej wojny światowej." *Psychologia Wychowawcza*: 1–2 (1948): 6–24.
Banasiak, Stefan. *Działalność osadnicza PUR na ziemiach odzyskanych w latach 1945–1947*. Poznań: Instytut Zachodni, 1963.
Banfield, Edward C. *The Moral Basis of a Backward Society*. Glencoe, IL: Free Press, 1958.
Barański, Piotr. "Walka z chorobami wenerycznymi w Polsce w latach 1948–1949." MA thesis, Institute of History of the University of Warsaw, 2007.
Barszczewski, Zdzisław. *Przywrócone życiu. Rozminowywanie ziem Polski*. Warsaw: Bellona 1998.
Bartkowski, Jerzy. *Tradycja i polityka: Wpływ tradycji kulturowych polskich regionów na współczesne zachowania społeczne i polityczne*. Warsaw: Żak 2003.
Bartoszewski, Władysław, and Zofia Lewinówna. *Ten jest z ojczyzny mojej: Polacy z pomocą Żydom*. Warsaw: Świat Książki, 2007.
Baslez, Marie-Françoise. *Les persécutions dans l'Antiquité. Victimes, héros, martyrs*. Paris: Fayard, 2007.
Batawia, Stanisław. "Wpływ ostatniej wojny na przestępczość nieletnich." *Psychologia Wychowawcza* 1–2 (1948): 25–33.
Bauman, Zygmunt. *Liquid Fear*. Cambridge: Polity, 2006.
———. *Liquid Times: Living in an Age of Uncertainty*. Malden, MA: Polity, 2007.
———. *Modernity and the Holocaust*. Cornell University Press, 2001.
———. "Wytłumaczyć niewytłumaczalne." In *Wokół Strachu: Dyskusja o książce Jana T. Grossa*, edited by Mariusz Gądek, 201–15. Cracow: Znak, 2008.
Bazior, Grzegorz. *Armia Czerwona na Pomorzu Gdańskim 1945–1947*. Warsaw: IPN, 2003.
———. "Stacjonowanie jednostek Armii Czerwonej na terenie woj. gdańskiego w latach 1945–1947." *Dzieje Najnowsze* 4 (2000): 161–67.
Bechta, Mariusz. *Rewolucja, mit, bandytyzm: Komuniści na Podlasiu w latach 1939–1944*. Warsaw—Biała Podlaska: Oficyna Wydawnicza Rekonkwista, 2000.
Beck, Ulrich. *Risk Society. Towards a New Modernity*. New York: Sage Publications, 1992.
Beevor, Antony. *Berlin: The Downfall 1945*. London: Viking, 2002.
———. *D-Day: The Battle for Normandy*. London: Viking, 2009.
———. "They Raped Every German Female from Eight to 80." *The Guardian*, May 1, 2002.
Bełczewski, Bronisław. "Przyczółek." In *Takie były początki*, edited by Władysław Góra et al. Warsaw: KiW, 1965.
Berger, Peter L., and Thomas Luckmann. *The Social Construction of Reality: A Treatise in the Sociology of Knowledge*. London: Penguin, 1966.
Bessel, Richard. *Germany 1945: From War to Peace*. New York: HarperCollins, 2009.
———. "Hatred after War: Emotion and the Postwar History of East Germany." *History and Memory* 17 (2005): 195–216.
Bettelheim, Bruno. *The Uses of Enchantment: The Meaning and Importance of Fairy Tales*. New York: Alfred A. Knopf, 1976.
Bettelheim, Bruno, and Morris Janowitz. "Pozycja społeczna, degradacja społeczna i wrogość wobec mniejszości." In *Zagadnienia psychologii społecznej: Wybór z literatury amerykańskiej*, translated by J. Jacobson and D. Jedlicka, edited by Andrzej Malewski. Warsaw: PWN, 1962.
Bielik-Robson, Agata. "Horror, Horror!" *Res Publica Nowa* 11 (1998): 19–29.
Bikont, Anna. "Puścić Żyda na zajączka." *Gazeta Wyborcza. Duży Format*, February 17, 2011.
Bilewicz, Michał, and Bogna Pawlisz, eds. *Żydzi i komunizm. Jidele. Żydowskie Pismo Otwarte*, special issue, 2000.
Blobaum, Robert E. *Rewolucja. Russian Poland, 1904–1907*. Cornell University Press, 1995.
Bloch, Marc. *Strange Defeat: A Statement of Evidence Written in 1940*. Oxford University Press, 1949.
Bogner, Nahum. *At the Mercy of Strangers: The Rescue of Jewish Children with Assumed Identities in Poland*. Jerusalem: Yad Vashem, 2009.
Bojarski, Piotr. "Czołgi strzelają do katedry, Julian fotografuje." *Gazeta Wyborcza*, January 21, 2011.
Bojomir, Władysław. *Chrześcijaństwo a bolszewizm*. Warsaw: n.p., 1920.
Borkowski, E. *Choroby weneryczne szerzą się*. Warsaw: n.p., 1945.
Borodziej, Włodzimierz. *Od Poczdamu do Szklarskiej Poręby: Polska w stosunkach międzynarodowych 1945–1947*. London: Aneks, 1990.
Borodziej, Włodzimierz, and Artur Hajnicz, eds. *Kompleks wypędzenia*. Cracow: ZNAK, 1998.
Borowiec, Janusz. *Aparat bezpieczeństwa a wojskowy wymiar sprawiedliwości: Rzeszowszczyzna 1944–1954*. Warsaw: IPN, 2004.
Bourke, Joanna. *Fear: A Cultural History*. London: Virago, 2006.
Braudel, Fernand. *Civilization and Capitalism, 15th–18th Century*. Vol. I: *The Structure of Everyday Life: The Limits of the Possible*. New York: Harper & Row, 1979.
———. Vol. II: *The Mediterranean and the Mediterranean World in the Age of Philip II*. New York: Harper & Row, 1982.
Brenda, Waldemar. "O bandytyzmie na Warmii i Mazurach w pierwszych latach powojennych." In *Problemy bandytyzmu w okupowanej Polsce w latach 1939–1947*, 93–115. Warsaw: ISP PAN, 2003.
Bronsztejn, Szyja. "Stosunki polsko-żydowskie przed Holocaustem we wspomnieniach okresu międzywojennego." In *Z historii ludności żydowskiej w Polsce i na Śląsku*, edited by Krystyn Matwijowski. Wrocław: Wydawnictwo Uniwersytetu Wrocławskiego, 1994.
Brun-Zejmis, Julia. "National Self–Denial and Marxist Ideology: The Origin of the Communist Movement in Poland and the Jewish Question (1918–1923)." *Nationalities Papers* 22 (1994): 29–54, supplement 1.
Brzezina, Maria. *Polszczyzna Żydów*. Warsaw, Cracow: PWN, 1986.

Brzeziński, Bogdan et al., eds. *Polegli w walce o władzę ludową*. Warsaw: KiW, 1970.

Brzoza, Czesław. *3 V 1946 w Krakowie*. Cracow: Księgarnia Akademicka, 1996.

Buryła, Sławomir. "Wojna i alkohol. Zaproszenie do tematu." In *Wojna doświadczenie i zapis: Nowe źródła, problemy, metody badawcze*, edited by Sławomir Buryła and Paweł Rodak. Cracow: Universitas, 2006.

Caillois, Roger. *Man and the Sacred*. Glencoe, IL: Free Press, 1959.

Cała, Alina. *Wizerunek Żyda w Polskiej kulturze ludowej*. Warsaw: In Plus, 1988.

Cantril, Hadley et al. *The Invasion from Mars: A Study in the Psychology of Panic*. New York: Harper, 1966.

Caute, David. *The Great Fear: The Anti-Communist Purge under Truman and Eisenhower*. New York: Simon and Schuster, 1978.

Chałasiński, Józef. *Młode pokolenie chłopów*, vol. 1. Warsaw: LSW, 1984.

Chumiński, Jędrzej. *Ruch zawodowy w Polsce w warunkach kształtującego się systemu totalitarnego 1944–1956*. Wrocław: Wydawnictwo AE im. Oskara Langego, 1999.

Chwalba, Andrzej. *Kraków w latach 1939–1945*. Cracow: WL, 2002.

Cichopek, Anna. *Pogrom Żydów w Krakowie 11 sierpnia 1945*. Warsaw: ŻIH, 2000.

Cichy, Michał. "1945—koniec i początek." *Gazeta Wyborcza*, May 26, 1995.

Ciesielski, Stanisław, ed. *Przesiedlenie ludności polskiej z kresów wschodnich do Polski 1944–1947*. Warsaw: Neriton, IH UW, 2009

Ciesielski, Stanisław, Grzegorz Hryciuk, and Aleksander Srebrakowski. *Masowe deportacje ludności w Związku Radzieckim*. Toruń: Wydawnictwo Adam Marszałek, 2002.

Cohen, Stanley. *Folk Devils and Moral Panics: Creation of Moods and Rockers*. London: Routledge, 2002.

Connelly, John. "Why the Poles Collaborated so Little—And Why That Is No Reason for National Hubris." *Slavic Review* 64 (4) (2005): 771–81.

Courtois, Stéphane et al. *The Black Book of Communism: Crimes, Terror, Repression*. Harvard University Press, 1999.

Cowley, Geoffrey. "Our Bodies, Our Fears." *Newsweek*, March 2, 2003.

Czarnowski, Stefan. "Ludzie zbędni w służbie przemocy." In Czarnowski, Stefan. *Społeczeństwo, kultura. Prace z socjologii i historii kultury*. Warsaw—Poznań: Polski Instytut Socjologiczny, 1939.

"Czas niepewności, interview with Ulrich Beck." *Forum*, March 1–7, 2010.

Czech, Franciszek. "Polityka strachu. Nowy kierunek badań sceny politycznej." In *Emocje a kultura i życie społeczne*, edited by Piotr Binder et al, 34–51. Warsaw: IFiS PAN, 2009.

Czerski, Mieczysław. "Kryzys bolszewizmu w Rosji." *Falanga*, February 17, 1937.

Czocher, Anna. *W okupowanym Krakowie: Codzienność polskich mieszkańców miasta 1939–1945*. Gdańsk: Oskar, 2011.

Datner, Helena. "Dziecko żydowskie (1944–1968)." In *Następstwa zagłady Żydów: Polska 1944–2010*, edited by Feliks Tych and Monika Adamczyk-Garbowska. Lublin: Wydawnictwo Uniwersytetu Marii Curie-Skłodowskiej, ŻIH, 2011.

Dąbrowski, Marjan. *Prawda o bolszewikach*. Warsaw: Wydawnictwo red. Żołnierza Polskiego, 1920.

———. *Precz z carską i bolszewicką Rosją!* Warsaw: Wydawnictwo red. Żołnierza Polskiego, 1920.

Deák, István, Jan T. Gross, and Tony Just, eds. *The Politics of Retribution in Europe: World War II and Its Aftermath*. Princeton University Press, 2000.

Delacroix, J. *Masoneria i bolszewizm*. Warsaw: n.p., 1923.

Delumeau, Jean. *La peur en Occident XIVe–XVIIIe siècles*. Paris: Fayard, 1978.

De Zayas, Alfred-Maurice. *A Terrible Revenge: The Ethnic Cleansing of the East European Germans, 1944–1950*. New York: St. Martin's, 1994.

Dmitrów, Edmund. *Niemcy i okupacja hitlerowska w oczach Polaków. Poglądy i opinie z lat 1945–1948*. Warsaw: Czytelnik, 1987.

———. *Obraz Rosji i Rosjan w propagandzie narodowych socjalistów 1933–1945: Stare i nowe stereotypy*. Warsaw: ISP PAN, 1997.

Dmowski, Roman. *W kwestii komunizmu*. Poznań: Wydawnictwo Głosy, 1984.

Dobieszewski, Adolf. *Kolektywizacja wsi polskiej 1948–1956*. Warsaw: Fundacja im. Kazimierza Kelles-Krauza, 1993.

Dobrowolski, Kazimierz. *Studia nad życiem społecznym i kulturą*. Wrocław—Warsaw—Cracow: Ossolineum, 1966.

Dominiczak, Henryk. *Organy bezpieczeństwa PRL 1944–1990*. Warsaw: Bellona, 1997.

Donnan, Hastings, and Thomas M. Wilson, eds. *Border Identities: Nation and State at International Frontiers*. Cambridge University Press, 1998.

Dreszerowa, H., and J. Handelsman. "Alkoholizm u młodzieży szkolnej." *Zdrowie Psychiczne* 2–4 (1948).

Dróżdż, Zofia, and Władysław Milczarek. *Zakochani w Pomorzu*. Cracow: Czytelnik, 1945.

Drygas, Maciej J. "Perlustracja." *Karta* 68 (2011): 88–125.

Dudek, Antoni. *Państwo Kościół w Polsce*. Cracow: PiT, 1995.

Dudek, Antoni, and Ryszard Gryz. *Komuniści i Kościół w Polsce (1945–1989)*. Cracow: Znak, 2003.

Dudek, Bohdan. *Zaburzenia po stresie traumatycznym*. Gdańsk: Gdańskie Wydawnictwo Psychologiczne, 2003.

Dunin-Wąsowicz, Krzysztof. *Warszawa 1914–1918*. Warsaw: PWN, 1989.

Dutton, Donald G., and Arthur P. Aron. "Some Evidence for Heightened Sexual Attraction Under Conditions of High Anxiety." In *Readings About the Social Animal*, 9th ed., edited by Elliot Aronson. New York: Worth, 2004.

Dzieszyński, Ryszard. *Ciemna, węsząca, żerująca. Pitaval*. Rzeszów: KAW, 1986.

Dziurok, Adam, and Bogdan Musiał. "'Bratni rabunek': O demontażach i wywózce sprzętu z terenu Górnego Śląska w 1945 r." In *W objęciach Wielkiego Brata: Sowieci w Polsce 1944–1993*, edited by Konrad Rokicki and Sławomir Stępień, 321–49. Warsaw: IPN, 2009.

Eberhardt, Piotr. *Przemieszczenia ludności na terytorium Polski spowodowane II wojną światową*. Warsaw: Instytut Geografii i

Przestrzennego Zagospodarowania Instytut Geografii i Przestrzennego Zagospodarowania PAN, 2000.

Eliade, Mircea. *The Sacred and the Profane: The Nature of Religion*. Orlando, FL: Harcourt, 1987.

Ellman, Michael. "The 1947 Soviet Famine and the Entitlement Approach to Famines." *Cambridge Journal of Economics* 24 (2000): 603–30.

Engel, D. "Patterns of Anti-Jewish Violence in Poland, 1944–1946." *Yad Vashem Studies* 26 (1998): 43–85.

Engelking, Barbara. *Jest taki piękny słoneczny dzień... Losy Żydów szukających ratunku na wsi polskiej 1942–1945*. Warsaw: Stowarzyszenie Centrum Badań nad Zagładą Żydów, 2011.

———. *"Szanowny panie gistapo": Donosy do władz niemieckich w Warszawie i okolicach w latach 1940–1941*. Warsaw: Wydawnictwo IFiS PAN, 2003.

———. *Zagłada i pamięć: Doświadczenie Holocaustu i jego konsekwencje opisane na podstawie relacji autobiograficznych*. Warsaw: Wydawnictwo IFiS PAN, 1994.

Engelking, Barbara, and Jan Grabowski, eds. *Zarys krajobrazu: Wieś Polska wobec zagłady Żydów 1942–1945*. Warsaw: Stowarzyszenie Centrum Badań nad Zagładą Żydów, 2011.

Engelking, Barbara, Jacek Leociak, and Dariusz Libionka, eds. *Prowincja noc. Życie i zagłada Żydów w dystrykcie warszawskim*. Warsaw: Wydawnictwo IFiS, 2007.

Fiedorczyk, Piotr. *Komisja Specjalna do Walki z Nadużyciami i Szkodnictwem Gospodarczym*. Białystok: Temida 2, 2002.

Filar, Władysław. *Wydarzenia wołyńskie 1939–1944: W poszukiwaniu odpowiedzi na trudne pytania*. Toruń: Wydawnictwo Adam Marszałek, 2008.

Fisch, Bernhard. *Nemmersdorf, Oktober 1944: Was in Ostpreussen tatsächlich geschah*. Berlin: Edition Ost, 1997.

Foster, George M. "Peasant Society and the Image of Limited Good." *American Anthropologist* vol. 67, 2 (1965): 293–315.

Frączek, Adam, and Horst Zumkley, eds. *Socialization and Aggression*. Berlin: Springer, 1992.

Friedrich, Klaus-Peter. "Collaboration in a 'Land without a Quisling.' Patterns of Cooperation with the Nazi German Occupation Regime in Poland during World War II." *Slavic Review* 64 (4) (2005): 711–46.

———. "Problem polskiej kolaboracji podczas II wojny światowej (1939–1944/45)." *Res Publica Nowa* 11 (1998).

Friszke, Andrzej. *Adam Ciołkosz. Portret polskiego socjalisty*. Warsaw: Wydawnictwo Krytyki Politycznej, 2011.

———. *Losy państwa i narodu 1939–1989*. Warsaw: Iskry, 2003.

———. "Naród, państwo, system władzy w myśli politycznej Związku Ludowo-Narodowego w latach 1919–1926." *Przegląd Historyczny* 1 (1981): 51–73.

———. *Opozycja polityczna w PRL 1945–1980*. London: Aneks 1994.

———. "Publicystyka Polski Podziemnej wobec zagłady Żydów 1939–1944." In *Polska—Polacy—mniejszości narodowe*, edited by E. Grześkowiak-Łuczak, 193–213. Wrocław—Warsaw—Cracow: Ossolineum 1992.

Frommer, Benjamin. *National Cleansing. Retribution against Nazi Collaborators in Postwar Czechoslovakia*. Cambridge University Press, 2005.

Frontczak, Kazimierz. *Siły zbrojne Polski Ludowej: Przejście na stopę pokojową 1945–1947*. Warsaw: MON, 1974.

Furedi, Frank. *Politics of Fear*. London—New York: Continuum, 2005.

Gądek, Mariusz, ed. *Wokół strachu. Dyskusja o książce Jana T. Grossa*. Cracow: Znak, 2008.

Gałązka-Petz, Barbara, and Andrzej Jezierski. "Odbudowa gospodarki narodowej 1944–1946." In *Gospodarka Polski Ludowej 1944–1955*, edited by Janusz Kaliński and Zbigniew Landau. Warsaw: KiW, 1986.

Gałczyński, K. I. *Wiersze*. Warsaw: Czytelnik, 1956.

Gapiński, Bartłomiej. *Sacrum i codzienność: Prośby o modlitwę nadsyłane do Kalwarii Zebrzydowskiej w latach 1965–1979*. Warsaw: Trio, 2008.

Garlicki, Andrzej, ed. *Sąsiedzi i inni*. Warsaw: Czytelnik, 1978.

Gawor, Leszek. *Katastrofizm w polskiej myśli społecznej i filozofii 1918–1939*. Lublin: Wydawnictwo UMCS, 1999.

Geen, Russell G., David Stonner, and Gary L. Shope. "The Facilitation of Aggression by Aggression: Evidence against the Catharsis Hypothesis." *Journal of Personality and Social Psychology* 31, 4 (1975): 721–26.

Gellner, Ernest. *Nations and Nationalism*, 2nd ed. Cornell University Press, 2006.

Geremek, Bronisław. *Litość i szubienica: Dzieje nędzy i miłosierdzia*. Warsaw: Czytelnik, 2003.

———. *Ludzie marginesu w średniowiecznym Paryżu: XIV–XV wiek*. Poznań: Poznańskie Towarzystwo Przyjaciół Nauk, 2003.

Gerrits, André. "Antisemitism and Anti-Communism: The Myth of 'Judeo-Communism' in Eastern Europe." *East European Jewish Affairs* 25 (1995): 49–72.

Gibbs, Nancy. "Shadow of Fear." *Time*, October 22, 2001.

Giddens, Anthony. *Modernity and Self-Identity: Self and Society in the Late Modern Age*. Stanford University Press, 1991.

———. *Sociology*. 5th ed. Cambridge: Polity, 2006.

Giertych, Jędrzej. *O wyjście z kryzysu*. Warsaw: n.p., 1938.

Gniazdowski, Mateusz. "Ustalić liczbę zabitych na 6 milionów," Dyrektywa Jakuba Bermana, dla Biura Odszkodowań Wojennych przy Prezydium Rady Ministrów. *Polski Przegląd Dyplomatyczny* 1 (2008): 99–113.

Goeschel, Christian. "Suicide at the End of the Third Reich." *Journal of Contemporary History* 41 (1) (2006): 153–73.

Golon, Mirosław. "Polityka radzieckich władz na Kujawach i Pomorzu w 1945 roku. Aspekty społeczno-ekonomiczne." In *Rok 1945 na Kujawach i Pomorzu: Koniec wojny początek nowej rzeczywistości, Prace Komisji Historii Bydgoskiego Towarzystwa Naukowego*, vol. 19, edited by Zdzisław Biegański and Zbigniew Karpus. Bydgoszcz: Bydgoskie Towarzystwo Naukowe, 2006.

———. *Polityka radzieckich władz wojskowych i policyjnych na Pomorzu Nadwiślańskim w latach 1945–1947*. Toruń: n.p., 2001

Gołębiowski, Janusz W. *Nacjonalizacja przemysłu w Polsce*. Warsaw: KiW, 1965.

Gomułka, Władysław. *Artykuły i przemówienia*, vol. 1: *Styczeń 1943–grudzień 1945*. Warsaw: n.p., 1962.

Gondek, Leszek. *Polska karząca 1939–1945: Polski podziemny wymiar sprawiedliwości w okresie okupacji niemieckiej*. Warsaw: PAX, 1988.

Gozdowski, Krzysztof. "Wielkopolski ataman." *Karta* 10 (1993).

Górecki, Wojciech. "Strajki robotnicze w Łodzi w latach 1945–1947." *Polska 1944/45–1989. Studia i Materiały* 2 (1997): 93–121.

Grabiec, Joachim. "Postępowanie Armii Czerwonej wobec miejscowej ludności w świetle pisemnych sprawozdań sytuacyjnych wojewody śląsko-dąbrowskiego z 1945 r." *Prace Historyczno-Archiwalne* 11 (2002): 207–16.

Grabowski, Jan. *Hunt for the Jews: Betrayal and Murder in German-Occupied Poland*. Indiana University Press, 2013.

———. "*Ja tego Żyda znam!" Szantażowanie Żydów w Warszawie 1939–1943*. Warsaw: Wydawnictwo IFiS PAN, 2004.

———. *Judenjagd. Polowanie na Żydów 1942–1945: Studium dziejów pewnego powiatu*. Warsaw: Stowarzyszenie Centrum Badań nad Zagładą Żydów, 2011.

Grabski, August. "Żydzi a polskie życie polityczne (1944–1949)." In *Następstwa zagłady Żydów: Polska 1944–2010*, edited by Feliks Tych and Monika Adamczyk-Garbowska, 157–88. Lublin: Wydawnictwo Uniwersytetu Marii Curie-Skłodowskiej, ŻIH, 2011.

Greenblum, Joseph, and Leonard I. Pearlin. "Ruchliwość pionowa a uprzedzenia etniczne: analiza socjologiczno-psychologiczna." In *Zagadnienia psychologii społecznej: Wybór z literatury amerykańskiej*, translated by J. Jacobson and D. Jedlicka, edited by Andrzej Malewski. Warsaw: PWN, 1962.

Greiner, Bernard et al., eds. *Angst im kalten Krieg*. Hamburg: Hamburger Edition, 2009.

Gross, Jan T. *Fear: Anti-Semitism in Poland after Auschwitz*. New York: Random House, 2006.

———. "Geneza społeczna demokracji ludowych o konsekwencja II wojny światowej w Europie Środkowej." In *Komunizm. Ideologia, system, ludzie*, edited by Tomasz Szarota, 40–58. Warsaw: Neriton, IH PAN, 2001.

———. *Neighbors: The Destruction of the Jewish Community in Jedwabne*. Princeton University Press, 2001.

———. "O kolaboracji." *Zagłada Żydów: Studia i Materiały* 2 (2006): 407–16.

———. *Polish Society under German Occupation: The Generalgouvernement 1939–1944*. Princeton University Press, 1979.

———. "The Social Consequences of War, Preliminaries to the Study of Imposition of Communist Regimes in East Central Europe." *East European Politics and Societies* 2 (1989): 198–214.

———. *Upiorna dekada: Trzy eseje o stereotypach na temat Żydów, Polaków, Niemców i komunistów 1939–1948*. Cracow: Universitas, 1998.

———. "War as Revolution." In *The Establishment of Communist Regimes in Eastern Europe, 1944–1949*, edited by Norman Naimark and Leonid Gibianskii, 17–35. Boulder, CO: Westview, 1997.

Gross, Jan T., and Irena Grudzińska-Gross. *Golden Harvest: Events at the Periphery of the Holocaust*. Oxford University Press, 2012.

Grossmann, Atina. "Question of Silence: The Rape of German Women by Occupation Soldiers." Special issue, *October: Berlin 1945; War and Rape "Liberators Take Liberties"* 72 (1995): 42–63.

Grudzińska-Gross, Irena. *The Scar of Revolution: Custine, Tocqueville and the Romantic Imagination*. University of California Press, 1991.

Guldon, Zenon, and Jacek Wijaczka. *Procesy o mordy rytualne w Polsce w XVI–XVIII wieku*. Kielce: DCF, 1995.

Guriewicz, Aron. *Problemy średniowiecznej kultury ludowej*. Warsaw: PIW, 1987.

Gutowski, Maciej. *Komizm w polskiej sztuce gotyckiej*. Warsaw: PWN, 1973.

Hagen, William W. "The Moral Economy of Popular Violence: The Pogrom of Lwów, November 1918." In *Antisemitism and Its Opponents in Modern Poland*, edited by Robert Blobaum, 124–47. Cornell University Press, 2005.

Hall, Edward T. *The Hidden Dimension*. New York: Penguin Random House, 1990.

Haynes, John Earl. "Tło amerykańskiego antykomunizmu." *Pamięć i Sprawiedliwość* 1 (2010): 37–55.

Hejger, Maciej. *Polityka narodowościowa władz polskich w województwie gdańskim w latach 1945–1947*. Słupsk: WSP w Słupsku, 1998.

Heller, Michał. *Maszyna i śrubki. Jak hartował się człowiek radziecki*. Warsaw: Pomost, 1989.

Hempel, Adam. *Pogrobowcy klęski: Rzecz o policji "granatowej" w Generalnym Gubernatorstwie 1939–1945*. Warsaw: PWN, 1990.

Hirsch, Helga. *Zemsta ofiar: Niemcy w obozach w Polsce 1944–1950*. Warsaw: Volumen 1999.

Hirszowicz, Maria. *Pułapki zaangażowania: Intelektualiści w służbie komunizmu*. Warsaw: Scholar, 2001.

Hobsbawm, Eric J. *Bandits*. New York: Pantheon, 1981.

———. *Primitive Rebels: Studies in Archaic Forms of Social Movement in the 19th and 20th Centuries*. New York: Frederick A. Praeger, 1963.

———. *The Age of Extremes: A History of the World, 1914–1991*. New York: Pantheon, 1994.

Horney, Karen. *The Neurotic Personality of Our Time*. Abingdon: Routledge, 1999.

Hryciuk, Grzegorz. "'Ciężkie dni Lwowa.' Akcja masowych aresztowań we Lwowie w styczniu 1945." In *Studia z historii najnowszej*, edited by K. Ruchniewicz et al., 21–33. Wrocław: Gajt, 1999.

———. *Polacy we Lwowie 1939–1944: Życie codzienne*. Warsaw: KiW, 2000.

Humphreys, Margaret. "Tuberculosis: The 'Consumption' and Civilization." In *Plague, Pox and Pestilence: Disease in History*, edited by Kenneth F. Kiple, 160–65. London: Weidenfeld and Nicholson, 1997.

Hurwic-Nowakowska, Irena. *Żydzi polscy (1947–1950): Analiza więzi społecznej ludności żydowskiej*. Warsaw: Wydawnictwo IFiS PAN, 1996.

Hytrek-Hryciuk, Joanna. *"Rosjanie nadchodzą": Ludność niemiecka a żołnierze Armii Radzieckiej (Czerwonej) na Dolnym Śląsku w latach 1945–1948*. Wrocław: IPN, 2010.

Iwaniak, Stefan. *Migracje chłopów kieleckich (1945–1949)*. Kielce: Kieleckie Towarzystwo Naukowe, 1988.

———. *Reforma rolna w województwie kieleckim w latach 1944–1945*. Warsaw: LSW, 1975.

———. *Służba zdrowia w województwie kieleckim (1944–1974)*. Kielce: Wydawnictwo Akademii Świętokrzyskiej, 2003.

Jackowska, Ewa. *Psychiczne następstwa deportacji w głąb ZSRR w czasie drugiej wojny światowej: Przyczyny, moderatory, uwarunkowania*. Szczecin: Uniwersytet Szczeciński, 2004.

Jakubowski, Zenon. *Milicja Obywatelska 1944–1948*. Warsaw: PWN, 1988.

Jankowski, Stanisław. "Warunki bytu ludności." In *Gospodarka Polski Ludowej 1944–1955*, edited by Janusz Kaliński and Zbigniew Landau. Warsaw: KiW, 1986.

Jarosińska, Izabela. *Było i tak. Życie codzienne w Polsce w latach 1946–1989*. Warsaw: KiW 2009.

Jarosz, Dariusz. "Bieda polska 1944–1956." In *Przeciw biedzie: Programy, pomysły, inicjatywy*, edited by Elżbieta Tarkowska. Warsaw: Oficyna Naukowa 2002.

———. "Kriegsgerüchte in Polen, 1946–1956." In *Angst im Kalten Krieg*, edited by Bernd Greiner et al. Hamburg: Hamburger Edition, 2009.

———. *Mieszkanie się należy... Studium z peerelowskich praktyk społecznych*. Warsaw: Oficyna Wydawnicza Aspra-Jr, 2010.

———. *Polacy a stalinizm 1948–1956*. Warsaw: IH PAN, 2000.

———. *Polityka władz komunistycznych w Polsce w latach 1948–1956 a chłopi*. Warsaw: DiG, 1998.

Jarosz, Dariusz, and Maria Pasztor. *W krzywym zwierciadle: Polityka władz komunistycznych w świetle plotek i pogłosek z lat 1949–1956*. Warsaw: Wydawnictwo Fakt, 1995.

Jarowiecki, Jerzy et al. *Prasa polska w latach 1939–1945*. Warsaw: PWN, 1980.

Jasieński, Juliusz. *Problemy mieszkalnictwa Krakowa*. Cracow: Wydawnictwo Naukowe WSP w Krakowie, 1974.

Jasiewicz, Krzysztof. *Lista strat ziemiaństwa polskiego 1939–1956*. Warsaw: Archiwum Wschodnie, IH PAN, 1995.

———. *Zagłada polskich Kresów: ziemiaństwo polskie na Kresach Północno-Wschodnich Rzeczypospolitej pod okupacją sowiecką 1939–1941. Studium z dziejów zagłady dawnego narodu politycznego*. Warsaw: Volumen, ISP PAN, 1998.

Jasińska-Kania, Aleksandra. "Socjologiczne odkrywanie emocji." *Kultura i Społeczeństwo* 1–2 (2006): 41–53.

Jastrząb, Mariusz. "Cuda podwarszawskie." *Więź* 12 (1998): 147–57.

Jastrzębowski, Wacław. *Gospodarka niemiecka w Polsce 1939–1944*. Warsaw: Czytelnik, 1946.

Jezierski, Andrzej, and Cecylia Leszczyńska. *Pierwsze lata działalności Narodowego Banku Polskiego: Narodziny systemu finansowego PRL*. Warsaw: Narodowy Bank Polski, 1996.

Jezierski, Andrzej, and Barbara Petz. *Historia gospodarcza Polski Ludowej 1944–1985*. Warsaw: PWN, 1988.

Jędruszczak, Hanna. "Miasta i przemysł w okresie odbudowy." In *Polska Ludowa 1944–1955. Przemiany społeczne*, edited by Franciszek Ryszka. Wrocław—Warszawa: Ossolineum, 1974.

J. K. *Bolszewizm a mesjasz żydowski*. Biblioteka Chrześcijańsko-Społeczna, 3. Cracow: Związek Chrześcijańsko-Społeczny, 1922.

Jońca, Karol, and Alfred Konieczny. *Upadek Festung Breslau*. Wrocław: Ossolineum, 1963.

Judt, Tony. "Aż strach się bać." *Forum*, May 17–23, 2010.

———. *Reappraisals: Reflections on the Forgotten Twentieth Century*. New York: Penguin, 2008.

Kacprzak, Lech. *Przemoc i agresja a oddziaływania społeczno-wychowawcze. Źródła—przyczyny—zapobieganie*. Piła: Państwowa Wyższa Szkoła Zawodowa im. St. Staszica, 2005.

Kaczmarski, Krzysztof. *Pogrom, którego nie było: Rzeszów, 11–12 czerwca 1945 r. Fakty, hipotezy, dokumenty*. Rzeszów: IPN 2008.

Kaczyńska, Maria. "Psychiczne skutki wojny wśród dzieci i młodzieży." *Zdrowie Psychiczne* 1–2 (1946): 50–70.

Kajetanowicz, Jerzy. *Polskie wojska lądowe w latach 1945–1960: Skład bojowy, struktury organizacyjne i uzbrojenie*. Wrocław: Wyższa Szkoła Oficerska im. T. Kościuszki, 2002.

Kalabiński, Stanisław, and Feliks Tych. *Czwarte powstanie czy pierwsza rewolucja. Lata 1905–1907 na ziemiach polskich*. Warsaw: Wiedza Powszechna, 1976.

Kalbarczyk, S. "Sowieckie represje wobec polskiego podziemia niepodległościowego w Warszawie i okolicach na przełomie 1944 i 1945 roku." *Pamięć i Sprawiedliwość* 2 (2002): 139–55.

Kalicki, Włodzimierz. "Z deszczu pod klucz." *Gazeta Wyborcza. Duży Format*, July 21, 2011.

Kaliński, Janusz. *Bitwa o handel 1947–1948*. Warsaw: KiW, 1970.

Kaliński, Janusz, and Zbigniew Landau, eds. *Gospodarka Polski Ludowej 1944–1955*. Warsaw: KiW, 1986.

Kaliński, Janusz, and Zygmunt Landau. *Gospodarka Polski w XX wieku*. Warsaw: PWE, 2003.

Kałużny, R., ed. *Wielka operacja rozminowania terytorium Polski: 60-lecie jej rozpoczęcia*. Wrocław: Stowarzyszenie Saperów Polskich, Wyższa Szkoła Oficerska Wojsk Lądowych, 2005.

Kamińska-Szmaj, Irena. *Judzi, zohydza, ze czci odziera: Język propagandy politycznej w prasie 1919–1923*. Wrocław: Towarzystwo Przyjaciół Polonistyki Wrocławskiej, 1994.

Kamiński, Łukasz. *Polacy wobec nowej rzeczywistości 1944–1948*. Toruń: Wydawnictwo Adam Marszałek, 2000.

———. *Strajki robotnicze w Polsce w latach 1945–1948*. Wrocław: Gajt, 1999.

Kamiński, Łukasz, and Jan Żaryn, eds. *Wokół pogromu kieleckiego*. Warsaw: IPN, 2006.

Kamiński, Łukasz, et al. *Opór społeczny w Europie Środkowej w latach 1948–1953 na przykładzie Polski, NRD i Czechosłowacji*. Wrocław: Oficyna Wydawnicza Atut, 2004.

Kamiński, Marek K. *Polsko-czechosłowackie stosunki polityczne 1945–1948*. Warsaw: PWN, 1990.

Kamosiński, Sławomir. "Przyczynek do badań nad postrzeganiem nowej rzeczywistości gospodarczej i postawami wobec niej urzędników, pracowników i przedsiębiorców województwa pomorskiego w 1945 roku." In *Rok 1945 na Kujawach i*

Pomorzu: Koniec wojny—początek nowej rzeczywistości, Prace Komisji Historii BTN, vol. 19, edited by Zdzisław Biegański and Z. Karpus. Bydgoszcz: n.p., 2006.

Kapralski, Sławomir. "Trauma i pamięć zbiorowa. Przypadek Jedwabnego." In *Stawanie się społeczeństwa. Szkice ofiarowane Piotrowi Sztompce z okazji 40-lecia pracy naukowej*, edited by Andrzej Flis. Cracow: Universitas, 2006.

Karłowicz, Jan, Adam Kryński, and Władysław Niedźwiedzki, eds. *Słownik języka polskiego*, vol. 6. Warsaw: nakładem prenumeratorów i Kasy im. Mianowskiego, 1915.

Karwacki, Arkadiusz. *Błędne Koło. Reprodukcja kultury społecznej*. Toruń: Wydawnictwo Uniwersytetu Mikołaja Kopernika, 2006.

Kazdin, Alan E., ed. *Encyclopedia of Psychology*. New York: Oxford University Press, 2000.

Kenney, Padraic. *Rebuilding Poland. Workers and Communists 1945–1950*. Cornell University Press, 1997.

Kępiński, Andrzej. *Lach i Moskal. Z dziejów stereotypu*. Warsaw—Cracow: PWN, 1990.

Kępiński, Antoni. *Lęk*. Warsaw: PZWL, 1977.

———. *Rytm życia*, rozdz. *KZ-syndrom*. Cracow: WL, 2000.

Kersten, Krystyna. *Między wyzwoleniem a zniewoleniem. Polska 1944–1956*. London: Aneks, 1993.

———. "Migracje w Polsce: Próba klasyfikacji i ogólna charakterystyka zewnętrznych ruchów ludności." *Polska Ludowa*, vol. 2, 1963, 3–26.

———. "Osadnictwo wojskowe w 1945 roku. Próba charakterystyki." *Przegląd Historyczny* 4 (1964): 640–59.

———. *Pisma rozproszone*. Toruń: Wydawnictwo Adam Marszałek, 2005.

———. "Początki stabilizacji życia społecznego w środowisku wiejskim na Pomorzu Zachodnim (1945–1947)." *Polska Ludowa*, vol. 4, 1965, 3–42.

———. *Polacy, Żydzi, komunizm: Anatomia półprawd 1939–68*. Warsaw: Niezależna Oficyna Wydawnicza, 1992.

———. "Polityczny i propagandowy obraz zbrojnego podziemia w latach 1945–1947 w świetle prasy komunistycznej." In Krystyna Kersten, *Pisma rozproszone*, 162–69. Toruń: Wydawnictwo Adam Marszałek, 2005.

———. "Polska—państwo narodowe. Dylematy i rzeczywistość." In *Narody. Jak powstawały i jak wybijały się na niepodległość?*, edited by Marcin Kula, 442–47. Warsaw: PWN, 1989.

———. "Polskiego inteligenta życie po śmierci." In Krystyna Kersten, *Pisma rozproszone*, 50–67. Toruń: Wydawnictwo Adam Marszałek, 2005.

———. *Repatriacja ludności po II wojnie światowej*. Wrocław—Warsaw—Cracow: Ossolineum, PAN, 1974.

———. "Ruchliwość w Polsce po II wojnie światowej jako element przeobrażeń społecznych i kształtowania postaw." In Krystyna Kersten, *Pisma rozproszone*, 175–97. Toruń: Wydawnictwo Adam Marszałek, 2005.

———. "Społeczeństwo polskie wobec władzy komunistów." In *Między wyzwoleniem a zniewoleniem. Polska 1944–1956*. London: Aneks, 1993.

———. *The Establishment of Communist Rule in Poland, 1943–1948*. University of California Press, 1991.

Kierkegaard, Søren. *The Concept of Anxiety*. Edited, translated, and with an introduction and notes by Alastair Hannay. New York: W. W. Norton, 2014.

Kiwerska, Jadwiga. "Niemcy w polityce PPR/PZPR." In *Polacy wobec Niemców: Z dziejów kultury politycznej Polski 1945–1989*, edited by Anna Wolff-Powęska, 45–93. Poznań: Instytut Zachodni, 1993.

Kładoczny, Piotr. "Kara śmierci jako wykładnik polityki karnej państwa w latach 1944–1956." In *Przestępstwa sędziów i prokuratorów w Polsce lat 1944–1956*, edited by Witold Kulesza and Andrzej Rzepliński, 67–84. Warsaw: IPN, UW, 2001.

Klich-Kluczewska, Barbara. *Przez dziurkę od klucza. Życie prywatne w Krakowie (1945–1989)*. Warsaw: Trio, 2009.

Klichowski, Longin. *Lęk, strach, panika: Przyczyny i zapobieganie*. Poznań: Printer, 1994.

Kłoskowska, Antonina. *Kultury narodowe u korzeni*. Warsaw: PWN, 1996.

Kochanowicz, Jacek. "Gospodarcze dzieje strachu." *Res Publica Nowa* 11 (1998): 34–36.

Kochanowski, Jerzy. "Do raportu!" *Polityka*, February 12, 2000.

———. "Dziesięć dni, które wstrząsnęły portfelem." *Polityka*, October 30, 2010.

———. "Listonosz nie doniósł." *Polityka*, April 15, 1995.

———. "Lubelskie czarne gabinety. Sprawozdania cenzury wojennej z 1944 roku." *Polska 1944/1945-1989: Studia i Materiały* 4 (1999): 325–37.

———. "'Niepewne czasy, pewny dolar,' czyli szkic do portretu warszawskiego czarnego rynku." *Przegląd Historyczny* 100 (2009): 29–46.

Kochański, Aleksander. *Polska 1944–1991: Informator historyczny*, vol. 1. Warsaw: Wydawnictwo Sejmowe, 1996.

Kochavi, Arieh J. "The Catholic Church and Antisemitism in Poland Following World War II as Reflected in British Diplomatic Documents." *Gal-Ed* 11 (1989): 116–28.

Kociszewski, J. *Zasiedlanie i zagospodarowanie Dolnego Śląska w latach 1945–1949 ze szczególnym uwzględnieniem regionu sudeckiego*. Wrocław—Warsaw—Cracow: Ossolineum, PAN, 1983.

Kołakowski, Leszek. *Metaphysical Horror*. University of Chicago Press, 2001.

———. *Obecność mitu*. Wrocław: Wydawnictwo Dolnośląskie, 1994.

Konczyński, Józef. *Stan moralny społeczeństwa polskiego*. Warsaw: Gebethner i Wolff, 1911.

Konieczny, Feliks. *Żydzi w Polsce i ich wrogi stosunek do narodu*. Cracow: Drukarnia "Powściągliwość i Praca," 1936.

Konopka, Tomasz. "Śmierć na ulicach Krakowa w latach 1945–1947 w materiale archiwum krakowskiego Zakładu Medycyny Sądowej." *Pamięć i Sprawiedliwość* 2 (8) (2005): 143–57.

Kopciowski, Adam. "Zajścia antyżydowskie na Lubelszczyźnie w pierwszych latach po drugiej wojnie światowej." *Zagłada Żydów. Studia i Materiały* 3 (2007): 178–207.

Kopstein, Jeffrey S., and Jason Wittenberg. "Who Voted Communist? Reconsidering the Social Bases of Radicalism in Interwar Poland." *Slavic Review* 62 (1) (2003): 87–109.

Kornat, Marek. *Polska szkoła sowietologiczna 1930–1939*. Cracow: Arcana, 2003.

Korsch, Rudolf. *Żydowskie ugrupowania wywrotowe w Polsce*. Warsaw: n.p., 1925.

Korzeniewski, Bogusław. "Wróg nadchodzi—polska propaganda polityczna w obliczu bitwy warszawskiej." *Przegląd Historyczny* 4 (2004): 467–84.

Kosiński, Krzysztof. *Historia pijaństwa w czasach PRL: polityka, obyczaje, szara strefa, patologie*. Warsaw: Neriton, Instytut Historii PAN, 2008.

Kossak-Szczucka, Zofia. *Pożoga: Wspomnienia z Wołynia 1917–1919*. Cracow: Krakowska Spółka Wydawnicza, 1927.

Kossobudzka, Margit. "Straszne życie bez strachu." *Gazeta Wyborcza*, December 20, 2010.

Kostewicz, Tadeusz. "Terror i represje." In *Polacy wobec przemocy 1944–1956*, edited by Barbara Otwinowska and Jan Żaryn. Warsaw: Editions Spotkania, 1996.

Kowalczyk, Elżbieta. "Obraz partyzantki sowieckiej na terytorium północno-wschodniej Rzeczypospolitej Polskiej w świetle meldunków Delegatury Rządu na Kraj." In *W objęciach wielkiego brata. Sowieci w Polsce 1944–1993*, edited by Konrad Rokicki and Sławomir Stępień, 377–99. Warsaw: IPN, 2009.

Kowalska-Leder, Justyna. "Szaber." In *Obyczaje polskie: Wiek XX w krótkich hasłach*, edited by M. Szpakowska. Warsaw: W.A.B., 2008.

Krajewski, Stanisław. "Problem żydowski—problem polski." *Więź* special issue, *Pod wspólnym niebem: Tematy polsko-żydowskie*, 1998.

Krajewski, Władysław. "Fakty i mity: O roli Żydów w okresie stalinowskim." *Więź* special issue, *Pod wspólnym niebem. Tematy polsko-żydowskie*, 1998.

Krakowski, Shmuel. *The War of the Doomed: Jewish Armed Resistance in Poland, 1942–1944*. New York—London: Holmes & Meier Publishers, 1984.

Kramer, Roderick M. "Collective Paranoia: Distrust Between Social Groups." In *Distrust*, Russell Sage Trust Series, VIII, edited by Russell Hardin, 136–66. New York: Russell Sage Foundation, 2004.

Krasucki, Eryk. *Międzynarodowy komunista: Jerzy Borejsza. Biografia polityczna*. Warsaw: PWN, 2009.

Król, Edmund C. *Polska i Polacy w propagandzie narodowego socjalizmu w Niemczech 1919–1945*. Warsaw: ISP PAN, Collegium Civitas, Rytm, 2006.

Kruk, Erwin. *Spadek: Zapiski mazurskie 2007–2009*. Dąbrówno: Retman, 2009.

Krzyk, Józef. "Uderzeni palcem Stalina." *Gazeta Wyborcza*, April 13, 2011.

Krzywiec, Grzegorz. *Szowinizm po polsku: Przypadek Romana Dmowskiego (1886–1905)*. Warsaw: Neriton, IH PAN, 2009.

Kselman, Thomas, A. *Miracles and Prophecies in Nineteenth-Century France*. Rutgers University Press, 1983.

Kula, Marcin. *Narodowe i rewolucyjne*. London—Warsaw: Aneks and Więź, 1991.

Kula, Marcin, and Krzysztof Smolana. "Echa meksykańskiego konfliktu religijnego w lat 1926–1929 w Polsce." *Ameryka Łacińska* 4 (2009).

Kułak, Jerzy. *Pierwszy rok sowieckiej okupacji. Białystok 1944–1945*. Białystok: Awadom, 1996.

———. *Rozstrzelany oddział: Monografia 3. Wileńskiej Brygady NZW—Białostocczyzna 1945–1946*. Białystok: Godruk, 2007.

Kulczyńska, Maria. *Lwów—Donbas 1945*. Warsaw: Biblioteka "Tygodnika Demokratycznego," 1988.

Kupiecki, Robert. *"Natchnienie milionów": Kult Józefa Stalina w Polsce 1944–1956*. Warsaw: WSiP, 1993.

Kurcz, Ida. *Zmienność i nieuchronność stereotypów*. Warszaw: Wydawnictwo Instytutu Psychologii, 1994.

Kurczewski, Jacek, Mariusz Cichomski, and Krzysztof Wiliński. *Wielkie bazary warszawskie*. Warsaw: Trio, 2010.

Kurka, A., ed. *Słownik mowy złodziejskiej*. Lvov: n.p., 1907.

Kwiek, Julian. *Nie chcemy Żydów u siebie. Przejawy wrogości wobec Żydów w latach 1944-1947*. Warsaw: Wydawnictwo Nieoczywiste, 2021.

Kwiatkowski, Franciszek. *Źródła dzisiejszego bezbożnictwa*. Cracow: Wydawnictwo Apostolstwa Modlitwy, 1937.

Kwiatkowski, Piotr T. "II wojna światowa jako doświadczenie narodowe." In Kwiatkowski, Piotr T. et al. *Między codziennością a wielką historią: Druga wojna światowa w pamięci zbiorowej społeczeństwa polskiego*. Gdańsk—Warsaw: Scholar, 2010.

Kwiatkowski, Piotr T. et al., *Między codziennością a wielką historią. Druga wojna światowa w pamięci zbiorowej społeczeństwa polskiego*. Gdańsk-Warsaw: Wydawnictwo Naukowe Scholar, 2010.

Kwilecki, Andrzej. "Migracje pionierskie na Ziemiach Odzyskanych." *Studia Socjologiczne* 1 (1986): 5–29.

Łach, Stanisław. *Osadnictwo miejskie na ziemiach odzyskanych w latach 1945–1950*. Słupsk: WSP w Słupsku, 1996.

———. *Pomorze zachodnie w latach 1945–1949. Studium społeczno-gospodarcze*. Słupsk: WSP w Słupsku, 1980.

Landau, Ludwik. Jerzy Pański, and Edward Strzelecki, eds. *Bezrobocie wśród chłopów*. Warsaw: Instytut Gospodarstwa Społecznego, 1939.

Landau, Zbigniew. *Gospodarka Polski Ludowej*. Warsaw: WSiP, 1994.

Landau-Czajka, Anna. *W jednym stali domu . . . Koncepcje rozwiązania kwestii żydowskiej w publicystyce polskiej lat 1933–1939*. Warsaw: Neriton, IH PAN, 1998.

Langmuir, Gavin I. *Toward a Definition of Antisemitism*. University of California Press, 1990.

Łatyński, Marek. *Nie paść na kolana: Szkice o opozycji lat czterdziestych*. Warsaw: "Piechur," 1987.

Leary, Mark, and Robin M. Kowalski. *Social Anxiety*. New York: Guilford, 1997.

Lechowski, Andrzej. *W służbie stolicy: Wojsko polskie w odbudowie Warszawy 1945–1949*. Warsaw: Ergos, 2002.

Lefebvre, Georges. *The Great Fear of 1789: Rural Panic in Revolutionary France*. New York: Schocken, 1989.

Lembeck, Andreas, and Klaus Wessels. *Befreit aber nicht in Freiheit: Displaced Persons im Emsland 1945–1951*. Bremen: Temmen, 1997.

Lewandowska, Stanisława. *Życie codzienne Wilna w latach II wojny światowej*. Warsaw: Neriton, IH PAN, 1997.

Lewin, Kurt. *A Dynamic Theory of Personality*. New York—London: McGraw Hill, 1935.

Libionka, Dariusz. "Biedni AK-owcy opisują Zagładę na prowincji." *Więź* 4 (April 2009): 118–29.

———. "Polska ludność chrześcijańska wobec eksterminacji Żydów—dystrykt lubelski." In *Akcja Reinhardt. Zagłada Żydów w Generalnym Gubernatorstwie*, edited by Dariusz Libionka, 306–33. Warsaw: IPN, 2004.

Ligarski, Sebastian. *W zwierciadle ogłoszeń drobnych: Życie codzienne na Śląsku w latach 1945–1949*. Wrocław: IPN, 2007.

Lipset, Seymour Martin. *Political Man: The Social Bases of Politics*. Johns Hopkins University Press, 1981.

Lipski, Jan Józef. *Antysemityzm ONR "Falangi."* N.p.p.: Wydawnictwo Myśl, 1986.

Lisiak, Henryk. "Propaganda obronna w Polsce w rozstrzygającym okresie wojny polsko-sowieckiej 1920 r." *Dzieje Najnowsze* 4 (1997): 3–25.

Lis-Turlejska, Maria. *Traumatyczny stress: Koncepcje i badania*. Warsaw: Instytut Psychologii PAN, 1998.

Lutosławski, Wincenty. *Bolszewizm i Polska*. Vilna: Księgarnia Józefa Zawadzkiego w Wilnie, 1920.

Łuczak, Czesław. *Polityka ekonomiczna Trzeciej Rzeszy w latach drugiej wojny światowej*. Poznań: Wydawnictwo Poznańskie, 1979.

———. *Polska i Polacy w drugiej wojnie światowej*. Poznań: Wydawnictwo Naukowe UAM, 1993.

———. "Szanse i trudności bilansu demograficznego Polski w latach 1939–1945." *Dzieje Najnowsze* 2 (1994): 9–14.

Łukaszewicz, Piotr. "Funkcje domu w okresie okupacji niemieckiej." *Kultura i Społeczeństwo* 2 (1989): 67–82.

MacDonogh, Giles. *After the Reich: The Brutal History of the Allied Occupation*. New York: Basic, 2007.

Machcewicz, Anna. "Tajemnica liberatora." *Newsweek Polska*, October 8, 2006.

Machcewicz, Paweł. *Wokół Jedwabnego*. In *Wokół Jedwabnego*, edited by Paweł Machcewicz and Krzysztof Persak. Warsaw: IPN, 2002.

Machcewicz, Paweł, and Krzysztof Persak, eds. *Wokół Jedwabnego*. Warsaw: IPN, 2002.

Machiavelli, Niccolò. "XVII. Of Cruelty and Clemency, and Whether It Is Better to Be Loved or Feared." In *The Prince*. Harvard Classics, 1909–14.

Mack, Arien, ed. *Fear: Its Political Uses and Abuses*. *Social Research* 4 (2004).

Maćkowiak, Tomasz. "Panika w mieście? O, to nic trudnego." *Newsweek Polska*, November 28, 2004.

Madajczyk, Czesław. "Kann man in Polen 1939–1945 von Kollaboration sprechen?" In *Okkupation und Kollaboration 1938–1945: Beiträge zu Konzepten und Praxis der Kollaboration in der deutschen Okkupationspolitik*. Berlin, Heidelberg: Werner Röhr, 1994.

———. "Między współpracą a kolaboracją." In *Faszyzm i okupacja 1938–1945*, vol. 2. Poznań: Wydawnictwo Poznańskie, 1984.

———. *Polityka III Rzeszy w okupowanej Polsce*, 2 vols. Warsaw: PWN, 1970.

Madajczyk, Piotr. *Czystki etniczne i klasowe w Europie XX wieku: Szkice do problemu*. Warsaw: ISP PAN, 2010.

———. *Niemcy polscy 1944–1989*. Warsaw: Oficyna Naukowa, 2001.

Magierska, Anna. "Ziemie Zachodnie i Północne w okresie komendantur wojennych i kształtowanie się polskiej administracji cywilnej." *Dzieje Najnowsze* 4 (1973).

———. *Ziemie zachodnie i północne w 1945 roku. Kształtowanie się podstaw polityki integracyjnej państwa polskiego*. Warsaw: KiW, 1978.

Majer, Piotr. "Zapomniana formacja. MO w walce z przestępczością kryminalną w pierwszych latach powojennych." *Gazeta Policyjna* 4 (2004).

Majzner, Robert. "Bilans radzieckiej obecności w Częstochowie w latach 1945–1946." In *Życie codzienne w Częstochowie w XIX i XX wieku*, edited by Ryszard Szwed and Waldemar Palus, 275–300. Częstochowa: n.p., 1999.

Malinowski, Bronisław. *Magic, Science and Religion, and Other Essays*. Garden City, NY: Anchor, 1954.

Marcinkowski, M. Interview with Z. Mach. "Kresowe życie na walizkach." *Gazeta Wyborcza*, December 24–26, 2010.

Mark, Eduard. "The War Scare of 1946 and Its Consequences." *Diplomatic History* 3, vol. 21 (1997): 383–415.

Mark, James. "Remembering Rape: Divided Social Memory and the Red Army in Hungary 1944–1945." *Past and Present Society* 188 (2005).

Markiewicz, Tomasz. *Prywatna odbudowa Warszawy*. In *Zbudować Warszawę piękną... O nowy krajobraz stolicy (1944–1956)*. Edited by Jerzy Kochanowski, 213–57. Warsaw: Trio, 1997.

Marszałkowski, Tomasz *Zamieszki, ekscesy i demonstracje w Krakowie 1918–1939*. Cracow: Arcana, 2006.

Marwick, Artur. *War and Social Change in the Twentieth Century: A Comparative Study of Britain, France, Germany, Russia and the United States*. London: Macmillan, 1974.

Massalski, Adam, and Stanisław Meducki. *Kielce w latach okupacji hitlerowskiej 1939–1945*. Wrocław—Warsaw—Cracow: Kieleckie Towarzystwo Naukowe, Ossolineum, 2007.

Materski, Wojciech. *Na widecie. II Rzeczpospolita wobec Sowietów 1919–1943*. Warsaw: ISP PAN, RYTM, 2005.

Materski, Wojciech, and Tomasz Szarota, eds. *Polska 1939–1945 straty osobowe i ofiary represji pod dwiema okupacjami*. Warsaw: IPN, 2009.

Mazower, Mark. *Dark Continent: Europe's Twentieth Century*. London: Penguin, 1999.

Mazowiecki, Wojciech. *Pierwsze starcie: Wydarzenia 3 V 1946*. Warsaw: PWN, 1998.

M. B. *Jak powstała armja bolszewicka?* Warsaw: n.p., July 1920.

McGovern, James R. *Anatomy of a Lynching*. Louisiana State University Press, 1982.

Melchior, Małgorzata. "Uciekinierzy z gett po 'stronie aryjskiej' na prowincji dystryktu warszawskiego—sposoby przetrwania." In *Prowincja noc: Życie i zagłada Żydów w dystrykcie warszawskim*, edited by Barbara Engelking et al., 321–72. Warsaw: Wydawnictwo IFiS, 2007.

Merridale, Catherine. *Ivan's War: Life and Death in the Red Army 1939–1945*. New York: Picador, 2006.

Michlic, Joanna. *Poland's Threatening Other: The Image of the Jew from 1880 to the Present*. University of Nebraska Press, 2006.

Miernik, Grzegorz. "Losy Żydów i nieruchomości pożydowskich w Szydłowcu po II wojnie światowej." In *Żydzi szydłowieccy*, edited by Jacek Wijaczka, 135–214. Szydłowiec: Takt, 1997.

———. *Opór chłopów wobec kolektywizacji w województwie kieleckim 1948–1956*. Kielce: Takt, 1999.

Minc, Hilary. "Wytyczne w sprawie naszego ustroju gospodarczego i społecznego." *Nowe Drogi* 10 (1948): 83–105.

Mironowicz, Eugeniusz. *Białorusini w Polsce 1944–1949*. Warsaw: PWN, 1993.

———. *Polityka narodowościowa PRL*. Białystok: Białoruskie Towarzystwo Historyczne, 2000.

Mishkinsky, Moshe. "The Communist Party of Poland and the Jews." In *The Jews of Poland between Two World Wars*, edited by Yisrael Gutman, Ezra Mendelsohn, and Jehuda Reinharz, 56–74. University Press of New England/Brandeis University Press, 1989.

Misiło, Eugeniusz. *Pawłokoma 3 III 1945 r.* Warsaw: Ukar, 2006.

Mitarski, Jan. "Demonologia lęku." In Kępiński, A. *Lęk*. Warsaw: Sagittarius, 1995.

Młynarczyk, Jacek A. "Bestialstwo z urzędu: Organizacja hitlerowskich akcji deportacyjnych w ramach 'Operacji Reinhard' na przykładzie likwidacji kieleckiego getta." *Kwartalnik Historii Żydów* 3 (September 2002): 354–79.

Mochocki, Wojciech. "Przestępstwa pospolite A. Czerwonej na Środkowym Nadodrzu (1945–1947) w przekazach urzędowych administracji terenowej i centralnej." *Studia Zachodnie* 5 (2000): 37–52.

Montefiore, Simon Sebag. *Stalin: The Court of the Red Tsar*. New York: Knopf, 2004.

Mosdorf, Jan. "U źródeł. Pokolenie Niepodległej Polski." *Prosto z mostu*, August 2, 1936.

Mosse, George L. *Fallen Soldiers: Reshaping the Memory of the World Wars*. Oxford University Press, 1990.

Motyka, Grzegorz. *Od rzezi wołyńskiej do akcji "Wisła": Konflikt polsko-ukraiński 1943–1947*. Cracow: WL, 2011.

Naimark, Norman M. *The Russians in Germany: A History of the Soviet Zone of Occupation, 1945–1949*. Harvard University Press, 1995.

Nalewajko-Kulikov, Joanna. *Obywatel Jidyszlandu: Rzecz o żydowskich komunistach w Polsce*. Warsaw: Neriton, IH PAN, 2009.

Nash, Gary B. *The Great Fear: Race in the Mind of America*. New York: Rinehart and Winston, 1970.

Neier, Aryeh. "America's New Nationalism." *Social Research* 4 (2004).

Neja, Jarosław. "Problemy z sojusznikami." *Biuletyn IPN* 1–2 (2005).

Nelson, Todd D. *The Psychology of Prejudice*. Boston: Allyn & Bacon, 2002.

Nolte, Ernst. "Auschwitz zrodził się z gułagu." *Gazeta Wyborcza*, June 26–27, 2004.

Nowak, Edmund. *Cień Łambinowic: Próba rekonstrukcji dziejów obozu pracy w Łambinowicach, 1945–1946*. Opole: Centralne Muzeum Jeńców Wojennych w Łambinowicach-Opolu, Uniwersytet Opolski, 1991.

———. *Obozy na Śląsku Opolskim w systemie powojennych obozów w Polsce (1945–1956): Historia i implikacje*. Opole: Centralne Muzeum Jeńców Wojennych w Łambinowicach-Opolu, Uniwersytet Opolski, 2002.

Nowosad, Witold. "Timiakow i trockiści." *Prosto z Mostu*, February 14, 1937.

Nurek, Mieczysław. *Gorycz zwycięstwa: Los Polskich Sił Zbrojnych na Zachodzie po II wojnie światowej 1945–1949*. Gdańsk: Wydawnictwo Uniwersytetu Gdańskiego, 2009.

"O, i tak, z profesor Marią Janion rozmawia Barbara N. Łopieńska." *Wysokie Obcasy*, 16 Oct. 2004.

"O kraju, gdzie ludzie zapomnieli się śmiać. Wywiad z człowiekiem, który wydobył się z piekła." *Ilustrowany Kuryer Codzienny*, 14 Oct. 1931.

O męczeńskim Meksyku. Garść faktów i myśli. Cracow: Wydawnictwo Księży Jezuitów, 1928.

"O tym, jak z wewnątrz getta patrzono na stronę aryjską. Z profesorem Israelem Gutmanem rozmawia Barbara Engelking." *Zagłada Żydów: Studia i materiały* 1 (2005): 230–33.

Oatley, Keith, and Jennifer M. Jenkins. *Understanding Emotions*. Hoboken, NJ: Wiley, 1996.

Odziemkowski, Janusz. *15 wiorst od Warszawy. Radzymin 1920*. Warsaw: Micromax 1990.

Ogrodowczyk, Arkadiusz. *Nad Odrą i Bałtykiem: Osadnictwo wojskowe na zachodnich i północnych ziemiach Polski po drugiej wojnie światowej*. Warsaw: Wydawnictwo MON, 1979.

Orczewski, Tadeusz. *Rządy bolszewickie*. Warsaw: Biblioteka "Żołnierza Polskiego," 1920.

Osęka, Piotr. "Spekulancie, nie chowaj twarzy!" *Gazeta Wyborcza*, December 3–4, 2005.

Osękowski, Czesław. *Pionierzy w mundurach na Ziemi Lubuskiej*. Zielona Góra: Lubuski Komitet Upowszechniania Prasy, 1985.

———. *Społeczeństwo Polski zachodniej i północnej w latach 1945–1956: Procesy integracji i dezintegracji*. Zielona Góra: WSP im. T. Kotarbińskiego, 1994.

Osiński, Zbigniew M. *Lęk w kulturze społeczeństwa polskiego w XVI–XVII wieku*. Warsaw: Wydawnictwo DiG, 2009.

Ostrowska, Joanna, and Marcin Zaremba. "Kobieca gehenna." *Polityka*, March 7, 2009.

Pace, David. "'Voila les atomes qui arrivent': The Fear of Science and the Great Atomic Panics of 1946." *French Cultural Studies* 3 (1992): 157–77.

Paczkowski, Andrzej. *Od sfałszowanego zwycięstwa do prawdziwej klęski: Szkice do portretu PRL*. Cracow: WL, 1999.

———. "Poland: The 'Enemy Nation.'" In Courtois, Stéphane et al. *The Black Book of Communism: Crimes, Terror, Repression*. Harvard University Press, 1999.

———. "Polska ofiarą dwóch totalitaryzmów 1939–1945," *Zeszyty Historyczne* 140 (2002): 3–38.

———. *Prasa polska w latach 1918–1939*. Warszaw: PWN, 1980.

———. *Trzy twarze Józefa Światły: Przyczynek do historii komunizmu w Polsce*. Warsaw: Prószyński i S-ka, 2009.

———. "Żydzi w UB. Próba weryfikacji stereotypu." In *Komunizm. Ideologia, system, ludzie*, edited by Tomasz Szarota, 192–204. Warsaw: Neriton, IH PAN, 2001.

Paczyńska, Irena. "Dekret o Nadzwyczajnej Komisji Mieszkaniowej i jego realizacja w Krakowie (1946–1947)." *Przegląd Historyczny* 3 (1993).

Palska, Hanna. *Bieda i dostatek: O nowych stylach życia w Polsce końca lat dziewięćdziesiątych*. Warsaw: Wydawnictwo IFiS PAN, 2002.

Pałys, Piotr. *Kłodzko, Racibórz i Głubczyce w stosunkach polsko-czechosłowackich w latach 1945–1947*. Opole: n.p., 1997.

"Panic Disorder." *New York Times Health Guide*, February 23, 2016.

Panz, Karolina. "Zagłada sztetl Grice." *Zagłada Żydów. Studia i Materiały* 3 (2007): 15–41.

Parandowski, Jan. *Bolszewizm i bolszewicy w Rosji*. Lvov: n.p., 1920.

Patočka, Jan. "Wojna XX wieku oraz wiek XX jako wojna." *Res Publica* 4 (1988).

Patton, Michael Quinn. *Qualitative Research and Evaluation Methods: Integrating Theory and Practice*, 4th ed. Thousand Oaks, CA: Sage, 2015.

Paulsson, Gunnar S. *Secret City: The Hidden Jews of Warsaw 1940–1945*. Yale University Press, 2002.

Petersen, Roger D. *Understanding Ethnic Violence: Fear, Hatred, and Resentment in Twentieth-Century Eastern Europe*. New York: Cambridge University Press, 2002.

Piasecki, Stanisław. "Front sowiecki i front Polski." *Prosto z Mostu*, June 7, 1936.

Piesowicz, Kazimierz. "Demograficzne skutki II wojny światowej." *Studia Demograficzne. Materiały Archiwalne* 1 (1987).

Pietrzak, Henryk. *Agresja indywidualna i zbiorowa w sytuacji napięć i konfliktów społecznych*. Rzeszów: WSP w Rzeszowie, 1992.

Pinker, Steven. "Żegnaj przemocy." *Gazeta Wyborcza*, July, 7–8, 2007.

Pipes, Daniel. *Conspiracy: How the Paranoid Style Flourishes and Where It Comes From*. New York: Free Press, 1997.

Piskorski, Jan M. *Wygnańcy. Przesiedlenia i uchodźcy w dwudziestowiecznej Europie*. Warsaw: PIW, 2010.

Piwońska, Iwona. "Dokwaterowanie jako temat listów do władz w latach 1945–1956 (komunikat z badań)." *Polska 1944/45-1989: Studia i materiały* 10 (2011).

Pobóg-Malinowski, Władysław. *Najnowsza historia polityczna Polski, 1864–1945*, vol. 3. London: Gryf Printers, 1960.

———. *Najnowsza historia polityczna Polski, 1964–1945*, vol. 2, part 1. London: Gryf Printers, 1956.

Po-chia Hsia, R. *The Myth of Ritual Murder: Jews and Magic in Reformation Germany*. Yale University Press, 1988.

Podgórecki, Adam et al. *Poglądy społeczeństwa polskiego na prawo i moralność*. Warsaw: KiW, 1971.

———. *Polish Society*. Westport, CT: Praeger, 1994.

Pogonowska, Ewa. "Pożoga Zofii Kossak-Szczuckiej, czyli rzecz o utracie Kresów." In *Formy dyskursu w powieści*, edited by Maria Woźniakiewicz-Dziadosz, 23–45. Lublin: Wydawnictwo UMCS, 1996.

Poliakov, Léon. *The History of Anti-Semitism, 4: Suicidal Europe, 1870–1933*. University of Pennsylvania Press, 2003.

Pollok, Ewald S. *Śląskie tragedie*. Przedbórz: Żyrowa, 2002.

Pragier, Ruta. *Żydzi czy Polacy*. Warsaw: Rytm, 1992.

Pratkanis, Anthony, and Elliot Aronson. *Age of Propaganda: The Everyday Use and Abuse of Persuasion*, chapter 24: "The Fear Appeal." New York: Henry Holt, 2001.

Prus, Bolesław. *Kroniki*, vols. 2, 18. Warsaw: PIW, 1956.

Przemyski, Andrzej P. *Ostatni Komendant. Generał Leopold Okulicki*. Lublin: Wydawnictwo Lubelskie, 1990.

Przestępstwa zameldowane Policji w latach 1924–1938 oraz przestępstwa zameldowane Milicji Obywatelskiej w latach 1945–1983. Warsaw: KG MO, 1984.

Pufelska, Agnieszka. *Die "Judäo-Kommune" ein Feindbild in Polen: Das polnische Selbverständnis im Schatten des Antisemitismus 1939–1948*. Paderborn: Schöningh, 2007.

Puławski, Adam. "Postrzeganie żydowskich oddziałów partyzanckich przez Armię Krajową i Delegaturę Rządu RP na Kraj." *Pamięć i Sprawiedliwość* 2 (2003).

Pytlakowski, Piotr. "Jak na Kujawach zabijano Niemców." *Polityka*, February 24, 2001.

Rabij, Bartłomiej. "Sprawiedliwość czy hańba." *Focus Historia* 1 (2007).

Radzinowicz, Leon. *Przestępczość w Polsce w latach 1924–1933: Studjum statystyczno-kryminalne*. Warsaw: F. Hoesick, 1935.

Rak, Stanisław. *Reforma rolna w Polsce*. London: n.p., 1946.

Ramachabdran, Vilayanur S., ed. *Encyclopedia of Human Behavior*. San Diego: Academic Press, 1994.

"Rasizm to zwykły lęk przed obcym?" *Gazeta Wyborcza*, April 18, 2010.

Reber, Arthur S. *Słownik psychologii*. Warsaw: Wydawnictwo Naukowe Scholar, 2000.

Redding, Kimberly A. *Hitler's Shadow: Remembering Youth in Postwar Berlin*. Westport, CT, and London: Praeger 2004.

Robin, Corey. *Fear: The History of a Political Idea*. Oxford University Press, 2004.

Rocznik statystyczny 1947. Warsaw: GUS, 1947.

Rocznik Statystyczny 1948. Warsaw: GUS, 1949.

Rokicki, Czesław. *Bolszewizm wobec kultury i cywilizacji i ludzkość wobec bolszewizmu*. Warsaw, 1920.

Rokuszewska-Pawełek, Alicja. *Chaos i przymus: Trajektorie wojenne Polaków—analiza biograficzna*. Łódź: Wydawnictwo Uniwersytetu Łódzkiego, 2002.

Rolicki, Henryk. *Zmierzch Izraela*. Warsaw: Skład Główny w Administracji "Myśli Narodowej," 1933.

Romaniak, Andrzej. "Powstanie, działalność i likwidacja antykomunistycznego oddziału partyzanckiego NSZ pod dowództwem Antoniego Żubryda." In *Powiat sanocki w latach 1944–1956*, edited by Krzysztof Kaczmarski and Andrzej Romaniak. Rzeszów—Sanok: Muzeum Historyczne w Sanoku, IPN, 2007.

———. "Publiczne egzekucje w Sanoku—maj—czerwiec 1946 r." *Zeszyty Historyczne WiN-u* 24 (2005): 73–86.

Rudnicki, Kazimierz. *Cuda i objawienia w Polsce 1949–1986*. Warsaw: Sawa, 1990.

Rudnicki, Szymon. "Mogą żyć, byle nie u nas... Propaganda NSZ wobec Żydów." *Więź*, April 2006.

Rusiniak, Martyna. *Obóz zagłady Treblinka II w pamięci społecznej (1943–1989)*. Warsaw: Neriton, IH PAN, 2008.

Rychard, Andrzej. *Komu potrzebna jest legitymizacja? Legitymacja klasyczne teorie i polskie doświadczenia*. Edited by Andrzej Rychard and Antoni Sułek. Warsaw: PTS, IS UW, 1988.

Sakson, Andrzej. *Stosunki narodowościowe na Warmii i Mazurach 1945–1997*. Poznań: Instytut Zachodni, 1998.

Samsonowicz, Henryk. "Głód i władza w Polsce w XIV–XVI w." In *Władza i społeczeństwo w XVI i XVII w. Prace ofiarowane Antoniemu Mączakowi*, edited by Marcin Kamler et al., 73–81. Warsaw: PWN, 1989.

Schatz, Jaff. "Świat mentalności i świadomości komunistów polsko-żydowskich—szkic do portretu." In *Społeczność żydowska w PRL przed kampanią antysemicką lat 1967–1968 i po niej*, edited by Grzegorz Berendt. Warsaw: IPN, 2009.

———. *The Generation. The Rise and Fall of the Jewish Communists of Poland*. University of California Press, 1991.

Scott, James C. *Weapons of the Weak: Everyday Forms of Peasant Resistance*. Yale University Press, 1985.

Shlapentokh, Vladimir. *Fear in Contemporary Society: Its Negative and Positive Effects*. New York: Palgrave Macmillan, 2006.

Shore, Marci. *Caviar and Ashes: A Warsaw Generation's Life and Death in Marxism, 1918–1938*. Yale University Press, 2006.

Siemaszko, Andrzej, ed. *Geografia występku i strachu*. Warsaw: Instytut Wymiaru Sprawiedliwości, 2008.

Siemaszko, Władysław, and Ewa Siemaszko. *Ludobójstwo dokonane przez nacjonalistów ukraińskich na ludności polskiej Wołynia 1939–1944*. 2 vols. Warsaw: Wydawnictwo Von Borowiecky, 2000.

Sienkiewicz, Witold, and Grzegorz Hryciuk, eds. *Wysiedlenia, wypędzenia i ucieczki 1939–1945. Atlas ziem polskich*. Warsaw: Demart, 2008.

Sitek, Aneta, and Michał Trębacz. "Życie codzienne w Łodzi w 1945 r." In *Rok 1945 w Łodzi. Studia i szkice*, edited by Joanna Żelazko, 171–86. Łódź: IPN, 2008.

Siuta, Jerzy, ed. *Słownik psychologii*. Cracow: Zielona Sowa, 2005.

Skibińska, Alina, and Jakub Petelewicz. "Udział Polaków w zbrodniach na Żydach na prowincji regionu świętokrzyskiego." *Zagłada Żydów: Studia i Materiały* 1 (2005): 114–47.

Skoczylas, Michał. *Wybory do Sejmu Ustawodawczego z 19 stycznia 1947 r. w świetle skarg do ludności*. Warsaw: Trio, 2003.

Skrudlik, Mieczysław. *Agentury obce*. Warsaw: Druk. Techniczna, 1929.

———. *Sekty żydujące w Polsce*. Warsaw: Wydawnictwo "Szczerbiec", 1927.

Skrzypek, Andrzej. *Mechanizmy uzależnienia: Stosunki polsko-radzieckie 1944–1957*. Pułtusk: Wyższa Szkoła Humanistyczna im. Aleksandra Gieysztora w Pułtusku, 2002.

Słabek, Henryk. *Dzieje polskiej reformy rolnej 1944–1948*. Warsaw: Wiedza Powszechna, 1972.

Szymczak, M., ed. *Słownik języka polskiego*. Warsaw: PWN, 1995.

Smelser, Neil J. *Theory of Collective Behavior*. New York: Free Press of Glencoe, 1963.

Snyder, Timothy. *Bloodlands: Europe between Hitler and Stalin*. New York: Basic, 2010.

Socha, Łukasz (Maria Turlejska). *Te pokolenia żałobami czarne... Skazani na śmierć i ich sędziowie 1944–1954*. Warsaw: *Krytyka*, 1986.

Sołtysiak, Grzegorz. "Komisja Specjalna do Walki." *Karta* 1 (1991).

Sorokin, Pitirim A. *Man and Society in Calamity: The Effects of War, Revolution, Famine, Pestilence upon Human Mind, Behavior, Social Organization and Cultural Life*. New York: E. P. Dutton and Co., 1942.

Spisek niemiecko-bolszewicki: Dokumenty dotyczące związku bolszewików z niemieckim naczelnym dowództwem, wielkim przemysłem i finansami, oraz reprodukcja fotograficzna dokumentów. Warsaw: n.p., 1919.

Starodworski, Antoni (A.W. Kwiatkowski). *Bolszewizm a masoneria*. Warsaw: Archidiecezja "Polak-Katolik," 1927.

Stein, Conrad R. *The Great Red Scare*. Parsippany, NJ: New Discovery, 1998.

Steinlauf, Michael. *Bondage to the Dead: Poland and the Memory of the Holocaust*. Syracuse University Press, 1997.

Stola, Dariusz. "Nieudana próba Grossa, rozmowa Marcina Wojciechowskiego z Dariuszem Stolą." In *Wokół* Strachu. *Dyskusja o książce Jana T. Grossa*, edited by Mariusz Gądek, 266–73. Cracow: Znak, 2008.

Stouffer, Samuel A. et al. *The American Soldier*, vol. 2. Princeton University Press, 1949–1950.

Strelau, Jan. "Miejsce lęku i zbliżonych konstruktów w badaniach nad temperamentem." In *Lęk: geneza, mechanizmy, funkcje*, edited by Małgorzata Fajkowska and Błażej Szymura. Warsaw: Scholar, 2009.

Strzelecki, Jan. *Próby świadectwa*. Warsaw: Czytelnik, 1971.

Strzembosz, Tomasz. "Przestępczość i okupacja." In *Problemy bandytyzmu w okupowanej Polsce w latach 1939–1947*, 7–24. Warsaw: ISP PAN, 2003.

Styś, Leszek. *Osadnictwo wojskowe na Dolnym Śląsku w latach 1945–1948*. Wrocław: Dolnośląskie Towarzystwo Społeczno-Kulturalne, 1978.

Szacka, Barbara. *II wojna światowa w pamięci rodzinnej*. In Kwiatkowski, P. T. et al., eds. *Między codziennością a wielką historią. Druga wojna światowa w pamięci zbiorowej społeczeństwa polskiego*. Gdańsk—Warsaw: Scholar 2010.

Szajkowski, Zosa. *Jews, Wars, and Communism: The Impact of the 1919–1920 Red Scare on American Jewish Life*. New York: KTAV, 1974.

Szapiro, Paweł. *Wojna żydowsko-niemiecka: Polska prasa konspiracyjna 1943–1944 o powstaniu w getcie Warszawy*. London: Aneks, 1989.

Szarota, Piotr. "Polaków zmagania z uśmiechem." In Skarżyńska, Krystyna, and Urszula Jakubowska, *Społeczeństwo po przejściach. Polityka a jakość życia, 143–56. Warsaw: Wydawnictwo Instytutu Psychologii, 2009.

Szarota, Tomasz. *Karuzela na Placu Krasińskich. Studia i szkice z lat wojny i okupacji.* Warsaw: Rytm, Fundacja "Historia i Kultura," 2007.

———. *Okupowanej Warszawy dzień powszedni.* Warsaw: Czytelnik, 1988.

———. *Osadnictwo miejskie na Dolnym Śląsku w latach 1945–1948.* Wrocław—Warsaw—Cracow: Ossolineum, 1969.

———. "Upowszechnienie kultury." In *Polska Ludowa 1944–1955: Przemiany społeczne,* edited by Franciszek Ryszka. Wrocław—Warsaw: Ossolineum, 1974.

Szaynok, Bożena. *Pogrom Żydów w Kielcach 4 lipca 1946.* Wrocław: Bellona, 1992.

———. "Społeczeństwo żydowskie w Polsce wobec referendum 30 VI 1946 r. i wyborów do Sejmu 19 I 1947 r." *Wrocławskie Studia z Historii Najnowszej,* vol. 7 (1997).

Szaynok, Bożena, and Zenon Wrona. "Pogrom kielecki w dokumentach." *Dzieje Najnowsze* 3 (1991): 75–117.

Sztompka, Piotr. *Socjologia analiza społeczeństwa.* Cracow: Znak, 2002.

———. *Trauma wielkiej zmiany. Społeczne koszt transformacji.* Warsaw: ISP PAN, 2000.

Sztompka, Piotr, and Małgorzata Boguni-Borowska, eds. *Socjologia codzienności.* Cracow: Znak, 2008.

Szwagrzyk, Krzysztof. "Przestępstwa funkcjonariuszy Urzędów Bezpieczeństwa na Dolnym Śląsku w latach 1945–1953." In *"Zwyczajny" resort: Studia o aparacie bezpieczeństwa 1944–1956,* edited by Kazimierz Krajewski and Tomasz Łabuszewski, 61–70. Warsaw: IPN, 2005.

Szymański, Antoni. *Bolszewizm.* Wrocław: Księgarnia św. Wojciecha, 1921.

Śmietanka-Kruszelnicki, Ryszard. "Problem 'bandycenia się' podziemia na przykładzie Kielecczyzny." *Polska 1944/45–1989: Studia i Materiały* 4 (1999).

Śmietanka-Kruszelnicki, Ryszard, and Edyta Wróbel. "Przestępstwa żołnierzy Armii Czerwonej na Kielecczyźnie 1945–1946." *Zeszyty Historyczne WiN-u* 25 (2006): 121–28.

"Świadków ubywa, pamięć słabnie, rozmowa W. Szackiego z P.T. Kwiatkowskim." *Gazeta Wyborcza,* September 1, 2009.

Świda-Ziemba, Hanna. *Człowiek wewnętrznie zniewolony: Mechanizmy i konsekwencje minionej formacji—analiza psychosocjologiczna.* Warsaw: Zakład Socjologii Moralności i Aksjologii Ogólnej Instytut Stosowanych Nauk Społecznych UW, 1997.

———. *Urwany lot.* Cracow: WL, 2003.

Tarkowska, Elżbieta, ed. *Przeciw biedzie. Programy, pomysły, inicjatywy.* Warsaw: Oficyna Naukowa, 2002.

Tarkowska, Elżbieta, and Jacek Tarkowski. "'Amoralny familizm' czyli o dezintegracji społecznej w Polsce lat osiemdziesiątych." In Tarkowski, Jacek. *Socjologia świata polityki: Władza i społeczeństwo w systemie autorytarnym,* vol. 1. Warsaw: ISP PAN, 1994.

Thiele-Dohrmann, Klaus. *Unter dem Siegel der Verschwiegenheit—Zur Psychologie des Klatsches.* Hamburg: Claassen, 1975.

Ther, Philipp, and Ane Siljak, eds. *Redrawing Nations: Ethnic Cleansing in East-Central Europe, 1944–1948.* Lanham, MD: Rowman & Littlefield, 2001.

Thomas, W. I., and Florian Znaniecki. *The Polish Peasant in Europe and America: Monograph of an Immigrant Group,* vol. IV: *Disorganization and Reorganization in Poland.* Boston: Richard G. Badger, Gorham Press, 1920.

Thompson, Kenneth. *Moral Panics.* London: Routledge, 1998.

Tkaczew, Władysław. *Organa Informacji Wojska Polskiego 1943–1956: Kontrwywiad wojskowy.* Warsaw: Bellona, 2007.

Tokarska-Bakir, Joanna. *Legendy o krwi. Antropologia przesądu.* Warsaw: W.A.B., 2008.

———. "Obrazy sandomierskie." *Res Publica Nowa* 1 (2007): 18–63.

Tomaszewski, Jerzy, ed. *Najnowsze dzieje Żydów w Polsce.* Warsaw: PWN, 1993.

Tomaszewski, Jerzy, and Andrzej Żbikowski, eds. *Żydzi w Polsce. Dzieje i kultura. Leksykon.* Warsaw: Cyklady, 2001.

Topiński, Jan. "Nacjonalizacja przemysłu w Polsce." *Polska Ludowa,* vol. 6, 1967.

Torańska, Teresa. *Śmierć spóźnia się o minutę. Trzy rozmowy: Brystygier, Głowiński, Rotfeld.* Warsaw: Biblioteka Gazety Wyborczej, 2010.

Tracz, Bogusław. *Rok ostatni—rok pierwszy. Gliwice 1945.* Gliwice: Muzeum w Gliwicach, 2004.

Trevelyan, George M. *English Social History.* London: Book Club Associates for Longman, 1973.

Turkowski, Roman. "Polskie Stronnictwo Ludowe—model oporu politycznego (1945–1947)." In *Represje wobec wsi i ruchu ludowego (1944–1956),* vol. 1. Warsaw: Muzeum Historii Polskiego Ruchu Ludowego, 2003.

———. *Polskie Stronnictwo Ludowe w obronie demokracji 1945–1949.* Warsaw: Wydawnictwo Sejmowe, 1992.

———. "Władza komunistyczna wobec przejawów religijności w Polsce w schyłku lat 40-tych XX wieku." In *Propaganda antykościelna w Polsce w latach 1945–1978,* edited by Stanisław Dąbrowski and Barbara Rogowska, 75–91. Wrocław: Arboretum, 2001.

Tuszyńska, Agata. *Rodzinna historia lęku.* Cracow: WL, 2005.

Twardochleb, Bogdan. "Prolegomena do ethosu pioniera." *Przegląd Zachodniopomorski* 1–2 (1988): 171–83.

Ułaszyn, Henryk. *Język złodziejski.* Łódź: Łódzkie Towarzystwo Naukowe, 1951.

———. *Przyczynki leksykalne: Gwara złodziejska z około roku 1840.* Cracow: Akademia Umiejętności, 1913.

Ungar, Sheldon. "Moral Panic versus the Risk Society: The Implications of the Changing Sites of Social Anxiety." *The British Journal of Psychology* 2 (June 2001), vol. 52.

Urbanek, Joanna. *Lęk i strach warszawiaków wobec zagrożeń Września 1939 r.* Master's thesis, Institute of History, University of Warsaw, 2008.

Urbanek, Mariusz. "Wielki szaber." *Polityka,* April 29, 1995.

Urynowicz, Marcin. "Stosunki polsko-żydowskie w Warszawie w okresie okupacji hitlerowskiej." In *Polacy i Żydzi pod okupacją* niemiecką 1939–1945: Studia i materiały, edited by Andrzej Żbikowski, 537–689. Warsaw: IPN, 2006.

Voglis, Polymeris. "Surviving Hunger: Life in the Cities and the Countryside during the Occupation." In *Surviving Hitler and Mussolini: Daily Life in Occupied Europe*, edited by Robert Gildea and Olivier Wieviorka, 16–41. Oxford: Berg, 2007.

Walewski, Paweł. "Epidemia strachu." *Polityka*, October 1, 2005.

Wańkowicz, Melchior. "Ogniem i mieczem." *Tygodnik Ilustrowany*, February 12–March 26, 1921.

———. *W kościołach Meksyku*. Warsaw: Rój, 1927.

Wawer, Zbigniew. "Miasto niepokonane." *Mówią Wieki* (special issue on the Battle of Warsaw of 1920) 5 (2005).

Wawrzyniak, Joanna. "W cieniu śmierci." *Polityka*, September 29, 2005.

Węgrzynek, Hanna. *"Czarna legenda" Żydów: Procesy o rzekome mordy rytualne w dawnej Polsce*. Warsaw: Bellona, 1995.

Weil, Simone. *Simone Weil: An Anthology*. Edited and with an introduction by Siân Miles. New York: Grove, 2000.

Weiner, Amir. *Making Sense of War*. Princeton University Press, 2001.

Werka, Tomasz, and Jolanta Zagrodzka. "Strach i lęk w świetle badań neurobiologicznych." In *Lęk: geneza, mechanizmy, funkcje*, edited by Małgorzata Fajkowska and Błażej Szymura. Warsaw: Scholar, 2009.

Werner, Andrzej. "Katastrofizm." In *Słownik literatury polskiej XX wieku*, edited by Alina Brodzka, Mirosława Puchalska, et al. Wrocław, Warsaw, Cracow: Ossolineum, 1993.

Wierzbicki, Marek. *Polacy i Białorusini w zaborze sowieckim: Stosunki polsko-białoruskie na ziemiach północno-wschodnich II Rzeczypospolitej pod okupacją sowiecką 1939–1941*. Warsaw: Volumen, 2000.

———. *Polacy i Żydzi w zaborze sowieckim*. Warsaw: Biblioteka Frondy, 2001.

Wilkinson, Iain. *Anxiety in a Risk Society*. London: Routledge, 2001.

Wnuk, Rafał, ed. *Atlas polskiego podziemia niepodległościowego 1944–1956*. Warsaw—Lublin: IPN, 2007.

———. "Problem bandytyzmu wśród żołnierzy antykomunistycznego podziemia w Polsce (1945–1947)." In *Komunizm. Ideologia, system, ludzie*, edited by Tomasz Szarota, 67–79. Warsaw: Neriton, IH PAN, 2001.

Wodecka, Dorota. "I nadeszli barbarzyńcy." *Gazeta Wyborcza*, Opole edition, January 25, 2011.

Wojnowska, Bożena. "Katastrofizm." In *Literatura polska: Przewodnik encyklopedyczny*, vol. 1. Warsaw: PWN, 1984.

Wolf, Eric R. *Peasant Wars of the Twentieth Century*. New York: Harper & Row, 1969.

Wolff-Powęska, Anna, ed. *Polacy wobec Niemców: Z dziejów kultury politycznej Polski 1945–1989*. Poznań: Instytut Zachodni, 1993.

Woźniczka, Zygmunt. *Trzecia wojna światowa w oczekiwaniach emigracji i podziemia w kraju w latach 1944–1953*. Katowice: Wydawnictwo Uniwersytetu Śląskiego, 1999.

Wróbel, Janusz. *Na rozdrożu historii: Repatriacja obywateli polskich z Zachodu w latach 1945–1949*. Łódź: IPN, 2009.

———. "Wyzwoliciele czy okupanci? Żołnierze sowieccy w Łódzkiem 1945–1946." *Biuletyn IPN* 8 (2001): 39–42.

Wróbel, Piotr. "The Seeds of Violence: The Brutalization of an East European Region, 1917–1921." *Journal of Modern European History* 1 (2003): 125–49.

Wtorkiewicz, Jarosław. *Wojsko Polskie w akcji propagandowej i wyborach do Sejmu Ustawodawczego w 1947 roku*. Warsaw: Trio, 2002.

Wust, Peter. *Niepewność i ryzyko*. Translated by Karol Toeplitz of *Ungewissheit und Wagnis*. Munich: Koesel-Pustet, 1937. Warsaw: PWN, 1995.

Wyka, Kazimierz. *Wspomnienie o katastrofizmie*. In Wyka, Kazimierz. *Rzecz o wyobraźni*. Warsaw: PIW, 1959.

———. *Życie na niby*. Cracow: WL, 1984.

Wyrobisz, Andrzej. "'Wielki strach' w Wenecji i we Florencji w XV wieku i jego możliwe przyczyny." *Przegląd Historyczny* 4 (2004).

"Z Olgą Tokarczuk rozmawia Miłada Jędrysik." *Gazeta Wyborcza*, May 8–9, 2010.

Ząbek, W. L. *Dzieje Makowa Mazowieckiego: Saperzy w operacji rozminowywania terytorium kraju na Ziemi Makowskiej*. Maków Mazowiecki: Stowarzyszenie Saperów Polskich, Towarzystwo Miłośników Ziemi Makowskiej, 2006.

Zackiewicz, Grzegorz. *Polska myśl polityczna wobec systemu radzieckiego 1918–1939*. Cracow: Arcana, 2004.

Zagrodzka, Jolanta, and Monika Kowaleczko-Szumowska, eds. *Psychospołeczne i neurobiologiczne aspekty agresji*. Warsaw: Wydawnictwo Instytutu Psychologii PAN, 2005.

Zaremba, Marcin. *Communism-Legitimacy-Nationalism: Nationalist Legitimization of the Communist Regime in Poland*. Berlin: Peter Lang, 2019.

———. "'Człowiek drży jak liść'—trwoga przed bandytyzmem w okresie powojennym (1945–1947)." In *Niepiękny wiek XX*, edited by B. Brzostek et al., 363–88. Warsaw: IH UW, IPN, 2010.

———. "Gorączka szabru." *Zagłada Żydów. Studia i Materiały* 5 (2009): 193–220.

———. "'Jak nie urok, to . . .' Strach przed czerwonoarmistami 1944–1947." In *W objęciach wielkiego brata: Sowieci w Polsce 1944–1993*, edited by Konrad Rokicki and Sławomir Stępień, 235–62. Warsaw: IPN, 2009.

———. "Jest marszałek, wyszedł cukier." *Gazeta Wyborcza*, November 9, 2009.

———. *Komunizm, legitymizacja, nacjonalizm: Nacjonalistyczna legitymizacja władzy komunistycznej w Polsce*. Warsaw: Trio, ISP PAN, 2001.

———. "Malborków wiele," *Polityka*, February 21, 2009.

———. "Milicja Oprychów." *Polityka*, November 16–22, 2011.

———. "O polskiej banalności zła." *Polityka*, March 19, 2011.

———. "Oni mają, a my głodujemy." *Polityka*, October 11, 2008.

———. "Oni mordują nasze dzieci! Mit mordu rytualnego w powojennej Polsce." Part 1: *Archeologia*, *Więź*, October 2007, 90–109. Part 2: *Hipotezy*, *Więź*, November–December 2007, 96–112.

———. "Polityka strachu i jej konsekwencje. Polska 1944–1947." In *Od Piłsudskiego do Wałęsy. Studia z dziejów Polski w XX wieku*, edited by Krzysztof Persak et al., 113–40. Warsaw: IPN, ISP PAN, 2008.

———. "Sąd nieostateczny." *Polityka*, January 19, 2008.

———. "Smalec strategiczny." *Polityka*, November 2, 2002.

———. "Trauma Wielkiej Wojny. Psychospołeczne konsekwencje drugiej wojny światowej." *Kultura i Społeczeństwo* 2 (2008): 3–42.

———. "Trzej jeźdźcy: strach przed głodem, drożyzną, chorobami zakaźnymi w Polsce 1944–1947." In *Gospodarka i społeczeństwo w czasach PRL-u (1944–1989)*, edited by Elżbieta Kościk and Tomasz Głowiński, 182–206. Wrocław: Gajt 2007.

Zaremba, Marcin, and Jolanta Zarembina. "1945 rok kobiet upodlonych." *Newsweek Polska*, July 24, 2005.

Zaremba, Zygmunt et al. "O Żydach i antysemityzmie," free supplement to *Myśl Socjalistyczna* 12–13. Warsaw, 1936.

Zarembina, Jolanta. "Strach się bać." *Rzeczpospolita—Magazyn*, May 13, 1999.

Zawadka, Grażyna, and Piotr Nisztor. "Polska lista strachów." *Rzeczpospolita*, February 27, 2009.

Żbikowski, Andrzej, ed. *Polacy i Żydzi pod okupacją niemiecką 1939–1945: Studia i materiały*. Warsaw: IPN, 2006.

Zdziarski, Stanisław. *Dżingis-Chan zmartwychwstały: Studia z psychopatologii rosyjskiej*. Poznań: Księgarnia św. Wojciecha, 1919.

Żaryn, Jan. "Hierarchia Kościoła katolickiego wobec relacji polsko-żydowskich w latach 1945–1947." In *Wokół pogromu kieleckiego*, edited by Łukasz Kamiński and Jan Żaryn. Warsaw: IPN, 2006.

———. *Kościół a władza w Polsce (1945–1950)*. Warsaw: DiG, 1997.

Żbikowski, Andrzej. "Antysemityzm, szmalcownictwo, współpraca z Niemcami a stosunki polsko-żydowskie pod okupacją niemiecką." In *Polacy i Żydzi pod okupacją niemiecką 1939–1945: Studia i materiały*, edited by Andrzej Żbikowski, 429–535. Warsaw: IPN, 2006.

———. "Morderstwa popełniane na Żydach w pierwszych latach po wojnie." In *Następstwa zagłady Żydów: Polska 1944–2010*, edited by Feliks Tych and Monika Adamczyk-Garbowska, 71–93. Lublin: Wydawnictwo Uniwersytetu Marii Curie-Skłodowskiej, ŻIH, 2011.

———. *Zabójstwa osób narodowości żydowskiej na ziemiach polskich w pierwszych latach po zakończeniu II wojny światowej* (typescript).

Łach, Stanisław, ed. *Ziemie Odzyskane pod wojskową administracją radziecką po II wojnie światowej: Materiały z konferencji*. Słupsk: n.p., 2000.

Zimbardo, Philip. *The Lucifer Effect: Understanding How Good People Turn Evil*. New York: Random House, 2008.

Zgółkowa, H., ed. *Praktyczny słownik współczesnej polszczyzny*. Poznań: Wydawnictwo Kurpisz, 2003.

Zweiniger-Bargielowska, Ina. *Austerity in Britain: Rationing, Controls and Consumption, 1939–1955*. Oxford University Press, 2000.

Żuradzki, Tomasz. "Strach się bać." *Gazeta Wyborcza*, December 16, 2003.

Żyndul, Jolanta. *Kłamstwo krwi: Legenda mordu rytualnego na ziemiach polskich w XIX i XX wieku*. Warsaw: Cyklady, 2011.

Websites

Marx, K., and F. Engels. *Manifesto of the Communist Party*, Chapter I. Accessed July 16, 2019. https://www.Marxists.org.

"Statystyki Urzędu Stanu Cywilnego w Szczecinie [Szczecin Registry Office statistics]." Accessed February 12, 2012. https://www.bip.um.szczecin.pl.

INDEX

abortion, 81, 83
Adamowicz, Bogusław, 25
Adamski, Tadeusz, 169
adolescents, 50, 54, 56, 57, 60, 95, 107, 223
A gdy komunizm zapanuje (Jezierski), 19, 25–26
aggression, 48–50. *See also* ethnic violence; pogroms; violence
Aggressive Behavior (Huesmann), 14
Ajdukiewicz, Kazimierz, 211
Alarm, 186
alcohol/alcoholism, 50–51, 74, 87, 102, 127, 185, 255, 305
Allport, Gordon W., 15, 116, 233
Anczarski, Józef, 278, 285
Andrzejewski, Jerzy, 35
anger, relationship between fear and, 14
Angstträger, 11
anti-clericalism, 52
anti-Semitism: alcohol and violence related to, 51; call to rid Poland of Jews and, 307; concealment of Jewish identity and, 277; as cultural effect of war trauma, 57; demobilized troops and, 98, 101; economic anxiety and, 15; encountered by returning Holocaust survivors, 277; German models of political culture and, 57; hunger and accusations against Jews and, 261; increase in Christian religiosity and, 239–40; increase of as cultural effect to wartime conditions, 57; messages opposing, 58–59; modernization and, 15; Nazi propaganda and, 57–58; political as part of Polish fear, 19; profiteering and, 122–23; psychic numbing and, 59; psychosocial condition of the Poles and, 59; transferred fear and, 14; unemployment and, 116; war invalids and, 102–4
anxiety, 12–14, 77. *See also* fear
apathy, 11
Archer, Dane, 48–49
art, 47
Asians, 25

Atlas polskiego podziemia niepodległościowego (Atlas of the pro-independence underground), 124
atomic bomb, 212–13

Baczyński, Krzysztof Kamil, 40
Baley, Stefan, 39, 46–47
Balkanization, 6
bandits: demobilized troops and, 100, 166–70; fear of, 155–56; Jewish victims of, 169–70, 174n135; joining out of fear and, 17; other historical examples of, 157, 171; peasant, 159–62; as source of chaos, 68; urban, 162–66; wartime origins of, 157–59
Bandits (Hobsbawm), 156
bank robberies, 165
Baslez, Marie-Françoise, 15
Batawia, Stanisław, 46
Bauman, Janina, 307
Bauman, Zygmunt, 7, 58, 200, 204, 245
bazaars, 119–21
Beck, Józef, 29, 35
Beck, Ulrich, 11, 182
Beevor, Antony, 84
beggars, 105–10
Belorussians, 3, 15, 136, 275, 284, 288–89
Bérillon, Edgar, 20–21
Berlin crisis, 216
Berman, Jakub, 193, 308
Bień, Adam, 21
Bieniek, Juliusz, 313
Bieńkowski, Witold, 210
Bierut, Bolesław, 183, 226, 244, 318
Biuletyn Informacyjny, 58, 158, 161, 210
black market, 53, 117–18, 222
Bloch, Marc, 33
Błyskawica, 313
Bogusz, Marian, 75
Bolshevism, 19–20, 23–26, 78, 276. *See also* Red Army; Soviet Union
Bolszewizm i Polska (Bolshevism and Poland) (Lutosławski), 31
Borejsza, Jerzy, 202, 204, 211, 308

Borek, Czesław, 146
Borowski, Tadeusz, 187
Braudel, Fernand, 15
Budyonny, Semyon, 21–22
Byłem sołtysem w latach okupacji (I was a village administrator under the occupation) (Chustecki), 138

Cała, Alina, 313
cannibalism, 260, 304
Cantril, Hadley, 309, 313–14
capitalism, 27, 32
Caritas, 262
Castel, Robert, 94
Catholic Church: in *A gdy komunizm zapanuje*, 26; alienation from, 51; anti-Communist propaganda and, 23–24; apocalyptic mood and, 238–41; on atrophy of morals, 54–55; concordat with the Vatican and, 242; Jewish ritual murder myth (vampirism) and, 313; losses of intelligentsia and, 41; as postwar social institution, 43–44; in *Pożoga* (Conflagration), 25; state action against, 242; stereotype of anti-Christianity of Jews and, 30–31
Central Committee of Polish Jews, 308, 317
Chajn, Leon, 203
chaos, 65–68
Charszewski, Ignacy, 313
children: abandoned newborns, 81; abductions of for ransom, 317–18; alcohol and, 50; anti-Semitism and, 107; as beggars, 107–8; crime and, 54; currency exchange and, 223; disease and, 265–66; hidden Jewish, 317–18; hunger and, 253, 258, 260–62, 272n41; landmines and, 237; panics about disappearances of, 83; postwar trauma and, 47; as source of anxiety, 315–16; of wartime rape, 78. *See also* Jewish ritual murder myth
Chodakowski, Jan, 48, 150
cholera, 179
Churchill, Winston, 207, 213

347

Chustecki, Jan, 138, 162
Cichopek, Anna, 8, 297
Citizens' Militia: alcohol, 127; anti-Semitic violence and, 125–27, 291–92, 295, 298, 300–302; anti-Soviet attitudes of, 126; bandits and, 163–65; bitterness of, 125, 127; bribery and, 122, 127; corruption and, 157; crime and, 125; demobilized soldiers and, 100, 124; desertion and, 125; housing and, 234; looting and, 153n50; makeup of, 124, 133n236; murder and, 128; profiteers and, 122; recruitment of expendables for, 96; Security Office vs, 125–26; theft and, 127; as type of expendable, 124–28; wages of, 125; wartime police and, 125
Cohen, Stanley, 11
Cold War, 216
collective fear, 11, 21–22
collective imagination, 3
collectivization, 2, 7, 27, 224–28, 249n185, 263
communal housing, 226
Communism, 19, 26–28, 30
Communist Manifesto, The, 94
Communist Party, 96, 275, 284, 309
concentration camps, 48, 79, 176, 205
Concept of Anxiety, The (Kierkegaard), 12
Conquest, Robert, 17
Coordination, 317
corruption, 53–54
Cracow, 8, 83, 108, 141, 270, 290, 294–99
crime, 54, 60, 63n109, 71, 156–58. *See also* bandits
Cukier, Mojżesz, 315
culture of fear, interwar, 24–28
currency exchange, 221–24, 228, 256
currency panics, 221, 224
cynicism, 53, 55
Cyrankiewicz, Józef, 192
Czarnowski, Stefan, 94, 124
Czechoslovakia, 84, 219
Czechowicz, Józef, 26
Czerski, Mieczysław, 32
Częstochowa, 299–300
Czuma, Stanisław, 169–70
Czuma, Walerian, 69
Czyż, Józef, 76

Dąbrowska, Maria, 4, 35, 45, 70, 72, 209–10, 212, 308
Dąmbski, Stefan, 100
death, 39–41
Delumeau, Jean, 8, 12, 16, 65
Dembiński, Henryk, 28
demobilized troops: anger of underground demobilized and, 100–101; anti-Semitism and, 98, 101; anxiety about the Red Army and, 97; as bandits, 166–70; bitterness of, 98–99; demobilization orders and, 97; as drifters, 108–9; housing and, 234; Jewish, 307; militia and, 124; numbers of, 96–97, 99; official troops, 96–97; promised conditions for, 97, 99; resettlement and, 97; Rzeszów pogrom and, 292; as source of chaos, 68; theft and, 99–100; underground fighters, 96, 100–101, 125; unemployment and, 98–99, 115
denunciations, 233
Department of the National Economy and Finances, 221
deportations/expulsions, 42, 46, 48, 61n31, 184, 187, 202
deserters, 96, 104–5, 166–70
diaries, 4, 47, 49
diphtheria, 266
disease: cholera, 179, 265; diphtheria, 266–67; dysentery, 266–68; fear of, 265–68; fears of from corpses, 40, 265; health insurance and, 266; hunger and, 259; internment camps and, 267; lice and, 267; malaria, 268; pediculosis, 266; as political tool, 254; quarantines, 267; scabies, 266; scarlet fever, 266; syphilis, 83, 267; travel conditions in mass movement and, 179; tuberculosis, 266; typhus, 2, 179, 254, 258, 259, 266–68; vaccinations, 267–68; venereal disease, 83–84
displaced persons camps, 177
Djilas, Milovan, 78–79
Dmitrów, Edmund, 276, 278
Dmowski, Roman, 30
Drang nach Osten, 19
dreams, 47
drifters, 108–9
drugs, 147
dysentery, 266
Dziennik Bałtycki, 102, 116, 119, 144, 205, 281
Dziennik Łódzki, 314
Dziennik Ludowy, 238
Dziennik Polski, 105, 112–13, 148, 235, 316
Dziennik Powszechny, 111, 135, 141, 259–60, 265, 298, 315
Dziennik Rzeszowski, 293
Dżingis-Chan zmartwychwstały (Zdziarski), 20
Dziś i Jutro, 210, 244

Echo Wieczorne, 95, 110, 317–18
economy, 263–65; challenges facing, 229–30; currency exchange, 221–24, 228, 256; food shortages and, 254–55, 255; inflation and, 6, 223, 230–31; nationalization and, 228–31; time between occupations and, 67
Edelman, Marek, 170
Eliade, Mircea, 296
Engel, David, 195
Engelking, Barbara, 158
Estreicher, Karol, 204
ethnic violence: against indigenous population, 276–77; alcohol and, 305; changes in social structure and, 311; fear of the "Other" and, 275; moral atrophy and, 305; nationalism and, 305; Nazism and, 306; Polish-Belorussian conflict and, 288–89; Polish-Ukrainian conflict and, 284–88; Stalinism and, 306; toward Germans, 276, 278–84. *See also* pogroms
exhumations, 40
expendables: beggars/hoboes, 105–10; deserters, 96, 104–5; drifters, 108–9; efforts to clear out, 109–10; Great Depression and, 95; housing shortages and, 95–96; militia members and, 124–28; othering of, 110; pogroms and, 312; postwar impoverishment and, 95; promotions by new regime and, 96; recruitment of by political movements and, 94, 96; recruitment of for militia, 96; terminology and, 94; thieves' gangs, 96; types of, 94–95; unemployment, 98–99, 110–16, 112; violence and, 96; wartime fluctuations of number of, 95. *See also* demobilized troops; invalids
Express Poznański, 240
Express Wieczorny, 106, 281, 317
Extraordinary Housing Commissions, 235

factories, 110–12, 131n144, 132n168, 228
Falanga, 28, 32, 34
family ties, 51, 55–56, 60, 63n119
farmers, 218
Fascism, 25
fear: acquisition of, 10; anger and, 14; of another war, 210–17; anxiety vs., 12; of bandits, 155–56, 159; as constant consequence of Second World War, 45–48, 314, 325; as contagious, 11; currency panics, 221, 224; death from, 10; distribution of in postwar Poland, 7–8; of hunger, 4, 254, 258–60; Jewish proximity and, 59; politics and, 182–83; positive effects of, 13; promotion of for political ends, 14; psychological definition of, 10; of rape, 78–84; of returning to Poland, 176–78; role of in society, 13; scholarship tradition and study of, 8; as source of aggression, 14–16; Stalin's lesson on, 183–84; template for studying, 4;

terror vs., 12; of unemployment, 115; "war syndrome" and, 46. *See also* collective fear; political terror
Fear (Gross), 8, 170, 290, 308
Fear in Contemporary Society (Shlapentokh), 13
First World War, 19, 25, 115, 157
food shortages, 179, 216, 254–56. *See also* hunger
forced exiles, 48, 61n31
forced labor camps, 79
Foster, George M., 135
freedom, between occupations, 66
Freedom and Independence Association, 82
Freud, Sigmund, 14
Frey-Bielecki, Jan, 295
Furedi, Frank, 182–83

Gałczyński, Konstanty Ildefons, 1, 204
Galician Slaughter of 1846, 17
gambling, street, 108, 121
Gapiński, Bartłomiej, 237
Gartner, Rosemary, 48–49
Gazeta Lubelska, 124, 141, 200
Gdyby pod Radzyminem (If near Radzymin) (Ligocki), 25
Gellner, Ernest, 15
Geremek, Bronisław, 108
Germans: anti-German kangaroo courts and, 283; chaos during invasion of, 65–66; currency exchange and, 222; disease and, 268; disease as political tool and, 254; employment of, 115–16; ethnic hatred in Germany and, 275–76; ethnic hatred of, 276, 278–84; ethnic violence and, 282–84; health insurance and, 266; hiding of German ethnicity and, 277–78; housing crisis and, 233; hunger and violence against, 270; Hunger Plan of, 253; language of political terror and, 193; legal reprisals against, 278–79; looting of, 142, 279; as "Other," 275; pogroms against, 282–84; policy of extermination, 157–58; Polish borders and, 219–20; Polish national solidarity and, 57; public executions by, 191; public executions of, 280–82; rumors about retreating, 283–84; slights of language and culture of, 278; suicide and, 276; uniting of Poles against, 3; wartime trauma and, 60
Gerrits, André, 29
Giddens, Anthony, 182
Giertych, Jędrzej, 32
Gil, Franciszek, 108
Girl in the Red Coat, The (Ligocka), 47
Głos Narodu, 143–44, 298

Głos Wielkopolski, 281
Głowiński, Michał, 277
Gobineau, Arthur de, 20
Godycka-Ćwirko, Janina, 79–80, 190
Goeschel, Christian, 276
Golden Harvest (Grudzińska-Gross and Gross), 312
Golon, Mirosław, 82
Gomułka, Władysław, 67, 151, 192–93, 202, 207, 218, 227
Górski, Walenty, 157
Grabowski, Jan, 158, 163
Great Depression, 19, 24–26, 45, 48, 57, 95
Great Fear, 15–16
Great Terror, 16–17
Greece, 215, 216
Gross, Jan T., 7–8, 96, 170, 233, 239, 290, 306, 308–9, 312, 320n92
Grossman, Vasily, 38, 70
Grot-Rowecki, Stefan, 57
Grudzińska-Gross, Irena, 312
Grzybowski, Faustyn, 147
guilt, 290, 306

Hagen, William W., 22
hearsay, 7, 11, 22, 210–17, 283–84. *See also* Jewish Communism stereotype; Jewish ritual murder myth (vampirism)
Heller, Michał, 182
Herbert, Zbigniew, 67
Herszenhorn, Szlomo, 290
Hirsch, Helga, 279
Hirszfeld, Ludwik, 304
Hirszowicz, Maria, 204
History of Anti-Semitism, The (Poliakov), 28–29
Hlond, August, 51
hoarding, 216, 325
Hobbes, Thomas, 182
hoboes, 105–10
Hobsbawm, Eric, 19, 156
Home Army: anti-Semitism and, 308; Jews in, 308
homelessness, 2, 94–95
homophobia, 16
Horney, Karen, 12
housing, 231–36
Huesmann, Rowell L., 14
hunger: accusations against Jews and, 261; black market and, 118; cannibalism and, 260; children and, 253, 258, 260–62; currency exchange and, 256; desertion and, 269; disease and, 259; drought and, 262–63; ethnic violence and, 270; fear of, 254, 258–60; flight and, 269; food aid and, 255, 259–62; food distribution system and, 256; German Hunger Plan of, 253; infant mortality and, 258, 267; landmines and, 236–37; mice and, 255, 261–63; pogroms and, 254, 270; as political tool, 253–54; profiteers and, 254, 270; prophecies and, 259; protests/strikes and, 254, 260, 269–70; rationing and, 255, 261; Red Army and, 255–57; Second World War and, 253; starvation and, 259; theft and, 256–57; unevenness of, 257–58; violent behavior and, 269
Hunt for the Jews (Grabowski), 163
Hurwic-Nowakowska, Irena, 277

I boję się snów (And I fear my dreams) (Półtawska), 47
Ilustrowany Kurier Polski, 98, 281
Ilustrowany Kuryer Codzienny, 27–28, 313
indifference, culture of, 54
indigenous population, ethnic violence against, 276–77
infant mortality, 258, 267
inflation, 6, 223, 230–31, 254, 263–65, 326
Informacji o przebiegu zajość antysemickich w Krakowie (Information about the course of the anti-Semitic incidents in Cracow), 295
insecuritas humana, 315
Institute of National Economy, 264
institutions, 38–43, 45
intelligentsia, 40–41, 70, 180, 204–5
internment camps, 184, 267
invalids, 96, 101–4
Iwaszkiewicz, Jarosław, 4, 49

Jackowska, Ewa, 48
Jakubaszek, Jan Maria, 176
Janion, Maria, 4
Jarosz, Dariusz, 225, 232
Jasienica, Paweł, 19, 21, 28
Jastrzębowski, Wacław, 117–18
Jedność, 120, 263
Jedwabne pogrom, 14, 35, 49, 306
Jewish Communism stereotype: culture of fear in interwar Poland and, 11, 308; international Jewish conspiracy and, 30–31; lack of truth to in Poland, 308–9; Masons and, 32–33; in Nazi propaganda, 58; prevalence of, 31–32, 34–35; Rzeszów pogrom and, 293; source of, 29–30; spread of belief in Europe in, 28–29; stereotype of anti-Christianity and, 30–31, 239–40; United States beliefs and, 29
Jewish Congregation, 317
Jewish Fighting Organization, 277

Index

Jewish ritual murder myth (vampirism): abduction of children for ransom and, 317–18; age of believer and, 310; agitators and, 309, 322n195; ancient roots of, 309, 312–13; anxieties and, 314–15; assaults of Jews tied to, 52, 1298, 291, 305; changing social norms and belief of, 314–15; connection to religion of, 290–91; Cracow pogroms, 294–99; Częstochowa and, 299–300; gender and, 310; Kielce pogrom and, 282, 300–303; lack of education and, 309–10; magical thinking and, 315–16; poverty and, 310; Rzeszów and, 291–94; spread through Poland of, 303–4; variations of, 303–4; Włocławek and, 299; women and, 310–11, 315–16

Jews: in *A gdy komunizm zapanuje*, 26; association of with fear, 306; conviction among Poles that Jews should leave Poland and, 307; disease and political tool against, 254; dissolution of social hierarchies and, 44; economic anxiety and, 15; ethnic violence against, 289–90; fear after pogroms of, 304–5; fear of cannibalism and, 6; fears of proximity to, 59; housing crisis and, 233–34; hunger and violence/accusations against, 261, 270; intermingles with fear of Bolsheviks and, 23–24; interwar press and, 28; legends about hidden treasures of, 149; militia and, 128; number of Communist in interwar Poland, 30; as "Other," 275; in Polish Army, 101; political terror and, 196; in *Pożoga* (Conflagration), 24–25; preying on of by bandits, 162–63; Stalinist Purges and, 32; suicide and, 277; surrender to Germans of, 277; thefts of property of, 54; time between occupations and, 66; transferred fear and, 15; transference of Jewish conspiracy onto Soviets and, 84; uniting of Poles against, 3. *See also* anti-Semitism; Jewish Communism stereotype; pogroms; Jewish ritual murder myth (vampirism)

Jezierski, Edmund, 19, 25
Judt, Tony, 29

Kaczmarski, Krzysztof, 293
Kaczyńska, Maria, 46, 52, 54
Kamieński, Kazimierz, 167
Kamińska-Szmaj, Irena, 23
Kamiński, Adam, 4
Kamiński, Łukasz, 8, 104
Kennkarten, 222
Kępiński, Antoni, 12, 14, 20, 59
Kersten, Krystyna, 4, 8, 57, 175, 180, 182, 184, 194, 201, 207, 238, 307

Kielce pogrom, 8, 51, 83, 208, 277, 282, 290, 292, 300–303
Kierkegaard, Søren, 12
Kiev pogrom, 60
Kisielewski, Stefan, 1
Kłoskowska, Antonina, 275
Klukowski, Zygmunt, 4, 66, 100, 140, 158, 166, 170, 185, 191
Kołakowski, Leszek, 200
Konieczny, Franciszek, 313
Konopińska, Joanna, 4, 119, 166
Kopciowski, Adam, 170
Kopecka, Olga, 307
Kopstein, Jeffrey S., 30
Kossak-Szczucka, Zofia, 24–25
Kotarbiński, Tadeusz, 35
Kott, Jan, 281
Kotus-Jankowski, Franciszek, 267
Kowalska, Anna, 4, 96, 218
Kowalska-Leder, Justyna, 152
Krajewski, Stanisław, 30, 33
Krasiński, Zygmunt, 29, 168
Krawczyńska, Jadwiga, 47
Kręglicki, Antoni, 300
Kroniki (Chronicles) (Prus), 136
Kruk, Erwin, 276
Kryński, Adam, 281
"Kryzys bolszewizmu w Rosji" (The crisis of Bolshevism in Russia), 32
Krzywicka, Irena, 142
Kubacki, Wacław, 4, 234
Kubina, Teodor, 313
Ku Klux Klan, 21
Kula, Witold, 253, 270
Kunert, Elisabeth, 145
Kurier Kaliski, 113, 235
Kurier Popularny, 118
Kurier Szczeciński, 109, 114, 192, 260
Kuroń, Jacek, 294
Kwiek, Julian, 170

Lambert, Charles, 231
Lanckorońska, Karolina, 52
Landau-Czajka, Anna, 34
Landau, Ludwik, 94–95, 137, 212
Landau, Zbigniew, 221
Landesmann, Jonas, 291–94
landmines, 101, 236–37
landowners, 44, 203, 226
Langmuir, Gavin I., 21, 30
Łatyński, Marek, 242
Lefebvre, Georges, 2, 8
Letters from Russia (Marquis de Custine), 20
Levi, Primo, 120, 278
Ligarski, Sebastian, 116

Ligocka, Roma, 47
Ligocki, Edward, 25
Lipicki, Stefan, 39
Lipski, Jan Józef, 32
Lisiak, Henryk, 23
Lithuanians, 67
Łódź, looting and, 142, 145
looting: alcohol and, 51; appropriation of German property by settlers vs., 147; causes of, 149–52; of cemeteries, 148; consequences of, 149–52; cultural looting, 147; drugs and, 147; in Europe at the end of the war, 150; of German property, 142, 279; Germans' tolerance of, 140; by institutions, 147; of Jewish property, 139–40, 142, 152n33, 152n399, 292, 301; legends about hidden Jewish treasures and, 149; militia and, 153n50; the "Other" and, 136; peasant mentality and, 135–36; in provinces, 143; relief supplies and, 146; scale of, 144; shame of and historical record, 135; stages of, 144–45; thefts and, 148; theory of smashed windows (chaos) and, 136–39; time between occupations and, 66, 68; types of, 146–49; in Warsaw at the end of the war, 141–43
Lorenz, Konrad, 14
Loth, Roman, 66
Lublin, looting and, 141
Lublin Castle prison, 189
Lubowicz, Włodzimierz, 74
Łuczak, Czesław, 42
Łukomski, Stanisław, 54
Lutosławski, Wincenty, 31
luxury goods, 118
Lvov, 141, 217–18, 284
Lvov Eaglets, 218
lynchings, 15, 87. *See also* public executions

Machcewicz, Anna, 140
Madajczyk, Czesław, 56
magical beliefs, 4, 7, 14, 51–52, 315–16
Main Trustee Office for the East (Haupttreuhandstelle Ost–HTO), 44
malaria, 268
Malinowski, Bronisław, 52
Mandalian, Andrzej, 101
manipulation, culture of, 53–54
Mark, James, 84
marriage, 242–43, 252n340
Marszałkowski, Tomasz, 48
Marwick, Arthur, 38
mass panic, 4, 309
Master and Margarita, The (Bulgakov), 28
Mayakovsky, Vladimir, 27

McCarthy, Joseph, 16
McCarthyism, 16, 28
Meducki, Stanisław, 8
memoirs: postwar trauma and, 47–48; as sources, 4
mental health, results of prolonged fear and, 46
Mexican boerder wall, 15
Mexican revolution, 241–42
Michlic, Joanna, 275
Mickiewicz, Adam, 204
Miedzierski, Tadeusz, 169
Mikołajczyk, Stanisław, 2, 207, 208, 227–28
Miłosz, Czesław, 26, 35, 162, 202
Minc, Hilary, 224, 229–30, 308
Minecki, Lieutenant Colonel, 59
Ministry of Health, 267
Ministry of Information and Propaganda, 110, 189
Ministry of Labor and Social Welfare, 262
Ministry of Provisions and Trade, 254, 255
Ministry of Public Security, 5
Ministry of Work and Social Welfare, 262
miracles, 239–40
Mironowicz, Eugeniusz, 288
Misler, Bronisław, 169
Miszewski, Józef, 243
Mitarski, Jan, 14
Moczarski, Kazimierz, 166
Montefiore, Simon, 184
moonshine, 50, 127
moral atrophy, 52–54, 305
moral panic, 11, 23
Moscow show trials, 19
Mosdorf, Jan, 32
Moskalewski, Stanisław, 22
Motyka, Grzegorz, 284, 287
movement of peoples, 175–80
Müller, Lucia, 278
Munich Conference, 28
murders, 48–49

Naimark, Norman M., 79, 82
Nałkowska, Zofia, 4
Narutowicz, Gabriel, 27
National Democratic Party, in interwar Poland, 27, 31, 35
National Economy Bank, 229
nationalism, 15, 305
nationalization, 228–29
National Radical Camp, 31–32
national solidarity, 51, 56–57, 60
newspapers, 6, 27–28. *See also* individual papers
New York Times, 215
Nie-Boska komedia (The undivine comedy), Krasiński, Zygmunt, 29
Niedziela, 299

Nienasycenie (*Insatiability*) (Witkiewicz), 26
Night of Saint Bartholomew (1572), 14
NKVD, 58, 75, 176, 184–88, 194
Nolte, Ernst, 32
Nowak, Stefan, 43
Nowy Kurier Warszawski, 58

Ochab, Edward, 220, 229, 242, 326
Office of Assistance to the Jewish Population, 290–91
Office of Information and Propaganda, 208, 225, 243
Office of War Compensation, 40
official documents, 6
Ogniem i mieczem (*With Fire and Sword*) (Sienkiewicz), 20
Okulicki, Leopold, 206
Origins of Totalitarianism, The (Arendt), 182
orphans, 107–8
orthodox communities, fear of Bolsheviks and, 21
Osmańczyk, Edmund, 200
Osóbka-Morawski, Edward, 282
Ossowski, Stanisław, 223, 281, 302
O wyjście z kryzysu (To emerge from the crisis) (Giertych), 32

Paczkowski, Andrzej, 8, 308
Paczyńska, Irena, 236
panic, 11–12. *See also* fear
panic buying, 4, 10
Pański, Jan, 94–95
Panufnik, Andrzej, 40
Parandowski, Jan, 21, 42
Parsons, Talcott, 13
Partitions, 8
Patočka, Jan, 60
patriotism, 56–57
payment, alcohol and, 50–51
Peasant Battalions, 45
peasant memoirs, 4–5
peasant mentality, fatalism and, 7
peasant strikes, 48
pediculosis, 266
Petersen, Roger D., 15
Piłsudski, Józef, 27
Pipes, Daniel, 30
Pobóg-Malinowski, Władysław, 29
Podgórecki, Adam, 326
poetry, nationalistic themes and, 56
Pogonowska, Ewa, 24–25, 36n40
pogroms: against Germans, 282–84; alcohol and, 51; associations of Jews with fear and, 306; Citizens' Militia and, 124; Cracow pogrom, 8, 83, 108, 270, 290, 294–99; expendables and, 312; fear as motivation

of, 3, 6–7; Great Terror and, 17; guilt and, 290, 306; housing and, 233–34, 235; hunger and, 254, 270; Jedwabne pogrom, 14, 35, 49, 306; Kielce pogrom, 8, 14, 51, 83, 208, 277, 282, 290, 292, 300–303; Kiev pogrom, 60; of landowners by Bolsheviks, 33; number of victims of, 320n92; panics about the disappearances of children and, 83; peasant mentality and, 7; Polish collaborators and, 306; Polish guilt and, 290; in *Pożoga* (Conflagration), 24–25; psychic numbing and, 59; Radziłów pogrom, 14, 35; as reaction to collective fear of Soviets, 22; Rzeszów pogrom, 83, 291–94; searching for motivations for, 289–90; wartime trauma as trigger for, 48, 305, 314
Polacy wobec nowej rzeczywistości (The Poles in the new reality), 104
Poliakov, Léon, 28–29
Polish Armed Forces, 97, 301. *See also* demobilized troops
Polish–Bolshevik War of 1919–20, 19, 21, 28, 31–33
Polish collaborators, 306
Polish Committee of National Liberation (Polski Komitet Wyzwolenia Narodowego), 67, 125, 141, 175, 202–3, 221, 226, 288
Polish Communist Party (interwar period), 26–28, 30
Polish Peasant Party (Polskie Stronnictwo Ludowe), 43, 195
Polish People's Party, 193, 205, 309
Polish Socialist Party, 205
Polish-Soviet War of 1920, 69, 157
Polish Workers' Party, 124, 193, 202, 205, 207, 218, 224, 309, 326
political terror: alcoholism and, 185; arrests and, 184–87, 189–90; class and, 183–84, 187; comparisons with Middle Ages and, 192; continuation of wartime strategies by people and, 195; death sentences and, 190; denunciations and, 233; deportations and, 184, 187; disease as political tool and, 254; fear of ruled and, 184; fear of rulers and, 184; Germans and, 191; hunger and, 253–54; internment camps and, 184; language of, 192–93; long-term anxiety and, 185, 326; mass rapes and, 191; NKVD and, 184–88, 194; pervasiveness of, 193–95; Polish Security Office and, 188–90, 192, 196; pretend executions and, 186; public executions, 19, 45, 190–91, 193; rural areas and, 195; scapegoating of and, 196; show trials, 190; Stalin's instruction on terror and, 183–84; torture and, 189–90
Półtawska, Wanda, 47

Index 351

Popel, Nikolai Kirillovich, 70
post-traumatic stress disorder, 46–47
Potsdam Agreement, 219
Pożoga (Conflagration) (Kossak-Szczucka), 24–25
Prawin, Jakub, 219
Próchnik, Adam, 35
profiteers: as analogous to the Jew in popular mythology, 116; anti-profiteer campaigns and, 116–17; anti-Semitic violence and, 122–23; bazaars and, 119–21; black market and, 117–19; crackdown on black market and, 122–23; currency exchange and, 118–19; fears of nationalization and, 119; hunger cause of accusations about, 254, 270; language of political terror and, 193; militia and, 122; scapegoating of, 116; social communication and, 121; as type of expendable, 96, 119
propaganda, 22–24, 26, 57–58, 117, 276
prophecies, 52, 243–44
Prosto z mostu, 32, 35
Protocols of the Elder of Zion, 30
Provincial Command of the Citizens' Militia, 125
Provincial Office of Information and Propaganda, 219
Provisional Government, 203
Prus, Bolesław, 136
Prussia, 8
Przedwiośnie (The Coming Spring) (Żeromski), 24
Przekrój, 281
Przemyski, Andrzej, 166
psychic numbing, 59
public executions, 19, 45, 190–91, 193, 280–82
Pułapki zaangażowania (The traps of engagement) (Hirszowicz), 204

racial theories, 20–21, 25
Radio France nuclear war simulation, 213
Radom, looting and, 141
Radziłów pogrom, 14, 35
rape: abandoned newborns and, 83; abortion and, 81, 83; alcohol and, 74, 80; by bandits in Second World War, 159; blinding and, 83; in concentration camps, 79; court martials of Polish soldiers accused of, 89; demobilization orders and, 82; estimating numbers of, 83–84; fears of Red Army, 71; in forced labor camps, 79; by Polish soldiers, 88–89; as political terror, 191; pregnancy from, 78, 81–82, 83; by Red Army soldiers, 72–75, 77–84; of returning prisoners, 81; suicide and, 83, 91n108; syphilis and, 83, 267; venereal disease and, 83–84

Red Army: alcohol and, 72, 74, 255; alcohol barter and, 50; anxieties about arrival of, 70–71, 315; assault and, 72–75; bazaars and, 120; chaos of liberation and, 66; confiscation of Polish property and supplies, 71–77; crimes while traveling, 75–76; disintegration of the Underground State and, 43; entrance in Poland (1939), 28; ethnic violence against Germans and, 282–84; fighting with, 86–88; First Cavalry Army and, 21–22; flight from, 86; fortressing as response to fear of, 85; hatred of in response to crimes, 84–85; hunger and, 255, 257; lynchings and, 87; mass flight and, 22; militia reports and, 88; murder and, 73, 75, 78–79, 81, 83; newspaper coverage and, 110; occupation stages of, 70; Polish feelings on the arrival of, 69–70; quartering of, 235; rape and, 72–75, 77–84; Regained Territories and, 72; returning prisoners of war and, 74; scapegoating of Germans in response to fear of, 85; stolen cattle and, 76–77; syphilis and, 83, 267
refugees, 96
Regained Territories, 72, 115, 151, 175–76, 219–22, 232, 262
religious beliefs: apocalyptic mood and, 238–41, 243; atrophy of morality and, 52–54; concerns about godlessness, 242–43; effect of Second World War on, 51; feelings of transience and, 237–44; fundamentalism and, 237–44; magical thinking and, 51–52; miracles and, 239–40, 243; myths about Jewish ritual murder of Christian children and, 52; prophecies and, 52, 243–44, 259; strengthening of, 51–52, 314
Ribbentrop-Molotov Pact, 137, 219
Risk Society, 11
Robin, Corey, 183
Rokossovsky, Konstantin, 88, 216
Rolicki, Henryk, 31–32
Różański, Józef, 308
Rusinek, Kazimierz, 234
Russian Revolution, fear of, 25
Russian Revolution of 1905, 157
Ruthenians, 24
Rychard, Andrzej, 204
Ryszka, Franciszek, 99, 188
Rzeszów pogrom, 83, 291–94
Rzętkowska, Maria, 34

scabies, 266
scarlet fever, 266
Schatz, Jeff, 30, 35
Sebyłowa, Sabina, 137

Second World War: cultural consequences of, 51–59, 60; global cultural effects from, 60; hunger and, 253; impressions of, 7; manifestation of trauma from, 45–51, 60; partisan movement and, 157; sociopsychological importance of to Polish Great Terror, 38–39; sources of trauma from, 39–45; violence against hiding Jews in, 158
Security Office, 100, 102, 125, 147, 157, 188, 234, 292–93, 308
Shlapentokh, Vladimir, 13
show trials, 190
Siemaszko, Andrzej, 164
Sienkiewicz, Henryk, 20
Simmons, William, 21
Słonimski, Antoni, 27, 32
Słowo Pomorskie, 313
SMERSH (military counterintelligence), 184
Social Construction of Reality, The (Berger and Luckmann), 13
social control, 3, 42–43
social hierarchies, 44–45
sociology of catastrophes (Sorokin), 39, 41
sociology of trauma (Sztompka), 39
Sołowiejczyk-Guter, Aleksandra, 277
sołtys (elected chair of village council), 44–45
Sorokin, Pitirim, 16, 39, 41, 51
Soviet military courts, 76
Soviet Union: in *A gdy komunizm zapanuje*, 26; anti-imperialist propaganda in, 28; connection of Jewish stereotypes with, 23; conspiracies about, 84; currency and, 221; disintegration of institutions/organizations and, 42–43; distrust of and deserters, 104; economic exploitation of Poland and, 87; ethnic purges and, 275; evocation of Germans with, 23; evocation of tsarist regime and, 23; fear of another war and, 210–17; fear of savage Russian stereotype and, 20–23, 326; fears of collectivization and, 2; Great Purge and, 32; hunger and, 263; Jews in, 32; Polish fears of Bolsheviks and, 20–21; in *Pożoga* (Conflagration), 25; pressure in the repatriation process, 178; prophecies and, 52; suppression of sexuality and, 78
Spengler, Oskar, 26
Srokowski, Lieutenant, 300
Stalinization, 7
Stalin, Joseph, 28, 78–79, 248n104
Starowieyski, Franciszek, 70
starvation, 259
State Institute of Mental Hygiene, 40
State National Council (KRN–Krajowa Rada Narodowa), 41
State Repatriation Office, 175, 262

Steinhaus, Hugo, 4, 72, 89, 283, 308
Steinlauf, Michael C., 59
Stola, Dariusz, 135, 143
Structure of Social Action (Parsons), 13
Stryjkowski, Julian, 46, 107
Strzelecki, Edward, 94–95
Strzelecki, Jan, 43
suicide, 8, 91n108, 276–77
surnames, 69
Świda-Zięba, Hanna, 210
Świda-Ziemba, Hanna, 279
Swieżawski, Stefan, 217
sympathetic nervous system, 10
syphilis, 83, 267
szaberplac, 119–21
Szarota, Tomasz, 4, 8, 45, 95, 118
Szaynok, Bożena, 8
Szczepański, Jan Józef, 2, 4, 34–35, 111
Szelburg-Zarembina, Ewa, 281
szmalcownictwo, 162–63
Sztandar Ludu, 97, 298
Sztompka, Piotr, 39, 53, 55
Szwalbe, Stanisław, 41
Szymański, Antoni, 23–24
Szyr, Eugeniusz, 288

Tarnowska, Dąbrowa, 205
terror, 12, 15–16
Thiele-Dohrmann, Klaus, 12
Third Reich, 8, 33, 42–43, 52, 110
Thompson, Kenneth, 11
Tischner, Józef, 66
Tomaszewski, Tadeusz, 117, 141
Topolewski, Jan Wojciech, 177
torture, 189–90
train stations, masses of people moving through, 176
transience, mood of: of borders, 217–21, 326; currency and, 221–24, 244–45; during the Second World War, 200–201; fear of collectivization and, 224–28, 249n185; fear of war and, 217; housing and, 231–36; Jews and, 245; landmines and, 236–37; nationalization and, 224, 228–29, 245; political, 201–5; religion and, 237–44; seesaw of moods in response to, 205–10
Trevelyan, George M., 3
Triumf żółtych (The triumph of the yellow race) (Adamowicz), 25
Truman, Harry, 216
tuberculosis, 266
Tukhachevsky, Mikhail, 22
Turkey, 216
Tuszyńska, Agata, 277
Tuwim, Julian, 27

Tygodnik Powszechny, 123, 281
typhus, 2, 179, 254, 258, 259, 266–67

Ukrainian Insurgent Army, 190
Ukrainians: appropriation at departure of, 147–48; fighting with, 192; hiding of ethnicity and, 227–28; hunger and, 263; interwar relations with, 284–85; militia and, 128; as "Other," 275; partisans directly after liberation, 67; Polish fears of at time of liberation, 70; Polish national solidarity and antipathy toward, 57; Polish-Ukrainian conflict and, 285–88; uniting of Poles against, 3
underground fighters, 96, 100–101, 125
Underground State, 38, 43, 45, 104, 186
unemployment, 2, 95, 98–99, 110–16, 112
Union of War Invalids, 101–2
United States, 29, 210–17
UNRRA assistance, 146, 229, 259, 262
Upadek cywilizacji zachodniej (The fall of Western civilization) (Znaniecki), 26
Urwany lot (Interrupted flight) (Świda-Ziemba), 279
US dollars, 221–23

venereal disease, 83–84
Vilna, 217–18
violence, 3, 7, 13, 51, 156. *See also* ethnic violence; murder; pogroms; rape
Volhynia, 284–85

Wańkowicz, Melchior, 21
war: fear of a another after Second World War, 210; frequency of rape in, 78; housing shortages and, 231–36; Polish fear of, 19; as stimulus for fear, 10; war panics and, 214–15
War Censorship Office, 5, 9n27, 80, 178, 201, 232
War of the Worlds, The (radio broadcast), 11, 309, 313–14
Warsaw Uprising, 40, 43, 165, 206
"war syndrome," 46–47
Wartime Censorship, 5
Wartime Censorship Office, 155
wartime hardship, 41
wartime police, 125
wartime schizophrenia, 52
Wat, Aleksander, 26, 36n51
Weil, Simone, 13–14
Wejsberger, Henryk, 277
Werfel, Roman, 308
Wiadomości Literackie, 32
Wieliczko, Anatol, 108–9
Wierzbicki, Marek, 136
Wilson, Woodrow, 29
Witkiewicz, Stanisław Ignacy, 26

Wittenberg, Jason, 30
Włocławek, 299
wójt (government clerk), 44–45
Wolf, Eric R., 160
Wolność, 194, 201
women: accusations of submission to occupiers and, 53; acknowledgment of fear and, 4, 9n19; alcohol and, 50; hunger and, 272n41; Jewish ritual murder myth (vampirism) and, 310–11, 315–16; looting and, 142, 146; mobilization for military service and, 212; selling on black market and, 117–18; syphilis and, 83, 267; time between occupations and accusations towards, 66; unemployment numbers and, 112–15
Workers' Housing Action, 232
Woźniczka, Zygmunt, 210–11
Wróblewska, Jadwiga, 201
W rodzinnej historii lęku (A family history of fear) (Tuszyńska), 277
Wrona, Zenon, 8
Współczesna Ambona, 237
Wust, Peter, 315
Wyka, Kazimierz, 42, 52, 55, 59–60, 95, 121, 208–9, 310
Wyrobisz, Andrzej, 16

xenophobia, 33, 57. *See also* Belorussians, anti-Semitism; Germans; Ukrainians

Yalta Conference, 206, 218

Zagórski, Jerzy, 123
Załuski, Zbigniew, 280–81
Zambrowski, Roman, 270, 308
Zaremba, Zygmunt, 242
Żaryn, Jan, 54
Zawadzki, Aleksander, 127, 256
Żebrowska, Maria, 46
Zelek, Roman, 300
Żeromski, Stefan, 24, 136
Ziemia Lubuska, 214
Ziemia Pomorska, 114, 260, 267
Zientara-Malewska, Maria, 145
Zimbardo, Philip, 138, 150
Zmierzch Izraela (The Twilight of Israel) (Rolicki), 31–32
Znaniecki, Florian, 26, 156
Zubek, Jerzy, 146
Żukrowski, Wojciech, 149
Życie Warszawy, 40, 106, 142–43, 222, 224
Żydul, Jolanta, 312–13
Żydzi i ich wrogi stosunek do Narodu (The Jews and their hostile attitude toward the Nation), 313

MARCIN ZAREMBA is Professor of History at the University of Warsaw. He is author of the award-winning *Wielka Trwoga: Polska 1944–1947* (2012) and more than fifty publications in periodicals and collective papers. He publishes in *Polityka*, one of the most popular opinion weeklies in Poland.